Dictionary of Literary Biography

1 *The American Renaissance in New England,* edited by Joel Myerson (1978)

2 *American Novelists Since World War II,* edited by Jeffrey Helterman and Richard Layman (1978)

3 *Antebellum Writers in New York and the South,* edited by Joel Myerson (1979)

4 *American Writers in Paris, 1920–1939,* edited by Karen Lane Rood (1980)

5 *American Poets Since World War II,* 2 parts, edited by Donald J. Greiner (1980)

6 *American Novelists Since World War II, Second Series,* edited by James E. Kibler Jr. (1980)

7 *Twentieth-Century American Dramatists,* 2 parts, edited by John MacNicholas (1981)

8 *Twentieth-Century American Science-Fiction Writers,* 2 parts, edited by David Cowart and Thomas L. Wymer (1981)

9 *American Novelists, 1910–1945,* 3 parts, edited by James J. Martine (1981)

10 *Modern British Dramatists, 1900–1945,* 2 parts, edited by Stanley Weintraub (1982)

11 *American Humorists, 1800–1950,* 2 parts, edited by Stanley Trachtenberg (1982)

12 *American Realists and Naturalists,* edited by Donald Pizer and Earl N. Harbert (1982)

13 *British Dramatists Since World War II,* 2 parts, edited by Stanley Weintraub (1982)

14 *British Novelists Since 1960,* 2 parts, edited by Jay L. Halio (1983)

15 *British Novelists, 1930–1959,* 2 parts, edited by Bernard Oldsey (1983)

16 *The Beats: Literary Bohemians in Postwar America,* 2 parts, edited by Ann Charters (1983)

17 *Twentieth-Century American Historians,* edited by Clyde N. Wilson (1983)

18 *Victorian Novelists After 1885,* edited by Ira B. Nadel and William E. Fredeman (1983)

19 *British Poets, 1880–1914,* edited by Donald E. Stanford (1983)

20 *British Poets, 1914–1945,* edited by Donald E. Stanford (1983)

21 *Victorian Novelists Before 1885,* edited by Ira B. Nadel and William E. Fredeman (1983)

22 *American Writers for Children, 1900–1960,* edited by John Cech (1983)

23 *American Newspaper Journalists, 1873–1900,* edited by Perry J. Ashley (1983)

24 *American Colonial Writers, 1606–1734,* edited by Emory Elliott (1984)

25 *American Newspaper Journalists, 1901–1925,* edited by Perry J. Ashley (1984)

26 *American Screenwriters,* edited by Robert E. Morsberger, Stephen O. Lesser, and Randall Clark (1984)

27 *Poets of Great Britain and Ireland, 1945–1960,* edited by Vincent B. Sherry Jr. (1984)

28 *Twentieth-Century American-Jewish Fiction Writers,* edited by Daniel Walden (1984)

29 *American Newspaper Journalists, 1926–1950,* edited by Perry J. Ashley (1984)

30 *American Historians, 1607–1865,* edited by Clyde N. Wilson (1984)

31 *American Colonial Writers, 1735–1781,* edited by Emory Elliott (1984)

32 *Victorian Poets Before 1850,* edited by William E. Fredeman and Ira B. Nadel (1984)

33 *Afro-American Fiction Writers After 1955,* edited by Thadious M. Davis and Trudier Harris (1984)

34 *British Novelists, 1890–1929: Traditionalists,* edited by Thomas F. Staley (1985)

35 *Victorian Poets After 1850,* edited by William E. Fredeman and Ira B. Nadel (1985)

36 *British Novelists, 1890–1929: Modernists,* edited by Thomas F. Staley (1985)

37 *American Writers of the Early Republic,* edited by Emory Elliott (1985)

38 *Afro-American Writers After 1955: Dramatists and Prose Writers,* edited by Thadious M. Davis and Trudier Harris (1985)

39 *British Novelists, 1660–1800,* 2 parts, edited by Martin C. Battestin (1985)

40 *Poets of Great Britain and Ireland Since 1960,* 2 parts, edited by Vincent B. Sherry Jr. (1985)

41 *Afro-American Poets Since 1955,* edited by Trudier Harris and Thadious M. Davis (1985)

42 *American Writers for Children Before 1900,* edited by Glenn E. Estes (1985)

43 *American Newspaper Journalists, 1690–1872,* edited by Perry J. Ashley (1986)

44 *American Screenwriters, Second Series,* edited by Randall Clark, Robert E. Morsberger, and Stephen O. Lesser (1986)

45 *American Poets, 1880–1945, First Series,* edited by Peter Quartermain (1986)

46 *American Literary Publishing Houses, 1900–1980: Trade and Paperback,* edited by Peter Dzwonkoski (1986)

47 *American Historians, 1866–1912,* edited by Clyde N. Wilson (1986)

48 *American Poets, 1880–1945, Second Series,* edited by Peter Quartermain (1986)

49 *American Literary Publishing Houses, 1638–1899,* 2 parts, edited by Peter Dzwonkoski (1986)

50 *Afro-American Writers Before the Harlem Renaissance,* edited by Trudier Harris (1986)

51 *Afro-American Writers from the Harlem Renaissance to 1940,* edited by Trudier Harris (1987)

52 *American Writers for Children Since 1960: Fiction,* edited by Glenn E. Estes (1986)

53 *Canadian Writers Since 1960, First Series,* edited by W. H. New (1986)

54 *American Poets, 1880–1945, Third Series,* 2 parts, edited by Peter Quartermain (1987)

55 *Victorian Prose Writers Before 1867,* edited by William B. Thesing (1987)

56 *German Fiction Writers, 1914–1945,* edited by James Hardin (1987)

57 *Victorian Prose Writers After 1867,* edited by William B. Thesing (1987)

58 *Jacobean and Caroline Dramatists,* edited by Fredson Bowers (1987)

59 *American Literary Critics and Scholars, 1800–1850,* edited by John W. Rathbun and Monica M. Grecu (1987)

60 *Canadian Writers Since 1960, Second Series,* edited by W. H. New (1987)

61 *American Writers for Children Since 1960: Poets, Illustrators, and Nonfiction Authors,* edited by Glenn E. Estes (1987)

62 *Elizabethan Dramatists,* edited by Fredson Bowers (1987)

63 *Modern American Critics, 1920–1955,* edited by Gregory S. Jay (1988)

64 *American Literary Critics and Scholars, 1850–1880,* edited by John W. Rathbun and Monica M. Grecu (1988)

65 *French Novelists, 1900–1930,* edited by Catharine Savage Brosman (1988)

66 *German Fiction Writers, 1885–1913,* 2 parts, edited by James Hardin (1988)

67 *Modern American Critics Since 1955,* edited by Gregory S. Jay (1988)

68 *Canadian Writers, 1920–1959, First Series,* edited by W. H. New (1988)

69 *Contemporary German Fiction Writers, First Series,* edited by Wolfgang D. Elfe and James Hardin (1988)

70 *British Mystery Writers, 1860–1919,* edited by Bernard Benstock and Thomas F. Staley (1988)

71 *American Literary Critics and Scholars, 1880–1900,* edited by John W. Rathbun and Monica M. Grecu (1988)

72 *French Novelists, 1930–1960,* edited by Catharine Savage Brosman (1988)

73 *American Magazine Journalists, 1741–1850,* edited by Sam G. Riley (1988)

74 *American Short-Story Writers Before 1880,* edited by Bobby Ellen Kimbel, with the assistance of William E. Grant (1988)

151 *British Prose Writers of the Early Seventeenth Century*, edited by Clayton D. Lein (1995)

152 *American Novelists Since World War II, Fourth Series*, edited by James R. Giles and Wanda H. Giles (1995)

153 *Late-Victorian and Edwardian British Novelists, First Series*, edited by George M. Johnson (1995)

154 *The British Literary Book Trade, 1700–1820*, edited by James K. Bracken and Joel Silver (1995)

155 *Twentieth-Century British Literary Biographers*, edited by Steven Serafin (1995)

156 *British Short-Fiction Writers, 1880–1914: The Romantic Tradition*, edited by William F. Naufftus (1995)

157 *Twentieth-Century Caribbean and Black African Writers, Third Series*, edited by Bernth Lindfors and Reinhard Sander (1995)

158 *British Reform Writers, 1789–1832*, edited by Gary Kelly and Edd Applegate (1995)

159 *British Short-Fiction Writers, 1800–1880*, edited by John R. Greenfield (1996)

160 *British Children's Writers, 1914–1960*, edited by Donald R. Hettinga and Gary D. Schmidt (1996)

161 *British Children's Writers Since 1960, First Series*, edited by Caroline Hunt (1996)

162 *British Short-Fiction Writers, 1915–1945*, edited by John H. Rogers (1996)

163 *British Children's Writers, 1800–1880*, edited by Meena Khorana (1996)

164 *German Baroque Writers, 1580–1660*, edited by James Hardin (1996)

165 *American Poets Since World War II, Fourth Series*, edited by Joseph Conte (1996)

166 *British Travel Writers, 1837–1875*, edited by Barbara Brothers and Julia Gergits (1996)

167 *Sixteenth-Century British Nondramatic Writers, Third Series*, edited by David A. Richardson (1996)

168 *German Baroque Writers, 1661–1730*, edited by James Hardin (1996)

169 *American Poets Since World War II, Fifth Series*, edited by Joseph Conte (1996)

170 *The British Literary Book Trade, 1475–1700*, edited by James K. Bracken and Joel Silver (1996)

171 *Twentieth-Century American Sportswriters*, edited by Richard Orodenker (1996)

172 *Sixteenth-Century British Nondramatic Writers, Fourth Series*, edited by David A. Richardson (1996)

173 *American Novelists Since World War II, Fifth Series*, edited by James R. Giles and Wanda H. Giles (1996)

174 *British Travel Writers, 1876–1909*, edited by Barbara Brothers and Julia Gergits (1997)

175 *Native American Writers of the United States*, edited by Kenneth M. Roemer (1997)

176 *Ancient Greek Authors*, edited by Ward W. Briggs (1997)

177 *Italian Novelists Since World War II, 1945–1965*, edited by Augustus Pallotta (1997)

178 *British Fantasy and Science-Fiction Writers Before World War I*, edited by Darren Harris-Fain (1997)

179 *German Writers of the Renaissance and Reformation, 1280–1580*, edited by James Hardin and Max Reinhart (1997)

180 *Japanese Fiction Writers, 1868–1945*, edited by Van C. Gessel (1997)

181 *South Slavic Writers Since World War II*, edited by Vasa D. Mihailovich (1997)

182 *Japanese Fiction Writers Since World War II*, edited by Van C. Gessel (1997)

183 *American Travel Writers, 1776–1864*, edited by James J. Schramer and Donald Ross (1997)

184 *Nineteenth-Century British Book-Collectors and Bibliographers*, edited by William Baker and Kenneth Womack (1997)

185 *American Literary Journalists, 1945–1995, First Series*, edited by Arthur J. Kaul (1998)

186 *Nineteenth-Century American Western Writers*, edited by Robert L. Gale (1998)

187 *American Book Collectors and Bibliographers, Second Series*, edited by Joseph Rosenblum (1998)

188 *American Book and Magazine Illustrators to 1920*, edited by Steven E. Smith, Catherine A. Hastedt, and Donald H. Dyal (1998)

189 *American Travel Writers, 1850–1915*, edited by Donald Ross and James J. Schramer (1998)

190 *British Reform Writers, 1832–1914*, edited by Gary Kelly and Edd Applegate (1998)

191 *British Novelists Between the Wars*, edited by George M. Johnson (1998)

192 *French Dramatists, 1789–1914*, edited by Barbara T. Cooper (1998)

193 *American Poets Since World War II, Sixth Series*, edited by Joseph Conte (1998)

194 *British Novelists Since 1960, Second Series*, edited by Merritt Moseley (1998)

195 *British Travel Writers, 1910–1939*, edited by Barbara Brothers and Julia Gergits (1998)

196 *Italian Novelists Since World War II, 1965–1995*, edited by Augustus Pallotta (1999)

197 *Late-Victorian and Edwardian British Novelists, Second Series*, edited by George M. Johnson (1999)

198 *Russian Literature in the Age of Pushkin and Gogol: Prose*, edited by Christine A. Rydel (1999)

199 *Victorian Women Poets*, edited by William B. Thesing (1999)

200 *American Women Prose Writers to 1820*, edited by Carla J. Mulford, with Angela Vietto and Amy E. Winans (1999)

201 *Twentieth-Century British Book Collectors and Bibliographers*, edited by William Baker and Kenneth Womack (1999)

202 *Nineteenth-Century American Fiction Writers*, edited by Kent P. Ljungquist (1999)

203 *Medieval Japanese Writers*, edited by Steven D. Carter (1999)

204 *British Travel Writers, 1940–1997*, edited by Barbara Brothers and Julia M. Gergits (1999)

205 *Russian Literature in the Age of Pushkin and Gogol: Poetry and Drama*, edited by Christine A. Rydel (1999)

206 *Twentieth-Century American Western Writers, First Series*, edited by Richard H. Cracroft (1999)

207 *British Novelists Since 1960, Third Series*, edited by Merritt Moseley (1999)

208 *Literature of the French and Occitan Middle Ages: Eleventh to Fifteenth Centuries*, edited by Deborah Sinnreich-Levi and Ian S. Laurie (1999)

209 *Chicano Writers, Third Series*, edited by Francisco A. Lomelí and Carl R. Shirley (1999)

210 *Ernest Hemingway: A Documentary Volume*, edited by Robert W. Trogdon (1999)

211 *Ancient Roman Writers*, edited by Ward W. Briggs (1999)

212 *Twentieth-Century American Western Writers, Second Series*, edited by Richard H. Cracroft (1999)

213 *Pre-Nineteenth-Century British Book Collectors and Bibliographers*, edited by William Baker and Kenneth Womack (1999)

214 *Twentieth-Century Danish Writers*, edited by Marianne Stecher-Hansen (1999)

215 *Twentieth-Century Eastern European Writers, First Series*, edited by Steven Serafin (1999)

216 *British Poets of the Great War: Brooke, Rosenberg, Thomas. A Documentary Volume*, edited by Patrick Quinn (2000)

217 *Nineteenth-Century French Poets*, edited by Robert Beum (2000)

218 *American Short-Story Writers Since World War II, Second Series*, edited by Patrick Meanor and Gwen Crane (2000)

219 *F. Scott Fitzgerald's* The Great Gatsby: *A Documentary Volume*, edited by Matthew J. Bruccoli (2000)

220 *Twentieth-Century Eastern European Writers, Second Series*, edited by Steven Serafin (2000)

221 *American Women Prose Writers, 1870–1920*, edited by Sharon M. Harris, with the assistance of Heidi L. M. Jacobs and Jennifer Putzi (2000)

222 *H. L. Mencken: A Documentary Volume*, edited by Richard J. Schrader (2000)

223 *The American Renaissance in New England, Second Series*, edited by Wesley T. Mott (2000)

224 *Walt Whitman: A Documentary Volume*, edited by Joel Myerson (2000)

225 *South African Writers*, edited by Paul A. Scanlon (2000)

226 *American Hard-Boiled Crime Writers*, edited by George Parker Anderson and Julie B. Anderson (2000)

227 *American Novelists Since World War II, Sixth Series*, edited by James R. Giles and Wanda H. Giles (2000)

228 *Twentieth-Century American Dramatists, Second Series*, edited by Christopher J. Wheatley (2000)

229 *Thomas Wolfe: A Documentary Volume*, edited by Ted Mitchell (2001)

230 *Australian Literature, 1788–1914*, edited by Selina Samuels (2001)

Dictionary of Literary Biography Documentary Series

Dictionary of Literary Biography Yearbooks

1980 edited by Karen L. Rood, Jean W. Ross, and Richard Ziegfeld (1981)

1981 edited by Karen L. Rood, Jean W. Ross, and Richard Ziegfeld (1982)

1982 edited by Richard Ziegfeld; associate editors: Jean W. Ross and Lynne C. Zeigler (1983)

1983 edited by Mary Bruccoli and Jean W. Ross; associate editor Richard Ziegfeld (1984)

1984 edited by Jean W. Ross (1985)

1985 edited by Jean W. Ross (1986)

1986 edited by J. M. Brook (1987)

1987 edited by J. M. Brook (1988)

1988 edited by J. M. Brook (1989)

1989 edited by J. M. Brook (1990)

1990 edited by James W. Hipp (1991)

1991 edited by James W. Hipp (1992)

1992 edited by James W. Hipp (1993)

1993 edited by James W. Hipp, contributing editor George Garrett (1994)

1994 edited by James W. Hipp, contributing editor George Garrett (1995)

1995 edited by James W. Hipp, contributing editor George Garrett (1996)

1996 edited by Samuel W. Bruce and L. Kay Webster, contributing editor George Garrett (1997)

1997 edited by Matthew J. Bruccoli and George Garrett, with the assistance of L. Kay Webster (1998)

1998 edited by Matthew J. Bruccoli, contributing editor George Garrett, with the assistance of D. W. Thomas (1999)

1999 edited by Matthew J. Bruccoli, contributing editor George Garrett, with the assistance of D. W. Thomas (2000)

2000 edited by Matthew J. Bruccoli, contributing editor George Garrett, with the assistance of George Parker Anderson (2001)

2001 edited by Matthew J. Bruccoli, contributing editor George Garrett, with the assistance of George Parker Anderson (2002)

Concise Series

Concise Dictionary of American Literary Biography, 7 volumes (1988–1999): *The New Consciousness, 1941–1968; Colonization to the American Renaissance, 1640–1865; Realism, Naturalism, and Local Color, 1865–1917; The Twenties, 1917–1929; The Age of Maturity, 1929–1941; Broadening Views, 1968–1988; Supplement: Modern Writers, 1900–1998.*

Concise Dictionary of British Literary Biography, 8 volumes (1991–1992): *Writers of the Middle Ages and Renaissance Before 1660; Writers of the Restoration and Eighteenth Century, 1660–1789; Writers of the Romantic Period, 1789–1832; Victorian Writers, 1832–1890; Late-Victorian and Edwardian Writers, 1890–1914; Modern Writers, 1914–1945; Writers After World War II, 1945–1960; Contemporary Writers, 1960 to Present.*

Concise Dictionary of World Literary Biography, 4 volumes (1999–2000): *Ancient Greek and Roman Writers; German Writers; African, Caribbean, and Latin American Writers; South Slavic and Eastern European Writers.*

American Philosophers, 1950–2000

Dictionary of Literary Biography® • Volume Two Hundred Seventy-Nine

American Philosophers, 1950–2000

Edited by
Philip B. Dematteis
Saint Leo University
and
Leemon B. McHenry
California State University, Northridge

A Bruccoli Clark Layman Book

GALE®

THOMSON
━━━━━✦━━━━━ ™
GALE
ST. PHILIP'S COLLEGE LIBRARY

Detroit • New York • San Diego • San Francisco • Cleveland • New Haven, Conn. • Waterville, Maine • London • Munich

B
935
.A45
2003

Dictionary of Literary Biography
Volume 279: American Philosophers, 1950–2000
Philip B. Dematteis and Leemon B. McHenry

Advisory Board
John Baker
William Cagle
Patrick O'Connor
George Garrett
Trudier Harris
Alvin Kernan
Kenny J. Williams

Editorial Directors
Matthew J. Bruccoli and Richard Layman

© 2003 by Gale. Gale is an imprint of The Gale Group, Inc., a division of Thomson Learning, Inc.

Gale and Design™ and Thomson Learning™ are trademarks used herein under license.

For more information, contact
The Gale Group, Inc.
27500 Drake Rd.
Farmington Hills, MI 48331-3535
Or you can visit our Internet site at
http://www.gale.com

ALL RIGHTS RESERVED
No part of this work covered by the copyright hereon may be reproduced or used in any form or by any means—graphic, electronic, or mechanical, including photocopying, recording, taping, Web distribution, or information storage retrieval systems—without the written permission of the publisher.

For permission to use material from this product, submit your request via Web at http://www.gale-edit.com/permissions, or you may download our Permissions Request form and submit your request by fax or mail to:

Permissions Department
The Gale Group, Inc.
27500 Drake Rd.
Farmington Hills, MI 48331-3535
Permissions Hotline:
248-699-8006 or 800-877-4253, ext. 8006
Fax: 248-699-8074 or 800-762-4058

While every effort has been made to ensure the reliability of the information presented in this publication, The Gale Group, Inc. does not guarantee the accuracy of the data contained herein. The Gale Group, Inc. accepts no payment for listing; and inclusion in the publication of any organization, agency, institution, publication, service, or individual does not imply endorsement of the editors or publisher. Errors brought to the attention of the publisher and verified to the satisfaction of the publisher will be corrected in future editions.

LIBRARY OF CONGRESS CATALOGING-IN-PUBLICATION DATA

American philosophers, 1950–2000 / edited by Philip B. Dematteis and Leemon B. McHenry.
    p. cm. — (Dictionary of literary biography ; v. 279)
"A Bruccoli Clark Layman book."
Includes bibliographical references and index.
    ISBN 0-7876-6023-X
    1. Philosophy, American—20th century—Bio-bibliography—Dictionaries.
    I. Dematteis, Philip Breed. II. McHenry, Leemon B., 1950– III. Series.

B935.A45 2003
191—dc21
                              2003005949

Printed in the United States of America
10 9 8 7 6 5 4 3 2 1

To the memories of Philip Thomas Anthony Dematteis and Virginia Harriet Breed Dematteis
and
to the memory of Willard Van Orman Quine, whose genius inspired many
and whose ideas provided shape and direction to philosophy
in the twentieth century

Contents

Plan of the Series

. . . Almost the most prodigious asset of a country, and perhaps its most precious possession, is its native literary product—when that product is fine and noble and enduring.

Mark Twain*

The advisory board, the editors, and the publisher of the *Dictionary of Literary Biography* are joined in endorsing Mark Twain's declaration. The literature of a nation provides an inexhaustible resource of permanent worth. Our purpose is to make literature and its creators better understood and more accessible to students and the reading public, while satisfying the needs of teachers and researchers.

To meet these requirements, *literary biography* has been construed in terms of the author's achievement. The most important thing about a writer is his writing. Accordingly, the entries in *DLB* are career biographies, tracing the development of the author's canon and the evolution of his reputation.

The purpose of *DLB* is not only to provide reliable information in a usable format but also to place the figures in the larger perspective of literary history and to offer appraisals of their accomplishments by qualified scholars.

The publication plan for *DLB* resulted from two years of preparation. The project was proposed to Bruccoli Clark by Frederick G. Ruffner, president of the Gale Research Company, in November 1975. After specimen entries were prepared and typeset, an advisory board was formed to refine the entry format and develop the series rationale. In meetings held during 1976, the publisher, series editors, and advisory board approved the scheme for a comprehensive biographical dictionary of persons who contributed to literature. Editorial work on the first volume began in January 1977, and it was published in 1978. In order to make *DLB* more than a dictionary and to compile volumes that individually have claim to status as literary history, it was decided to organize volumes by topic, period, or

*From an unpublished section of Mark Twain's autobiography, copyright by the Mark Twain Company

genre. Each of these freestanding volumes provides a biographical-bibliographical guide and overview for a particular area of literature. We are convinced that this organization—as opposed to a single alphabet method—constitutes a valuable innovation in the presentation of reference material. The volume plan necessarily requires many decisions for the placement and treatment of authors. Certain figures will be included in separate volumes, but with different entries emphasizing the aspect of his career appropriate to each volume. Ernest Hemingway, for example, is represented in *American Writers in Paris, 1920–1939* by an entry focusing on his expatriate apprenticeship; he is also in *American Novelists, 1910–1945* with an entry surveying his entire career, as well as in *American Short-Story Writers, 1910–1945, Second Series* with an entry concentrating on his short fiction. Each volume includes a cumulative index of the subject authors and articles.

Since 1981 the series has been further augmented by the *DLB Yearbooks,* which update published entries, add new entries to keep the *DLB* current with contemporary activity, and provide articles on literary history. There have also been nineteen *DLB Documentary Series* volumes, which provide illustrations, facsimiles, and biographical and critical source materials for figures, works, or groups judged to have particular interest for students. In 1999 the *Documentary Series* was incorporated into the *DLB* volume numbering system beginning with *DLB 210: Ernest Hemingway.*

We define literature as the *intellectual commerce of a nation:* not merely as belles lettres but as that ample and complex process by which ideas are generated, shaped, and transmitted. *DLB* entries are not limited to "creative writers" but extend to other figures who in their time and in their way influenced the mind of a people. Thus the series encompasses historians, journalists, publishers, book collectors, and screenwriters. By this means readers of *DLB* may be aided to perceive literature not as cult scripture in the keeping of intellectual high priests but firmly positioned at the center of a nation's life.

DLB includes the major writers appropriate to each volume and those standing in the ranks behind them. Scholarly and critical counsel has been sought in deciding which minor figures to include and how full their entries should be. Wherever possible, useful references are made to figures who do not warrant separate entries.

Each *DLB* volume has an expert volume editor responsible for planning the volume, selecting the figures for inclusion, and assigning the entries. Volume editors are also responsible for preparing, where appropriate, appendices surveying the major periodicals and literary and intellectual movements for their volumes, as well as lists of further readings. Work on the series as a whole is coordinated at the Bruccoli Clark Layman editorial center in Columbia, South Carolina, where the editorial staff is responsible for accuracy and utility of the published volumes.

One feature that distinguishes *DLB* is the illustration policy–its concern with the iconography of literature. Just as an author is influenced by his surroundings, so is the reader's understanding of the author enhanced by a knowledge of his environment. Therefore *DLB* volumes include not only drawings, paintings, and photographs of authors, often depicting them at various stages in their careers, but also illustrations of their families and places where they lived. Title pages are regularly reproduced in facsimile along with dust jackets for modern authors. The dust jackets are a special feature of *DLB* because they often document better than anything else the way in which an author's work was perceived in its own time. Specimens of the writers' manuscripts and letters are included when feasible.

Samuel Johnson rightly decreed that "The chief glory of every people arises from its authors." The purpose of the *Dictionary of Literary Biography* is to compile literary history in the surest way available to us–by accurate and comprehensive treatment of the lives and work of those who contributed to it.

The *DLB* Advisory Board

Introduction

Analytic philosophy was the dominant philosophical movement in the English-speaking world for most of the twentieth century. It is generally referred to as Anglo-American philosophy; the reader of this volume and of *DLB 262: British Philosophers, 1800–2000* will find that the American and British analytic philosophers form a unified tradition in pursuit of rigor and clarity of thought. In the United States, analytic philosophy gained prominence in the latter half of the twentieth century with the work of such thinkers as Donald Davidson, Saul Kripke, Hilary Putnam, W. V. Quine, and John Searle.

William James, the most influential American philosopher of the classical period and one of the founders of pragmatism (James and the other leading pragmatists are treated in *DLB 270: American Philosophers Before 1950*), remarked that American philosophy at the outset of the twentieth century "lacks logical rigour, but it has the tang of life." What came in the next hundred years was anything but a lack of logical rigor; but as American analytic philosophy developed in complexity and technical detail, it became more remote and incomprehensible to the nonprofessional. The philosophy that flourished at midcentury was far removed from the emphasis on concrete lived experience that one finds in James or in the other leaders of the "classical period" of American philosophy such as Charles Sanders Peirce, Josiah Royce, George Santayana, and John Dewey.

The British philosopher Bertrand Russell expressed the view that logic is the essence of philosophy and thereby set the pattern for the technical orientation of analytic philosophy. The monumental *Principia Mathematica* (1910–1913) of Russell and Alfred North Whitehead (both of whom are treated in *DLB 262*) provided much of the technical apparatus for logical positivism and the analytic movement. A synthesis of developments in nineteenth-century mathematics and logic, *Principia Mathematica* was the first serious advance in logic since Aristotle. Russell said that the advances in modern logic "gave thought wings," whereas the older Aristotelian logic caused it to flutter. Quine and the positivist Rudolf Carnap (treated in *DLB 270*) both regarded the logic of *Principia Mathematica* as the basis for developing a philosophical system that sought truth

in the manner of a scientific investigator. Quine's classic *Word and Object* (1960), for example, develops a canonical notation—that is, a logical language that is clearer and simpler than a natural one—to regiment ordinary language and lay bare its ontological commitments (its assumptions about the nature of reality). Quine and C. I. Lewis (treated in *DLB 270*) at Harvard University and Kripke and David Lewis at Princeton University continued to make contributions to the modern logic that is indispensable to the formulation and attempted solution of problems by analytic philosophy.

The careful attention given to language in analytic philosophy parallels the focus on logic. As the movement developed, it became less concerned with the sort of attempt to provide a comprehensive description of the world that is found in Russell's early work and more concerned with the pursuit of conceptual clarity. Traditional philosophical problems were thus recast as problems of language. Like the pragmatists, many of the early linguistic philosophers were skeptical of grand metaphysical claims, and this skepticism was reinforced by logical positivism with its verifiability criterion of meaning: for both the pragmatists and the positivists, concepts whose truth or falsity would make no difference in human experience are meaningless. The more extreme linguistic philosophers saw philosophy as a kind of linguistic therapy aimed at avoiding metaphysical quandaries caused by the misuse of language. The work of Paul Grice, developed at the University of Oxford and continued after his move to the University of California at Berkeley, exemplifies this "linguistic turn" in analytical philosophy.

Although a quintessential linguistic philosopher, Quine resurrected metaphysics with his critique of logical positivism. His philosophy is a systematic attempt to answer the question: How do we acquire our theory of the world? As Quine came to recognize the failure of positivism's attempt to demarcate the theoretical and experimental aspects of modern science, he became committed to a holism in which both hang together; for Quine, metaphysics is the general and abstract end of a continuum with the natural sciences. It is not the transcendent or speculative metaphysics of previous rationalistic systems but a naturalized metaphysics that originates in the natural sciences and forms an essential part of our view of the world. For Quine, the problem with many linguistic philosophers was that they neglected the role of science in the shaping of worldviews.

Quine's naturalism shared some of the insights of the early pragmatists in rejecting traditional "foundationalism" in epistemology (the theory of knowledge). Since philosophy has failed to find foundations for knowledge outside of science, Quine says, the basis must be found within science itself. Quine uses the positivist Otto Neurath's metaphor of the busy sailor who must rebuild his ship while staying afloat: we must make do with our inherited theory of the world and adjust it from within. Furthermore, Quine recognized in his famous "underdetermination" thesis that since theory always outruns its evidential support, human beings are "makers of truth" in the sense that they choose the theories that guide the direction of scientific inquiry. Pragmatism and realism are compatible, in Quine's view, because as the authors of theories we create truth, and as believers of theories we must view the theories as the truth about a reality that is external to them. Our choice of a conceptual scheme is pragmatic; but once the choice has been made, the objects of the theoretical framework must be treated as ultimate—at least, until evidence to the contrary requires a revision.

Antifoundationalism takes a more radical turn in the work of Thomas S. Kuhn, a philosopher of science who ended his career at the Massachusetts Institute of Technology. Educated at Harvard as a theoretical physicist, Kuhn turned his attention to the history and philosophy of science in such classics as *The Copernican Revolution* (1957) and *The Structure of Scientific Revolutions* (1962). While Kuhn is not analytic in his approach to philosophy, he agrees with Quine in rejecting the simple incrementalism of the positivist model of science, according to which science is the slow but continuous accumulation of theories that approximate more and more closely to "the truth." Instead, Kuhn proposes that science goes through "normal" and "revolutionary" periods, the latter occurring when the generally accepted "paradigm" of normal science breaks up from within under the weight of an increasing number of "anomalies," puzzles that it cannot solve. The domain of inquiry undergoes a revolution during which the fundamental theoretical principles are replaced by new ones, leading to another paradigm and period of normal science. For Kuhn, the later periods of normal science are not guaranteed to preserve the "truths" of the earlier periods; the notion of "progress" only makes sense within an accepted paradigm, not from one paradigm to another. Kuhn's view of science is compatible with the negative theses of pragmatism in that no absolute, foundational "superparadigm" is available from

which the correctness of the ones that dominate any particular period of science may be judged. Later theories will be better than their predecessors in explanatory and predictive power, but Kuhn rejects the idea of scientific progress as growing ever closer to some ultimate and objective truth.

In the late twentieth century, analytic philosophy found a new direction in dealing with some of the traditional problems of metaphysics. "Analytic metaphysics" is a combination of philosophy of mind, philosophy of science, and philosophy of language and has connections to linguistics, physiological psychology, evolutionary biology, and the fledgling interdisciplinary field of cognitive science. The most important development in this area was a revival of interest in the mind-body problem stimulated by the development of computers and advances in cognitive psychology, artificial intelligence, and neuroscience. Davidson, Putnam, Searle, and Thomas Nagel have made important contributions here. Another fertile area is the metaphysics of possible worlds and the powerful new formalism of modal logic that is essential to such theories. While the seventeenth-century German rationalist Gottfried Wilhelm Leibniz is credited with introducing the concept of possible worlds into philosophy, the Americans Kripke, David Lewis, and Alvin Plantinga have made significant advances in possible-world theory—in Plantinga's case, in defense of traditional Christian theism. A third area that has received a great deal of attention is the realist/antirealist debate that raises questions about the extent of mind-independent reality. Much of this debate has been conducted within the context of the philosophy of mind. Putnam has led the way in the formulation of the problem and its attempted solution.

Against the grain of Anglo-American analytical philosophy, postmodern philosophy developed in the United States with influences from Continental philosophy in the nineteenth and twentieth centuries. While analytical philosophy focuses on logical and philosophical method in the manner of a scientist seeking truth, postmodern philosophy adopts a more historical, rhetorical, and literary approach. Although originally associated with existentialism and phenomenology, and especially German philosopher Friedrich Nietzsche's critique of modernism, postmodernism in the United States is more closely allied with contemporary French and German philosophy. Generally, the term *postmodernism* is used in a number of disciplines to emphasize a plurality of styles and methods and a shared disdain for the pretensions of modernist culture. In philosophy, however, postmodernism begins with the rejection of the ideal of rationality extolled by the Enlightenment. It shares with neopragmatists, such as Richard Rorty, the general critique of philosophy as a privileged, truth-telling discourse and advances relativism in place of any foundational role logic or science previously held in the quest for knowledge.

If James was the ambassador of American philosophy in the nineteenth century, Rorty played this role in the twentieth. Like James, he attracted a wide audience outside of philosophy and the academic world more generally. He revived certain strains of pragmatism found in James's and John Dewey's work, pushed their doctrines to a more consistently antimetaphysical stance, and denounced what he considered the high-minded hubris of professional philosophy. Rorty announced the end of philosophy–or, at least, the end of a certain type of philosophy in the epistemological vein–in his widely read *Philosophy and the Mirror of Nature* (1979) and put theory into practice by resigning his position as professor of philosophy at Princeton. He identifies Dewey, the Austrian-born Cambridge logician Ludwig Wittgenstein, and the German phenomenologist/existentialist Martin Heidegger as his allies in the revolution against traditional philosophy. From various standpoints these philosophers, he contends, arrived at similar conclusions about the type of philosophical activity that must be abandoned: that which involves the notion of some transcendental, objective viewpoint from which one could judge the correctness of one's beliefs. In place of this traditional epistemology, Rorty proposes that philosophy adopt a more humble role of edifying conversation similar to that of literary criticism.

While most of the analytic mainstream continues to resist Rorty's view of philosophy, he has opened the doors to a much more pluralistic stance and allowed many Continental thinkers to gain a hearing. The schism between analytic philosophy and Continental philosophy in the contemporary philosophical scene can be traced to a rebellion in the 1960s regarding a perceived narrowness in the analytic approach and a neglect of the relevance of philosophy to everyday life. In Rorty's wake, Arthur C. Danto has produced a more inclusive philosophy by combining analytic and Continental approaches.

Many analysts believe that the traditional value-oriented branches of philosophy, such as ethics, political philosophy, and aesthetics, are outside their professional purview–or, at least, that they can do no more than clarify the language used in such fields; they do not think that it is their place to make substantive statements in those areas. Russell, for example, wrote extensively on ethics and politics but explicitly separated those works from his philosophical ones. The logical positivists claimed that since value judgments are not verifiable or falsifiable, they have no cognitive content; and the position known as emotivism holds that so-called value statements are not really statements at all but expression of the speaker's feelings: "Murder is wrong," for example, is equivalent to "Murder, boo!"

These considerations do not mean, however, that philosophers have no personal opinions about such matters; most of them do, and those opinions are often quite strongly held. In politics, in particular, most philosophers tend to be on the Left–at least liberal, often socialist, in many cases Marxist. They are generally disdainful of free-market capitalism, which they view as disorderly, wasteful of natural resources, rooted in and reinforcing such antisocial motivations as greed and materialism, and, perhaps worst of all, as producing unjust economic inequality. Contempt for business can, perhaps, be traced back to the pre-Socratic philosopher Pythagoras in the sixth century B.C., who is said to have divided those who attended the Olympic games into three classes: the lowest are those who come to buy and sell; above them are the athletes, who compete not for money but for honor and glory; but highest of all are the spectators, who only want to observe–they are, obviously, a metaphor for the philosopher, who desires only to know. And Plato's ideal state in the *Republic* is ruled by philosopher-kings with the assistance of the "auxiliaries," a combination police and military force who live a Spartan and communal lifestyle; at the bottom are the "artisans"–the economic sector of society, the only class that is allowed to own precious metals and jewelry.

Three of the philosophers treated in this volume are, however, dramatic exceptions to this rule: they are exponents of libertarianism, a political philosophy that holds that individuals are the sole legitimate owners of their own minds and bodies and that they should be free to do as they please, provided that they do not infringe on the rights of others to life, liberty, and property. These rights are considered to be "natural" or innate, not granted by government; and they are "negative" rights in that they do not impose positive duties of assistance but only duties of forbearance or leaving others alone. The only legitimate function of government is to enforce these rights more effectively than individuals, left to themselves, could do; it is not a legitimate function of the government to redistribute wealth to promote equality, to operate the educational system, or to prohibit individuals from consuming recreational drugs, viewing pornography, gambling, or engaging in prostitution (whether as customer or provider). Capitalism is seen as a natural and spontaneous result of the free interaction of individuals, although many libertarians consider that the actual form it has taken in the United States and other countries has been distorted by forcible government interventions such as price con-

Introduction

DLB 279

trols, subsidies, import tariffs and quotas, and occupational licensing.

The Russian immigrant Ayn Rand extolled capitalism and egoism in her lengthy philosophical novels *The Fountainhead* (1943) and *Atlas Shrugged* (1957) and nonfiction works such as *The Virtue of Selfishness: A New Concept of Egoism* (1964) and *Capitalism: The Unknown Ideal* (1966). She founded a philosophical movement known as Objectivism, purportedly based on Aristotelian logic, that has continued since her death in 1982 and given rise to at least two research institutes; during her lifetime she was the center of a virtual cult that at one point included future Federal Reserve Board Chairman Alan Greenspan. Regarded as the grandmother of the libertarian movement, she inspired many people to become libertarian thinkers and activists, even though not all of them agreed with all of her positions, and some even reacted rather strongly against them.

One of those who was attracted to libertarianism by personal contact with Rand, though without ever becoming one of her disciples, is John Hospers. Widely credited with bringing British ordinary-language philosophy to the attention of American philosophers with his *An Introduction to Philosophical Analysis* (1953), Hospers is also well regarded for his work in ethics and, especially, aesthetics. But he is also the author of *Libertarianism: A Political Philosophy for Tomorrow* (1971), a nontechnical presentation of and argument for the libertarian position intended for general readers; and in 1972 he became the first presidential candidate of the recently formed Libertarian Party, gaining one vote from a member of the Electoral College who had been pledged to Richard M. Nixon but had become disenchanted with the former vice president.

Among professional philosophers, the exposition and defense of libertarianism that is considered the strongest is that presented by Robert Nozick in his blockbuster (within the philosophical community, at any rate) 1974 treatise *Anarchy, State, and Utopia*. Using rigorous argumentation, including highly technical procedures from decision theory, Nozick showed how a minimal government, or "night-watchman state," would evolve naturally from independent self-defense agencies in a "state of nature" without violating anyone's rights. Using his famous "Wilt Chamberlain" example, he attacked the various "patterned" theories of distribution, such as "to each an equal share," "to each according to his or her needs," "to each according to his or her effort," and so on, and asserted his own "historical entitlement" theory, according to which someone is entitled to own a thing if he or she makes it from previously unowned resources, trades for it, or receives it as a gift. If the distribution of goods resulting from such voluntary transactions is massively unequal,

Nozick says, so be it. Nozick's position was criticized in an outpouring of dissertations, articles, and books; how successful these critiques have been is open to debate. Nozick himself, famous for his intellectual restlessness—he is said to have taught only one course a second time during his years at Harvard—resisted attempts to make him a spokesperson for libertarianism and largely abandoned political philosophy for other interests, such as epistemology; he said that he "did not want to spend my life writing 'The Son of Anarchy, State, and Utopia,' 'The Return of the Son of . . . ,' etc."

One who did, in essence, spend most of his life writing the same book over and over was the nonlibertarian John Rawls, whose *A Theory of Justice* (1971) was almost universally hailed as one of the greatest works of political philosophy of the twentieth century; even Nozick, who disagreed with much of what his Harvard colleague had to say, praised Rawls's book in *Anarchy, State, and Utopia*. Rawls developed the central thesis of the book, "justice as fairness," in articles that preceded its publication, in several revised editions of the book itself, and in the last book he published before his death, *Justice as Fairness: A Restatement* (2001). Rawls modernizes the classic social-contract approach to political philosophy as found in the works of Thomas Hobbes, John Locke, and Jean-Jacques Rousseau by using the techniques of game theory, such as the "maximin" principle. Instead of placing his parties in a hypothetical pregovernment "state of nature," he places them behind a "veil of ignorance" in which they are not allowed to know what roles they will play in the society whose basic principles of justice they are deciding; they do not know what their talents, interests, races, or sexes will be. Under such conditions of procedural fairness, where each is trying to do the best for himself or herself as possible, Rawls thinks that they will agree that certain basic freedoms must be guaranteed but that economic inequality must be permitted only insofar as, through providing incentives to productivity, it benefits the least-advantaged group in the society.

At the beginning of the twenty-first century, analytical philosophy continues to dominate professional academic philosophy in the United States, but nonanalytic approaches, or pluralism, such as Continental philosophy, speculative metaphysics, process philosophy, absolute idealism, Catholic philosophy, personalism, existentialism, and non-Western philosophy, are gaining momentum. The pluralism in philosophical approaches and schools of thought has developed concurrently with the emphasis on multiculturalism and the increasing awareness of racial and gender-based exclusion in the profession of philosophy.

—Leemon B. McHenry and Philip B. Dematteis

xx

Acknowledgments

This book was produced by Bruccoli Clark Layman, Inc. Philip B. Dematteis and Michael Allen were the in-house editors.

Production manager is Philip B. Dematteis.

Administrative support was provided by Ann M. Cheschi and Carol A. Cheschi.

Accountant is Ann-Marie Holland.

Copyediting supervisor is Sally R. Evans. The copyediting staff includes Phyllis A. Avant, Caryl Brown, Melissa D. Hinton, Philip I. Jones, Rebecca Mayo, Nancy E. Smith, and Elizabeth Jo Ann Sumner.

Editorial associates are Amelia B. Lacey, Michael S. Martin, Catherine M. Polit, and William Mathes Straney.

In-house prevetting is by Nicole A. La Rocque.

Permissions editor and database manager is Amber L. Coker.

Layout and graphics supervisor is Janet E. Hill. The graphics staff includes Zoe R. Cook and Sydney E. Hammock.

Office manager is Kathy Lawler Merlette.

Photography supervisor is Paul Talbot. Photography editor is Scott Nemzek.

Digital photographic copy work was performed by Joseph M. Bruccoli.

Systems manager is Donald Kevin Starling.

Typesetting supervisor is Kathleen M. Flanagan. The typesetting staff includes Patricia Marie Flanagan, Mark J. McEwan, and Pamela D. Norton. Freelance typesetters are Wanda Adams and Rebecca Mayo.

Walter W. Ross did library research. He was assisted by Jo Cottingham and the following other librarians at the Thomas Cooper Library of the University of South Carolina: circulation department head Tucker Taylor; reference department head Virginia W. Weathers; reference department staff Brette Barron, Marilee Birchfield, Paul Cammarata, Gary Geer, Michael Macan, Tom Marcil, Rose Marshall, and Sharon Verba; interlibrary loan department head John Brunswick; and interlibrary loan staff Robert Arndt, Hayden Battle, Alex Byrne, Bill Fetty, Marna Hostetler, and Nelson Rivera.

American Philosophers, 1950–2000

Dictionary of Literary Biography

Peter Anthony Bertocci

(13 May 1910 – 13 October 1989)

John Howie
Southern Illinois University at Carbondale

BOOKS: *The Empirical Argument for God in Late British Thought* (Cambridge, Mass.: Harvard University Press, 1938);

The Human Venture in Sex, Love, and Marriage (New York: Association Press, 1949);

Introduction to the Philosophy of Religion (New York: Prentice-Hall, 1951);

Facing the Facts about Sex (New York: Association Press, 1953; revised, 1967);

Free Will, Responsibility, and Grace (New York: Abingdon Press, 1957);

Religion as Creative Insecurity (New York: Association Press, 1958);

Education and the Vision of Excellence (Boston: Boston University Press, 1960);

Why Believe in God? (New York: Association Press, 1963);

Personality and the Good: Psychological and Ethical Perspectives, by Bertocci and Richard M. Millard (New York: McKay, 1963);

Sex, Love, and the Person (New York: Sheed & Ward, 1967);

The Person God Is (London: Allen & Unwin / New York: Humanities Press, 1970);

Is God for Real? (New York: Thomas Nelson, 1971);

The Goodness of God (Washington, D.C.: University Press of America, 1981);

The Person and Primary Emotions (New York: Springer, 1988).

Peter Anthony Bertocci in the 1970s

OTHER: "Attributes of God," "Bruno, Giordano," "Conservation of Value," "Creation," "Creationism," "Datum," "Immanence," "Immediacy," "Leibniz, Gottfried Wilhelm," "Lotze, Rudolf Herman," "Martineau, James," "Monadism or Monadology," "Panpsychism," "Pringle-Pattison, Andrew Seth," "Realism, Moral," "Religious Datum," "Santayana, George," "Sorley, William Ritchie," "Taylor, Alfred Edward," "Temporality of God," "Tennant, Frederick Robert," and

3

ST. PHILIP'S COLLEGE LIBRARY

"Ward, James," in *An Encyclopedia of Religion,* edited by Vergilius Ferm (Paterson, N.J.: Littlefield, Adams, 1945), pp. 45, 90, 198, 207, 217, 359–360, 439, 453, 473, 502, 557, 609–610, 636, 647, 688, 727, 762, 772, 818;

"Personality," in *Encyclopedia of Psychology,* edited by P. L. Harriman (New York: Philosophical Library, 1946), p. 477;

"Problems of Philosophy," in *College Reading and Religion: A Survey of College Reading Materials* (New Haven: Yale University Press, 1948), pp. 28–79;

"Bases for Developing Religious Community," in *Crucial Issues in Education: An Anthology,* edited by Henry J. Ehlers (New York: Holt, 1955), pp. 124–130;

Edgar Sheffield Brightman, *Person and Reality: An Introduction to Metaphysics,* edited by Bertocci, Jannette E. Newhall, and Robert S. Brightman (New York: Ronald Press, 1958);

"A Critique of Gordon W. Allport's Theory of Motivation" and "The Psychological Self, the Ego, and Personality," in *Understanding Human Motivation,* edited by Chalmers L. Stacey and Manfred F. DeMartino (Cleveland: Howard Allen, 1958), pp. 82–105, 174–183;

"A Temporalistic View of Mind," in *Theories of the Mind,* edited by Jordan M. Scher (New York: Free Press, 1962), pp. 398–421;

"The Logic of Creationism, Advaita, and Visistadvaita: A Critique," in *Essays in Philosophy Presented to Dr. T. M. P. Mahadevan on His Fiftieth Birthday,* edited by C. T. K. Chari (Madras, India: Ganesh, 1962), pp. 26–42;

"The Person, the Ego, and Personality in the Light of Recent Psychology," in *El problema del hombre: Comunicaciones sobre el tema 1. Le problème de l'homme. Problem of Man,* Memorias del XIII Congreso Internacional de Filosofía, volume 3 (Mexico City: Universidad Nacional Autónoma de México, 1963), pp. 43–58;

"Mind," in *The Encyclopedia of Mental Health,* volume 4, edited by Albert Deutsch (New York: Watts, 1963), pp. 1231–1234;

"Personalism: Borden Parker Bowne," in *Masterpieces of Christian Literature in Summary Form,* volume 2, edited by Frank N. Magill and Ian P. McGreal (New York: Salem Press, 1963), pp. 851–856;

Philosophical Interrogations: Interrogations of Martin Buber, John Wild, Jean Wahl, Brand Blanshard, Paul Weiss, Charles Hartshorne, Paul Tillich, edited by Sydney Rome and Beatrice Rome, contributions by Bertocci (New York: Holt, Rinehart & Winston, 1964);

"Foundations of Personalistic Psychology," in *Scientific Psychology: Principles and Approaches,* edited by Benjamin B. Wolman and Ernest Nagel (New York: Basic Books, 1965), pp. 293–316;

"Is There a System of Human Rights?" in *Proceedings of the Twenty-First Annual Meeting of the Philosophy of Education Society (April 11–14, 1965),* edited by Maxine Greene (Lawrence, Kans.: Ernest Bayles, 1965), pp. 53–68;

"Free Will, the Creativity of God, and Order," in *Current Philosophical Issues: Essays in Honor of Curt John Ducasse,* edited by Frederick C. Dommeyer (Springfield, Ill.: Thomas, 1966), pp. 213–235;

"The Co-Responsive Community," in *The Knowledge Explosion: Liberation and Limitation,* edited by Francis Sweeney (New York: Farrar, Straus & Giroux, 1966), pp. 49–60;

"Borden Parker Bowne" and "George Holmes Howison," in *The Encyclopedia of Philosophy,* 8 volumes, edited by Paul Edwards (New York: Macmillan, 1967), I: 356–357; IV: 66;

"Free Will, Creativity of God, and Order," in *East-West Studies on the Problem of the Self,* edited by P. T. Raju and Alburey Castell (The Hague: Nijhoff, 1968), pp. 44–60;

"The Person and His Body: Critique of Existentialist Responses to Descartes," in *Cartesian Essays: A Collection of Critical Studies,* edited by Bernd Magnus and James B. Wilbur (The Hague: Nijhoff, 1969), pp. 116–144;

"The Person God Is," in *Talk of God,* edited by G. N. A. Vesey, Royal Institute of Philosophy Lectures, volume 2 (London: Macmillan / New York: St. Martin's Press, 1969), pp. 185–206;

"The Perspective of a Teleological Personalist," in *Contemporary American Philosophy: Second Series,* edited by John E. Smith (London: Allen & Unwin / New York: Humanities Press, 1970), pp. 248–272;

"Creation in Religion," in *Dictionary of the History of Ideas: Studies of Selected Pivotal Ideas,* volume 1, edited by Philip P. Wiener (New York: Scribners, 1970), pp. 571–577;

"Psychological Interpretations of Religious Experience," in *Research on Religious Development,* edited by Merton P. Strommen (New York: Hawthorn Books, 1971), pp. 3–41;

Mid-Twentieth Century American Philosophy: Personal Statements, edited by Bertocci (New York: Humanities Press, 1974);

Gordon W. Allport, *Waiting for the Lord: Thirty-Three Meditations on God and Man,* edited by Bertocci (New York: Macmillan / London: Collier-Macmillan, 1978);

"Does Blanshard Escape Epistemic Dualism?" in *The Philosophy of Brand Blanshard,* edited by Paul Arthur Schilpp, The Library of Living Philosophers, volume 15 (La Salle, Ill.: Open Court, 1980), pp. 601–617;

"The Scholar, the Liberal Ideal, and the Philosophy of Science," in *Hegel and the Sciences,* edited by Robert S. Cohen and Marx W. Wartofsky (Dordrecht & Boston: Reidel, 1984), pp. 3–10;

"Borden Parker Bowne and His Personalistic Theistic Idealism" and "Reflections on the Experience of 'Oughting,'" in *The Boston Personalist Tradition in Philosophy, Social Ethics, and Theology,* edited by Paul Deats and Carol Robb (Macon, Ga.: Mercer University Press, 1986), pp. 55–80, 209–220;

"Theism," in *The Encyclopedia of Religion,* volume 14, edited by Mircea Eliade (New York: Macmillan / London: Collier-Macmillan, 1987), pp. 421–427.

SELECTED PERIODICAL PUBLICATIONS–
UNCOLLECTED: "The Authority of Ethical Ideals," *Journal of Philosophy,* 33 (1936): 269–274;

"We Send Them to College–to Be Confused," *Journal of Higher Education,* 8 (October 1937): 343–350;

"An Empirical Critique of the Moral Argument for God," *Journal of Religion,* 3 (November 1938): 275–288;

"The Perplexing Faith of a Moralist," *Review of Religion,* 3 (November 1938): 38–51;

"Is Wieman Empirical Enough?" *Personalist,* 19 (Winter 1938): 56–67;

"Comments and Criticisms: Concerning Empirical Philosophy," *Journal of Philosophy,* 36 (1939): 263–269;

"Tennant's Critique of Religious Belief," *Religion in Life,* 8 (1939): 248–259;

"Sentiments and Attitudes," *Journal of Social Philosophy,* 11 (May 1940): 245–257;

"The Focus of Religious Education," *Religion in Life,* 10 (1941): 54–63;

"The Man Neglected by Science and Education," *Crozer Quarterly,* 19 (1942): 209–217;

"A Critique of Professor Cantril's Theory of Motivation," *Psychological Review,* 49 (July 1942): 365–385;

"The Personal and Social Roots of Democracy," *Personalist,* 23 (Summer 1942): 253–266;

"Macintosh's Theory of Natural Knowledge," *Journal of Religion,* 23 (July 1943): 164–172;

"The Crucible of Religion and the Pastoral Function," *Crozer Quarterly,* 21 (1944): 25–29;

"An Analysis of Macintosh's Theory of Religious Knowledge," *Journal of Religion,* 24 (January 1944): 42–55;

"Faith and Reason: The Implications of Dr. Ferré's View," *Review of Religion,* 8 (May 1944): 359–369;

"The Moral Outlook of the Adolescent in War Time," *Mental Hygiene,* 28 (July 1944): 353–367;

"A Reinterpretation of Moral Obligation," *Philosophy and Phenomenological Research,* 6 (December 1945): 270–282;

"William James' Psychology of Will: An Evaluation," *Philosophical Forum,* 4 (1946): 2–13;

"The Logic of Naturalistic Arguments against Theistic Hypotheses," *Philosophical Review,* 56 (January 1947): 82–87;

"A Sixth Conception of Christian Strategy," *Christendom,* 13, no. 1 (1948): 45–55;

"Spiritual Summons to Marriage," *National Parent-Teacher,* 43 (February 1949): 30–32;

"Brightman's View of the Self, the Person, and the Body," *Philosophical Forum,* 8 (1950): 21–28;

"Fulbright Scholar in Italy," *Boston University Graduate Journal,* 1 (1952): 57–59;

"Ramsey's *Basic Christian Ethics:* A Critique," *Crozer Quarterly,* 29 (January 1952): 24–38;

"Edgar Sheffield Brightman, 1884–1953," *Bostonia,* 26 (July 1953): 15–17;

"Edgar Sheffield Brightman," *Personalist,* 34 (October 1953): 358–360;

"The Nature of Cognition," *Review of Metaphysics,* 8 (1954): 49–60;

"Edgar Sheffield Brightman, through His Students' Eyes," by Bertocci and M. Alicia Corea, *Philosophical Forum,* 12 (1954): 53–67;

"Edgar Sheffield Brightman," *Philosophical Forum,* 12 (1954): 92–94;

"Religious Diversity and American Education," *School and Society,* 80 (21 August 1954): 55–56;

"Gordon W. Allport's *The Nature of Prejudice* and *The Problem of Choice,*" *Pastoral Psychology,* 5 (November 1954): 31–37;

"The Juncture between Creative Art and Creative Science," *Main Currents in Modern Thought,* 11 (January 1955): 51;

"Philosophy as Wisdom," *Boston University Graduate Journal,* 4 (September 1955): 5–7;

"Is God a Fool?" *Motive,* 4 (January 1956): 7–8, 27–29;

"Marriage Demands Maturity," *Christian Action,* 11 (January–March 1956): 1–5;

"A Vacuum in Educational Theory," *School and Society,* 82 (18 February 1956): 59–61;

"Unless Educators Be Philosophers, and Philosophers Be Educators," *Harvard Educational Review,* 26 (Spring 1956): 158–161;

"What Makes a Philosophy Christian? A Liberal Speaks," *Christian Scholar,* 39 (June 1956): 102–112;

"Credo for *CP*," *Contemporary Psychology*, 1 (July 1956): 222;

"The Person as the Key Metaphysical Principle," *Philosophy and Phenomenological Research*, 17 (December 1956): 207–225;

"Is an Existentialist Christian Approach to Sex Adequate?" *Pastoral Psychology*, 8 (March 1957): 15–27;

"Comment on 'What Can Philosophy of Religion Accomplish?' by Horace L. Friess," *Review of Religion*, 21 (March 1957): 145–155;

"Can the Goodness of God Be Empirically Grounded?" *Journal of Bible and Religion*, 25 (April 1957): 99–105;

"Free Will, Responsibility, and Grace," *Faculty Forum* (May 1957): 1–2;

"Croce's Aesthetics in Context," *Personalist*, 38 (Summer 1957): 248–259;

"Is a Humanistic Grounding of Democracy Adequate?" *Religion in Life*, 26 (Fall 1957): 550–559;

"Does the Concept of Christian Love Add Anything to Moral Philosophy?" *Journal of Religion*, 38 (January 1958): 1–11;

"Toward a Clarification of the Christian Doctrine of Grace and the Moral Life," *Journal of Religion*, 38 (April 1958): 85–94;

"The Goodness of God and Two Conceptions of Value Objectivity," *Journal of Bible and Religion*, 26 (July 1958): 232–240;

"Philosophy and the Philosophy of Education," by Bertocci and Richard M. Millard, *Journal of Education*, 141 (October 1958): 7–13;

"The Person, Obligation, and Value," *Personalist*, 40 (Spring 1959): 141–151;

"What Makes a Christian Home?" *Christian Century*, 76 (7 May 1959): 544–546;

"Borden Parker Bowne: Philosophical Theologian and Personalist," *Religion in Life*, 29 (Fall 1960): 587–591;

"The Renaissance of Bowne: A Symposium," by Bertocci, Millard, John H. Lavely, and Walter G. Muelder, *Bostonia*, 34 (Fall 1960): 23–27;

"The Moral Structure of the Person," *Review of Metaphysics*, 14 (1961): 369–388;

"Edgar Sheffield Brightman," *Bostonia*, 35 (Summer 1961): 28;

"Tagore," *Religion in Life*, 30 (Fall 1961): 555–561;

"In Defense of Metaphysical Creation," *Philosophical Forum*, 19 (May 1962): 3–15;

"A New Area of Concentration for Women?" *Boston University Graduate Journal*, 10 (June 1962): 143–150;

"God: Creator and Redeemer," *Workers with Youth*, 15 (August 1962): 2–5;

"Three Visions of Perfection and Human Freedom," *Psychologia*, 5 (1962): 59–67;

"Of Pattern and Purpose," *Christian Century*, 80 (9 January 1963): 50;

"Edgar S. Brightman–Ten Years Later," *Philosophical Forum*, 20 (May 1963): 3–10;

"Extramarital Sex and the Pill," *Christian Century*, 81 (26 February 1964): 267–270;

"The 'Self' in Recent Psychology of Personality: A Philosophical Critique," *Philosophical Forum*, 21 (June 1964): 19–31;

"Toward a Metaphysics of Creation," *Review of Metaphysics*, 17 (1964): 493–510;

"Reply to Elmer Lear's Review of *Personality and the Good*," *Studies in Philosophy and Education*, 4 (Spring 1965): 62–65;

"Change and Creation: Reply to Dr. Frazier" and "Values and Ethical Principles: Comment on Professor Reck's Review of *Personality and the Good*," *Philosophical Forum*, 22 (May 1965): 79–81, 82–86;

"Existential Phenomenology and Psychoanalysis," *Review of Metaphysics*, 28 (1965): 629–646;

"An Impasse in Philosophical Theology," *International Philosophical Quarterly*, 5 (September 1965): 379–396;

"The Cosmological Argument–Revisited and Revised," *Proceedings of the American Catholic Philosophical Association*, 41 (March 1967): 33–43;

"The Freedom to Be Free!" *Faculty Forum*, 42 (November 1967): 1–3;

"Descartes and Marcel on the Person and His Body: A Critique," *Proceedings of the Aristotelian Society*, new series 68 (1968): 207–226;

"Susanne K. Langer's Theory of Feeling and Mind," *Review of Metaphysics*, 23 (1970): 527–551;

"The Scholar, the Liberal Ideal, and Freedom," *Journal of Social Philosophy*, 2 (October 1971): 13–17;

"The Partners That Cannot Be Divorced: Psychology and Philosophy," *Psychologia*, 14 (1971): 148–152;

"Hartshorne on Personal Identity: A Personalistic Critique," *Process Studies*, 2 (Fall 1972): 216–221;

"John Lukacs, *The Passing of the Modern Age*," *Philosophy Forum*, 13 (1973): 111–124;

"Man: Responsible Agent, Not Reactor!" *Contemporary Psychology*, 18 (July 1973): 307–310;

"A Life Good to Live: A Psycho-Ethical Perspective," *Military Chaplains' Review* (Winter 1974): 47–66;

"Creative Insecurity: A Style of Being-Becoming," *Humanitas*, 10 (May 1974): 127–139;

"Love and Reality in E. A. Burtt's Philosophy: A Personalistic Critique," *Idealistic Studies*, 5 (September 1975): 269–289;

"Rationale for a Cosmoteleological Argument for God," *Journal of Religion,* 56 (October 1976): 323–337;

"Keeping Quality in Sexual Experience," *Christian Century,* 93 (8 December 1976): 1096–1098;

"Idealistic Temporalistic Personalism and Good-and-Evil," *Proceedings of the American Catholic Philosophical Association,* 51 (1977): 56–65;

"A Personalistic Philosophy of Education," *Teachers College Record,* 80 (February 1979): 483–506;

"The Person, His Personality, and Environment," *Review of Metaphysics,* 32 (1979): 605–621;

"Does Elusive Becoming in Fact Characterize H. D. Lewis' View of the Mind?" *Religious Studies,* 15 (September 1979): 399–405;

"Le conception du Moi, de son identité et de l'immortalité selon H. D. Lewis," *Archives de Philosophie,* 43 (July–September 1980): 363–383;

"Why Personalistic Idealism?" *Idealistic Studies,* 10 (September 1980): 181–198;

"The Search for Meaning in Adolescent Sexuality and Love," *Teachers College Record,* 84 (Winter 1982): 379–390;

"The Personalism of Edgar S. Brightman and Ultimate Reality," *Ultimate Reality and Meaning,* 6 (March 1983): 32–50;

"Autobiographical Reflections," *Personalist Forum,* 7 (Spring 1991): 5–50.

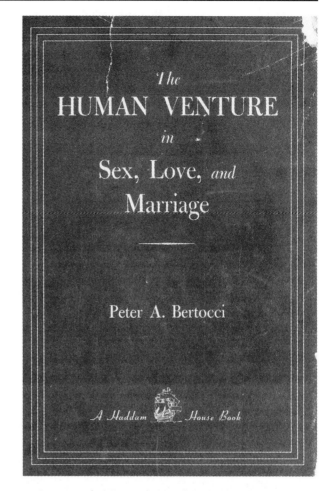

Dust jacket for Bertocci's 1949 defense of traditional monogamy, written in reaction to Alfred C. Kinsey's 1948 study Sexual Behavior in the Human Male *(Bruccoli Clark Layman Archives)*

Peter Anthony Bertocci succeeded Borden Parker Bowne and Edgar Sheffield Brightman as the leader of the school of Boston personalism, a philosophical-theological perspective influenced by the philosophies of Gottfried Wilhelm Leibniz and George Berkeley that regards reality as ultimately personal in nature. According to this view, personality is a basic category of existence that cannot be reduced to or explained by any more-fundamental concepts, such as mechanistic ones. The ultimate person, and the creator of all other persons, is God.

Bertocci was born on 13 May 1910 in Gaeta, Italy. A few months later his mother, Annunziata Guglietta Bertocci, moved with him and his brother, Angelo Philip, to Somerville, Massachusetts, where their father, Gaetano, had settled and was working in a meat-packing plant. Of the thirteen Bertocci children, only three boys and three girls survived childbirth. The family worked hard and lived frugally, and despite financial strain Bertocci's parents were able to earn sufficient money to provide an education for their children. From age seven Peter worked at odd jobs, such as selling newspapers at his father's workplace, tending a shoemaker's shop, collecting and repairing barrels, and cleaning a neighbor's barn; he also procured kindling, cooking wood, and coal for the family.

The greatest single influence on Peter and Angelo Bertocci during their youth was the Italian Christian Mission. Leaders of the mission organized sports and other activities that especially appealed to the younger immigrants. The most devoted of these leaders in the opinion of the Bertocci brothers was Ruth Bidmead; in his autobiography, *Teacher from Little Italy* (1990), Angelo calls her "Lady Bountiful." Bidmead arranged for her boys to have a baseball team and bought most of the equipment with her own money; she also paid their way to football games and took them, a pair at a time and again at her own expense, to some of the better restaurants in Boston. In his "Autobiographical Reflections" (1991) Peter Bertocci says that Bidmead "won" him to Christ well before he decided to "take his stand" for Jesus at a church service at the age of twelve. Also when he was twelve, Bertocci began working during the summers as an assistant to a carpenter, mason, and plasterer; the job continued through his high-school years. Bertocci's early life was, thus, an education in working-class realities; no critic could later claim that the philosophical idealist Bertocci had no acquaintance with the real world.

Bertocci enrolled in the "commercial" track in high school, but midway through the program, after he had made the honor roll and been elected to the honor society, he switched to the college track. He wanted to follow Angelo into the College of Liberal Arts at Boston University; but by the time he graduated from high school he had saved less than $200, and the university offered no first-year scholarships. The mission leaders, however, persuaded the Boston Rotary Club to provide him with a loan and summer jobs.

During his first year at Boston University, Bertocci became acquainted with a liberal religious perspective, exemplified by his professors Edgar Sheffield Brightman and William G. Aurelio and the Reverend William F. Warren of Marsh Chapel, that contrasted with the fundamentalist views of the mission workers. His resulting doubts about the infallibility of the Bible almost led to a permanent rift between him and Angelo. He recalls in his 1986 essay "Reflections on the Experience of 'Oughting'" that he was himself reluctant to relinquish his belief in the literal truth of the Bible.

During Bertocci's junior year an Augustus Howe Buck Scholarship relieved him of the need to work to pay for his education and allowed him to participate in extracurricular activities such as the philosophy club, whose members called themselves the "Neoalchemists." He also joined the YMCA (Young Men's Christian Association) and was elected president of his local division in 1930. A training school for YMCA leaders at Union Theological Seminary in New York City during the summer of that year introduced him to the work of such Christian teachers as Henry P. Van Dusen, Henry Sloane Coffin, and W. G. T. Shedd.

Bertocci received his B.A. in philosophy with honors in 1931. He then studied under Gordon W. Allport, Alfred North Whitehead, and Ralph Barton Perry at Harvard University, earning an M.A. in psychology in 1932, and returned to Boston University to work on a Ph.D. in philosophy. Although he was still working through many philosophical questions, he had already begun to accept the viewpoint of Boston personalism.

At Brightman's urging, Bertocci used money from the Buck Scholarship and personal loans to spend the 1934–1935 academic year studying with Frederick Robert Tennant at the University of Cambridge. His dissertation, supervised by Tennant, was an exploration of the ideas of Tennant and four other British philosophers of religion: James Martineau, Andrew Seth Pringle-Pattison, James Ward, and William Ritchie Sor-

ley. Bertocci had the benefit of Tennant's guidance in regard to Tennant's own views and those of Tennant's teacher, Ward, while Sorley explained his and Pringle-Pattison's ideas.

Bertocci received his Ph.D. from Boston University in 1935 and became an instructor in psychology and philosophy at Bates College in Lewiston, Maine. That same year he married Lucy Soldani, whom he had met seven years earlier at a freshman reception. They had three children: Peter John, Stephen Paul, and Richard Anthony.

Bertocci's dissertation served as the basis for his first book, *The Empirical Argument for God in Late British Thought* (1938). His own ideas are expressed in the final chapter, "An Empirical View of God's Goodness"; he later developed them at length in *The Goodness of God* (1981). Also in 1938 Bertocci became secretary-treasurer of the Personalistic Discussion Group; he held the position until 1975. In 1939 he was promoted to assistant professor at Bates College.

In 1944 Bertocci became a professor of philosophy at Boston University. Among his first publications after moving to Boston were twenty-two articles for *An Encyclopedia of Religion* (1945) and the entry "Personality" for the *Encyclopedia of Psychology* (1946).

In 1948 Alfred C. Kinsey and fellow researchers at Indiana University published *Sexual Behavior in the Human Male,* a controversial work popularly known as "the Kinsey Report." Bertocci responded the following year with *The Human Venture in Sex, Love, and Marriage,* in which he defends the traditional ideal of monogamous sexual relations on the bases of psychological fulfillment and social stability.

Bertocci was a Fulbright Research Scholar in Italy in 1950–1951. His third book, *Introduction to the Philosophy of Religion* (1951), includes one of his chief contributions to philosophy: his adaptation of the classical teleological argument, or "argument from design," for the existence of God. Bertocci's "cosmo-teleological-ethical argument" is a more sophisticated version of the last of the five proofs of God's existence formulated by St. Thomas Aquinas in the *Summa Theologiae* in the thirteenth century and echoed by later thinkers such as Joseph Butler, William Paley, and Tennant. The argument holds that the vast and intricate order observed in nature could only have been brought about by a wise and powerful being. Unlike Aquinas, Bertocci does not claim to provide irrefutable proof of God's existence; his more modest goal is to supply a reasonable warrant for belief.

Bertocci's argument is presented in chapters 13 to 15 of *Introduction to the Philosophy of Religion*. He begins by noting that although life depends on inanimate matter, it is not reducible to matter: the selectivity of living organisms, their maintenance of their equilibrium within their environment, and their capacity for reproduction cannot be adequately explained on the basis of chemical reactions or physical processes. The harmonious interactions of living organisms with inert matter can be better explained by postulating the presence of purpose. The theory of evolution, as commonly understood, cannot account for the coming into existence and continuation of new beings; calling them "emergents," "accidents," or "mutations" is merely a confession of ignorance. By contrast, the notion of mind or intelligence employing creative purpose makes the physical evolution of the universe and the biological evolution of species intelligible. The positing of an intelligence that employs ordered means to accomplish its ends enables one to understand the laws of physics, chemistry, biology, and psychology.

Bertocci next examines the relationship of thought to reality. Mind is related to the objects it knows in a way analogous to that in which a road map is related to the arrangement of highways it depicts. The map is not the highways themselves nor even a copy of them; rather, it is a representation of the arrangement of the highways that is accurate enough to allow drivers to find their way. The map did not come into being by accident or happenstance but through the purposive action of the mapmaker. Similarly, to suppose that a cosmic mind created what the human mind can apprehend is, Bertocci argues, more credible than to suppose that inert matter did so.

Next, Bertocci points out that the order and regularity of nature justify moral effort. The environment draws the boundaries of the consequences of human choices and permits some of those consequences to be predictable. Nature and value are likewise interrelated, in that human experience corroborates the suitability of nature for the realization of value. Value is a joint product of human action and the environment: the environment contains "value-possibilities" that await their realization through human effort and thought. A materialistic-mechanistic explanation cannot account for the correlation of moral effort and value-realization with the order of nature; a more "empirically coherent" supposition is that a creative, intelligent "purposer" is responsible for the interconnectedness of inanimate matter, life, rational beings, and the moral development of such beings. The universe is good for human beings in that it makes possible not only intellectual satisfaction and moral achievement but also friendship, aesthetic experience, and religious experience. Bertocci asks what or who could have made the universe such that it is good for human beings, and answers: "the Person God is." Only a consciousness could connect matter and living organisms in such a way as to make moral effort, value, and

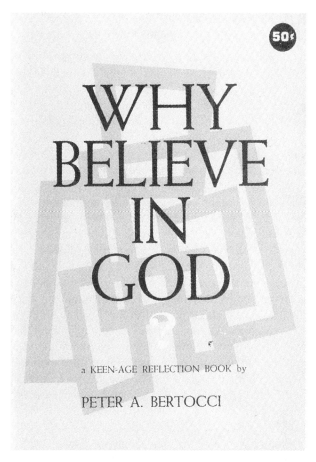

Cover of Bertocci's 1963 defense of theism
(Bruccoli Clark Layman Archives)

aesthetic and religious experience possible. These interrelationships and possibilities for human beings are not the result of accident or chance but of the design of God.

Although the universe is, on the whole, good for human beings, it does seem to contain a large amount of evil—both "natural evils," such as disease, floods, and tornadoes, and "moral evil," which results from human free will. In *Introduction to the Philosophy of Religion* Bertocci defines evil as "any condition which keeps the individual and the commonwealth of individuals from the self-fulfillment of which each is capable." By this definition, a hardship is not necessarily an evil: it may be an occasion for insight, a goad to courage, a challenge to one's inner resources, or a provocation to mutual sympathy. Even when actual evil does exist, human beings can restrict and contain its effects through their attitude toward it. They may, additionally, force evil to contribute to good: for example, the blind and deaf Helen Keller transformed her handicaps through patience, courage, and discipline; she experienced natural evil but forced it to yield good—if not to her directly, as an achievement over seemingly insurmountable obstacles, then for others as an example of incredible courage.

Some natural evils are the result of moral evils: the starvation and disease that are the aftermath of war and the droughts and floods that arise from human exploitation of the land are obvious examples. In Bertocci's view, the real difficulty for traditional theism lies in what he calls "nondisciplinary evil"—"unnecessary" or "excess" evil, an action or condition "whose destructive effect, so far as we know, is greater than any good which may come from it." The problem posed by this sort of evil is: "If God is all-powerful and all-knowing, he could have framed a universe in which the unnecessary afflictions of evil were absent. If God is omnipotent and therefore the creator of so much evil, how can he be good? Or, if he is good, and did not intend evil, can he be omnipotent in the sense defined?" Limitations of memory and intelligence cripple human efforts to adjust to nature and to cure physical and mental illnesses; these hindrances cannot be the best an omnipotent and omniscient God could have done. The traditional view of God also cannot explain the "radical disproportion" between human faults and the consequences that result from them: human beings do commit wrongs and injure each other, but one is hard pressed to understand why the effects of such wrongdoing should be disproportionately painful or should fall so heavily on the innocent. These consequences serve no pedagogical purpose and are, therefore, nondisciplinary. Finally, the traditional view cannot explain the suffering produced by natural evils such as tidal waves and earthquakes or that which is undergone by animals in the evolutionary struggle for existence. If such phenomena are part of the intention of an omnipotent God, then one can question whether God's power is controlled by his love.

On the other hand, Bertocci says, God's goodness is sufficiently attested to in the world that one has no adequate grounds for supposing him to be perverse. This goodness of God, along with the difficulties and paradoxes presented by the notion of omnipotence, suggest that a limitation on or impediment to God's power exists. Such an impediment could result either from an external constraint—an uncreated environment coeternal with God—or from "a recalcitrant aspect of God's own nature." Following Brightman, Bertocci chooses the second option as the most plausible one.

Bertocci and Brightman identify an aspect of God that God cannot completely control; they call it "The Given." It comprises a rational part—the laws of logic and ethical principles or ideals—and a nonrational part comparable to human desires, pains, and sensations. In its basic structure, thus, God's experience does not differ essentially from that of human beings. The nonra-

tional aspect of God gives rise to the unnecessary and excess evil, both natural and moral, in the world.

Bertocci maintains that this concept of a God with limitations is acceptable to the religious consciousness, because it provides for growth in God and in God's relationship to human beings. If God had no unrealized goals, no change or growth in God's experiences would be possible. Yet, since God has created human beings with the freedom to choose and to act, goals God has not yet realized through these cocreators must exist. God's moral perfection is not a static one but, rather, one that thrives on building, fulfilling, and sustaining. This energizing of growth is God's major function.

In 1953 Bertocci was a visiting professor at San Jose State College in California. On 25 February of that year Brightman died, and Bertocci was chosen to succeed him as Borden Parker Bowne Professor of Philosophy at Boston University. He was a visiting professor at the University of Vermont in 1956. In 1958 he, Jannette Elthina Newhall, and Brightman's son, Robert, published their edition of Brightman's unfinished last work, *Person and Reality: An Introduction to Metaphysics*.

Bertocci was a Fulbright Research Scholar in India in 1960–1961 and served as president of both the American Theological Society and the Metaphysical Society of America in 1963–1964. In 1963 he collaborated with Richard M. Millard on *Personality and the Good: Psychological and Ethical Perspectives*. According to their ethical perspective, which they call "normative universalism," the norms for value experience are not in human beings alone nor in the structure of things outside them. Rather, "norms" are hypotheses about the best way or ways for human beings, in interaction with the total environment, to preserve and increase values. "The life good to live," Bertocci and Millard remark, is "a symphony of values."

In part 1 of *Personality and the Good* Bertocci and Millard explain theories of personality proposed by such psychologists as Allport, Abraham Maslow, and Harry Stack Sullivan, focusing on their philosophical implications for the nature of the good life. In part 2 they assess problems about human wants, freedom, and obligation that are linked with ethical theory and offer solutions. A pivotal conception for Bertocci and Millard is the uniqueness of the experience of "oughting." The experience of an "ought" is not reducible to the experience of either a "want" or a "must," they explain, and an adequate psychology will recognize its irreducible character. Moreover, an adequate ethical theory of the good must not insist that the "ought" has no connection with the "is."

In part 3 Bertocci and Millard offer a theory of value and of the good life that is supported by their psychological and ethical analyses. In part 4 they discuss and offer fresh support for the "moral laws" postulated by Brightman. Finally, in part 5 they indicate the application of this view of duty, virtues, values, and the good life to the choices a person makes in regard to the social order, love and sex, and religion.

Bertocci was appointed a Guggenheim Fellow for 1967–1968. In *Sex, Love, and the Person* (1967) he elaborates on the "ventures" of love and sex as aspects of the larger "symphony of values." The meanings of sex, love, and personhood are determined, he says, not in isolation but by their place in the context of one's life as a whole. For the relationship between a man and a woman to be refreshing and creative, the commitment of love, marriage, and home is required. In this framework, love and sex contribute to the development and growth of persons. Home, in particular, provides the "creative matrix" that makes possible those "unfinished symphonies" that bestow quality and meaning on living.

Bertocci elaborates his personalist view of the divine in *The Person God Is* (1970). His understanding of God's personhood is derived in part from Brightman's philosophy and in part from his own rethinking of why this "symbol" or "model" of God is more appropriate than others. Central to his conception are the ideas of God as a purposive designer, of God having only finite power, and of God suffering because of human abuses of freedom.

To call God a person, Bertocci explains, is to say that God is "self-identical"; self-identity entails having a unity of being that abides, while the particular content or quality of one's experience changes. As a person, God is capable of knowing, remembering, imagining, reasoning, feeling, wanting, willing, and caring; throughout these diverse activities he remains a "unity-in-continuity." As a "cosmic Knower," God is the source of unity and continuity in the universe; human beings can be assured of coming to know the interconnections of nature because they are the expression of a mind not wholly unlike their own. As a person, God is self-conscious: he knows the difference between himself and the world and is capable of acting in terms of rational ideals. By analogy with human experiences and human actions, one can ascribe to God the actions of thinking and loving, which constitute the "creative matrix" for all goodness. God is committed to the growth of human persons within a community of which he is a member.

Bertocci refers to the interaction between God and human beings as "creative insecurity," which means that God loves people "unto forgiveness." Even from the perspective of human experience, Bertocci points out, this sort of love describes how persons achieve self-fulfillment in their relationships with one another. Forgiveness makes possible improvement,

Dust jacket for Bertocci's 1967 book, in which he places love, sex, marriage, and home in a "symphony of values" (Bruccoli Clark Layman Archives)

growth, and creativity by bringing people into a community of mutual concern. Loving another person brings into being new dimensions in one's own life and in the life of the other. Through loving, one learns about oneself and one's fellow human beings. The highest good is realized in a community in which persons respect and care for each other.

Bertocci maintains that the traditional doctrine that God created the universe ex nihilo does not imply that he made something literally out of "nothing," which is not even thinkable. Instead, it means that God is the creative ground of all that is. To say that God creates out of nothing is to reject the notion that independent, coeternal entities exist along with God and is also to reject the pantheistic position that God is identical with the universe. Created beings depend on God's will for whatever independence they have, and God's continuous activity and involvement make the orderliness of the universe possible. This conception protects the individuality and freedom both of human beings and of God.

Bertocci complains that alternative accounts of creation, which fail to acknowledge God as a creator of cocreators, are incompatible with human beings' genuine power of choosing within the range of their possibilities. Humans have a delegated responsibility for the "subcreations" that result from their choices; the chief of these subcreations is the individual's own character. God's purpose requires "a community of responsive-responsible persons as the norm of creation and history." Only a God whose power is finite and whose quality of life is inextricably linked to the freedom of created beings, Bertocci concludes, is worthy of worship.

During his years at Boston University, Bertocci lectured at more than 175 other institutions. He officially retired in 1975 but continued to write and speak. He edited a volume of prayers by Allport, *Waiting for the Lord: Thirty-Three Meditations on God and Man* (1978), and wrote a seven-hundred-page manuscript on philosophical psychology. In 1981 he published *The Goodness of God,* in which he attempts to explain what he calls the "creative teleology" of personalistic theism through an analogy with a musical composition:

> The Composer, the Creator-Person, in accordance with comprehensive ideals intrinsic to His nature (the rational Given), envisages a tremendous symphony whose movements and motifs will be such that many orders of instrumentation will be required. The Composer, let us say, has selected the compatible orders without which finite composers and musicians cannot function . . . and these orders require His, the Composer-Conductor's, contemporaneous attention as the basis for continuity and for further creativity.

Goodness consists in this symphony of values; it is the continual realization in harmonious activity of all of one's capabilities, the achievement of self-fulfillment in interactive relationships with other beings, including God, within a communal context. A perfect being would experience no inconsistency among its purposes, actions, and feelings; all would blend harmoniously. This ideal can never be reached, but it can serve as a source of inspiration and as a goal.

Returning to the theodicy of *Introduction to the Philosophy of Religion,* Bertocci reiterates the distinction between the rational and nonrational Given within God's complex but unified nature. The recalcitrant elements within the nonrational Given limit God's power, and his knowledge is limited because he cannot foresee the consequences of his struggle with these recalcitrant aspects. Because he does not know for certain what will happen, his delegation of creativity to human beings carries risks for both God and humans. God's goodness and love lie, in part, precisely in his willingness to subject himself to these risks: "It is the relentless care of the Creator-Person Who, unflinchingly facing resistance within His own being, creates and participates in the risky co-creativity of persons in every dimension of their lives."

God's creating is, thus, bound up with what Bertocci calls "the 'tragic' goodness of God." The tragic aspect is the inevitable pain that God inflicts on himself by his commitment to allow cocreation at the human level, since this cocreation inevitably results in the production of nondisciplinary evil. Since "*to be creative is to be insecure, be it in God or persons,*" realization of the "symphony of values" is inseparable from creative insecurity. Because of his delegation of genuine freedom to human agents, God must work through the consequences that result from their abuse of this freedom. Nonetheless, this "insecure" situation is precisely the context in which God "realizes Himself." The orchestration of mutually enhancing values in community is "the lure and task of every creative factor in the Creator-Person's world."

Creativity at the human level is manifested in the bringing into being of character, which is a joint production of divine and human activity. Like God's creativity, it is not devoid of hardship and even of suffering; indeed, suffering is integral to it. At its best, however, this suffering is characterized by "blessedness" in that the human interchange with "the More," as Bertocci sometimes refers to God, in religious experience revitalizes the individual. Commitment to "the God who cares" is commitment to cocreativity of an "unfinished symphony of values." Bertocci offers "a minimal interpretation of prayer" as an instance of "religious co-creation": "Prayer becomes the occasion for God's creative response in ways, conscious and unconscious, relevant to the suppliant's preparation for change and growth."

Bertocci's final book was *The Person and Primary Emotions* (1988), in which he outlines some of his work on philosophical psychology. Weakened by Parkinson's disease, he died in his sleep at his home in Arlington, Massachusetts, on 13 October 1989. The January 1990 issue of *Proceedings and Addresses of the American Philosophical Association* included a tribute from his Boston personalist colleague Erazim V. Kohák: "Most of all, Peter Bertocci was a teacher, actively and genuinely committed to the nurture of the persons who were his students and his colleagues. All of us who remember him as a colleague remain grateful for his unfailing willingness to hear, to encourage, to comfort, to support and, in gentle ways, to teach us what moral personhood is all about."

Bibliographies:
John Howie, "Bibliography of Peter Anthony Bertocci," in *Contemporary Studies in Philosophical Idealism,*

edited by Howie and Thomas O. Buford (Cape Cod, Mass.: Claude Stark, 1975), pp. 263–282;

Howie and Peter J. Bertocci, "Bibliography of Peter Anthony Bertocci," *Personalist Forum,* 7 (Spring 1991): 91–113.

References:

Gordon W. Allport, "Motivation in Personality: Reply to Peter A. Bertocci," in *Understanding Human Motivation,* edited by Chalmers L. Stacey and Manfred F. DeMartino (Cleveland: Howard Allen, 1958), pp. 105–120;

Allport, "Peter Bertocci: Philosopher-Psychologist," *Philosophical Forum,* 21 (1963–1964): 3–7;

Angelo P. Bertocci, *Teacher from Little Italy* (Washington, D.C.: Legation Press, 1990);

James J. Brummer, "Dignity and the Person: A Defense of Impartiality in Ethics," dissertation, Boston University, 1980;

J. H. Kentigern Connelly, "The Role of Self-Experience in Personality Theory: A Study of the Allport-Bertocci Debate," dissertation, University of Ottawa, 1974;

Thomas Edward Damer, "Value in the Thought of Peter A. Bertocci and A. Campbell Garnett: A Comparison of Two Theistic Theories," dissertation, Boston University, 1970;

Allie M. Frazier, "Creative Events," *Philosophical Forum,* 21 (1963–1964): 16–18;

Hywel David Lewis, "Reply to Professor Bertocci," *Religious Studies,* 15 (September 1979): 407–409;

Robert F. Milde, "The Influence of Personalism on the Laws of the Roman Catholic Church during and since the Second Vatican Council," dissertation, New York University, 1978;

J. B. Pratt, "Comments and Criticisms (Bertocci and Lamprecht)," *Journal of Philosophy,* 36 (1939): 263–274;

Ervin Smith, "The Role of Personalism in the Development of the Social Ethics of Martin Luther King, Jr.," dissertation, Northwestern University, 1976;

James E. Will, "Implications for Philosophical Theology in the Confrontation of American Personalism with Depth Psychology," dissertation, Columbia University, 1962.

Brand Blanshard

(27 August 1892 – 18 November 1987)

John Howie

Southern Illinois University at Carbondale

BOOKS: *The Church and the Polish Immigrant* (New York: A. C. Barnes, 1920);

The Nature of Thought, 2 volumes (London: Allen & Unwin, 1939; New York: Macmillan, 1940);

The Great Commandment (Philadelphia: Friends General Conference, 1944);

The Uses of a Liberal Education (Norton, Mass.: Wheaton College, 1949); enlarged as *The Uses of a Liberal Education, and Other Talks to Students,* edited by Eugene Freeman (La Salle, Ill.: Open Court, 1973);

On Philosophical Style (Manchester, U.K.: University of Manchester Press, 1954; Bloomington & London: Indiana University Press, 1954);

Sources of Serenity (Buck Hill Falls, Pa.: Foxhowe Association, 1954);

The Impass in Ethics—and a Way Out (Berkeley & Los Angeles: University of California Press, 1955);

Reason and Goodness (London: Allen & Unwin / New York: Macmillan, 1961);

Reason and Analysis (La Salle, Ill.: Open Court, 1962; London: Allen & Unwin, 1962);

On Sanity in Thought and Art (Tucson: University of Arizona Press, 1962);

The Life of the Spirit in a Machine Age (Northampton, Mass.: Smith College, 1967);

Reason and Belief (London: Allen & Unwin, 1974; New Haven: Yale University Press, 1975);

Four Reasonable Men: Marcus Aurelius, John Stuart Mill, Ernest Renan, Henry Sidgwick (Middletown, Conn.: Wesleyan University Press, 1984).

OTHER: *In Commemoration of William James, 1842–1942,* edited by Blanshard and Herbert W. Schneider (New York: Columbia University Press, 1942);

"The Climate of Opinion," "The Opportunity of Philosophy," "The Basic Courses in Philosophy: Ethics," and "The Basic Courses in Philosophy: Metaphysics," by Blanshard and C. J. Ducasse, in *Philosophy in American Education: Its Tasks and Oppor-*

Brand Blanshard (photograph © 1984 by Kelly Wise; from the dust jacket for Four Reasonable Men: Marcus Aurelius, John Stuart Mill, Ernest Renan, Henry Sidgwick, *1984)*

tunities (New York & London: Harper, 1945), pp. 3–42, 87–117, 221–224, 227–232;

"Personal Ethics," in *Preface to Philosophy,* edited by William Pearson Tolley (New York: Macmillan, 1946), pp. 103–195;

"Can Men Be Reasonable?" in *Our Emergent Civilization,* edited by Ruth Nanda Ashen (New York & London: Harper, 1947), pp. 25–48;

"The Escape from Philosophic Futility," in *Freedom and Experience: Essays Presented to Horace M. Kallen,* edited by Sidney Hook and Milton R. Konvitz

(Ithaca, N.Y. & New York: Cornell University Press, 1947), pp. 191–204;

"Speculative Thinkers," in *Literary History of the United States,* 2 volumes, edited by Robert E. Spiller, Willard Thorp, Thomas H. Johnson, and Henry Seidel Canby (New York: Macmillan, 1948), II: 1273–1296;

"The Heritage of Idealism," in *Changing Patterns in American Civilization* (Philadelphia: University of Pennsylvania Press, 1949), pp. 82–124;

"Philosophy Teaching, Past and Present," in *The Teaching of Philosophy,* edited by Frederick P. Harris (Cleveland: Western Reserve University Press, 1950), pp. 1–12;

"Psychology and Psychotherapy," in *The Nature of Man: His World, His Spiritual Resources, His Destiny,* edited by A. William Loos and Lawrence B. Chrow (New York: Church Peace Union and the World Alliance for International Fellowship through Religion, 1950), pp. 29–36;

"The Nature of Mind," in *American Philosophers at Work: The Philosophic Scene in the United States,* edited by Hook (New York: Criterion, 1956), pp. 183–193;

"Absolute," in *Encyclopaedia Britannica,* volume 1 (Chicago, London & Toronto: Encyclopaedia Britannica, 1956), p. 64;

"The Case for Determinism," in *Determinism and Freedom,* edited by Hook (New York: New York University Press, 1958), pp. 3–15;

Education in the Age of Science, edited by Blanshard (New York: Basic Books, 1959);

"Broad's Conception of Reason," in *The Philosophy of C. D. Broad,* edited by Paul Arthur Schilpp, The Library of Living Philosophers, volume 10 (New York: Tudor, 1959), pp. 233–262;

"Values: The Polestar of Education," in *The Goals of Higher Education,* edited by Willis D. Weatherford Jr. (Cambridge, Mass.: Harvard University Press, 1960), pp. 76–98;

"What Is Education For?" in *Education in a Free Society* (Pittsburgh: University of Pittsburgh Press, 1960), pp. 40–62;

"Symbolism," in *Religious Experience and Truth: A Symposium,* edited by Hook (New York: New York University Press, 1961), pp. 48–54;

"Conformity and Human Nature" and "Conformity and the Intellectual Task," in *Conformity* (Indianola, Iowa: Simpson College, 1962), pp. 11–21, 54–64;

"The Test of a University," in *Man, Science, Learning and Education: The Semicentennial Lectures at Rice University,* edited by Sanford Wilson Higginbotham, Rice University Studies, volume 49, supplement 2 (Houston: Rice University, 1963), pp. 21–40;

Arthur Pap, *Semantics and Necessary Truth,* foreword by Blanshard (New Haven: Yale University Press, 1966);

"A Verdict on Epiphenomenalism," in *Current Philosophical Issues: Essays in Honor of Curt John Ducasse,* edited by Frederick C. Dommeyer (Springfield, Ill.: Charles C. Thomas, 1966), pp. 105–126;

"In Defense of Metaphysics," in *Metaphysics: Readings and Reappraisals,* edited by W. E. Kennick and Morris Lazerowitz (Englewood Cliffs, N.J.: Prentice-Hall, 1966), pp. 331–355;

Warren Steinkraus, ed., *New Studies in Berkeley's Philosophy,* foreword by Blanshard (New York: Holt, Rinehart & Winston, 1966);

"Morality and Politics," in *Ethics and Society: Original Essays on Contemporary Moral Problems,* edited by Paul Kurtz (Garden City, N.Y.: Doubleday, 1966), pp. 1–23;

"Wisdom," in *The Encyclopedia of Philosophy,* 8 volumes, edited by Paul Edwards (New York: Macmillan & The Free Press / London: Collier-Macmillan, 1967), VIII: 322–324;

"Retribution Revisited," in *Philosophical Perspectives on Punishment,* edited by Edward H. Madden, Rollo Handy, and Marvin Farber (Springfield, Ill.: Charles C. Thomas, 1968), pp. 59–81;

"The Limits of Naturalism," in *Mind, Science, and History,* edited by Howard E. Kiefer and Milton K. Munitz (Albany: State University of New York Press, 1970), pp. 3–33;

Frances Margaret Blanshard, *Frank Aydelotte of Swarthmore,* edited and completed by Brand Blanshard (Middletown, Conn.: Wesleyan University Press, 1970);

"John Dewey," "William James," "Josiah Royce," and "George Santayana," in *The Penguin Companion to American Literature,* edited by Malcolm Bradbury, Eric Mottram, and Jean Franco (New York: McGraw-Hill, 1971), pp. 72–73, 134–135, 224, 227–228;

"Rationalism in Ethics and Religion," in *Mid-Twentieth Century American Philosophy: Personal Statements,* edited by Peter Anthony Bertocci (New York: Humanities Press, 1974), pp. 20–46;

"Reflections on Economic Determinism," in *Dialogues on the Philosophy of Marxism,* edited by John Somerville and Howard L. Parsons (Westport, Conn. & London: Greenwood Press, 1974);

"The Philosophic Enterprise," in *The Owl of Minerva: Philosophers on Philosophy,* edited by Charles J. Bontempo and S. Jack Odell (New York: McGraw-Hill, 1975), pp. 163–177;

"Democracy and Distinction in American Education," in *On the Meaning of the University,* edited by Sterling

M. McMurrin (Salt Lake City: University of Utah Press, 1976), pp. 29–49;

"Practical Reason: Reason and Feeling in 20th-Century Ethics," in *The Abdication of Philosophy: Philosophy and the Public Good,* edited by Eugene Freeman (La Salle, Ill.: Open Court, 1976), pp. 49–65;

"Autobiography of Brand Blanshard" and replies to critics, in *The Philosophy of Brand Blanshard,* edited by Schilpp, The Library of Living Philosophers, volume 15 (La Salle, Ill.: Open Court, 1980), pp. 3–185, 209–219, 237–246, 259–266, 288–296, 314–319, 341–353, 364–378, 402–419, 446–462, 471–477, 510–523, 540–547, 568–573, 589–600, 618–628, 636–645, 664–672, 686–695, 725–741, 756–773, 807–821, 832–841, 854–860, 869–877, 892–905, 930–943, 977–993, 1002–1014, 1040–1055, 1085–1099;

"Bradley on Relations," in *The Philosophy of F. H. Bradley,* edited by Anthony Manser and Guy Stock (Oxford: Clarendon Press, 1984), pp. 211–226;

Studies in Personalism: Selected Writings of Edgar Sheffield Brightman, edited by Warren E. Steinkraus and Robert N. Beck, foreword by Blanshard (Utica, N.Y.: Meridian, 1989).

SELECTED PERIODICAL PUBLICATIONS–
UNCOLLECTED: "Behaviorism and the Theory of Knowledge," *Philosophical Review,* 37 (July 1928): 328–352;

"The Nature of Mind," *Journal of Philosophy,* 38 (April 1941): 207–216;

"Current Strictures on Reason," *Philosophical Review,* 54 (July 1945): 345–368;

"Current Strictures on Reason: A Rejoinder," *Philosophical Review,* 55 (November 1946): 670–673;

"The New Subjectivism in Ethics," *Philosophy and Phenomenological Research,* 9 (March 1949): 504–511;

"Subjectivism in Ethics–a Criticism," *Philosophical Quarterly,* 1 (January 1951): 127–139;

"The Philosophy of Analysis," *Proceedings of the British Academy,* 38 (1952): 39–69;

"Can the Philosopher Influence Social Change?" *Journal of Philosophy,* 51 (November 1954): 741–753;

"The Objectivity of Moral Judgment," *Revue internationale de philosophie,* 18 (1964): 361–378;

"Reflections on Economic Determinism," *Journal of Philosophy,* 63 (March 1966): 169–178;

"Reason and Unreason in Religion," *Zygon,* 1 (June 1966): 200–204;

"The Problem of Consciousness–a Debate," by Blanshard and B. F. Skinner, *Philosophy and Phenomenological Research,* 27 (March 1967): 317–337;

"Internal Relations and Their Importance to Philosophy" and "Rejoinder to My Critics," *Review of Metaphysics,* 21 (December 1967): 227–236, 262–272;

"Current Issues in Education," *Monist,* 52 (January 1968): 11–17;

"The Liberal in Religion," *Humanist,* 28 (May–June 1968): 11–14;

"Rejoinder to Mr. Kearns," *Philosophy and Phenomenological Research,* 29 (September 1968): 116–118;

"Humanists Reply," *Humanist,* 34 (January–February 1974): 9;

"A Reply to My Critics," *Idealistic Studies,* 4 (May 1974): 107–130;

"Rationalism and Humanism," *Humanist,* 34 (November–December 1974): 24–27;

"On Rationalism: A Reply to Professor Harris," *Idealistic Studies,* 10 (May 1980): 95–106;

"One Man's Humanism," *Free Inquiry,* 3 (1983): 14–15;

"The Habit of Reason," *Free Inquiry,* 6 (1985): 22–25.

Widely acclaimed as "the philosopher's philosopher," Brand Blanshard was known for his original thinking about the role of reason in human life. He delivered both the Gifford Lectures and the Paul Carus Lectures–a distinction he shared with only one other American philosopher, John Dewey. The American Philosophical Association ranked Blanshard's first philosophical book, *The Nature of Thought* (1939), one of the ten outstanding books in the field published in the United States in the twentieth century. He won an international reputation for the clarity and grace of his literary style; in many philosophers' libraries his *On Philosophical Style* (1954) can be found alongside William Strunk and E. B. White Jr.'s *The Elements of Style* (1959).

Percy Brand Blanshard and his fraternal twin, Paul, were born on 27 August 1892 in Fredericksburg, Ohio, to Francis George Blanshard, the minister of a Congregational church, and Emily Coulter Blanshard. Both parents had emigrated from Canada. In the autobiography he contributed to the Library of Living Philosophers volume *The Philosophy of Brand Blanshard* (1980) Blanshard explains the spelling of his surname: "A few generations back in my father's line was a French Huguenot who had brought to England the good French name of Blanchard. He seems to have wanted to retain the French pronunciation, so he spelled his name in English with an 's'. . . . This spelling has been a nuisance. It pointlessly disguises the old French name, and since the 'c' form is almost universal, the variant is constantly misspelled, and people cannot find me in the telephone book." Before the boys were a year old, their mother died of burns from a kerosene fire while she and they were visiting her parents on a farm near Toronto. Shortly after her death, Francis Blanshard was diagnosed with tuberculosis. Taking his sons and his parents with him, he returned to Oberlin Seminary to finish his degree, then accepted the pastorate of a Congregational church in Grand Rapids, Michigan. In 1899 the family moved to Edinburg, Ohio. In 1902, on medical advice, Francis Blanshard left his sons with his mother, Orminda Adams Blanshard—his father had died in Oberlin—and took an extended trip west in search of a dry climate. He died in Albuquerque, New Mexico, in March 1904 without having been able to return to his family.

The twins were raised by their grandmother amid real poverty and with great strictness: a highly religious woman, she disapproved of dancing, theatergoing, smoking, drinking, playing on the Sabbath, swearing, reading novels (with some exceptions), and all but the most carefully regulated interest in the opposite sex. After a few years in Edinburg she purchased a small cabin in Bay View, Michigan, which had been founded in 1875 as a community for Methodist retreats that were similar to the Chautauqua assemblies in upstate New York. Each summer Bay View drew singers, actors, lecturers, and preachers; during these retreats Brand and Paul ran a newsstand, ordering newspapers from the hometowns of the summer visitors for two or three cents apiece and selling them for a nickel. Later, the brothers wrote columns about the retreats for the *Petoskey Daily Resorter,* a newspaper published in a nearby town.

In his autobiography Blanshard remarks that he was especially struck by the variety of rhetorical styles he encountered at the summer retreats: "This was the beginning of a lasting interest first in spoken, and then in written, style. With saw and hammer I made a speaker's stand, set it up in a clump of birch trees, and proceeded to read and speechify to the breezes, with the trees rustling their applause." Blanshard recalls hearing William Jennings Bryan deliver his talk "The Prince of Peace," in which he argued that God must exist because no other force could bring a watermelon into being through so small a stem. At the time Blanshard was planning to follow his father into the ministry.

In 1908 Orminda Blanshard and her grandsons moved to Detroit, where the boys finished high school. In 1910 the three moved to Ann Arbor so that the twins could attend the University of Michigan. For the next three years Brand Blanshard immersed himself in Greek and Latin literature. As a sophomore he took his first course in philosophy, an introductory class taught by Robert Mark Wenley, in the hope of finding certainty in religion; he could not accept his grandmother's fundamentalism. The following year Wenley selected him to grade students' papers for the course. Among Blanshard's favorite professors in the philosophy department were DeWitt Parker and Roy Wood Sellars,

whose son, Wilfrid, was later a colleague of Blanshard's at Yale University.

During his junior year Blanshard was awarded a Rhodes Scholarship. At the University of Oxford, Harold H. Joachim, a disciple of the idealist F. H. Bradley, was his tutor. Blanshard recalls in his autobiography that having Joachim read and comment on one's essay was "a chastening experience": he required exact expression, impeccable logic, and an absence of metaphor. At Oxford, Blanshard met the future poet T. S. Eliot; four years Blanshard's senior, Eliot was preparing a dissertation on Bradley with Joachim as his tutor.

Bradley himself had a reputation as a stern and crotchety recluse: he never lectured, did not take pupils, and would not discuss philosophy even with his peers at Oxford. When Blanshard wrote to him asking for clarification on certain points of his logic, however, Bradley granted the student an interview. Blanshard found Bradley a "Victorian gentleman" who spoke in "rounded paragraphs" of "neat, crisp sentences." He admired Bradley's insistence that human experience is woven with necessary connections and that thought, at its best, is a rational movement and not "a mere drifting along a line of associations." Blanshard was also drawn to a religious vein in Bradley's thought: in the preface to *Appearance and Reality: A Metaphysical Essay* (1893) Bradley says that for some people philosophy, particularly metaphysics, is a means of experiencing deity.

Other philosophers at Oxford who influenced Blanshard included C. C. J. Webb, who served as his thesis adviser, and Hastings Rashdall, who lectured on idealism and its critics. Blanshard also attended weekly conferences in the rooms of J. A. Smith, Waynflete Professor of Metaphysics and one of the editors of the Oxford translation of the works of Aristotle (1912–1954).

At the beginning of World War I in August 1914 Blanshard returned from a summer trip to Germany to find the tenor of life at Oxford changed. Most undergraduate activities were canceled, and many of his friends had enlisted. Blanshard joined the YMCA (Young Men's Christian Association), which sent him to India in August 1915. He was in Bombay for only a week before being transferred to the city of Basra in Mesopotamia (today Iraq), where he was appointed head of YMCA activities at the British base camp. He returned to Bombay in the late spring of 1916 and left for the United States in June 1917. On the steamship voyage from Japan to San Francisco he read Henry Sidgwick's *Methods of Ethics* (1874; revised, 1877). Although he did not agree with Sidgwick's hedonism, he admired the style in which the book was written.

On his return home, Blanshard discovered that he and his brother had each received $500 from their

THE NATURE
OF
THOUGHT

Muirhead Library of Philosophy

BRAND
BLANSHARD

LONDON : GEORGE ALLEN AND UNWIN
NEW YORK : THE MACMILLAN COMPANY

*Dust jacket for the third printing (1955) of the work, originally published
in two volumes in 1939, in which Blanshard elaborates his rationalistic
worldview. The American Philosophical Association designated this
work one of the ten outstanding twentieth-century American books
in the field (Bruccoli Clark Layman Archives)*

"The theory appeared in his educational work as a defense of learning by doing, in his ethics as a doctrine of growth as the end, in his philosophy of religion through an interpretation of faith as dedication to long-range ends, in the history of philosophy as a devaluation of the Greek philosophical tradition." For Blanshard, the chief error of Dewey's pragmatism can be traced to his theory of thought. Blanshard denied that the cognitive value of a thought and its practical significance are equivalent; he believed that the truth of a claim can be considered apart from its utility.

In the spring of 1918 Blanshard received his M.A. in philosophy from Columbia with a thesis on David Hume's theory of judgment. Around the same time the University of Michigan awarded him the B.A. degree Phi Beta Kappa, even though he had never completed his studies there.

That summer Blanshard took part in a research project funded by the wealthy pharmaceutical manufacturer and art collector Albert C. Barnes, a friend and admirer of Dewey's. Barnes, who had been sitting in on Dewey's class in social philosophy, proposed that Dewey and some of his graduate students undertake a study of a Polish immigrant community in Philadelphia that was resisting "Americanization." Each member of the group dealt with a particular aspect of the community's life; Blanshard's assignment was to examine its religious attitudes. His report, *The Church and the Polish Immigrant*, was published by Barnes in 1920.

Toward the end of the summer of 1918 Blanshard was drafted into the army. On 3 November he married Frances Margaret Bradshaw, whom he had met at Columbia and worked with on the Philadelphia project. Almost immediately after the wedding he was shipped out to France, where he managed paperwork for a military hospital. He was discharged ten months later and returned to Oxford, accompanied by his wife, for a final year of study. He completed a thesis on Dewey's theory of judgment, with W. D. (later Sir David) Ross and H. W. B. Joseph as his readers and examiners. In his autobiography Blanshard acknowledges his debt to Joseph for helping him to see that "mind at all its levels is irreducibly teleological."

Blanshard was awarded a Sears Scholarship at Harvard for the academic year 1920–1921; his wife was hired as an instructor in English at Wellesley College. With C. I. Lewis as his director and William Ernest Hocking as his second reader, Blanshard completed a dissertation on the nature of judgment in May 1921 and received his Ph.D.

In the fall of 1921 Blanshard took his first full-time teaching position as an assistant professor of philosophy at his alma mater, the University of Michigan. In 1925 he became an associate professor at Swarth-

father's insurance policy and that his share had compounded to $900 in fifteen years. Blanshard applied the money toward a year of study at Columbia University under Dewey, W. P. Montague, and Frederick J. E. Woodbridge. Blanshard was especially impressed by Montague's succinct, lucid, and orderly teaching style; by contrast, he was initially disappointed with Dewey's lectures. In his autobiography he says that Dewey gave the impression of simply thinking aloud in the presence of the students; later, however, when one looked over one's notes, one could see that the argument had progressed in an orderly manner. According to Blanshard, Dewey "biologized philosophy," holding that thought is an instrument of organic adjustment. Dewey developed his "instrumentalism" into a sweeping and multifaceted perspective, Blanshard notes in his autobiography:

more College; his wife took a job in the administration of the college, ultimately becoming academic dean. During his first year at Swarthmore, Blanshard helped to found the Fullerton Club, the members of which met regularly to deliver and discuss papers on philosophy; the club was named for George Stuart Fullerton, a University of Pennsylvania philosopher who had recently died.

In 1929 Blanshard received a Guggenheim Fellowship that provided him a free year to work on the manuscript for *The Nature of Thought*. He spent the summer in France and Vienna and the rest of the year in England and completed the first four hundred pages of the book.

In 1932 Blanshard joined the New York Philosophy Club, which met once a month at Columbia University. At that time its membership included Dewey, Woodbridge, Montague, and Herbert W. Schneider; Ernest Nagel, Irwin Edman, and John Herman Randall Jr. were among those who joined in later years. Faculty members of the Union Theological Seminary in New York, including Reinhold Niebuhr, William Adams Brown, and Paul Tillich, also attended the meetings.

Blanshard completed *The Nature of Thought* during another trip to England in 1938. By that time the work had become unwieldy in length, and Blanshard doubted whether any publisher would take it. On an impulse, however, he decided to take it to Allen and Unwin, whose London office he had often passed. *The Nature of Thought* appeared in two volumes the following fall as part of the Muirhead Library of Philosophy.

The Nature of Thought explores the rational movement of thought and the correlative rationality or intelligibility of the world. In his autobiography Blanshard provides a succinct account of how he arrived at his views. Influenced by the seventeenth-century rationalist philosopher Baruch Spinoza, as well as by Bradley and Joachim, he had come to believe that human nature includes a basic desire for "an understanding of the world, a vision of the whole, in which the nature and place of each thing is to be understood only by seeing its place in an overall inclusive order." He further profited from a study and critique of then-prominent psychological accounts of thought. In his view, neither associationism nor behaviorism could account for the contention that thought has its own end: understanding or rational insight. He explains that he came to this view through reading the works of L. T. Hobhouse and William McDougall and, more directly, through reflection on his own mental processes. Such introspection reveals that the mind is goal oriented in terms of both the range and the nature of options it considers. As examples he cites the thought involved in buying a birthday present or writing a poem with a given meter.

The teleological view of mind excludes the notion that mental processes can be explained mechanically, without reference to ends. Another major influence, Blanshard says, was Dewey, much of whose *How We Think* (1910) he accepted. Blanshard agreed with Dewey that thought was a biological instrument of adjustment and survival for primitive humans, but he was unwilling to concede that it had remained what it was in the beginning. In the study of geometry or history, for example, the emphasis is on knowing, not on doing. According to Blanshard, Dewey confused truth and utility. In primitive thought, practical motives took precedence over the desire for knowledge for its own sake; but even then, both concerns were present to some degree. An isolated fact will not provide the desired understanding; a context is required. Blanshard uses as an example the question "What is the Panama Canal?" To answer that it is a waterway with locks allowing ships to pass from one ocean to another is not sufficient. What must be described is the relationship between the Caribbean and Pacific mouths of the canal and the importance for ships of the shorter route provided by the canal as opposed to going around the tip of South America.

The relationships sought by human thinking are of many kinds; the ones most important to the philosopher are those that answer the question "Why?" Only a knowledge of the "why" relations can fully satisfy the natural desire for understanding. Blanshard identifies three relationships that provide explanations: the relationship of means to ends, cause-and-effect relationships, and logical (that is, necessary) relationships. Only the third kind of relationship can answer the "why" question so decisively that it cannot be raised again. Human reasoning is under the control of a framework of necessary relations that is independent of the thinking subject; through recourse to this framework a person is able to see the necessary connections among things and thereby to understand them. Blanshard uses the example of the series 1, 3, 9. . . . When one is asked how one knows that 27 will be the next number in the sequence, one cannot simply respond, "I saw that the rule required it"; for one could only see what the rule required if one already knew what number must come next, and the explanation would then be circular. The correct answer is not that one perceives the rule but simply that the rule exists. The key lies in the structure of the series, not in one's thinking. This observation, Blanshard explains, is "a metaphysical watershed," for it reveals the existence of a logical order external to individual thought processes. By extension, Blanshard argues, one must also postulate the existence of aesthetic standards and moral necessities. In each case, what is essential is to realize that "why" questions have answers, whether or not one has discovered the answers.

The Nature of Thought elaborates these ideas. In the first volume Blanshard explores the notion that thought is a movement toward an end of its own; the human mind is purposive, and the movement of thought is, therefore, teleological. In the first six chapters he shows that purpose is operative even below the reflective level of human mental processes. The lowest level of thought is perception, which Blanshard defines as "that experience in which, on the warrant of something given in sensation at the time, we unreflectingly take some object to be before us." Perception thus always involves inference, and inference receives its directive from purpose. Purpose is, therefore, present in even the simplest act of perception.

Blanshard notes that Dewey rejects this view, because for him thought is always reflective; and reflection only occurs, according to Dewey, when normal responses are blocked and one needs to circumvent the block: without an obstacle there is no problem, and without a problem there is no thought. Blanshard responds that Dewey's view cannot account for errors in perception. If perception entails no thought but amounts only to an unintelligent sensation, how could perception be in error? For example, how could a person looking at curtains rustling in a dark hallway think that he was seeing a ghost?

The difference between animal thought and human thought, according to Blanshard, is the achievement by human beings of "free ideas": in animals, ideas remain tethered to sense, while humans can think about objects that are not currently being perceived. Blanshard then devotes several chapters to the array of theories psychologists and philosophers have proposed to explain human ideas. On the "common sense" view, an idea is an image that copies a thing; Bertrand Russell holds that ideas can be reduced to sensations, which, for him, exist in the realms of both mind and matter; for the behaviorist, an act of thought is a bodily response, and consciousness as such does not exist; for the realist, by contrast, consciousness exists, but ideas are replaced by mental acts; the critical realist holds that the essence, or "whatness," of a thing replaces one's idea of it. Blanshard rejects each of these theories on the way to developing his own. He devotes chapter 9 to John B. Watson's version of behaviorism, which he defines as "the theory that the mind may be adequately studied in the reactions of the body." Blanshard shows the inadequacy of Watson's identification of thought with speech by asking a series of pointed questions: can language vary while the thought remains the same? Can thoughts vary while the language is the same? Can speech be present without thought, and thought with-

out speech? To answer such questions the behaviorist must appeal to relations that are ruled out by his own theory.

In the next chapter Blanshard points out the flaws in the pragmatist theory of thought. He concentrates on Dewey, whose perspective he considers more original and carefully argued than those of Charles Sanders Peirce, William James, or F. C. S. Schiller. He singles out for detailed criticism the pragmatist view that ideas are plans of action, instruments with which to change one's environment. First, he appeals to the history of science, which shows that knowledge is sometimes sought for its own sake and that this disinterested search often brings about profound changes in human life. Second, the notion that thought is a means to practice runs counter to one's personal experience: self-examination indicates that an inner motive and an outer motive can often be distinguished, and that the inner motive may change while the outer one remains the same. Third, Blanshard objects that the pragmatist misconstrues what ordinary people mean when they ascribe a quality to an object, such as "sugar is sweet." For the pragmatist, this statement really means that when a lump of sugar is placed in the mouth, a certain sensation will follow. But for the ordinary person the meaning of the statement is that the sweetness can be ascribed directly to the lump; the quality is a present attribute, not the expectation of a future event. Following Arthur O. Lovejoy and Sterling P. Lamprecht, Blanshard contends that pragmatism, with its orientation toward future consequences, cannot account for ideas of past events.

Blanshard proceeds to develop his own theory of the idea. First, he states the problem to be solved: "The idea is thus an X which must satisfy many conditions, positive and negative. What sort of thing must that be which refers to an object, yet is not the object; which calls words and images an aid, yet is itself neither word nor copy; which changes with bodily changes, but is more than any bodily change; which is always a means to an end, though not always to an end that is practical?" He answers that an idea is related to its object as a purpose is related to its full realization. "When we say that an idea is *of* an object, we are saying that the idea is a purpose which the object alone would fulfill, that it is a potentiality which this object alone would actualize, a content informed by an impulse to become this object." He goes on to show that this view escapes the difficulties that the rival theories cannot overcome, and that it accords with what is known about the nature of mind, knowledge, and the empirical facts of thinking.

In the final two chapters of volume one Blanshard applies his theory to the old problem of the nature of general ideas. He uses the example of the class of col-

Blanshard with his wife, Frances Margaret Bradshaw Blanshard, and their dog at Swarthmore College
(photograph by Roger Russell)

ors: one can think of such a class and employ the concept in identifying colored things, but defining color as such is much more difficult. The difficulty lies in abstracting the essence of a class from the individual members of the class. Blanshard suggests that in speaking of color, people simply mean that which, if developed and specified, would realize itself in the experienced variety and range of colors. In other words, a general idea such as "color" or "human being" is an effort to realize in some degree within experience a range of individuals or specific instances in which the idea could recognize itself as fulfilled. Blanshard thus parts company with Plato and the German idealist philosopher Georg Wilhelm Friedrich Hegel in his theory of universals, but he is not a nominalist—that is, he does not claim that universals are mere words. He distinguishes three types of universals: universals embodied by individuals, such as animality; "qualitative universals," such as the concept of color, which are formed for mental convenience; and "specific universals," such as the colors red or blue, which are presented in sensation. Blanshard is a realist insofar as he contends that "specific universals" actually exist; but they are the only kind of universal to which he ascribes existence.

In the second volume of *The Nature of Thought* Blanshard offers an analysis of reflective thinking. Thought, he says, develops in a continuous manner from perception toward understanding. On the basis of experience, thought attempts to construct a world that will satisfy the intellect. At its core, thought is "a drive toward system," whether in an advanced or a rudimentary form. While this drive might be obvious in a discipline such as geometry, Blanshard claims that even accounts of the world of everyday experience aim at systematization—though here the lines of connection are often only vaguely drawn. In this context a problem is a felt need to assimilate something foreign into the familiar world of common sense.

Blanshard believes that his account of reflection provides more adequately for such phenomena as the "leap of invention" than do the behaviorist or associationist psychologies. No random parade of ideas can account for the insight that resolves a difficult problem. When an able mind adds up a series of numbers or solves an equation, the process has nothing groping or experimental about it. Thought is guided in its advance by the implicit ideal of a more perfect order in which its search can find fulfillment. This order need not be an all-comprehensive system; in actual thinking it is usually some minor one—the system of number if one is performing arithmetic, or some aesthetic whole if one is composing fiction, poetry, or music.

The Nature of Thought appeared in Britain just as the country was entering World War II, and it was not a great success. During the bombing of London the publisher's warehouse was hit, destroying half of the copies of Blanshard's book. Moreover, in the years since Blanshard had begun the work the currents of philosophy had begun to change, chiefly under the influence of the analytic philosopher Ludwig Wittgenstein. Nonetheless, *The Nature of Thought* was not completely ignored. Its publication in the United States in 1940 led to Blanshard's election as president of the Eastern Division of the American Philosophical Association for 1942.

Around 1942 Blanshard met Russell, who was living near Swarthmore. Blanshard most valued Russell for his appeal to reason as the ultimate arbiter of differences of viewpoint. Russell always presented reasons for his beliefs and would reconsider them if the reasons were shown to be unsound. This "great grey virtue," as Blanshard called it, is central to Blanshard's own philosophy.

In 1943 the Armed Forces Institute in Washington, D.C., asked Blanshard and three other leading philosophers—Hocking, Randall, and Charles W. Hendel, the chairman of the philosophy department at Yale University—to write an introduction to philosophy for soldiers who were continuing their education. The collaboration with Hendel led to an invitation for Blanshard to join the Yale faculty, and he did so in 1945 as a full professor and chairman of the philosophy department. Edited by William Pearson Tolley, *Preface to Philosophy* was published in 1946; Blanshard contributed the section titled "Personal Ethics." Accompanied by a companion volume of readings selected by Tolley, Ross Earle Hoople, and Raymond Frank Piper, the book was used widely in the military and was adopted as an introductory text at many universities. Also in 1946 Blanshard delivered the Dudleian Lecture at Harvard University.

Blanshard notes in his autobiography that the tutorial method he had employed at Swarthmore had little prepared him for the demands of lecturing to large classes of undergraduates at Yale. He was eventually able to lecture without notes, however, and to conclude his classes exactly at the end of the period. He was immensely popular with students, his introductory philosophy course attracting as many as four hundred each semester.

In 1948 Blanshard delivered the William Belden Noble Lectures at Harvard; the following year he gave the Otis Lectures at Wheaton College in Norton, Massachusetts. These honors were followed by an invitation to deliver the prestigious Gifford Lectures at St. Andrews University in Scotland. The Gifford appointment called for two sets of ten lectures on the theme of religion and ethics over the course of two successive academic years. Yale granted Blanshard an eighteen-month leave of absence to meet the commitment. He delivered the first set of lectures, titled "Reason and Its Critics," between February and May 1952 and the second set, titled "Reason and Goodness," during the same period in 1953; in between the two series he gave the Adamson Lecture at the University of Manchester, which was published as *On Philosophical Style*. He presented the Dana Lecture at Carlton College in 1954 and the John William Graham Lecture at Brown University in 1955. He served as president of the American Theological Society in 1955–1956. In 1956 he delivered the Ingraham Lecture at Colby College; that same year Yale named him Sterling Professor of Philosophy. He gave the William J. Cooper Lectures at Swarthmore in 1958, the same year he received the Senior Award of the American Council of Learned Societies for work in the humanities. In 1959 he became chairman of the Yale philosophy department a second time, retaining the position until his retirement. That same year he was selected by the American Philosophical Association to deliver the twelfth series of the Paul Carus Lectures, which he devoted to an examination and critique of analytic philosophy. In 1960 he delivered the Pitcairn-Crabbe Foundation Lecture at the University of Pittsburgh. In 1961 he gave the Mahlon Powell Lecture at Indiana University and the Alfred North Whitehead Lecture at Harvard.

Blanshard retired from Yale in 1961, becoming Sterling Professor Emeritus. That same year he published *Reason and Goodness,* which was based mainly on his second series of Gifford Lectures with additional material from the 1948 Noble Lectures. Blanshard's focus in the book is the relationship between reason and feeling in ethics. His view includes elements drawn from the British philosophers G. E. Moore and A. C.

Ewing and the American philosopher Ralph Barton Perry. Blanshard rejects Moore's "ideal utilitarianism," explaining that he cannot discover in his own experience the simple, nonnatural quality that Moore claimed was intrinsic good. He agrees, however, with Moore's opposition to the emotivists, who hold that moral "judgments" are merely expressions of favor or disfavor. Moral judgments really are judgments, he says, pointing out that they can contradict each other, that people make mistakes in moral matters and defend their moral views with arguments, and that one can see certain experiences to be really better than others. Moral assertions must, therefore, have cognitive content. Furthermore, Blanshard says, emotivism (which he calls, in the title of a 1949 article, "the new subjectivism in ethics") would make it impossible to speak consistently of any event in the past as good or evil. All one could say is that a past event prompted a certain present feeling of attraction or repulsion. Blanshard argues that even those who espouse emotivism do not practice it. A notable example is Russell, an outspoken pacifist who always insisted that conduct should be governed by reason, whereas his ethical theory made rational standards meaningless.

Cultural relativists, Blanshard notes, claim that diversity in moral practices in various societies undermines the claim that certain rules apply universally. He responds that moral practices are means to ends, and that diverse moral practices are often directed toward similar or identical ends. All people seem to prefer pleasure to intense pain; order, beauty, and comfort to disorder, filth, and misery; health to disease; security to fear and anxiety; and friendship to hatred. This simple observation proves cultural relativism false.

In chapters 11 and 12 of *Reason and Goodness* Blanshard works out a definition of goodness. He rejects, on introspective grounds, the view of Moore and Ross that goodness is a nonnatural quality or property. For Blanshard, value or goodness exists only in the realm of experience. An intrinsically good experience will constitute fulfillment of some impulse or drive of human nature, and this fulfillment will bring satisfaction. These two features—fulfillment and satisfaction—are not merely "good-making characteristics," but, together, constitute goodness itself. Blanshard concludes by explaining how reason operates in the good life to order and harmonize human impulses in such a way as to make possible the greatest degree of their fulfillment.

Reason and Goodness evoked diverse critical reactions. F. E. Sparshott, reviewing the book in *Ethics* (April 1962), found the doctrinal portions of the book superficial and frivolous and complained in particular of weaknesses in Blanshard's criticism of emotivism. Errol E. Harris, on the other hand, predicted in the *Yale*

Dust jacket for the British edition of Blanshard's 1962 book, a revised version of his 1959 Paul Carus Lectures, in which he attacks some of the major theses of logical positivism (Bruccoli Clark Layman Archives)

Review (March 1962) that the book would become a "modern philosophical classic" because of "the range of its purview, the comprehensiveness of its subject matter, the meticulousness of its argument, the penetration of its insight, the breadth of its vision, and the clarity and elegance of its style."

In 1962 Blanshard gave the Annie W. Riecker Lecture at the University of Arizona and published *Reason and Analysis*. The book is a revision of Blanshard's Carus Lectures, which were themselves an elaboration of points he had made in "The Philosophy of Analysis," his 1952 Henriette Hertz Lecture to the British Academy. Blanshard also incorporated into the book material from his Gifford Lectures.

By World War II, Blanshard says, philosophy had come to be seen as the logic of science, and with this conception came a shift from a concern with traditional large issues in metaphysics, epistemology, ethics, and so on to the exact discussion of smaller and more precisely defined problems. Rigorous analysis was held in high esteem, and philosophers were sometimes paralyzed by the realization that they would be held accountable by acute and unsparing critics for a loosely used word or phrase.

Analytic philosophers in general differed widely among themselves and never formed a single well-defined school or movement. In *Reason and Analysis* Blanshard focuses on the logical positivists–or "logical empiricists," as they called themselves–who did hold a common set of beliefs. First, they employed a verifiability criterion of meaning, according to which no statement is meaningful–or, for that matter, even a statement at all–unless it refers to and can be confirmed by sense experience. Statements about God and immortality are, accordingly, ruled out as nonsensical. Blanshard turns the theory on itself: how, he asks, can the verifiability criterion itself be verified? That is, how can sense experience confirm or refute the claim that sense experience alone can confirm or refute? He examines seven interpretations of the verifiability criterion and shows each to be inadequate.

A second logical empiricist doctrine is that the deductive reasoning of speculative philosophers is merely analytic, linguistic, and conventional. An "analytic" statement is one in which the meaning of the predicate is "contained in" that of the subject; thus, such statements are necessarily true only in the trivial sense that the statement "All bachelors are unmarried men" is true. For Blanshard, however, not all necessary statements are analytic. As a counterexample he offers the statement "Whatever is red is extended." Being extended is not the same thing as being red, nor is it a part of the meaning of the latter, though it is entailed by it. Blanshard opposes the logical empiricists' description of a priori reasoning as inseparable from "linguistic necessity" by pointing out that, for example, what necessitates the geometric properties of the triangle is the reality itself and not simply the word *triangle,* for which any other word could be substituted. To claim that necessity inheres in language is to confuse verbal definition, which merely reports the way a word is used, with real definition, which describes the attributes of an object and is reached by analysis of that object or reflection on it. Finally, he says, the logical empiricists' claim–that the laws of logic are simply a convenience in the ordering of thought and not, as earlier philosophers had held, a clue to the nature of reality–would mean that Plato, St. Thomas Aquinas, René Descartes, Spinoza, Bradley, and J. M. E. McTaggart were all mistaken. Blanshard points out that logical empiricists themselves implicitly accept the objective validity of logic. He concludes that these new philosophers are so mired in skepticism that they cannot consistently state their own case.

Blanshard's wife died of a heart attack on 9 December 1966. In 1967 Blanshard gave the William Allan Nielsen Lectures at Smith College. On 6 June 1969 he married Roberta Yerkes, the daughter of the Yale psychologist Robert M. Yerkes. In 1970 he published his first wife's biography of Frank Aydelotte, the innovative former president of Swarthmore, who had died in 1956; Blanshard edited the work and wrote the final two chapters.

In 1974 appeared *Reason and Belief,* a second volume based on Blanshard's Gifford and Noble Lectures. Blanshard had delayed the publication of the work because he wanted to research certain theological matters more thoroughly. The book focuses on the function of reason in religious life. Parts 1 and 2 consider the relationship of reason and faith in Roman Catholic and Lutheran theology, respectively. Although Catholic theology respects reason and makes considerable use of it, Blanshard thinks that it still circumscribes the employment of reason. He lists several difficulties in accepting revelation, along with reason, as an avenue to truth and notes that the use of revelation casts doubt on the validity of reasoning. Blanshard argues that the revealed truths of Catholicism are in accord neither with reason nor with the generally accepted findings of biology, astronomy, and psychology and that the Church, therefore, has isolated itself from both philosophy and science. Thinkers in what he calls "The Lutheran Succession," which includes Martin Luther, Søren Kierkegaard, Karl Barth, and Emil Brunner, make faith discontinuous with natural knowledge; they accept "paradox" and repudiate the findings of reason. To accept paradox, Blanshard says, is to reject the logical principle of noncontradiction, which is fundamental to philosophy and science.

Part 3 examines the relationship of ethical principles to religious belief. In chapter 11, "The Ethics of Belief," based on lecture seven of his first Gifford series, Blanshard sketches contrasting scientific and religious approaches to belief. For the scientist, belief that goes beyond the evidence is an embarrassment; for the religious person, this kind of belief is often approved and even required. In agreement with Russell, Blanshard points out that feelings or the will to believe do not justify belief. Acceptance or rejection of dogmas should not be capricious.

Part 4 of *Reason and Belief,* "A Rationalist's Outlook," is an exposition of Blanshard's own views; it is divided into sections titled "Cosmology," "Human Nature and Its Values," "Goodness and the Absolute," and "Religion and Rationalism." For Blanshard, a rationalist outlook is one that considers the world as a coherent whole. The rationalist believes that the world does not harbor self-contradictions or include items that contradict other items. If one starts with the law of noncon-

*Dust jacket for Blanshard's final book: biographies of figures who lived their lives
in accordance with the principles of rationality (Richland County Public Library)*

tradiction, Blanshard argues, one comes to realize that traditional systems of religious dogma, if posited as revealed and certain, cannot be true, since they are internally inconsistent. Since the rationalist is concerned with truth above all else, he or she must, therefore, part company with traditional theologians.

Returning to the logical empiricist objection that the law of noncontradiction is merely a linguistic rule, Blanshard responds that the linguistic rule only exists because it reflects the way nature actually is. Against the similar objection that the law of noncontradiction is only a convention of thought, Blanshard points out that those who accept this theory never hold to it in practice. If such a philosopher proved that the laws of thought are arbitrary, what would he or she think if the audience accepted the argument but rejected the conclusion? Or if they both accepted and rejected the conclusion? Those, such as Rudolf Carnap, who insist on the arbitrariness of logic must

suppose that their own argument is itself arbitrary; but they do not seem to do so.

A third objection to Blanshard's rationalist view is that the laws of logic are laws of thought but not of things. According to this position, logical laws might only be necessary in the sense that one cannot escape from them mentally, insofar as one cannot think their opposites. Perhaps a thing could be both X and not-X at the same time in the same respect, regardless of the inability of the human mind to conceive of such a situation. According to Blanshard, however, this train of thinking breaks down: for as soon as one considers the possibility of the thing being both X and not-X, one is employing thought, and the thought that something could contradict itself is unthinkable and, therefore, meaningless. "For we have said both that the law of contradiction binds our thought and that it does not, since we have successfully thought its opposite. Thus, the theory that the law is a law of thought only, and not of things, cannot even be intelligibly stated."

For a rationalist such as Blanshard, the world is not only a coherent whole but a causal whole as well. Every event is causally connected with some other event, and every event must, therefore, be connected, albeit indirectly, with every other event. Blanshard notes that this view involves the assumptions that nature is uniform and that all events have causes. He believes that Hume's analysis of causality, which denies a real and necessary link between cause and effect, applies strictly to physical causality. In mental sequences and in rational thought, by contrast, an a priori, necessary element is always present.

Blanshard finds epistemological idealism (the claim that all one knows directly are one's own ideas) plausible–or, at least, more plausible than any form of realism (the claim that one knows objects that are independent of the mind). He argues that while epistemological idealism can account for errors in perception, realism, whether of the critical or the common-sense variety, cannot. He pulls back, however, from affirming ontological idealism: he sees no warrant for holding that because the world is a rational whole, it must also be mental in nature.

Similarly, Blanshard finds no warrant for conceiving of the Absolute as a conscious mind; therefore, the Absolute cannot be characterized as morally good, since the intrinsically good is that which satisfies or fulfills some consciousness. The Absolute, then, is not a substitute for God. Blanshard concludes that human beings live in a "neutral world," a universe that is indifferent to good and evil. The actual distribution of good and evil cannot be reconciled with the notion of a morally governed universe except by a leap of blind faith. Much of the foundation of human hope in the West, Blanshard says, the rationalist cannot accept.

Blanshard thinks that this admittedly "bleak" rationalism will supplant traditional Western supernaturalism. Although "tragic" in its import, it is salutary in its honesty. Rationalism dispels the biases inherent in nationalism, bigotry, and religious sectarianism. It discloses that no connection exists between supernaturalist theology and morality. What is more confidently asserted need not depend upon what is less assuredly affirmed: thus, to insist that morality depends on such central dogmas of supernaturalism as the Incarnation, Atonement, or the Trinity is to weaken morality rather than to give it added strength. The authority of reason and the reasonable temper can replace the authority of dogma and supernatural theology. Blanshard argues that the "two-storied cosmology," which divides the universe into natural and supernatural realms, and the "two-level anthropology," in which human beings are divided into spiritual and natural aspects, stand or fall together. In his judgment both views are untenable. What they purport to account for can increasingly be more adequately explained by science, supplemented by a philosophy that realizes its own limitations.

Blanshard's alternative to supernaturalism is reasonableness as a demanding ideal, a guide to belief, and a directive for conduct. The appeal to reasonableness does not mean abandoning all religion, if religion is properly conceived. On Blanshard's view religion is simply "man's attempt to live in the light of what he holds to be ultimately true and good." Reasonableness supplants faith; it is the disposition "to guide one's belief and conduct by the evidence, a bent of the will to order one's thought by the relevant facts, and to order one's practice in the light of the values involved." Integral to this rationalist outlook will be reverence, conceived as respect for the moral ideal and for examples of genuine human goodness; humility based on truth; and an attitude that is morally receptive and teachable.

Reason and Belief drew fire from Catholics and Protestants alike. Even those with less partial viewpoints hinted that Blanshard's treatment of liberal Christian theism was not entirely adequate. Other reviewers praised the book. "Blanshard writes lucidly, incisively and with profound scholarship over the entire range of his subject," wrote Robert Hoffman, "and the result is a contribution to the philosophy of religion which merits close study by all who take the subject seriously, whether laymen or professionals."

Blanshard's final book, *Four Reasonable Men: Marcus Aurelius, John Stuart Mill, Ernest Renan, Henry Sidgwick* (1984), consists of biographical studies of a Roman emperor, a freelance reformer, an orientalist, and a Cambridge philosophy professor who guided their lives by the "quiet habitual reasonableness" that Blanshard believes is the great need of humankind:

> For all of them conformity to reason was more than a special interest and delight. It was an integral part of duty and honor. For all of them prejudice was close to sin. All of them shared an ethics or belief that made carelessness in conviction or statement, surrender to superstition, fanaticism of any kind, personal attack in argument, dogmatism, the misstatement of an opponent's case or the concealment of weakness in their own seem like strains on their integrity.

Blanshard draws the lesson: "If our ills are inward, as they largely are, we should do well to listen to what these men say. We should do even better to catch something of the reasonable temper in which they sought with such success to live their lives." In the concluding chapter, "The Enemy: Prejudice," Blanshard lists the approaches to life that most threaten the "great grey virtue" of an open and reasonable mind: divided selves, failures of observation, perversions of logic, egoistic quirks, family biases, religious dogmas, rampant patriotism, and prejudgments fastened to race and sex.

Blanshard died on 18 November 1987. In a letter read at his memorial service at Yale, the philosopher Paul Weiss wrote: "He is a beacon to all who knew him, an exceptionally honest man, deeply concerned with being clear about fundamental issues, which he pursued with vigor and commitment, eminently civilized, hard working, a man deserving to be long remembered both for what he was and for what he had accomplished."

Brand Blanshard was, above all, a man of reason. He believed that rationalism provides a foundation for choices among values and, in the final analysis, a guide for practical living. What else, he asked, can provide solutions to the problems of racism, sexism, crime, the environment, and overpopulation? He once remarked in a talk to a group of Phi Beta Kappa members at Southern Illinois University: "Against the partisan slogans, the Pollyana faiths, the self-righteous nationalism of our time, the nightmare art and beatnik poetry, the erotic stage, the violent television, the perpetual adolescence of the screen, there is perhaps no full protection. But the best I know is that habit of detached and critical reflection which belongs to the philosophical spirit." Throughout his long career and life Blanshard's confidence in this "philosophical spirit" never faltered.

Interviews:

Louis C. Mink and others, "Interrogation of Brand Blanshard," in *Philosophical Interrogations: Interrogations of Martin Buber, John Wild, Jean Wahl, Brand Blanshard, Paul Weiss, Charles Hartshorne, Paul Tillich,* edited by Sydney Rome and Beatrice Rome (New York: Holt, Rinehart & Winston, 1964), pp. 201–257;

Israel Shenker, "At 80, Blanshard Twins Still Back the Unpopular," *New York Times,* 28 August 1972, section 2, pp. 1, 45.

Bibliographies:

John Howie, "Bibliography of the Writings of Brand Blanshard to 1980," in *The Philosophy of Brand Blanshard,* edited by Paul Arthur Schilpp, The Library of Living Philosophers, volume 15 (La Salle, Ill.: Open Court, 1980), pp. 1101–1127;

Howie, "Bibliography: Brand Blanshard, 1980–1987," *Idealistic Studies,* 20 (May 1990): 169–170.

References:

Bruce Aune, "Blanshard and Internal Relations," *Review of Metaphysics,* 27 (December 1967): 237–243;

Ivan Babić, "Blanshard's Reduction of Marxism," *Journal of Philosophy,* 63 (December 1966): 745–756;

Carroll R. Bowman, "Brand Blanshard's Philosophy of Education," *Educational Theory,* 21 (Spring 1971): 199–207;

Charles Arthur Campbell, "Blanshard's Gifford Lectures," *Philosophy,* 37 (July 1962): 263–268;

Milič Čapek, "Professor Blanshard on Kierkegaard," *Modern Schoolman,* 48 (November 1970): 44–53;

Peter Caws, "Coherence, System, and Structure," *Idealistic Studies,* 4 (January 1974): 2–17;

Marcus M. Clayton, "A Critical Study of Four Principal Theories in Brand Blanshard's Philosophical System," dissertation, Emory University, 1967;

Richard E. Creel, "Blanshard's Epistemology: A Clarification," *Southern Journal of Philosophy,* 9 (Winter 1971): 361–370;

Martin Cyril D'Arcy, "The Nature of Thought," *Thought,* 15 (December 1940): 665–680;

Bernard P. Dauenhauer, "On Kierkegaard's Alleged Nihilism," *Southern Journal of Philosophy,* 12 (Summer 1974): 153–163;

Willis Doney, "The Argument from Difference," *Review of Metaphysics,* 21 (December 1967): 244–249;

Paul Edwards, "The Logic of Moral Discourse (III)," in his *The Logic of Moral Discourse* (Glencoe, Ill.: Free Press, 1955), pp. 199–209;

Frederick Ferré, "Toward a Reasonable Ethics of Belief," *Philosophic Exchange,* 1 (Summer 1971): 95–102;

Robert J. Fogelin, "Blanshard's Reason and Goodness," *Review of Metaphysics,* 17 (September 1963): 91–97;

Walter Larry Fogg, "Experience and Order in Blanshard and Whitehead," dissertation, Boston University, 1963;

John M. Groth, "Current Strictures on Reason: A Criticism," *Philosophical Review,* 55 (November 1946): 668–669;

James Walter Gustafson, "Causality and Freedom in Jonathan Edwards, Samuel Alexander, and Brand Blanshard," dissertation, Boston University, 1967;

Errol Eustace Harris, "Goodness, Duty and Human Nature," *Yale Review,* 51 (March 1962): 489–495;

Harris, "On Reason: A Response to Professor Blanshard," *Idealistic Studies,* 12 (September 1982): 199–210;

Harris, "Reason and Rationalism," *Idealistic Studies,* 9 (May 1979): 93–114;

Thomas English Hill, "Recent Idealism," in his *Contemporary Theories of Knowledge* (New York: Ronald Press, 1961), pp. 42–59;

Yeager Hudson, "Metaphysical Causality in the Philosophies of Brand Blanshard, Roy Wood Sellars, and John Laird," dissertation, Boston University, 1965;

Idealistic Studies, special Blanshard issue, 4 (January 1974);

Idealistic Studies, special Blanshard issue, 20 (January 1990);

Charles Edwin Jones, "The Theory of Truth as Subjectivity in Kierkegaard Compared with Theories of Truth in Blanshard and Ayer," dissertation, University of Arkansas, 1973;

John T. Kearns, "Sameness or Similarity?" *Philosophy and Phenomenological Research,* 29 (September 1968): 105–115;

J. Calvin Keene, "Religion and Belief," *Philosophic Exchange,* 1 (Summer 1971): 103–110;

Walter H. Kehler Jr., "The Blanshard Entailment and the Madden Natural Necessity Views of Causality," *Idealistic Studies,* 10 (January 1980): 40–45;

William E. Kennick, "The Intelligibility of the World," *Review of Metaphysics,* 21 (December 1967): 250–255;

Jackie Kleinman, "Čapek on Blanshard on Kierkegaard," *Modern Schoolman,* 50 (January 1973): 209–219;

Elmer D. Klemke, "Blanshard's Criticisms of Wittgenstein's Tractatus," *Personalist,* 60 (July 1979): 305–311;

Klemke, "The Laws of Logic," *Philosophy of Science,* 33 (1966): 271–278;

John Knox Jr., "Blanshard on Causation and Necessity," *Review of Metaphysics,* 20 (March 1967): 518–532;

Clifford G. Kossel, "The Problem of Relation in Some Non-Scholastic Philosophies," *Modern Schoolman,* 23 (January 1946): 61–81;

Yervant H. Krikorian, "Brand Blanshard's Rationalistic Idealism," in his *Recent Perspectives in American Philosophy* (The Hague: Nijhoff, 1973), pp. 50–62;

Theodore T. Lafferty, "Inter-communication in Philosophy," *Journal of Philosophy,* 43 (August 1946): 449–465;

Charles Landesman, "Specific and Abstract Universals," *Idealistic Studies,* 4 (January 1974): 89–105;

Alice Ambrose Lazerowitz, "Internal Relations," *Review of Metaphysics,* 21 (December 1967): 256–261;

Hywel David Lewis, "The Philosophy of Brand Blanshard," *Philosophy,* 58 (January 1983): 110–117;

Alan Pierce MacAllister, "Metaphysical Propositions: The Views of Brand Blanshard and Charles Hartshorne," dissertation, University of Toronto, 1975;

Dickinson S. Miller, "An Event in Modern Philosophy," *Philosophical Review,* 54 (November 1945): 593–606;

Arthur E. Murphy, "Blanshard on Good in General," *Philosophical Review,* 72 (April 1963): 228–241;

Kai Nielsen, "Hume and the Emotive Theory," *Philosophical Studies* (Dublin), 19 (1970): 202–213;

Robert A. Oakes, "Professor Blanshard, Causality, and Internal Relations: Some Perspectives," *Idealistic Studies,* 1 (May 1971): 172–178;

Oakes, "Some Historical Perspectives on Professor Blanshard's Critique of Critical Realism as 'Objective Idealism in Disguise,'" *Personalist,* 51 (Spring 1970): 237–242;

Scott D. Palmer, "Blanshard, Rescher, and the Coherence Theory of Truth," *Idealistic Studies,* 12 (September 1982): 211–230;

LaMoyne Lloyd Pederson, "An Investigation of the Forms and Defenses of Teleological Ethical Theories, with Emphasis on the Ethical Theory of Brand Blanshard," dissertation, University of Southern California, 1970;

Andrew J. Reck, "Brand Blanshard: Idealism and Rationalism," in his *The New American Philosophers: An Exploration of Thought since World War II* (Baton Rouge: Louisiana State University Press, 1968), pp. 81–119;

Reck, "Idealism in American Philosophy since 1900," in *Contemporary Studies in Philosophical Idealism,* edited by John Howie and Thomas O. Buford (Cape Cod, Mass.: Stark, 1975), pp. 17–52;

Reck, "The Philosophy of Brand Blanshard," *Tulane Studies in Philosophy,* 13 (1964): 111–147;

Paul Arthur Schilpp, ed., *The Philosophy of Brand Blanshard,* The Library of Living Philosophers, volume 15 (La Salle, Ill.: Open Court, 1980);

Wilfrid Sellars, "Actions and Events," *Noûs,* 7 (May 1973): 179–202;

Robert Spiegelberg, "Phenomenology of Direct Evidence," *Philosophy and Phenomenological Research,* 2 (June 1942): 427–456.

Papers:

Brand Blanshard's correspondence and other materials are in Sterling Memorial Library at Yale University.

Justus Buchler
(27 March 1914 – 19 March 1991)

Kathleen A. Wallace
Hofstra University

BOOKS: *Charles Peirce's Empiricism* (London: Kegan Paul, Trench, Trübner, 1939; New York: Harcourt, Brace, 1939);

Philosophy: An Introduction, by Buchler and John Herman Randall Jr. (New York: Barnes & Noble, 1942; revised, 1971);

Toward a General Theory of Human Judgment (New York: Columbia University Press, 1951; revised edition, New York: Dover, 1979);

Nature and Judgment (New York: Columbia University Press, 1955);

The Concept of Method (New York: Columbia University Press, 1961);

Metaphysics of Natural Complexes (New York: Columbia University Press, 1966; enlarged edition, edited by Kathleen A. Wallace, Armen Marsoobian, and Robert S. Corrington, Albany: State University of New York Press, 1990);

The Main of Light: On the Concept of Poetry (New York, London & Toronto: Oxford University Press, 1974).

OTHER: George Santayana, *Obiter Scripta: Lectures, Essays, and Reviews,* edited by Buchler and Benjamin Schwartz (New York & London: Scribners, 1936);

The Philosophy of Peirce: Selected Writings, edited by Buchler (London: Kegan Paul, Trench, Trübner, 1940; New York: Harcourt, Brace, 1940); republished as *Philosophical Writings of Peirce* (New York: Dover, 1955);

"Russell and the Principles of Ethics," in *The Philosophy of Bertrand Russell,* edited by Paul Arthur Schilpp, The Library of Living Philosophers, volume 5 (Evanston, Ill. & Chicago: Northwestern University Press, 1944), pp. 511–535;

Introduction to Contemporary Civilization in the West, 2 volumes, edited by Buchler and others (New York: Columbia University Press, 1946);

Readings in Philosophy, edited by Buchler, John Herman Randall Jr., and Evelyn Shirk (New York: Barnes

Justus Buchler (photograph © 1979 by Dorothy McKenzie)

& Noble, 1946; revised, 1950; revised again, 1972);

"What Is the Pragmaticist Theory of Meaning?" in *Studies in the Philosophy of Charles Sanders Peirce,* edited by Philip P. Wiener and Frederic H. Young (Cambridge, Mass.: Harvard University Press, 1952), pp. 21–32;

"Reconstruction in the Liberal Arts," in *A History of Columbia College on Morningside* (New York: Columbia University Press, 1954), pp. 48–135;

Academic Due Process: A Statement of Desirable Procedures Applicable within Educational Institutions in Cases Involving Academic Freedom, anonymous, by Buchler and others (New York: American Civil Liberties Union, 1954);

Academic Freedom and Civil Liberties of Students in Colleges and Universities, anonymous (New York: American Civil Liberties Union, 1961; revised, 1963);

"One Santayana or Two?" in *Animal Faith and the Spiritual Life: Previously Unpublished and Uncollected Writings by George Santayana, with Critical Essays on His Thought,* edited by John Lachs (New York: Appleton-Century-Crofts, 1967), pp. 66–72;

"Ontological Parity," in *Naturalism and Historical Understanding: Essays on the Philosophy of John Herman Randall Jr.,* edited by John P. Anton (Albany: State University of New York Press, 1967), pp. 162–175;

Beth J. Singer, *The Rational Society: A Critical Study of Santayana's Social Thought,* foreword by Buchler (Cleveland & London: Press of Case Western Reserve University, 1970).

SELECTED PERIODICAL PUBLICATIONS–
UNCOLLECTED: "Note on Proust," *Lavender* (January 1934): 14–18;

"Dr. von Juhos and Physicalism," *Analysis,* 3 (August 1936): 88–92;

"Value-Statements," *Analysis,* 4 (April 1937): 49–58;

"Act and Object in Locke," *Philosophical Review,* 46 (September 1937): 528–535;

"Charles Sanders Peirce, Giant in American Philosophy," *American Scholar,* 8 (Fall 1939): 400–411;

Review of Charles Hartshorne, *Man's Vision of God and the Logic of Theism, Journal of Philosophy,* 39 (23 April 1942): 245–247;

"The Philosopher, the Common Man and William James," *American Scholar,* 2 (Autumn 1942): 416–426;

"Specialization or General Education," by Buchler and Lawrence H. Chamberlain, *Journal of General Education,* 6 (April 1952): 166–169;

"On the Problem of Liberal Education," *Columbia Spectator,* 31 October 1954, p. 7;

"What Is a Discussion?" *Journal of General Education,* 8 (October 1954): 7–17;

"Teacher Disclosure of Information about Students to Prospective Employers," anonymous, *School and Society,* 89 (7 October 1961): 319–321;

"Justus Buchler's Reply to A. Stafford Clayton," *Studies in Philosophy and Education,* 3 (1963): 42–44;

"On a Strain of Arbitrariness in Whitehead's System," *Journal of Philosophy,* 66 (2 October 1969): 589–601;

"Reply to Reck: The Structure of the Whole, the Location of the Parts," "Reply to Singer: Alleged Ambiguities in the Metaphysics of Natural Complexes," "Reply to Anton: Against 'Proper' Ontology," "Reply to Ross: Aspects of the Theory of Judgment," and "Reply to Kuhns: Poetry, Assertiveness, and Prevalence," *Southern Journal of Philosophy,* 14 (Spring 1976): 47–53.

Many of his contemporaries considered Justus Buchler the most distinguished living systematic philosopher in the United States. His ideas are elaborated in five books and several articles written over a span of thirty years. In regard to his themes Buchler was influenced by the classical American philosophers Charles Sanders Peirce, William James, Josiah Royce, George Santayana, and John Dewey; in regard to philosophical method he drew his inspiration chiefly from Aristotle, Baruch Spinoza, and Georg Wilhelm Friedrich Hegel. As a result, his work, while widely respected, falls outside the mainstream of Anglo-American analytic philosophy. His writings, especially *Metaphysics of Natural Complexes* (1966; enlarged, 1990), are notable for their elegantly spare style.

Buchler was born in New York City on 27 March 1914, the first of three children of Samuel and Ida Frost Buchler. Samuel Buchler had been born in Hungary, where he earned a Ph.D. in history and was ordained a rabbi. After immigrating to the United States in 1908, he had become a lawyer and served as deputy New York state attorney general. In 1920 he founded the Jewish Court of Arbitration, and in 1933 he published *"Cohen Comes First" and Other Cases: Stories of Controversies before the New York Jewish Court of Arbitration.* Ida Buchler, who was of Russian descent, died of a heart condition in 1948 at fifty-three; Buchler's brother, Harry, who also studied philosophy, died of the same cause six years later. Buchler's sister, Beatrice Buchler Gotthold, became the founding editor of *Working Woman* magazine, executive editor of *Family Circle,* and the first female vice president of the New York Times Company.

Buchler studied philosophy under Morris R. Cohen, Yervant Krikorian, and Abraham Edel at City College of New York; another major influence on Buchler was Bird Stair, a professor of English who taught critical writing. Because of the Great Depression, Buchler had to support his family in addition to pursuing his studies. He published his first article, "Note on Proust," in 1934 in *The Lavender,* a student publication; it is a five-page, single-paragraph essay written in imitation of Marcel Proust.

Buchler received a B.S.S. in 1934 and went on to Columbia University, where he earned his M.A. in 1935 with a thesis on John Locke directed by Frederick J. E. Woodbridge. At Columbia, Buchler formed a lasting friendship with the philosophers Milton Munitz and Lenore Munitz. In 1936 he and Benjamin Schwartz edited George Santayana's *Obiter Scripta: Lectures, Essays, and Reviews.* In 1937, while studying for his doctorate, Buchler became a part-time instructor of philosophy at both Brooklyn College and Columbia. He earned his Ph.D. in 1938 with a dissertation directed by Ernest Nagel and, while retaining his instructorship at Columbia, took a similar position at Brooklyn College. Published in 1939 as *Charles Peirce's Empiricism,* Buchler's dissertation became a classic in Peirce studies. In 1940 he edited a selection of Peirce's writings.

During his early years at Columbia, Buchler served as book editor of *The Journal of Philosophy.* Charles Hartshorne was so impressed by Buchler's review of his *Man's Vision of God and the Logic of Theism* (1941) that he sought Buchler out for two hours of discussion. In 1942 Buchler became a full-time instructor at Columbia, and he and his colleague and mentor John Herman Randall Jr. co-authored the textbook *Philosophy: An Introduction.*

From 1942 until 1960 Buchler participated in the Contemporary Civilization program at Columbia College, serving as administrative head from 1950 to 1956. He told Beth J. Singer in a 23 March 1972 letter that "The teaching, reading, editing and (in 1950) administering of CC (the great staff, the discussions, the *esprit*) was *the* most fundamental intellectual experience of my life." Buchler's colleagues in the program included the sociologist C. Wright Mills, the social historian Benjamin Nelson, and the philosophers Randall, Nagel, and Herbert Schneider.

In February 1943 Buchler married Evelyn Urban Shirk, a fellow philosophy instructor at Brooklyn College who was working on her doctorate at Columbia. Buchler relinquished his instructorship at Brooklyn College that year. A few years after their marriage the couple purchased a farm in the northeast corner of Vermont as a summer retreat. Work on the colonial farmhouse became a lifelong project for Buchler and Shirk, who did much of the carpentry themselves. The farm provided the solitude Buchler needed for his creative philosophical work.

In 1946 Buchler, Shirk, and Randall co-edited the introductory anthology *Readings in Philosophy,* which went through several editions. Buchler was promoted to assistant professor the following year. In 1949 Shirk received her Ph.D. from Columbia and joined the faculty of Hofstra University in Hempstead, on Long Island; the couple moved to nearby Garden City. In

Buchler's wife, the philosopher Evelyn Urban Shirk, whom he married in 1943

1950 Buchler advanced to the rank of associate professor at Columbia.

Buchler published the first of his books of systematic philosophy, *Toward a General Theory of Human Judgment,* in 1951. He wrote several articles on education, including "The Liberal Arts and General Education" (1952), "On the Problem of Liberal Education" (1954), "What Is a Discussion?" (1954), and "Reconstruction in the Liberal Arts," a history of the development of the Contemporary Civilization program for *A History of Columbia College on Morningside* (1954). During the 1950s Buchler, an opponent of McCarthyism, was active in the American Civil Liberties Union (ACLU). In 1954 he co-authored the paper *Academic Due Process: A Statement of Desirable Procedures Applicable within Educational Institutions in Cases Involving Academic Freedom.* He published the second of his systematic philosophical works, *Nature and Judgment,* in 1955. In 1956 he was promoted to full professor.

For many years Buchler taught a course at Columbia titled "Major Themes in Recent Philosophy,"

toward a general theory of human judgment

_by_

Justus Buchler

Dust jacket for Buchler's first book of systematic philosophy, published in 1951 (Bruccoli Clark Layman Archives)

in which he covered the concepts of experience, intuition, and common sense as dealt with by philosophers such as Aristotle, David Hume, Edmund Husserl, and Alfred North Whitehead. He devoted several terms of the course to philosophical method. He also taught courses on symbolism, language and meaning, Locke's _Essay Concerning Human Understanding_ (1689), major themes in twentieth-century philosophy, metaphysics, and metaphysical themes in literature.

Buchler and Shirk's only child, Katherine Urban Buchler, was born in 1958. That same year Buchler became vice chairman of the National Academic Freedom Committee of the ACLU, a position he held for the next seven years. In 1958, 1959, and 1960 he was a guest lecturer at the William Alanson White Institute of Psychiatry in New York City. He was named Johnsonian Professor of Philosophy at Columbia in 1959. He co-authored _Academic Freedom and Civil Liberties of Students in Colleges and Universities_ (1961; revised, 1963) and

"Teacher Disclosure of Information about Students to Prospective Employers" (1961), which was adopted as a policy statement of the ACLU. In 1961 he published his third major systematic work, _The Concept of Method_.

Buchler's three early books develop his metaphysics of human process. By _metaphysics_, Buchler means the construction of categories to frame one's thinking about a particular subject matter; the "metaphysics of human process" is the formulating of categories about the nature of human beings. According to Buchler, one way to formulate categories is to theorize about what must be the case if the world is what it is; but this method is just a starting point. Unlike the eighteenth-century philosopher Immanuel Kant, Buchler does not regard categories as necessary a priori conditions of thought; rather, metaphysical categories are invented— they are constructed as devices for interpreting the world and one's experience of it, and they are to be assessed in terms of their interpretive power. No sharp distinction exists for Buchler between reality as it is in itself (Kant's "noumenal reality") and reality as it appears to the human mind (Kant's "phenomenal reality"); Buchler assumes that categories are about the world itself, as well as about one's experience of it. While all metaphysical systems purport to be universal in at least some sense, none is a "view from nowhere," a "perspectiveless perspective," or the only necessary foundation for all possible thought. A metaphysical system is a conceivable way of thinking about its subject matter; it is necessary only to the extent that its underlying assumptions are indispensable to doing justice to its subject matter.

Buchler considers Plato the exemplar of the inventiveness required of any philosopher who attempts to change the terms in which people think about the world. Buchler, like Plato, Aristotle, and Hegel, critiques and synthesizes the views of his predecessors and moves beyond them to construct a new conceptual framework. His project in the metaphysics of human process is to develop a conception of experience that, as he says in _Toward a General Theory of Human Judgment,_ "should be able to encompass aspects of human life reflected by the sciences and arts, by moral and religious attitudes, and by what takes place psychologically, socially, technologically." A philosophical conception of experience has to be able to encompass and locate human experiences of communicating, discovering, and creating meaning and of interpreting and validating judgments in all their multiple forms.

If this goal is to be achieved, Buchler warns, several common philosophical assumptions about experience have to be avoided. One such assumption is that experience is subordinate to, or an inferior form of, knowledge. Another, which is a corollary of the first, is the assumption that knowledge is restricted to propositional, or what Buchler calls "assertive," judgments. For Buchler, some experiences may be cognitively negligible or have no discernible cognitive relevance or outcome, but they are not any the less experiences on that account. A third assumption Buchler rejects is that experience and judgment must be conscious. When one limits experience to that of which one is explicitly aware, one excludes too much from total experience and, ultimately, from judgment.

One standard way philosophers have conceptualized human being has been to parse it into two distinct kinds of being: mental and physical, or mind and body. Body is explained in terms of the same kinds of causal processes that determine any physical entity or event, while mind is defined as that which is distinctively human; all human functions have to be traceable to, or in some way an outcome of, mind or consciousness. Buchler contends that such a framework cannot do justice to experience, communication, and knowledge. The knowledge possessed by an athlete is just as much knowledge as that of a mathematician; thus, knowledge must involve more than purely "mental processes." Buchler's metaphysics of human process is a sustained argument that the conceptualization of experience and judgment requires the formulation of philosophical categories that can identify what goes on in experience and judgment, whatever their physiology or psychology turns out to be. In *Toward a General Theory of Human Judgment* he replaces *experience* with a broader concept that he calls *proception*. Buchler accepts the insight of idealists and pragmatists that the nature of meaning requires a breakdown of the traditional distinction between language and world, sign and existence, or symbol and symbolized, but he avoids the idealist conclusion that the world itself must be mental. Not only words or other human products but facts themselves can function as signs; therefore, meaning cannot be purely mental or linguistic. And if meaning is generated in proception, then proception must involve a similar breakdown between language and world. Proception cannot, then, be either merely mental or merely physical.

According to Buchler, judgment appraises and discriminates some feature or features of the world in one of three modes: "assertive," "active," or "exhibitive." "The world" includes whatever exists—trees, art objects, mathematical models, hypotheses, human relationships, social institutions, even fictional entities. Judgment is both an expression of some feature of the individual doing the judging and a discovery about an aspect of the world to which the individual is related at that moment. Judgment presupposes communication as a fundamental human process, whether linguistic or not, and moves toward "justification" or validation.

Judging is always done from a perspective; but perspectives are shareable and duplicatable, because a perspective is defined not exclusively by the one judging but by the entire context of judgment. Those who are judging are, therefore, not locked into intrinsically private, first-person perspectives. As a proceiver, one assimilates features of the world in which one is located and seeks to communicate both to oneself and to others aspects of oneself and of the world that is being proceived. For example, the heat of a summer day is assimilated not just physiologically but proceptively—that is, into the organization of one's past experiences, current activities, desires, and so on: a person is working on a manuscript, perspiring, having difficulty concentrating; he or she gets up and puts on a bathing suit to take a dip in the pool. In Buchler's terminology, the person is "located" in several perspectives or "orders"—the meteorological order, the order of his or her writing, the order of the house and how hot it becomes, and so forth. The action of going swimming is a judgment—an active judgment—about the heat, the person's state of mind vis-à-vis the manuscript, and the ordering of his or her desires at that time. While swimming, the person may try to perfect his or her stroke, not to be able to swim faster but simply to become more graceful. This action is an exhibitive judgment: the person discriminates the graceful form in the activity and tries to execute it simply for the sake of exhibiting it. According to Buchler, these active and exhibitive judgments are no less judgments than if the person had asserted the propositions "It's hot today" or "I'm going to take a swim."

One's judgment about the hotness of the day is made in the action of swimming. One is judging "the temperature-in-relation-to-human-functioning." One does not have a representation of the heat standing in between oneself and the actual heat; rather, the temperature itself is one's procept. Similarly, when one proceives a house, it is the house itself that one proceives, just as it is the house that one buys, sells, or bequeaths to one's heirs. In each case, the "object" is a complex in relation to the self, not a third thing posited between the self and the world. Hence, judgments are "in" and "of" the world.

Judgment can be appraised formally, expressively, socially, or personally. Assertive judgments are formally appraisable in terms of true and false, active judgments are formally appraisable in terms of moral attributes such as right and wrong, and exhibitive judgments are formally appraisable in terms of excellence of kind such as good and bad. These types of appraisal are not mutually exclusive: a judgment can comprise any combination of the three, albeit in different respects. Hence, a mathematical proof is both an assertive (true or false) and an exhibitive (elegant or clumsy) judg-

nature
and
judgment

by
_____ Justus Buchler

Dust jacket for the second of Buchler's systematic works,
published in 1955 (Bruccoli Clark Layman Archives)

ment. An athlete's performance may be both active (correct in terms of the standards of the sport) and exhibitive (graceful or beautifully executed). A teacher's utterances may be both assertive (true or false) and active (efficacious or inefficacious in producing learning in the students).

Buchler's view can be compared with Aristotle's. Aristotle recognized kinds of reason–theoretical, practical, and productive–that would seem to correspond roughly to Buchler's assertive, active, and exhibitive judgments. In Aristotle's system, however, the kinds of reason are hierarchically arranged and valued, with theoretical as the highest and best. In Buchler's system, by contrast, the assertive judgments of a philosopher or mathematician are no higher or better than the active or exhibitive judgments of an athlete or dancer. Any mode of judgment may be preferable in a specific context or with respect to a particular purpose, but none is intrinsically superior to another.

Buchler served as chairman of the Columbia philosophy department from 1964 to 1967. His fourth systematic work, *Metaphysics of Natural Complexes,* appeared in 1966. It deals not with the metaphysics of human being but with the wider field of "general ontology," which Buchler defines as the metaphysics of being in general.

If Buchler's earlier systematic works are driven by the goal of reconstructing the concepts of experience and judgment on metaphysical and not merely epistemological grounds, *Metaphysics of Natural Complexes* derives its impetus from what he calls the "principle of ontological parity." This principle asserts the equal reality of whatever is: attributes are as real as substances, relations as real as entities, the impermanent as real as the fixed, the mental as real as the physical, human beings and the human order as real as God and the divine order, fictional entities as real as physical ones, and so on. Buchler's metaphysical orientation is, thus, nonreductionistic, nonhierarchical, and all-inclusive. It sets the stage for the development of the specific categories of Buchler's "ordinal metaphysics," or "metaphysics of natural complexes." Ontological parity completes the critiques of metaphysics advanced by Friedrich Nietzsche, the logical positivists, Martin Heidegger, Dewey and other pragmatists, Richard Rorty, and the postmodernists. Such critiques usually end either in an attempt to formulate an alternative set of concepts, as with Nietzsche, Heidegger, and Dewey, or in a rejection of the possibility of metaphysics altogether, as with the logical positivists, Rorty, and the postmodernists. Buchler falls into the former group. His system of general ontology is guided by an interest in addressing such metaphysical issues as identity, determinateness, relation, possibility, meaning, and the nature of being as such. In other words, he believes that there are substantive metaphysical issues that need to be rethought, not just abandoned as unsolvable. One of his aims is to provide categories that allow for the adequate conceptualization of such issues.

Buchler's first task in *Metaphysics of Natural Complexes* is to formulate a generic term of identification for whatever exists. The term he chooses is *natural complex,* or *complex* for short. *Natural* is intended to convey the notion of nature as all-inclusive; for Buchler, *nonnatural* and *supernatural,* as designations of intrinsically lower or higher, better or worse, less- or more-real kinds of being, are not metaphysically meaningful. No being, he says, is, in principle, inaccessible to other beings. On this view, God is a natural complex and is ontologically comprehensible in terms of the same categories as any other being. Whatever is special or unique about God as a kind of being or complex would require a more specific set of categories, just as the distinctiveness of human being or process is not captured by the categories of general ontology but requires a distinct set of categories—the metaphysics of human process. (Buchler does not pursue philosophical theology beyond a brief section on God in the first part of *Metaphysics of Natural Complexes*.) On the other hand, specific categories must be consistent with and encompassed by the categories of general ontology if the latter is to be truly general.

Buchler's second task is to formulate a way to recognize the being of anything that is, including relations, possibilities, fictional characters, processes, changes, and novelty. The thrust of his first pair of ontological categories is to conceptualize the being of change, as well as of permanence; the being of possibilities, as well as of actualities; and the being of societies, individuals, dreams, poems, and death, as well as of brains, books, and bodies. If entities are not the only realities, then *existence* is not a broad enough category to capture the being of any being; if not all beings change, then *becoming* is not broad enough. Buchler's categories for the predicative sense of *is* are the pair *prevalence* (derived from *prevail*) and *alescence* (derived from *coalescence*, "a coming together of complexes"). They are designed to encompass all possible ways of being—that is, the being or "thatness" of any natural complex.

Buchler's third task is to provide categories to define the "whatness" of any being or natural complex. Categories are needed that specify the ways in which a natural complex is constituted by its particular characteristics and that specify its similarities to and differences from other natural complexes. In Buchler's view, metaphysical complexity is irreducible. A natural complex is not a traitless "it" that is ontologically prior to its attributes or relations; instead, it is—or, in Buchler's terminology, it "prevails"—insofar as it is its traits, that is, insofar as it prevails as related, as actual, as possible, and so forth. The key categories here are *order* and *relation*. Buchler defines *order* as a "sphere of relatedness." Every complex—whether entity, process, relation, or possibility—is what it is in virtue of its locatedness in orders, or "ordinal locations." Every complex shares traits or locations with other complexes. Moreover, every complex is itself an order and, hence, is uniquely determinate, that is, different from every other complex. For example, a university is a university in virtue of its location in the order of universities; it is related to other universities in virtue of shared traits such as educational and research goals, departmental organization, and principles of faculty governance. A university qua university is thus located, or prevails, in the order of universities, which is, in turn, located in the orders of educational institutions, social institutions, and the like. A university qua this particular university is itself an order and, as such, locates other complexes, such as its

type of student body, its particular principles of faculty governance, and so on. A complex, then, is irreducibly complex, shares traits (relations) with other complexes, and is distinguishable as a distinct complex; and no complex is more or less complex than another, because there is no fixed limit to possible relatedness.

In anticipation of the objection that some relations or traits are important and others trivial, Buchler distinguishes two kinds of relation or location: "strongly relevant" and "weakly relevant" ones. The former constitute the very character of a complex, while the latter affect the scope or reach of the complex. For example, a particular faculty member may be a weakly relevant trait of a university in that he or she does not contribute to the character of the university but is still a constituent of the scope of the university. On the other hand, a faculty member who played a role in the formation of the structure of government at the university might be strongly relevant to the university—that is, a constituent of its character as this particular university. Each trait is identifiable as a trait of this university, but each is determinate in a different way. Finally, every complex and every trait is related to some other complex or trait, and no complex or trait reaches or affects every other complex or trait. This conclusion is entailed by the distinct location of each complex. If every complex were related to every other, then either complexes would be indistinguishable from each other, or a single overarching complex would exist. The metaphysics of natural complexes is premised on a rejection of the monistic commitment entailed by the latter possibility. It also endorses the principle of the "identity of identicals" of the German philosopher Gottfried Wilhelm Leibniz (1646–1716), according to which multiplicity entails discernibility.

The final set of categories has to do with the issue of the limit, or boundary, of any particular complex. If determinateness entails a boundary, but that boundary is itself indeterminate, then both boundary and indeterminateness need to be conceptualized. Buchler's solution is to define *boundary* in terms of the categories *actuality* and *possibility*: a boundary is determinate insofar as it contains actualities and indeterminate insofar as it contains possibilities. The indeterminateness of a boundary is "determinately indeterminate," because every possibility is determinate—that is, every possibility prevails in a particular ordinal location. Not just anything is a possibility for a complex; but insofar as there is possibility, its boundary is indeterminate, pending actualization. For example, the number of lines that can be drawn from a given point is indefinite; but this indeterminate possibility is determined by the initial point and, more generally, by the entire spatial order. The boundary of a possibility or set of possibilities becomes

Dust jacket for Buchler's 1966 book, in which he develops his "general ontology" (Bruccoli Clark Layman Archives)

determinate on actualization; but because actualization itself becomes the condition for new possibilities, boundaries or determinateness of complexes cannot be wholly fixed.

In 1971 Buchler was hired away from Columbia by Patrick Heelan, who was establishing a Ph.D. program in philosophy at the University of New York at Stony Brook. As a systematic philosopher he enabled the program to distinguish itself as a pluralistic one rather than being dominated by the then ascendant analytic tradition, and his presence facilitated the approval of the program by the state board of education. At Stony Brook, Buchler, who held the title Distinguished Professor of Philosophy, taught only graduate courses. At the M.A. level he offered courses in the history of philosophy (the focus of the master's program at Stony Brook), such as modern moral philosophy, philosophy of religion, and ancient moral philosophy. At the doctoral level he taught courses on Locke, classical and contemporary

metaphysics, experience, meaning, and conceptions of philosophy. In 1972 Buchler and Shirk were among the founders of the Society for the Advancement of American Philosophy. In 1973 Buchler was awarded the Butler Silver Medal by Columbia University.

Aside from philosophy, one of Buchler's major interests was photography. He owned an Exakta camera, and, with his friend and former student Sidney Gelber, who became provost at Stony Brook, he frequently took pictures around New York City; he also took pictures during his summers in Vermont. He developed and printed all of the photographs himself. Another of his passions was baseball: the rhythm of the game, the complex systems of communication that developed among the players, and the timelessness inherent in the structure of baseball fascinated him. He also had a great appreciation for the beauty in athleticism and the human body in general and had as much admiration for the graceful leap of the outfielder reaching for a ball as for the dancer's pirouette. Such catholicity and respect for the multiplicity of forms of human activity were not only characteristic of Buchler's personal relationships—he could evince as much interest in the publishing ideas of his sister or in the intricacies of carpentry as in the arguments for and against an abstract philosophical thesis—but also were embodied in his theory of human judgment.

Buchler was also a great lover of the arts, in particular Baroque music, Italian Renaissance art (especially the sculptures of Donatello), dance, and poetry. In a 1971 interview with Earl Lane, Buchler remarked that "the whole history of art, especially poetic art, has been apologetic" and that philosophy and, in particular, "an adequate metaphysics of judgment" could establish the autonomy and value of art. He endeavored to carry out this project in his last book, *The Main of Light: On the Concept of Poetry* (1974).

In *The Main of Light* Buchler returns to the theory of judgment, which he believes is necessary for an adequate understanding of the range of actual and possible human experience. Buchler chooses poetry to show how the theory of judgment can better frame a philosophical understanding of a specific type of human experience. The book is divided into four parts: a critique of prevailing theories of poetry in chapters 1 through 4, the classification of poetry as a species of exhibitive judgment in chapter 5, the development of categories to identify the distinguishing features of poetry as a literary art in chapter 6, and an analysis of the conditions of meaning and interpretation in poetry in chapter 7. The book incorporates the categories of Buchler's entire system, both the theory of judgment and the general ontology. Buchler's thesis is that poetry can be created, but cannot be understood philosophically, without an adequate metaphysics of general ontology.

In 1978 Buchler published two major articles that complete his system: "On the Concept of 'the World'" and "Probing the Idea of Nature." Both were republished in an enlarged edition (1990) of *Metaphysics of Natural Complexes*. In these final articles Buchler takes up the question of whether there is an order of orders that can be designated "the world" or "nature." He argues that according to the principles of ordinality and noncontradiction, there is no such order, and he shows that attempts by such philosophers as Whitehead, Thomas Hobbes, R. G. Collingwood, and Ludwig Wittgenstein to argue for the notion of totality fail.

Buchler suffered a serious stroke in March 1979, a few days before he was to deliver his paper "Probing the Idea of Nature" to the Metaphysical Society of America. He recovered sufficiently to return to teaching and dissertation supervision in January 1980. He retired the following year. His health steadily declined, and he died in a nursing home in Chambersburg, Pennsylvania, near the home of his daughter, on 19 March 1991. Shirk wrote an account of his final years titled *After the Stroke: Coping with America's Third Leading Cause of Death* (1991). She died on 24 August 1997.

Buchler's work was somewhat out of step with the dominant analytic trends in philosophy; even so, it has been studied since it first appeared. In 1959 a double issue of *The Journal of Philosophy* devoted to Buchler's work was edited by Gelber and Matthew Lipman. In the early 1960s some former students and colleagues of Buchler's began meeting informally to discuss his ideas; they came to be known as the New York Philosophical Group. The membership of the group included, at various times, Edel, Singer, Gelber, Lipman, Lynne Belaief, Gail Belaief, Robert Olsen, George Kline, Douglas Greenlee, Stephen Ross, Arnold Berleant, Patrick Hill, Victorino Tejera, and Marjorie C. Miller. Buchler himself sometimes attended.

While Buchler's work has not had wide influence, the daring nature of his system guarantees him a place in the history of philosophy. In *Creativity in American Philosophy* (1984) Hartshorne comments on Buchler's central concept of natural complexes: "I think almost the entire history of philosophy is against such an idea. . . . Only considerable courage could have made it seem worth while to challenge this tradition." Others see Buchler's work in relation to the American pragmatist tradition. In *A Stroll with William James* (1983) Jacques Barzun remarks that "among the very few contemporary thinkers who have attempted to fashion an entire philosophy as James did, Justus Buchler may be regarded as taking up empiricism where James left it and restoring to pragmatism the breadth and flexibility

that its first followers restricted." However one reads Buchler's works, one cannot help but be impressed by the originality and depth of his insights and the economy and rigor of expression of his literary style.

Interviews:
Earl Lane, "Is Philosophy the Answer?" *Newsday*, 26 November 1971, p. 3A;

Robert S. Corrington, "Conversation between Justus Buchler and Robert S. Corrington," *Journal of Speculative Philosophy*, 3, no. 4 (1989): 261–274.

Bibliographies:
Beth J. Singer, "Bibliography: The Writings of Justus Buchler," in her *Ordinal Naturalism: An Introduction to the Philosophy of Justus Buchler* (Lewisburg, Pa.: Bucknell University Press / London & Toronto: Associated University Presses, 1983), pp. 221–225;

Armen Marsoobian, Kathleen A. Wallace, and Robert S. Corrington, "Bibliography of Secondary Works on Justus Buchler," in their *Nature's Perspectives: Prospects for Ordinal Metaphysics* (Albany: State University of New York Press, 1991), pp. 371–379.

Biography:
Evelyn Shirk, *After the Stroke: Coping with America's Third Leading Cause of Death* (Buffalo, N.Y.: Prometheus, 1991).

References:
Monroe Beardsley, "Categories," *Review of Metaphysics*, 8 (September 1954): 3–29;

Robert S. Corrington, "Justus Buchler's Ordinal Metaphysics and the Eclipse of Foundationalism," *International Philosophical Quarterly*, 25 (September 1985): 289–298;

Roland Garrett, "The Limits of Generalization in Metaphysics: The Case of Justus Buchler," *Southern Journal of Philosophy*, 27 (Spring 1989): 1–28;

Sidney Gelber, "Toward a Radical Naturalism," *Journal of Philosophy*, 56, no. 5 (1959): 193–199;

Gelber and Kathleen A. Wallace, "Justus Buchler: Nature, Power, and Prospect," *Process Studies*, 15 (Summer 1986): 106–119;

Douglas Greenlee, "Buchler and the Concept of Poetry," *British Journal of Aesthetics*, 20 (Winter 1980): 54–66;

Greenlee, "Particulars and Ontological Parity," *Metaphilosophy*, 5 (July 1974): 216–231;

Peter H. Hare and John Ryder, "Buchler's Ordinal Metaphysics and Process Theology," *Process Studies*, 10 (Fall–Winter 1980): 120–129;

Charles Hartshorne, "Neville on Creation and Buchler on Natural Complexes," in his *Creativity in American Philosophy* (Albany: State University of New York Press, 1984), pp. 265–276;

Journal of Philosophy, special Buchler double issue, edited by Gelber and Matthew Lipman, 61 (February 1959);

Charles Landesman, "Metaphysics and Human Nature," *Review of Metaphysics,* 15 (June 1962): 656–671;

Armen Marsoobian, "Meaning in the Arts: Considerations for a General Theory," in *Frontiers in American Philosophy,* volume 2, edited by Robert W. Burch and Herman J. Saatkamp Jr. (College Station: Texas A&M University Press, 1996), pp. 338–346;

Marsoobian, Kathleen A. Wallace, and Robert S. Corrington, eds., *Nature's Perspectives: Prospects for Ordinal Metaphysics* (Albany: State University of New York Press, 1991);

Michael J. McGandy, "Buchler's Notion of Query," *Journal of Speculative Philosophy,* 11, no. 2 (1997): 203–224;

Marjorie C. Miller, "The Concept of Identity in Justus Buchler and Mahayana Buddhism," *International Philosophical Quarterly,* 16 (March 1976): 87–107;

Miller, "Method and System in Justus Buchler and Chu Hsi: A Comparison," *Journal of Chinese Philosophy,* 14 (1987): 209–225;

Beth J. Singer, "Art, Poetry and the Sense of Prevalence: Some Implications of Buchler's Theory of Poetry," *International Philosophical Quarterly,* 24 (September 1985): 267–282;

Singer, "Intersubjectivity without Subjectivism," *Man and World* (July 1991): 321–338;

Singer, "Introduction to the Philosophy of Justus Buchler," *Southern Journal of Philosophy,* 14 (Spring 1976): 3–30;

Singer, *Ordinal Naturalism: An Introduction to the Philosophy of Justus Buchler* (Lewisburg, Pa.: Bucknell University Press / London & Toronto: Associated University Presses, 1983);

Singer, "Substitutes for Substances," *Modern Schoolman,* 53 (1975): 19–38;

Southern Journal of Philosophy, special Buchler issue, edited by Singer and Joseph G. Grassi, 14 (Spring 1976);

Wallace, "Justus Buchler," in *The Blackwell Guide to American Philosophy,* edited by Marsoobian and Ryder (Oxford & Malden, Mass.: Blackwell, forthcoming 2003);

Wallace, "Making Categories or Making Worlds," *Journal of Speculative Philosophy,* 2, no. 4 (1988): 322–327;

Wallace, "Making Categories or Making Worlds, II," in *Frontiers in American Philosophy,* volume 1, edited by Burch and Saatkamp (College Station: Texas A&M University Press, 1992), pp. 147–156;

Wallace, "Ontological Parity and/or Ordinality?" *Metaphilosophy,* 30, no. 4 (1999): 302–318;

Wallace, "Reconstructing Judgment: Emotion and Moral Judgment," *Hypatia,* 8, no. 3 (1993): 61–83;

Phil Weiss, "Possibility: Three Recent Ontologies," *International Philosophical Quarterly,* 20 (June 1980): 199–219.

Papers:

Justus Buchler's papers are at the Center for Dewey Studies, Southern Illinois University at Carbondale.

Arthur C. Danto

(1 January 1924 –   )

D. Seiple

BOOKS: *Analytical Philosophy of History* (Cambridge: Cambridge University Press, 1965); revised as *Narration and Knowledge: Including the Integral Text of Analytical Philosophy of History* (New York: Columbia University Press, 1985);

Nietzsche as Philosopher (London: Macmillan, 1965; New York: Macmillan, 1965);

Analytical Philosophy of Knowledge (London: Cambridge University Press, 1968);

What Philosophy Is: A Guide to the Elements (New York: Harper & Row, 1968);

Mysticism and Morality: Oriental Thought and Moral Philosophy (New York: Basic Books, 1972);

Analytical Philosophy of Action (Cambridge: Cambridge University Press, 1973);

Jean-Paul Sartre (New York: Viking, 1975; Glasgow: Fontana, 1975);

Handlungstheorie, by Danto and others, Neue Hefte für Philosophie, Heft 9 (Göttingen: Vandenhoeck & Ruprecht, 1976);

The Transfiguration of the Commonplace: A Philosophy of Art (Cambridge, Mass.: Harvard University Press, 1981);

The Philosophical Disenfranchisement of Art (New York: Columbia University Press, 1986);

The State of the Art (New York: Prentice-Hall, 1987);

The Politics of Imagination (Lawrence: Department of Philosophy, University of Kansas, 1988);

Connections to the World: The Basic Concepts of Philosophy (New York: Harper & Row, 1989);

Encounters and Reflections: Art in the Historical Present (New York: Farrar, Straus & Giroux, 1990);

Beyond the Brillo Box (New York: Farrar, Straus & Giroux, 1992);

Embodied Meanings: Critical Essays and Aesthetic Meditations (New York: Farrar, Straus & Giroux, 1994);

Playing with the Edge: The Photographic Achievement of Robert Mapplethorpe (Berkeley: University of California Press, 1996);

Art on the Edge and Over: Searching for Art's Meaning in Contemporary Society, 1970s–1990s, by Danto, Linda

Arthur C. Danto (from the dust jacket for After the End of Art: Contemporary Art and the Pale of History, *1997)*

Weintraub, and Thomas McEvilley (Litchfield, Conn.: Art Insights, 1996);

After the End of Art: Contemporary Art and the Pale of History (Princeton: Princeton University Press, 1997);

Anything Goes: The Work of Art and the Historical Figure, by Danto, Charles Altieri, Anthony J. Cascardi, and Anne M. Wagner, Doreen B. Townsend Center Occasional Papers, no. 14 (Berkeley, Cal.: Doreen B. Townsend Center for the Humanities, 1998);

The Body/Body Problem: Selected Essays (Berkeley: University of California Press, 1999);

Philosophizing Art: Selected Essays (Berkeley: University of California Press, 1999);

The Madonna of the Future: Essays in a Pluralistic Art World (New York: Farrar, Straus & Giroux, 2000).

OTHER: *Philosophy of Science: Readings,* edited by Danto and Sidney Morgenbesser (New York: Meridian, 1960);

"The End of Art," in *The Death of Art,* edited by Berel Lang, Art and Philosophy, volume 2 (New York: Haven, 1984), pp. 5–35;

Art/Artifact: African Art in Anthropology Collections, text by Danto and others, photographs by Jerry L. Thompson (New York: Center for African Art / Munich: Prestel / New York: Distributed by te Neueus, 1988);

397 Chairs, text by Danto, photographs by Jennifer Lévy (New York: Abrams, 1988);

J. S. G. Boggs, *Smart Money (Hard Currency): An Exhibition Organized by the Tampa Museum of Art, Sponsored by Sunbank of Tampa Bay,* text by Danto and Bruce W. Chambers (Tampa, Fla.: Tampa Museum of Art, 1990);

Angel Chairs: New Works by Wendell Castle, text by Danto, Peter T. Joseph, and Emma T. Cobb (New York: Peter Joseph Gallery, 1991);

Masterworks, text by Danto, Joseph, and Witold Rybczynski (New York: Peter Joseph Gallery, 1991);

Cindy Sherman, *History Portraits,* text by Danto (New York: Rizzoli, 1991);

Ludwig Wittgenstein, *Über Gewissheit/On Certainty,* edited by G. E. M. Anscombe and G. H. von Wright, translated by Anscombe and Denis Paul, introduction by Danto (San Francisco: Arion Press, 1991);

Mark Tansey, *Visions and Revisions,* edited by Christopher Sweet, notes and comments by Danto (New York: Abrams, 1992);

Robert Mapplethorpe, *Mapplethorpe,* text by Danto (New York: Random House, 1992);

From the Inside Out: Eight Contemporary Artists, organized by Susan Tumarkin Goodman, text by Danto (New York: Jewish Museum, 1993);

Sean Scully, *The Catherine Paintings,* text by Danto, Carter Ratcliff, and Steven Henry Madoff (Fort Worth: Modern Art Museum of Fort Worth, 1993);

"Responses and Replies," in *Danto and His Critics,* edited by Mark Rollins (Oxford & Cambridge, Mass.: Blackwell, 1993), pp. 191–215;

Steven S. High, George Cruger, and Randee Humphrey, eds., *Repicturing Abstraction,* text by Danto (Richmond: Anderson Gallery, Virginia Commonwealth University, 1995);

Joshua Neustein, *Light on the Ashes: August 10–October 2, 1996, Southeastern Center for Contemporary Art,* text by Danto, Jeff Fleming, and Susan Labrowsky Talbott (Winston-Salem, N.C.: Southeastern Center for Contemporary Art, 1996);

Betty Woodman, *Stedelijk Museum Amsterdam 21/9/96–10/11/96, Calouste Gulbenkian Foundation Lissabon June–August 1997, Musée d'Art Contemporain, Dunkerque September–December 1997,* introduction by Liesbeth Crommelin, text by Danto (Amsterdam: Stedelijk Museum, 1996);

Henry James, *The Madonna of the Future,* photogravure by Jim Dine, introduction by Danto (San Francisco: Arion Press, 1997);

Cy Twombly: Catalogue Raisonné of Sculpture, edited by Nicola Del Roscio, text by Danto (Munich: Schirmer/Mosel, 1997);

The Art of John Cederquist: Reality of Illusion, text by Danto and Nancy Princenthal, introduction by Kenneth R. Trapp (Oakland: Oakland Museum of California, 1997);

Ida Applebroog: Nothing Personal, Paintings 1987–1997, text by Danto, Terrie Sultan, and Dorothy Allison (Washington, D.C.: Corcoran Gallery of Art in association with Distributed Art Publishers, 1998);

Sherman, *Untitled Film Stills,* text by Danto (London: Schirmer Art Books, 1998);

Francesc Torres, *The Repository of Absent Flesh,* text by Danto (Cambridge, Mass.: MIT List Visual Arts Center, 1998);

Neal Benezra and Olga M. Viso, *Regarding Beauty: A View of the Late Twentieth Century,* text by Danto (Washington, D.C.: Hirshhorn Museum and Sculpture Garden, Smithsonian Institution, 1999);

Howard Ben Tré, text by Danto, Mary Jane Jacob, and Patterson Sims (New York: Hudson Hills Press, 1999);

Choice from America: Modern American Ceramics, text by Danto and Janet Koplos ('s-Hertogenbosch, Netherlands: Kruithuis Museums Collection, 1999);

Neustein, *Five Ash Cities,* text by Danto, Hilary Putnam, and Kristine Stiles (Chicago: Olive Production in association with Academy Chicago Publishers, 2000);

"Formation, Success, and Mastery: Eric Fischl through Three Decades," in *Eric Fischl, 1970–2000* (New York: Monacelli Press, 2000), pp. 11–24;

Jean-Marie Schaeffer, *Art of the Modern Age: Philosophy of Art from Kant to Heidegger,* translated by Steven Rendall, foreword by Danto (Princeton: Princeton University Press, 2000);

Honoré de Balzac, *The Unknown Masterpiece; and, Gambara,* translated by Richard Howard, introduction by Danto (New York: New York Review Books, 2001);

Jun Kaneko, *Susan Peterson,* foreword by Danto (London: Laurence King / Trumbull, Conn.: Distributed by Weatherhill, 2001);

Made in Oakland: The Furniture of Garry Knox Bennett, text by Danto, Edward S. Cooke Jr., and Ursula Ilse-Neuman (New York: American Craft Museum, 2001);

Peter G. Meyer, ed., *Brushes with History: Writing on Art from* The Nation, *1865–2001,* introduction and contributions by Danto (New York: Thunder Mouth Press, 2001);

Testimony: Vernacular Art of the African-American South. The Ronald and June Shelp Collection, text by Danto, Grey Gundaker, Edmund Barry Gaither, Judith M. McWillie, and Kinshasha Conwill (New York: Abrams, 2002).

SELECTED PERIODICAL PUBLICATIONS–
UNCOLLECTED: "The Artworld," *Journal of Philosophy,* 61 (1964): 571–584;

"Basic Actions," *American Philosophical Quarterly,* 2 (1965): 141–148.

The philosopher and art critic Arthur C. Danto has produced a body of work of a breadth that is unusual in an era of specialization. To the overriding philosophical question of the twentieth century–"What is philosophy?"–he has devoted two major texts: *What Philosophy Is: A Guide to the Elements* (1968) and *Connections to the World: The Basic Concepts of Philosophy* (1989). To the pop-art phenomenon Danto has addressed his groundbreaking essay "The Artworld" (1964), his book *The Transfiguration of the Commonplace: A Philosophy of Art* (1981), and several of the essays collected in *The Philosophical Disenfranchisement of Art* (1986). His art criticism proper, produced regularly for *The Nation* magazine since 1984 and collected in several volumes, including *The State of the Art* (1987) and *The Madonna of the Future: Essays in a Pluralistic Art World* (2000), as well as his essays in exhibition catalogues, have carried many of his ideas into popular discussion and won him wider recognition than is generally afforded professional philosophers in the United States. Danto is anything but a mere popularizer, however, and his professional recognitions include election as president of the American Philosophical Association in 1983 and literary awards such as the Lionel Trilling Book Prize in 1982 and the National Book Critics Circle Award in 1990 for *Encounters and Reflections: Art in the Historical Present.*

Arthur Coleman Danto was born in Ann Arbor, Michigan, on 1 January 1924 to Samuel Budd Danto, a dentist, and Sylvia Gittleman Danto. He spent much of his childhood in Detroit. During World War II he served in the army in North Africa and Italy. He married Shirley Rovetch on 9 August 1946; they had two children, Elizabeth Ann and Jane Nicole.

Originally intending to pursue a career as a painter, Danto received a B.A. in art and history at Wayne University (now Wayne State University) in 1948 and an M.A. in philosophy at Columbia University in 1949. At Columbia he studied with Ernest Nagel, Suzanne K. Langer, and Justus Buchler. A Fulbright fellowship enabled him to study at the University of Paris in 1949–1950. He became an instructor in philosophy at the University of Colorado, Boulder, in 1950; in 1951 he accepted a similar position at Columbia, where he completed his doctorate in 1952 with a dissertation on the philosophy of history. He was promoted to assistant professor in 1954, associate professor in 1959, and full professor in 1966. He became Johnsonian Professor of Philosophy in 1975. His wife died in July 1978; on 15 February 1980 he married Barbara Westman, an artist. Danto retired in 1992 and is now Johnsonian Professor Emeritus.

For most of his career Danto was situated in the tradition of Anglo-American analytic philosophy, as is indicated by the titles of three of his books: *Analytical Philosophy of History* (1965), *Analytical Philosophy of Knowledge* (1968), and *Analytical Philosophy of Action* (1973). In *Nietzsche as Philosopher* (1965) and *Jean-Paul Sartre* (1975) he uses analysis to uncover the philosophical substance beneath the continental European style of these two figures. In *Mysticism and Morality: Oriental Thought and Moral Philosophy* (1972) he attempts to treat East Asian ethics in a similar way, though he is less sanguine about that project because the factual beliefs of those cultures are so different from those of the West that "their moral belief systems are unavailable to us." Danto's current work, however, like Richard Rorty's, emerges out of the convergence near the end of the twentieth century of the analytic and Continental traditions. As Jürgen Habermas observed in his review of Hans-Georg Gadamer's *Wahrheit und Methode: Grundzüge einer philosophischen Hermeneutik* (Truth and Method: Chraracteristics of a Philosophical Hermeneutics, 1960; translated as *Truth and Method,* 1975), Danto had already come to some of the same hermeneutic conclusions as Gadamer by the orthodox analytic route of examining the logical form of narrative sentences. "Logical form" refers to the implicit limits of any such sentence. Historical narratives are stories: they have a beginning and an end that are threaded together by human action. Actions are intentional, and no account that ignores this fact can properly qualify as an

Painting by Danto's wife, Barbara Westman, of herself and Danto with their dogs, Charlotte and Emilio (photograph © 1988 by Barbara Westman; from Mark Rollins, ed., Danto and His Critics, *1993)*

historical one. A physicist describing a past event is not giving an historical account, because such a description lacks reference to human intentions. Gadamer's point, however, is that the meaning of historical events far surpasses the historical narratives that provide the raw materials for historians' larger assessments, and Danto makes the same point. For example, the conflict between Prussia and Austria that began in 1756 is today called "the Seven Years' War"; but the Prussian king Frederick II certainly did not march into Dresden that year and proclaim the opening of a seven-year conflict. Historical explanations, for Danto, are not reducible to the explanations typically offered by empirical science, because they cannot be exhaustively rendered in purely physical language. This contrast between the understanding of human culture and theories about the physical world has become a hallmark of Continental thought, and *Analytical Philosophy of History* is an analytic philosopher's argument for a Continental philosopher's perspective. Habermas commented to Danto in a private communication that the book, the impact of which was widely felt in Europe,

had overcome the prevailing divide between those two major schools of thought. If Danto had never written anything beyond *Analytical Philosophy of History,* his place in the history of philosophy would have been assured. But he contributed, as well, to the discussions about action theory that arose in the early 1970s, and in the early 1980s he applied those results to develop an original view of art history.

Throughout his work Danto makes use of "the method of indiscernibles." Indiscernibles—instances that are categorically distinct but empirically indistinguishable—provide the essential paradigm of what, in Danto's view, philosophy is supposed to do: look beneath the surface of things to discern their essential natures. He applies the method in *Analytical Philosophy of Action,* an expansion of his influential 1965 essay "Basic Actions," which did much to make the concept of action a major concern of Anglo-American philosophy. Danto asks his readers to consider the difference between the intentional raising of an arm—an action—and a physically indiscernible reflex motion. A "basic action" is a bodily movement that is caused by an intention, which excludes reflexes, and that "satisfies" that intention, which excludes instances where a person intends to raise an arm but a cerebral misfunction triggers the twitching of the shoulder instead. Ever since Plato in the fourth century B.C., and even more since René Descartes in the seventeenth century, discussion of indiscernibles has been the standard starting point for distinguishing genuine knowledge from seductive but false claimants to that status. Danto has devoted considerable attention to the problem, most prominently in *Analytical Philosophy of Knowledge* and *Connections to the World,* and he has applied the method of indiscernibles to posit what he takes to be the essential questions of art theory.

For Danto, the method of indiscernibles operates as half of a methodological pair; the other half is representation. Considered from a physical point of view, an historically significant event would be indistinguishable from a trivial episode in the universal molecular flux. What makes it a human event at all is that a mode of representation—an intention—supervenes to raise its status above that of a mere atomic happening, and by being placed in a wider framework of intentionality the event becomes comprehensible. For example, Martin Luther might have initiated the Protestant Reformation by his intransigence before the Diet of Worms on 18 April 1521, when he said, "Here I stand; I can do no other"; but that utterance is of little interest if it was only the result of his chronic constipation. The difference lies in how Luther's action is represented to himself, to his contemporaries, and to posterity.

For a nonphilosophical audience Danto's concern with indiscernibles and representation may not command much interest; but his art criticism in *The Nation* provides ready access to his general philosophical views. The historicism of the nineteenth-century German idealist philosopher Georg Wilhelm Friedrich Hegel grounds almost all of Danto's writings on art. What art is, for Danto, depends on its historical context of production, and what the aesthetician can notice about art depends on his or her station along the trajectory of art history. These points might, at first sight, seem trivial: of course, one might say, art objects have an historical genesis, and of course, questions about a work's aesthetic properties are raised in response to what artists have actually produced. But Danto's Hegelian historicism puts a radical spin on these seemingly banal observations. That everyday objects such as Marcel Duchamp's ready-mades and Andy Warhol's *Brillo Boxes* (1964) have entered the field of art opens questions that not only have not actually been posed but also could not, even in principle, have been posed previously. What counts as "art" varies from one historical moment to the next. The point is not just the obvious one that one's understanding of art is not fixed; art itself is not fixed. Standards of "good" art, and even the criteria for "art" itself, do not eternally await human discernment. Once

this point is understood, one can see that the use of such categories must appeal to some historical narrative tethered to the contemporary moment and, also, that productive discussions about past art must respect the art-historical vocabulary available to the culture of that day. Otherwise, Danto says, one would be in the absurd position of an historian, present at the defenestration of two Catholic councillors and their secretary in Prague on 23 May 1618, reporting that he had just witnessed the beginning of the Thirty Years' War.

According to Danto, the history of modern art until Warhol was an experimental expansion of creative horizons, achieving ever bolder results. But history does not go on in one direction forever: narratives have a natural structure that includes closure. In Warhol, art reaches a peculiar kind of end point in which a wooden reproduction of an ordinary box of Brillo scouring pads is "made" into an art object without any obvious perceptual alteration. Art, which had always been recognizably representational, suddenly became "indiscernibly" representational: Warhol's Brillo box is not "about" Brillo boxes, kitchen chores, or grocery-store shelves; it is about a further possibility that no one—except, perhaps, Duchamp—had exploited until then. It is not about how to make better, more beautiful, or more true-to-life works of art; it is about what distinguishes art from non-art. Art, with Warhol, became fully self-representational. For Danto, Warhol shows that a point has been reached at which anything can be "art"; therefore, nothing can be identified as art apart from "an atmosphere of artistic theory" that the eye or ear alone cannot negotiate.

One of the main complaints against pop art was that an achievement such as Warhol's does nothing for aesthetic sensibility; instead, it wins the viewer over only at the level of an intellectual tease. For Danto, that is precisely the point: one can appreciate this movement in art only by confronting the philosophical questions it raises. And because it raises the most perplexing and exciting question about art, further innovations cannot convincingly serve as the grand historical impetus to the next wave of the avant-garde. The last conceivable radical moment in art history has been accomplished. Previously, the avant-garde—Edouard Manet, Auguste Renoir, Paul Gaugin, Pablo Picasso, or Jackson Pollock—had been concerned with "moving beyond" where others had already been. But, Danto asks, how could an artist ever "move beyond" Warhol? Nothing more radical can even be imagined than the collapse of the perceptual difference between art and nonart. The creation of art objects has taken on a "transfigurational" aspect: at this point in history the artistic act can, for the first time, consist of nothing more than the construction of a perception-altering context, as when Warhol gives the impression of having simply moved the Brillo box from the supermarket to the exhibit space.

Dust jacket for Danto's 1989 study of the nature of philosophy (Richland County Public Library)

And, Danto says in a nod to Hegel, this phenomenon suggests that by the mid 1960s the spirit of philosophy itself must have entered the art world: only the philosophically sophisticated could divine what transformed the modest Brillo box into an epoch-shattering artwork, and only the philosophically sophisticated could recognize the sense in which art had come to an "end." With Duchamp, Warhol, and Robert Rauschenberg, art production is no longer preoccupied with specifically artistic questions; Warhol could have displayed a real Brillo box, rather than a replica of one. Doing so would have no specifically "artistic" point, which is what outraged the conservative critics. But doing it has a philosophical point that, for Danto, provides an almost uncanny illustration of his own methodological themes. Questions about indiscernibility generate philosophical reflection. At the "end" of art, according to Danto, lies philosophy–though he does not mean that philosophy replaces art.

Danto's "end of art" claim has probably been more misunderstood than any of his other theses; popular commentators have protested that galleries have not, after all, ceased acquiring new works. Even some of

Danto's sophisticated critics portray him as proclaiming that everything produced under the name of "art" since 1964 is not art but philosophy. Danto's point is not that the production of art has stopped but that the modernist narrative about art has reached its culmination. Meanwhile, neoconservative rear-guard efforts to reinstate this narrative are a product of embittered nostalgia, like that of an historian who could not admit that the Thirty Years' War lasted only thirty years.

Warhol has frequently been interpreted as a cultural mirror in which the boredom of late-twentieth-century cultural life is reflected. This claim, whatever its merits, does not capture Danto's point about the "end of art." That moment in art history signals neither the termination of art production nor its enervation but, rather, its closure and consummation, "where the need for constant self-revolutionizing of art is now past." The remaining prospects for art may strike some as boring, and the resulting transformation of museum space may offend critics such as Hilton Kramer, who has denounced both Warhol and Danto. Danto sees the end of art as an era of great promise in which artists have finally been freed from the onus of membership in the latest avant-garde movement. Excesses will still be committed by artists entranced by media attention and commercial prospects; the result will be what Danto has called "Importance Art." But the "end of art" lifts artists out from under the burden of history: "There can and should never again be anything like the astonishing sequence of convulsions that have defined the history of art of our century," with "its vertiginous succession of movements and its waspish intolerances." This "post-historical atmosphere of art" will bring art back to where it belongs, as the vehicle for the satisfaction of those "human ends" that define the legitimate preoccupations of cultural life and redefine the social function of museums.

Thus, as an art critic Danto is not, as some of his critics suppose, an academic brandishing his cleverness in the popular press. He is a humanist who has always tried to place art in a wider context than the one the isolated art world provides. In his contributions to the left-leaning *Nation* magazine he has reflected on a wider range of topics than art criticism has typically presented. His aim has been to connect art to the concerns of educated ordinary people and to describe the moral and philosophical considerations that illuminate a world that produces the art he addresses. He has not shrunk from dealing with some of the more unseemly issues that have found their way into postmodern culture. At a time when most academic commentators were keeping their distance, he began to address the efforts of AIDS activists to find a voice through displays of art that were meant to inspire a political response as well as to express their personal agony. Danto points out that these two aims can be incompatible, since the rapport required for political inspiration is often shattered by the shrillness of the personal testimony: "activist art should fulfill itself through convincing those it reaches to attack its targets, not itself."

Danto's boldness is especially evident in the attention he has given to the controversial late gay photographer Robert Mapplethorpe, resulting in the publication of *Playing with the Edge: The Photographic Achievement of Robert Mapplethorpe* (1996). Here, Danto describes a body of work that is virtually inaccessible to anyone uninterested in or upset by sadomasochism or gay culture in general, and he does so through a vocabulary and sensibility that few outside or even inside the gay world have mastered. He makes apparent why Mapplethorpe's kind of art, which approaches what Danto earlier called "disturbational art," deserves to be respected rather than vilified: though it appears to sanctify practices that inflict suffering on willing recipients, such as the insertion of a fist or a whip handle into a rectum, it imbues those acts with "an edge of meaning" that sets them apart from the meaningless horrors that headline the nightly news. Its power confirms the enduring function of at least one element of the modernist repertoire: its capacity to challenge people's most sacred preconceptions. The effect of Mapplethorpe's work is all the more poignant when the images are disclosures of the trust that can hold between lovers and even of the dark fantasy side at work in the psychology of the astounded viewer. Whether the viewer is brought to the edge of sexual excitement or to moral revulsion is an individual response to the content of Mapplethorpe's photographs; Danto takes the reader beyond that kind of response so that he or she can begin to view those photographs as artistic accomplishments that "beautify what is initially remote from beauty." Mapplethorpe's work does what is characteristic of art as a human activity: it exploits its mode of representing its content, and so, in Hegelian terms, the content is *aufgehoben* (transcended and raised to a higher level).

Even so, given the social considerations that many believe override purely artistic merit, the question remains why one should concern oneself with such images—as well as why public funding should be provided for their exhibition, as the National Endowment for the Arts had initially done. The venom that greeted Mapplethorpe's work on the floor of the U.S. Senate in the late 1980s had not yet surfaced when Danto reviewed the Mapplethorpe retrospective at the Whitney Museum of American Art in New York City in 1988; the press had not yet addressed the explicitly sexual side of the work. In the years that followed, the questions of government subsidy and censorship of the arts took on a political edge not matched since the publication of James Joyce's *Ulysses* in 1922. Danto has expressed himself forcefully on both issues, holding that government should subsidize art because it promotes

Dust jacket for the 2000 collection of Danto's art criticism for The Nation *magazine (Richland County Public Library)*

social good and that censorship has a chilling effect on the healthy pluralism that art promotes. Thus, art, like philosophy, leads one to a consideration of politics, history, and philosophical method. For Danto, as for Hegel and the American pragmatist philosopher John Dewey, what one can interestingly say about art becomes both a testing ground for and a stepping stone to other concerns.

Inspired by the parallels between his theories of art and certain issues in the psychology of perception and cognition, Danto for years team-taught several courses at Columbia with members of the psychology department. The result has appeared at various points in his writings. To make plausible his observations on historical narrative as they apply to art history, Danto needs to allow for one's ability to view past artworks relatively uncorrupted by subsequent culture. What is required for historical narrative in general also applies, according to Danto, to art history. A painter's work must be explainable in vocabulary that is translatable into terms the artist could plausibly have used. Thus, the paintings of Annibale Carracci (1560–1609) are explained through those of Antonio Alle-

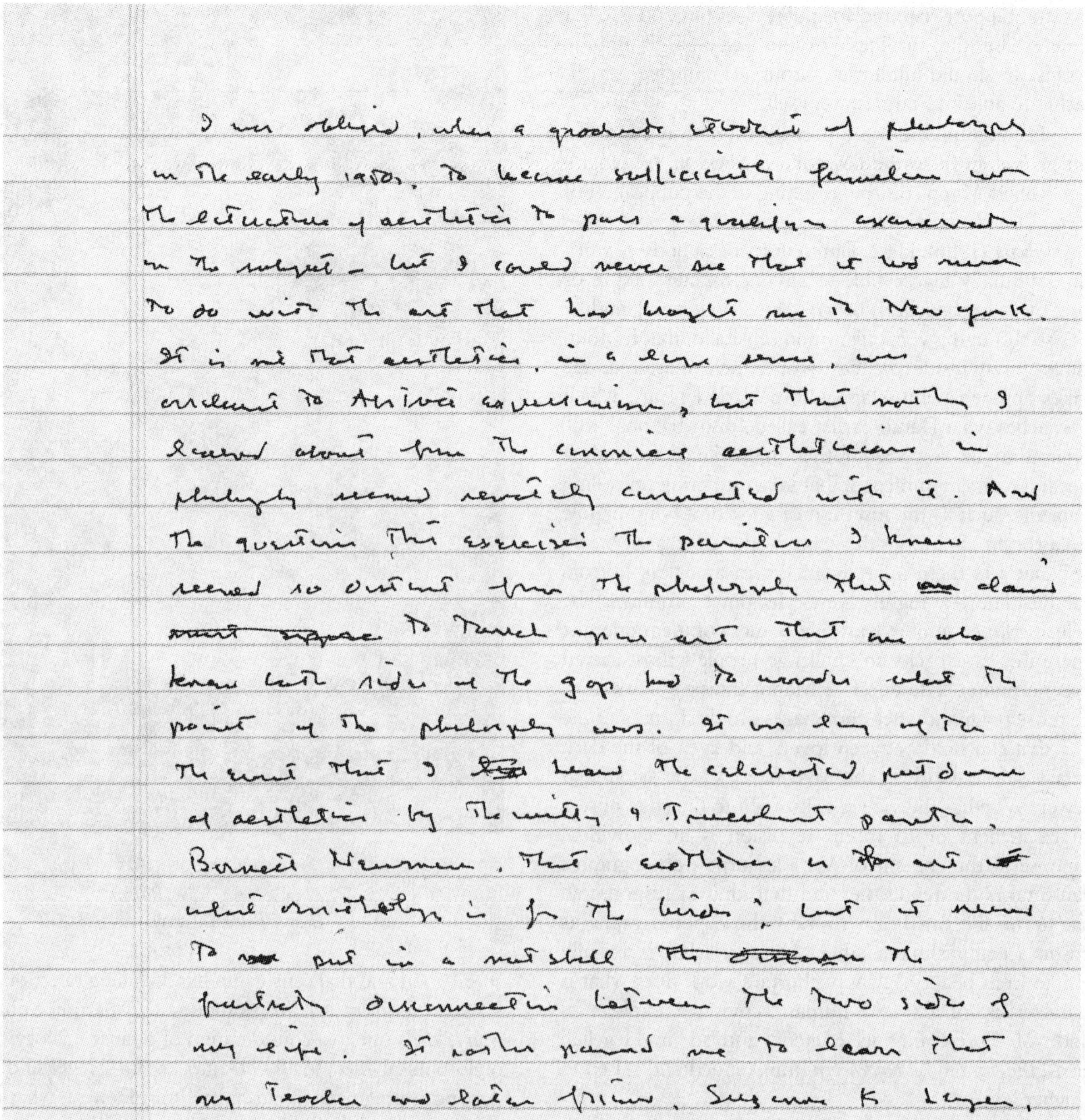
I was obliged, when a graduate student of philosophy in the early 1950s, to become sufficiently familiar with the literature of aesthetics to pass a qualifying examination on the subject – but I could never see that it had much to do with the art that had brought me to New York. It is not that aesthetics, in a large sense, was irrelevant to artistic experience, but that nothing I learned about from the American aestheticians in philosophy seemed remotely connected with it. And the questions that exercised the painters I knew seemed so distant from the philosophy that ~~one~~ claimed ~~must suppose~~ to touch upon art that one who knew both sides of the gap had to wonder what the point of the philosophy was. It was long after the event that I first heard the celebrated put down of aesthetics by the witty and truculent painter, Barnett Newman, that 'aesthetics is for the artist what ornithology is for the birds,' but it seems to put in a nutshell the perfect disconnection between the two sides of my life. It rather pained me to learn that my teacher and later friend, Suzanne K. Langer, had been Newman's particular target on the occasion when he fired an audience of artists and aestheticians gathered at Woodstock, New York, that no ornithologist ever supposed that ornithology was 'for the birds' – but I thought the meeting must have been animated by the somewhat patronizing conviction

First two pages of the draft for the introduction to Danto's forthcoming book "The Abuse of Beauty" (Collection of Arthur C. Danto)

on the part of the aesthetician. There that they do of true sensibly of experience 'for the artist' of this were true. The Texts in which such inquire knowledge on neither done were totally unknown to me.

The second issue among the analytic philosophers I hoped to impress, when I began with philosophy, was that aesthetics it was one for the birds, to one that deepens expression, and such I used in brief piece on the philosophy of art in 1964. I modelled it on the kind of thinking that belonged to the philosophy of science & of language that defined the most respectable philosophy at the time. Abstract Expressionism was giving way just then to a very different movement in the visual arts, one in which the philosophical question that excited me had, or seemed to have, almost nothing to do with aesthetics at all. Pop Art was attempting to overcome the gap between fine and revealed art — between the elevated and the coarse, the high and the low. The latter exemplified by comic strips and commercial art. And I was in particular bewildered by an exhibition I had since written about aesthetics, in which Andy Warhol displayed a number of wooden boxes painted to resemble the cartons in which Brillo

gri di Correggio (1494–1534), and not vice versa, because of their relative positions in history: no painter could have an historical impact on his or her predecessor. On the other hand, people today occupy even more distance from Correggio than Caracci's contemporaries did, and if the forms that appear in Correggio's paintings were unavailable to culturally unimpacted perception, no interesting account of Correggio could even be written. If those forms are available, then some level of human perception, at the innate level, has to be impervious to cultural influence. A body of psychological literature offers support for Danto's thesis: pigeons, monkeys, and sheep respond by innate programming to environmental features, and humans are subject to optical illusions such as the Muller-Lyer illusion, in which the observer cannot see two lines, one above the other, as identical in length, even though he or she knows by measuring them that they are identical. There may be more to perceptual constancy than humans acquire from their culture alone and, if Danto is right, enough to outweigh the more-radical historicist arguments that achieved prominence in the last quarter of the twentieth century.

Danto's views on art are emblematic of his overall philosophy: he has managed to reconcile apparently conflicting philosophical sensibilities without slighting either of them. Though he appreciates historicism in general and postmodernism specifically, his views are a good deal less radical than those of most postmodernists. Though he agrees with Hegel that not all things are possible at all times, and that historical circumstances prepare the way for consciousness to represent reality in new ways, he holds that such representations attain a connection to a world that was there all along but simply hidden from view. Thus, Danto rejects the idealism implicit in deconstructionism: the world is more than the linguistic web that is presupposed in describing it. In this sense, Danto denies that philosophy is a radically historicist enterprise. Its genuine options are limited by more than the linguistic habits of its practitioners: they are also limited by the ways in which the world really could not be, whether those limits are entirely apparent at any historical moment. Ascertaining those limits is the task of philosophy. Danto regards the most important philosophical problems as truly deep and their solutions as genuine discoveries, and he remains an "unabashed essentialist." Even now, he thinks, intriguing findings may remain to be made–such as his own thesis about the end of art, which, he claims, follows "almost" as a logical necessity once the priority of the narrative form has been established for art history, "since narratives cannot be endless." As he puts it in the "Responses and Replies" section of Mark Rollins's *Danto and His Critics*

(1993), philosophy remains "always the same and always totally present to itself–a finite array of positions on representation, truth, and causality." Though unperturbed by the notion of art's "end," Danto does not follow Rorty and Jacques Derrida in consigning philosophy to the same fate.

In the view of many who know him, Arthur C. Danto manifests his philosophy in his personal qualities. Among these qualities is the generosity he displays toward critics. To those who contend that his treatment of art is too self-consciously clever, lacking–as one critic put it–sufficient "aesthetic passion," Danto replies that in the scale of human joys and agonies, art itself is not all that important; after Warhol, especially, it is certainly not important enough to bear the world-historical significance that was once thought to be its peculiar burden. To those who complain about his "reductionistic" treatment of Continental or East Asian thought, Danto in a way concedes the point but challenges its impact by replying that philosophy itself is not all that there should be, even within the domain of the professional philosopher. Danto is a humanist and offers a balanced view of the place of philosophy in human life. Philosophy, like art, has an indispensable, but by no means the only, privileged role in human thinking, and any cultural feature that fails–even as a philosophical category–is not rendered inconsequential to those for whom it still has meaning.

Interview:

Giovanna Borradori, "The Cosmopolitan Alphabet of Art: Arthur C. Danto," in her *The American Philosopher: Conversations with Quine, Davidson, Putnam, Nozick, Danto, Rorty, Cavell, MacIntyre, and Kuhn,* translated by Rosanna Crocitto (Chicago & London: University of Chicago Press, 1994), pp. 86–102.

References:

David Carrier, ed., *Danto and His Critics: Art History, Historiography and after the End of Art* (Middletown, Conn.: Wesleyan University, 1998);

Dominique Chateau, *La question de la question de l'art: Note sur l'esthétique analytique. Danto, Goodman et quelques autres* (Saint-Denis: Presses universitaires de Vincennes, 1994);

Arto Haapala, Jerrold Levinson, and Veikko Rantala, eds., *The End of Art and Beyond: Essays after Danto* (Atlantic Highlands, N.J.: Humanities Press, 1997);

Berel Lang, ed., *The Death of Art,* Art and Philosophy, volume 2 (New York: Haven, 1984);

Mark Rollins, ed., *Danto and His Critics* (Oxford & Cambridge, Mass.: Blackwell, 1993).

Donald Davidson

(6 March 1917 –   )

Ernest Lepore
Rutgers University

BOOKS: *Decision Making: An Experimental Approach,* by
  Davidson, Patrick Suppes, and Sidney Siegel
  (Stanford, Cal.: Stanford University Press, 1957);
Essays on Actions and Events (Oxford: Clarendon Press /
  New York: Oxford University Press, 1980;
  enlarged, 2001);
Inquiries into Truth and Interpretation (Oxford: Clarendon
  Press / New York: Oxford University Press,
  1984; enlarged, 2001);
Plato's Philebus (New York: Garland, 1990);
*Reflecting Davidson: Donald Davidson Responding to an Inter-
  national Forum of Philosophers,* by Davidson and oth-
  ers, edited by Ralf Stoecker (Berlin & New York:
  De Gruyter, 1993);
Subjective, Intersubjective, Objective (Oxford: Clarendon
  Press, 2001).

OTHER: "The Method of Intension and Extension,"
  in *The Philosophy of Rudolf Carnap,* edited by Paul
  Arthur Schilpp, The Library of Living Philoso-
  phers, volume 11 (La Salle, Ill.: Open Court,
  1963), pp. 311–349;
Words and Objections: Essays on the Work of W. V. Quine,
  edited by Davidson and Jaakko Hintikka (Dor-
  drecht, Netherlands: Reidel, 1969)–includes "On
  Saying That," by Davidson, pp. 158–174;
"The Individuation of Events," in *Essays in Honor of Carl
  G. Hempel: A Tribute on the Occasion of His Sixty-fifth
  Birthday,* edited by Nicholas Rescher (Dordrecht,
  Netherlands: Reidel, 1969), pp. 216–234;
"Mental Events," in *Experience and Theory,* edited by
  Lawrence Foster and J. W. Swanson (Amherst:
  University of Massachusetts Press, 1970; Lon-
  don: Duckworth, 1970), pp. 79–99;
"Agency," in *Agent, Action, and Reason,* edited by Robert
  Binkley, Richard Bronaugh, and Ausonio Marras
  (Toronto & Buffalo, N.Y.: University of Toronto
  Press, 1971), pp. 3–37;
Semantics of Natural Language, edited by Davidson and
  Gilbert Harman (Dordecht, Netherlands & Bos-
  ton: Reidel, 1972);

Donald Davidson (photograph by Steve Pyke, London)

"Freedom to Act," in *Essays on Freedom of Action,* edited
  by Ted Honderich (London: Routledge & Kegan
  Paul, 1973), pp. 137–156;
"The Material Mind," in *Fourth International Congress for
  Logic, Methodology, and Philosophy of Science, Bucharest,
  Romania: Proceedings,* edited by Patrick Suppes, L.
  Henkin, G. C. Moisil, and A. Joja (Amsterdam:
  North-Holland / New York: American Elsevier,
  1973), pp. 709–722;
"Psychology as Philosophy," in *Philosophy of Psychology,*
  edited by S. C. Brown (New York: Barnes &
  Noble, 1974; London: Macmillan, 1974), pp. 41–
  52;
"Thought and Talk," in *Mind and Language,* edited by
  Samuel Guttenplan (Oxford: Oxford University
  Press, 1975), pp. 7–23;
The Logic of Grammar, edited by Davidson and Harman
  (Encino, Cal.: Dickenson, 1975);
"Paradoxes of Irrationality," in *Philosophical Essays on
  Freud,* edited by Richard Wollheim and James

Hopkins (Cambridge & New York: Cambridge University Press, 1982), pp. 289–305;

"Adverbs of Action," in *Essays on Davidson: Actions and Events,* edited by Bruce Vermazen and Merrill B. Hintikka (Oxford: Clarendon Press / New York: Oxford University Press, 1985), pp. 230–241;

"Deception and Division," "Reply to Quine on Events," and "Rational Animals," in *Actions and Events: Perspectives on the Philosophy of Donald Davidson,* edited by Ernest Lepore and Brian P. McLaughlin (Oxford & New York: Blackwell, 1985), pp. 138–148, 173–176, 317–327;

"A Coherence Theory of Truth and Knowledge," "Empirical Content," and "A Nice Derangement of Epitaphs," in *Truth and Interpretation: Perspectives on the Philosophy of Donald Davidson,* edited by Lepore (Cambridge: Blackwell, 1986), pp. 307–332, 433–446;

"Judging Interpersonal Interests," in *Foundations of Social Choice Theory,* edited by Jon Elster and Aanund Hylland (Cambridge & New York: Cambridge University Press, 1986), pp. 195–211;

"Problems in the Explanation of Action," in *Metaphysics and Morality: Essays in Honour of J. J. C. Smart,* edited by Philip Pettit, Richard Sylvan, and Jean Norman (Oxford & New York: Blackwell, 1987), pp. 35–49;

"What Is Present to the Mind?" and "The Conditions of Thought," in *The Mind of Donald Davidson,* edited by Johannes Brandl and Wolfgang L. Gombocz (Amsterdam & Atlanta: Rodopi, 1989), pp. 3–18, 193–200;

"The Myth of the Subjective," in *Relativism: Interpretation and Confrontation,* edited by Michael Krausz (Notre Dame, Ind.: University of Notre Dame Press, 1989), pp. 159–172;

"Meaning, Truth and Evidence," in *Perspectives on Quine,* edited by Robert B. Barret and Roger F. Gibson (Cambridge, Mass.: Blackwell, 1990), pp. 68–79;

"Turing's Test" and "Representation and Interpretation," in *Modelling the Mind,* edited by K. A. Mohyeldin Said, W. H. Newton-Smith, and K. V. Wilkes (Oxford: Clarendon Press / New York: Oxford University Press, 1990), pp. 1–11, 12–26;

"Three Varieties of Knowledge," in *A. J. Ayer: Memorial Essays,* edited by A. Phillips Griffiths (Cambridge & New York: Cambridge University Press, 1991), pp. 153–166;

"What Is Present to the Mind," in *Consciousness,* edited by Enrique Villanueva (Atascadero, Cal.: Ridgeview, 1991), pp. 197–213;

"The Socratic Conception of Truth," in *The Philosophy of Socrates: Elenchus, Ethics and Truth,* edited by K. J. Boudouris, Studies in Greek Philosophy, no. 5 (Athens, Greece: International Center for Greek Philosophy and Culture, 1991), pp. 51–58;

"Locating Literary Language," in *Literary Theory after Davidson,* edited by Reed Way Dasenbrock (University Park: Pennsylvania State University Press, 1993), pp. 295–308;

"Thinking Causes," in *Mental Causation,* edited by John Heil and Alfred Mele (Oxford: Clarendon Press / New York: Oxford University Press, 1993), pp. 3–17;

"Dialectic and Dialogue," in *Language, Mind, and Epistemology: On Donald Davidson's Philosophy,* edited by Gerhard Preyer, Frank Siebelt, and Alexander Ulfig (Dordrecht, Netherlands & Boston: Kluwer, 1994), pp. 429–437;

"The Social Aspect of Language," in *The Philosophy of Michael Dummett,* edited by Brian McGuinness and Gianluigi Oliveri (Dordrecht, Netherlands & Boston: Kluwer, 1994), pp. 1–16;

"Pursuit of the Concept of Truth," in *On Quine: New Essays,* edited by Paolo Leonardi and Marco Santambrogio (Cambridge & New York: Cambridge University Press, 1995), pp. 7–21;

"Subjective, Intersubjective, Objective," in *Current Issues in Idealism,* edited by Paul Coates and Daniel D. Hutto (Bristol, U.K.: Thoemmes Press, 1996), pp. 155–177;

"Seeing through Language," in *Thought and Language,* edited by John Preston (Cambridge & New York: Cambridge University Press, 1997), pp. 15–28;

"Intellectual Autobiography of Donald Davidson" and replies to critics, in *The Philosophy of Donald Davidson,* edited by Lewis Edwin Hahn, The Library of Living Philosophers, volume 27 (Chicago: Open Court, 1999), pp. 3–70, 80–86, 105–108, 123–126, 137–138, 162–166, 192–194, 207–210, 225–228, 251–254, 286–288, 305–310, 330–332, 342–344, 357–360, 378–380, 402–406, 422–424, 443–446, 460–462, 480–482, 497–500, 529–530, 571–574, 595–600, 619–622, 653–656, 667–670, 687–690, 715–718, 729–732;

Ben Mou, ed., *Two Roads to Wisdom? Chinese and Analytic Philosophical Traditions,* foreword by Davidson (Chicago: Open Court, 2001).

SELECTED PERIODICAL PUBLICATIONS–
UNCOLLECTED: "Outlines of a Formal Theory of Value I," by Davidson, J. C. C. McKinsey, and Patrick Suppes, *Philosophy of Science,* 22 (1955): 140–160;

"Action and Reaction," *Inquiry,* 13 (1970): 140–148;

"Toward a Unified Theory of Meaning and Action," *Grazer Philosophische Studien,* 11 (1980): 1–12;

"Incoherence and Irrationality," *Dialectica,* 39 (1985): 345–354;

"A New Basis for Decision Theory," *Theory and Decision,* 18 (1985): 87–98;

"The Structure and Content of Truth," *Journal of Philosophy,* 87 (1990): 279–328;

"James Joyce and Humpty Dumpty," *Midwest Studies in Philosophy,* 16 (1991): 1–12;

"The Third Man," *Critical Inquiry,* 19, no. 4 (1993): 607–616;

"On Quine's Philosophy," *Theoria,* 60 (1994): 184–192;

"What Is Quine's View of Truth?" *Inquiry,* 37 (1994): 437–440;

"Radical Interpretation Interpreted," *Philosophical Perspectives,* 8 (1994): 121–128;

"Could There Be a Science of Rationality?" *International Journal of Philosophical Studies,* 3, no. 1 (1995): 1–16;

"Laws and Cause," *Dialectica,* 49 (1995): 263–279;

"The Problem of Objectivity," *Tijdschr Filosof,* 57, no. 2 (1995): 203–220;

"The Folly of Trying to Define Truth," *Journal of Philosophy,* 93 (1996): 263–278.

Davidson in 1980 (from the cover for Essays on Actions and Events, *1980)*

Donald Davidson is widely regarded as one of the most important and influential philosophers of the second half of the twentieth century. He is an analytic philosopher in the tradition of Ludwig Wittgenstein and W. V. Quine, and his formulations of action, truth, and communicative interaction have generated considerable debate in philosophical circles around the world. He has never attempted a systematic exposition of his philosophical program, and so there is no single place where a student, interpreter, or critic can seek its official formulation. His published essays, taken together, form a mosaic that must be viewed all at once to discern an overall pattern. In addition, many of them include subtleties, complexities, and cross-references that cannot be entirely appreciated except in conjunction with one another.

Davidson was born on 6 March 1917 in Springfield, Massachusetts, to Clarence Herbert Davidson, an engineer, and Grace Cordelia Anthony Davidson. The family lived in the Philippines from shortly after Davidson was born until he was about four. They then returned to the United States. They lived for about a year in Amherst, Massachusetts, where Davidson's father taught elementary mathematics at Amherst College, then in suburban Philadelphia. When Davidson was about nine, they settled in Staten Island, New York, where he attended the Staten Island Academy. As a high-school student he read the works of Friedrich Nietzsche, Plato's *Parmenides,* and Immanuel Kant's *Kritik der reinen Vernunft* (1781; revised, 1787; translated as *Critique of Pure Reason,* 1855). In the fall of 1935 he entered Harvard University,

where he was regularly invited to afternoon tea in the apartment of the philosopher Alfred North Whitehead. Davidson became acquainted with most of the people in the philosophy department, including Quine, C. I. Lewis, and Raphael Demos.

After graduating with a B.A. in philosophy and classics in the spring of 1939, Davidson spent the summer in Hollywood writing scripts for *Big Town,* a weekly private-eye radio program starring Edward G. Robinson. He returned to Harvard in the fall on a graduate scholarship to study philosophy with an emphasis in classics. Among his fellow graduate students were Roderick Chisholm, Roderick Furth, Henry Aiken, and Arthur Smullyan. Davidson left graduate school in November 1942 to enlist in the navy. Before going overseas he married Virginia Baldwin on New Year's Eve; they had one child, Elizabeth. He participated in the invasions of Sicily, Salerno, and Anzio before being discharged in the summer of 1945.

Davidson returned to Harvard in March 1946. After completing the first draft of his dissertation on Plato's *Philebus,* he was hired in September as an instructor at Queens College in New York City. He completed the dissertation early in 1949 and received his Ph.D. (The dissertation was published in 1990.) He and his wife spent the summer of 1950 bicycling through France; during the trip he read and commented on the manuscript for Quine's "Two Dogmas of Empiricism" (1953).

In January 1951 Davidson joined the philosophy department at Stanford University. His work on decision theory and measurement theory with his colleagues Patrick Suppes and J. C. C. McKinsey culminated in a joint paper, "Outlines of a Formal Theory of Value I," which appeared in the journal *Philosophy of Science* in 1955.

While directing a dissertation in the late 1950s, Davidson identified a mistake in the literature of action theory. This discovery led to his classic paper "Actions, Reasons, and Causes," which he presented at the American Philosophical Association meeting in Washington, D.C., on 29 December 1963; it was published in *The Journal of Philosophy* that year and was later collected in his *Essays on Actions and Events* (1980). Prior to Davidson's paper, a near consensus had formed among philosophers that whatever the relationship between reasons and actions might be, it could not be causal: an alleged "logical connection" between reasons and actions excluded any causal relation between them. Davidson's purpose in his paper, he says, is "to defend the ancient—and common-sense—position that rationalization is a species of causal explanation." Much of the essay is devoted to refuting various then-popular arguments that purported to show that reasons could not cause the actions that they rationalize. Many philosophers believed that the eighteenth-century British philosopher David Hume had established that if event A is causally related to event B, A and B cannot be logically connected. In Hume's example, when a billiard ball moving with a certain momentum hits another ball, the movement of the second ball occurs not as a matter of logic but as a matter of the physical nature of the universe; and it is logically possible that causal interaction could have been different from what it actually is. One intuition behind the denial that reasons can be causes of actions, then, is that reasons and actions are logically related: for example, if a person believes that smoking is harmful and desires not to be harmed, he or she must, as a matter of logic alone, intend not to smoke. The person's reasons for intending not to smoke, therefore, could not be the cause of the intention.

Davidson replies that a logical connection between the description of a cause and the description of an effect does not, by itself, preempt causation, as is evident in the statement "The cause of event E caused event E." No one would infer from the fact that an event could not logically be described as "the cause of E" without being the cause of E that the first event did not cause the second. Similarly, even if no one could have a belief that smoking is harmful and have a desire not to do anything harmful without having an intention not to smoke, it does not follow that there is no causal relation between the reasons and the intentional action that ensues.

"Actions, Reasons, and Causes" resulted from Davidson's realization that no one had a good argument against causal theories of action. He then began to think about the nature of events. In "The Individuation of Events," first published in a 1969 Festschrift for Carl G. Hempel and collected in *Essays on Actions and Events,* he points out that the same action can be described in various ways. If not, one could not make sense of perfectly natural statements such as "Jones managed to apologize by saying 'I apologize,'" in which a single action is described both as managing to apologize and as saying "I apologize." But, Davidson asks, what sort of entities are these actions that admit of such redescriptions? Tables, chairs, and people are concrete, dated particulars—unique entities with locations in space and time. But what about actions and events—for example, the action of Bob shooting Bill or the event of the stock market crash of October 1929? Davidson claims that actions and events, like tables and chairs, are concrete, dated particulars that can be described in various nonlogically equivalent and nonsynonymous ways. What distinguishes them from other sorts of concrete, dated particulars is their potential for causal interaction; thus, part of the nature of being an event is to be able to stand in a causal relationship. Two events are identical if they have the same causes and effects. Since causation is a relation between events, and action is a type of event, events comprise the subject matter of action theory, as well as of science and ethics.

Davidson holds that events related by causation must be subsumable under a law; a law, in turn, is a generalization that is confirmable by its positive instances, and, if it is true, it supports counterfactual statements; finally, an event is subsumed by a law if it instantiates that law. For example, according to Boyle's law, the pressure of a fixed mass of gas at a constant temperature is inversely proportional to the volume. An instance of this law would be the statement "If A is the pressure of a fixed mass of gas at a constant temperature, then A is inversely proportional to the volume of that gas," and the law is confirmed if the consequent of this statement is true whenever its antecedent is. To say that the law "supports its counterfactual instances" means that even if A is not the pressure of a fixed mass of gas at a constant temperature, if it *were,* then it would be inversely proportional to the volume of that gas.

Around this time Davidson read the Polish American logician Alfred Tarski's article "Der Wahreitsbegriff in den formalisierten Sprachen" (1935; translated as "The Concept of Truth in Formalized Languages" in Tarski's *Logic, Semantics, Mathematics,* 1956). Davidson's work on decision theory had given him an appreciation for what a serious theory was; others who were working in philosophy of language did not have that appreciation. On the other hand, Tarski knew what a serious theory was but was not concerned with the semantics of natural languages. Davidson put these two interests together in

"Theories of Meaning and Learnable Languages," read at the 1964 International Congress for Logic, Methodology, and Philosophy of Science and published in 1965 in the proceedings of that congress, and "Truth and Meaning," published in the journal *Synthèse* in 1967; both are collected in his *Inquiries into Truth and Interpretation* (1984). In these papers he identifies an adequacy criterion for theories of meaning of natural languages, applies the criterion to several analyses of aspects of natural language that were prominent in the mid 1960s, and sketches a program in which a certain austere style of meaning theory meets the criterion.

What a theory of meaning should seek to accomplish, Davidson says, depends on what aspect of language the theorist wants to explain. For example, though natural languages are spoken by finite speakers without magical abilities, they are "unbounded": that is, they potentially include an infinite number of meaningful nonsynonymous sentences, any one of which such a speaker could understand. For example, from any indicative sentence of English a new one can be formed by prefacing the original sentence with "It is believed that"; any two indicative sentences can be joined with the word *or* to form a new sentence; and so on. The novel sentences to which these mechanisms give rise are intelligible to normal speakers of the language if the components of the sentences are. This capacity seems to require that speakers have learned a finite number of rules that determine from a finite set of "semantic primitives" what counts as a meaningful composition; an expression is semantically primitive, Davidson says in "Theories of Meaning and Learnable Languages," if the "rules which give the meaning for the sentences in which it does not appear do not suffice to determine the meaning of the sentences in which it does appear." On the basis of these considerations, Davidson lays down as a requirement of a theory of meaning that the theory specify what every sentence in a language means by exhibiting that meaning as a function of the meanings of the significant parts of the sentence: such a theory he calls "a compositional meaning theory." Davidson's "Theories of Meaning and Learnable Languages" first brought to prominence the requirement that a theory of meaning of a language exhibit the language as compositional. The requirement focuses attention on the need to uncover structure in natural languages. While philosophers from time immemorial have engaged in this activity, until Davidson the project had not been clearly separated from conceptual analysis.

Davidson's positive suggestion for a compositional meaning theory for a language L uses no concept of meaning that goes beyond truth. His theory of meaning takes the form of a finite theory of truth that, for each sentence S of language L, entails a "T-sentence" of form T: "S is true in L if and only if p"; p is the specification in a

Cover for the collection that includes Davidson's "Mental Events," in which he argues that every mental event is identical with some physical event (Bruccoli Clark Layman Archives)

"metalanguage" of conditions under which S is true in L. For example, an adequate compositional meaning theory for German should issue in a theorem such as "'Schnee ist weiss' is true in German if and only if snow is white." Davidson chooses this rather austere form of theory over one that explicitly invokes meaning by issuing in theorems of the form M: "S in L means that p," where p specifies in a metalanguage what S means in L. His reasons do not, as is sometimes suggested, have anything to do with replacing the complex notion of meaning with one that is more easily understood. His inquiry is guided solely by the goal of devising a compositional meaning theory, and he argues in "Truth and Meaning" that this aim can be achieved with a theory that issues in theorems of the form T but not with one that issues in theorems of the form M because, unlike the locution "is true if and only if," the locution "means that" is "semantically opaque" and, thus, hinders the development of a compositional meaning theory. A compositional theory of meaning for a language L that issues in interpretive T-sentences such as S is such that anyone who knows the theory can understand every sentence of L; that is, anyone who understands the language in which the specification is given—the metalanguage—can understand the sentence S in the language being analyzed (the "object language").

In September 1958 Quine visited the Center for Behavioral Studies at Stanford and asked Davidson to read the manuscript for his *Word and Object* (1960). Davidson did virtually nothing that term except read and reread the manuscript, trying to understand it. He saw that Quine was dealing with problems in the philosophy of language that no one else had considered. After reading Tarski's essay he went back and reread Quine's *Word and Object* with fresh eyes. This experience brought Davidson to his project of "radical interpretation," which he discusses in an article of that title published in the journal *Dialectica* in 1973 and collected in *Inquiries into Truth and Interpretation*.

Since, Davidson says, it is impossible to know a priori how to interpret the expressions of a natural language or how to assign truth conditions to them, an adequate compositional meaning theory must be empirical. In the case of one's own language, no difficulty arises in identifying which sentences of form T are interpretive. The problem for a theorist in regard to a language he or she already understands is to formulate the axioms of the theory and construct proofs of them. A quite different problem confronts a theorist in dealing with a language he or she does not understand. An adequate compositional meaning theory must be empirically warranted under the practice of radical interpretation, which means that specific empirical considerations must be respected in choosing between true compositional meaning theories. For example, a compositional meaning theory for German might issue in W: "'Schnee ist weiss' is true in German if and only if grass is green." This statement is, as a matter of fact, true; but unlike S, it fails to interpret "Schnee ist weiss." Thus, no compositional meaning theory for German that issues in W can be adequate. But for languages one does not understand, a compositional meaning theory must be selected on the basis of "evidence plausibly available to an interpreter . . . who does not already know how to interpret utterances the theory is designed to cover." Davidson claims that nothing can be a language unless a correct compositional meaning theory, which issues in a true and interpretive sentence such as S for each sentence of that language, can be selected on the basis of the sorts of observations plausibly available to a "radical interpreter." A radical interpreter is defined as one who is ignorant of the language he or she is trying to interpret and lacks access to bilingual informants, dictionaries, and the like. A radical interpreter is able to determine when an informant holds a sentence to be true, even

though the interpreter fails to understand the sentence. The primary data for radical interpretation are formulable in singular sentences held to be true, such as E: "Kurt belongs to the German speech community, and Kurt holds true 'Es regnet' on Saturday at noon, and it is raining near Kurt on Saturday at noon." Data such as E can be collected from a variety of speakers across a variety of times by someone who does not understand German, and these data will eventually confirm a generally held true sentence such as GE: "For any speaker of the German speech community and for any time, that speaker holds true 'Es regnet' at that time if and only if it is raining near him or her at that time." Claims such as GE provide evidence for a radical interpreter that speakers of the German speech community take some form of words to express a specific truth. But, Davidson asks, what licenses inferring from data such as GE a theorem such as R: "'Es regnet' is true in German of a speaker S at a time T just in case it is raining near that speaker at that time"? Could all German speakers be wrong about such a matter? Davidson denies any such possibility, arguing that the inference from GE to R is legitimate if a "principle of charity" is presupposed. According to this principle, the favored compositional meaning theory for a language L must entail sentences of form T such that most sentences speakers of L hold to be true are, in fact, true.

Under radical interpretation, sentences speakers hold to be true continually turn out to be true. This result is not an accident but occurs because radical interpretation is a special sort of project, one that is constituted by the principle of charity. So, once data such as GE are collected, one can infer the corresponding T-sentence R via the principle of charity. Furthermore, by virtue of securing a set of interpretive T-sentences for context-sensitive sentences such as "Es regnet," a truth theory automatically assigns interpretive T-sentences to context-insensitive sentences such as "Schnee ist weiss." Thus, for example, on the basis of what a radical interpreter collects, he or she may devise for the context-sensitive sentences "Es schneit" and "Es ist weiss" the interpretive T-sentences a and b: (a) "For any speaker and time, if the speaker utters 'Es schneit' at that time, then the speaker's utterance of 'Es schneit' is true just in case it is snowing near him or her at that time"; (b) "For any speaker, time, and object, if the speaker utters 'Es ist weiss' at that time, then his or her utterance of 'Es ist weiss' is true at that time of that object if and only if that object is white at that time." On the basis of these generalizations, a radical interpreter may conjecture "application conditions" c and d for subsentence expressions such as *schnee* and *weiss:* (c) "For any object and time, *schnee* is true of that object at that time if and only if that object is snow at that time"; (d) "For any object and time, *weiss* is true of that object at that time if and only if that object is white at that time." Such information can be

Davidson (left) with the philosophers W. V. Quine and Dagfinn Føllesdal in Oxford, 1984

imagined as exploited in attributing truth-condition e to a context-insensitive sentence such as "Schnee ist weiss": (e) "'Schnee ist weiss' is true if and only if snow is white." Davidson concludes that only those compositional meaning theories that entail T-sentences licensed by radical interpretation are adequate.

Davidson's embrace of truth theories as the correct form for compositional meaning theories, and of radical interpretation as their presumed manner of confirmation, has philosophical ramifications. His strongest argument that events exist and have a certain nature is not a piece of pure metaphysical reasoning but, rather, derives from the constraints he places on compositional meaning theories. Any theory of meaning for a language must embody a view of the relationship between language and reality. Davidson holds that a compositional meaning theory, by providing a view about this relationship, offers substantive answers to metaphysical questions about reality and its nature. The best compositional meaning theory for English, for example, will require positing events to explain sentences about actions, events, and singular causal relationships such as sentence 1: "John hit Bill." An obvious candidate for its interpretive truth-condition would be 2: "'John hit Bill' is true if and only if John hit Bill." In 2, linguistic expressions are both used and mentioned: the words *hit, John,* and *Bill* and the corresponding aspects of the world—that is, the people and the action

that relates them—are discussed. In this limited sense, 2 could be said to "hook up" language and reality. The hookup remains silent, though, on the nature of reality, since it tells one nothing more than what the English sentence 1 requires for its truth—that John hit Bill. Since an adequate compositional meaning theory must be finite, however, in constructing a compositional meaning theory for English—an unbounded language—one must read a structure into its sentences. Action sentences: "John hit Bill at six o'clock," "John hit Bill at six o'clock in the bedroom," and "John hit Bill at six o'clock in the bedroom with the stick" are examples of how adverbial modifiers in the form of prepositional phrases can be added to an English sentence without compromising its grammaticality or intelligibility. No obvious upper limit exists on the number of modifiers English allows to be attached sensibly to these sorts of sentences—one could add "after dark," "on his ear," "on a Tuesday," and so on. Therefore, any compositional meaning that treats each such sentence as involving a distinct primitive relation threatens to violate the condition that a compositional meaning theory must be finite. Were one to try to devise a compositional meaning theory for English according to which "John hit Bill at six o'clock" is true just in case the three-place relation of hitting obtains between John and Bill and six o'clock, Davidson asks, what would one say about "John hit Bill at six o'clock in the bedroom with the stick"? Is it true just in case the distinct four-place relation of hitting obtains among two people, a time, and a place, and so on? This strategy for devising interpretive T-sentences treats each adverbial modifier as introducing a distinct and novel relation with a distinct number of relata. Since the aim of a compositional meaning theory is to explain how indefinitely many nonsynonymous sentences can exist, given a finite basis of meaningful components, such a theory prohibits positing indefinitely many distinct primitive predicates in a language.

In 1967 Davidson moved to Princeton University. He became chairman of the philosophy department there in 1968 but spent the academic year 1969–1970 at the Stanford Center for Social and Behavioral Sciences. During that year he wrote six of his best-known papers in the philosophy of language, all but one of which were collected in *Inquiries into Truth and Interpretation*. In September 1970 he was named a professor of philosophy at Rockefeller University in New York City. A research institution, Rockefeller University has no undergraduate students and no classes, but while holding the appointment at Rockefeller, Davidson was invited to teach one semester each year at Princeton. The paper that was omitted from *Inquiries into Truth and Interpretation*, "On the Very Idea of a Conceptual Scheme," became his first American Philosophical Association presidential address; it was delivered in Atlanta, Georgia, on 28 December 1973 and was added to the second edition of *Inquiries into Truth and Interpretation*, published in 2001. Davidson and his wife had separated in 1970; in 1975 they were divorced, and Davidson married Nancy Hirshberg.

In "Thought and Talk," a 1974 Wolfson College Lecture published in Samuel Guttenplan's *Mind and Language* (1975) and collected in *Inquiries into Truth and Interpretation*, and in "Rational Animals," published in *Dialectica* in 1982, collected in *Actions and Events: Perspectives on the Philosophy of Donald Davidson* (1985), and republished in *Inquiries into Truth and Interpretation*, Donaldson investigates the question of which comes first–language or thought? Intuition seems to cut both ways on this matter. It would be hard to find a pet owner who believed that his or her pet is a thoughtless brute, even though the animal has no facility with language. If this intuition is correct, then language and thought are independent. Yet, it seems equally intuitive that when people think, they think in their native tongue. So, at least for those who have language, it seems as if the two are mutually dependent. Davidson's position is that only creatures with a language can think. In "Rational Animals" he begins his argument for this thesis by noting that the ascription to others of psychological states such as belief, desire, and intention exhibit "semantic opacity." In attributing to a dog the belief that a cat it was chasing went up a particular tree, he asks whether the propriety of this ascription would be affected were one to substitute for "the

tree" another expression that refers to the same tree, such as "the oak tree in the backyard." Given that the tree under which the dog is barking is the oak tree in the backyard, would one be inclined to ascribe to the dog the belief that "the cat went up the oak tree in the backyard"? If one would not be so inclined, this reluctance would disclose that the attribution of belief to the dog falls short of literalness: that is, it is semantically opaque.

Davidson's contention is that semantic opacity–failure to preserve truth when words with the same referent are substituted–exists only when language is tied to thought. He advances two arguments for this conclusion. The first appeals to a holistic thesis about belief ascription, which holds that one could never have grounds for ascribing a belief to an organism except against the background of a wide array of other beliefs. Since, Davidson argues, one could never have grounds for ascribing the required array of background beliefs to creatures that do not have a language, one would never be warranted in ascribing to such creatures any thought at all. That is, belief ascription exhibits semantic opacity; semantic opacity requires that one regard beliefs as possessing some definite intentional content; the possession of a belief with a definite intentional content presupposes "endless" further beliefs (holism); therefore, a creature to whom one is warranted in ascribing a belief must possess a sophisticated behavioral repertoire; but the only behavior that exhibits the sort of complex pattern that might warrant such ascription is linguistic behavior.

This argument, even if sound, at most establishes that one is unlikely ever to have decisive evidence that a speechless creature has beliefs. But the views for which one can collect decisive evidences, on the one hand, and what one can establish as truth, on the other hand, can differ. Davidson wants to draw the stronger conclusion that "unless there is actually such a complex pattern of behavior, there is no thought." He does so by arguing that propositional attitudes require a dense network of beliefs (holism), that "in order to have a belief, it is necessary to have the concept of belief," and that "in order to have the concept of belief one must have language"–that is, one must be a member of a "speech community."

Even if thought requires language, one might ask, is it not possible that different people, communities, cultures, or periods view, conceptualize, or make the world in different ways? Could not another thinker have concepts or beliefs radically different from one's own? In "On the Very Idea of a Conceptual Scheme" Davidson identifies conceptual schemes with sets of intertranslatable languages; in so doing, he transforms the question of whether alternative conceptual schemes could exist into the question of whether nonintertranslatable languages could exist. But, one might ask, why should questions about conceptual relativity have anything to do with translation? Davidson's identification requires the assumptions that speakers alone have thoughts and that any concept a speaker possesses and any thought he or she can entertain is expressible in his or her language. These assumptions entail that a difference in the conceptual schemes of two people requires that a portion of the language that one speaks is not translatable into any portion of the other's language.

Once conceptual schemes are identified with sets of intertranslatable languages, the question of whether sense can be made of radically different conceptual schemes reduces to the question of whether sense can be made of two nonintertranslatable languages—or, what is much the same thing, to whether a "significant range of sentences in one language could be translated into the other." Davidson argues that making sense of such talk requires a criterion for when a form of behavior can be counted both as speech behavior and as speech that is untranslatable into one's own language. He then argues that no sense can be made of a total failure of translatability between languages, and so one could never be in a position to judge that others had concepts or beliefs radically different from one's own.

Davidson's view of the nature of events and their relation to laws brought him to a conclusion about the relationship between minds and bodies that he calls "the thesis of anomalous monism." Various philosophers have advanced three claims that are inconsistent with one another: that the mental and the physical are distinct; that the mental and the physical causally interact; and that the physical order is causally closed. The first claim is that no mental event is a physical event. The second is that some mental events cause physical events and vice versa; for example, a loud noise reaching Tom's ear may cause in him a desire to turn down his radio, and his desire to turn down the radio may cause his arm to move in such a way as to result in the volume of the radio being lowered. The third claim is that all the causes of physical events are themselves physical events. The combination of the plausibility of each of these claims with their apparent incompatibility results in the traditional "mind-body problem." Davidson's solution of the problem is articulated in three papers, all of which are collected in *Essays on Actions and Events:* "Mental Events," delivered during the academic year 1968–1969 at the University of Massachusetts and first published in 1970; "The Material Mind," delivered at an international congress in Bucharest in 1971 and first published in 1973; and "Psychology as Philosophy," delivered at the University of Kent in 1971 and first published in 1973. This solution consists of three claims that, taken together, comprise anomalous monism: there are no exceptionless psychological or psychophysical laws, and, in fact, all exceptionless laws can be expressed in a purely physical

Cover for Davidson's 1984 collection, which includes his essay "Radical Interpretation" (Bruccoli Clark Layman Archives)

vocabulary (an exceptionless law is one that under no conditions admits of exceptions; Boyle's law is not such a law); mental events causally interact with physical events; and event C causes event E only if an exceptionless causal law subsumes C and E. The thesis is monistic, since it assumes that only physical "stuff" exists; but it is also anomalous, since, although its monism commits it to physical and mental stuff being the same, it denies that a strict reduction of the one to other is possible.

Davidson's claim that there are no exceptionless psychological or psychophysical laws and that all exceptionless laws can be expressed in a purely physical vocabulary is a version of the traditional claim that no mental event is a physical event. It is commonly held that whatever property a mentalistic predicate M expresses is reducible to one expressed by a physical predicate P—where M and P are not logically connected—only if an exceptionless law links them. According to Davidson's first claim, mental and physical properties are distinct.

Cover for the 2001 collection that includes articles by Davidson
originally published between 1982 and 1997
(Bruccoli Clark Layman Archives)

Davidson bases his argument against the possibility of exceptionless laws linking mental and physical predicates on their distinct "constitutive principles." Measurability of length, mass, temperature, and time are constitutive of the physical; for example, anything physical must have length. If, on investigation, one discovered that of three physical items, though the first is longer than the second and the second is longer than the third, the first is not longer than the third, one would assume that either the measurements are mistaken or the lengths changed during the course of measurement. One would not conclude that the transitivity of length is false because no physical predicate could be true of three things unless their lengths respect transitivity: that is, respecting this constraint is constitutive of being physical.

The constitutive principles of mental items, on the other hand, include principles of rationality—that is, constraints in regard to consistency and rational coherence.

For example, the principle of the transitivity of desire holds that if a person desires a over b and b over c, he or she ought to desire a over c; the principle of consistency of belief holds that if a person believes that p, he or she ought not also believe that not-p. These principles tie in with Davidson's earlier discussions of reasons and actions: interpreting the behavior of another person requires attributing desires and beliefs to that person. These attributions are intended to provide an agent's rationale for acting, but they fail in this task unless a degree of rational choice is presumed. By virtue of this presumption, the constitutive principles of the mental include norms of rationality. Davidson says in "Psychology as Philosophy" that such constitutive principles have "no echo in physical theory." Therefore, he concludes in "The Material Mind" that "There is no important sense in which psychology can be reduced to the physical sciences": exceptionless laws cannot link the two sorts of sciences, because the normative relationships among mental states cannot be expressed in a physicalistic language.

In "Causal Relations," published in *The Journal of Philosophy* in 1967 and collected in *Essays on Actions and Events,* Davidson argues that the most plausible interpretation of singular causal statements such as "The short circuit caused the fire" treats them as two-place predicate statements with their singular terms ("the short circuit" and "the fire") designating events. The third of Davidson's three claims that make up anomalous monism is that an event C causes an event E only if there are singular descriptions D of C and D' of E, and an exceptionless causal law L such that L and "D occurred" entail that "D caused D'." But this claim and the second part of Davidson's first claim entail that physical events have only physical causes and that all causation of events is physically grounded.

Given the parallels between the three traditional claims and Davidson's three claims, and the fact that the former are incompatible with one another, it may seem that the latter, too, are incompatible. Davidson, however, argues in "Mental Events" and in "Psychology as Philosophy" that they can all be true if and only if individual mental events are identical with individual physical ones. Suppose, he says, that an event E is physical just in case E satisfies a predicate of basic physical science, where such predicates are those that occur in exceptionless laws. Since Davidson assumes that only physical predicates or predicates expressing properties reducible to physical properties occur in exceptionless laws, it follows that every event that enters into causal relations satisfies a physical predicate. But then it also follows that a mental event that enters into a causal relation must satisfy some physical predicate and so is itself a physical event. His argument establishes that every concrete mental event is identical with some concrete physical one.

In 1976 Davidson left his dual appointment at Princeton and Rockefeller to move to the University of Chicago. His second wife died in 1979. In 1981 he moved to the University of California at Berkeley, where he still holds the title Distinguished Professor. He married Marcia Cavell on 4 July 1994.

Of the many consequences of radical interpretation, a quite striking one is antiskepticism; that is, the claim that massive error is impossible. "The Method of Truth in Metaphysics" (published in *Midwest Studies in Philosophy* in 1977 and collected in *Inquiries into Truth and Interpretation*), "Empirical Content" (published in *Grazer Philosophische Studien* in 1982 and collected in *Truth and Interpretation: Perspectives on the Philosophy of Donald Davidson* [1986]), "A Coherence Theory of Truth and Knowledge" (first published in *Truth and Interpretation*), "What Is Present to the Mind?" and "The Conditions of Thought" (both published in *The Mind of Donald Davidson* [1989]), "Three Varieties of Knowledge" and "Epistemology Externalized" (published in *Dialectica* in 1991 and republished in Davidson's *Subjective, Intersubjective, Objective* [2001]), Davidson argues on the basis of his principle of charity that an interpreter cannot find speakers to have largely false beliefs, even if the interpreter himself or herself has no opinion as to the general truth and falsity of these beliefs. Given what beliefs are and how their contents are determined, Davidson is committed, as he says in "Epistemology Externalized," to the impossibility of the claim that "all our beliefs about the world might be false." A radical interpreter must have beliefs about the world in order to succeed in ascribing such beliefs to others. But radical interpretation holds that the interpreter must also find others largely in agreement with him or her in those beliefs.

Davidson's antiskeptical argument from radical interpretation rests on two assumptions: that to be a speaker is to be interpretable by others, and that to be interpretable by others requires being largely correct not only in one's general beliefs but also in beliefs about the local environment. On the assumption that radical interpretation is possible, the proper way to state the requirement on a speaker is that his or her beliefs about his or her environment be mostly true. The crucial aspect of radical interpretation is the importance of causality in determining what someone means or believes. In "A Coherence Theory of Truth and Knowledge" he says that one cannot "in general fix what someone means independently of what he believes and independently of what caused the belief. . . . The causality plays an indispensable role in determining the content of what we say and believe." Therefore, the central role of causation in fixing the contents of beliefs ensures that the truth of everything one believes is not, in general, "logically independent" of having those beliefs and that others cannot differ too much from oneself in what they believe. Davidson's central claim is that how the contents of beliefs are determined limits the extent of falsity and diversity discriminable in a coherent set of beliefs. In interpreting another, a radical interpreter ventures hypotheses as to what, in the given circumstances, causes a speaker to hold the sentence in question to be true; this process is supposed to provide the interpreter with the meaning of that sentence. In every case, various causal chains will lead to the same utterance, and the radical interpreter must choose one of them. He or she does so by responding to something in the environment and so converges on something that is a common cause both of the interpreter's own response and of the utterance of the speaker, thereby correlating the two and giving the content of the speaker's utterances. Davidson refers to this process as "triangulation." The method of radical interpretation "enforces" on any successful interpreter the conclusion that a speaker's beliefs are largely true and largely like the interpreter's own. Thus, global skepticism is ruled out.

A central feature of the Cartesian tradition in modern philosophy is that at the foundation of the structure of one's justified beliefs about the world are one's beliefs about one's own mental states, attitudes, experiences, and sensations. Since he rejects this assumption, Davidson's approach to meaning and interpretation and to central issues in epistemology is anti-Cartesian. A radical interpreter is restricted to behavioral evidence in interpreting the statements of another. From this standpoint, Davidson treats the central concepts employed in interpreting another's statements as theoretical concepts introduced to keep track of behavior. The role of a theory of interpretation is to identify and systematize patterns in the behavior of speakers in relation to their environment. One does not first have access to facts about speakers' meanings and attitudes, including one's own.

How to reconcile his treatment of the central concepts of interpretation as theoretical with the presumption of first-person authority–that is, with the fact that speakers are necessarily more authoritative about their own attitudes and sensations than others are–is a central topic in Davidson's later writings. It seems scarcely intelligible that another could be as well placed as oneself with respect to whether one is hungry or in pain. This asymmetry in epistemic position is connected with a difference in the way one knows one's own mental states and the way others know them: in ascribing mental states to others, one relies on their behavior or records of their behavior; but in the case of first-person ascription, one does not. Indeed, in one's own case one does not rely on evidence at all. Although knowing something not on the basis of evidence does not guarantee that what is known is better known, one would expect that this difference in how one knows one's own mental states (first-person knowledge) and how others do underlies first-person authority.

Caricature of Davidson by David Levine (© by David Levine; courtesy of Forum Gallery, New York City)

Davidson first takes up the challenge that first-person authority presents to his assumption of the theoretical character of the concepts of interpretation in "First-Person Authority," published in *Dialectica* in 1984 and collected in *Subjective, Intersubjective, Objective*. Here he explains the presumption that "a speaker is right when he sincerely attributes a belief, desire, or intention to his present self" by grounding it in the assumptions that an interpreter must make to succeed at interpretation. He aims to explain the asymmetry between one's knowledge of one's own mental states and one's knowledge of the mental states of others (or, alternatively, the asymmetry between one's knowledge of one's own mental states and the knowledge others have of those mental states) by explaining a closely related asymmetry: why there is a "presumption that a speaker is right when he sincerely attributes a belief, desire, or intention to his present self, while there is no such presumption when others make similar attributions to him." His explanation of first-person authority rests on an explanation of an asymmetry between the knowledge a speaker and interpreter have of the meanings of the speaker's words. This asymmetry between the knowledge

one has of one's own words and an interpreter's knowledge of the meanings of one's words is most striking in the case of an interpreter who is not a member of one's speech community. Davidson argues that one speaks a language only if one is interpretable; one is interpretable only if one is mostly right about the meanings of one's words; therefore, one speaks a language only if one is mostly right about the meanings of one's words.

Davidson's central methodological assumption is that a third-person point of view on others' utterances and psychological states is primary, in the sense that behavioral evidence forms one's only evidence for the application of linguistic and psychological concepts and terms to others and that their content is to be understood wholly in terms of their role in accounting for the behavioral evidence available to one from this standpoint. His shift of viewpoint is so fundamental that, once adopted, the whole landscape of the philosophy of language and mind is changed. If Davidson is correct, the central mistake of the Western philosophical tradition is the assumption of the Cartesian standpoint and, in particular, the central place the tradition accords to the epistemic priority of knowledge of one's own mental states to knowledge of the world and other minds. Once this assumption is relinquished, each domain in which one has knowledge will be seen as necessary for the others; but knowledge of the world and, by extension, of other minds will turn out to be autonomous from knowledge of one's own mind in the sense that it is not explicable by appeal to inferences from a basis in knowledge of one's own mind. Davidson's picture is attractive: part of its interest and power lies in its promise to lay to rest what have, perhaps, been the central problems of the Western tradition from the beginning of the modern period in the seventeenth century.

Another consequence of Davidson's taking a "third-person perspective" on the radical interpreter as methodologically fundamental is the rejection of all forms of traditional empiricism. Essential to traditional empiricism is the attempt to account for knowledge of the world exclusively by appeal to sensory experience. What is distinctive about empiricism is not the claim that sensory experience can play a role in justifying beliefs about the world but the claim that it is the foundation of such knowledge. This claim entails that the first-person point of view is fundamental, since each person's experience is treated as his or her own foundation for his or her empirical knowledge. In adopting the third-person point of view as fundamental, Davidson rejects a central tenet of all forms of empiricism and the traditional project of explaining empirical knowledge by appeal to experience. Rather, in Davidson's view, knowledge of the world, of other minds, and of one's own mind has a unified source in the nature of human beings as rational beings capable of communicating with one another.

Donald Davidson, then, argues that language, mind, and action are inseparable. To account for language—that is, to answer the question "What is meaning?"—he advances the radical idea that a theory of meaning can be satisfactory only if it discovers a finite basic vocabulary and rules of composition in the language to be interpreted. His goal of providing a comprehensive understanding of natural languages led him to a treatment of the theory of truth for a language as an empirical theory and to the adoption of the stance of the radical interpreter as the standpoint for confirmation, linking the structure of a rich theory with its basic evidence and placing the theory of meaning in the context of a theory of rational agency. Adopting this stance as fundamental is tantamount to the rejection of Cartesianism and empiricism and so to the abandonment, among other philosophical mainstays, of conceptual relativism, global skepticism, and representationalism. Theories frequently yield insight into problems that they were not specifically designed to solve. A careful reading of Davidson's writings will bear out both how broad in scope his philosophical accomplishments are and, more important, how well they cohere.

Interview:

Giovanna Borradori, "Post-Analytic Visions: Donald Davidson," in her *The American Philosopher: Conversations with Quine, Davidson, Putnam, Nozick, Danto, Rorty, Cavell, MacIntyre, and Kuhn*, translated by Rosanna Crocitto (Chicago & London: University of Chicago Press, 1994), pp. 40–54.

Bibliography:

"Bibliography of Donald Davidson," in *The Philosophy of Donald Davidson*, edited by Lewis Edwin Hahn, The Library of Living Philosophers, volume 27 (Chicago: Open Court, 1999), pp. 733–758.

References:

Samuel Louis Bayer, *Confessions of a Lapsed Neo-Davidsonian: Events and Arguments in Compositional Semantics* (New York: Garland, 1977);

Johannes Brandl and Wolfgang L. Gombocz, eds., *The Mind of Donald Davidson* (Amsterdam & Atlanta: Rodopi, 1989);

Filip Buekens, *Kritiek van de interpreterende rede: Grondslagen van Donald Davidsons filosofische project* (Louvain: Universitaire Pers, 1996);

Mario De Caro, ed., *Interpretations and Causes: New Perspectives on Donald Davidson's Philosophy* (Dordrecht, Netherlands & Boston: Kluwer, 1999);

Reed Way Dasenbrock, ed., *Literary Theory after Davidson* (University Park: Pennsylvania State University Press, 1993);

Pascal Engel, *Davidson et la philosophie du langage* (Paris: Presses universitaires de France, 1994);

Gareth Evans and John McDowell, eds., *Truth and Meaning: Essays in Semantics* (Oxford: Clarendon Press, 1976);

Simon Evnine, *Donald Davidson* (Stanford, Cal.: Stanford University Press, 1991);

Jerry Fodor and Ernest Lepore, *Holism: A Shopper's Guide* (Oxford & Cambridge, Mass.: Blackwell, 1992);

Lewis Edwin Hahn, ed., *The Philosophy of Donald Davidson*, The Library of Living Philosophers, volume 27 (Chicago: Open Court, 2000);

Manuel Hernández Iglesias, *La semántica de Davidson: Una introducción crítica* (Madrid: Visor, 1990);

Petr Kotatko, Peter Pagin, and Gabriel Segal, eds., *Interpreting Davidson* (Stanford, Cal.: CSLI, 2001);

Peter Lanz, *Menschliches Handeln zwischen Kausalität und Rationalität* (Frankfurt am Main: Athenäum, 1987);

Ernest Lepore, ed., *Truth and Interpretation: Perspectives on the Philosophy of Donald Davidson* (Oxford: Blackwell, 1986);

Lepore and Brian P. McLaughlin, eds., *Actions and Events: Perspectives on the Philosophy of Donald Davidson* (Oxford: Blackwell, 1986);

Ben H. Letson, *Davidson's Theory of Truth and Its Implications for Rorty's Pragmatism*, American University Studies, Series V: Philosophy, volume 178 (New York: Peter Lang, 1997);

Kirk Ludwig, ed., *Donald Davidson* (Cambridge & New York: Cambridge University Press, forthcoming, 2003);

J. E. Malpas, *Donald Davidson and the Mirror of Meaning: Holism, Truth, Interpretation* (Cambridge & New York: Cambridge University Press, 1992);

Gerhard Preyer, Frank Siebelt, and Alexander Ulfig, eds., *Language, Mind, and Epistemology: On Donald Davidson's Philosophy* (Dordrecht, Netherlands & Boston: Kluwer, 1994);

Bjørn T. Ramberg, *Donald Davidson's Philosophy of Language: An Introduction* (Oxford & New York: Blackwell, 1989);

Matthias Schaedler-Om, *Der soziale Charakter sprachlicher Bedeutung und propositionaler Einstellungen: Eine Untersuchung zu Donald Davidsons Theorie der radikalen Interpretation* (Würzburg: Königshausen & Neumann, 1997);

Bruce Vermazen and Merrill B. Hintikka, eds., *Essays on Davidson: Actions and Events* (Oxford: Clarendon Press / New York: Oxford University Press, 1985);

Samuel C. Wheeler III, *Deconstruction as Analytic Philosophy* (Stanford, Cal.: Stanford University Press, 2000);

Urszula M. Żegleń, ed., *Donald Davidson: Truth, Meaning and Knowledge* (London & New York: Routledge, 1999).

Nelson Goodman

(7 August 1906 – 25 November 1998)

Curtis L. Carter
Marquette University

BOOKS: *The Structure of Appearance* (Cambridge, Mass.: Harvard University Press, 1951; revised edition, Dordrecht, Netherlands & Boston: Reidel, 1977);

Fact, Fiction, and Forecast (London: Athlone Press, 1954; Cambridge, Mass.: Harvard University Press, 1955);

Languages of Art: An Approach to a Theory of Symbols (Indianapolis: Bobbs-Merrill, 1968; London: Oxford University Press, 1969);

Problems and Projects (Indianapolis: Bobbs-Merrill, 1972);

Basic Abilities Required for Understanding and Creation in the Arts: Final Report, by Goodman, David Perkins, Howard Gardner, Jeanne Bamberger, and others (Cambridge, Mass.: Harvard University Press, 1972);

Ways of Worldmaking (Indianapolis: Hackett, 1978; Hassocks, U.K.: Harvester Press, 1978);

Of Mind and Other Matters (Cambridge, Mass.: Harvard University Press, 1984);

Reconceptions in Philosophy and Other Arts and Sciences, by Goodman and Catherine Z. Elgin (Indianapolis: Hackett, 1988; London: Routledge, 1988);

A Study of Qualities (New York: Garland, 1990).

OTHER: "A World of Individuals," in *The Problem of Universals* (Notre Dame, Ind.: University of Notre Dame Press, 1956), pp. 398–412;

Catherine Z. Elgin, *With Reference to Reference,* foreword by Goodman (Indianapolis: Hackett, 1983);

"Art in Action," in *Encyclopedia of Aesthetics,* volume 2, edited by Michael Kelly (New York: Oxford University Press, 1998), pp. 322–326.

SELECTED PERIODICAL PUBLICATIONS–
UNCOLLECTED: "The Calculus of Individuals and Its Uses," by Goodman and Henry S. Leonard, *Journal of Symbolic Logic,* 5 (1940): 45–55;

"Elimination of Extra-logical Predicates," by Goodman and W. V. Quine, *Journal of Symbolic Logic,* 5 (1940): 104–109;

Nelson Goodman

"On the Simplicity of Ideas," *Journal of Symbolic Logic,* 8 (1943): 107–121;

"The Problem of Counterfactual Conditionals," *Journal of Philosophy,* 44 (1947): 113–128;

"Sense and Certainty," *Philosophical Review,* 61 (1952): 160–167;

"The Way the World Is," *Review of Metaphysics,* 14 (1960): 48–56;

"Languages of Art," by Goodman, Joseph Margolis, F. E. Sparshott, Alan Tormey, Søren Kjørup,

Goodman in 1941, the year he earned his Ph.D. at Harvard University

Kendall Walton, John G. Bennett, David Carrier, Stephanie Ross, and V. A. Howard, *Monist,* 58 (1974): 175–381;

"The Philosophy of Nelson Goodman: Part I," by Goodman, Kjørup, Rolf A. Berle, Marx W. Wartofsky, J. Robinson, V. A. Howard, Mark Sagoff, Monroe Beardsley, Stefan Morawski, and Richard Rudner, *Erkenntnis,* 12 (1978): 1–179;

"The Philosophy of Nelson Goodman: Part II," by Goodman, Wilhelm K. Essler, Franz Von Kutschera, G. Hellman, Alfred Breitkopf, and Ivan Fox, *Erkenntnis,* 13 (1979): 182–291;

"The End of the Museum?" *New Criterion* (October 1983): 9–14;

"Probing into Reconceptions," by Goodman, Catherine Z. Elgin, Guido Küng, Rosemarie Rheinwald, Wolfgang Heydrich, Oliver R. Scholz, Wolfgang Künne, and Dirk Koppelberg, *Synthèse,* 95 (1993): 1–128;

"On Some Worldly Worries," *Synthèse,* 95 (1993): 9–12.

Nelson Goodman is widely acknowledged as one of the most important analytic philosophers of the post–World War II era. He made penetrating original contributions to logic, philosophy of science, aesthetics, the theory of symbols, epistemology, and metaphysics. Rather than engaging his philosophic predecessors in debates of historic interest or becoming sidetracked by ideological concerns, Goodman developed his own approach to symbol systems. He held that science and the arts alike contribute to understanding. In *Ways of Worldmaking* (1978) Goodman claimed that there are many correct, even conflicting, versions of the world; yet, he vigorously denied that "anything goes." He acknowledged that wrong versions exist, which he referred to as "not well made." A major portion of his work was devoted to differentiating among the various types of symbols according to their syntactic and semantic features and sorting out their respective contributions to knowledge. He approached value questions not to formalize them but to suggest that the particular value dimension in question be specified. Value questions require a good deal of specification, he held, as a way of sharpening perception.

Henry Nelson Goodman was born on 7 August 1906 in Somerville, Massachusetts, to Henry L. and Sarah Elizabeth Woodbury Goodman; his Jewish father owned a paper factory. In 1924 Goodman enrolled at Harvard University, where he studied philosophy and art history. The distinguished British philosopher

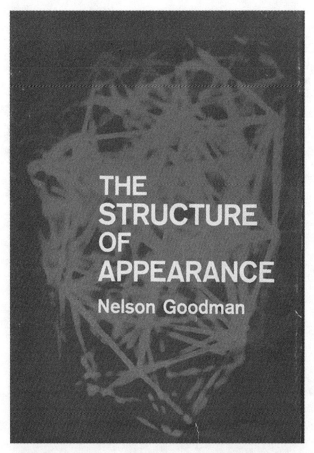

Dust jacket for the second edition (1966) of Goodman's first book,
originally published in 1951, in which he argues that, contrary
to the commonsense view, the temporal characteristics of a
thing are more static than its spatial ones
(Collection of Curtis L. Carter)

Alfred North Whitehead came to Harvard from the University of Cambridge that same year. Only tangential references to Whitehead's logical theories appear in Goodman's work on logical definition, *The Structure of Appearance* (1951), and in his collection *Problems and Projects* (1972), but they demonstrate his familiarity with Whitehead's views. In the preface to *The Structure of Appearance* Goodman cites James Haughton Woods, who was chairman of the Harvard philosophy department and a specialist in Asian philosophy, "for the indispensable initial spark of encouragement"; he may well have influenced Goodman's decision to become a philosopher. Among Goodman's other teachers at Harvard was Paul Sachs, the associate director of the Fogg Art Museum, whose influence helped foster Goodman's lifelong interest in art.

After graduating Phi Beta Kappa and magna cum laude with a B.S. in 1928, Goodman directed the Walker-Goodman Art Gallery in Boston for the next twelve years while working on his doctorate. He and

fellow graduate student Henry S. Leonard had to invent a "part-whole" logic to do their work. The logic that was developed by Goodman and Leonard around 1930 (it had been formulated in 1916 and was revised between 1927 and 1931 by Stanisław Leśniewski in Poland, but his work had not been translated into English) is known as mereology. Their part-whole logic was not a general logic like that of Whitehead and Bertrand Russell's *Principia Mathematica* (1910–1913) but a system to deal with a special class of overlapping relations. Their approach was, in part, a response to Rudolf Carnap's *Der logische Aufbau der Welt* (1928; translated as "The Logical Structure of the World," 1967).

In a characteristically offbeat manner, Goodman always cited as his first and most widely distributed publication in logic and philosophy a puzzle, "The Truth-tellers and the Liars," that he contributed anonymously to the front page of the 8 June 1931 issue of the *Boston Post:*

> All the men of a certain country are either nobles or hunters, and no one is both a noble and a hunter. The male inhabitants are so nearly alike that it is difficult to tell them apart, but there is one difference: nobles never lie, and hunters never tell the truth. Three of the men meet one day and Ahmed, the first, says something. He says either, "I am a noble," or "I am a hunter." (We don't know yet which he said.)
>
> Ali, the second man, heard what Ahmed said, and in reply to a query, answered, "Ahmed said, 'I am a hunter.'" Then Ali went on to say, "Azab is a hunter."
>
> Azab was the third man. He said, "Ahmed is a noble."
>
> Now the problem is, which is each? How do you know?

Goodman's solution was published in the *Post* the next day. The solution hinges on the second speaker's having uttered two separate sentences, rather than a single sentence with those two sentences as conjoined clauses: "the falsity of the conjunction of the two sentences does not imply the falsity of the components separately." His puzzle has circulated around the world, from logicians in Warsaw to *Esquire* magazine, taking on many variations in the process.

Goodman met Carnap in 1936 at the home of W. V. Quine. Goodman and Leonard published their new logic in "The Calculus of Individuals and Its Uses" in *The Journal of Symbolic Logic* in 1940. That same year Goodman and Quine jointly published a further development of the new logic in "Elimination of Extralogical Postulates" in the same journal.

Goodman was awarded the Ph.D. in philosophy in 1941. His dissertation, "A Study of Qualities," was directed by C. I. Lewis.

During World War II Goodman served in the United States Army; he was assigned to psychological testing of troops. The experience gave him an interest in questions of intelligence, perception, and cognition. His article "On the Simplicity of Ideas" was published in *The Journal of Symbolic Logic* in 1943. On 13 April 1944 he married Katharine Sturgis of Cambridge, whom he had met when she brought her watercolors of New England scenes to exhibit at his gallery; they had no children. Throughout their years together Goodman was devoted to advancing his wife's career. When she exhibited her works, he actively participated in the details of the arrangements, including the selection and installation of the paintings.

Goodman began his academic career in 1945 as an instructor in philosophy at Tufts College in Medford, Massachusetts, and moved to the University of Pennsylvania as an associate professor in 1946. He received a Guggenheim Fellowship for 1946–1947. His students in a class on induction offered between 1949 and 1951 included the future linguist Noam Chomsky, with whom Goodman later broke over the theory of innate ideas; John Fisher, who edited *The Journal of Aesthetics and Art Criticism* during the 1980s; and Israel Scheffler. Scheffler became a lifelong friend and colleague. Goodman served as vice president of the Association for Symbolic Logic from 1950 to 1952. He was promoted to full professor in 1951.

In his first book, *The Structure of Appearance,* Goodman applies his and Leonard's part-whole logic to create a phenomenalist system–that is, one in which physical objects are reducible to sensory experiences. The primitive elements of his system are "qualia"–the subjective qualities of conscious experience, such as particular tastes, sounds, and feelings. He defends Carnap against critics who attacked the phenomenalist account of experience in the latter's *Der logische Aufbau der Welt* but denies that phenomenalism has any epistemological superiority over rival physicalist (materialist) systems and disavows any commitment to either type of system. He reverses a commonsense notion by arguing that the temporal characteristics of a thing are more static than its spatial characteristics: "The location, or the color, or the shape of a thing may change, but not its time."

In his second book, *Fact, Fiction, and Forecast* (1954), Goodman radically alters the eighteenth-century Scottish philosopher David Hume's theory that predictions are grounded solely in observed past regularities; he points out that regularities can be found anywhere, but not all observed regularities result in valid projections. His "new riddle of induction" states that, under the regularity theory, the same evidence that supports a prediction equally supports the exact opposite prediction. He illustrates the riddle by presenting his well-known "grue

Dust jacket for Goodman's 1968 book, in which he approaches aesthetics in the context of a general theory of symbols (Collection of Curtis L. Carter)

paradox." A "grue" object is one that is green if it is examined before some specific future date and blue if it is examined after that date. If generalizations are confirmed by past regularities, then the fact that all emeralds observed so far have been green confirms the generalization that all emeralds are grue just as much as it confirms the generalization that all emeralds are green; but this result seems counterintuitive. Goodman's answer to the riddle is that habits of adopting and projecting certain predicates, rather than Hume's regularities alone, are the basis of valid generalization.

Goodman delivered the Sherman Lecture at the University of London in 1953. A warm and stimulating man, filled with energy and bubbling with ideas when with friends, Goodman had a gruff manner and penetrating mind that could be intimidating to those who did not know him well. He did not suffer fools gladly and had little patience for small talk. Yet, he inspired

NELSON GOODMAN

problems and projects

Dust jacket for the 1972 collection of Goodman's articles on philosophy of language, philosophy of science, and aesthetics (Richland County Public Library)

had been firmly established in this field. The program provided a laboratory to test the theories of cognition and symbol differentiation he had presented in his John Locke Lectures, which were revised and enlarged to become his third book, *Languages of Art: An Approach to a Theory of Symbols* (1968).

In *Languages of Art* Goodman approaches aesthetics in the context of a general theory of symbols that accommodates art, science, and language. Through careful individuation of the kinds of symbolism represented in painting, music, dance, and the other arts he offers a fresh structure for addressing key problems in aesthetics. His theory is based on the view that the use of symbols beyond immediate practical needs is for the sake of understanding—of "cognition in and for itself." Understanding draws on the urge to know or to delight in discovery and leads to enlightenment; the use of symbols for communication and other practical or pleasurable purposes is secondary. Goodman's criterion for judging symbols, whether in the arts or the sciences, is how well they serve their cognitive purposes; pictures, music, dance, literary texts, and architecture are partners with the sciences in the pursuit of understanding. Goodman distinguishes representational, exemplificational, and expressive forms of reference: representation is a form of denotation, or pointing to objects; exemplification is the relationship between a sample and the features to which it refers (for example, the relationship between a swatch of cloth and the color, texture, weave, or other properties of the bolt); and expression implies metaphorical exemplification (for example, a painting expressing sadness metaphorically exemplifies the property of being sad). Goodman replaces the question "What is Art?" with the question "When is Art?". By doing so, he shifts the focus to the functions of art symbols. Goodman finds the attempt to identify uniquely aesthetic qualities to be without significance; he prefers to search for clusters of symbolic features that result in an understanding that is peculiar to artworks. He considers scientific understanding and the arts complementary means for making and understanding worlds. *Languages of Art* begins with terms from ordinary language and proceeds systematically to clear away confusion by making increasingly fine distinctions and developing the connections necessary to advance understanding of the arts and other symbol systems. Precision is achieved by restricting the use of ordinary-language terms, purging them of their ambiguities and vagueness so that they can be used in a system where new connections can be forged.

In 1968 Goodman became professor of philosophy at Harvard. Some of his supporters believed that anti-Semitism was a factor in blocking earlier efforts to secure his appointment. He served as producer of the

his students and opened new paths of thought for them while demanding from them precision and clarity.

In 1962 Goodman delivered the Alfred North Whitehead Lecture at Harvard University and the John Locke Lectures at the University of Oxford. In 1964 he was named Harry Austryn Wolfson Professor of Philosophy at Brandeis University. He served as president of the Eastern Division of the American Philosophical Association in 1967. That same year Goodman founded and became the first director of Project Zero, a pioneering interdisciplinary program for research in arts education in the Harvard University Graduate School of Education; Goodman was a research associate of the school. Project Zero was created to investigate the nature of artistic knowledge and how arts programs in schools and museums can enhance students' artistic skills and understanding; its name derived from Goodman's conviction that "zero"

Goodman in 1978 (photograph by Wayne Moore; from the dust jacket for Ways of Worldmaking, *1978)*

Harvard Arts Orientation Series from 1969 to 1971, as consultant to the Harvard Arts Summer School from 1971 to 1977, and as founding director of the Harvard Dance Center. He turned over the directorship of Project Zero to Howard Gardner and David Perkins in 1972. That year Goodman published *Problems and Projects,* a collection of his articles that includes "Steps toward a Constructive Nominalism" (1947), co-authored with Quine; "On Likeness of Meaning" (1949); "On Some Differences about Meaning" (1953); "The Significance of *Der logische Aufbau der Welt*" (1963); and "Art and Inquiry" (1967). Goodman wrote and–in collaboration with the choreographer Martha Gray, the composer John Adams, and his wife, Sturgis–produced *Hockey Seen,* a multimedia event that was performed at Harvard in 1972 and in Knokke-le Zoute, Belgium, in 1980; Goodman's text, notes, a motion picture of the Harvard performance, and props used in the production are in the permanent collection of the Haggerty Museum of Art at Marquette University. He also produced *Rabbit, Run,* a dance piece adapted from the 1960 novel by John Updike in collaboration with Gray and

the composer Joel Kabakov. It was performed at Harvard and at the University of Pennsylvania in 1973. Goodman delivered the Miller Lectures at the University of Illinois in 1974 and the Immanuel Kant Lectures at Stanford University in 1976. He assumed emeritus status at Harvard in 1977.

The year after his retirement Goodman published *Ways of Worldmaking.* In the foreword he states concisely the radical nature of his approach to philosophical concerns: "Few familiar philosophical labels fit comfortably a book that is at odds with rationalism and empiricism alike, with materialism and idealism, with mechanism and vitalism, with mysticism and scientism, and with most other ardent doctrines." He envisions his work as part of the mainstream of modern philosophy; yet, he proposes to replace the views of major theorists, such as Immanuel Kant's on the structure of the mind and Lewis's on the structure of concepts, with his own theory of symbol systems. The symbol systems of the sciences, philosophy, the arts, perception, and everyday discourse constitute the "ways of worldmaking" that comprise understanding.

*Dust jacket for the book in which Goodman claims that human
beings create various versions of the world and that
even conflicting versions can be equally correct
(Richland County Public Library)*

With Quine, Goodman challenges two of the principal "dogmas of empiricism": the distinction between analytic and synthetic propositions and a reductionist/foundationalist account of knowledge.

Perhaps the most radical claim in *Ways of Worldmaking* is that no "objective" world exists apart from the versions constructed through such symbol-making processes as language, science, and art. His key argument is that apart from symbolic frames of reference there is nothing else with which to compare versions of the world. Goodman does not consider every version of the world to be of equal significance, but he says that both the constructed versions of the world and the criteria one uses to test them are dependent on human making. This position set Goodman at odds with his predecessor at Harvard, Charles Sanders Peirce, who argued that science depends on the premise that a real world exists independent of particular theories or beliefs, and with his former student and longtime col-

league Scheffler, who believed that some features of the world must be independent of all versions. Their debate on this issue continued, with neither changing his views, right up until Goodman's ninety-first birthday.

In *Of Mind and Other Matters* (1984) Goodman says that his principal aim in philosophy is to advance understanding by "removing confusions, discerning distinctions and connections, perceiving more sensitively and fully, gaining new insights"; he leaves social betterment and technological progress to others. He says that whereas Ludwig Wittgenstein treated a topic "as a cat does a mouse, teasing it, leaving it, pouncing again," his own approach is bulldog-like, intended to "follow through with certain insights, with certain techniques, and make systematic connections."

Goodman delivered the Howison Lecture at the University of California at Berkeley in 1985. In collaboration with the composer David Alpher he produced *Variations: An Illustrated Lecture Concert,* which featured Pablo Picasso's variations on Diego Rodríguez da Silva Velásquez's painting *Las Meninas* (1656–1657); it was performed at a philosophy of music conference at the Helsinki Music Festival in 1985 and at Harvard in 1986. His dissertation was published in 1990. That year he received honorary doctorates from the University of Pennsylvania, Adelphi University, and the Technische Universität Berlin. In 1991 international colloquia on his work were held by the Zentrum für Interdisciplinare Forschung der Universität Bielefeld in Germany and jointly by the University of Rome and the University of Tuschia-Viterbo in Viterbo, Italy. In 1992 his ideas were also discussed at a colloquium held by the Musée National de l'Art Moderne at the Centre Georges Pompidou in Paris and a seminar at the fiftieth anniversary meeting of the American Society for Aesthetics in Philadelphia.

Goodman's lifelong pursuit of art collecting began when he was a student, and his acute eye and talent for rigorous bargaining were well known among the major art dealers and auction houses of New York and London and at the Maastricht, Netherlands, art fair, which he visited regularly until illness prevented him from traveling in his final years. At his home in Weston, Massachusetts, treasures were abundant in every closet and drawer, as well as on the walls. Among the works he collected were seventeenth-century Dutch Old Master paintings and prints, drawings by Picasso and the American artist Charles Demuth, Asian sculptures, and Native American arts of the Northwest coast and the Southwest. Hanging on opposite walls one might see a Dutch Old Master painting by Abel Grimmer and a pristine naive work by Peter Petronzio, an unknown twentieth-century

Goodman and his wife, the artist Katharine Sturgis, at the exhibition "The Art of Hockey: Sixty Drawings and Other Works by Katharine Sturgis" and "Hockey Seen," an exhibition of the props from their multimedia production Hockey Seen *at the Haggerty Museum of Art, Marquette University (photograph © by Curtis L. Carter, all rights reserved)*

Italian immigrant farmer. Donations from Goodman's art collections benefited various institutions, including the Harvard University Art Museums, the Worcester Museum, and the Haggerty Museum of Art at Marquette University.

Goodman also cared deeply about animals. As a member of the World Society for the Protection of Animals and other societies dedicated to animal welfare, he sponsored projects throughout the world to rescue animals caught in war zones, including the Persian Gulf area and Bosnia, and in natural disasters such as volcanic eruptions in Montserrat and fires in Borneo.

After Goodman's wife died in 1996, he arranged for the permanent care and display of her art at the Cape Ann Historical Association in Gloucester, Massachusetts. He was a fellow of the American Academy of Arts and Sciences and a corresponding fellow of the British Academy. In 1997 he received an honorary doctorate from the Université de Nancy in France, where an international colloquium was

being held on his work; yet another colloquium was held in Heidelberg, Germany, in 1998. Goodman died on 25 November of that year.

Whatever garnered his attention–philosophy, art, or animal welfare; lecturing, writing, or engaging in discussion with a friend–Nelson Goodman pursued with uncommon intelligence and enthusiasm. As one of the major thinkers of the twentieth century, he may well have altered thinking in logic, epistemology, aesthetics, and philosophy of science for generations to come.

Bibliography:
Sigrid Berka, *An International Bibliography of Works by and Selected Works about Nelson Goodman* (Champaign-Urbana: University of Illinois Press, 1991).

References:
Curtis L. Carter, Jean-Pierre Cometti, Catherine Z. Elgin, Howard Gardner, Peter Kivy, Dominic M. Lopes, and Jenefer Robinson, "The Legacy of

Nelson Goodman," *Journal of Aesthetics and Art Criticism,* 58, no. 3 (2000): 213–254;

Mary Douglas and David Hull, eds., *How Classification Works: Nelson Goodman among the Social Sciences* (Edinburgh: Edinburgh University Press, 1992);

Elgin, *With Reference to Reference* (Indianapolis: Hackett, 1983);

Elgin, ed., *The Philosophy of Nelson Goodman,* 4 volumes (New York & London: Garland, 1997);

Hans Rudi Fischer and Siegfried J. Schmidt, eds., *Wirklichkeit und Welterzeugung: In Memoriam Nelson Goodman* (Heidelberg: Carl Auer Systeme, 2000);

Howard Gardner and David Perkins, *Art, Mind, and Education* (Carbondale: Southern Illinois University Press, 1989);

Dietfried Gerhardus and B. Phillipi, *Kunst als Erkenntnis: Zur Diskission um Nelson Goodman's Buch, Sprachen der Kunst* (Frankfurt am Main: Suhkamp, forthcoming);

Alan Hausman and Fred Wilson, *Carnap and Goodman: Two Formalists,* Iowa Publications in Philosophy, volume 3 (Iowa City: University of Iowa / The Hague: Nijhoff, 1967);

V. A. Howard, *Artistry* (Indianapolis: Hackett, 1982);

Peter J. McCormick, ed., *Starmaking* (Cambridge, Mass.: MIT Press, 1996);

W. T. J. Mitchell, "Vim and Rigor (Remembering Nelson Goodman)," *Art Forum,* 37 (May 1999): 17–20;

Jacques Morizot, *La philosophie de l'art de Nelson Goodman* (Nîmes: Editions Jacqueline Chambon, 1996);

Israel Scheffler, *The Anatomy of Inquiry* (New York: Knopf, 1963);

Scheffler, *Symbolic Worlds: Art, Science, Language, Ritual* (Cambridge: Cambridge University Press, 1997);

Scheffler and Richard Rudner, eds., *Logic and Art: Essays in Honor of Nelson Goodman* (Indianapolis: Bobbs-Merrill, 1972);

Douglas Stalker, *Grue: The New Riddle of Induction* (Chicago: Open Court, 1994);

"Symposium: The Legacy of Nelson Goodman," *Journal of Aesthetics and Art Criticism,* 58, no. 3 (2000): 213–254;

Richard Wollheim, "Nelson Goodman's Languages of Art," *Journal of Philosophy,* 67, no. 16 (1970): 531–539.

Papers:

Nelson Goodman's papers are in the Harvard University Libraries and in Special Collections and Archives at Marquette University Library. Documents of the performance of *Hockey Seen* are in the Haggerty Museum of Art at Marquette University.

Paul Grice

(13 March 1913 – 28 August 1988)

Stephen L. Thompson
William Paterson University

BOOKS: *Intention and Uncertainty* (London: Oxford University Press, 1972);
Studies in the Way of Words (Cambridge, Mass.: Harvard University Press, 1989);
The Conception of Value, edited by Judith Baker (Oxford: Clarendon Press / New York: Oxford University Press, 1991);
Aspects of Reason, edited by Richard Warner (Oxford: Clarendon Press / New York: Oxford University Press, 2001).

OTHER: "Vacuous Names," in *Words and Objections: Essays on the Work of W. V. Quine,* edited by Donald Davidson and Jaakko Hintikka (Dordrecht, Netherlands: Reidel, 1969), pp. 118–145;
"Reply to Richards," in *Philosophical Grounds of Rationality: Intentions, Categories, Ends,* edited by Richard E. Grandy and Richard Warner (Oxford: Clarendon Press / New York: Oxford University Press, 1986), pp. 45–106.

SELECTED PERIODICAL PUBLICATION–
UNCOLLECTED: "Personal Identity," *Mind,* 50 (1941): 330–350.

Paul Grice

Paul Grice's work greatly influenced both arcs of the so-called linguistic turn of twentieth-century philosophy. The first arc–the variety of attempts to recast the traditional problems of philosophy as problems of language–includes ordinary-language philosophy, which Grice helped to develop. The second arc–full-blown attempts to understand linguistic phenomena–includes philosophical semantics, a field that Grice's work continues to define. Specialists generally regard his approaches to questions of meaning and the logic and grammar of conversation as among the most valuable and enduring in the philosophy of language. His theory of meaning continues to attract the attention of philosophers of language for its ambitious attempt to bring together a pair of epochal claims that, prior to Grice, were generally taken to be mutually exclusive: Ludwig

Wittgenstein's insight that meaning must be pegged to how ordinary speakers use language, and Gottlob Frege's observation that such linguistic units as sentences possess meaning-conferring features, or senses, that are not wholly determined by conventions of use. For this reason alone, Grice's theory of meaning is itself considered an epochal account within the field.

In addition to his work in the philosophy of language, Grice's writings on knowledge and value are well regarded. Epistemologists concerned with the role of the senses in knowledge and belief must contend with his defense of causal theories of perception. Problems he pursued toward the end of his life on the nature of value helped to revive interest in metaphysical issues in ethics. In all his work, though, Grice is as much noted for his philosophical method as for the content of his views. As few have been able to do, he approached the problems of the generalist with the tools of the specialist and scored an enviable record of successes. While his meticulous turns of argument may be formidable in detail and complexity, given their dependence on the tools of technical logic and linguistics, his conclusions illuminate the great problems of meaning, truth, and knowledge associated with such traditional philosophers as Plato, Aristotle, and René Descartes. Like Plato's, his example-counterexample-proposal style of inquiry intrigues and invites rather than obscures and excludes. Navigating Grice's examples and counterexamples is valuable in itself; a mere summary of his proposals for explaining phenomena of ordinary language misses some of the strength of his thought.

Grice is also widely renowned among linguists working in the field of pragmatics. His ideas on the contribution of speakers to the meanings of utterances in conversation are regarded as part of the foundational and theoretical core of pragmatics. His papers on the subject are reprinted in texts in the field, as well as in those of such related fields as conversational analysis and sociolinguistics. Work on metaphor, irony, satire, and humor in these fields tends to pivot on Grice's views.

Though Grice wrote much during his career of more than fifty years, many of his most important papers were not widely published, or even remained unpublished, until just after his death in 1988. His reluctance to publish stemmed from the critical acuity that allowed him to see the flaws in the arguments not only of others but also in his own: he did not want to put his ideas in print until he had refined them to the point of invulnerability to attack, and he was rarely able to regard them as having reached that level of perfection. The views addressed in *Philosophical Grounds of Rationality: Intentions, Categories, Ends* (1986), a major anthology of critical essays on his work, were probably unfamiliar to many readers of the book when it was first published. The dust jacket of his first collection of essays, *Studies in the Way of Words* (1989), which finally brought many of his papers together, includes the notice of his death. The views Grice began to develop during the last decade of his life on the subject of value did not appear in print until *The Conception of Value* (1991).

Herbert Paul Grice was born in Birmingham, England, on 13 March 1913. He studied philosophy at Clifton and Corpus Christi Colleges of the University of Oxford, earning first-class honors in classical honor moderations ("Mods") in 1935 and in *literae humaniores*

("Greats") in 1936 at Corpus Christi. He held a Harmsworth Senior Scholarship at Merton College, Oxford, from 1936 to 1938. He later recalled that one of his professors, W. F. R. Hardie, taught him "just about all the things which one can be taught by someone else"–most important, how to argue. Hardie's tutorials, which were notorious among his students for their unrelenting rigor, left an unmistakable stamp on Grice's own sometimes agonizing philosophical work. Grice taught for a year as assistant master at the Rossall boarding school in Lancashire before being elected to a fellowship in philosophy at St. John's College, Oxford, in 1939.

Grice's main concerns during his early years at Oxford dealt with two quintessential issues of British philosophy: how philosophy can do justice to common sense and–a special case of the first issue–how philosophy of language can do justice to ordinary language. The idea that common sense ought to be a key datum for philosophical theories has long played an important role in English-language philosophy, but philosophers of language were less clear about how to regard common forms of language use. Frege had pronounced against ordinary language in his influential 1892 paper "Über Sinn und Bedeutung" (On Sense and Reference; translated as "On Sense and Nominatum," 1949), claiming that the "looseness" of natural languages–languages actually used, such as German or English–makes problems of meaning and belief difficult to solve. As a result, formal semantics and logic came to dominate the agendas of philosophers such as Bertrand Russell and Rudolf Carnap. Another major influence on British philosophy at the time was A. J. Ayer's logical positivism–or, as Ayer preferred to call it, logical empiricism–which held that any statement that is not, at least in principle, empirically verifiable is empty and meaningless; this criterion not only ruled out all metaphysical and theological claims but also removed from the philosopher's purview problems about what people actually say or hearers take to be implied in ordinary communication.

Grice served for nearly five years in the Royal Navy during World War II, first on destroyers in the Atlantic and then in Admiralty intelligence. In 1943 he married Kathleen Watson; they had two children, Tim and Karen. After the war Grice returned to St. John's College, where he retained his fellowship and served as lecturer, tutor, and, finally, university lecturer. At various times he lectured and conducted seminars in the United States at Harvard, Brandeis, Stanford, and Cornell Universities.

By the time he returned to Oxford after the war, Grice had decided that neither Frege's formalist semantics nor Ayer's positivism was hospitable to his concerns about common sense and everyday language. In the late 1940s and the 1950s, in contrast to positivist thinkers such as Carnap who were constructing formal languages intended to facilitate the understanding of meaning, Grice developed a powerful account of meaning centered on the intricacies of ordinary language. At this time Oxford–largely because of the presence of Gilbert Ryle, editor of the influential journal *Mind*–was emerging as a world philosophical center, thereby setting the stage for the rise and spread of ordinary-language philosophy.

One of Grice's earliest papers, "Common Sense and Skepticism," written between 1946 and 1950 and first published in *Studies in the Way of Words,* begins with a survey of the philosophy of G. E. Moore. Moore's defenses of common sense against skeptical challenges early in the century were stunning in their baldness. In his lecture "Proof of an External World," first published in *Proceedings of the British Academy* in 1939, he offered his own hands as proof against the skeptic who doubts that a world outside the mind exists:

> I can prove now, for instance, that two human hands exist. How? By holding up my two hands, and saying, as I make a certain gesture with the right hand, "Here is one hand," and adding, as I make a certain gesture with the left, "and here is another." And if, by doing this, I have proved *ipso facto* the existence of external things, you will all see that I can also do it now in numbers of ways: there is no need to multiply examples.

Grice points out that while Moore does not claim that no commonsense beliefs are beyond philosophical challenge, he accuses skeptics of sinning against common sense by questioning or denying things that they–the skeptics–know to be true. Grice, however, takes the principled skeptical challenge to empirical propositions to be the most crucial form of skepticism. That form of skepticism denies that any empirical proposition is ever known with certainty to be true, though it allows that the truth of such propositions may be a matter of high probability. He restates Norman Malcolm's objection in his contribution to the Library of Living Philosophers volume *The Philosophy of G. E. Moore* (1942) that this sort of skeptic is making an a priori argument that any claim such as the ordinary expression "I know that there is cheese on the table" will fail tests of certainty, regardless of the circumstances of its utterance. This argument, Malcolm says, asserts that some perfectly ordinary expression is actually a self-contradiction. But this claim is absurd: any expression that is self-contradictory or otherwise incoherent would not be uttered in ordinary contexts. Grice points out that the skeptic can urge that, if one reflects adequately, one may see that one needs to correct one's use of the word *know* with regard to empirical statements: one is only entitled to claim certainty

when one can say one is using *know* correctly. Grice thus argues that philosophical paradoxes of the sort that preoccupy Moore are, ultimately, matters of ordinary language in use.

At Oxford, Grice participated in informal Saturday-morning discussions of "the Playgroup," begun in the late 1940s and led by J. L. Austin. Most of the participants were younger philosophers; regular attendees included P. F. Strawson, G. J. Warnock, R. M. Hare, Stuart Hampshire, and David F. Pears. Though not committed to any particular doctrinal views, members of the group found common ground in the broad claim that the detailed features of ordinary discourse ought to be carefully examined as a foundation for philosophical thinking; the group thus came to be identified as ordinary-language philosophers. Grice and his colleagues tended to avoid pat summaries of what the ordinary-language approach entails, however. "To my mind," Grice observes, "getting together with others to do philosophy should be very much like getting together with others to make music: lively yet sensitive interaction is directed towards a common end, in the case of philosophy a better grasp of some fragment of philosophical truth; and if, as sometimes happens, harmony is sufficiently great to allow collaboration as authors, then so much the better."

Grice's main collaborator was Strawson, who was one of his former students. The two conducted joint seminars on meaning, categories, and logical form; they also pursued systematic and unsystematic explorations, including a long but uncompleted work on predication and Aristotelian categories. Grice recalled in 1986 that their "method of collaboration was laborious in the extreme; work was constructed together sentence by sentence, nothing being written down until agreement had been reached, which often took quite a time"; the "rigours of this procedure eventually led to its demise." The most striking feature of this approach, to Grice, was not so much a convergence of views as "the extraordinary closeness of the intellectual *rapport*" that developed. These collaborative efforts continued throughout Grice's life; he went on to work with Austin on Aristotle's *Categories* and *De Interpretatione,* with Warnock on perception, with Pears and James Thomson on the philosophy of action, with Frits Staal on philosophical-linguistic questions, with George Myro on metaphysics, with Judith Baker on ethics, and with John Haugeland on personal identity.

Grice's chief collaboration with Strawson was their widely read "In Defense of a Dogma," published in *The Philosophical Review* in 1956 and collected in *Studies in the Way of Words.* The article is a response to the Harvard University philosopher W. V. Quine's attack on the traditional distinction between analytic and syn-

*The British philosopher P. F. Strawson, a fellow participant with Grice,
G. J. Warnock, R. M. Hare, Stuart Hampshire, and David F.
Pears in the Saturday-morning discussions of "the Playgroup"
led by J. L. Austin at the University of Oxford
in the late 1940s*

thetic statements. The distinction, which dates back at least to Immanuel Kant in the eighteenth century, is between statements that are true solely because of the meanings of their terms and statements that are true because of facts about the world. The first sort of truths are called "analytic" and include such statements as "All bachelors are unmarried men." This statement is true because the meaning of the term *bachelor* accords with the meaning of the term *unmarried man*. Analytic truths thus depend on the "intensional," or internal, features of words and are independent of features of the world; one need only examine definitions to verify their truth. The second sort of truths are called "synthetic" and include such statements as "Some bachelors are bald" (*some,* in logic, means "at least one"). Synthetic truths depend on the "extensional" features of the words in them—that is, how the words "extend over" features of the world; one has to look at the world to verify their truth. The first statement is true because a married

bachelor is an impossibility; the second statement is verified by the observation of even one bald man who is not married. Carnap's *Meaning and Necessity: A Study in Semantics and Modal Logic* (1947) updated Kant's account using the tools of symbolic logic. Carnap says that analytic truths are true in virtue of the synonymy of the terms contained in them: for example, *bachelor* and *unmarried man* are synonyms—they are identical in meaning. Meanings, then, underwrite the analytic/synthetic distinction. If the distinction is implausible, then meanings cannot be intensional, and so they cannot do what philosophers since Frege have taken them to do.

The analytic/synthetic distinction came into serious question when Quine's Harvard colleague Nelson Goodman published a paper on it in 1949, followed a year later by a paper by Morton White; with Quine's attack in "Two Dogmas of Empiricism" (1951) the case against the distinction was widely regarded as having been persuasively made. Quine argues that the standard view of analyticity is circular: rather than synonymy providing an independent basis for analyticity, analyticity presupposes synonymy; to say that two terms are synonymous is simply to say that they can be used to form analytic statements. Synonymy and analyticity lie within the same "intensional circle," encompassing facts about the intensions of words and statements; Quine argues that the terms within this circle are not acceptable for explanations of other such terms. One must, instead, advert to terms outside the intensional circle, terms that encompass facts about the extensions of words and statements—that is, the things and facts in the world to which the words and statements refer. Thus, no intensional facts exist to be explained; only extensional ones do, and the analytic/synthetic distinction cannot be defended.

Grice and Strawson reply that when ordinary speakers say "All bachelors are unmarried men," they take the utterance to be true by definition. Holding that it means that *bachelor* and *unmarried man* have the same extension—refer to the same things—does not capture the strength of this common intuition. Grice and Strawson cite the statements "My neighbor's three-year-old child understands Russell's theory of types" and "My neighbor's three-year-old child is an adult." One who hears the first statement might, after initial disbelief, ultimately concede that the child is a genius—rare, even unique, but not logically impossible. But no hearer would concede the truth of the second statement. Regardless of what sort of creature might be presented as proof, it could not be brought within the extensions of the words *child* and *adult* at the same time without changing the meaning of one or both of the words. Thus, some intensional facts resist extensional explanation, and the distinction between analytic and synthetic truths remains intact.

Though no consensus about analytic statements has emerged, Quine is widely taken to have won the debate in that all theories posed since his 1951 paper have had to take account of his criticisms. Grice and Strawson's article, while not as influential as Quine's, is, nonetheless, valuable in helping to demarcate the territory of ordinary language with respect to philosophical semantics. While Quine is largely concerned with a problem in semantics–how an item in a lexical system is to be individuated–Grice and Strawson are asking a different question: what do ordinary speakers think?

In 1957 Grice published in *The Philosophical Review* a short article, "Meaning," that he had written in 1948; it is collected in *Studies in the Ways of Words*. The arguments presented in it dominated much of the philosophy of language in the 1960s and 1970s, and the paper continues to be cited as one of the two or three serious contenders for solving philosophical problems about meaning. Grice attempts to bypass a thorny problem in the philosophy of language about the meanings of arbitrary sounds and marks. Frege had argued that a linguistic unit such as a sentence has a "sense" that is distinct both from the image one has in mind on uttering the sentence and from the things in the world to which it refers. Frege's discovery of sense led many philosophers to take the intensional features of language to be primary and directed attention away from the ways language is used. Wittgenstein, however, argued in *Philosophical Investigations* (1953) that the meaning of an expression is simply the use to which it is put by participants in "language games." This "meaning-is-use" view suggests that theorists need to study the use of language rather than futilely pursue its intensional features. Grice seeks to reconcile the two positions by reducing the problem to what speakers intend when they use sounds and marks meaningfully–an approach that has been dubbed "intention-based semantics." He thus interweaves what speakers mean with what expressions mean, appealing to psychological facts to determine semantic facts.

Grice begins by dividing statements of the form "*x* means *p*" into two groups. The first group includes statements such as "Those spots mean measles" and "The recent budget means that we shall have a hard year." Several logical features are common to these statements. First, when they are true, they entail that *p*. For example, if a certain kind of spot on the skin means measles, then, if such spots are present, the patient has measles. This sense of meaning reflects a "tight fit" between a fact about what something means and a state of affairs in the world; the two, so to speak, "travel together." Another feature of statements in this group is

that one cannot rephrase them as "What is meant by *x* is *p*" nor as "So-and-so meant *p* by *x*." That is, "Those spots mean measles" is distinct both from "What is meant by those spots is measles" and from "By those spots he means measles," and "The recent budget means that we shall have a hard year" is distinct both from "What is meant by the recent budget is that we shall have a hard year" and "He meant by the recent budget that we shall have a hard year." The last two statements in each case seem to depend on the meaning of *x* having an "internal" character that it clearly does not have. Finally, one cannot paraphrase any statement in this group by placing a sentence or phrase in quotation marks after the verb *mean:* "Those spots mean measles" is not the same as "Those spots mean 'measles.'" On the other hand, one can restate them using the phrase "the fact that . . . ," as in "The fact that he has those spots means that he has measles."

Grice's second group includes statements such as "Those three rings on the bell of the bus mean that the bus is full" and "The remark 'Jones could not get on without his trouble and strife' means (in Cockney rhyming slang) that Jones found his wife indispensable." In the case of these statements, even if "*x* means *p*" is true, *p* is not entailed. Even if three rings on the bell does mean that the bus is full, the bus's being full is not entailed by the fact that the bell is rung three times. The bell might have been rung in error because the driver was not able to see an empty seat; or it might have been rung with the intention to deceive–perhaps the driver wanted to prevent an obnoxious would-be passenger from boarding. Second, one can rephrase these statements in the form "What is meant by *x* is *p*" and "So-and-so means by *x* that *p*": "What is meant by those three rings is that the bus is full," "He means by those three rings that the bus is full." Finally, these sentences do permit restatement in which the verb *mean* is followed by an expression in quotation marks: the first statement can be paraphrased as "Those three rings mean 'the bus is full.'" These statements cannot, however, be restated by using the phrase "the fact that. . . ."

These differences between group-one and group-two statements hinge on the relevance of what the meaningful sound or mark in question means in itself to how it is intended to be meant on some particular occasion. What Grice calls "natural meaning" is exemplified in group one, while "nonnatural meaning" is exemplified in group two. Much of what makes language interesting lies in its ability to mean nonnaturally; Grice, therefore, focuses on this sort of meaning.

One might be tempted to think that nonnatural meaning is simply a speaker's intention to communicate something, but, Grice notes, this view presents difficulties. Someone may communicate something by using an object as a signal, so that an audience might draw a particular conclusion, without the object itself meaning what the audience concludes. A chalk outline showing where a body has been discovered sends a signal to members of a crime-scene team, as well as to onlookers, not because chalk outlines in themselves mean "a body was found here" but because those who perceive the outline discern that this signal is intended. It would be better–though, Grice argues, it is still insufficient–to say that nonnatural meaning requires both that a speaker intend to communicate something and that the targeted audience recognize this intention. When Herod Antipas presented Salome with John the Baptist's head on a platter, he intended to induce in her the belief that John the Baptist was dead and also intended her to recognize his intention to induce that belief, and she recognized these intentions; but the decapitated head itself did not "mean" anything. Grice argues that such situations, in which one deliberately and openly lets someone know something, should be distinguished from those in which one gets someone to think something. For example, Grice says, if he shows Mr. X a photograph of Mr. Y showing undue familiarity to Mrs. X, the photograph itself does not nonnaturally mean anything. But if Grice draws a picture of Mr. Y showing undue familiarity to Mrs. X and shows it to Mr. X, the drawing does nonnaturally mean something. The difference is that with the photograph, Mr. X need not recognize Grice's intention in order to draw the intended conclusion; the same effect would be produced if Grice had simply left the photo where Mr. X would find it. The example of the photograph is, thus, a case of deliberately and openly letting someone know something. With the drawing, however, intention does matter: Grice might have intended to produce a work of art or might simply have been doodling on a cocktail napkin. This example illustrates getting someone to think something. Grice concludes that in nonnatural meaning a speaker must intend by uttering a sentence to induce a belief in an audience and must intend that utterance to be recognized as so intended. These intentions are not independent; the speaker must also intend that the recognition play its part in inducing the belief. In uttering "I'm tired," a speaker intends, first, that the audience believe that he or she is tired; second, that the audience recognize that intention; and third, that this recognition be part of the audience's reason for believing that the speaker is tired. Grice calls what the speaker intends "speaker meaning" (the term "utterer's meaning" has been used by others to designate the same phenomenon). The three intentions together form what Grice calls a "meaning intention"; it has become customary to refer to it as an "m-intention." Formally, then, speaker *A* means that *p* by uttering *x* if and only if

A m-intends that *p* by uttering *x*. Speaker meaning is thus a function of a potentially complex m-intention.

Several important objections appeared following the publication of Grice's paper. Strawson argued in "Intention and Convention in Speech Acts" (1964) that the account fails to provide a sufficient condition for meaning that *p*. For example, even if Smith does something as overt as smearing lipstick on Mr. Jones's shirt in front of Mrs. Jones to try to get her to believe that her husband is unfaithful, the act of smearing does not mean that he is unfaithful. Strawson's point is that it is necessary to add a higher level of deliberate intention to a speaker's m-intention: the intention that the hearer recognize the speaker's intention to get the hearer to recognize the m-intention to get that hearer to think that *p*.

Stephen R. Schiffer presses the point further in his *Meaning* (1972), observing that no set of jointly sufficient conditions will result simply by adding some further condition that a speaker intend this higher-level intention, since one can always construct a Strawson-style counterexample. For someone to mean something, Schiffer asserts, "all of his meaning-constitutive intentions must in some appropriate sense be entirely out in the open." To avoid such problems, Schiffer says, one might suggest that a speaker, in addition to m-intending, further intend that there be a special kind of shared knowledge between speaker and hearer that the speaker uttered *x* with that intention. Schiffer calls this shared knowledge "mutual knowledge*"; the asterisk indicates the qualified sense of the term *knowledge*. To say that "*A* and *B* mutually know* that *p*" is, then, to suppose an infinite continuation of the sequence "*A* knows that *p*; *B* knows that *p*; *A* knows that *B* knows that *p*; . . ." Were this condition built into m-intending, one could avoid the need for higher Strawson-style intentions and thus avoid any regress.

Schiffer identifies two problems with this suggestion. First, it fails to address certain kinds of deceitful situations, including those where Grice's original three conditions of a speaker's m-intention and the new condition of mutual knowledge* are met but the speaker has the further intention that the hearer mistakenly think that the speaker did not intend those m-intention conditions. Mrs. Jones can recognize Smith's intention, and Smith can intend this recognition, with both Mrs. Jones and Smith all the while aware of these facts, up to any number of levels; yet, Smith could still be intending everything to be a ruse. There would be no end to the second-guessing. The second reason that this amendment will not work is that it is doubtful that two people ever actually have mutual knowledge*; the idea seems psychologically unreal.

Schiffer's overall objection is that Grice "may be saying what meaning is, but he can hardly be unpacking anyone's *concept* of meaning." Near the end of "Meaning" Grice anticipates this kind of objection. He is not explicating what speakers and hearers actually think as they communicate; the theory of speaker meaning is intended to reconstruct what speakers and hearers know. Grice's theory of meaning, like the linguist Noam Chomsky's theory of transformational-generative grammar, attempts to make explicit a cognitive activity of which those who engage in it are not consciously aware. Even if pressed, they would scarcely recognize the three-part conjunction that constitutes m-intending as their own.

Grice's "Meaning" is not confined to the notion of speaker meaning. He also argues that "expression meaning," the meanings of expressions themselves, can be analyzed entirely in terms of a speaker's m-intentions—hence the label "intention-based semantics." The importance of intention-based semantics is that it can clarify what meanings finally are in a way that does not already presume meanings. If expressions mean one of the three conjuncts of what speakers m-intend, then Grice's theory of meaning will have reduced the internal features of expressions—the concepts they express, that is, their meanings—to the intentions of speakers. While the primacy of speaker meaning to expression meaning in the theory contrasts with Wittgenstein's view that intentions do not fix semantic facts, it simultaneously agrees with Wittgenstein's central tenet that meaning is use. M-intending, whatever else it may be, comes under the heading of the use of language. At the same time, Grice's intention-based semantics accounts for Frege's concern about the senses of sentences.

Intention-based semantics is an instance of philosophical reduction. Such reductions have been proposed for many topics: what they generally accomplish, when successful, is an exhaustive translation. That is, all of the terms of a less-well-understood analysandum are translated, without residue, into the terms of a better-understood analysandum. In the case of intention-based semantics, semantic features such as the intensional-meaning properties of an expression are translated into psychological features such as a speaker's beliefs and intentions. Reducing the semantic to the psychological does not complete the theory of meaning; instead, it connects the theory to the more promising project of psychological explanation. While philosophers have not fully explicated the nature of psychological intentions to communicate, a sufficiently robust neuroscience may someday accomplish this goal. The theory of language will then inherit that explication.

Intention-based semantics requires the differentiation of the concepts expressed by two potentially confusing terms: the homonyms *intensional* and *intentional*. Intensionality is a property of expressions with internal

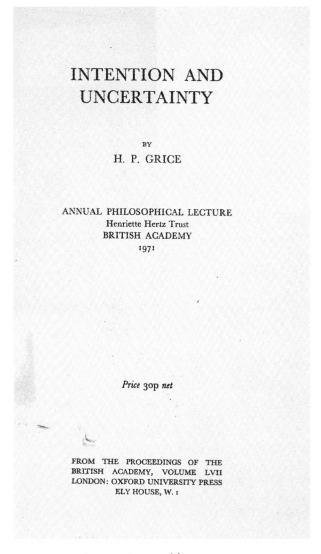

INTENTION AND
UNCERTAINTY

BY
H. P. GRICE

ANNUAL PHILOSOPHICAL LECTURE
Henriette Hertz Trust
BRITISH ACADEMY
1971

Price 30p *net*

FROM THE PROCEEDINGS OF THE
BRITISH ACADEMY, VOLUME LVII
LONDON: OXFORD UNIVERSITY PRESS
ELY HOUSE, W. 1

*Cover for Grice's first book (Thomas Cooper Library,
University of South Carolina)*

features—that is, features that are specifiable by taking only the expressions themselves into account, apart from their extensions (the objects to which they refer). Their importance in the theory of meaning is evident in discussions of analyticity. Intentionality, on the other hand, is a property of sentences, words, and thoughts—of anything that can be *about* something other than itself. For example, a thought or phrase about tourism in Greece is about something going on in that country, which, of course, is utterly unlike the thought or words in question. Since its formulation by Franz Brentano in the nineteenth century, intentionality has been taken as "the mark of the mental." Neither homonym, though, fully captures the sense of Grice's m-intending. His sense certainly includes the "aboutness" property integral to intentionality, in that a speaker intends some particular thing—that a hearer believe such-and-such or recognize that the speaker intends such-and-such and so on. (Paraphrasing m-intentions using that-clauses is usually a decisive sign of intentionality.) But his term also expresses something about a speaker's motivation. When a speaker m-intends, he or she is moved by an ulterior motive—to communicate to a hearer. Gricean intending thus expands the sense of intentionality.

Grice typically left it to others to flesh out his ideas. David K. Lewis's influential *Convention: A Philosophical Study* (1969) is generally regarded as presenting the most promising sustained analysis of the role convention plays in accomplishing the reduction of expression meaning to speaker meaning for a given group of speakers. The definitive statement of intention-based semantics appeared in Schiffer's 1972 book, fifteen years after Grice's original article. Their accounts of intention-based semantics are commonly discussed along with Grice's own.

Grice was elected to the British Academy in 1966. The following year he delivered the William James Lectures at Harvard University; revised versions of the lectures appear as the first seven essays in *Studies in the Way of Words*. In the second, "Logic and Conversation," he lays out the concept of "conversational implicature," a key notion in communication. To understand a conversation one must follow more than the simple meaning of each utterance, since utterances routinely imply things that are left unspoken. In saying "Smith has not yet been arrested," for example, Jones is not only stating that Smith is not being detained by the authorities but is also implying that one might expect him to be detained. Grice argues that conversation is regulated by a set of presuppositions. Primarily, the parties are to follow "the Cooperative Principle," which requires that each contribute to the conversation in turn and at the appropriate time, in accordance with "the accepted purpose or direction" of the exchange. The principle implies several maxims, which Grice arranges—echoing Immanuel Kant, he says—under four categories. Under the category of Quantity the maxims are "Make your contribution as informative as is required (for the current purpose of the exchange)" and "Do not make your contribution more informative than is required." Under the category of Quality are a "supermaxim"—"Try to make your contribution one that is true"—and two more-specific maxims: "Do not say what you believe to be false" and "Do not say that for which you lack adequate evidence." The category of Relation comprises only one maxim: "Be relevant." Finally, under the category of Manner one finds another supermaxim, "Be perspicuous," and four maxims: "Avoid Obscurity of expression," "Avoid ambiguity," "Be brief (avoid unnecessary prolixity)," and "Be orderly." Grice is not prescribing an etiquette of conversation but is explicat-

ing maxims that, he claims, participants in conversation tacitly presuppose. Thus, Jones's comment that Smith has not yet been arrested would violate the condition of relevance unless it is meant to "implicate" something beyond what it literally states. This level of communication is that of conversational implicature.

The theory of implicature influenced a generation of linguists by showing that they must appeal to implied meaning and presumed maxims to explain such dimensions of speech as irony, satire, and humor. Dan Sperber and Deirdre Wilson's *Relevance: Communication and Cognition* (1986) is a wide-ranging discussion of such applications of the theory.

In the following essay, "Indicative Conditionals," Grice explores the way in which grammatical devices stand in, in ordinary conversation, for logical operators. Ordinary uses of the word *if* are not identical to the logical operator symbolized by the horseshoe, he says, but everyday speech does reflect formal logic to a considerable extent.

The next two essays, "Utterer's Meaning and Intentions" and "Utterer's Meaning, Sentence-Meaning, and Word-Meaning," are responses to the attention Grice's theory had received in the 1960s. In "What Is a Speech Act?" (1965) John R. Searle produced a counterexample to intention-based semantics. During World War II an American soldier is captured by Italian troops. He reasons that his best chance to avoid imprisonment is to persuade his captors that he is not, in fact, an American but a German. He does not speak Italian well enough to lie to them directly in their own language. Though he does not speak German, either, he does recall the first line of a German poem he learned in grade school: "Kennst du das Land, wo die Zitronen blühen?" (Knowest thou the land where the lemon trees bloom?). He utters it, intending them to recognize his intention to tell them something; to recognize that he is speaking German, even (and especially) if they do not understand German; and to take him to mean "I am a German soldier." Searle points out that these conditions count as m-intending, which suggests that the speaker means by the German sentence that he is a German soldier. Searle argues that whatever the intentions of the speaker, he does not change the meaning of the expression in virtue of them; "Kennst du das Land, wo die Zitronen blühen?" does not on this occasion come to mean "I am a German soldier." Searle concludes that Grice's account is insufficient.

In "Utterer's Meaning and Intentions" Grice responds that, though the American soldier intends for the Italians to believe that he is a German, he does not intend that they recognize this intention. Rather, he intends that they reason in a certain way: he is speaking German; no one but a German would do so; therefore, he must be a German. The American speaker no more means by the sentence "Kennst du das Land, wo die Zitronen blühen?" that he is a German soldier than, say, an Arabian merchant, smiling and saying in Arabic to a British customer "You pig of an Englishman," would mean "Please come in," even if the customer took the latter to be his meaning. To argue otherwise is to confuse the meanings of utterances with any effects they may precipitate. The American, then, does not mean by his utterance that he is a German soldier; thus, Searle has failed to provide a genuine counterexample.

Grice proposes several revisions to the theory he put forward in his 1957 paper. Introducing the concept of an "m-intended effect," he applies it to utterances in the imperative and indicative moods. The m-intended effect of an imperative utterance is that the hearer intend to do something. For instance, Jones tells Smith to pass the peas; Jones's m-intention has as its m-intended effect that Smith intend to perform that action. Smith responds with the indicative utterance, "There are no peas left"; the m-intended effect of this utterance is not to get Jones to believe that there are no peas but to get Jones to think that Smith believes that there are no peas. Grice concludes that the mood of an utterance plays an essential and systematic role in specifying what the utterance means, and that moods are represented in the underlying syntactic structures of utterances. An utterance thus has both a content and a "mood-operator."

In 1967 Grice accepted an appointment as professor of philosophy at the University of California at Berkeley. "The need for greater contact with experts in logic and in linguistics than was then available in Oxford," he later wrote, "was one of my main professional reasons for moving to the United States."

In 1971 Grice served briefly as chairman of the Berkeley philosophy department. That same year he participated in a summer institute on the philosophy of language at the University of California at Irvine, lecturing on formal semantics. In 1975 he was elected president of the Pacific Division of the American Philosophical Association; his presidential address, "Methodological Issues in the Philosophy of Psychology (From the Banal to the Bizarre)," is collected in *The Conception of Value*. In 1977 he delivered the Immanuel Kant Lectures at Stanford University on communicative rationality; he gave the same four lectures, with the addition of a fifth, for the John Locke Lectures at Oxford two years later; Grice was one of the few philosophers ever invited to give both the William James and the John Locke Lectures. Revised versions of the Locke lectures, based on a manuscript Grice worked on during the last decade of his life, were published posthumously in 2001 as *Aspects of Reason*. Here Grice says that in reasoning one uses, even if only implicitly, a set

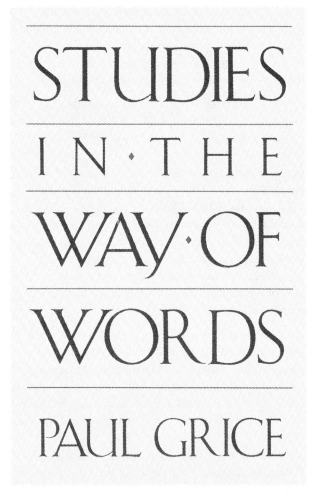

STUDIES
IN·THE
WAY·OF
WORDS
PAUL GRICE

Cover for the 1991 paperback edition of Grice's first collection of essays, originally published in 1989. It includes "Common Sense and Skepticism," in which he argues that some seemingly intractable philosophical problems result from the misuse of words (Bruccoli Clark Layman Archives).

of procedures to infer, from some claim *A,* some other claim *B*. On being asked by Jones to pass the peas, Smith may reason: "Jones wants me to pass the peas, but she is a meat lover; therefore, she will probably ask for the ham, too." Smith may be employing a suppressed premise such as "Meat lovers normally ask for ham" or "Some people of Jones's age and description ask for ham provided they are meat lovers"; such suppressed premises may not be obvious and may be multiplied indefinitely. A second and unsettling possibility is that Smith is not employing a suppressed premise but merely coming to a conclusion on the strength of some brute irrational conviction. Grice's answer is that in any case of a speaker reasoning from *A* to *B* the speaker must intend for there to be some formally valid argument from *A* to *B*. The speaker need not actually entertain, even implicitly, any premises that would secure formal validity; he or she must merely intend that some such linking premises exist. Communication is, therefore, rational whenever speakers at least intend that a logical sequence exist from one claim to another, even if they can neither construct nor report that sequence.

In "Meaning Revisited," first published in 1982 and collected in *Studies in the Way of Words,* Grice defines expression as "having a procedure in one's repertoire"—gestures, marks, or sounds—that may be used to mean that *p*. A particular wave of the hand, for example, may be taken by those who see it to mean "the waver knows the route to follow." Such a hand-wave procedure would be in the repertoire of those who use and interpret it. In the case of utterances, speakers have a finite stock of primary procedures that they use to generate a potentially infinite set of secondary procedures. The task of a complete theory of expression meaning is to specify such procedures.

Grice retired in 1979 but continued to teach as professor emeritus. He delivered the Paul Carus Lectures to the American Philosophical Association in 1983; they are published in *The Conception of Value.* In the lectures he attempts to show how value judgments may be said to be objective by indicating how such judgments are constructed. Following the eighteenth-century British empiricist philosopher David Hume, he appeals to the power of the mind to project onto the world features that, properly speaking, belong only to minds. Humean projection, as this power is called, provides a plausible account of how mental attitudes come to intervene in the objective world. Grice goes on to show how what is originally regarded as an accidental feature of a thing can come to be regarded as one of its essential features. This shift takes place as a result of a change not in the thing itself but in people's attitudes toward it. Once such a "metaphysical transubstantiation" has taken place, the projection of value onto the thing is legitimate. Thus, according to Grice, values are real, and value relativism is avoided.

In addition to being a philosopher, Grice was, in his younger years, an avid cricket player; he was also adept at bridge and chess, played the piano, and composed music. Health problems forced him to cease teaching at Berkeley in 1986, but he continued to lead discussion groups at his home, present papers at professional meetings, and work on the manuscript for *Studies in the Way of Words.* He died on 28 August 1988.

Few thinkers have brought as rich a palette of techniques to so broad a range of concerns as Paul Grice. He combined the utmost in philosophical rigor with an ear for ordinary speech. The technical sophistication of his thought ensures that his ideas will continue to engage philosophers of language and linguists. His concerns with such perennial problems as meaning, knowledge, and value give his work an enduring importance. Perhaps the most vital aspect of Grice's thinking is his dogged search for final answers to such problems.

References:

Anita Avramides, *Meaning and Mind: An Examination of a Gricean Account of Language* (Cambridge, Mass.: MIT Press, 1989);

Richard E. Grandy and Richard Warner, eds., *Philosophical Grounds of Rationality: Intentions, Categories, Ends* (Oxford: Clarendon Press / New York: Oxford University Press, 1986);

David K. Lewis, *Convention: A Philosophical Study* (Cambridge, Mass.: Harvard University Press, 1969);

Stephen R. Schiffer, *Meaning* (Oxford: Clarendon Press, 1972);

Schiffer, *Remnants of Meaning* (Cambridge, Mass.: MIT Press, 1987);

John R. Searle, *Speech Acts: An Essay in the Philosophy of Language* (London: Cambridge University Press, 1969);

Searle, "What Is a Speech Act?" in *Philosophy in America,* edited by Max Black (Ithaca, N.Y.: Cornell University Press, 1965), pp. 221–239;

Dan Sperber and Deirdre Wilson, *Relevance: Communication and Cognition* (Cambridge, Mass.: Harvard University Press, 1986);

P. F. Strawson, "Intention and Convention in Speech Acts," *Philosophical Review,* 73 (1964): 439–460;

Strawson and David Wiggins, "Herbert Paul Grice: 1913–1988," *Proceedings of the British Academy,* 111 (2001): 515–528.

Papers:

The Paul Grice Archives are at the Bancroft Library of the University of California at Berkeley.

Errol E. Harris

(19 February 1908 –   )

Philip T. Grier
Dickinson College

BOOKS: *The Survival of Political Man: A Study in the Principles of International Order* (Johannesburg: Witwatersrand University Press, 1950);

"White" Civilization: How It Is Threatened and How It Can Be Preserved in South Africa (Johannesburg: South African Institute of Race Relations, 1952);

Nature, Mind and Modern Science (London: Allen & Unwin / New York: Macmillan, 1954);

Objectivity and Reason: Inaugural Lecture (Johannesburg: Witwatersrand University Press, 1955);

Revelation through Reason: Reason in the Light of Science and Philosophy (New Haven: Yale University Press, 1958);

The Foundations of Metaphysics in Science (London: Allen & Unwin, 1965; New York: Humanities Press, 1965);

Annihilation and Utopia: The Principles of International Politics (London: Allen & Unwin, 1966);

Fundamentals of Philosophy: A Study of Classical Texts (New York: Holt, Rinehart & Winston, 1969); republished as *Fundamentals of Philosophy* (London: Allen & Unwin, 1969);

Hypothesis and Perception: The Roots of Scientific Method, Muirhead Library of Philosophy (London: Allen & Unwin / New York: Humanities Press, 1970);

Salvation from Despair: A Reappraisal of Spinoza's Philosophy (The Hague: Nijhoff, 1973);

Perceptual Assurance and the Reality of the World (Worcester, Mass.: Clark University Press, with Barre Publishers, 1974);

The Problem of Evil (Milwaukee: Marquette University, 1977);

Atheism and Theism (New Orleans: Tulane University, 1977);

An Interpretation of the Logic of Hegel (Lanham, Md.: University Press of America, 1983);

Formal, Transcendental, and Dialectical Thinking: Logic and Reality (Albany: State University of New York Press, 1987);

The Reality of Time (Albany: State University of New York Press, 1988);

Errol E. Harris in 1976

Cosmos and Anthropos: A Philosophical Interpretation of the Anthropic Cosmological Principle (Atlantic Highlands, N.J. & London: Humanities Press, 1991);

Cosmos and Theos: Ethical and Theological Implications of the Anthropic Cosmological Principle (Atlantic Highlands, N.J. & London: Humanities Press, 1992);

Spinoza's Philosophy: An Outline (Atlantic Highlands, N.J. & London: Humanities Press, 1992);

One World or None: Prescription for Survival (Atlantic Highlands, N.J. & London: Humanities Press, 1993);

The Spirit of Hegel (Atlantic Highlands, N.J. & London: Humanities Press, 1993);

The Substance of Spinoza (Atlantic Highlands, N.J. & London: Humanities Press, 1995);

Apocalypse and Paradigm: Science and Everyday Thinking
  (Westport, Conn.: Praeger, 2000);
The Restitution of Metaphysics (Amherst, N.Y.: Humanity
  Books, 2000).

OTHER: Harold H. Joachim, *Descartes's Rules for the
  Direction of the Mind,* edited by Harris (London:
  Allen & Unwin, 1957; Westport, Conn.: Green-
  wood Press, 1979);
Friedrich Wilhelm Joseph von Schelling, *Ideas for a Phi-
  losophy of Nature,* translated by Harris and Peter
  Heath (Cambridge & New York: Cambridge Uni-
  versity Press, 1988);
*Toward Genuine Global Governance: Critical Reactions to "Our
  Global Neighborhood,"* edited by Harris and James
  A. Yunker (Westport, Conn.: Praeger, 1999).

SELECTED PERIODICAL PUBLICATIONS–
UNCOLLECTED: "Scientific Philosophy," *Philosophi-
  cal Quarterly,* 2 (1952): 153–165;
"Objectivity and Reason," *Philosophy,* 31 (1956): 55–73;
"Political Power," *Ethics,* 68 (1957): 1–10;
"Teleology and Teleological Explanation," *Journal of
  Philosophy,* 56 (1959): 5–25;
"The Neural-Identity Theory and the Person," *Interna-
  tional Philosophical Quarterly,* 6 (1966): 515–537;
"Method and Explanation in Metaphysics," *Proceedings
  of the Catholic Philosophical Association,* 41 (1967):
  124–133;
"The Power of Reason," *Review of Metaphysics,* 22
  (1969): 621–639;
"Coherence and Its Critics," *Idealistic Studies,* 5 (1975):
  208–230;
"Time and Eternity," *Review of Metaphysics,* 29 (1976):
  464–482;
"Natural Law and Naturalism," *International Philosophical
  Quarterly,* 23 (1983): 115–124;
"John Niemeyer Findlay (1903–1987)," *Owl of Minerva,*
  19 (Spring 1988): 252–253.

Errol E. Harris is widely recognized for his innovative neo-Hegelian approach to problems in the philosophy and history of science and the philosophy of nature.
His career serves as a connecting link between British
neo-Hegelianism of the early twentieth century and the
resurgent Hegelianism of the last decades of the twentieth century in North America, Britain, and Europe. He is
best known for exploring the philosophical implications
of modern scientific theory. The dialectical and holistic
conception of nature and of the relationship of the mind
to nature discerned by Harris in the results of contemporary science is strongly reminiscent of the thought of the
nineteenth-century German idealist philosopher Georg
Wilhelm Friedrich Hegel.

Harris has also been an influential contributor to
the interpretation of Hegel's philosophy, as well as that
of the seventeenth-century Dutch rationalist Baruch
Spinoza. In the 1930s, when scarcely any attention was
being paid by scholars to Hegel's philosophy of nature,
Harris began to argue for its central role in his system.
This view came to be widely appreciated only in the late
twentieth century. Harris's own philosophical contribution is one of the most cogent recent demonstrations of
the possibility and necessity of a contemporary philosophy of nature. Harris has also made original contributions to the philosophy of religion and to political
philosophy. As these various elements of his thought
emerged over the years, the internal coherence and systematic nature of his thought became increasingly evident; the result is one of the most comprehensive and
substantive philosophical systems produced in the twentieth century.

Errol Eustace Harris was born on 19 February
1908 in Kimberley, South Africa, to Samuel Jacob Harris, a merchant, and Dora Gross Harris, both of whom
had immigrated to South Africa from England. He had
two older sisters: Esther Gwendolyn and Muriel Enid.
He grew up in Kimberley, Capetown, and Port Elizabeth. He earned a B.A. in 1927 and an M.A. in 1929
from Rhodes University College (now Rhodes University). He was a lecturer in philosophy at Fort Hare University College (now the University of Fort Hare) in
1930. From 1931 to 1933 he attended Magdalen College at the University of Oxford, obtaining a B.Litt. with
a thesis on Samuel Alexander and Alfred North Whitehead. From 1937 to 1941 he was an education officer in
Basutoland and Zanzibar for the British Colonial Service, and from 1941 to 1946 he served in the South African and then the British army in Egypt, Beirut,
Lebanon; and Haifa, Palestine (today Israel). After his
discharge he became a member of the executive council
of the South African Institute of Race Relations and
was one of the founders of the anti-apartheid South
African Liberal Party. He married Sylvia Mundahl on
11 July 1946; they had four children: Jonathan, Nigel,
Hermione, and Martin.

In 1946 Harris became a lecturer in the philosophy
department of the University of the Witwatersrand. He
received the D.Litt. from that institution in 1950 for the
work that was published in 1954 as *Nature, Mind and
Modern Science.* In 1950 he published his first book, *The
Survival of Political Man: A Study in the Principles of International Order,* in which he argues that the introduction of
nuclear weapons threatens global catastrophe in the
event of a third world war and that the only means of
securing the future of civilization is the formation of a
world government, the feasibility of which he defends on
the basis of the theories of sovereignty found in the writ-

ings of Thomas Hobbes, John Locke, Jean-Jacques Rousseau, Spinoza, and Hegel and the theories of the supremacy of world law advanced by Georg Jellinek, Hugo Krabbe, and Hans Kelsen.

Harris was appointed senior lecturer at the University of the Witwatersrand in 1951. The following year he published his second work, *"White" Civilization: How It Is Threatened and How It Can Be Preserved in South Africa* (1952), in which he argues that the concept of a "civilization" founded on racism is incoherent and unacceptable.

Harris became a full professor at Witwatersrand in 1953. In 1954 he published *Nature, Mind and Modern Science,* in which he adopts the British philosopher R. G. Collingwood's thesis that the history of Western philosophy can be regarded as a sustained attempt to understand the relationship of mind to nature. Examining the formulations and attempted solutions of the problem from the ancient Greek pre-Socratics to the twentieth century, Harris contends that the seventeenth-century French rationalist René Descartes's separation of mind from nature was a product of Renaissance thought. He treats the positions of the seventeenth- and eighteenth-century British empiricists Locke, George Berkeley, and David Hume and the eighteenth-century German "critical" philosopher Immanuel Kant on this problem as belonging to the Renaissance tradition, insofar as the Cartesian conception of mind can still be traced in their work, and he regards treatments of the mind/nature problem in the twentieth-century variants of empiricism—logical positivism and linguistic analysis—as a continuation of the Renaissance conception. Harris stipulates five conditions that any adequate solution of the problem would have to satisfy: "(i) that mind is immanent in all things; (ii) that reality is a whole, self-sufficient and self-maintaining, and that coherence is the test of truth of any theory about it; (iii) that the subject and object of knowledge are ultimately one—the same thing viewed from opposite (and mutually complementary) standpoints; (iv) that events and phenomena can adequately be explained only teleologically; and (v) that the ultimate principle of interpretation is, in consequence, the principle of value." According to Harris, a philosophical conception answering to all of these requirements and freed of the defects of the Renaissance view did, in fact, emerge in the history of modern philosophy: elements of the solution can be found in the thought of Spinoza and the seventeenth- and early-eighteenth-century German rationalist Gottfried Wilhelm Leibniz, but only in Hegel does the solution emerge more or less fully developed. Harris expounds Hegel's solution to the problem, comparing and contrasting it with various more recent philosophies, finding none that deal with it as comprehensively or as successfully. The solution is a conception of mind developing itself out of physical

nature through successive phases of a hierarchy of forms, first natural and subsequently "spiritual"–psychological, social, and rational–ones. Hegel, he says, is the first philosopher to have worked out this conception in detail, but Harris attempts to reestablish the cogency of the position through his sequential analysis of the failures of all the significant alternatives in the history of philosophy–above all, of the Renaissance conception of the separation of mind from nature.

By the mid 1950s Harris had concluded that the liberal cause was doomed to failure in South Africa, and in the atmosphere of increasing violence he found it impossible to continue the program of political activity he had pursued during the previous decade. In 1956 he accepted a professorship at Connecticut College; but even after moving to the United States, he continued to work with international organizations dedicated to ending apartheid.

In 1957 Harris delivered the Terry Lectures at Yale University; they were published the following year as *Revelation through Reason: Reason in the Light of Science and Philosophy.* In the lectures Harris attacks the notion that conflict between science and religion is inevitable, arguing that neither outlook is wholly coherent when considered in isolation from the other. All scientific pursuits, he says, presuppose faith in the rational intelligibility of natural phenomena; and religion, which claims ultimate truth, cannot ignore or deny the validity of scientific discoveries.

In 1962 Harris became Roy Roberts Distinguished Professor of Philosophy at the University of Kansas. In his next book, *The Foundations of Metaphysics in Science* (1965), he argues that the major theoretical developments in twentieth-century physics, biology, and psychology support the dialectical and holistic viewpoint he defended in *Nature, Mind and Modern Science* rather than the reductionist logical atomism that was often presented as the only valid philosophical position for modern science. He claims, further, that the atomistic empiricist position is internally incoherent. The work concludes with a systematic presentation of his own Hegelian-inspired cosmology.

In 1966 Harris moved to Northwestern University. With the Cold War at its height, he wrote *Annihilation and Utopia: The Principles of International Politics* (1966). He argues that the 1962 Cuban Missile Crisis shows that the threat of nuclear annihilation has become even more likely and reiterates the message of *The Survival of Political Man* that only a world government can avert such a catastrophe. Referring to Western and Soviet sources on international law, he also argues that the ideological conflict that underlies the Cold War is not irreconcilable.

In *Hypothesis and Perception: The Roots of Scientific Method* (1970) Harris defends his epistemology and philosophy of science against empiricist accounts. He concludes that

THE PROBLEM OF EVIL

I   The Problem for Theology.

'The treatment of evil by theology', writes Brand Blanshard, 'seems to me an intellectual disgrace'.[1] My aim in this lecture

[1] Reason and Belief (Yale University Press, 1970) p.546.

is to ensure, so far as I am able, that the same indictment shall not be brought against philosophy. In so doing, I hope incidentally to show cause why in the case of at least two outstanding theologians, it may not justly be brought against all theology, which at least has been aware of the problem virtually from its beginnings.

Since biblical times the experience of evil has presented theists and theologians with what seemed an insuperable obstacle to belief in the existence of a benevolent and all-powerful God. Unmerited misfortune and suffering, catastrophic disasters, and human malevolence have always seemed irreconcilable with an omnipotent creator of supreme justice and mercy. With this mystery Job and his admonitors wrestled; and their reasonings and protestations were finally silenced only by a declaration of the inscrutability of the divine wisdom. But in that pronouncement the question is begged, for to accede to divine wisdom we must understand the principle of its justice, and what remains inscrutable to us we recognize neither as wise nor sensible. There must be some securer foundation for faith in the justice of the inscrutable than its unintelligibility.

In his progress to conversion St. Augustine encountered and overcame this hurdle; but his solution of the difficulty has proved less convincing to many than his statement of the problem.

First pages of the manuscript and typescript for Harris's Aquinas Lecture at Marquette University in 1977 (Collection of Errol E. Harris)

THE PROBLEM OF EVIL

I. The Problem for Theology.

"The treatment of evil by theology," writes Brand Blanshard, "seems to me an intellectual disgrace."[1] My aim in this lecture is to ensure, so far

[1] Reason and Belief, (Yale University Press, 1975), p. 546.

as I am able, that the same indictment shall not be brought against philosophy. In so doing, I hope incidentally to show cause why in the case of at least two outstanding theologians, it may not justly be brought against all theology, which at least has been aware of the problem virtually from its earliest beginnings.

Since biblical times the experience of evil has presented theists and theologians with what seems an insuperable obstacle to belief in the existence of a benevolent and all-powerful God. Unmerited misfortune and suffering, catastrophic disasters, and human malevolence have always seemed irreconcilable with an omnipotent creator of supreme justice and mercy. With this mystery Job and his admonitors wrestled; and their reasonings and protestations were finally silenced only by a declaration of the inscrutability of divine wisdom. But in that pronouncement the question is begged, for to accede to divine wisdom we must understand the principle of its justice, and what remains inscrutable to us we recognize neither as wise nor sensible. There must be some securer foundation for faith in the justice of the inscrutable than its unintelligibility.

Cover for Harris's 1987 book, in which he critiques the atomistic metaphysical presuppositions of modern logic and argues for a more holistic approach (Thomas Cooper Library, University of South Carolina)

even if it could solve the notorious problem of induction—how one can argue that future instances will resemble those observed in the past without assuming, in a circular fashion, that nature is uniform—empiricism cannot supply an account of the rationality of the procedures of scientific reasoning. He shows that the history of scientific reasoning and theory construction is better explained by a dialectical logic of question and answer derived from Collingwood and, ultimately, from Hegel. He argues that an adequate conception of scientific reasoning cannot be represented in terms of the standard predicate calculus of formal logic because, contrary to the usual claims made for it, that logic is not metaphysically neutral: it presupposes an atomism of contingently related particulars that seemed appropriate to the worldview of Newtonian mechanics but that is inappropriate for the relativist and quantum physics of the twentieth century.

Harris was named John Evans Professor of Moral and Intellectual Philosophy in 1973. That year he pub-

lished *Salvation from Despair: A Reappraisal of Spinoza's Philosophy,* which led to many invitations to give papers at international conferences on Spinoza. Also in 1973 he delivered the Heinz Werner Lectures at Clark University in Worcester, Massachusetts; they were published the following year as *Perceptual Assurance and the Reality of the World.* In this work he examines one of the most fundamental problems of epistemology: the criterion of truth in perception. Scientific knowledge is ultimately based on perception; at the same time, science claims to be able to provide a causal account of perception. But, Harris argues, "If perception is to be explained as a causal relation between the physical world and human sensibility, some account must be forthcoming, which is free from circularity, of the self-revelatory character of the causal process." Naturalistic accounts fail in this task because they treat perception as an effect of certain physicochemical and neurophysiological processes, but such an end product could not simultaneously constitute an awareness of its own causes. Harris considers the phenomenology of Edmund Husserl and Maurice Merleau-Ponty, particularly the latter's notion of the "lived body," more fruitful directions of inquiry, and incorporates elements of their approach in his own theory of "perceptual assurance," according to which coherence is the criterion of truth.

Harris retired from Northwestern University in 1976. He was a visiting distinguished professor at Marquette University in 1976–1977 and delivered the Aquinas Lecture there in 1977; it was published that same year as *The Problem of Evil.* Harris argues that evil is inseparable from finitude. Finitude, in turn, is partiality, or inadequacy to the whole; it is a factor or moment, a lower phase on the dialectical scale of forms that is in the process of being overcome in the realization of the whole. Evil is, then, inevitable in the world, since a world without finitude would be no world at all. At the same time, the infinite whole, the perfection of the finite world, is immanent in each of its finite moments and destined to transcend each. Thus, finitude, or evil, is not the ultimate reality, but it cannot be eliminated from any actual creation. Harris's treatment of the problem of evil is developed in part from his discussion of Spinoza in *Salvation from Despair* and in part from his interpretation of Hegel's logic.

Also in 1977 Harris's 1975 Matchette Lectures at Tulane University were published as *Atheism and Theism.* His strategy is to take the phenomenon of atheism as a stimulus to submit the claims of religious faith to skeptical questioning and thereby transform uncritical faith into rationally grounded belief. He counters the atheistic arguments of Karl Marx, Friedrich Nietzsche, and Sigmund Freud with arguments from Spinoza, Hegel, and Pierre Teilhard de Chardin that show the rationality of theism. According to Harris, God is immanent in the hierarchy of finite forms, the unfolding of which constitutes successive stages in the perfecting of the whole: he is "an infinite, omniscient, self-conscious, spiritual being, actualizing the potencies of physical and biological nature, supra-personal in character and including in his single unity a multiplicity of spirits—a kingdom of ends, an integral union of all minds in one transcendent individuality."

Harris's wife died on 22 June 1983. His next book, *An Interpretation of the Logic of Hegel,* appeared that year. It was followed four years later by a more general exploration of logic, *Formal, Transcendental, and Dialectical Thinking: Logic and Reality* (1987). As he had in *Hypothesis and Perception,* Harris rejects the claim of metaphysical neutrality usually advanced on behalf of formal logic and describes its atomistic presuppositions. He then examines the transcendental logic of Kant, Johann Gottlieb Fichte, and Husserl, focusing on their criticisms of formal logic. Finally, drawing on Hegel and Collingwood, he shows how the limitations of transcendental logic can be resolved dialectically. The book itself exhibits a dialectical structure in that the argument for each successive form of logic emerges from the critique of its predecessor.

In *The Reality of Time* (1988) Harris shows that the standard "refutations" of the late-nineteenth- and early-twentieth-century British idealist philosopher J. M. E. McTaggart's arguments for the unreality of time are failures, thereby revealing the power of McTaggart's position. He develops his own response to McTaggart, arguing that the reality of time is presupposed by physics, biology, psychology, and history and that experience itself is unintelligible without this presupposition. Harris goes on to demonstrate that the reality of time and change in the world of experience implies the reality of a nontemporal and eternal whole. The elegance and lucidity of Harris's argument in *The Reality of Time* have led some professors to use the work as an introduction to metaphysics for their students.

The evolutionary cosmology sketched at the conclusion of *The Reality of Time* is developed more fully in *Cosmos and Anthropos: A Philosophical Interpretation of the Anthropic Cosmological Principle* (1991) and its companion volume, *Cosmos and Theos: Ethical and Theological Implications of the Anthropic Cosmological Principle* (1992). In the first book Harris examines various forms of the "anthropic cosmological principle" espoused by contemporary physicists such as R. H. Dicke, Brandon Carter, John Barrow, and Frank Tipler: essentially, the principle holds that the existence of just the right combination of conditions in the universe needed for the existence of human beings is not a surprising coincidence, nor does it require a divine designer, since if those conditions did not exist, people would not exist to wonder about them. Harris argues that while several of the formulations most frequently encountered are significantly flawed, when properly

Cover for Harris's 1988 book, in which he argues that the reality of time is presupposed by science and ordinary experience (Thomas Cooper Library, University of South Carolina)

stated the principle encapsulates an important cosmological implication of contemporary science: the unity or wholeness of physical nature. Exploring the characteristics of that wholeness, Harris points to its necessarily dialectical and teleological form and shows how such a cosmology inevitably culminates in the emergence from nature of mind and, ultimately, of science itself as a reflective awareness of nature. He points to some strong resemblances between his cosmology and Teilhard de Chardin's "Omega" theory, including their similar theological implications.

The theological and ethical implications of Harris's scheme are pursued in detail in *Cosmos and Theos.* The alleged conflict between religion and science has no rational basis: a conception of God as an infinite suprapersonal self-consciousness is inherent in the cosmological process presented in the previous volume, which is itself grounded in the results of contemporary science. Harris concludes by discussing the traditional proofs of the

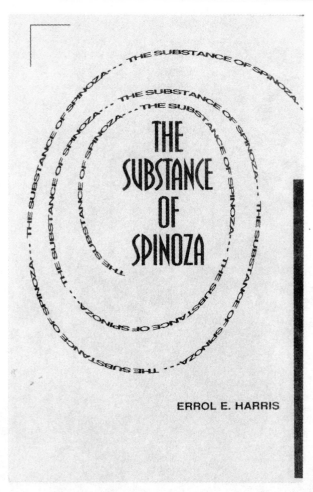

*Cover for Harris's 1995 collection of his essays on the
seventeenth-century Dutch rationalist philosopher
Baruch Spinoza (Thomas Cooper Library,
University of South Carolina)*

existence of God and the problem of evil in the light of his theology.

In 1992 Harris also published *Spinoza's Philosophy: An Outline*. Written some fifteen years previously, the work is a briefer introduction to Spinoza than his earlier *Salvation from Despair*. The following year he published a collection of his articles on Hegel, *The Spirit of Hegel*. The book provides an overview of the interpretation of Hegel's philosophy that informs most of Harris's work and defends the relevance of Hegel for contemporary philosophical debate.

In *One World or None: Prescription for Survival* (1993) Harris points out that the dangers inherent in the existence of sovereign nation-states have not diminished and that the recently recognized threat of global ecological crisis has increased the urgency of a transformation of the international political order. He defends the feasibility and desirability of the "Federation of Earth" program put forward by the World Constitution and Parliament Association.

In 1995 Harris put together a collection of his previously published and new articles titled *The Substance of Spinoza*. His interpretation of the philosopher is distinctive in emphasizing that Spinoza's method is as much dialectical as geometric and that Hegel and Spinoza are more similar than is usually perceived, especially on the doctrine of negation. In *Apocalypse and Paradigm: Science and Everyday Thinking* (2000) he argues that the contemporary world crisis cannot be remedied as long as the Newtonian scientific paradigm persists in disciplines other than physics. *The Restitution of Metaphysics* (2000) is a comprehensive statement of his claim that the modern rejection of metaphysics is itself based on a metaphysics—empiricism—that has been rendered obsolete by twentieth-century physics and biology.

Errol E. Harris has produced a wide-ranging body of philosophical work that is marked by a consistent approach and founded on a common core of philosophical insight. He has persistently advanced the claims of reason, both theoretical and practical, in an age in which the "death of reason" is widely proclaimed. His work is grounded in a conviction of the continuity and vitality of the Western philosophical tradition, of the possibility of objective scientific knowledge of nature, of the reality of the world described therein, of the continuity of mind with nature, and of the compatibility of a rational religious faith with science and philosophy. Though he is not alone in advocating any single one of these viewpoints, the breadth of his vision and the vigor and learning with which he presents and defends it have had few equals.

Bibliographies:

Errol E. Harris, "Complete Bibliography to July 1984," *Teilhard Review and Journal of Creative Evolution,* 19 (Autumn 1984): 83–86;

Philip T. Grier, "Bibliography of Works by Errol E. Harris," in *Dialectic and Contemporary Science: Essays in Honor of Errol E. Harris,* edited by Grier (Lanham, Md.: University Press of America, 1989), pp. 219–227.

References:

D. E. Christiansen, "Der universelle Systemgedanke bei Errol Harris," *Wiener Jahrbuch für Philosophie,* 8 (1975): 195–211;

Philip T. Grier, ed., *Dialectic and Contemporary Science: Essays in Honor of Errol E. Harris* (Lanham, Md.: University Press of America, 1989);

Giacomo Rinaldi, *A History and Interpretation of the Logic of Hegel* (Lewiston, N.Y.: Edwin Mellen Press, 1992), pp. 478–483;

Rinaldi, *Saggio sulla metafisica di Harris* (Bologna: Li Causi, 1984).

Carl G. Hempel

(8 January 1905 – 9 November 1997)

James H. Fetzer
University of Minnesota, Duluth

BOOKS: *Beiträge zur logischen Analyse des Wahrscheinlich-keitsbegriffs* (Jena: Universitäts-Buchdruckerei G. Neuenhahn, 1934);

Der Typusbegriff im Lichte der Neuen Logik: Wissenschaftstheo-retische Untersuchungen zur konstitutions forschung und Psychologie, by Hempel and Paul Oppenheim (Leiden: Sijthoff, 1936);

Fundamentals of Concept Formation in Empirical Science, International Encyclopedia of Unified Science, volume 2, no. 7 (Chicago: University of Chicago Press, 1952); translated into German and enlarged by Hempel as *Grundzüge der Begriffsbildung in der empirischen Wissenschaft* (Düsseldorf: Bertelsmann Universitätsverlag, 1974)–includes "Theoretische Begriffe und Theoriewandel: Ein Nachwort," pp. 72–89, 97–98;

Aspects of Scientific Explanation and Other Essays in the Philosophy of Science (New York: Free Press, 1965; London: Collier-Macmillan, 1965);

Philosophy of Natural Science (Englewood Cliffs, N.J.: Prentice-Hall, 1966);

The Isenberg Memorial Lecture Series, 1965–1966, by Hempel and others (East Lansing: Michigan State University Press, 1969);

Methodology of Science: Descriptive and Prescriptive Facets, Pamphlet no. IAS 814-84 (Tel Aviv: Mortimer and Raymond Sackler Institute of Advanced Studies, Tel Aviv University, 1984);

Selected Philosophical Essays, edited by Richard Jeffrey (Cambridge: Cambridge University Press, 2000);

The Philosophy of Carl G. Hempel: Studies in Science, Explanation, and Rationality, edited by James H. Fetzer (Oxford & New York: Oxford University Press, 2001).

OTHER: "L'importance en logique de la notion de type," by Hempel and Paul Oppenheim, in *Actes du Congrés International de Philosophie Scientifique, Paris, 1935,* volume 2 (Paris: Hermann, 1936), pp. 41–49;

Carl G. Hempel

"The Theoretician's Dilemma," in *Concepts, Theories, and the Mind-body Problem,* edited by Herbert Feigl, Michael Scriven, and Grover Maxwell, Minnesota Studies in the Philosophy of Science, volume 2 (Minneapolis: University of Minnesota Press, 1958), pp. 37–98;

"Deductive-Nomological vs. Statistical Explanation," in *Scientific Explanation, Space, and Time,* edited by Feigl and Maxwell, Minnesota Studies in the Philosophy of Science, volume 3 (Minneapolis: University of Minnesota Press, 1962), pp. 98–169;

"Explanation in Science and in History," in *Frontiers of Science and Philosophy*, edited by Robert Garland Colodny (Pittsburgh: University of Pittsburgh Press, 1962), pp. 9–33;

"Implications of Carnap's Work for the Philosophy of Science," in *The Philosophy of Rudolf Carnap*, edited by Paul Arthur Schilpp, The Library of Living Philosophers, volume 11 (La Salle, Ill.: Open Court, 1963; London: Cambridge University Press, 1963), pp. 685–709;

"Recent Problems of Induction," in *Mind and Cosmos*, edited by Colodny (Pittsburgh: University of Pittsburgh Press, 1966), pp. 112–134;

"Reduction: Ontological and Linguistic Facets," in *Philosophy, Science, and Method: Essays in Honor of Ernest Nagel*, edited by Sidney Morgenbesser, Patrick Suppes, and Morton White (New York: St. Martin's Press, 1969), pp. 179–199;

"On the Structure of Scientific Theories," in *The Isenberg Memorial Lecture Series 1965–1966*, edited by Ronald Suter (East Lansing: Michigan State University Press, 1969), pp. 11–38;

"On the 'Standard Conception' of Scientific Theories," in *Analyses of Theories and Methods of Physics and Psychology*, edited by Michael Radner and Stephen Winokur, Minnesota Studies in the Philosophy of Science, volume 4 (Minneapolis: University of Minnesota Press, 1970), pp. 142–163;

"Homage to Rudolf Carnap," in *PSA 1970: In Memory of Rudolf Carnap*, edited by Roger C. Buck and Robert S. Cohen (Dordrecht, Netherlands: Reidel, 1971), pp. xvii–xix;

"The Meaning of Theoretical Terms: A Critique of the Standard Empiricist Construal," in *Logic, Methodology, and Philosophy of Science: Proceedings of the Fourth International Congress for Logic, Methodology, and Philosophy of Science, Bucharest, Romania, 1971*, edited by Suppes, Studies in Logic and the Foundations of Mathematics, volume 74 (Amsterdam: North-Holland / New York: American Elsevier, 1973), pp. 367–378;

"Formulation and Formalization of Scientific Theories: A Summary-Abstract," in *The Structure of Scientific Theories*, edited by Frederick Suppe (Urbana: University of Illinois Press, 1974), pp. 244–254;

"Die Wissenschaftstheorie des analytischen Empirismus im Lichte zeitgenössischer Kritik," in *Kongressberichte des XI. Deutschen Kongresses für Philosophie, 1975* (Hamburg: Meiner, 1977), pp. 20–34;

"Selección de una teoría en la ciencia: perspectivas analíticas vs. pragmáticas," in *La filosofía y las revoluciones científicas: Segundo Coloquio Nacional de Filosofía, Monterrey, Nuevo Leon, México* (Mexico City: Grijalbo, 1979), pp. 115–135;

"Scientific Rationality: Analytic vs. Pragmatic Perspectives" and discussion remarks, in *Rationality Today/La Rationalité Aujourd'hui*, edited by Theodore F. Geraets (Ottawa: University of Ottawa Press, 1979), pp. 46–58, 59–66;

"Der Wiener Kreis–eine persoenliche Perspektive," in *Wittgenstein, the Vienna Circle, and Critical Rationalism: Proceedings of the Third International Wittgenstein Symposium, August 1978*, edited by Hal Berghel, Adolf Hübner, and Eckehart Koehler (Vienna: Hölder-Pichler-Tempsky, 1979), pp. 21–26;

Methodology, Epistemology, and Philosophy of Science: Essays in Honour of Wolfgang Stegmüller on the Occasion of His 60th Birthday, June 3rd, 1983, edited by Hempel, Hilary Putnam, and Wilhelm K. Essler (Dordrecht, Netherlands & Boston: Reidel, 1983);

"Valuation and Objectivity in Science," in *Physics, Philosophy, and Psychoanalysis: Essays in Honor of Adolf Grünbaum*, edited by Robert S. Cohen and Larry Laudan (Dordrecht, Netherlands & Boston: Reidel, 1983), pp. 73–100;

"Wissenschaft, Induktion und Wahrheit," in *Verleihung der Würde eines Ehrendoktors der Wirtschaftswissenschaft an Prof. Dr. Phil. Carl G. Hempel (University of Pittsburgh) am 10. Dezember 1984* (Berlin: Fachbereich Wirtschaftswissenschaft der Freien Universität Berlin, 1985);

"Provisoes: A Problem Concerning the Inferential Function of Scientific Theories," in *The Limitations of Deductivism*, edited by Adolf Grünbaum and Wesley C. Salmon (Berkeley: University of California Press, 1988), pp. 19–36;

"Limits of a Deductive Construal of the Function of Scientific Theories," in *Science in Reflection*, edited by Edna Ullmann-Margalit, Boston Studies in the Philosophy of Science, volume 110; The Israel Colloquium: Studies in History, Philosophy, and Sociology of Science, volume 3 (Dordrecht, Netherlands & Boston: Kluwer, 1988), pp. 1–15.

SELECTED PERIODICAL PUBLICATIONS–
UNCOLLECTED: "Über den Gehalt von Wahrscheinlichtkeitsaussagen," *Erkenntnis*, 5 (1935/1936): 228–260; translated by Christopher Erlenkamp, revised by Olaf Helmer, as "On the Content of Probability Statements," in Hempel's *Selected Philosophical Essays*, edited by Richard Jeffrey (Cambridge: Cambridge University Press, 2000), pp. 89–123;

"Vagueness and Logic," *Philosophy of Science,* 6 (1939): 163–180;

"A Purely Syntactical Definition of Confirmation," *Journal of Symbolic Logic,* 8 (1943): 122–143;

"Problems and Changes in the Empiricist Criterion of Meaning," *Revue Internationale de Philosophie,* no. 11 (1950): 41–63;

"A Note on Semantic Realism," *Philosophy of Science,* 17 (1950): 169–173;

"The Concept of Cognitive Significance: A Reconsideration," *Proceedings of the American Academy of Arts and Sciences,* 80, no. 1 (1951): 61–77;

"General System Theory and the Unity of Science," *Human Biology,* 23 (1951): 313–322;

"Reflections on Nelson Goodman's *The Structure of Appearance,*" *Philosophical Review,* 62 (1952): 108–116;

"Comments on Goodman's 'Ways of Worldmaking,'" *Synthèse,* 45 (1980): 193–199;

"Kuhn and Salmon on Rationality and Theory Choice," *Journal of Philosophy,* 80 (1983): 570–572;

"Thoughts on the Limitations of Discovery by Computer," in *Logic of Discovery and Diagnosis in Medicine,* edited by Kenneth F. Schaffner (Berkeley: University of California Press, 1985), pp. 115–122.

Hempel circa 1933

The primary proponent of the "covering law" theory of explanation and of the paradoxes of confirmation, Carl G. Hempel was among the most important philosophers of science of the twentieth century. With Rudolf Carnap and Hans Reichenbach he was a leader in the transformation of the rigid, somewhat simplistic, and doctrinaire philosophical movement known as logical positivism into its more subtle and nuanced successor, logical empiricism. His ideas on induction, confirmation, and scientific explanation exerted a profound influence on more than a generation of philosophers.

Carl Gustav Hempel (known since his youth as "Peter" to his friends) was born in Eden, near Berlin, on 8 January 1905 to Karl Friedrich and Charlotte Kessler Hempel. His father owned a fruit orchard. Hempel was educated at a village school until his father became a civil servant for the city of Berlin; the family then moved to a suburb of the city, where Hempel studied Latin, French, English, mathematics, and physics at the Realgymnasium. In 1923 he began the study of philosophy, mathematics, physics, chemistry, and psychology at the University of Göttingen, transferring to the University of Heidelberg in 1924 and to the University of Berlin in 1925. At Berlin he studied under Reichenbach. Influenced by the works of the mathematicians David Hilbert and Paul Bernays, he became interested in symbolic logic and the foundations of

mathematics, and Reichenbach introduced him to the application of symbolic logic to science. Reading Carnap's *Der logische Aufbau der Welt* (1928; enlarged, 1961; translated as "The Logical Structure of the World," 1967) and *Scheinprobleme in der Philosophie* (1928; translated as "Pseudoproblems in Philosophy," 1967), he became convinced that the method detailed there held the key to the solution of all problems in philosophy. Carnap held that to be meaningful or cognitively significant, assertions had to be either logical or semantical truths, on the one hand, or either directly accessible to experience through observation or reducible to those that were directly accessible to experience, on the other hand. This approach was intended to qualify principles of logic and mathematics as logical truths and hypotheses and theories in science as empirical truths, while other assertions, such as those of metaphysics and theology, were neither. Questions about the existence of a soul, a supreme being, or an afterlife were taken to be "pseudo-questions," grammatically proper but cognitively meaningless. Hempel later demonstrated that this approach was too strict, because it excluded hypotheses and theories that were central to science and denied cognitive significance to theories about values, morality, and aesthetics.

In 1929 Hempel passed examinations in mathematics, physics, and philosophy that were required for prospective high-school teachers. Then, on Reichenbach's advice, he spent the fall semester of 1929 at the University of Vienna, where he studied with Carnap, Moritz Schlick, and Frederick Waismann and met Otto Neurath, Herbert Feigl, and Hans Hahn. All of these men were members of the logical positivist "Vienna Circle"; Hempel also encountered Ludwig Wittgenstein, who did not belong to the group but influenced the thinking of its members. One of the issues debated by the Vienna Circle was the possibility of formulating a language that would be able to describe the contents of experience and thereby function as the foundation of science. The controversy centered on whether the "protocol," or "basic," sentences of such a language—sentences that would express the results of observations and serve as the basis for confirming or disconfirming other scientific statements—should report the intersubjectively observable properties of objects or describe the subjective perceptions of individuals. Hempel allied himself with the former group.

Returning to Berlin, Hempel took on substitute-teaching jobs while undergoing two years of pedagogical training. He received his Ph.D. summa cum laude from the University of Berlin in 1934 with a dissertation on the logical form and empirical testability of probability hypotheses about limiting frequencies. He had begun the dissertation under Reichenbach, but the latter had been dismissed after Adolf Hitler became chancellor of Germany in 1933; he completed it with the philosopher Nicolai Hartmann and the Gestalt psychologist Wolfgang Koehler as his advisers. Also in 1934 Hempel married Eva Ahrends.

After receiving his Ph.D., Hempel wanted to leave Germany because of the rise of Nazism. He accepted an invitation from Paul Oppenheim, a German chemist with an interest in philosophy to whom he had been introduced by Reichenbach around 1930, to move to Brussels. The two men worked together there from 1934 to 1937. At Carnap's invitation Hempel spent the academic year 1937–1938 at the University of Chicago, assisting with Carnap's seminar and giving lectures on induction and probability. In 1938 he went back to Brussels, where he and Oppenheim completed their work on the logic of confirmation. The results appeared in 1945 as "A Definition of 'Degree of Confirmation'"; the article is collected in his *Selected Philosophical Essays* (2000), edited by Richard Jeffrey.

Returning to the United States, Hempel taught summer and evening courses at the City College of New York in 1939–1940 and eventually became a naturalized citizen. In 1940 he was hired as an instructor at Queen's College in New York City; by the time he left in 1948 he had risen to the rank of assistant professor. Some of his most important early papers were published during this period. In "The Function of General Laws in History" (1942), which is collected in his *Aspects of Scientific Explanation and Other Essays in the Philosophy of Science* (1965), he says that laws establish causal connections between events, and that although these laws may be implicit, in their absence no historical explanations—as opposed to mere chronological summaries—are possible. The paper generated an enormous literature, not all of which reflected understanding of the points Hempel had made. In "Geometry and Empirical Science" (1945), which is collected in *The Philosophy of Carl G. Hempel: Studies in Science, Explanation, and Rationality* (2001), edited by James H. Fetzer, Hempel distinguishes between pure and applied mathematics and explains that a formal calculus such as geometry, which is certain but vacuous, must be combined with an empirical interpretation to produce a scientific theory, which is informative but fallible. In "On the Nature of Mathematical Truth" (1945; collected in *The Philosophy of Carl G. Hempel*) Hempel defines *logicism* as consisting of the theses that mathematical concepts can be reduced to logical ones, that mathematical reasoning can be reduced to logical reasoning, and that logical reasoning is tautological—that is, necessarily true but devoid of content—and defends it as an alternative to intuitionism. According to intuitionism, mathematical claims are significant only when they are capable of proof on the basis of ordinary thought and immediate experience. Hempel's reservations about intuitionism included the inapplicability to it of the logical law of excluded middle, which maintains that every assertion or its negation must be true: an example would be the hypothesis "Either every number greater than two can be expressed as the sum of two primes or not"; since inspecting every number greater than two involves an infinite number of mental operations, which could never be finished, an intuitionist would suspend judgment until one alternative or the other could be subjected to proof. Most important, Hempel wanted to establish the foundations of mathematics in logic and set theory rather than in psychology, thereby advancing the conception of mathematical objectivity. In "Hempel's Logicist Philosophy of Mathematics: Background and Sequel" in *Science, Explanation, and Rationality: Aspects of the Philosophy of Carl G. Hempel* (2000), edited by Fetzer, Jaakko Hintikka argues that although "the logicist approach to the foundations of mathematics has fallen into disrepute since the days of Hempel's classic exposition," his "philosophy of mathematics is . . . on the right track much more than most of its later critics have acknowledged."

Hempel's best-known work from this period is "Studies in the Logic of Confirmation" (1945; collected in *Aspects of Scientific Explanation and Other Essays in the Phi-*

Extr 10

5.   Extremal Axioms.

$R(M)$

If '$F(M)$' is structural sent.

there we understand by the *maximal* axiom belonging to 'F':

" There is no extension N of M, such that $F(N)$ "

minimal axiom:

There is no N such that $F(N)$ and M are extension of N.

Model Extension
Structural Extension

$\left\{ \begin{array}{l} < \text{in} \{1,2,3,\ldots\} \\ \text{a model is not a structural} \\ \text{Ext of } < \text{in} \{2,4,6,\ldots\} \end{array} \right.$

$Ext_m (N, M) \equiv \{M \supset N\} \cdot M \neq N$

$Ext_{st} (N, M) \equiv \{M \supset N\} \cdot \sim Isom (M, N)$

Hence, there are 4 extremal axioms belonging to '$F(M)$':
Structure-ext contains Model-Ext; see Figure p176
The second cond'l for M implies the first, and not vice versa.

Page from Hempel's notes taken during a seminar given by Rudolf Carnap at the University of Chicago in 1937 (published with special permission, Carl Hempel Papers [unprocessed], Archives of Scientific Philosophy in the 20th Century, University of Pittsburgh Library System; all rights reserved)

*Rudolf Carnap at around the time Hempel served as his
assistant at the University of Chicago*

losophy of Science). Here he points out that a generalization such as "All ravens are black" can be translated into the logically equivalent statement "All nonblack things are nonravens." But then, since logically equivalent sentences are confirmed by the same observations, the absurd result arises that observations of white shoes, which are not ravens, must confirm the hypothesis that "All ravens are black." This puzzle, which has come to be known as "the paradox of confirmation," or "the Raven Paradox," is still being discussed by philosophers.

Hempel's wife died in 1944, soon after the birth of their only child, Peter Andrew. Two years later Hempel married Diane Perlow. In 1948 he became an associate professor at Yale University. His daughter, Miranda Toby Anne, was born in 1949.

Hempel's publications during his years at Yale were relatively sparse but highly influential. In "Problems and Changes in the Empiricist Criterion of Meaning" (1950) and "The Concept of Cognitive Significance: A Reconsideration" (1951) he declared that logical positivism was theoretically indefensible, because on its principles sentences that express the most basic scientific

claims—general laws—have no cognitive significance. He pointed out that the negation of a significant sentence must also be significant, but that the existential generalization "Some storks are red-legged" (where *some* means "at least one") would be verifiable on the basis of a finite number of observations, but its negation, "Not even one stork is red-legged," whose truth would span the universe past, present, and future, would not be; that, similarly, the universal generalization "All ravens are black" could not be verified but its negation, "Some ravens are nonblack," could be; and that some hypotheses, such as "Every metal has a melting point," could neither be verified, because "every metal" means every past, present, or future instance, nor falsified, because even if an instance of a metal had not melted at some temperature, it would be necessary to test every higher temperature before concluding that the statement was false. The approach Hempel recommends, which has become known as "logical empiricism," continues to search for methods to insure the cognitive significance of scientific hypotheses and theories but understands the issues to be far more subtle and complex than logical positivism had recognized. Hempel proposes that the cognitive significance of a theory is "a matter of degree" based on multiple criteria, including the clarity and precision of the language in which it is formulated, its explanatory and predictive power, its degree of confirmation by the empirical evidence, and its simplicity, economy, and elegance.

In *Fundamentals of Concept Formation in Empirical Science* (1952) Hempel elaborates on the criticisms of the analytic/synthetic distinction made by Carnap in his two-part article "Testability and Meaning" (1936, 1937) and by W. V. Quine in "Two Dogmas of Empiricism" (1951). He notes, for example, that so-called dispositional predicates, which attribute nonobservable properties to observable entities, encounter problems of definability when conditional statements of the form "If ___ then . . ." are understood, according to the ordinary rules of symbolic logic, as equivalent in meaning to "either not-___ or . . ." If having an IQ of 150 is defined in terms of taking an IQ test and scoring 150, then that IQ—and every other—would be applicable to anything that never took the test, including brown cows and red roses, since it would satisfy the definition of either not taking the test or scoring 150. To circumvent this problem, Hempel follows Carnap in using "reduction sentences," which restrict the range of applicability of such attributions to only those things that satisfy the test condition. "If something takes an IQ test, then it has an IQ of 150 if and only if it scores 150" does not apply to things that do not take the test, even if they happen to have IQs of 150. Moreover, there are presumably other manifestations of IQ that could be used as components of other reduction sentences, such as "If

N2 II

II Induction, Valuation, and Rationality in Scientific Inquiry

1. The problem of induction.

In the course of its long history, scientific inquiry has vastly broadened man's knowledge and deepened his understanding of the world he lives in; and the striking successes in the far-reaching applications of scientific findings bear eloquent testimony to the basic soundness of scientific modes of research.

In view of these achievements, scientific inquiry has come to be widely acknowledged as the exemplar of rationality in the search for dependable knowledge.

But there is no unanimity among scientists, methodologists, and historians of science when it comes to the question whether scientific inquiry can be said to be governed by a set of clearly stateable rules or standards of procedure, which characterize "the scientific method", and adherence to which makes science that exemplar of rationality in the pursuit of reliable knowledge about the world.

First page of the draft for an article by Hempel (published with special permission, Carl Hempel Papers [unprocessed], Archives of Scientific Philosophy in the 20th Century, University of Pittsburgh Library System; all rights reserved)

Cover for Hempel's 1965 collection. In the title essay he develops his "covering law" notion of scientific explanation (Collection of James H. Fetzer).

is public, i.e., which can be secured by different observers and does not depend essentially upon the observer," is promoted by the use of physicalistic language, especially if such language includes measurable magnitudes.

In 1955, after a semester as a visiting professor, Hempel was appointed Stuart Professor of Philosophy at Princeton University. During his two decades at Princeton his ideas dominated the philosophy of science. His publications included "The Theoretician's Dilemma" (1958), "Inductive Inconsistencies" (1960; collected in *Aspects of Scientific Explanation and Other Essays in the Philosophy of Science*), "Deductive-Nomological vs. Statistical Explanation" (1962), "Explanation in Science and in History" (1962), "Rational Action" (1962; collected in *The Philosophy of Carl G. Hempel*), and the collection *Aspects of Scientific Explanation and Other Essays in the Philosophy of Science*, in which the articles "Problems and Changes in the Empiricist Criterion of Meaning" and "The Concept of Cognitive Significance: A Reconsideration" were merged as "Empiricist Criteria of Cognitive Significance: Problems and Changes" and the 165-page title essay appeared for the first time. According to Hempel, scientific explanations subsume the events they explain by "covering laws" that link the initial conditions attending the occurrence of the events with the events themselves. He elaborates the notion of the covering law for explanations involving both causal and noncausal laws and for universal and statistical laws. His deductive-nomological ("D-N") and inductive-statistical ("I-S") models of explanation have been widely discussed and highly influential, though later statistical-relevance ("S-R") and causal-relevance ("C-R") models have been able to solve problems that Hempel's models were not. Nevertheless, but for Hempel's contributions, it is virtually inconceivable that scientists would have come to accept the notion that science not only explains how events occur but why.

In 1966 he published *Philosophy of Natural Science*, which was translated into ten languages between 1967 and 1986 and became the most widely used introductory textbook in the subject in the world. He continued to produce important articles, including "Recent Problems of Induction" (1966), "Maximal Specificity and Lawlikeness in Probabilistic Explanation" (1968; collected in *The Philosophy of Carl G. Hempel*), and a series of studies of the structure of and relationships among scientific theories that includes "Reduction: Ontological and Linguistic Facets" (1969), "On the Structure of Scientific Theories" (1969), "On the 'Standard Conception' of Scientific Theories" (1970), and "The Meaning of Theoretical Terms: A Critique of the Standard Empiricist Construal" (1973).

Hempel remained Stuart Professor until his mandatory retirement in 1973 but continued to lecture at

someone were to make change, then if their IQ is 150, then they would make correct change." These manifestations, when combined with the original hypothesis, imply that "If you take an IQ test and score 150, then if you were to make change, you would make it correctly," which no longer has the character of a definition but appears to have the standing of an empirical law. Yet, Hempel observes, one would hardly want to maintain that analytic sentences can have synthetic consequences. He also says that the choice between a phenomenalistic language of sense-data, such as "looks-brighter-than" and "appears-to-be-blue," and a physicalistic language of objects and their properties, such as "is brighter than" and "is blue," is not capable of a definitive solution. He agrees, however, with the philosopher of science Karl Popper that the intersubjectivity of science, which requires "that all statements of empirical science be capable of test by reference to evidence that

Hempel with his wife, Diane Perlow Hempel, in his office at the University of Pittsburgh in 1982

Princeton until 1975. In 1977 he was appointed University Professor at the University of Pittsburgh. He continued to publish significant articles, including "Scientific Rationality: Analytic vs. Pragmatic Perspectives" (1979), "Turns in the Evolution of the Problem of Induction" (1981; collected in *The Philosophy of Carl G. Hempel*), and "Valuation and Objectivity in Science" (1983).

Hempel retired from the University of Pittsburgh in 1985 and returned to live in Princeton, New Jersey. In "Wissenschaft, Induktion und Wahrheit" (Science, Induction and Truth, 1985) he explains why observation cannot, strictly speaking, verify or falsify hypotheses or theories but can confirm or disconfirm them, provided that the observations are taken in conjunction with "a huge set of other premises." Verification and falsification involve deducing the truth or falsity of hypotheses from a finite set of observation sentences, which Hempel had shown could not be done for significant classes of hypotheses and theories, including existential generalizations, which are verifiable but not falsifiable, and universal generalizations, which are falsifiable but not verifiable. The weaker requirements of confirmability and disconfirmability substitute conditions of partial verification and partial falsification, mak-

ing scientific hypotheses and theories inductive rather than deductive consequences of available data and, therefore, empirically testable, amenable to comparative evaluations with respect to their probability, and subject to change with the acquisition of more evidence. He reviews several criteria for evaluating scientific hypotheses and theories and notes that the difficulty of formalizing them does not make the choice of theories subjective. He also explains why, although science tries to discover true hypotheses and theories, it is limited to the establishment of comprehensive, systematic, and elegant "pictures of the world," the truth of which it cannot guarantee. The fallibility of scientific knowledge has multiple explanations, including the possibility of misdescriptions of experience, errors of measurement, mistaken assumptions about the conditions under which experiments are conducted, and the circumstances that will actually obtain when predicted events occur. One can never guarantee that all of the properties whose presence or absence makes a difference to the truth of an explanation or prediction have been taken into account. The reliability of observation itself must be established by empirical means, he says. One's senses can be enhanced by various forms of technology—eyesight by the use of eyeglasses, magnifying

Hempel in the 1990s (photograph by Julius Cohen)

glasses, microscopes, and telescopes and hearing by the use of hearing aids, for example. Reliable perceptions will withstand further scrutiny with the accumulation of additional evidence, which should yield compatible results—unless the original observations were mistaken, as in the case of seeing a form in the distance and recognizing it as one's friend, only to discover as he draws closer that it is someone else.

Some of the articles Hempel published after returning to Princeton constitute major revisions of his previous positions. In "Provisoes: A Problem Concerning the Inferential Function of Scientific Theories" (1988) and "Limits of a Deductive Construal of the Function of Scientific Theories" (1988) Hempel reconsiders deductive predictions made on the basis of a theory when the conditions that affect the phenomena include properties whose presence or absence might not be explicitly encompassed by the theory—for example, the motion of metal objects whose behavior may be affected by thermodynamic, electromagnetic, and gravitational factors. If the application of a theory presupposes variables that are not logically required by the theory, he says, then the falsification of theories is more complex than has been supposed, the goal of eliminating theoretical terms from scientific language is illusory,

the "instrumentalist" conception that regards theories as mere calculating devices is implausible, and the notion of the empirical content of a theory is far more problematic than has typically been thought.

In "On the Cognitive Status and the Rationale of Scientific Methodology" (1988; collected in *Selected Philosophical Essays*) Hempel asks whether the philosophy of science should be interpreted as a descriptive study of actual research or as a quasi-normative discipline directed at formulating the standards of rational scientific inquiry. In the latter case, he says, even if the standards are regarded as conventions, they are not arbitrary but require justification; and the justifications will include empirical claims about actual scientific practice. After discussing the views of Carnap, Popper, and Thomas S. Kuhn, he concludes that the first interpretation is not purely descriptive and the second is not purely normative. Both interpretations lead to a conception of science according to which the bearing of evidence on hypotheses remains open to critical appraisal on the basis of normative standards.

Carl G. Hempel died on 9 November 1997. Beyond his vastly influential publications, Hempel's scholarly legacy includes many distinguished philosophers of science who studied with him, including Adolf

Grünbaum, Nicholas Rescher, Larry Laudan, Robert Nozick, Lawrence Sklar, Philip Kitcher, and Jaegwon Kim. Among the three most important philosophers of science of the twentieth century, Popper exerted the strongest influence on natural scientists and Kuhn, Hempel's colleague at Princeton, on social scientists and humanists; but Hempel had the strongest impact on the profession itself by virtually defining its problems and its methods. In one of his last essays on the philosophy of science, "The Spirit of Logical Empiricism: Carl G. Hempel's Role in Twentieth-Century Philosophy of Science" (1999; collected in *Science, Explanation, and Rationality: Aspects of the Philosophy of Carl G. Hempel*, 2000), Wesley C. Salmon notes that at the beginning of the twentieth century the dominant attitude among scientists and philosophers of science was that explanation lies beyond the scope of science, which can describe how things happen but cannot explain why they happen; by the end of the century the discovery of natural laws and the explanations they provide were considered the greatest contribution science can supply. According to Salmon, this profound change in outlook resulted mainly from two factors: the development of quantum mechanics, which made appeals to nonobservable entities scientifically respectable, and the development by Hempel of the covering-law model of scientific explanation. In advancing this conception of scientific explanation, Hempel made one of the most significant philosophical contributions of the twentieth century and one whose influence is destined to endure.

Interview:

Richard Nollan, "An Intellectual Autobiography: Carl G. Hempel," in *Science, Explanation, and Rationality: Aspects of the Philosophy of Carl G. Hempel*, edited by James H. Fetzer (Oxford & New York: Oxford University Press, 2000), pp. 3–35.

Bibliographies:

Carl G. Hempel, "Publications (1934–1969) by Carl G. Hempel," in *Essays in Honor of Carl G. Hempel: A Tribute on the Occasion of His Sixty-fifth Birthday*, edited by Nicholas Rescher (Dordrecht, Netherlands: Reidel, 1970), pp. 266–270;

Richard Jeffrey and James H. Fetzer, "A Bibliography of Carl G. Hempel," in Hempel, *The Philosophy of Carl G. Hempel: Studies in Science, Explanation, and Rationality*, edited by Fetzer (Oxford & New York: Oxford University Press, 2001), pp. 397–403.

References:

Donald Davidson, Frederic B. Fitch, Adolf Grünbaum, and others, *Essays in Honor of Carl G. Hempel: A Tribute on the Occasion of His Sixty-fifth Birthday*, edited by Nicholas Rescher (Dordrecht, Netherlands: Reidel, 1969);

Wilhelm K. Essler, Hilary Putnam, and Wolfgang Stegmüller, eds., *Epistemology, Methodology, and Philosophy of Science: Essays in Honor of Carl G. Hempel* (Dordrecht, Netherlands: Kluwer, 1985);

James H. Fetzer, ed., *Science, Explanation, and Rationality: Aspects of the Philosophy of Carl G. Hempel* (Oxford & New York: Oxford University Press, 2000);

Wesley C. Salmon, *Four Decades of Scientific Explanation* (Minneapolis: University of Minnesota Press, 1990).

Papers:

Carl G. Hempel's papers, including his dissertation, are in the Philosophy of Science Archives at the University of Pittsburgh.

Sidney Hook

(20 December 1902 – 12 July 1989)

Robert B. Talisse
Vanderbilt University

BOOKS: *The Metaphysics of Pragmatism* (Chicago & London: Open Court, 1927);

Towards the Understanding of Karl Marx: A Revolutionary Interpretation (New York: John Day, 1933; London: Gollancz, 1933);

The Political and Social Doctrine of Communism: Report of the Work of the Central Committee of the Communist Party of the Soviet Union, by Joseph Stalin; The Democratic and Dictatorial Aspects of Communism, by Sidney Hook (Worcester, Mass. & New York: Carnegie Endowment for International Peace, 1934);

The Meaning of Marx, by Hook, Bertrand Russell, John Dewey, Morris Raphael Cohen, and Sherwood Eddy, edited by Hook (New York: Farrar & Rinehart, 1934);

From Hegel to Marx: Studies in the Intellectual Development of Karl Marx (New York: John Day, 1936; London: Gollancz, 1936; republished with new introduction, Ann Arbor: University of Michigan Press, 1962);

John Dewey: An Intellectual Portrait (New York: John Day, 1939);

Reason, Social Myths, and Democracy (New York: John Day, 1940; republished with new introduction, New York: Harper & Row, 1965);

The Hero in History: A Study in Limitation and Possibility (New York: John Day, 1943; London: Secker & Warburg, 1945);

Education for Modern Man (New York: Dial, 1946); revised and enlarged as *Education for Modern Man: A New Perspective* (New York: Knopf, 1963; enlarged edition, New York: Humanities Press, 1973);

Religion and the Intellectuals, by Hook, John Dewey, Ernest van den Haag, and others (New York: Partisan Review, 1950);

Democracy and Desegregation (New York: Tamiment Institute, 1952);

Heresy, Yes—Conspiracy, No (New York: John Day, 1953; republished with new introduction, Westport, Conn.: Greenwood Press, 1973);

Sidney Hook

Dialectical Materialism and Scientific Method (Manchester, U.K.: Committee on Science and Freedom, 1955);

Marx and the Marxists: The Ambiguous Legacy (Princeton: Van Nostrand, 1955);

Common Sense and the Fifth Amendment (New York: Criterion, 1957);

John Dewey: His Philosophy of Education and Its Critics (New York: Tamiment Institute, 1959);

Political Power and Personal Freedom: Critical Studies in Democracy, Communism, and Civil Rights (New York: Criterion, 1959);

The Quest for Being, and Other Studies in Naturalism and Humanism (New York: St. Martin's Press, 1961);

The Paradoxes of Freedom (Berkeley: University of California Press, 1962; republished with new introduction, Buffalo, N.Y.: Prometheus, 1987);

Education for Modern Man: A New Perspective (New York: Knopf, 1963; enlarged edition, Atlantic Highlands, N.J.: Humanities Press, 1973);

The Fail-Safe Fallacy (New York: Stein & Day, 1963);

Religion in a Free Society (Lincoln: University of Nebraska Press, 1967);

Contemporary Philosophy (Chicago: American Library Association, 1968);

Academic Freedom and Academic Anarchy (New York: Cowles, 1970);

Education and the Taming of Power (La Salle, Ill.: Open Court, 1973; London: Alcove Press, 1974);

Pragmatism and the Tragic Sense of Life (New York: Basic Books, 1974);

Revolution, Reform, and Social Justice: Studies in the Theory and Practice of Marxism (New York: New York University Press, 1975; Oxford: Blackwell, 1976);

Philosophy and Public Policy (Carbondale & Edwardsville: Southern Illinois University Press / London: Feffer & Simons, 1980);

Marxism and Beyond (Totowa, N.J.: Rowman & Littlefield, 1983);

Soviet Hypocrisy and Western Gullibility, by Hook, Vladimir Bukovsky, and Paul Hollander (Washington, D.C.: Ethics and Public Policy Center, 1987; London: Ethics and Public Policy Center, 1988);

Out of Step: An Unquiet Life in the Twentieth Century (New York: Harper & Row, 1987);

Convictions (Buffalo, N.Y.: Prometheus, 1990);

Sidney Hook on Pragmatism, Democracy, and Freedom: The Essential Essays, edited by Robert B. Talisse and Robert Tempio (Amherst, N.Y.: Prometheus, 2002).

OTHER: *Collected Works of Vladimir Ilyich Lenin,* translated by Hook and David Kvitko (New York: International Publishers, 1927);

"A Pragmatic Critique of the Historico-Genetic Method," in *Essays in Honor of John Dewey on the Occasion of His Seventieth Birthday, October 20, 1929* (New York: Holt, 1929), pp. 156–174;

"Bauer, Bruno," "Büchner, Ludwig," "Determinism," "Dietzgen, Joseph," "Engels, Friedrich," "Feuerbach, Ludwig Andreas," "Materialism," "Ruge, Arnold," and "Violence," in *Encyclopaedia of the Social Sciences,* 15 volumes, edited by Edwin R. A. Seligman and Alvin Johnson (New York: Macmillan, 1930–1935); II (1930): 481; III (1931): 30; V (1931): 110–114, 139, 540–541; VI (1931): 221–222; X (1933): 209–220; XIII (1934): 462–463; XV (1935): 264–267;

"Experimental Naturalism," in *American Philosophy Today and Tomorrow,* edited by Hook and Horace M. Kallen (New York: Lee Furman, 1935), pp. 205–225;

"The Philosophical Implications of Economic Planning," in *Planned Society: Yesterday, Today, Tomorrow; a Symposium by Thirty-five Economists, Sociologists, and Statesmen,* edited by Findlay MacKenzie (New York: Prentice-Hall, 1937), pp. 663–677;

Richard Lowenthal, *What Is Folksocialism? A Critical Analysis,* introduction by Hook (New York: League for Industrial Democracy, 1937);

"Naturalism and Democracy," in *Naturalism and the Human Spirit,* edited by Yervant H. Krikorian (New York: Columbia University Press, 1944), pp. 40–64;

"Democracy and Education. I: Introduction," in *The Authoritarian Attempt to Capture Education* (New York: King's Crown Press, 1945), pp. 10–12;

"Illustrations," in *Theory and Practice in Historical Study: A Report of the Committee on Historiography* (New York: Social Science Research Council, 1946), pp. 108–130;

Karl Kautsky, *Social Democracy versus Communism,* edited and translated by David Shub and Joseph Shaplen, introduction by Hook (New York: Rand School Press, 1946);

"Does Private Industry Threaten Freedom of Scientific Research?" and "The Role of Science in Determination of Democratic Policy," by Hook and others, in *Science for Democracy,* edited by Jerome Nathanson (New York: King's Crown Press, 1946), pp. 54–170;

"Intelligence and Evil in Human History," in *Freedom and Experience: Essays Presented to Horace M. Kallen,* edited by Hook and Milton R. Konvitz (Ithaca, N.Y.: Cornell University Press, 1947), pp. 25–45;

"Academic Freedom and Communism," in *The People Shall Judge: Readings in the Formation of American Policy,* volume 2 (Chicago: University of Chicago Press, 1949), pp. 705–714;

"Nature and the Human Spirit," in *Proceedings of the Tenth International Congress of Philosophy* (Amsterdam: North-Holland, 1949), pp. 153–155;

"The Desirable and Emotive in Dewey's Ethics," in *John Dewey: Philosopher of Science and Freedom,* edited by Hook (New York: Dial, 1950), pp. 194–216;

"John Dewey and His Critics," in *Pragmatism and American Culture,* edited by Gail Kennedy (Boston: Heath, 1950), pp. 92–94;

"The Place of John Dewey in Modern Thought," in *Philosophic Thought in France and the United States: Essays Representing Major Trends in Contemporary French and American Philosophy,* edited by Marvin

Farber (Buffalo: University of Buffalo Press, 1950), pp. 483–505;

"General Education: Its Nature and Purposes. Part II," in *General Education in Transition: A Look Ahead*, edited by Horace T. Morse (Minneapolis: University of Minnesota Press, 1951), pp. 68–82;

"Nature and the Human Spirit," in *Freedom and Reason: Studies in Philosophy and Jewish Culture, in Memory of Morris Raphael Cohen*, edited by Salo W. Baron, Ernest Nagel, and Koppel S. Pinson (Glencoe, Ill.: Free Press, 1951), pp. 142–156;

"Bertrand Russell's Philosophy of History," in *The Philosophy of Bertrand Russell*, edited by Paul Arthur Schilpp, The Library of Living Philosophers, volume 5, second edition (New York: Tudor, 1952), pp. 645–678;

"The Role of Intelligence in Our Moral Awakening," by Hook and others, in *Needed: A Moral Awakening in America; a Symposium by Walter P. Reuther and Others*, edited by Harry W. Laidler (New York: League for Industrial Democracy, 1952), pp. 14–16;

"Academic Freedom and Its Values for Higher Education," in *Current Issues in Higher Education 1952*, edited by the National Conference on Higher Education (Washington, D.C.: Association for Higher Education, 1952), pp. 70–75;

"Atheism," in *Collier's Encyclopedia*, volume 2 (New York: Collier, 1952), p. 418;

"The Philosophical Basis of Marxian Socialism in the United States," in *Socialism and American Life*, edited by Donald Drew Egbert and Stow Persons (Princeton: Princeton University Press, 1952), pp. 427–451;

"The Ethics of Academic Freedom," by Hook and George Boas, in *Academic Freedom, Logic, and Religion*, edited by Morton G. White (Philadelphia: University of Pennsylvania Press, 1953), pp. 19–37;

"The Quest for 'Being,'" in *Proceedings of the XIth International Congress of Philosophy, Brussels, 1953*, volume 14 (Amsterdam: North-Holland, 1953), pp. 17–25;

Paul Edwards, *The Logic of Moral Discourse*, introduction by Hook (Glencoe, Ill.: Free Press, 1955);

"Science and Dialectical Materialism," in *Science and Freedom: The Proceedings of a Conference Convened by the Congress for Cultural Freedom and Held in Hamburg on July 23rd–26th, 1953* (London: Published for the Congress for Cultural Freedom by Secker & Warburg, 1955), pp. 182–195; contributions to discussions, pp. 47–48, 114–115, 144–146, 263–264;

"Naturalism and First Principles" in *American Philosophers at Work: The Philosophic Scene in the United States*, edited by Hook (New York: Criterion, 1956), pp. 236–258;

"Outlook for Philosophy," in *New Frontiers of Knowledge: A Symposium by Distinguished Writers, Notable Scholars and Public Figures*, edited by M. B. Schnapper (Washington, D.C.: Public Affairs Press, 1957), pp. 18–21;

"Necessity, Indeterminism, and Sentimentalism," in *Determinism and Freedom in the Age of Modern Science*, edited by Hook (New York: New York University Press, 1958; London: Collier-Macmillan, 1961), pp. 167–180;

"A Pragmatic Note," in *Dimensions of Mind*, edited by Hook (New York: New York University Press, 1960; London: Collier, 1961), pp. 202–207;

"The Atheism of Paul Tillich," in *Religious Experience and Truth*, edited by Hook (New York: New York University Press, 1961; Edinburgh & London: Oliver & Boyd, 1962), pp. 59–64;

World Communism: Key Documentary Material, edited by Hook (Princeton: Van Nostrand, 1962);

"The Humanities and the Taming of Power," in *The Role of the Humanities in Ordering a Peaceful World* (New Britain: Central Connecticut State College, 1962), pp. 5–21;

Raphael R. Abramovitch, *The Soviet Revolution, 1917–1939*, introduction by Hook (New York: International Universities Press, 1962; London: Allen & Unwin, 1962);

"Philosophy and Human Conduct," in *Philosophy and Culture–East and West*, edited by Charles A. Moore (Honolulu: University of Hawaii Press, 1962), pp. 15–32;

"Objectivity and Reconstruction in History," in *Philosophy and History*, edited by Hook (New York: New York University Press, 1963), pp. 250–275;

"Summary of the Symposium," in *The Health Care Issues of the 1960's* (New York: Group Health Insurance, 1963), pp. 179–199;

Eric Hoffer, *The True Believer: Thoughts on the Nature of Mass Movements*, introduction by Hook (New York: Time, 1963);

"Law, Justice, and Obedience," in *Law and Philosophy: A Symposium*, edited by Hook (New York: New York University Press, 1964), pp. 56–60;

"The Death Sentence," in *The Death Penalty in America: An Anthology*, edited by Hugo Adam Bedau (Chicago: Aldine, 1964), pp. 146–164;

Walter Lippmann, *A Preface to Morals*, new edition, introduction by Hook (New York: Time-Life, 1964);

Hook with his second wife, Ann E. Zinken Hook, circa 1940

"Intelligence and Human Rights," in *Memorias del XIII Congreso Internacional de Filosofía,* volume 7 (Mexico City: Universidad Nacional Autónoma de México, 1964), pp. 101–102;

"Religious Liberty from the Viewpoint of a Secular Humanist," in *Religious Conflict in America: Studies of the Problems beyond Bigotry,* edited by Earl Raab (Garden City, N.Y.: Doubleday, 1964), pp. 138–151;

Rebecca West, *The New Meaning of Treason,* new edition, introduction by Hook (New York: Time-Life, 1965);

"Academic Freedom and the Rights of Students," in *The Berkeley Student Revolt: Facts and Interpretations,* edited by Seymour Martin Lipset and Sheldon S. Wolin (Garden City, N.Y.: Doubleday/Anchor, 1965), pp. 432–442;

"The Political Aspects of General and Complete Disarmament," in *The Prospects for Arms Control,* edited by James E. Dougherty and John F. Lehman Jr. (New York: Macfadden-Bartell, 1965), pp. 153–163;

"Are There Universal Criteria of Judgments of Excellence in Art?" in *Art and Philosophy,* edited by

Hook (New York: New York University Press, 1966), pp. 49–55;

"A Philosopher's View," in *Man's Quest for Security: A Symposium,* edited by Edwin J. Faulkner (Lincoln: University of Nebraska Press, 1966), pp. 1–17;

"Basic Values and Economic Policy," in *Human Values and Economic Policy: A Symposium,* edited by Hook (New York: New York University Press, 1967), pp. 246–255;

"The Democratic Challenge to Communism," in *Fifty Years of Communism in Russia,* edited by Milorad M. Drachkovitch, Hoover Institution Publication no. 77 (University Park: Pennsylvania State University Press, 1968), pp. 284–292;

Comment on speech by Robert M. Hutchins and "The University Law School," in *The Law School of Tomorrow: The Projection of an Ideal,* edited by David Haber and Julius Cohen (New Brunswick, N.J.: Rutgers University Press, 1968), pp. 5–24, 38–55;

"Empiricism, Realism, and Innate Ideas," in *Language and Philosophy: A Symposium,* edited by Hook (New York: New York University Press / London: London University Press, 1969), pp. 160–167;

The Essential Thomas Paine, edited by Hook (New York: New American Library, 1969);

"The Long View," "Conflict and Change in the Academic Community," and "From the Platitudinous to the Absurd," in *In Defense of Academic Freedom,* edited by Hook (New York: Pegasus, 1971), pp. 11–20, 106–119, 249–266;

"Academic Freedom and the Supreme Court: The Court in Another Wilderness," in *On Academic Freedom,* edited by Valerie Earle (Washington, D.C.: American Enterprise Institute for Public Policy Research, 1971), pp. 31–46;

"How Democratic Is America? A Response to Howard Zinn," in *How Democratic Is America? Responses to the New Left Challenge,* edited by Robert A. Godwin (Chicago: Rand McNally, 1971), pp. 61–75;

"Ideals and Realities of Academic Tenure," in *Twenty-eighth Annual Utah Conference on Higher Education* (Logan: Utah State University, 1971), pp. 13–24;

Marvin Zimmerman, *Contemporary Problems of Democracy,* introduction by Hook (New York: Humanities Press, 1972);

Cornelius J. Troost, ed., *Radical School Reform: Critique and Alternatives,* foreword by Hook (Boston: Little, Brown, 1973);

"Marxism," in *Dictionary of the History of Ideas,* volume 3, edited by Philip P. Wiener (New York: Scribners, 1973), pp. 146–161;

"The Relevance of John Dewey's Thought," in *The Chief Glory of Every People: Essays on Classic American Writers,* edited by Matthew J. Bruccoli (Carbondale: Southern Illinois University Press, 1973), pp. 53–75;

"Introduction: The Rationale of the Problem" and "Democracy and Higher Education," in *The Idea of a Modern University,* edited by Hook, Paul Kurtz, and Miro Todorovich (Buffalo, N.Y.: Prometheus, 1974), pp. xvii–xix, 33–40;

"The Modern Quarterly: Baltimore and New York, 1923–1932, 1938–1940. The Modern Monthly: New York. 1933–1938," in *The American Radical Press,* volume 2, edited by Joseph R. Conlin (Westport, Conn.: Greenwood Press, 1974), pp. 596–605;

"General Education: The Indispensable Minimum" and "On Sharpening the Horns," in *The Philosophy of the Curriculum: The Need for General Education,* edited by Hook, Kurtz, and Todorovich (Buffalo, N.Y.: Prometheus, 1975), pp. 27–36, 211–215;

John Dewey, *Moral Principles in Education,* preface by Hook (Carbondale & Edwardsville: Southern Illinois University Press/Arcturus Books, 1975);

James Gouinlock, *The Moral Writings of John Dewey,* foreword by Hook (New York: Macmillan, Hafner Press, 1976);

"Academic Freedom and Professional Responsibilities" and "Dr. Hibbs and the Ethics of Discussion," in *The Ethics of Teaching and Scientific Research,* edited by Hook, Kurtz, and Todorovich (Buffalo, N.Y.: Prometheus, 1977), pp. 117–123, 187–190;

The University and the State: What Role for Government in Higher Education? edited by Hook, Kurtz, and Todorovich (Buffalo, N.Y.: Prometheus, 1978);

"Are There Alternatives to Collective Bargaining?" in *Landmarks in Collective Bargaining in Higher Education,* edited by Aaron Levenstein (New York: National Center for the Study of Collective Bargaining in Higher Education, 1978), pp. 150–154;

"The Conceptual Structure of Power–an Overview," in *Power: Its Nature, Its Use, and Its Limits,* edited by Donald W. Harward (Boston: G. K. Hall, 1979), pp. 3–19;

The Middle Works of John Dewey 1899–1924, volume 9, edited by Jo Ann Boydston, introduction by Hook (Carbondale & Edwardsville: Southern Illinois University Press, 1980);

James H. Wentzel, *Countdown to 1984: A Review of Federal Government "Minority" Group Preference in Small Business and Public Works Programs,* preface by Hook (Washington, D.C.: National Legal Center for the Public Interest, 1980);

"On Western Freedom," in *Solzhenitzyn at Harvard,* edited by Ronald Berman (Washington, D.C.: Ethics and Public Policy Center, 1980), pp. 85–97;

The Later Works of John Dewey, 1925–1933, volume 1, edited by Boydston, introduction by Hook (Carbondale & Edwardsville: Southern Illinois University Press, 1981);

Bertram D. Wolfe, *A Life in Two Centuries,* afterword by Hook (New York: Stein & Day, 1981);

"General Education in a Free Society," in *Freedom, Order, and the University,* edited by James R. Wilburn (Malibu, Cal.: Pepperdine University Press, 1982), pp. 31–41;

Gary Bullert, *The Politics of John Dewey,* foreword by Hook (Buffalo: N.Y.: Prometheus, 1983);

"Pluralistic Societies at Stake," in *Challenges to the Western Alliance,* edited by Joseph Godson (London: Times Books, 1984), pp. 177–181;

James Burnham, *The Machiavellians: Defenders of Freedom,* introduction by Hook (Washington, D.C.: Regnery Gateway, 1988);

Philosophy, History, and Social Action: Essays in Honor of Lewis Feuer, edited by Hook, William L. O'Neill, and Roger O'Toole, Boston Studies in the Philosophy of Science, volume 107 (Dordrecht, Netherlands, Boston & London: Kluwer Academic, 1988).

SELECTED PERIODICAL PUBLICATION–UNCOLLECTED: "The Future of Socialism," *Partisan Review,* 14 (January–February 1947): 23–36.

Although Sidney Hook's academic work spans the gamut of philosophical inquiry, from metaphysics and epistemology to ethics, aesthetics, and philosophy of education, a set of central concerns runs through all of his work. These concerns, which reflect the influence John Dewey exerted on Hook's thinking, are democracy, freedom, and intelligence. They coalesce in the question that Hook endeavored to answer throughout his career: how can the best available methods of inquiry be applied to the most pressing problems of human life in a way that both responds to those problems and establishes and nurtures the conditions that enable further progress in the amelioration of human ills?

Saul Hook was born in the Williamsburg area of Brooklyn, New York, on 20 December 1902, the fourth child of the Jewish immigrants Isaac Hook, a factory worker from Moravia in the present-day Czech Republic, and Jennie Halpern Hook, from Galicia in present-day Poland. His mother changed his first name to Sidney when he enrolled in public school at age five. Hook earned his B.S. at the City College of New York, where he studied principally under the philosopher Morris Raphael Cohen, in 1923 and began teaching in the New York public school system. He married Carrie Katz on 31 March 1924; they had one child, John Bertrand.

Hook received his M.A. in 1926 and his Ph.D. in 1927 at Columbia University under the tutelage of Dewey. His dissertation was published in 1927 as *The Metaphysics of Pragmatism.* He was appointed an instructor in the philosophy department of Washington Square College of New York University in 1927 but continued to teach in the public schools for another year. He was a Guggenheim fellow in 1928–1929. In 1932 he was promoted to assistant professor.

Much of Hook's earliest work focused on technical philosophical issues stemming from the pragmatic naturalism and instrumentalism he learned from Dewey. The fundamental pragmatist thesis that ideas are fundamentally instruments and plans for action holds important implications for all of the standard areas of philosophy: metaphysics, epistemology, logic, and value theory. Although *The Metaphysics of Pragmatism* is an important contribution to the literature on the metaphysical and epistemological commitments of pragmatism, Hook found his own distinctive philosophical voice in value theory, especially in social and politi-

Hook with his daughter, Susan, and his son Ernest in August 1942

cal philosophy. In the early years of his career Hook was an unabashed Marxist. He taught the first college course on Marxism ever presented in the United States, and his *Towards the Understanding of Karl Marx: A Revolutionary Interpretation* (1933) remains a classic in Marx scholarship. In this work Hook seeks to synthesize Marx's dialectical materialism with Dewey's experimental naturalism, contending that the jewel of Marx's philosophy was the attempt to bring scientific methods of inquiry and practice to bear on social problems. Hook maintained that the Marxian theory of class conflict driven by disparities in control over material forces provided a fully scientific theory of society that not only could explain observed social phenomena but could also direct social action aimed at the reformation of social conditions. In this way, Hook saw deep continuities in the projects of Marx and Dewey: both eschewed supernaturalism and sought to bring scientific methods to bear on present problems, and both aimed to reform society by means of the application of cooperative social intelligence. Thus, in *Towards the Understanding of Karl Marx* Hook promotes a thoroughly Deweyan reading of Marx according to which Marx was fundamentally a philosopher of democracy. This reading of Marx was then and continues to be unorthodox, since it resolutely de-emphasizes the role of historical determinism in Marx's system in favor of a focus on social practice and open experimentalism.

Hook was promoted to associate professor and named chairman of the philosophy department at New York University in 1934. His first marriage having

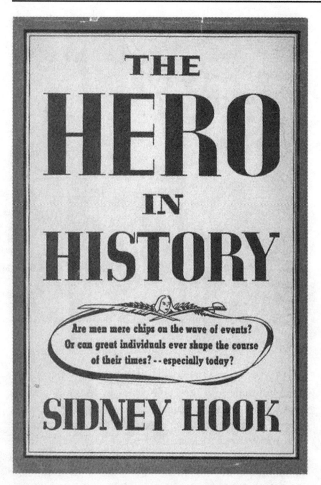

THE HERO IN HISTORY

Are men mere chips on the wave of events? Or can great individuals ever shape the course of their times? -- especially today?

SIDNEY HOOK

Dust jacket for Hook's 1943 book, in which he argues that history is created by the actions of individuals and not by immutable Marxist laws of development (Reason Alone Books)

ended in divorce, he married Ann E. Zinken on 25 May 1935; they had two children: Ernest Benjamin and Susan Ann.

As early as 1934 it had become apparent to Hook that Marxism as understood by the Communist Party was nothing more than a dogmatic justification for the tyranny of the party over the people, rather than a scientific method of democratic social reconstruction. Hence, that year Hook included the essay "Marxism without Dogmas" in his *The Meaning of Marx* (it became famous under the title "Why I Am a Communist"). His sympathy for communism waned even further as news of the Moscow purge trials of 1936–1937 reached the West. In 1936 he was the principal catalyst behind the formation of the Commission of Inquiry into the Truth of the Moscow Trials, which secured an opportunity for Leon Trotsky to defend himself against Joseph Stalin's charges; the commission, led by Dewey, exonerated Trotsky. The case confirmed Hook's suspicion that the

American Communist Party was actually a conspiratorial organization under the direct control of Stalin that aimed to infiltrate and ultimately to dismantle the political structure of the United States. This realization led Hook to make what many see as a drastic shift to the political Right: in 1938 he adopted the vehement anti-Communist and anti-Soviet stance that he sustained until his death. Hook's anti-Communism drove him to defend positions that were unpopular with the Left on issues such as academic freedom, the employment of Communist Party members by public colleges and universities, the rights of student war protesters, and affirmative action.

In "Democracy as a Way of Life," published in *The Southern Review* in the summer of 1938, revised in the fall of the same year as "The Democratic Way of Life" in the *Menorah Journal,* and collected under the latter title in *Reason, Social Myths, and Democracy* (1940), Hook gives a Deweyan analysis of democracy. He begins by defining a democratic society as "one where the government rests upon the freely given consent of the governed," which means that political mechanisms exist by which the governed may register approval or disapproval of government actions and policies at regular intervals, and the government acknowledges a prima facie duty to conduct itself according to the consent of the governed. Furthermore, the consent of the governed must be "freely given": for example, "A threat to deprive the governed of their jobs or means of livelihood, by a group which has the power to do so, would undermine a democracy." Hook concludes: "Where the political forms of democracy function within a society in which economic controls are not subject to political control, there is always a standing threat to democracy." Democracy requires not only protection of the populace from the direct domination of the economically powerful; it also requires that steps be taken to ensure that economic power is not employed to control or undermine democratic procedures. Democracy also requires that the access of the governed to information be unrestricted: "The expression of consent by the majority is not free if it is deprived of access to sources of information, if it can read *only* the official interpretation, if it can hear *only* one voice in the classroom, pulpit, and radio." Without such minimal provisions, consent is not free, since "the individual has no more freedom of action when his mind is deliberately tied by ignorance than when his hands are tied with rope." Hook says that

those who believe in democracy . . . must distinguish between honest opposition *within* the framework of the democratic process and the opposition, subsidized and controlled by the totalitarian enemies of democracy, which is a form of treason to everything democrats hold dear. Opposition of the first kind, no matter how mistaken, must be tolerated, if for no other reason than that we cannot be sure that it is not we who are mistaken. Opposition of the second kind, no matter what protective coloration it wears . . . must be swiftly dealt with if democracy is to survive.

In any political controversy, the first objective must always be to preserve the processes of democracy. When considered at the level of an entire community, the radical implications of Deweyan experimentalism are revealed. Hook points out

how revolutionary the impact would be of giving the method of intelligence institutional force in education, economics, law and politics. Policies would be treated as hypotheses, not as dogmas; customary practices as generalizations, not as God-given truths. A generation trained in schools where emphasis was placed upon method, method, and more method, could hardly be swayed by current high-pressured propaganda.

Although Hook rejected what he considered the Stalinist perversion of communism in the Soviet Union, he continued to regard himself as a Marxist. In the chapter "What Is Living and Dead in Marxism" in *Reason, Social Myths, and Democracy* he goes so far as to say, "The most outstanding figure in the world today in whom the best elements of Marx's thought are present is John Dewey."

In 1939 Hook was promoted to full professor. He was awarded the Nicholas Murray Butler Silver Medal by Columbia University in 1945 for his book *The Hero in History: A Study in Limitation and Possibility* (1943). In this book Hook undertakes a detailed study of political history with a view to refuting the Marxist contention that history is a predetermined progression by means of class struggle toward a classless society. He argues that pivotal episodes in history are the products not of a metaphysical "historical dialectic" but of the actions and efforts of human individuals.

By the mid 1940s Hook had clearly disassociated himself from Marxism and turned his efforts fully toward the theory and defense of democracy. Among the most important works he produced in this vein is *Education for Modern Man* (1946), in which he follows Dewey in opposing both strictly traditionalist theories of education typified by the "Great Books" program modeled at St. John's University and the naively progressivist, neo-Rousseauian views that focus on the spontaneity of the child. Hook proposes, instead, a democratic form of education that includes the traditional curriculum of history, science, literature, and mathematics but sees education as involving more than simply mastery of the past. According to Hook, proper

Hook, at his summer home in Vermont with his son Ernest, circa 1943

education involves the application of knowledge to new contexts; more specifically, he advocates a view of education according to which students master the methods by which old knowledge is applied and new knowledge is gained. Hence, proper education serves as a guard against dogmatism, traditionalism, and authoritarianism. In short, Hook sees education as the cultivation of the skills and capacities necessary for citizenship in a democratic society.

Hook's growing concern over the dogmatism and authoritarianism of Soviet Communism and his consequent focus on the defense of democratic, anti-authoritarian ideals led him to advocate the staunch anticommunism for which he is now well known. He finally ceased to refer to himself as a Marxist in 1947. In "The Future of Socialism," published that year in *Partisan Review,* he says: "It would appear that if I were justified in my interpretation of Marx's meaning, I would be perhaps the last Marxist left in the world. This is too much for my sense of humor, and so I have decided to abandon the term as a descriptive epithet of my position."

*Hook and the British philosopher Bertrand Russell at the International
Congress of Philosophy in Amsterdam in August 1948*

Hook was head of the Department of Philosophy
of the Graduate School at New York University from
1948 to 1967 and chairman of the Division of Philosophy and Psychology of the Graduate School from 1949
to 1955. He received a second Guggenheim Fellowship
in 1953. In his 1953 book *Heresy, Yes—Conspiracy, No*
Hook distinguishes between "internal" and "external"
opponents of democracy. Internal critics honor the
democratic "rules of the game" in their attempts to
generate social change. Hook maintains that such
opponents must be vehemently protected and engaged.
External critics, on the other hand, exploit the freedoms of a democratic society to engage in activity that
undermines the very processes of democratic discourse, as when a group uses the freedom of speech to
drown out dissident voices; such opponents need not
be tolerated. Hook characterizes the Communist Party
as an "external" opponent of democracy and holds that
confirmed members of the Communist Party should
be removed from public educational institutions and
other sensitive posts. To the charge that such a policy
violates the key democratic value of academic freedom,
Hook replies that academic freedom is the freedom to
follow evidence and argument wherever they lead, not

the freedom to use the classroom for indoctrination
and Communist recruitment. He does not say that all
believers in communism should be removed: a responsible communist would be willing to engage in the
democratic activity of exchanging reasons and hence
open to refutation. But membership in the Communist
Party, according to Hook, is sufficient evidence that
person has given up on the project of supporting communism with reasons and had adopted communism as
a dogma.

In "The Ethics of Controversy," published in *The
New Leader* in February 1954 and collected in *Philosophy
and Public Policy* (1980), Hook notes that "democratic society cannot exist without free discussion," since such discussion is a necessary condition for free consent. But, he
points out, "Some kinds of discussion tend to undermine
democratic society," since "wherever discussion flour-
ishes, controversy is sure to arise." Certain modes of controversy tend to silence debate, generate confusion,
discredit dissenters rather than their views, suppress relevant information, encourage dogmatism, and establish,
on the basis of an appeal to loyalty to tradition, that
which cannot be established by an appeal to evidence
and analysis. Following Dewey, Hook offers what he

calls the "method of intelligence," or "experimental method," derived from the experimentalist epistemology embodied in the methods of science. On this basis he offers ten "ground rules" for democratic discourse:

1. Nothing and no one is immune from criticism.

2. Everyone involved in a controversy has an intellectual responsibility to inform himself of the available facts.

3. Criticism should be directed first to policies, and against persons only when they are responsible for policies, and against their motives or purposes only when there is some independent evidence of their character.

4. Because certain words are legally permissible, they are not therefore morally permissible.

5. *Before* impugning an opponent's motives, even when they legitimately may be impugned, answer his arguments.

6. Do not treat an opponent of a policy as if he were therefore a personal enemy of the country or a concealed enemy of democracy.

7. Since a good cause may be defended by bad arguments, after answering the bad arguments for another's position present positive evidence for your own.

8. Do not hesitate to admit lack of knowledge or to suspend judgment if evidence is not decisive either way.

9. Only in pure logic and mathematics, not in human affairs, can one demonstrate that something is strictly impossible. Because something is logically possible, it is not therefore probable. "It is not impossible" is a preface to an irrelevant statement about human affairs. The question is always one of the balance of probabilities. And the evidence for probabilities must include more than abstract possibilities.

10. The cardinal sin, when we are looking for truth of fact or wisdom of policy, is refusal to discuss, or action which blocks discussion.

Hook admits that these principles may sound like truisms, but he points out that what is often not apprehended is that experimentalism presupposes a community that is committed to the project of cooperatively inquiring into common problems to reach tentative but workable solutions.

Hook was head of the All-University Department of Philosophy at New York University from 1957 to 1972. He served as vice president of the American Philosophical Association, Eastern Division, in 1958

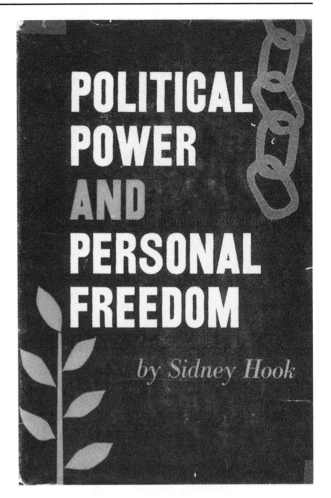

Dust jacket for the 1959 book in which Hook analyzes the concept of free consent and discusses the various impediments to it (Reason Alone Books)

and as president in 1959–1960. In 1959 he published *Political Power and Personal Freedom: Critical Studies in Democracy, Communism, and Civil Rights.* In the first chapter, "The Philosophical Heritage of the Atlantic Democracies," he notes that since "there are few things to which a starving man will not consent," one may speak of economic obstructions to free consent. More important are epistemological impediments to free consent: "Even in the absence of physical and economic coercion, consent is not free if it is bound or blinded by ignorance." Hook concludes that "what is required to live prosperously and peacefully together is not a fixed common doctrine or a fixed body of truths, but a common method or set of fixed rules under which we can live with our differences." Democracy is "a perpetual invitation to sit down in the face of differences and reason together, to consider the evidence, explore alternative proposals, assess the consequences, and let the decision rest—when matters of human concern are at stake—with the consent of those affected by the propos-

Dust jacket for Hook's 1962 book, in which he recognizes the imperfections of democracy but argues that it contains the mechanisms necessary to improve itself (Bruccoli Clark Layman Archives)

als." In the chapter "Are There Two Kinds of Democracy?" Hook notes that consent is freely given only when it is "voluntary" and "not subject to coercion," since "An election held in the shadow of bayonets, or in which one can vote only 'Yes,' or in which no opposition candidates are permitted is obviously one which does not register freely given consent." He elaborates: "If one is kept ignorant of alternatives, denied access to information, deprived of the opportunity to influence and be influenced by the opinions of others, consent is not free." Furthermore, "Differences in economic power make it possible for the more powerful economic group to exercise a much greater influence upon decisions that affect public welfare than their numbers or deserts warrant." Hook fears that unchecked economic power will be employed to "render nugatory even legislative action." Moreover, the economically powerful enjoy "greater advantages in mobilizing resources to influence public opinion and consent."

Nevertheless, "democracy, with all its imperfections, possesses the instruments by which it can move towards the realization of the promise of equality and freedom it contains."

Hook received a Doctorate of Hebrew Letters (D.H.L.) from the University of Maine in 1960. He was a visiting professor at Harvard University in 1961 and a fellow of the Center for Advanced Study in the Behavioral Sciences in 1961–1962. In *The Paradoxes of Freedom* (1962) he recognizes that a democratic community is "sometimes foolish, sometimes callous and hostile to the underprivileged." Nevertheless, the instruments and processes of experimentalism that are the essential agencies of the democratic way of life must be most widely adopted and most vehemently protected, for they alone constitute the difference between an open but imperfect society that is able to improve, on the one hand, and tyranny, on the other hand.

Hook was a fellow of the American Academy of Arts and Sciences in 1965 and of the National Academy of Education in 1966; also in 1966 he received an honorary LL.D. from the University of California. His opposition to Supreme Court decisions of the early 1960s banning voluntary prayer and Bible reading in public schools was not based on a belief that prayer is wholesome or necessary for the cultivation of virtue. Instead, Hook objected to the process by which the secular position was secured. In *Religion in a Free Society* (1967) he pointed out that "Since what one Court can do, another can undo, in the long run it seems to me that those who wish to keep religion out of the public life of a free society should look primarily to the educational processes of democracy itself rather than to the decrees of the Court to strengthen and extend the secular position." He opposed the student anti–Vietnam War movement not because he supported American intervention in Vietnam but because, as he says in *Academic Freedom and Academic Anarchy* (1970), he considered the protests an attack on the democratic process. Similarly, he attacked the employment of Communist Party members in public educational institutions not because of his opposition to communism but because they belonged to an organization that dictated beliefs to its members and tolerated no opposition.

Hook assumed professor emeritus status at New York University in 1970. He received a second D.H.L. from the University of Utah that year and LL.D. degrees from Rockford College and the University of Florida in 1971. In "How Democratic Is America? A Response to Howard Zinn" (1971) he maintains that the essential feature of a democratic community is its commitment to the methods and processes of experimentalism rather than its commitment to any specific

Hook at the Hoover Institution in 1984, flanked by pictures of his lifelong inspiration, John Dewey, and the hero of his youth, Karl Marx (photograph © 1984 by Victoria Rouse; all rights reserved)

principles derived therefrom. For a democracy, the epistemological method of deciding policy and resolving conflict is supreme.

In 1973 Hook became a senior research fellow at the Hoover Institution of War, Revolution, and Peace at Stanford University. He received an LL.D. from the University of Vermont in 1977 and a third D.H.L. from Hebrew Union College in 1978. In 1985 he was awarded the Medal of Freedom by President Ronald Reagan. Nevertheless, in his autobiography, *Out of Step: An Unquiet Life in the Twentieth Century* (1987) Hook makes the striking claim that Reagan's policies regarding Soviet Communism were "irresolute." Despite his shift from radical Marxist to neoconservative cold warrior, Hook maintains in the autobiography that he is "not aware of having undergone any serious conversions from the days of my youth, or of having abandoned my basic ideals." Those "basic ideals" were the democratic ones he inherited from Dewey. Hook's overriding commitment lies not with any given political party or platform but with democratic processes themselves and the way of life they require. His dedication to democracy as process led him to some positions that today are associated with the Right; but he was at all times motivated by a radical conception of democracy

and a concern for its continued expansion. Accordingly, Hook's life was characterized by a willingness to follow an argument to wherever it led, even if doing so required that some most cherished belief be revised or abandoned, or some revered allegiance be dissolved, or some unfashionable view be adopted. Hence, despite his endorsement of many views paradigmatic of neoconservatism, Hook affirms in his autobiography that "I am an unreconstructed believer in the welfare state and in a steeply progressive income tax, a secular humanist, and a firm supporter of freedom of choice with respect to abortion, voluntary euthanasia, and other domestic measures" that contemporary conservatives oppose. Hook rightly observed that his thought was perpetually "out of step" with intellectual fashion and prevailing opinion; his life was, therefore, as the subtitle of his autobiography indicates, "unquiet." Hook's primary commitments–which he did, indeed, uphold throughout his life–are best captured in the remarks that close the autobiography:

> The test of whether a human being has enjoyed a happy life is whether, if it were possible, he or she would accept another round of it. By this test I have had a happy life. But of the specific forms of happiness

(as well as of unhappiness) in the human experience, one must say that they more truly befall us than they result from anything we contrive. The greatest and most enduring source of happiness in my life—aside from the bittersweet joys of personal and parental life, about which I am sure few would care to hear—have been the experience and excitement of clarifying ideas, of battling in a good cause, and of teaching a bright and questioning class of students. Paradoxical as it may sound, I have always regarded political life as a diversion from my primary interests. I would regard a professional life in politics as an unendurable sacrifice. And yet indifference to the political life of one's times I deem a flagrant expression of moral irresponsibility. Those who profess such indifference owe the intellectual and cultural freedoms in which they luxuriate to the commitment and sacrifices of others.

Sidney Hook died in Stanford of congestive heart failure on 12 July 1989. Despite his importance during his lifetime, today his philosophy is almost completely neglected by scholars. Neither John Murphy's *Pragmatism: From Peirce to Davidson* (1990) nor H. O. Mounce's *The Two Pragmatisms: From Peirce to Rorty* (1997) includes a substantial treatment of Hook. Michael Brint and William Weaver's collection *Pragmatism in Law and Society* (1991) includes no examination of Hook's major contribution to legal philosophy, *The Paradoxes of Freedom*. James Campbell's *The Community Reconstructs: The Meaning of Pragmatic Social Thought* (1992), Matthew Festenstein's *Pragmatism and Political Theory: From Dewey to Rorty* (1997), and Richard E. Hart and Douglas R. Anderson's collection *Philosophy in Experience: American Philosophy in Transition* (1997) ignore Hook completely, and Richard Rorty's *Achieving Our Country: Leftist Thought in Twentieth-Century America* (1998) mentions him only in passing. A rare exception is John J. Stuhr, who says in a footnote in his collection *Philosophy and the Reconstruction of Culture: Pragmatic Essays after Dewey* (1993) that it is "unfortunate" that Hook's work "now is generally neglected and not well-known." A revival of interest in Hook's work, however, may have been signaled by the publication in 1997 of Christopher Phelps's *Young Sidney Hook: Marxist and Pragmatist* and by a conference, "Sidney Hook Reconsidered: A Centennial Celebration," held on 25–26 October 2002 at the City University of New York.

Letters:

Letters of Sidney Hook: Democracy, Communism, and the Cold War, edited by Edward S. Shapiro (Armonk, N.Y. & London: M. E. Sharpe, 1995).

Interviews:

Ethics, National Ideology, Marxism and Existentialism: Discussions with Sidney Hook, edited by Harsja W. Bachtiar (Jakarta: Djambatan, 1976);

"An Interview with Sidney Hook at Eighty," *Free Inquiry,* 2 (Summer 1983): 3.

Bibliographies:

John Dennis Crowley, "Sidney Hook: A Bibliography," *Modern Schoolman: A Quarterly Journal of Philosophy,* 44 (May 1967): 331–374;

Jo Ann Boydston and Kathleen Poulos, "A Complete Bibliography of Sidney Hook," in *Sidney Hook: Philosopher of Democracy and Humanism,* edited by Paul Kurtz (Buffalo, N.Y.: Prometheus, 1983), pp. 311–347;

Barbara Levine, *Checklist of Writings by Sidney Hook* (Carbondale & Edwardsville: Southern Illinois University Press, 1989).

References:

Max Eastman, *Last Stand of Dialectic Materialism: A Study of Sidney Hook's Marxism* (New York: Polemic, 1934);

Paul Kurtz, ed., *Sidney Hook: Philosopher of Democracy and Humanism* (Buffalo, N.Y.: Prometheus, 1983);

Kurtz, ed., *Sidney Hook and the Contemporary World: Essays on the Pragmatic Intelligence* (New York: John Day, 1968);

Paul Mattick, *The Inevitability of Communism: A Critique of Sidney Hook's Interpretation of Marx* (New York: Polemic, 1935);

Christopher Phelps, *Young Sidney Hook: Marxist and Pragmatist* (Ithaca, N.Y.: Cornell University Press, 1997);

Danny Postel, "Sidney Hook, an Intellectual Street Fighter, Reconsidered," *Chronicle of Higher Education,* 49 (8 November 2002): A18;

Richard Rorty, *Achieving Our Country: Leftist Thought in Twentieth-Century America* (Cambridge, Mass.: Harvard University Press, 1998), p. 24;

John J. Stuhr, ed., *Philosophy and the Reconstruction of Culture: Pragmatic Essays after Dewey* (Albany: State University of New York Press, 1993), p. 56n;

Robert B. Talisse, "Sidney Hook Reconsidered," *Pragmatism Cybrary* <www.pragmatism.org/genealogy/hook.htm>.

Papers:

"The Sidney Hook Papers, 1902–1996" are in the Hoover Institution Archives at Stanford University.

John Hospers

(9 June 1918 –   )

J. P. Moreland
Biola University

BOOKS: *Meaning and Truth in the Arts* (Chapel Hill: University of North Carolina Press, 1946);

An Introduction to Philosophical Analysis (New York: Prentice-Hall, 1953; London: Routledge & Kegan Paul, 1956; revised edition, Englewood Cliffs, N.J.: Prentice-Hall, 1967; London: Routledge & Kegan Paul, 1970; revised again, Englewood Cliffs, N.J.: Prentice Hall, 1988; London: Routledge, 1990; revised again, Upper Saddle River, N.J.: Prentice Hall, 1997; London: Routledge, 1997);

Human Conduct: An Introduction to the Problems of Ethics (New York: Harcourt, Brace & World, 1961; London: Hart-Davis, 1962); revised as *Human Conduct: Problems of Ethics* (New York: Harcourt Brace Jovanovich, 1982; revised edition, Fort Worth, Tex.: Harcourt Brace College Publishers, 1996);

Libertarianism: A Political Philosophy for Tomorrow (Los Angeles: Nash, 1971);

Understanding the Arts (Englewood Cliffs, N.J.: Prentice-Hall, 1982);

Anarchy or Limited Government? (San Francisco: Gutenberg Press, 1982);

Law and the Market (Johannesburg: Free Market Foundation of Southern Africa, 1985).

OTHER: *Readings in Ethical Theory,* edited by Hospers and Wilfrid Sellars (New York: Appleton-Century-Crofts, 1952; revised, 1970);

"What Means This Freedom?" in *Determinism and Freedom in the Age of Modern Science: A Philosophical Symposium,* edited by Sidney Hook (New York: New York University Press, 1958), pp. 113–130;

"Art and Reality," in *Art and Philosophy,* edited by Hook (New York: New York University Press, 1966), pp. 121–152;

"Aesthetics, Problems of," in *The Encyclopedia of Philosophy,* volume 1, edited by Paul Edwards (New York: Macmillan, 1967), pp. 35–56;

John Hospers (from dust jacket for Human Conduct: An Introduction to the Problems of Ethics, *1961)*

Readings in Introductory Philosophical Analysis, edited by Hospers (Englewood Cliffs, N.J.: Prentice-Hall, 1968; London: Routledge & Kegan Paul, 1969);

Introductory Readings in Aesthetics, edited by Hospers (New York: Free Press / London: Collier-Macmillan, 1969);

"The Croce-Collingwood Theory of Art," in *Artistic Expression,* edited by Hospers (New York: Appleton-Century-Crofts, 1971), pp. 51–71;

"What Libertarianism Is," in *The Libertarian Alternative: Essays in Social and Political Philosophy,* edited by Tibor R. Machan (Chicago: Nelson-Hall, 1974), pp. 3–20;

"Art, Problems of," in *The New Encyclopaedia Britannica,* fifteenth edition, volume 12 (Chicago: Encyclopaedia Britannica, 1974), pp. 40–56;

"Punishment, Protection, and Retaliation," in *Justice and Punishment,* edited by J. B. Cederblom and William L. Blizek (Cambridge, Mass.: Ballinger, 1977), pp. 15–50;

"The Ethics of Punishment," in *Assessing the Criminal: Restitution, Retribution, and the Legal Process,* edited by Randy E. Barnett and John Hagel III (Cambridge, Mass.: Ballinger, 1977), pp. 181–211;

"Free Enterprise and Social Justice," in *Ethics, Free Enterprise, and Public Policy: Original Essays on Moral Issues in Business,* edited by Richard T. De George and Joseph A. Pichler (New York: Oxford University Press, 1978), pp. 70–96;

Ethics and the Modern World, edited by Hospers (La Salle, Ill.: Hegeler Institute, 1984);

Descartes and His Contemporaries, edited by Hospers (La Salle, Ill.: Hegeler Institute, 1988);

"Hartshorne's Aesthetics," in *The Philosophy of Charles Hartshorne,* edited by Lewis E. Hahn, The Library of Living Philosophers, volume 20 (La Salle, Ill.: Open Court, 1991), pp. 113–134;

"What Libertarianism Is," in *Liberty for the Twenty-First Century: Contemporary Libertarian Thought,* edited by Machan and Douglas B. Rasmussen (Lanham, Md.: Rowman & Littlefield, 1995), pp. 5–17.

SELECTED PERIODICAL PUBLICATIONS–
UNCOLLECTED: "What Is Explanation?" *Journal of Philosophy,* 43 (June 1946): 337–356;

"Meaning and Free-Will," *Philosophy and Phenomenological Research,* 10 (March 1950): 307–330;

"The Concept of Artistic Expression," *Proceedings of the Aristotelian Society,* 55 (1954–1955): 313–344;

"Literature and Human Nature," *Journal of Aesthetics and Art Criticism,* 17 (September 1958): 45–57;

"Implied Truths in Literature," *Journal of Aesthetics and Art Criticism,* 19 (September 1960): 36–46;

"Baier and Medlin on Ethical Egoism," *Philosophical Studies,* 12 (January–February 1961): 10–16;

"Ethical Egoism," *Personalist,* 51 (Spring 1970): 190–195;

"Collingwood and Art Media," *Southwestern Journal of Philosophy,* 2 (Fall 1971): 43–44;

"Property," *Personalist,* 53 (Summer 1972): 263–273;

"Rule-Egoism," *Personalist,* 54 (Autumn 1973): 391–395;

"Art and Morality," *Journal of Comparative Literature and Aesthetics,* 1 (Summer 1978): 27–54;

"The Nature of the State," *Personalist,* 58 (Autumn 1978): 398–404;

"The Multiplicity of Aesthetic Criteria," *Philosophical Inquiry,* 2 (November 1979): 311–326;

"Truth and Fictional Characters," *Journal of Aesthetic Education,* 4 (July 1980): 5–17;

"Artistic Creativity," *Journal of Aesthetics and Art Criticism,* 43 (Spring 1985): 243–256;

"Humanity vs. Nature," *Liberty,* 3 (March 1990): 26–36;

"Conversations with Ayn Rand," *Liberty,* 3 (July 1990): 23–36; 4 (September 1990): 42–52;

"Some Unquestioned Assumptions," *Journal of Social Philosophy,* 22, no. 3 (1991): 42–51;

"The American Educational Establishment, 1993," *Freeman,* 43 (December 1993): 464;

"Regulation and Productivity," *Freeman,* 44 (July 1994): 373;

"Nuclear Power: Our Best Option," *Freeman,* 45 (January 1995): 40;

"A Libertarian Argument against Open Borders," *Journal of Libertarian Studies,* 13 (Summer 1998): 153–165;

"Rand's Aesthetics: A Personal View," *Journal of Ayn Rand Studies,* 2 (Spring 2001): 311–334.

John Hospers was a central figure in American ordinary-language philosophy in the twentieth century. His academic interests have mainly been in the fields of aesthetics, ethics, and social and political philosophy. Neither his life nor his writings exemplify an "ivory-tower" approach: he is also an art critic and a political activist who in 1972 ran as the first presidential candidate of the Libertarian Party.

John G. Hospers Jr. was born in Pella, Iowa, on 9 June 1918 to John and Dena Verhey Hospers. The town had been founded in the mid eighteenth century by immigrants from Holland, including Hospers's great-grandparents, who were seeking religious freedom from the Dutch Reformed state church. It was a conservative, Dutch-speaking community–Dutch was Hospers's first language–steeped in Reformed Presbyterian Christianity. Hospers's childhood study of Calvinist theology fostered his interest in philosophy–although at the time he was not aware that such a subject existed–and the history of the founding of the town gave him a sense of the importance of liberty. In the sixth grade he became fascinated with astronomy and read every article on the subject in the *World Book Encyclopedia* and every book he could find in the local library. When he entered Central College (now the Central University of Iowa) in Pella at seventeen, the dean, who taught astronomy, turned the classes over to Hospers, claiming that the freshman knew more about the subject.

Believing that opportunities for a career in astronomy were limited, and influenced by a cousin who was planning to study English at Harvard University, Hos-

pers majored in that subject. He also took the few philosophy courses that were available at the college.
Hospers already had doubts about religion based on
the problem of evil: how, he wondered, could a good
and all-powerful deity allow such suffering of human
beings and animals? David Hume's *Dialogues Concerning
Natural Religion* (1779), which he still considers the greatest book ever written on the subject, showed him that
he was not alone in having such thoughts.

Hospers graduated with a B.A. in 1939 and
earned an M.A. in English at the University of Iowa in
1941. Offered a scholarship at Columbia University, he
changed his focus to philosophy. At Columbia he studied for a year under the British analytic philosopher G. E.
Moore, who was a visiting professor. In 1944 he
received his Ph.D. in philosophy and accepted a position at Columbia as an instructor in the subject.

Hospers's dissertation was published in 1946
under the title *Meaning and Truth in the Arts*. Finding the
common notion of the "meaning" of a work of art
vague and unhelpful, Hospers stipulates his own definition: a work of art means to a person whatever effect it
evokes in that person. An evocation counts as an artistic
expression, however, only when what is expressed is
felt in, and is a quality of, the artistic object, as joy can
be felt in a piece of music. Much of the controversy
about artistic meaning revolves around the relationship
of the formal element in art—the balance, symmetry,
and organic unity in the arrangement of the parts of the
object—to its expressive content: one school of thought
limits meaning to the former and eschews talk about,
say, the sadness of a painting; a second school holds
that art is not isolated from life but makes contact with
it and expresses its values. Hospers sides with the second school.

Moving from meaning to truth, Hospers argues
that art does not primarily communicate propositional
truths. A novel set in Paris might include true statements
about the city, but such truths would only be incidental
to the work as a work of art. Artistic truths are, in Hospers's terminology, "true-to": for example, art may be
"true-to" human nature in that it reveals the universal
characteristics of the human condition; art may also be
"true-to" the felt qualities of experience, as when a poem
evokes the feeling of love. Art is true when it breaks people out of their standard ways of seeing and feeling and
makes them aware of the world in new ways. *Meaning and
Truth in the Arts* was widely recognized as an important
contribution to aesthetic theory.

In 1948 Hospers moved to the University of Minnesota as an assistant professor; he was promoted to
associate professor in 1950. That same year he published "Meaning and Free-Will," an influential article on
the perennial issue of free will versus determinism. Hos-

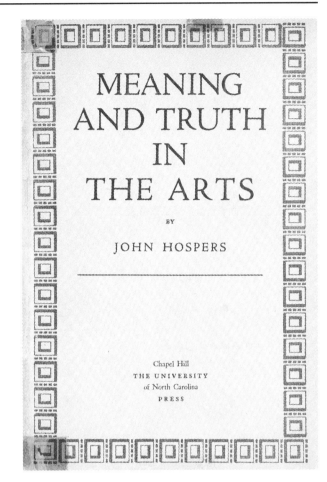

MEANING
AND TRUTH
IN
THE ARTS

BY

JOHN HOSPERS

Chapel Hill
THE UNIVERSITY
of North Carolina
PRESS

*Dust jacket for the published version (1946) of Hospers's 1944
Columbia University dissertation, which is recognized
as an important contribution to aesthetic theory
(Bruccoli Clark Layman Archives)*

pers points out that what a person does depends on his
or her character, and one's character is determined by
factors outside one's control. Furthermore, he notes,
psychoanalytic theory holds that one's conscious life is
merely a mouthpiece for the unconscious. Thus, in a
strict sense, one is not responsible for one's actions; but
punishment is still legitimate: to protect society by
removing the criminal from it, to deter other potential
criminals from committing the same actions, and to
reform the offender. Hospers was widely understood as
upholding "hard determinism," the position that all
human actions are the result of causative factors and
that free will is illusory. Hospers, however, contends
that people are free to do what they want, but what
they want to do is not a matter of their free choice. He
does not claim that all human actions are determined
but that, often, what people take to be a free act is actually determined by character or by unconscious drives.

In 1953 Hospers published *An Introduction to Philosophical Analysis,* his major work in ordinary-language

AN
INTRODUCTION
TO
PHILOSOPHICAL
ANALYSIS

John Hospers

*Associate Professor of Philosophy
University of Minnesota*

*Dust jacket for Hospers's 1953 book, which was largely responsible for
acquainting American philosophers with the ordinary-language
approach (Bruccoli Clark Layman Archives)*

philosophy. By 2003 the book had gone through four revised editions and sold more than one hundred thousand copies. The ordinary-language approach, which had risen to prominence in England in the 1940s and was inspired by the ideas of Moore, Ludwig Wittgenstein, Gilbert Ryle, J. L. Austin, Norman Malcolm, and John Wisdom, holds that attention to everyday discourse can enable one to clarify philosophical problems and, sometimes, to show that they are not problems at all but result from the misuse of words. The one-hundred-page first chapter, "Words and the World," is devoted to the clarification of meaning and the nature of definition. The remainder of the work applies the techniques of ordinary-language philosophy to traditional issues such as free will versus determinism, causation, religion, the nature of truth, and knowledge of the external world. For example, if one were trying to understand the nature of moral duty, an ordinary-language

approach would focus on the use of the phrase "moral duty" in day-to-day talk. Certain facts about the ordinary use of "moral duty" would become apparent: moral duties are more binding than legal duties, and the former are associated with deeper, more pervasive forms of social shame and praise than the latter; if one has a moral duty, then one has the responsibility to perform some action (for example, keeping a promise) in regard to someone (for example, to keep one's promise to a specific individual or group); if one has a moral duty, then one has the ability to perform that duty, and there can be no external constraints on the person who attempts to honor the duty; and a duty is always correlated with a rule that universalizes that duty. Under the ordinary-language approach, philosophical analyses of an issue should preserve its ordinary-language usage when possible and not revise it in the interests of some philosophical agenda—for example, it should not reduce moral language to mere expressions of emotions in keeping with the logical positivist criterion that only propositions verifiable by the five senses are true or false and that since moral assertions cannot be so verified, they are neither true nor false but are mere expressions of emotion. The importance of the book lies less in the topics treated or the conclusions reached, however, than in its exemplification of ordinary-language techniques. The work was largely responsible for introducing a generation of American philosophers to the ordinary-language approach.

In 1956 Hospers left the University of Minnesota to become a full professor at Brooklyn College of the City University of New York. He was a visiting professor at the University of California, Los Angeles, in 1960–1961. After returning to New York he met Ayn Rand, the author of the philosophical novels *The Fountainhead* (1943)—for which she also wrote the screenplay for the 1949 movie adaptation—and *Atlas Shrugged* (1957) and the nonfiction *For the New Intellectual: The Philosophy of Ayn Rand* (1961). Hospers said in a 1998 interview that at the time he encountered Rand he was suffering from philosophical "tired blood," but "She renewed my confidence in my profession." In discussions in her apartment that often lasted from the evening into the early morning, as well as in their correspondence, he challenged some of her ideas; such effrontery usually resulted in the offender being banished from her circle, but she tolerated and even welcomed criticism from Hospers. Hospers was never part of the "Objectivist" cult that grew up around Rand, but her influence was decisive in moving him toward the libertarian position in political philosophy.

In 1961 Hospers published *Human Conduct: An Introduction to the Problems of Ethics,* which was widely adopted as a textbook. The work is characterized by a

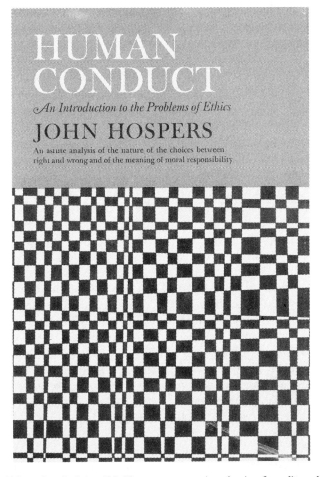

Dust jacket for the widely used textbook in which Hospers surveys various theories of morality and advocates a modified hedonism according to which the value of an action or object depends on whether it contributes to the production of happiness (Bruccoli Clark Layman Archives)

realistic approach to the moral life and a readable, almost novel-like literary style. It deals with a wide range of topics, including theories of the good; the nature of moral responsibility; egoistic, utilitarian, and deontological (duty-based) ethical theories; rights; justice; and morality and the state. Hospers himself advocates a modified hedonism similar to that of the nineteenth-century British utilitarian John Stuart Mill, according to which the value of an action or object depends on whether it contributes to the production of happiness. Critics of this view claim that some things, such as knowledge, have intrinsic value irrespective of their connection with happiness.

Human Conduct appeared at a time when rule utilitarianism was being distinguished from act utilitarianism. Both forms of utilitarianism aim at producing the most happiness and the least suffering for the greatest number of sentient beings; but while act utilitarianism focuses on the consequences of particular actions, rule utilitarianism endeavors to formulate a system of moral rules that would promote happiness if generally followed. While

Hospers does not advocate either form of utilitarianism, his discussion of rule utilitarianism in *Human Conduct* was a major contribution to the development and dissemination of that mode of moral reasoning.

A controversial aspect of the book was Hospers's treatment of a fundamental question of ethics that dates back at least to Plato's *Republic:* "Why should I be moral?" For Hospers the answer is not that God commands one to be moral, that morality pays, or any other external motivation; the answer is that one should be moral simply because being moral is the right thing to do. Critics such as Kai Nielsen have claimed that Hospers misunderstands the question, thinking that it is being asked from within "the moral point of view" itself; so understood, it requires a moral reason for accepting moral reasons. But, Nielsen argues, the question is actually seeking a rational justification of the moral point of view itself. To adopt that point of view and assert that it is right to be moral is, thus, to beg the question.

In 1966 Hospers moved to California State University at Los Angeles and two years later to the University of Southern California, where, in addition to teaching, he served as director of the School of Philosophy until 1974 and as editor of the journal *The Personalist* (in 1978 the journal changed its name to *Pacific Philosophical Quarterly;* Hospers continued as editor until 1984).

In 1971 Hospers published *Libertarianism: A Political Philosophy for Tomorrow,* which remains one of the definitive statements of the libertarian political philosophy. Hospers argues that government is the hired servant of the people and that its sole legitimate function is to protect individuals' natural rights to life, liberty, and property from infringement by direct physical interference, or the threat of such interference, by other individuals. According to Hospers, these rights are "negative" ones–that is, they impose a duty on others to refrain from acting in certain ways. Alleged "positive rights," such as rights to a guaranteed income, medical care, or education, would impose duties on others to act in certain ways and would, in effect, make them the slaves of the person who claimed the rights. Further, only individuals have rights, because only individuals exist: collectivist notions such as "the common good," "the people," "society," and "public ownership" are vacuous. Accordingly, the government ought to be limited to operating the courts and penal system and maintaining police and military forces. Laws against such "victimless crimes" as prostitution, pornography, gambling, and the taking of "illicit" drugs–activities in which people engage voluntarily–should be repealed; only actions that harm others against their will should be punishable.

The only economic system compatible with liberty is free-market capitalism, a system of voluntary exchange; it is also the only system that guarantees prosperity. Socialism, on the other hand, is an immoral system that violates individual rights and an inefficient one that will lead to a lower standard of living for all except the bureaucrats who operate it. To those who say that government should subsidize art and culture and sports stadiums, Hospers replies: let those who enjoy such things support them with their own money. Taxation is equivalent to robbery, since it involves taking the citizen's money through the threat of force and using it for purposes that he or she has not chosen to support. Welfare not only violates the rights of those who are taxed to fund it but also ultimately harms everyone by making the poor dependent and removing their incentive to work and contribute to the general prosperity; in addition, a portion of the money is siphoned off to pay the bureaucrats who run the tax and welfare systems. To the objection that libertarianism has no compassion for the poor and no way to help them, Hospers responds that most poverty is caused by such government interventions in the market as minimum-

wage laws, price controls, and occupational licensing and that what remained after these distortions were removed could easily be dealt with by private charity. In a libertarian society functions such as roads, coinage, and education would be provided by private enterprise; when government manages these functions, they are inefficient and inherently coercive.

In the same year that Hospers's book appeared, the Libertarian Party was founded in Colorado; Hospers and others started a California branch of the party shortly thereafter. At the national convention in Denver in June 1972 Hospers was nominated as the party's first candidate for president of the United States. He campaigned widely against Republican Richard M. Nixon and Democrat George S. McGovern, and he and his running mate, Theodora "Toni" Nathan, received 3,673 votes and one electoral vote cast by a disillusioned Nixon elector in Virginia (that elector, Roger Lea McBride, became the Libertarian presidential candidate in 1976)–and helped bring national attention to libertarian ideas.

Hospers's 1973 article "Rule-Egoism" outlines the ethical basis for his libertarian political philosophy. Rejected by most philosophers but defended by a few, such as the ancient Epicurean school, Thomas Hobbes in the seventeenth century, and Rand in the twentieth century, ethical egoism is the principle that each individual should strive to advance his or her best long-term interests. Like utilitarianism, it is a consequentialist theory, in that it makes the rightness or wrongness of an action dependent on its consequences or results; deontological theories, in contrast, maintain that certain actions are right or wrong in themselves, regardless of the consequences to which they lead. Egoism differs from utilitarianism, however, in that the latter takes overall well-being, not just that of the agent, as the goal at which one ought to aim. Like utilitarianism, egoism takes both "act" and "rule" forms. According to act egoism, an act is morally right if no alternative act has better consequences for the agent's self-interest. Act egoism and act utilitarianism are open to the objection that, for instance, they would hold stealing or lying to be morally acceptable–even obligatory–if such acts advance the agent's self-interest or the general happiness, respectively. Hospers argues that certain rules, such as "Do not steal" or "Be beneficent in dealings with others," would be in everyone's self-interest if they were generally followed. Such rules, therefore, ought to be adopted. To the objection that rule egoism would collapse into act egoism if one were faced with a situation in which following a rule would not, in fact, advance one's self-interest, Hospers responds that abandoning the rules would lead to chaos and behavioral unpredictability, which would not be in anyone's self-interest.

*Cover for Hospers's 1971 anthology of articles on aesthetics by literary authors, philosophers, and artists
(Thomas Cooper Library, University of South Carolina)*

In the monograph *Anarchy or Limited Government?* (1982) Hospers responds to objections to his limited-government version of libertarianism raised by more-extreme libertarians who call themselves anarchists or anarchocapitalists and favor no government at all. They claim that the monopolization of force by the state is morally unjustifiable and that even the courts, the police, and the military would be more efficiently run by the private sector. Hospers responds that to be effective in protecting individual rights, laws must be uniform throughout a geographical area and enforced by a single entity–the state.

In 1982 Hospers published *Understanding the Arts*, which became a widely used textbook in aesthetics. Hospers discusses the nature of a work of art; how to classify the arts; the role of form, representation, expression, and truth in the arts; and the relationship between art and morality. *Understanding the Arts* includes a developed statement of Hospers's chief contribution to the field, his theory of artistic expression. He rejects

views, such as those of Benedetto Croce and R. G. Collingwood, according to which artistic expression is a process in the artist's mind; for Hospers, expression is a feature of the work of art itself, not of the artist. For example, by being slow, low, or soft, music can express sadness just as a person's facial features can. In art, all qualities, such as sound or color, are suffused with affect or "feeling-tone." Aesthetic qualities are objective, relational properties of works of art.

Hospers assumed emeritus status at the University of Southern California in 1988; he continues to teach part-time at UCLA and other colleges in the Los Angeles area. Hospers has also continued to write, mostly for the libertarian magazines *The Freeman*, *Liberty*, and *Reason*. In 1991 the Libertarian Party of Los Angeles County honored Hospers with its Champion of Freedom Award, presented to an individual who has made an outstanding contribution to the cause of liberty.

Hospers is still highly regarded for his contributions to aesthetics, ordinary-language philosophy, and ethics. Most philosophers, however, tend to be of the left politically and have little respect for Hospers's libertarian views; they much prefer the welfare-state liberalism of John Rawls's *A Theory of Justice,* which was published the same year as Hospers's *Libertarianism.* Hospers's work was, in any case, overshadowed by the publication in 1974 of Robert Nozick's *Anarchy, State, and Utopia,* which advocated the same sort of limited-government libertarianism as Hospers had but met Rawls on his own ground by using sophisticated arguments drawn from decision theory. As a result, Nozick became the target of attacks on libertarianism, and Hospers's book tended to be ignored.

Interview:

Karen Minto, "Interview with John Hospers," *Full Context,* 10 (May 1998).

References:

Robert Berg, "Rule-Egoism?" *Personalist,* 60 (April 1979): 211–215;

Myron Brendon, "Hospers on Psychoanalysis: A Critique," *Philosophy of Science,* 32 (January 1965): 73–83;

Donald Burrill, "The Rule-Egoism Principle," *Personalist,* 57 (Autumn 1976): 408–410;

Peter A. Carmichael, "Collingwood and Art Media," *Southwestern Journal of Philosophy,* 2 (Spring–Summer 1971): 37–42;

F. F. Centore, "Hospers' Understanding of 'Necessary Being,'" *New Scholasticism,* 43 (Summer 1969): 449–453;

Alan Donagan, "The Croce-Collingwood Theory of Art," *Philosophy,* 33 (April 1958): 162–167;

Antony Flew, "Splitting Hairs before Starting Hares," *Personalist,* 53 (Winter 1972): 84–93;

Gary L. Foulk, "The Relation between Normative Ethics and Metaethics," *Personalist,* 54 (Spring 1973): 171–175;

W. Dwaine Greer, "Hospers on Artistic Creativity," *Journal of Aesthetic Education,* 20 (Winter 1986): 62–64;

Richard G. Henson, "Responsibility for Character and Responsibility for Conduct," *Australasian Journal of Philosophy,* 43 (December 1965): 311–320;

Bernard C. Heyl, "Artistic Truth Reconsidered," *Journal of Aesthetics and Art Criticism,* 9 (January 1950): 251–258;

Daniel Kading and Martin Kramer, "Mr. Hospers' Defense of Impersonal Egoism," *Philosophical Studies,* 15 (1964): 44–45;

John Nelson, "Hospers' 'Ultimate Moral Equality,'" *Reason Papers,* 13 (Spring 1988): 35–47;

Kai Nielsen, "On Being Moral," *Philosophical Studies,* 16 (1965): 1–3;

Mary Sirridge, "Hospers on the Artist's Intentions," *Reason Papers,* 13 (Spring 1988): 143–151;

Charles Taliaferro, "The Ideal Aesthetic Observer Revisited," *British Journal of Aesthetics,* 30 (January 1990): 1–13;

Arnulf Zweig, "The Questions We Ask," *Personalist,* 59 (October 1978): 410–414.

Papers:

A collection of John Hospers's papers from 1971 to 1974 is at the University of Virginia Library.

Walter Kaufmann
(1 July 1921 – 4 September 1980)

Walter W. Ross

BOOKS: *Nietzsche: Philosopher, Psychologist, Antichrist* (Princeton: Princeton University Press, 1950; revised edition, New York: Meridian, 1956; revised and enlarged edition, Princeton: Princeton University Press, 1968; revised, 1974);

Critique of Religion and Philosophy (New York: Harper, 1958; London: Faber & Faber, 1959; republished with a new preface, Princeton: Princeton University Press, 1978);

From Shakespeare to Existentialism: Studies in Poetry, Religion, and Philosophy (Boston: Beacon, 1959; enlarged edition, Garden City, N.Y.: Doubleday, 1960); republished as *The Owl and the Nightingale: From Shakespeare to Existentialism* (London: Weidenfeld & Nicolson, 1960); republished, with a new introduction by Kaufmann, as *From Shakespeare to Existentialism: An Original Study: Essays on Shakespeare and Goethe, Hegel and Kierkegaard, Nietzsche, Rilke, and Freud, Jaspers, Heidegger, and Toynbee* (Princeton: Princeton University Press, 1980);

The Faith of a Heretic (Garden City, N.Y.: Doubleday, 1961; republished with a new introduction, New York: New American Library, 1978);

Cain and Other Poems (Garden City, N.Y.: Doubleday, 1962; enlarged edition, New York: Vintage, 1971);

Hegel: Reinterpretation, Texts, and Commentary (Garden City, N.Y.: Doubleday, 1965; London: Weidenfeld & Nicolson, 1966);

Tragedy and Philosophy (Garden City, N.Y.: Doubleday, 1968; republished with a new introduction, Princeton: Princeton University Press, 1979);

Without Guilt and Justice: From Decidophobia to Autonomy (New York: Wyden, 1973);

Religions in Four Dimensions: Existential and Aesthetic, Historical and Comparative (New York: Reader's Digest Press, 1976);

Existentialism, Religion, and Death: Thirteen Essays (New York: New American Library, 1976);

The Future of the Humanities (New York: Reader's Digest Press, 1977);

Walter Kaufmann (from the dust jacket for Discovering the Mind, *1980)*

Man's Lot: A Trilogy. Photographs and Text, 3 volumes (New York: Reader's Digest Press, distributed by McGraw-Hill, 1978)—comprises *Life at the Limits, Time Is an Artist,* and *What Is Man?;*

Discovering the Mind, 3 volumes (New York: McGraw-Hill, 1980)—comprises volume 1, *Goethe, Kant, and Hegel;* volume 2, *Nietzsche, Heidegger, and Buber;* and volume 3, *Freud versus Adler and Jung.*

RECORDINGS: *Oedipus Rex,* lecture by Kaufmann, Norton 23116, 1963;

Aeschylus and the Death of Tragedy, lecture by Kaufmann, Norton, 1963;

The Will to Power Re-examined, discussion by Kaufmann, Denis O'Donovan, Heinz Ludwig Ansbacher, and Helene Papanek, Big Sur 648, 1972;

Existentialism: Sartre, Jaspers, Heidegger, Kierkegaard, lecture by Kaufmann, Center for Cassette Studies, 1973.

OTHER: *Existentialism from Dostoevsky to Sartre,* edited and translated by Kaufmann (New York: Meridian, 1956; London: Thames & Hudson, 1957; revised and enlarged edition, New York: New American Library, 1975);

"Existentialism and Death," in *The Meaning of Death,* edited by Herman Feifel (New York: McGraw-Hill, 1959), pp. 39–63;

Malcolm Hay, *Europe and the Jews: The Pressure of Christendom on the People of Israel for 1900 Years,* preface by Kaufmann (Boston: Beacon, 1960);

Philosophic Classics: Basic Texts, 2 volumes, edited by Kaufmann (Englewood Cliffs, N.J.: Prentice-Hall, 1961; revised, 1968)—comprises volume 1, *Thales to Saint Thomas;* revised as *Thales to Ockham;* volume 2, *Bacon to Kant;*

Religion from Tolstoy to Camus, edited by Kaufmann (New York: Harper, 1961; enlarged, 1964);

Søren Kierkegaard, *The Present Age; and, Of the Difference between a Genius and an Apostle,* translated by Alexander Dru, introduction by Kaufmann (New York: Harper, 1962);

"Educational Development from the Point of View of a Normative Philosophy," in *Philosophy and Educational Development,* edited by George Barnett (Boston: Houghton Mifflin, 1966), pp. 23–45;

"Literature and Reality," in *Art and Philosophy,* edited by Sidney Hook (New York: New York University Press, 1966), pp. 250–261;

"Nietzsche, Friedrich," in *The Encyclopedia of Philosophy,* volume 5, edited by Paul Edwards (New York: Macmillan & The Free Press / London: Collier-Macmillan, 1967), pp. 504–514;

Rudolph Binion, *Frau Lou: Nietzsche's Wayward Disciple,* foreword by Kaufmann (Princeton: Princeton University Press, 1968);

Ivan Soll, *An Introduction to Hegel's Metaphysics,* foreword by Kaufmann (Chicago: University of Chicago Press, 1969);

"The Hegel Myth and Its Method," in *Hegel's Political Philosophy,* edited by Kaufmann (New York: Atherton, 1970), pp. 137–171;

Richard Schacht, *Alienation,* introductory essay by Kaufmann (Garden City, N.Y.: Doubleday, 1970; London: Allen & Unwin, 1971);

John T. Wilcox, *Truth and Value in Nietzsche: A Study of His Metaphysics and Epistemology,* foreword by Kaufmann (Ann Arbor: University of Michigan Press, 1974);

"Hegel's Conception of Phenomenology," in *Phenomenology and Philosophical Understanding,* edited by Edo Pivčević (Cambridge: Cambridge University Press, 1975), pp. 211–230;

Philosophy and Truth: Selections from Nietzsche's Notebooks of the Early 1870's, edited and translated by Daniel Breazeale, foreword by Kaufmann (Atlantic Highlands, N.J.: Humanities Press, 1979).

TRANSLATIONS: *The Portable Nietzsche,* edited and translated by Kaufmann (New York: Viking, 1954; London: Chatto & Windus, 1971);

Leo Baeck, *Judaism and Christianity: Essays* (Philadelphia: Jewish Publication Society of America, 1958);

Johann Wolfgang von Goethe, *Goethe's Faust: The Original German and a New Translation. Part One and Sections from Part Two* (Garden City, N.Y.: Doubleday, 1961);

Twenty German Poets: A Bilingual Collection (New York: Random House, 1962); revised and enlarged as *Twenty-five German Poets: A Bilingual Collection* (New York: Norton, 1975);

Friedrich Nietzsche, *Beyond Good and Evil: Prelude to a Philosophy of the Future,* translated with commentaries by Kaufmann (New York: Vintage, 1966);

Nietzsche, *Thus Spoke Zarathustra: A Book for All and None* (New York: Viking, 1966);

Nietzsche, *The Birth of Tragedy, and The Case of Wagner,* translated with commentary by Kaufmann (New York: Vintage, 1966);

Nietzsche, *On the Genealogy of Morals; Ecce homo,* edited with commentary by Kaufmann (New York: Vintage, 1967)—*On the Genealogy of Morals* translated by Kaufmann and R. J. Hollingdale; *Ecce homo* translated by Kaufmann;

Nietzsche, *The Will to Power: A New Translation,* translated by Kaufmann and Hollingdale, edited with commentary by Kaufmann (New York: Vintage, 1967; London: Weidenfeld & Nicolson, 1968);

Basic Writings of Nietzsche (New York: Modern Library, 1968); republished with introduction by Peter Gay (New York: Modern Library, 2000);

Martin Buber, *I and Thou: A New Translation* (New York: Scribners, 1970; Edinburgh: Clark, 1970)—includes a prologue, "I and You," by Kaufmann, pp. 9–48;

Nietzsche, *The Gay Science: With a Prelude in Rhymes and an Appendix of Songs,* translated with commentary by Kaufmann (New York: Vintage, 1974).

SELECTED PERIODICAL PUBLICATIONS—UNCOLLECTED: "Faust and Jacob," *Germanic Review,* 26 (April 1951): 124;

"Nietzsche and the Seven Sirens," *Partisan Review,* 19 (May–June 1952): 372–376;

"Existentialism Tamed," *Kenyon Review,* 16 (Summer 1954): 486–490;

"The Stature of Martin Buber," *Commentary,* 26 (October 1958): 355–359;

"Nietzsche and Existentialism," *Symposium,* 28 (Spring 1974): 7–16.

Walter Kaufmann was one of the leading authorities on the philosophy of Friedrich Nietzsche. Many scholars consider his *Nietzsche: Philosopher, Psychologist, Antichrist* (1950) the most profound interpretation of the German thinker ever written; the historian of ideas Peter Gay says of it in his introduction to the 2000 edition of Kaufmann's *Basic Writings of Nietzsche* (1968) that "in the course of the twentieth century no American academic study has had a wider, and more fully deserved, impact." Kaufmann also translated many of Nietzsche's works, and his *The Portable Nietzsche* (1954) had the largest sales of any of the volumes in the Portable Viking series. His 1961 translation of Johann Wolfgang von Goethe's *Faust* (1808, 1832) and his 1970 translation of Martin Buber's *Ich und Du* (1923) as *I and Thou* are widely considered to be unexcelled. In addition to Nietzsche, Kaufmann wrote extensively on the German idealist philosopher Georg Wilhelm Friedrich Hegel and introduced English-speaking readers to existentialism. Beyond such scholarly endeavors in exegesis and translation, Kaufmann also did important original work in philosophy, particularly in the philosophy of religion and ethics.

Walter Arnold Kaufmann was born in Freiburg, Germany, on 1 July 1921 to Bruno Paul Kaufmann, a lawyer, and Edith Seligsohn Kaufmann. He grew up in Berlin. At eleven, because of doubts concerning the Holy Trinity and the divinity of Jesus, he converted from Lutheranism to Judaism. Kaufmann recalls in *The Faith of a Heretic* (1961) that his parents pleaded with him to reconsider, since the Nazis were then coming to power in Germany—Adolf Hitler became chancellor in 1933—but "I insisted that one could not change one's mind for a reason like that."

In the spring of 1938 Kaufmann graduated from the gymnasium in Berlin and entered the Academy for the Science of Judaism, where he studied under Leo Baeck and began reading the Talmud in Hebrew. In January 1939 he immigrated to the United States and enrolled at Williams College, planning to become a rabbi. Kaufmann's father was interned in a concentration camp but released on the condition that he leave the country, and both parents spent the World War II years in London.

Since Williams did not offer a major in religion, Kaufmann chose philosophy as the nearest alternative. James Bissett Pratt, whom Kaufmann always regarded as

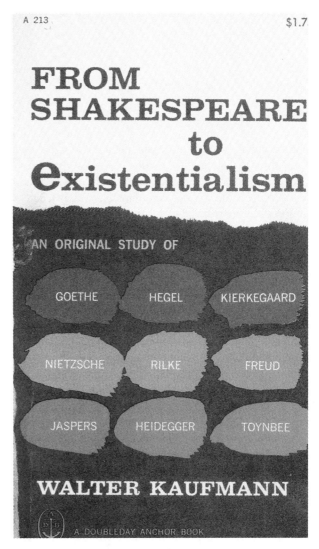

A 213 $1.7

FROM SHAKESPEARE to existentialism

AN ORIGINAL STUDY OF

GOETHE   HEGEL   KIERKEGAARD

NIETZSCHE   RILKE   FREUD

JASPERS   HEIDEGGER   TOYNBEE

WALTER KAUFMANN

A DOUBLEDAY ANCHOR BOOK

Cover for the enlarged 1960 edition of Kaufmann's collection of articles on writers who were able to rise above the obstacles placed in their way by the eras in which they lived and produce great works (Thomas Cooper Library, University of South Carolina)

the most influential teacher he had in college or graduate school, introduced him to Eastern religions. Kaufmann graduated Phi Beta Kappa in 1941, entered Harvard University on a fellowship, and received his M.A. in 1942. That year he married Hazel Irene Dennis. Their first child, Dinah Hazel, was born in 1944. Also in 1944 Kaufmann interrupted his studies for the Ph.D. to join the army, serving in military intelligence and spending fifteen months in Germany. He returned to Harvard on a scholarship in 1946. In 1947 he earned his Ph.D. with a dissertation on Nietzsche's theory of values and took a job as an instructor at Princeton University. His and his wife's second child, David Felix, was born in 1947. Kaufmann was promoted to assistant professor in 1950.

Kaufmann's first book, *Nietzsche: Philosopher, Psychologist, Antichrist,* appeared in 1950. The German philosopher was in eclipse in the English-speaking world, and misunderstandings abounded regarding his philosophy. Kaufmann shows that an erroneous legend about Nietzsche had been propagated chiefly by the philosopher's sister, Elizabeth Förster-Nietzsche. After her brother lapsed into insanity in 1889, she acquired control over his writings and restricted access to them by scholars. Although she had only a rudimentary knowledge of philosophy, she rearranged the texts and made additions and deletions that often rendered the meanings the opposite of what Nietzsche had intended. Nietzsche's autobiography, *Ecce homo* (translated, 1911), had clarified many of his ideas, but Förster-Nietzsche had deliberately delayed publication of it until 1908–eight years after Nietzsche's death–and then published it only in an expensive edition that was out of the reach of many scholars. She added further confusion by passing off Nietzsche's desultory notes and musings, often made while hiking in the Alps or elsewhere, as his finished thoughts on a subject. Her meddling, Kaufmann demonstrates, produced an impression that Nietzsche's philosophy was incoherent and riddled with contradictions. She also made him appear to be an anti-Semite, as she and her husband, in fact, were, but Nietzsche was not, and a glorifier of German culture, when he was actually harshly critical of it. These distortions allowed the Nazis to adopt Nietzsche as a "house philosopher."

Drawing on the Förster-Nietzsche "scholarship," Kaufmann notes, the writers Stefan George and Ernst Bertram solidified the Nietzsche legend. George developed a highly personal and romantic image of Nietzsche, often misinterpreting his meaning and never addressing his overall philosophy. George's disciples, known as the George Circle, perpetuated their master's ideas in books, articles, and lectures. Leaning on the writings of the George Circle, Bertram added to the myth in his influential *Nietzsche: Versuch einer Mythologie* (Nietzsche: Test of a Mythology, 1918), which went through seven editions. In Bertram's view, Nietzsche's insanity resulted from loneliness and dejection, an agony comparable in Bertram's mind to the intensity of Christ's crucifixion. Like George, Bertram emphasized Nietzsche's contradictions.

Challenging the established view, Kaufmann contends that Nietzsche thought of himself first and foremost as a philosopher in the Western tradition of Plato and Aristotle. But, he says, Nietzsche was also a profound psychologist, and he cites Sigmund Freud's comments that "he had a more penetrating knowledge of himself than any other man who ever lived or who was ever likely to live" and that many of Freud's own psychoana-

lytical theories were prefigured in Nietzsche's writings. Finally, Nietzsche was an "Antichrist" in that he was an outspoken critic of Christianity's endorsement of meekness and pity as virtues, its emphasis on the afterlife at the expense of the earthly one, its condemnation of sex as sinful, and its valuing of faith over reason. Kaufmann notes that the many specialized studies of Nietzsche's relationship to existentialism, analytic philosophy, Goethe, and so on have failed to arrive at an understanding of Nietzsche's general philosophy. What is needed, he says, is a total reconstruction of that philosophy: "Nietzsche's books are easier to read but harder to understand than those of almost any other thinker. . . . we find that practically every sentence and every page of his writings presents far less trouble than the involved and technical periods of Kant, Hegel, and even Schopenhauer"; yet, "it is perhaps easier to form an opinion of the general meaning of Kant's *Critique of Pure Reason* than to grasp the precise significance of any number of sentences in that work–while in Nietzsche's books the individual sentences seem clear enough and it is the total design that puzzles us." The essence of Nietzsche's thought cannot be found in any one of his works, Kaufmann says; instead, the development of his philosophy must be traced over a period of seventeen years, beginning with *Die Geburt der Tragödie* (1872; revised, 1874; revised, 1886; translated as *The Birth of Tragedy,* 1909), written in 1871, and ending with *Ecce homo,* written in 1888. Nietzsche himself, Kaufmann points out, had said in his *Zur Genealogie der Moral* (1887; translated as *The Genealogy of Morals,* 1910), "If this writing is incomprehensible for anybody or will not go into his head, the fault it seems to me is not necessarily mine. It is plain enough, assuming–as I do assume–that one has first read my earlier writings and not spared some trouble in doing this."

At the core of Nietzsche's philosophy Kaufmann finds the "will to power," a concept that is applicable not only to human beings but also to all of nature. Some earlier scholars, he notes, had argued that the will to power is central to Nietzsche's thought, but they believed that he had confined the idea to the military and political spheres. In his early writings Nietzsche places little emphasis on power, and when he does allude to it, he does so negatively: power is identified with unbridled ambition, the attainment of worldly success at the expense of one's personality, or the amassing of wealth. But in the late 1870s Nietzsche discovered that in ancient Greek civilization power was regarded as a positive force. Nietzsche sees manifestations of power in all elements of Greek life, including the Olympic games, the depiction of Socrates in Plato's dialogues, and the competition of playwrights such as Euripides, Sophocles, and Aristophanes for literary prizes. The discovery of this principle in classical antiquity, Kaufmann argues, was the turning point in Nietzsche's thought that finds fruition in his major work, *Also sprach Zarathustra: Ein Buch für Alle und Keinen* (1883–1885; translated as *Thus Spake Zarathustra: A Book for All and None*, 1896).

Because of the importance and complexity of the will to power, Kaufmann devotes three chapters to a close study of the concept. Inherent in it, he says, is the element of self-overcoming, which is manifested in the transformation of raw impulses into art and literature by the force of reason:

> Reason and the sex drive are both forms of the will to power. The sex drive, however, is an impulse, and in yielding to it in its unsublimated form, man is still the slave of his passions and has no power over them. Rationality, on the other hand, gives man mastery over himself. . . . Reason is the "highest" manifestation of the will to power, in the distinct sense that through rationality it can realize its objective most fully.

Kaufmann argues that admirers of Nietzsche such as Bertram and George erred in labeling him an irrationalist, as did scholars who claimed that Freud had first used the term *sublimation* in its modern form when the credit should have gone to Nietzsche. Self-overcoming is achieved by the rare individual who, through constant inner striving, achieves the status of the *Übermensch* (Overman; frequently mistranslated as "Superman"), a higher level of existence evident in such figures as Socrates, Leonardo da Vinci, and Goethe. The Overman is a person who has attained near perfection and would gladly welcome the "eternal recurrence"–another famous Nietzschean concept, according to which each person is fated to relive his or her life in all of its details, including the misery and suffering, over and over again forever.

Kaufmann not only restores the will to power to the center of Nietzsche's philosophy but also introduces a revolutionary view concerning Nietzsche's interpretation of Socrates. For decades Nietzsche scholars had claimed that he had all but repudiated Socrates or that, at best, his position on the Greek philosopher was ambiguous. Having reread everything Nietzsche wrote on the subject, Kaufmann asserts that from beginning to end Nietzsche regarded Socrates in a positive light and even viewed the Athenian gadfly as the model for his own philosophy. Without the example of Socrates and his famous epigram that the "unexamined life is not worth living," Nietzsche believed, the whole course of Western civilization would have been different.

Ultimately, the philosophy Kaufmann finds in Nietzsche's writings resembles the ideals of the Founding Fathers of the United States. Nietzsche, he says, stressed the good life, took a dim view of those who yearned for the afterlife at the expense of the here and now, and urged the individual to become all that he or she could be.

Dust jacket for Kaufmann's 1961 book, in which he elaborates his concept of an "ethic of openness" (Reason Alone Books)

In the 1950s Kaufmann wrote many articles for such journals as *Partisan Review, Kenyon Review, Commentary,* and *The Philosophical Review.* He was promoted to associate professor in 1954. In 1956 he contributed entries on Goethe and Nietzsche to the *Encyclopedia of Morals* and edited the anthology *Existentialism from Dostoevsky to Sartre.* The latter work, which included a forty-page introduction and new translations of writings by such key figures as Nietzsche, Søren Kierkegaard, Jean-Paul Sartre, Martin Heidegger, and Karl Jaspers, introduced existentialism to the educated American public.

Kaufmann's next major work, *Critique of Religion and Philosophy* (1958), is a sustained polemic on philosophers from Plato to G. E. Moore and theologians from St. Thomas Aquinas to Paul Tillich; as he says in the introduction, the subtitle of the work could have been "The Need for Negative Thinking." No thinker is studied comprehensively; Kaufmann's goal is to focus on one or two points of each subject's thought: "To present everything is impossible; but one can present several images, each boldly etched to bring out what truth there is in it, untouched, as sharp as possible."

The first fourth of the book deals with philosophy. Plato's doctrine of the Forms, William James's pragmatism, and the psychologist Erich Fromm's humanism are all found wanting. Kaufmann treats positivism, or analytic philosophy, and existentialism at some length, not only because they are the dominant philosophies of the twentieth century but also because, he says, features of each can be found in philosophies from the earliest times. Using Socrates as a model of the ideal philosopher, Kaufmann finds both positivism and existentialism incomplete. Positivists such as Moore and Rudolf Carnap are rigorous in their methodology; but the subject matter to which they apply it is confined to trivialities such as everyday language and symbols, while themes such as theodicy, morality, and determinism versus free will are ignored. Existentialists, on the other hand, are preoccupied with such vital issues as dread, the absurdity of life, and suffering but fail to address these problems with precision. Kierkegaard, often regarded as a protoexistentialist, upheld subjectivity over close reasoning and endorsed the "leap of faith."

The rest of *Critique of Religion and Philosophy* deals with Judaism, Buddhism, and Christianity; lack of space forced Kaufmann to omit Hinduism from consideration. All religions, Kaufmann argues, are deficient to the extent that truth is relegated to a secondary role. In Buddhism, salvation and detachment from the things of this world are of paramount importance. In Zen Buddhism "The experience of a good slap is more substantial than all speculation." Truth in Judaism is relevant only within its own tradition and chosen texts; what is of supreme value in this faith is a way of life.

Christianity is given the most extensive and most negative treatment as Kaufmann attacks St. Paul, Aquinas, Martin Luther, Reinhold Niebuhr, and Harry Emerson Fosdick. He holds Luther up as the archenemy of reason, supporting the charge with such quotations from the writings of the Reformation leader as "Whoever wants to be a Christian should tear the eyes out of his reason" and "You must part with reason and not know anything of it and even kill it; else one will not get into the kingdom of heaven."

Kaufmann summarizes the seventeenth-century French philosopher and mathematician Blaise Pascal's "wager" argument for belief in the existence of God: "If we wager that God exists and we are right, we win everything; if we are wrong we lose nothing. . . . Anybody who is not out of his mind will bet that God exists." Pascal, says Kaufmann, has overlooked the possibility that "God might punish those whose faith is prompted by prudence. Perhaps God prefers the abstinent to those who whore around with some denomination he despises.

Perhaps he reserves special rewards for those who deny themselves the comfort of belief. Perhaps the intellectual ascetic will win all while those who compromised their intellectual integrity lose everything."

Kaufmann takes issue with the nineteenth-century Liberal Protestant movement, which claimed that the true message of Christianity—charity—is elucidated in the four Gospels. According to Kaufmann, this interpretation ignores 1,900 years of history, including the perennial schisms in church councils over dogma and the sacraments. Only in the last 150 years, he says, has love become a central tenet of Christianity.

In the end, drawing on his former teacher Baeck, Kaufmann declares that whatever cannot be criticized in religion is not worth having and that aspiration is at the heart of religion. But an anonymous reviewer in *The Times Literary Supplement* (31 July 1959) asked, "aspiration for what?" and went on to comment: "In Victorian times we might have been content to praise Professor Kaufmann not only for his vigorous style but as a genuine seeker after truth. But there have been too many seekers after truth who have found nothing, and the phrase has gone bad on us. We ask for something more from a contemporary writer on the philosophy of religion." The review made such an impression on Kaufmann that he wrote *The Faith of a Heretic* partly as a response to the reviewer's challenge.

From Shakespeare to Existentialism: Studies in Poetry, Religion, and Philosophy (1959) is a collection of twenty articles; three are new, while the rest were originally published during the previous ten years in journals such as *Partisan Review* and *Kenyon Review* or in encyclopedias. Although the volume begins and ends with studies of two English writers—William Shakespeare and Arnold Toynbee, respectively—most of the book deals with authors who wrote in German: Goethe, Hegel, Nietzsche, Freud, Jaspers, Heidegger, and Rainer Maria Rilke; the only other exception is the Dane Kierkegaard.

In the two opening chapters, which appear for the first time in this volume, Kaufmann lambastes twentieth-century writers who blame their inability to produce great literature on the age in which they live. In Kaufmann's view, Gertrude Stein's cry of a "lost generation" and T. S. Eliot's poem *The Waste Land* (1922) are exercises in self-deception and self-pity. Each era—classical antiquity, the Renaissance, the Enlightenment, or any other—has its own set of problems. The true writer—a Cicero, a Michel de Montaigne, or a Voltaire—is self-sufficient and able to rise above the deficiencies of the time.

In the first chapter Kaufmann compares the treatment of character, action, and place in Shakespeare's *Hamlet* (circa 1600–1601), *Othello* (1604?), and *Macbeth* (1606?) with the same elements in Goethe's *Faust*. The heroes of Shakespeare's plays are of a higher stature and

NIETZSCHE FRIEDRICH (1844-1900).

~~The life of few, if any, other major philosophers has attracted such due attention~~

~~Nietzsche's life has probably attracted more attention~~

~~No other philosopher's life has attracted more attention, both from interpreters of his thought and~~

Nietzsche's life has attracted more attention than the life of any other major philosopher--from interpreters of his thought, ~~from~~ major novelists ~~(including Thomas Mann, Andre Malraux, and Stefan Zweig), from~~ psychiatrists, and ~~from~~ others. Misrepresentations of almost every facet of his life have been considered crucial for an understanding of his ~~historic role.~~ significance ~~By now it is easier to determine what he said (reading one of his books shows that)~~ than to get reliable information on ~~the~~ relative ~~weight to be attached to his books, on~~ and importance the authenticity of ~~several~~ works ~~published over his name, on the significance of~~ and the the posthumously published notes, on his relation to Wagner, and on his madness. ~~Therefore, a large part of this article will be devoted to questions of this sort.~~

First page of the corrected typescript for Kaufmann's entry on Nietzsche for The Encyclopedia of Philosophy, *published in 1967 (Walter Kaufmann Philosophy Manuscripts, Manuscript Division, Department of Rare Books and Special Collections, Princeton University Library)*

Kaufmann, circa 1977 (from the dust jacket for
The Future of the Humanities, *1977)*

less understandable than Faust, whose familiar longings, joys, and sorrows are easier for the ordinary person to fathom. Even Mephistopheles is less the incarnation of evil than "a projection of human qualities—call them inhuman if you will; it is still a peculiarly human inhumanity, one that we encounter in ourselves and our fellow men."

In a later chapter Kaufmann finds the key to Goethe to be his never-ending capacity for development. While still relatively young, Goethe mastered the drama, the novel, and lyric poetry, illustrating in all of these forms Nietzsche's dictum: "Only those who continue to change remain my kin." Goethe's early works, such as the play *Götz von Berlichingen mit der eisernen Hand* (1773; translated as *Goetz von Berlichingen,* 1799) and *Die Leiden des jungen Werthers* (1774; translated as *The Sorrows of Werther,* 1779), reflect Romanticism; but the mature Goethe found fault with the otherworldliness, pining over the past, and unconditional striving of the writing of such contemporary Romantics as Novalis, August Wilhelm Schlegel, Friedrich Schlegel, and Friedrich Wilhelm Joseph von Schelling. He came to believe that one should live one's life within the bounds of limitation and self-discipline.

The volume includes three essays on Hegel. In the first Kaufmann addresses the emerging myth about Hegel's work that was reinforced and given wide cur-

rency by Karl Popper's highly acclaimed *The Open Society and Its Enemies* (1945). Popper identifies a totalitarian strain in thinkers from Plato to Toynbee, and he considers Hegel one of the chief offenders; he also claims that Hegel resorted to hysterical historicism and lacked talent and originality. Kaufmann says that Popper's interpretation is marred by his relying primarily on Jacob Loewenberg's *Hegel: Selections* (1929), while ignoring much of the rest of Hegel's writing as well as seminal critical pieces by Wilhelm Dilthey and Franz Rosenzweig. The other two articles on Hegel were incorporated into Kaufmann's major 1965 study of the German philosopher.

Kaufmann analyzes Kierkegaard as a stylist, religious writer, psychologist, and philosopher and finds him to have little distinction in any category. His claim that "truth is subjectivity" is, in Kaufmann's view, "a multiple confusion." In "How Nietzsche Revolutionized Ethics" Kaufmann discusses Nietzsche's challenge to the notion that morality is fixed. Other chapters deal with similarities between Rilke's poetry and Nietzsche's philosophy, Jaspers's relation to Nietzsche, Heidegger's lack of vision, and German thought after World War II.

The final two chapters are a sustained attack on Toynbee, who was then at the pinnacle of his fame as an historian. According to Kaufmann, Toynbee presents history in a quirky, unintelligible fashion. For example, he fails to identify the Renaissance familiar to most historians, instead setting forth a collection of many smaller renaissances; in his treatment of "the renaissance of visual arts" Leonardo da Vinci, Michelangelo, and Titian are not even mentioned. Also, he describes the Napoleonic period as a time of peace lasting from 1797 until 1814, despite the revolutions and wars that were endemic to those years. Kaufmann agrees with the assessment of the British historian A. J. P. Taylor: "Professor Toynbee's method is not that of scholarship, but of the lucky dip, with emphasis on the luck."

The Faith of a Heretic might be described as a sequel to *Critique of Religion and Philosophy.* Many of the themes of the earlier work are present, including the limitations of analytic philosophy, existentialism, and utilitarianism; the shallowness of organized religion; Christianity in Luther, John Calvin, and Albert Schweitzer; suffering and Job; and death. Here, however, Kaufmann proposes answers to the criticisms he raises and, in so doing, reveals his own philosophy. After demonstrating that morality cannot be based on religion and that it is impossible to formulate an absolute morality, he sets forth his own ethical system that he calls an "ethic of openness." It consists of four cardinal virtues: honesty; "humbition," a combination of humility and ambition; courage; and love. He says that although he developed this ethic over many years, beginning in his youth, he does not consider it fixed and unalterable. He quotes Leo Tolstoy: "I do not believe my faith to be the one indubitable truth for all time, but I see no other that is plainer, clearer, or answers better to all the demands of my reason and my heart; should I find such a one I shall at once accept it." Of the four virtues, honesty stands above the others and provides the guiding thread throughout the book. On the basis of this ethic Kaufmann analyzes the teachings of theologians such as Aquinas and Rudolf Bultmann and finds them wanting. Above all, he thinks, theological writing lacks fairness and precision in addressing issues. Theologians often adopt the tactics of the legal profession, setting forth reasoned arguments to defend their positions but leaving out critical evidence that might cast doubt on their case; embarrassing notions such as eternal torment are sidestepped, as if they are unworthy of attention. In summary, Kaufmann says that theology "involves a deliberate blindness to most points of view other than one's own, a refusal to see others as they see themselves and to see oneself as one appears to others—a radical insistence on applying different standards to oneself and others."

Organized religion fares no better than theology. Kaufmann finds that although the majority of Americans claim to believe that the Bible is the word of God, few bother to open its covers. To point up the superficiality of the religious views of political leaders, Kaufmann cites President Dwight D. Eisenhower's comment in December 1952: "Our government makes no sense unless it is founded in a deeply felt religious faith—and I don't care what it is." Kaufmann searches for truth in Christianity, Judaism, Buddhism, and Hinduism and in the philosophies of the ancient Greeks, Kant, Kierkegaard, and Nietzsche. All influence him in varying degrees, but he finally decides that he feels most at home as a heretic. Near the end of *The Faith of a Heretic* Kaufmann states his own credo in simple terms: "The life I want is a life I could not endure in eternity. It is a life of love and intensity, suffering and creation, that makes life worth-while and death welcome. There is no other life I would prefer. Neither should I like not to die."

Kaufmann was one of the most popular professors ever to teach at Princeton. It was not unusual for an undergraduate to change his or her strong religious convictions after taking a course from him on existentialism or Nietzsche. He became a full professor in 1962; that year he was chosen by the undergraduate council to deliver the spring Witherspoon Lecture series, an honor bestowed only on professors who were highly regarded by the student body. In the series, which was titled "Existentialism and the Modern Crisis," Kaufmann delivered three lectures to overflowing crowds of students and faculty: "The Crisis in Religion," "The Crisis in Morality," and "The Crisis in Philosophy"; the lectures have not been published. Kaufmann also served as a visiting professor at many universities, including

Columbia, Cornell, the Hebrew University of Jerusalem, and the University of Michigan.

Kaufmann's *Hegel: Reinterpretation, Texts, and Commentary* appeared in 1965; he envisioned the work, which was intended, he says in the preface, "to establish a comprehensive reinterpretation of Hegel—not just of one facet of his thought but of the whole phenomenon of Hegel," as the counterpart to his 1950 study of Nietzsche. The book combines Kaufmann's own ideas about Hegel's philosophy with a careful study of recent scholarship on his thought. Kaufmann tries to destroy the long-established view of Hegel as a lonely, isolated thinker by translating letters and documents, many for the first time. He also endeavors to overturn the two usual approaches to Hegel's philosophy. The first, mainly used by German critics, begins by analyzing Hegel's precursors, sometimes as far back as Aristotle. This circuitous method, Kaufmann observes, often goes on for hundreds of pages before reaching Hegel's books and then often treats them superficially. The other approach, generally undertaken in the English-speaking world, is to launch into Hegel's mature writings, usually his *Wissenschaft der Logik* (1812–1813, 1816; translated as *Science of Logic*, 1929)—a practice that, because of his obscure style, often results in serious misreadings. Inspired by Goethe's observation that "Works of nature and art one does not get to know as they are finished: one has to catch them in their genesis to comprehend them to some extent," Kaufmann suggests an analysis of Hegel's youthful writings, which were posthumously published as *Hegels theologische Jugendschriften* (1907; translated as *Early Theological Writings*, 1948); the title is misleading, Kaufmann notes, since they were written in the spirit of the Enlightenment and are actually antitheological in character. In these writings, Hegel's view is that the highest form of religion is one that is not hampered by the dogmas of any church but is based on reason: "Pure reason, incapable of any limitation, is the deity itself." The mature Hegel incorporated this outlook into his major works, although he also accepted more-orthodox doctrines than he had as a young man. Kaufmann shows the influence on Hegel's youthful thought of Sophocles' *Antigone,* Goethe's *Faust,* Friedrich Schiller's "Über die ästhetische Erziehung des Menschen in einer Reihe von Briefen" (On the Aesthetic Education of Man in a Series of Letters, 1795), and Gotthold Ephraim Lessing's play *Nathan der Weise* (1779; translated as *Nathan the Wise,* 1781), the theme of which is that one cannot know if one religion is better than another and that one should try to lead a life of high personal morality.

One of the principal reasons Kaufmann gives for undertaking his reappraisal of Hegel is that too many critics, as he sees it, have been mired in detailed analyses that fail to do justice to Hegel's comprehensive worldview. Citing authorities who claim that if the reader can master the

THE FUTURE OF THE HUMANITIES

A NEW APPROACH TO TEACHING ART, RELIGION,
PHILOSOPHY, LITERATURE AND HISTORY

Walter Kaufmann

*Dust jacket for the book in which Kaufmann bemoans the
sorry state of humanities education in an age of
specialization and proposes solutions to it
(Bruccoli Clark Layman Archives)*

preface to Hegel's first book, *Die Phänomenologie des
Geistes* (1807; translated as *The Phenomenology of Mind*,
1910), he or she will understand Hegel's philosophy as a
whole, Kaufmann offers a new translation of the preface.
Since the terminology Hegel uses in the preface has contributed to confusion about his ideas, Kaufmann accom-
panies the translation with a copious commentary. He
also includes a translation of the essay *Wer denkt abstract?*
("Who Thinks Abstractly?") to illustrate Hegel's capacity
for clear prose and sense of humor—qualities rarely associated with the philosopher. An annotated bibliography
traces individual works of Hegel's through their various
editions and translations into English.

Reviewers generally agreed that the study provides
valuable biographical information in the form of letters
and documents and that fresh treatment of Hegel's early
writings and a new translation of the preface to *Die
Phänomenologie des Geistes* were much needed. W. H. Walsh
said in *The Philosophical Review* that Kaufmann had shown
that "Hegel was no dry-as-dust pedant, but both a man of

feeling and a man who laid stress on feeling, as might
have been expected of a close friend of Hölderlin." Otherwise, the reviews were less favorable. They said that
Kaufmann had cleared up some points, especially in
regard to the frequent mangling by commentators of the
word *Geist* and other terminology and by showing that
the stereotypical view of the thesis-antithesis-synthesis
triad cannot be found anywhere in Hegel's works. They
agreed, however, that a new interpretation of Hegel's philosophy was yet to come. Kaufmann himself says in the
book that this study "is plainly not the place for an effort
to demonstrate philosophical acuity," but many critics
hoped for more acuity and less background.

Tragedy and Philosophy (1968), a volume that origi-
nated in lectures Kaufmann delivered at the Hebrew University of Jerusalem in 1962–1963, ranges beyond the
conventional boundaries of philosophical analysis into literary criticism, history, and philology. Kaufmann's goal is
"to develop a sound and fruitful approach to tragedy, try
it out, and thus illuminate Greek tragedy and some problems relating to the possibility and actuality of tragedy in
our time." His starting point is Plato, whose treatment of
tragedy is surprisingly limited and mainly negative.
Plato's views on the subject, Kaufmann notes, are to be
found mainly in *The Republic* and *The Laws,* in both of
which tragedy is seen as detrimental to the public good.
According to Plato, tragedy is harmful to morality
because it undermines the virtues of self-control, courage,
and reverence for a higher power; to preserve the integrity of the state, the young should be protected from the
influence of the tragic poets.

While Kaufmann's discussion of Plato's views on
tragedy is somewhat perfunctory, his treatment of Aristotle's
treatise *The Poetics* is minutely detailed and exhaustive.
Kaufmann devotes a full chapter to Aristotle's definition
of tragedy as he tries to come up with a satisfactory definition of his own. Aristotle says that a tragedy should
arouse pity and fear in the observer, so as to cause a
catharsis, or purgation, of these emotions. Kaufmann
argues that one should not pity Oedipus, for example, but
should feel compassion for him. Searching for a better
term than *pity,* Kaufmann finds it in the somewhat archaic
ruth, which means compassion for the misery of others
(one who lacks such compassion is *ruthless*). *Fear* also fails
to convey the intended emotion, and for it Kaufmann
substitutes *terror.* Proceeding in this manner, analyzing one
Aristotelian tragic element after another, Kaufmann
arrives at his own definition of tragedy: it is a form of literature that presents a symbolic action performed by
actors and moves into the center of immense human suffering in such a way that it brings to one's mind one's
own forgotten and repressed sorrows, as well as those of
one's kin and of humanity in general, and releases the
spectator with some sense that suffering is universal and

not a mere accident in one's experience; that courage and endurance in suffering and nobility in despair are admirable, not ridiculous; and usually also that fates worse than one's own can be experienced as exhilarating. Performances range from slightly less than two hours to about four, and the experience is highly concentrated.

Analyzing Sophocles' *Oedipus Tyrannus,* Kaufmann isolates the themes of humanity's radical insecurity, blindness to family and friends, and, above all, the curse of honesty. Because of this curse, Oedipus is unwilling to settle for anything less than the truth–despite the warnings of the blind seer Teiresias and of Oedipus's mother/wife, Jocasta. In the course of his analysis Kaufmann exposes what he considers the superficial ideas of Plato and Aristotle. Plato's claim that after one eliminates his colorful poetry, the poet leaves nothing of substance behind, was hardly true of Sophocles, since his tragedies–especially *Oedipus Tyrannus*–combine poetic diction with depth of thought. Aristotle says that Oedipus is "not specially virtuous, not specially wise" and that his downfall occurs because of hamartia, a fatal flaw or error in judgment. Kaufmann demonstrates that, in fact, Oedipus is no ordinary individual but would be quite exceptional–"first among men"–in any period of history and that he does not possess a fatal flaw or commit an error in judgment.

In subsequent chapters of *Tragedy and Philosophy* Kaufmann discusses the birth of tragedy in Homer and the works of other major Greek writers. He does not attempt to impose his definition of tragedy on these writers but is "prepared to discover a variety of visions–one in Sophocles, another in Homer, a third in Aeschylus, a fourth in Euripides. In addition, the sense of life in the *Iliad* is very different from that in the *Odyssey,* and what is found in Sophocles' late tragedies is not quite the same as what is found in *Oedipus Tyrannus.*"

Toward the end of the book Kaufmann addresses the question of whether tragedy can be written in the twentieth century. He notes that in the previous two centuries many thinkers, including Nietzsche, had maintained that the growth of rationalism and optimism and the fading of religious faith had rendered the writing of tragedy impossible; the critic George Steiner had even written *The Death of Tragedy* (1961), in which he argued that "tragedy requires the intolerable burden of God's presence"–a burden no longer felt by most people. Other critics accounted for the demise of tragedy by invoking the disappearance of great men and the widespread preoccupation with success. None of these claims convince Kaufmann, who finds in Rolf Hochhuth's *The Deputy* (1963) all of the elements for a modern-day tragedy. The subject of the play is the agony of the Jews under Nazi rule. Hochhuth not only condemns many of his countrymen for Nazi atrocities but also underlines the indifference of the Catholic Church to the Jews' plight; Pope Pius XII, he charges, actually aided and abetted the Nazis. The hero of the play is a priest who refuses to obey Pius XII's orders and sacrifices his life for another in the Auschwitz death camp. The play illustrates one of Kaufmann's main points in *Tragedy and Philosophy:* that tragedy takes various forms in various countries and times.

In *Without Guilt and Justice: From Decidophobia to Autonomy* (1973) Kaufmann maps out a new morality in which older ideas of justice and guilt are eliminated. To have a full life, Kaufmann argues, a person must achieve "creative autonomy." Hurdles that impede one's progress toward this goal include what Kaufmann calls "decidophobia," the fear of making important decisions; pedantry, the condition of being so preoccupied with minutiae that one fails to address major issues; and drifting, the tendency–exemplified by the antihero Meursault in Albert Camus's novel *The Stranger* (1942)–to accept whatever comes along.

The major obstacle, however, is the "old morality":

> The road to autonomy is blocked by a two-headed dragon. One head is Guilt, the other Justice. Justice roars: "You have no right to decide for yourself; you have been told what is good, right, and just. There is one righteous road, and there are many unrighteous ones. Turn back and seek justice!" . . . Frightened man stops and marvels at his own presumption, when Guilt cries: "Those who succeed in getting past Justice are devoured by Guilt. Seek the road to which Justice directs you and dare not to strike out on paths of your own. Guilt has a thousand eyes to swallow you, and the lids above and below each are lined with poison fangs. Turn back: autonomy is sacrilege."

Kaufmann says that justice has passed through many phases: in classical antiquity it was identical with tradition; later it evolved into the sum of all virtues, then one virtue, and finally, in modern times, into "retributive justice"–a combination of rewards and punishments. But retributive justice is on its deathbed for several reasons: increasing skepticism about authority; compassion for the criminal, who, according to Freud, is in many ways similar to the ordinary person; and a repugnance for the often sadistic motives behind punishment. Earlier conceptions of justice had had strong associations with Christianity, particularly the concepts of the Last Judgment and hell; but with the decline in religious belief it has formed closer ties with the emphasis on reason that has come down from the Enlightenment. Distributive justice, on the other hand, is alive and flourishing in the contemporary period, although it is in no better condition conceptually than its "siamese twin," retributive justice. This form of justice involves getting what one deserves, but, Kaufmann points out, what one deserves is almost always incalculable

*Dust jacket for the first volume of Kaufmann's final work,
a trilogy in which he deals with nine important thinkers
(Reason Alone Books)*

except in extremely elementary cases: it is not possible to determine whether what is deserved depends on ability, need, merit, or treating everyone equally. If justice belongs to an outdated morality, Kaufmann argues, then guilt, the internalized punishment one inflicts on oneself for violating the dictates of justice, is also outmoded. The new morality calls for the virtues that Kaufmann had introduced more than a decade earlier in *The Faith of a Heretic:* honesty, "humbition," courage, and love.

The new morality comes with a price, however: because of the high demands autonomy places on the individual, alienation—or, as Kaufmann terms it, "estrangement"—from one's fellow human beings, from oneself, and from the universe is not a byproduct but is inherent in it. Individuals who have achieved full creative autonomy include Eleanor Roosevelt, Martin Luther King Jr., and Aleksandr Solzhenitsyn, to whom Kaufmann dedicates the book. But one should not infer that only a select few have access to this higher consciousness. Not everyone can be a great artist, writer, or political leader; but that every individual is born with innate cre-

ativity is evident when one watches a child at play. Although many lose this creativity during their formative years, it can be recovered. Creative autonomy is not only available to all but is, in Kaufmann's view, essential if one is to live life fully.

Religions in Four Dimensions: Existential and Aesthetic, Historical and Comparative (1976) is a study of ten religions with two chapters each on Judaism, Christianity, Islam, Hinduism, and Buddhism and one chapter on Zoroastrianism; religions such as Sikhism and Jainism are treated more briefly. The "aesthetic dimension" of each religion consists of a selection of photographs taken by Kaufmann, many of simple street scenes and works of art, during his travels in Europe, the Middle East, India, and the Far East. The "existential dimension" Kaufmann defines as a concern "not with beliefs and speculations, with theology and metaphysics, but with humanity." The "historical dimension" consists of the story of the development of each religion, the "comparative dimension" of a comparison of the central doctrines of the various religions.

In a short book, *The Future of the Humanities* (1977), Kaufmann notes a decline in interest among college students in philosophy, art, music, history, and religion. Part of the problem, he says, is job availability: the post–World War II "baby boom" had produced a need for more professors in the 1960s, when the postwar generation was reaching college age; but by the end of the decade fewer openings were available, and many new Ph.D. recipients were facing the prospect of not finding positions in their chosen fields. Furthermore, since the war the natural and social sciences had gained in prestige, resulting in an increase of government grants to those fields at the expense of the humanities. Another problem, Kaufmann contends, is the mentality of the faculty in the humanities. Kaufmann divides academic minds into four categories: visionary, scholastic, journalistic, and Socratic. The visionary, represented by such figures as Freud, Albert Einstein, and Max Planck, is responsible for original ideas; such a person is usually a loner and is seldom found in the classroom. The scholastic—the type with which most undergraduates come into contact—is characterized by adherence to the consensus of thought in his or her field and narrow specialization; such people are rigorous and careful in their research but often lack imagination. The least desirable category in Kaufmann's typology is the journalistic mind: this type is anxious to appear up-to-date, interesting, and fashionable and values speed above accuracy and thoroughness.

The type of academic mind Kaufmann celebrates is the Socratic, which is the rarest but, with proper training, can be developed in anyone. Exemplifying the give-and-take method of Socrates, this type is unwilling to join any school of thought or uncritically accept any current point of view. One of the chief functions of this type is to confront prevailing ideas with objections and alternatives: "What I mean by the Socratic type is the type committed to the rigorous examination of the faith and morals of the time, giving pride of place to those convictions which are widely shared and rarely questioned. Reliance on consensus and prestigious paradigms are prime targets . . . for people of this type it is a point of honor to swim against the stream." Other undesirables, according to Kaufmann, include reviewers, who often compare with journalists in the number of errors and misrepresentations they perpetrate; translators who fail to capture the voice of the original; and editors who churn out critical editions in which the scholarly notes overwhelm the text itself. Perhaps the greatest problem, however, is that students, as well as many of their professors, have never mastered the subtle art of reading deeply and proficiently. Kaufmann furnishes several examples of what he considers poor reading, followed by his own interpretations of the same texts. He calls his method of reading "dialectical":

> One does not endow the text with authority, one is not committed to making it come out right, one is not predisposed to agree with it. One *is* committed to trying to hear and understand it, and one assumes in all probability it will not agree with us and not be agreeable at every point. The dialectical reader allows himself to be questioned, but he also questions the text.

Kaufmann's solution to the poor state of education in the humanities is, first, the teaching of comparative religion through the Socratic method. Students should be exposed to a one-year course in Christianity, Buddhism, and Islam, followed by an intense study of a single text: "I can't think of a better choice than Genesis. Nor do I know a book that is greater or more beautiful, profound, and influential." Other courses should take an interdisciplinary approach, combining art, literature, history, and philosophy. A philosophy course, for example, might concentrate on the plays of Euripides or Sophocles, since each of those tragedians had a unique conception of the world. Furthermore, learning need not be confined to the classroom: students could study punishment or dying by visiting prisons or nursing homes. Above all, Kaufmann says, the goal is to provide an education free of overspecialization, one in which the learner is not indoctrinated but comes to see that there is not necessarily a single truth.

In 1978 Kaufmann published three volumes of his photographs under the title *Man's Lot: A Trilogy*. His final work, another trilogy, represents a return to more-traditional philosophy. Each volume of *Discovering the Mind* (1980) deals with three important thinkers: volume 1 is titled *Goethe, Kant, and Hegel;* volume 2,

Nietzsche, Heidegger, and Buber; and volume 3, *Freud versus Adler and Jung.* Kaufmann's intent is to show how these figures advanced or impeded an understanding of the mind. Some of them did both: Kant's obscure and convoluted prose set a ruinous example for philosophers for a hundred years, Kaufmann says, while some of his concepts have proven to be of inestimable value. The first-named thinker in each volume–Goethe, Nietzsche, and Freud, respectively–is considered the exemplary one; the others are assessed as having varying degrees of value in the progress of knowledge, with one, Carl Gustav Jung, offering nothing of merit, according to Kaufmann. The preeminent figure of the entire work is Goethe, who laid the groundwork for the ideas of Nietzsche and Freud. Goethe's concept of autonomy, his assertion that a human being is the sum total of his or her actions ("man is his deeds"), and, above all, his belief that the mind can only be understood in developmental terms were his key contributions. Nietzsche contributed the will to power and the diagnosis of the role that resentment plays in traditional morality. Freud's contributions include the Oedipus complex and infantile sexuality. All three of these major figures, Kaufmann notes, had a clear and unencumbered writing style, an undogmatic approach to issues, and a willingness to subject their ideas to objections and alternatives–characteristics that were shared by Kaufmann himself.

Walter Kaufmann died of a ruptured aorta on 4 September 1980. In the final chapter of *Discovering the Mind* he wrote:

> We are our lives and works. We are unfinished as long as we live and work and can add a few lines that could place the whole picture in a new perspective. We are unfinished until we are dead. While we live we are like a speaker in midsentence who cannot be understood fully until he has had a chance to finish.

Now that Kaufmann's life is over, this principle can be applied to the evaluation of his own achievement.

References:

Thomas Jovanovski, "Critique of Walter Kaufmann's 'Nietzsche's Attitude toward Socrates,'" *Nietzsche Studien,* 20 (1991): 329–358;

Ivan Soll, *An Introduction to Hegel's Metaphysics* (Chicago: University of Chicago Press, 1969);

James Woelfel, "Religious Empiricism as '-ism': The Critical Legacy of Walter Kaufmann," *American Journal of Theology and Philosophy,* 15 (May 1994): 181–196.

Papers:

Many of Walter Kaufmann's manuscripts, including his translations, are at the Princeton University Library.

Saul Kripke

(13 November 1940 –)

Jeff Buechner
Rutgers University

BOOKS: *Naming and Necessity* (Oxford: Blackwell, 1980; Cambridge, Mass.: Harvard University Press, 1980);

Wittgenstein on Rules and Private Language: An Elementary Exposition (Oxford: Blackwell, 1982; Cambridge, Mass.: Harvard University Press, 1982).

OTHER: "Semantical Analysis of Intuitionistic Logic I," in *Formal Systems and Recursive Functions,* edited by John N. Crossley and Michael A. E. Dummett (Amsterdam: North-Holland, 1963), pp. 92–129;

"Semantical Analysis of Modal Logic II, Non-Normal Modal Propositional Calculi," in *The Theory of Models,* edited by J. W. Addison, Léon Henkin, and Alfred Tarski (Amsterdam: North-Holland, 1965), pp. 20–220;

"Identity and Necessity," in *Identity and Individuation,* edited by Milton K. Munitz (New York: New York University Press, 1971), pp. 135–164;

"Is There a Problem about Substitutional Quantification?" in *Truth and Meaning: Essays in Semantics,* edited by Gareth Evans and John McDowell (Oxford: Clarendon Press, 1976), pp. 325–419;

"A Puzzle about Belief," in *Meaning and Use: Papers Presented at the Second Jerusalem Philosophical Encounter, April 1976,* edited by Avishai Margalit (Dordrecht, Netherlands & Boston: Reidel, 1979), pp. 239–283;

"Nonstandard Models of Peano Arithmetic," by Kripke and Simon Kochen, in *Logic and Algorithmic: An International Symposium Held in Honour of Ernst Specker,* edited by Hans Lauchli, L'Enseignement mathématique, monograph no. 30 (Geneva: University of Geneva, 1982), pp. 277–295;

"A Problem in the Theory of Reference: The Linguistic Division of Labor and the Social Character of Naming," in *Philosophy and Culture: Proceedings of the XVIIth World Congress of Philosophy* (Montreal: Editions du Beffroi, Editions Montmorency, 1986), pp. 241–247.

Saul Kripke

SELECTED PERIODICAL PUBLICATIONS–UNCOLLECTED: "A Completeness Theorem in Modal Logic," *Journal of Symbolic Logic,* 24 (1959): 1–14;

"Abstract: Distinguished Constituents," "Abstract: Semantical Analysis of Modal Logic," and "Abstract: The Problem of Entailment," *Journal of Symbolic Logic*, 24 (1959): 323–324;

"'Flexible' Predicates of Formal Number Theory," *Proceedings of the American Mathematical Society*, 13, no. 4 (1962): 647–650;

"The Undecidability of Monadic Modal Quantification Theory," *Zeitschrift für mathematische Logik und Grundlagen der Mathematik*, 8 (1962): 113–116;

"Semantical Considerations on Modal Logic," *Acta Philosophica Fennica*, 16 (1963): 67–96;

"Semantical Analysis of Modal Logic I, Normal Propositional Calculi," *Zeitschrift für mathematische Logik und Grundlagen der Mathematik*, 9 (1963): 67–96;

"Abstract: Transfinite Recursions on Admissible Ordinals, I," "Abstract: Transfinite Recursions on Admissible Ordinals, II," and "Abstract: Admissible Ordinals and the Analytic Heirarchy," *Journal of Symbolic Logic*, 29 (1964): 161–162;

"Research Announcement: Deduction-Preserving 'Recursive Isomorphisms' between Theories," by Kripke and Marian Boykan Pour-El, *Bulletin of the American Mathematical Society*, 73 (1967): 145–148;

"An Extension of a Theorem of Gaifman-Hales-Solovay," *Fundamenta Mathematicae*, 61 (1967): 29–32;

"Deduction-Preserving 'Recursive Isomorphisms' between Theories," by Kripke and Pour-El, *Fundamenta Mathematicae*, 61 (1967): 141–163;

"Review of E. J. Lemmon, 'Algebraic Semantics for Modal Logic I,'" and "Review of E. J. Lemmon, 'Algebraic Semantics for Modal Logic II,'" *Mathematical Reviews*, 34 (November 1967): 1021–1022;

"Outline of a Theory of Truth," *Journal of Philosophy*, 72, no. 19 (1975): 690–716;

"Abstract: A Theory of Truth, I, Preliminary Report," and "Abstract: A Theory of Truth, II, Preliminary Report," *Journal of Symbolic Logic*, 41, no. 2 (1976): 556–557;

"Speaker's Reference and Semantic Reference," *Midwest Studies in Philosophy*, 2 (1977): 255–276;

"Review of Kit Fine, 'Failures of the Interpolation Lemma in Quantified Modal Logic,'" *Journal of Symbolic Logic*, 48 (June 1983): 486–488;

"Critical Review of Three Papers by Kit Fine, All Entitled 'Model Theory for Modal Logic,'" *Journal of Symbolic Logic*, 50 (December 1985): 1083–1093;

"Individual Concepts: Their Logic, Philosophy, and Some of Their Uses," *Proceedings and Addresses of the American Philosophical Association*, 66 (October 1992): 70–73.

Many philosophers consider Saul Kripke to be among the most important contributors to the subject in the twentieth century. Particularly during three phases of exceptional productivity that he has characterized as "golden" periods–1956 to 1958 (when he was still in high school), 1962 to 1964, and 1972 to 1975–he has done groundbreaking work in most major areas of philosophy. His seminal papers and books have overturned received views and redefined and rejuvenated philosophy of language, epistemology, metaphysics, philosophy of science, philosophy of mind, and philosophical logic. His discussion of truth exemplifies a new way of doing philosophy that is an amalgam of mathematical precision and intuitive simplicity. He made modal logic an honest and mathematically rigorous discipline. Although he does not adopt the style of a grand theorist, Kripke's work–much of which was presented in the form of lectures and seminars that have been recorded and transcribed but remain unpublished–constitutes a unified and seamless whole. Almost all contemporary analytic philosophers comment on Kripke; the late Robert Nozick called him the "one true genius of our profession." In person he radiates intellectual energy, and his lectures and seminars are rich with jokes and bons mots. A liberal in politics and a conservative Jew, he has a knowledge of national and international politics, constitutional law, and organized religion–especially Judaism and Christianity–that is profound and detailed.

Saul Aaron Kripke was born on 13 November 1940 in Bay Shore, New York, on Long Island, to Rabbi Myer Samuel Kripke and Dorothy Evelyn Karp Kripke; Bay Shore had the closest hospital to Patchogue, where the family lived. Within the year the Kripkes moved to New London, Connecticut, and soon afterward to Omaha, Nebraska, where they were neighbors and friends of investor Warren Buffett; Saul Kripke retains a strong interest in Buffett's career and in financial matters in general. His parents had met as students at the Jewish Theological Seminary in New York City; in 1998 they helped defray the cost of rebuilding a thirteen-story tower at the seminary that had burned down in 1966, and it is called the Kripke Tower in their honor. Dorothy Kripke, who died on 30 September 2000, wrote several books for children, the most popular of which is *Let's Talk about God* (1953). Samuel Kripke, the author of *Insight and Interpretation: Reflections on the Weekly Sidrah* (1988), is rabbi emeritus of Beth El Synagogue in Omaha and an emeritus adjunct associate professor of theology at Creighton University. Saul Kripke has two younger sisters, Madeleine and Netta.

Kripke's genius manifested itself early. He discovered a good deal of algebra on his own; he told his mother that the subject came to him so naturally that he would have invented it himself had it not already existed. He taught himself Hebrew when he was six, read all of William Shakespeare's works in the fourth grade, and had read the major works of most of the great philosophers by the eighth grade. Lois Croft, his eighth-grade teacher at the Dundee School, exerted the greatest influence on him during his precollege years. She recommended several popular books on mathematics to him, including one on the nature of numbers and James Newman and Eric Kastner's *Mathematics and the Imagination* (1940), in which he was exposed for the first time to the logical paradoxes. Without any guidance he discovered Morris Raphael Cohen and Ernest Nagel's classic *An Introduction to Logic and Scientific Method* (1934) and Alice Ambrose and Morris Lazerowitz's *Fundamentals of Symbolic Logic* (1948) in the local library. As a bar mitzvah present an uncle gave him a copy of W. V. Quine's *Mathematical Logic* (1940). Around this time he read Stephen Cole Kleene's *Introduction to Metamathematics* (1952), thinking—mistakenly—that it was a text in David Hilbert-style metamathematics. He next mastered J. Barkley Rosser's *Logic for Mathematicians* (1953), which was used as a textbook in graduate courses in mathematical logic.

At sixteen Kripke read a paper by Arthur Prior about a problem that had stymied logicians for more than forty years: finding semantics and completeness proofs for modal logics. He soon invented a solution: a method for constructing completeness theorems for arbitrary systems of modal logic. Modal notions figure centrally in people's thoughts about the world: they say such things as "It is possible that she will arrive late" and "It is necessary that water is H_2O." But people's intuitions about modalities are insecure. In the early twentieth century C. I. Lewis formulated systems of modal logic as responses to the inadequacy of the material conditional in classical logic. A material conditional is a sentence of the form "If P, then Q" and is true if the antecedent (P) is false or the consequent (Q) is true; it is false only if the antecedent is true and the consequent is false; it is inadequate because it cannot express the idea of a necessary connection between the antecedent and the consequent and cannot distinguish between two sentences that exhibit a necessary connection, on the one hand, and two sentences that are entirely unrelated to each other, on the other hand. Logic characterizes the abstract structure of objects and relations; different objects and different relations can be characterized by the same logic if they share the same structure. To show that a logic "fits" particular objects and relations is to provide a semantics for it. Justifying a logic consists in showing that it is sound (that all of the sentences provable in the logic are true) and complete

(that all of the truths the logic is supposed to "fit" are provable). A semantics is necessary to demonstrate the completeness of a logic. Lewis could not show that his modal logics were complete because he had no semantics for them. After Lewis, several other logicians, including Rudolf Carnap, failed to solve the puzzle of completeness. Kripke's method for proving completeness theorems in modal logic lies in his invention of modal model structures. Model structures—today known as "frames"—consist of three elements: a set of abstract objects, called "worlds"; a relation, R, between the worlds, called the "accessibility relation"; and a distinguished member of the set of worlds—the actual world. When a valuation system determining the truth of a nonmodal sentence in a given world is added to a model structure, a full-blown model results. The sentence "Necessarily P" (where "P" stands for any declarative sentence) is true in the actual world provided that it is true in every world that is "R-related" to the actual world; "Possibly P" is true in the actual world provided that a world R-related to it exists in which it is true. The accessibility relation is the key to unifying the motley of modal logics: different accessibility relations define different modal logics.

While he was working on his proof, Kripke asked the logician Haskell Curry whether his ideas were interesting and new; Curry affirmed that they were. At that time Kripke had a completeness theorem only for the modal system known as "S5"; it was complicated, he had not yet hit upon the notion of an accessibility relation, and he did not even know whether his proof was correct. Curry recommended that he read papers on semantic tableaux methods. In these papers he saw how to get completeness proofs for modal predicate logics that employ the quantifiers *all* and *some*. Even in the professional logic texts of the day, such as Quine's, Kleene's, and Rosser's, completeness proofs were given only for propositional logics. Finding a semantics and proving completeness for quantified modal logics is more difficult than doing so for propositional modal logics because of the problem of comparing objects across various possible worlds. If one says, "Necessarily, every object x has property F," one needs to know whether the object x in the actual world is the same object x in those worlds that are accessible to the actual world. J. C. C. McKinsey had written several papers on the subject in the late 1940s in an algebraic vein. In 1950 Chandler Davis wrote a dissertation at Harvard University under Garrett Birkhoff in which he proved an algebraic representation theorem for the modal system S5; Davis had a completeness proof, but it was tailored to that specific system. In 1951 Barni Jonsson and Alfred Tarski also proved algebraic theorems; though they did not realize it, they were also doing modal logic

(Tarski told Kripke that he could not see the connection, even after Kripke pointed it out to him at a conference in Finland in 1962). Stig Kanger and C. A. Meredith both had fragments of modal logic but not a completeness proof. Jaakko Hintikka had a Byzantine system of modal logic; though he had the technique of semantic tableaux, he had no proof that they are equivalent to models of a modal logic. Kripke's quantificational models are flexible: decisions can be made as to whether the domain over which quantifiers range is fixed ("possibilist" or "constant domain" quantification) or varies from world to world ("actualist" or "varying domain" quantification).

In February 1958 Kripke submitted a paper, "The System LE," on refutability in classical propositional logics in the Gentzen style, to the Westinghouse Science Talent Search; he was a finalist. He also did work in several other Gentzen-style systems, none of which has been published; it became known to the logic community through Curry's efforts.

By the time Kripke's work on the completeness and semantics of modal logics finally appeared, as the lead article in *The Journal of Symbolic Logic* in January 1959, he was a freshman at Harvard. During his freshman year Hintikka visited him several times to hear his views on modal logic. Before Kripke, chaos had reigned in modal logic: inclusion relations were invisible, and no one knew whether different logics would require radically different kinds of completeness proofs. After Kripke's watershed paper, the field of modal logic underwent wildfire growth. Kripke catalogued relations between different modal logics, provided decision procedures for some of them, and devised the distinction between normal and nonnormal modal logics lacking a rule of necessitation, such as Lewis's modal logics.

Before 1959, logicians thought of necessity, in crude Leibnizian terms, as "truth in all possible worlds." Modal models—called "Kripke structures"—reveal how different kinds of accessibility relations generate different kinds of necessity and possibility. Kripke structures have been employed outside the field of logic in the technology of artificial intelligence, distributed computer systems, computer-aided verification methods such as model checking, and parallel-processing algorithms. In mathematical economics they are used to formulate game theory. When used properly they have eliminated much philosophical obfuscation. The only other twentieth-century idea to have such a profound influence in philosophy, scientific theory, and technology was Albert Einstein's special theory of relativity.

An abstract of Kripke's contribution to relevance logic also appeared in 1959. Relevance logics are nonclassical logics in which "unsavory" classical theorems cannot be proved. An unsavory classical theorem that

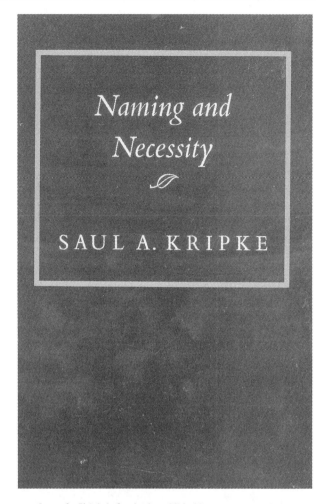

Cover for Kripke's first book, published in 1980, transcriptions of three lectures he delivered at Princeton University in 1970 (Bruccoli Clark Layman Archives)

relevantist logicians abjure is that a true proposition is materially implied by any proposition; another is that a false proposition materially implies any proposition. Kripke discovered decision procedures for implicational fragments in which only the implication connective occurs in formulas. He also devised a lemma for the proofs that has an analogue in number theory proved in 1913 by Leonard Dickson. The leading relevantist logician Nuel Belnap wrote in an unpublished 28 September 1959 letter to Kripke: "Manifold congratulations! *That*, sir, is a splendid piece of work. Hats off to you."

At nineteen Kripke improved on an important generalization of Kurt Gödel's first incompleteness theorem. Gödel's 1931 theorem says that any system of logic that is strong enough to reason about elementary arithmetic is deficient, in that it cannot prove truths of arithmetic that are expressible in the system. This discovery shattered the dream of the rationalist philosopher Gottfried Wilhelm Leibniz (1646–1716) of settling all questions by mechanical reasoning. Andrzej Mostowski had proved a generalization of this theorem in 1960, and Kripke strengthened Mostowski's result by proving that predicates exist in a formal system whose extensions as sets cannot be fully determined within it. For example, one would not be able to determine the extension of the predicate "is red" if it were formalized in such a system and if it were the appropriate kind of predicate for which the results hold.

Kripke majored in mathematics, taking courses with many of the renowned Harvard mathematicians—he particulary enjoyed John Tate's algebra course—and with Hartley Rogers Jr. at the Massachusetts Institute of Technology. His fellow students included Fields Medal winner David Mumford, Theodore John Kaczynski (now serving a life sentence for murder as the Unabomber), Daniel Stroock, Gene Lewis, Nicholas Goodman, Joseph Kadane, and Laurence Tribe, who went on to become an expert in constitutional law. Kripke took four philosophy courses: a year of ancient, medieval, and modern philosophy; epistemology with visiting professor David Pears; Ludwig Wittgenstein's *Philosophical Investigations* (1953) with Rogers Albritton; and Quine's course on his recently published *Word and Object* (1960). He won the Detur prize, awarded to the top 10 percent of students of the sophomore classes as determined by the grade-point average earned in their first year in Harvard College; he was elected to Phi Beta Kappa during his junior year; he received the Charles Wister prize, awarded to a senior in mathematics with the highest record in the field, and the Palfrey Exhibition, for the most distinguished scholar in the senior class who is the recipient of a stipendiary scholarship. He graduated summa cum laude in 1962; at the ceremony a Harvard College dean told Kripke's father that Kripke was the smartest student Harvard ever graduated. He has never pursued a master's degree or a doctorate.

Kripke's 1962 article "The Undecidability of Monadic Modal Quantification Theory" delivered unexpected results. Classical first-order predicate logic restricted to monadic formulas is decidable, and the prevailing opinion was that the same holds for modal predicate logic with monadic formulas. Monadic formulas contain only one-place predicates, such as "is round"; dyadic predicates, such as "loves," have two places. Kripke proved that a fragment of modal predicate logic with monadic formulas having just two predicates is undecidable. To get the startling result, Kripke reduced a decision problem for first-order predicate logic shown to be unsolvable to a decision problem for modal predicate logic with monadic formulas. Since the former decision problem is undecidable, so is the latter. He also provided reasons why no reasonable system of modal predicate logic can escape his undecidability theorems.

Kripke was a Fulbright scholar at the University of Oxford for the 1962–1963 academic year. At Oxford he spent a great deal of time with G. E. M. Anscombe and her husband, Peter Geach; H. Paul Grice; and Michael A. E. Dummett. He also associated with Peter Strawson and Phillipa Foot. Kripke was the only person who was not an Oxford faculty member who was ever invited to attend meetings of the Oxford Philosophical Society.

In 1962–1963 Kripke discovered how to generalize the theory of computability, or recursion theory, which studies functions on the natural numbers computable by procedures whose moves are finite in number and finitary. A procedure is finitary if it requires little or no intelligence to execute and it makes no appeals to extraordinary capacities. For example, moving a pebble on a ruled tape one square to the right or one square to the left is a finitary procedure. The mathematical theory of computation was invented by Gödel, Alan Turing, and Jacques Herbrand in the 1930s. Several distinct frameworks for defining computations were devised, all of which were shown to be equivalent. The equivalence fails, however, when recursion theory is generalized. A generalization of recursion theory provides mathematically precise statements about the power of taking infinitely many steps in executing computations. Gaisi Takeuti, Georg Kreisel, and Gerald Sacks, who initiated the project of generalizing recursion theory, could not demarcate a limited domain of ordinals for it. They took the domain to be vast, including either all ordinals or all ordinals up to the first nonrecursive ordinal. Two problems loom large in generalizing recursion theory: choosing a framework defining the computable functions and defining quantitatively distinct resource measures other than "omega-many" resources (such as omega-many time steps), where "omega" is the first infinite ordinal. Kripke asked what a computation theory would look like for infinitary procedures or over objects other than the natural numbers and went on to invent alpha-recursion theory, which studies recursion on "admissible" ordinals. Computable functions defined over an ordinal must be closed over it—that is, must take range values over the domain of ordinals governed by it. Kripke selected the framework of an equation calculus, thereby solving the vexing problem of finding the analogue in alpha-recursion theory of the notion of "finite" in ordinary recursion theory. To demonstrate which set-theoretic objects are computable, he applied alpha-recursion theory to set theory. He proved an equivalence between ordinal admissibility and an axiom of set theory—the axiom of replacement—whose definition is relativized to an existentially quantified formula. His theory of admissible ordinals spans the three pillars of logic: set theory, recursion theory, and model theory.

Kripke's Harvard senior thesis, an exposition of the logical and philosophical ideas underlying his semantics for quantified modal logic, was published in 1963 as "Semantical Analysis of Modal Logic I, Normal Propositional Calculi." In 1963 Kripke also published "Semantical Analysis of Intuitionistic Logic I"; an abstract of the paper had appeared in 1959, and the work had been done between 1956 and 1958. The Dutch mathematician, philosopher, and mystic L. E. J. Brouwer had articulated the principles of intuitionistic mathematics early in the twentieth century. Historically, intuitionistic mathematics banned any mathematical entities that were not explicitly constructed—that is, it said that mathematical objects that cannot be constructed do not exist. Proof by contradiction is unacceptable to an intuitionist, since such proofs assert that mathematical entities exist solely on the ground that their nonexistence is contradictory. The fundamental logical law of excluded middle fails when neither a mathematical object nor its contradictory can be constructed. Brouwer and his students, especially Arend Heyting, constructed logics for intuitionism, and Mostowski and Evert Beth attempted to develop a semantics for those logics in the early 1950s. No viable semantics existed, however, until Kripke invented it. In "Kripke structures" for intuitionistic logics the objects are not worlds, as in modal logics, but evidential situations. The intuitionistic analogue of the actual world is the present evidential situation.

Two results appear in "Semantical Analysis of Intuitionistic Logic I" that were not announced in the 1959 abstract. One is an elegant exposition of Paul J. Cohen's method of "forcing" in terms of Kripke's semantics. In 1963 Cohen proved that the continuum hypothesis framed by Georg Cantor nearly one hundred years earlier is independent of the axioms of set theory by inventing the method of forcing to construct a model of the axioms of set theory in which the hypothesis is false. Years earlier Gödel had constructed a model of the axioms in which it is true. Kripke's second new result is a proof of the undecidability of monadic intuitionistic quantification theory.

Brouwer had introduced into intuitionistic mathematics the mystical idea of a "creating subject" to give full meaning to his interpretation of the notion of a sequence: since sequences in mathematics can be infinitely long, he argued, they cannot be constructed by a finite human mathematician. Brouwer's creating subject is an idealized mathematician. Since the creating subject thinks sequentially, it is held hostage to time—thus, a physical element enters into mathematics, and mathe-matics becomes a branch of physics. In lectures Kripke presented a principle, known as "Kripke's Schema"—for each proposition P there exists an increasing binary sequence a_n such that P holds if and only if $a_n = 1$ for some value of n—that eliminates time by eliminating the creating subject. The creating subject is eliminated by defining any sequence in tandem with asserting P.

In 1964 Kripke was elected to a three-year appointment to Harvard's Society of Fellows. At about this time he solved an important problem posed by Burton Dreben and Marian Boykan Pour-El; the solution was published in 1967 in a joint paper by Kripke and Pour-El, "Deduction-Preserving 'Recursive Isomorphisms' between Theories." The question was whether a recursive isomorphism exists between theories that preserves their deductive structure—that is, that preserves deducibility, negation, and implication. An isomorphism takes every element of one structure and maps it into a unique element of the other structure; property preservation means that elements in one structure that have some property are mapped into elements of the other structure having that property. If the isomorphism can be computed, it is recursive. Dreben believed that the answer was negative: it seemed incredible to him that recursive isomorphisms that preserve deductive structure could exist between formal systems. Kripke and Pour-El proved that they could. Their paper shows how to transfer between theories computable results about theoremhood, refutability, and undecidability. Recursive isomorphism between theories is not universal, however: between some theories the isomorphism is noncomputable; between others there is none at all.

Also around 1964 Kripke used Gödel's second incompleteness theorem, which says that a system of logic strong enough to reason about arithmetic cannot prove its consistency, in a theorem proving Löb's Theorem (proposed by M. H. Löb in "Solution of a Problem of Leon Henkin," *The Journal of Symbolic Logic*, 1955): if it is provable that A follows from the provability of A, then A is provable. Kripke's theorem was never published but has the status of a folklore result.

Kripke gave several lectures on admissible ordinals at Harvard between 1964 and 1967; Jon Barwise attended one lecture, and his report on it inspired Richard Platek to devote his 1966 dissertation at Stanford University to it. Platek independently rediscovered many of Kripke's results, as well as proving theorems on higher-type objects such as recursive functionals. In the spring of 1964 Kripke gave a seminar at Princeton University in which he aired a new interpretation of Wittgenstein's *Philosophical Investigations* that he had conceived in 1962–1963. In the spring of 1965 he taught another seminar at Princeton in which he advanced a critique of alternative logics, such as quantum logic, that has never been published and a critique of Quine's demolition of the analytic/synthetic distinction that is discussed in Alan Berger's 1979 doctoral dissertation. Kripke also taught a course, Mathematics 282, at Princeton in the spring of 1967. His lectures were transcribed by Thomas Tymoczco and John Muller as "The Theory of Transfinite Recursion"; the 118-page transcription has not been published.

Kripke remained at Harvard as a lecturer for two years after his appointment to the Society of Fellows ended. In the fall of 1968 he moved to Rockefeller University in New York City, an elite graduate school primarily for the sciences that had launched a Ph.D. program in philosophy. In addition to Kripke, the university recruited Nozick, Donald Davidson, Hao Wang, Harry Frankfurt, Leslie Tharp, Joel Feinberg, John Dolan, John Wallace, John Earman, and the set theorists Robert Solovay, Tony Martin, and William Mitchell. The students were similarly illustrious: Berger, Michael Bratman, Jules Coleman, Robert Hambourger, Michael Jubien, Jonathan Lear, David Malament, and Scott Weinstein; Kripke supervised the dissertations of Berger, Hambourger, Jubien, Lear, and Weinstein.

The three lectures Kripke delivered at Princeton on 20, 22, and 29 January 1970 have been called the most significant contributions to philosophy of the twentieth century. Each lecture was about three hours long; Kripke, as usual, did not use notes. Tape recordings of the lectures were transcribed by Gilbert Harman, Thomas Nagel, and Davidson; the transcriptions were published in 1980 with a preface, footnotes, and an addendum by Kripke, as *Naming and Necessity*. The lectures, Richard Rorty said in a review of *Naming and Necessity* in *The London Review of Books* (4 September 1980), "stood analytic philosophy on its ear."

A stalking horse in *Naming and Necessity* is the theory, proposed by Gottlob Frege and Bertrand Russell, that proper names are disguised descriptions. The view appeals to common sense: surely, one would think, names refer because they are associated with traits of the referent. One successfully refers to John Smith by the name *John Smith* because various traits Smith possesses—red hair, blue eyes, snub nose—are associated with that name. Kripke attacks this view, resuscitating John Stuart Mill's contention that all that there is to a proper name is its referent. His attack employs simple ideas on the metaphysics of identity statements and reveals how a failure to appreciate these ideas sustains descriptivism. Kripke points out that the traditional dichotomy between the necessary and the contingent is metaphysical, while that between the a priori and a posteriori is epistemological; philosophers such as Russell,

he contends, have collapsed these dichotomies by infusing epistemological concerns into metaphysical ones and thereby have come to identify necessity with the a priori and contingency with the a posteriori. Kripke restores the two dichotomies by citing examples of truths that are a priori but contingent and necessary but a posteriori. Even Quine and Ruth Barcan Marcus conflate necessity with epistemological notions.

The a priori-but-contingent example is that of the standard meter. One knows a priori that the standard meter stick in Paris is one meter long, because it has been stipulated to be that length; one does not have to measure the stick to determine that it is a meter in length. At the time the stipulation was made, however, the stick might have been a different length than it actually is.

The necessary-but-a posteriori example is that of Hesperus and Phosphorus. These names were given by astronomers to what they thought were two different stars. Later astronomers discovered that the two names refer to the same object—the planet Venus. This discovery was a posteriori, or empirical: it was made by observing the object, not by thinking about it. Since both names refer to the same object, and a thing must be identical to itself, Hesperus is necessarily Phosphorus. The epistemic means by which Hesperus was recognized differed from the epistemic means by which Phosphorus was recognized, but that epistemic difference is irrelevant to the planet's metaphysical status. According to Kripke, the mistaken idea that the epistemic means used to recognize an entity determine its metaphysical status tainted metaphysics with epistemology and resulted in a false semantic theory of the reference of proper names: the Frege-Russell description theory.

A proper name, Kripke holds, refers to the same thing in all possible worlds in which it refers at all. On the description theory of proper names, the referent of the name *John Smith* in a possible world is the person who most resembles the actual John Smith. On Kripke's view, on the other hand, the referent of *John Smith* is John Smith himself, whatever he may look like in that possible world. That is, essential properties are preserved across possible worlds: whatever is taken to be constitutive of being John Smith must be a property of John Smith in any possible world in which he exists; having red hair, blue eyes, and a snub nose are not essential properties of him. Kripke observes that the epistemic means by which the referent of a proper name is fixed in the actual world can be much less austere than a description of the referent. A causal chain from speaker to speaker satisfying the speakers' intention to refer to the object preserves reference. This notion is the germ of Kripke's "causal" theory of reference.

Kripke invents the phrase *rigid designator* for linguistic items, such as proper names, that refer to the same thing in any given possible world in which the referent exists. His insight that proper names are rigid designators is a powerful idea that can dissolve various confusions that had been rampant in philosophy of language and in linguistics, and *Naming and Necessity* includes several important exercises of this power. One that had explosive effect is Kripke's demonstration that the mind is not identical to any material thing, which means that the materialist claim that the mind is identical to the body's neurophysiology is mistaken. He shows that the commonsense intuition that pain is not the same thing as the firing of nerve fibers is, in fact, true by contrasting that intuition with the false one that heat might not be mean molecular motion. Once heat is identified with mean molecular motion—an empirical discovery—imagining heat not to be mean molecular motion is imagining something that is not heat. Any intuition that heat might not be mean molecular motion badly confuses how one comes to recognize the true nature of heat. If one imagines something that is not mean molecular motion but affects one as heat does, one cannot say that it is heat. Epistemic means by which one accesses that thing—such as sensations on the skin or thermometer readings—do not reveal its metaphysical status. This insight explains the falsity of the intuition that heat might not be mean molecular motion. One cannot, in the same way, explain as false the intuition that pain might not be the firing of nerve fibers. If one imagines pain behavior not caused by the firing of nerve fibers, one cannot say that what one imagines is not pain, because one's epistemic access to pain ("it feels like pain") is essential to pain; that is, how pain is recognized determines what it is. Anything to which one is epistemically related in the way one is epistemically related to pain must be pain. It follows that one can, after all, imagine pain not being the firing of nerve fibers. Hence, pain is not identical with neurophysiology, since identities are necessary.

Naming and Necessity has spawned an enormous critical literature, in which a common misinterpretation of Kripke's argument is that it is intended to prove that the mind is some sort of spirit. What it actually proves, however, is that the mind is not identical to any material thing; the argument is not, for example, incompatible with the notion that the mind supervenes on the brain. Mind-brain supervenience is a dependency relation such that if the brain did not exist, the mind would not exist; but the mind is not identical to the brain. Similarly, Jack's existence is supervenient on his father's existence: if his father had not existed, Jack would not exist; but this fact does not mean that Jack is identical to his father. Critics have also contended that possibility

WITTGENSTEIN
ON RULES
AND PRIVATE
LANGUAGE

Saul A. Kripke

Dust jacket for Kripke's 1982 book, a radical reinterpretation of some of the theories of the Austrian-born philosopher Ludwig Wittgenstein (Bruccoli Clark Layman Archives)

claims do not immediately follow from intuitions about conceivability. Intuitions play a paramount role in Kripke's philosophical methodology: they serve as the basis for adjudication of philosophical theories. Otherwise known as "epistemological" or "basic prejudices"—terms he employs in his unpublished 1978 Cornell University lectures on time and identity—they are, he says, subject to revision only when the price of maintaining them becomes much too high. Many philosophers resist, if they do not reject outright, the centrality of epistemological prejudices.

Kripke was a visiting professor at Cornell University in 1970. In 1971 he remarked on the limitations of Gödel's theorems in disproving computational functionalism—the view that the human mind is a computer program—at the Chapel Hill Colloquium in Philosophy. In 1972 he was a visiting professor at the University of California at Berkeley and at UCLA.

Kripke did much of his work on intensional logics between 1970 and 1972, though he had done some as early as 1966. Many varieties of quantified modal logic exist, corresponding to various choices concerning the objects of quantification. An intensional logic that employs quantification over individual concepts is called Q2. An example of an individual concept is the descriptive phrase "the card on top of the deck." In different possible worlds, the identity of the top card on the deck might differ: in one world it might be the eight of hearts, in another the ace of spades. Whether or not Q2 is axiomatizable depends on its underlying modal propositional logic. Kripke shows that Q2 is axiomatizable in the system S5—overturning the folklore view attributed to David Kaplan that it is nonaxiomatizable. On the other hand, Q2 is nonaxiomatizable in the system S4. In the system S4.3 the nonaxiomatizability of Q2 depends on assuming the continuum hypothesis in set theory. These results have not been published but are cited in correspondence; they are discussed by James Garson in his "Quantification in Modal Logic" (2001).

Kripke was a visiting professor at the University of London in 1973. That year he was invited to give the prestigious John Locke lectures at Oxford; at thirty-two, he was the youngest Locke lecturer since the series began in 1950. His topic was the problem—which he has said might be the most difficult one in philosophy—of referring to nonexistent objects. An example of a true singular negative existential is the sentence "Hamlet does not exist," which contains the nonreferring name *Hamlet*. Kripke argued that the name *Hamlet* used by William Shakespeare in his play of that title lacks a referent of any kind. Instead, Shakespeare pretends to refer to a person whenever he employs the name *Hamlet* in his play. It is a name only in a make-believe world. But when someone occupying a point of view external to the fictional world of the play discusses the character Hamlet, he or she semantically endows the word *Hamlet* with the status of a name. It is no longer a fictional name but names a fictional character—Hamlet. *Hamlet* is, thus, ambiguous. On the "pretense" reading, it names nothing; on the external reading, it names an abstract object—that is, it names a fictional character. The six lectures were transcribed by Henry Hardy from tape recordings; the manuscript of more than two hundred pages, titled "Reference and Existence," has not been published.

In 1974 Kripke gave two presentations on alternative logics: a lecture at the University of Pittsburgh titled "The Nature of Logic" and a seminar at Princeton. In these presentations Kripke showed that abandoning the distributive law, as Hilary Putnam proposed for quantum logic, allows one to prove set-theoretically that $2 \times 2 = 5$ (or even more than 5). Allen Stairs discusses Kripke's views on alternative logics in his 1978 doctoral dissertation.

In June 1975 Kripke delivered three lectures on truth at Princeton. Hans Herzberger, Graeme Hunter, and William Seager made a 136-page transcription of the tapes of the lectures; it has not been published. The problem of the nature of truth is one of the oldest and most important in philosophy. In the late 1930s Alfred Tarski mathematically defined truth for logical languages. The correspondence theory of truth—that truth consists in a correspondence between one's words and the states of affairs in the world—underlies his work. Tarski eliminated the vague phrase "correspondence between," which hides the notion of truth within it: one cannot know when there is a correspondence between words and reality unless one already knows what truth is. He demonstrated that defining truth within a language leads to paradox. In his lectures Kripke noted, tongue in cheek, that Pontius Pilate set the problem by asking "What is truth?" He also pointed out that St. Paul's Epistle to Titus mentions a problem any theory of truth must address: the semantic paradoxes, such as the liar paradox. Someone utters the sentence "I am lying"; if the sentence is true, it is false; if it is false, it is true. Tarski avoided semantic paradoxes by defining truth outside the language to which it applies. This solution is unnatural, however: people generally ascribe the predicate "true" (or its equivalent) to sentences in a natural language within the language. Kripke blocked this strategy by devising semantic paradoxes that arise naturally in ordinary conversation. At the height of the Watergate scandal, for example, President Richard Nixon was under investigation by the Senate. If his chief of staff, H. R. Haldeman, had testified that "Most [that is, a majority] of Nixon's assertions about Watergate are false," the utterance would not have been strange; it is not self-referential like the sentence "I am lying." The Senate committee might have taken Haldeman literally and looked at every assertion Nixon made about Watergate, assigning truth-values to all of the assertions except one and finding the number of true assertions to equal the number of false ones. If the Nixonian assertion not assigned a truth-value had been "Everything Haldeman says about Watergate is true," a liar-like paradox would have occurred in an ordinary conversation.

Kripke went on to note that if empirical conditions are unfavorable, assertions using the terms *true* and *false* will be paradoxical. Liar-like paradoxes cannot be separated from ordinary talk, since one will not always know, as one is talking, when empirical conditions are unfavorable. Kripke described the desiderata for a mathematically precise theory of truth: it should be a precise semantic description of a language that is rich enough to speak of its own elementary syntax and contain its own truth predicate; it should be applicable to arbitrarily rich languages, no matter what their "ordinary" predicates, other than truth, might be; it should be formally precise, so that one can speak of a theory of the semantic paradoxes; and it should provide the means necessary for a mathematical definition of truth. He then formulated the first theory of truth to satisfy these desiderata. His theory avoids paradoxes by not assigning them a truth-value, thereby jettisoning the principle of classical logic that a declarative sentence must be true or false. His theory, in other words, allows "truth-value gaps." A common misunderstanding of his gap proposal is that it is a new truth-value; he has taken pains to deflect that misreading, pointing out that the element "undefined" in Kleene truth-tables is not a new truth-value but a marker that no proposition has been expressed: paradoxical sentences do not express genuine propositions.

Kripke invented a monotonic inductive procedure that captures the process by which one grounds sentences to which one applies the predicate *true*. Grounded sentences are assigned a truth-value before the construction closes off. Inductive definitions are indispensable in precisely constructing families of mathematical objects. Kripke iterates his monotonic inductive procedure until it yields no more new sentences to which the term *true* can be meaningfully applied. This stage in the inductive construction of the truth-predicate is called a "fixed-point." Ungrounded sentences in the fixed-point fail to express genuine propositions. The model Kripke most emphasizes is the minimal fixed-point, because it defines the notion of a grounded sentence. He notes that different models emphasize different and often conflicting intuitions about the nature of truth. Truth-value gaps differ, depending on the kind of truth-table that is used to define truth-functions. Different kinds of truth-tables yield different fixed-points and different sentences that are grounded or ungrounded in those fixed-points. Different fixed-points reflect distinct philosophical intuitions.

Kripke returned to UCLA as a visiting professor in 1975. In December of that year he delivered a three-hour talk on truth at the Eastern Division meeting of the American Philosophical Association in New York City. The room originally scheduled for the talk was too small for the number of people who wanted to hear Kripke, so the event was relocated to a ballroom with a seating capacity of several thousand. It was still not large enough.

Kripke's "Is There a Problem about Substitutional Quantification?" (1976) is widely agreed to have effectively ended a subtle but intense debate over quantification. The standard referential view of quantification as it occurs in first-order logic is that the quantifiers *all* and *some* range over objects. The propositional form "(x)Fx"—in English, "For all x, x has the property F,"

or, more simply, "Everything has F"—is true provided that every object in the "universe of objects" over which the quantifier ranges has the property F. An alternative to referential quantification is substitutional quantification: linguistic expressions, not objects, are the range of a substitutional quantifier, and an existentially quantified sentence is true provided that the sentence obtained by deleting the existential quantifier and replacing its variables by names is true. The philosophical appeal of substitutional quantification is that it appears to block thorny "opacity problems." Opacity problems are generated by "opaque contexts," which are linguistic contexts in which substitution of coreferential terms need not preserve truth. For example, "John believes David Lewis is a metaphysician" is true, but "John believes Bruce LeCatt is a metaphysician" is false, even though *David Lewis* and *Bruce LeCatt* name the same person—David Lewis, who has used LeCatt as a pseudonym.

Between 1971 and 1974 Kripke's Rockefeller University colleagues Tharp and Wallace had published a series of papers, some jointly, in which they claimed that the distinction between referential and substitutional quantification is untenable and that there is a problem about substitutional quantification. In conversation they made the even stronger claims that substitutional quantification is unintelligible and that a truth definition for it is impossible. Davidson endorsed the latter view in print, writing that the failure of substitutional theories to satisfy Convention T is enough to disqualify them from useful employment. (Convention T is the general pattern Tarski took a theory of truth to embody: x is true if and only if p. A specific instance of Convention T would be: "Roses are red" is true if and only if roses are red.) His imprimatur helped fuel the dispute, which was soon joined on Tharp and Wallace's side by the powerful University of Pittsburgh group: Belnap, Joseph Camp, and Dorothy Grover.

Kripke's 1976 paper, which he had begun in early 1972, provides a clear overview of the issue and refutes Tharp's and Wallace's claims. He works within the standard framework of ontological commitment encapsulated in Quine's slogan, "To be is to be the value of a variable" of quantification, though he does not endorse it. Kripke concludes that no problem of substitutional quantification exists. Tharp and Wallace claimed that they had established the possibility that there might be no determinate truth-conditions for substitutional quantifiers; Kripke proves, as a mathematical fact that cannot be changed by philosophical argumentation, that there are such truth-conditions.

Tharp threatened a lawsuit for libel against Oxford University Press, whose Clarendon Press had published the book in which Kripke's paper appeared.

The impetus for the suit might have been Kripke's admonition at the end of his paper to beware of those who misuse technical results in mathematical logic to make philosophical claims. He recounts the legendary nineteenth-century confrontation between Denis Diderot and Leonhard Euler at the St. Petersburg court of Catherine the Great when Euler and several courtiers, wishing to make a fool of Diderot because of his atheism, engaged him in a debate on the existence of God. In full view of the court, Euler declaimed: "(a + b^n)/n = x; therefore, God exists. Please respond, sir!" Diderot could not, and he left ignominiously. Kripke's moral is that technical results can be misused in philosophy and that philosophers should use them responsibly. (He also speculates that the Diderot-Euler confrontation never happened as reported.) Kripke is not denying that one can do rigorous and precise work in philosophy; his own work on truth is a paradigm of mathematical rigor and precision. Tharp did not pursue the lawsuit beyond the threat.

Speaking at a 1976 conference at Hebrew University in Jerusalem, Kripke staggered the philosophical world by inventing a puzzle that poses problems for any theory of belief. (He had had the idea for the puzzle in the late 1960s and had considered adding it to his *Naming and Necessity* lectures but decided not to do so because he thought that there would not be enough time to discuss it adequately.) Critics of *Naming and Necessity* argued that opaque contexts such as belief attribution and quotation are counterexamples to Kripke's view that proper names are not disguised descriptions. If the sentence "Jack believes Jill loves him" is true, they said, it does not follow that if a coreferential term is substituted for *Jill*–for example, *Sandra*–the resulting sentence is also true, since Jack may not know that Jill is also called Sandra. But, they asked, if names are logically proper, with no descriptive component, how can the sentences differ in truth-value? Only if each name has a descriptive component, and the descriptive components differ, will the sentences' truth-values differ, the critics said.

Kripke's puzzle responds to these critics. It concerns Pierre, who speaks only French. On the basis of what he has heard about London, Pierre says, "Londres est jolie." Hearing him, one would conclude that Pierre believes that London is pretty. Some years later, Pierre moves to a squalid section of London. He learns English from listening to Londoners, not by using a translation manual. After doing so, he says, "London is not pretty." He does not know that the London in which he lives is the same place as the Londres about which he heard years ago. Hearing Pierre now, one would conclude that Pierre believes that London is not pretty. But Pierre has not changed his mind: if he were conversing in French, he would still assert that "Londres est jolie." It cannot be the case, however, that "Pierre believes that London is pretty" and "Pierre believes that London is not pretty" are both true. After discussing and faulting various ways of disarming the puzzle, Kripke concludes that it is a genuine puzzle for any philosophical account of belief and proper names, that it arises on any semantic theory of proper names, and that it is not tied to substitution failures of coextensive terms. The puzzle has generated an enormous critical literature.

In 1976 Rockefeller University president Frederick Seitz decided that the institution could no longer afford a graduate program in philosophy. Kripke chose Princeton from among several universities that offered him positions, and in 1977 he was appointed McCosh Professor of Philosophy there.

In "Speaker's Reference and Semantic Reference" (1977), which is based on several talks he had given in the early 1970s, Kripke deals with a distinction that had been introduced by Keith Donnellan in 1966. Definite descriptions are singular noun phrases that have the form "the F" or "NP [Noun Phrase] Possessive marker F"; examples are "the soprano" and "Jack's spouse." A common view is that descriptive phrases refer to what they describe: "The guy by the railing holding the smelling salts" refers to the man who is standing next to the railing with a container of ammonium carbonate and ammonia water in his hand. In 1905 Russell shattered this view, arguing that descriptive phrases do not refer but are quantifiers: a description such as "the F that is G" can be logically unpacked as "there is exactly one such F and all Fs have G." No mention of an object occurs in the Russellian analysis of a descriptive phrase. Donnellan argued that descriptive phrases are ambiguous and can be read either as attributive or as referential and claimed that Russell's analysis fails for referential uses, since that analysis holds that descriptions do not refer. Kripke defends Russell against Donnellan without committing himself to Russell's theory. He claims that there is no semantic distinction between the referential and attributive uses of descriptive phrases and, thus, no ambiguity in descriptive phrases. He defines the concept of "speaker's reference" and distinguishes it from semantic reference: the former is pragmatic (it concerns the relationship between linguistic expressions and their users), the latter semantic (it concerns the relationship between expressions and their referents). The linguistic data can thus be explained by introducing pragmatic facts. The controversy was ingeniously rekindled, though the consensus is that the ambiguity view of descriptions cannot be sustained.

In the late 1970s Kripke gave lectures at philosophical conferences–including a particularly important one in Banff, Alberta, in 1978—and a spring 1979 seminar at Princeton on Wittgenstein. Only then did his new interpretation of Wittgenstein become widely known. Kripke speculates that participants in his 1964 Princeton seminar, including a prominent Wittgenstein specialist, had a mistaken impression of his new interpretation.

Kripke gave five lectures titled "Time and Identity" in March and April 1978 as Andrew Dickson White Professor-at-Large at Cornell University, a position he held from 1977 to 1983 concurrently with his McCosh professorship at Princeton. These lectures were transcribed from tape recordings, and copies of the 252-page manuscript were circulated during the 1980s.

In 1978 Kripke lectured at Princeton and elsewhere on a model-theoretic method, "fulfillability," that he invented to construct independent sentences of arithmetic that—unlike the recherché Gödel sentences—are mathematically interesting truths. In the mid 1970s Jeff Paris and Leo Harrington had found such a truth: a finite form of Ramsey's Theorem that could not be proved within formal systems used to reason about arithmetic. The theorem, postulated by Frank P. Ramsey, a British philosopher who died at twenty-six in 1930, holds that infinite sets always exhibit a certain kind of order. The Paris-Harrington proof employed the metamathematical concept of consistency; Kripke wrote a paper in collaboration with his Princeton colleague Simon Kochen on constructing independent sentences of arithmetic that avoid metamathematical concepts, as well as Gödel's self-referential sentences. They returned to older model-building techniques to prove independence. Around this time Kripke invented the method of fulfillability for constructing independent sentences of mathematics. Fulfillability is model-theoretic, but it is closely connected to Hilbert's proof-theoretic ideas. Model theory examines the interpretations or structures that satisfy a given formal language, while proof theory examines the provability relation defined within the formal language. Model-theoretic independence proofs work by finding a structure in which a sentence in the formal language is true and a structure in which that sentence is false. Kripke also invented a proof-theoretic version of his model-theoretic proof. Fulfillability came to Kripke from trying to abstract the "combinatorial" or Ramsey-type features of the Kripke-Kochen construction from its more purely formal model-theoretic features. He has never written up the method of fulfillability and does not even have many notes on it; almost all of the work was done in his head. Joseph Quinsey's 1980 Oxford dissertation on the method of fulfillability, which Kripke was supervising at the time he gave the 1978 lectures, proved several

Kripke in 1983 (photograph by Robert P. Matthews)

results that Kripke cited in his lectures, revealing the scope and power of the method and generalizing it to omega-models of analysis. Quinsey never published his dissertation, however, and it is not well known. On the basis of the 1978 lectures, Warren Goldfarb wrote up Kripke's proof-theoretic method for constructing independent sentences. In unpublished correspondence Kripke has said that some machinery in Goldfarb's proof—Herbrand's Theorem and the cut-elimination theorem—is not needed.

In a fall 1978 seminar Kripke adumbrated his view that philosophical theories of criteria of identity are both ill defined and ill justified. He employed a variety of geometrical-physical arguments to argue against standard views of criteria of identity over time for material objects and invented imaginary examples to illustrate his claims. One of these examples is a universe that consists entirely of a disk of homogeneous material rotating at a constant angular velocity. Photographs of the disk at various times cannot distinguish different sectors of it. If one used a Magic Marker to mark it, one could make that discrimination; but, Kripke pointed out, a criterion of identity over time cannot require the existence of a Magic Marker. (Even a Magic Marker may not do the job: Kripke envisioned coloring sectors of the disk, but how could one distinguish stationary colors on a moving disk from a stationary disk on which the pattern of colors changes?) The rotating-disk universe was intended to refute "holographic" theories of identity over time, which maintain that an identity criterion can be extracted from information available in a set of temporally successive pictures of an object. Kripke also considered complications that arise from postulating velocity, acceleration, and even higher derivatives as conceptual primitives in theories of criteria of identity over time; ultimately, he decided that there is no need for such criteria. An unpublished transcription of the fall 1978 seminar is more than six hundred pages in length. Also in the fall of 1978 Kripke delivered three Matchette Foundation Lectures at the University of Wisconsin on the "surprise exam" paradox. Jerrold Levinson's 174-page transcription of the lectures has not been published.

In fall 1979 Kripke gave a joint seminar at Princeton with his colleague Lewis on the foundations of modal logic. Lewis lectured on possible worlds, claiming that they are just as real as the actual world. Notes of the seminar were made by Nathan Salmon, a visiting professor at Princeton and an important philosopher in his own right. That he was note-taker for a debate on the foundations of modal logic between Kripke and Lewis, a great figure in twentieth-century philosophy, has a mythic quality to it. The notes have not been published.

In late December 1979 Kripke addressed the winter meeting of the American Philosophical Association in New York City on his work on identity over time. During the question period a member of the audience stated that if Kripke is right, the world is an unchanging Parmenidean unity. The questioner failed to see that refuting a theory of identity over time does not mean that nothing can change over time nor that objects cannot be identified and reidentified over time.

In 1979–1980 Kripke gave seminars on Russell; on Frege and Russell; on materialism and the mind-body problem; and on mathematical logic, emphasizing his new work on fulfillability. Salmon made notes of all four seminars. In the spring 1980 seminar Kripke discussed Kit Fine's views on *de dicto* and *de re* modalities. One can, in one's mind, either access an object through a proposition—a *dictum*—describing the object (*de dicto*), or access it directly by referring to it without a dictum to describe it (*de re*). Fine argued that in some circumstances *de re* modalities can be eliminated and "replaced" by *de dicto* modalities and, moreover, that philosophical objections to *de re* modalities are justified

by mathematical results. Fine also claimed that his technique for proving completeness of modal systems is optimal. Kripke found that Fine's claims about the possibility of eliminating *de re* modalities need to be carefully hedged, if not dismissed altogether. He also showed that Fine's results are more complex, but not stronger, than those obtained in an unpublished 1974 University of Pittsburgh dissertation by J. Broido. Kripke lamented that the connection between philosophy and mathematical logic is not as strong as Fine would have liked it to be. Finally, Kripke rejected Fine's claims that Fine-style completeness proofs are significantly different from his own and that Fine's modal completeness proof is optimal.

In his fall 1980 seminar Kripke investigated completeness and compactness theorems in quantified modal logic, as well as the use of infinitary modal logics to prove mathematically—that is, justify—Kripke semantics for modal logics. He showed how Kripke semantics can be deduced from modal systems rather than superimposed from the outside. He also showed how one can prove, using infinitary logic, that Kripke semantics is preferable to neighborhood semantics, a competing semantics for modal logics.

Kripke's lectures on Wittgenstein metamorphosed in 1982 into *Wittgenstein on Rules and Private Language: An Elementary Exposition.* The central topic of Wittgenstein's *Philosophical Investigations*—the rule-following considerations—is famously elusive, and his cryptic prose is notoriously hard to penetrate. Typical views of what he was trying to say simply rehearse his language, but Kripke proposes a novel, clear, and alarming interpretation of the work that takes Wittgenstein to have articulated the most radical and original skeptical problem ever posed: the "paradox of meaning skepticism." That the words one utters might mean almost anything at all is a disturbing thought; Kripke says that the "problem is insane and intolerable."

Kripke employs a simple example from arithmetic to illustrate meaning skepticism, making it both easy to see what it is and why proposed solutions to it are faulty. People are so familiar with addition that they would regard with incredulity anyone who proposed that they do not know what they mean when they say that they are adding two numbers. The meaning skeptic, however, asks one to add two natural numbers that one has never before added. The numbers will surely be quite large, since one has done many additions in the past, but for the sake of hypothesis the numbers can be stipulated to be 68 and 57. One would say without hesitation that their sum is 125. The meaning skeptic then informs one of another arithmetical function, "quus." The quus function behaves exactly like the plus function for all sums in which the numbers to be added are less than 57 but diverges from the plus function for all sums in which the numbers to be added are equal to or greater than 57. That is, if x and y are each less than 57, then x quus y is the same as x plus y; thus, 2 quus 2 equals 4, just as 2 plus 2 does. For all numbers x and y greater than or equal to 57, x quus y equals 5. Thus, 57 plus 68 equals 125, while 57 quus 68 equals 5. Is there anything in one's past additions or in one's mind, the meaning skeptic asks, that warrants the claim that one means plus, and not quus, when one says "plus"?

Anything one may adduce to support the claim that one means plus when one says "plus" can be appropriated by the meaning skeptic and turned against one. If a person says that he or she means "plus" because he or she can count the number of objects in a pile of 57 objects and in a pile of 68 objects, with the counting continuing until 125 is reached, the meaning skeptic will ask how the person knows that *count* means count and not "quont." Counting and "quonting" yield the same results for all numbers less than 57, but for all numbers equal to or greater than 57 the result of quonting 57 and 68 is 5. If one specifies in words any property that one might use to justify one's meaning plus, rather than quus, by "plus," the meaning skeptic can "qussify" it: that is, the meaning skeptic can show that the words expressing the property proposed for any justification of what one means are themselves in need of justification, because they are also susceptible of multiple interpretation. One might think that a few alternative readings of the meanings of one's words is no great cause for concern. The definition of the quus function, however, reveals a simple procedure for constructing any number of other alternatives to the plus function, any one of which might be meant when one uses the word *plus*.

A naive criticism of meaning skepticism is that it is self-defeating: meaning skepticism cannot even be expounded, since if it were true, no one would be able to understand it. Kripke dismisses this objection by employing a dialectical strategy in describing the paradox of meaning skepticism. The skeptic does not initially dispute how one presently uses the word *plus,* only whether past usage and present usage are the same. Past usage is what is put into question. Without employment of this strategy, the paradox could not be formulated. He also mounts a powerful attack on "dispositionalist" solutions to meaning skepticism, which claim that underlying mechanisms within people determine what they mean when they say "plus": they are disposed to answer "125" to the question "What is the sum of 57 and 68?" because a mechanism within them guarantees that answer. Kripke points to a fatal flaw in a dispositionalist analysis: it is common knowledge that people make mistakes when they add, especially when

adding large numbers. The dispositionalist is powerless to distinguish in someone's use of the word *plus* between meaning plus but making a mistake in addition, on the one hand, and meaning quus and making no mistake in "quaddition." How does one know that one has made a mistake? One would not be faced with this question if no alternatives existed to meaning plus. Dispositionalist solutions beg the question by assuming that one already knows that one means plus when one uses the word *plus.*

Elsewhere in *Wittgenstein on Rules and Private Language* Kripke argues, contrary to all previous Wittgenstein interpreters, that the "private-language argument" occurs well before paragraph 243 in *Philosophical Investigations.* The argument claims that a person could not construct his or her own private language. The claim seems absurd: does a child not sometimes do just that as a form of play? As Kripke interprets Wittgenstein, meaningful linguistic communication requires a language community that agrees to the responses given in their language. Community agreement blocks both the meaning skeptic and private languages. Kripke says: "The set of responses in which we agree, and the way they interweave with our activities, is our *form of life.*" The solution creates new difficulties, however. Kripke notes, for example, that accepting the private-language argument applied to one's own sensations has a strange consequence: one cannot know whether one is experiencing a certain sensory state, such as being in pain, unless the community affirms that one is. This idea flies in the face of common sense: surely, the individual having the experience is the only one who can affirm that he or she is in pain. But such affirmation presupposes that one can successfully identify a pain, and a lesson of meaning skepticism is that identification cannot be taken for granted.

Kripke includes a postscript on Wittgenstein's treatment of the problem of other minds: how can one know that people other than oneself have minds? According to Kripke, Wittgenstein takes the view that people have no real idea of their own minds (or selves). They do not, then, even know what it would mean to say that another person has a mind, since they cannot make sense of the idea of their own mind.

Kripke's interpretation of *Philosophical Investigations* is startling and terrifying. It is bad enough to think that speech might be nothing more than glossolalia. It is far worse to consider that there might be no comprehensible speaker or hearer of that speech. In Kripke's exegesis of *Philosophical Investigations* nothing remains hidden.

In the early 1980s Kripke wrote a manuscript in which he criticized, on philosophical, historical, and mathematical grounds, Hartry Field's proposals in *Science without Numbers: A Defence of Nominalism* (1980) for reviving nominalism in the philosophy of mathematics. Many varieties of nominalism have been proposed, but the core doctrine in all of them is that abstract mathematical objects do not exist. Inscriptions–that is, numeral systems–and rules for their employment exist, but nothing more. Kripke contends that Field commits elementary errors in logic and mathematics and claims ideas that preceded his work as his own. At the same time he weighed in on the Goodman-Zabludowski controversy. In *Fact, Fiction, and Forecast* (1955) Nelson Goodman had formulated a "new riddle of induction" known as the "grue paradox": *grue* is defined as the property of being green if examined before some future date, such as 1 January 3000, and blue if examined after that date. Then the fact that all emeralds examined before that date have been green is evidence for the generalization that all emeralds are grue and that they will turn blue after 1 January 3000. This result, however, seems bizarre. Goodman proposed as a solution to the paradox his theory of "predicate entrenchment." Among the projectible predicates–those that are supported, unviolated, and unexhausted–the best entrenched are those that have the highest frequency of past employment in hypotheses. In the late 1970s Andrezj Zabludowski claimed that he had found a logical error in Goodman's definition of entrenchment. A debate between Zabludowski and Goodman raged for several years in *The Journal of Philosophy*. Kripke drafted a fifty-page manuscript on the debate, tentatively concluding that the consensus view that Goodman was the winner was wrong.

In August 1983 Kripke gave a talk at the Seventeenth World Congress of Philosophy in Montreal in which he argued that Putnam's concept of the "linguistic division of labor" has no semantic role. Putnam pointed out that there are many words that people use meaningfully even though they know little about the referents of those words. Most English speakers, for example, know that *elm* and *beech* refer to different kinds of trees but cannot distinguish an elm from a beech. But if one cannot distinguish an elm from a beech, Putnam asked, does one really know what the words *elm* and *beech* mean? He argued that one does know, as long as there are experts in the community who do know how to distinguish elms from beeches. Language, that is, has a social dimension, outside the head of the speaker. The view that meaning has a social dimension is part of the ambitious program of "semantic externalism." Kripke did not deny that referential and historical connections play a role in determining meaning. In his unpublished paper "Fictional Entities," read at the Storrs Conference on the Philosophy of Language in 1973, he said that could not "tell, just by inspecting my own mental processes, whether given sentences of mine express propositions or not."

In 1983 Kripke received an offer from Indiana University; Princeton made a superior counteroffer, and he remained there. The department chairman, Paul Benacerraf, said in an unpublished 17 May 1983 letter that the package offered by Princeton "is a genuine tribute to the esteem in which you are held, and a real effort to help you advance the goals in your research and teaching, for the benefit of us all."

In a footnote in *Wittgenstein on Rules and Private Language* Kripke had argued that the philosophical theory of the mind known as functionalism–the view that mental states are defined by their causes and effects rather than by their intrinsic properties–is fatally flawed. He amplified the argument in lectures in 1984, two of which–one at the Wittgenstein Congress at Kirchberg am Wechsel in August and the other at Brown University in September–were transcribed but have not been published. The basic idea of the refutation is that a finite automaton computational model on which computer programs of the mind are based cannot successfully perform multiplication on inputs greater than a certain size. When inputs are longer than the bounding size, one must stipulate that it is multiplication and not another arithmetical function that the program computes; that is, an outside observer is needed to ascertain which program is implemented. If the program is that for human cognition, an outside observer is needed to ascertain which program a human mind implements. This result holds for all human minds–including the outside observer's. Kripke concludes that functionalism is mired in "a sophomoric relativism."

Kripke did additional work on semantics for modal and intensional logics in a fall 1984 seminar, a complete transcription of which was made by John Collins; the 134-page transcription has not been published. The contingent a priori was the subject of a talk Kripke gave at the "Themes from Kaplan" conference at Stanford University in the spring of 1984 and of a series of three Exxon Foundation Distinguished Lectures titled "Perspectives in Philosophy" at the University of Notre Dame in 1986. In the lectures Kripke addressed criticisms of and elaborated his views on the standard-meter example from *Naming and Necessity*. In response to a problem posed by Salmon he argued that if one did not stipulate *some* length, there could be no empirical–a posteriori–measurements. Measurement is not primitive; stipulation is primitive, and measurement requires it. He also discussed the relation between fixing a reference and Russellian acquaintance and its ramifications for Davidson's work on propositional attitudes and J. J. C. Smart's work on the identity theory of mind. The three lectures were transcribed by Howard Wettstein in a one-hundred-page manuscript that has not been published.

Between 1987 and 1989 Kripke conducted four seminars at Princeton on theories of truth. The first was devoted to clarifying and amplifying fixed-point constructions and nonclassical truth-tables. The second looked at alternative truth theories. The third seminar gave philosophical interpretations of theorems in hierarchy theory from computability and descriptive set theory within Kripkean truth theories. In the fourth seminar Kripke defended Russell against the consensus charge that the axiom of reducibility nullifies his ramified theory of types. Kripke's research assistant, James Cain, transcribed the tapes of most of the seminars; the still-unpublished manuscript is more than 1,500 pages in length.

Two alternative theories of truth, one by Herzberger and the other by Belnap and Anil Gupta, eliminated Kripke's truth-value gaps. Herzberger notes in his paper on naive semantics that Kripke's seminal work made all subsequent work possible. In his spring 1989 Princeton seminar on truth theories Kripke exhaustively analyzed Belnap and Gupta's revision theory of truth, finding mathematical and conceptual errors in its motivating ideas and in its counterexamples to his minimal fixed-point theory. Kripke devised his own revision theory that avoids these errors. There is a technical correspondence between the logical languages in which the truth-predicate is defined and hierarchies of recursion theory (which classify logical formulas by the amount of information required to compute their truth-values). Kripke gave philosophical interpretations of theorems in recursion and descriptive set theory, such as the Kleene-Souslin theorems, in his seminars.

Kripke delivered the lead talk, "No Fool's Red? Some Comments on the Primary, Secondary Quality Distinction," at a University of Michigan Philosophical Conference on Color and Secondary Qualities in the spring of 1989. Philosophers had always thought that there could not be a color that appeared under normal conditions of observation to be red but that was, in fact, not red, whereas there is such a thing as fool's gold—metals that appear to the eye to be the element gold but are not. Kripke put considerable pressure on the view that there is no fool's red.

Kripke gave several lectures on counterfactual theories of knowledge during the 1980s and wrote a still-unpublished monograph of more than 150 pages on the topic. In a 1963 article in *Analysis* Edmund Gettier had overturned the 2,500-year-old view, originating with Plato, that knowledge is justified true belief by giving an example of such a belief that no one would want to call "knowledge." In his wake, epistemologists have

Kripke, Moscow State University computer scientist and mathematician Sergei N. Artemov, and Cornell University mathematician Anil Nerode at the New York Logic Colloquium at the City University of New York in 1999

sought a fourth condition, in addition to justification, truth, and belief, that provides genuine knowledge. An important response to Gettier was made in the mid-to-late 1970s by Nozick in lectures at Harvard and in manuscript versions of his *Philosophical Explanations* (1981) that he circulated. Nozick proposed a counterfactual theory of knowledge in which a subject "tracks" the truth under various counterfactual epistemic conditions. Nozick's theory was widely regarded as a viable solution to Gettier's problem, but Kripke finds it irreparably flawed. One difficulty with Nozick's theory, he claims, is that knowledge is not closed under existential generalization: for example, one can know that there is a blue barn but not know that there is a barn. Ordinarily, it is thought that knowledge is closed under existential generalization: that is, if one knows that there is a blue barn, it follows that one knows that there is a barn. But someone may visit an area where there is a genuine blue barn and many nonblue barn facades built by a mischievous millionaire. One would not know that there is a blue barn since one would not know whether what appears to be a blue barn is genuine or a facade. But on Nozick's theory one would know, since one would not believe that there was a blue barn if one did not see one. The millionaire did not build any blue barn facades; but one might believe that one sees a barn, since there are many barn facades. It is not true that one would not believe that one sees a barn if one did not see a barn. Thus, on Nozick's theory, one would know that there is a blue barn without thereby knowing that there is a barn.

In the fall of 1987 and again in the fall of 1991 Kripke gave seminars on the metaphysics of primary and secondary qualities, an issue that has relevance to the philosophy of mind. Primary qualities are those properties of an object that are thought actually to inhere in the object itself, such as size and shape; secondary qualities are those that exist in the mind of the perceiver, such as color and taste. He questioned whether strict boundaries between the types of quality can be meaningfully maintained and concluded that the distinction is not as clear-cut as most philosophers had thought it to be. He introduced the example of "killer yellow"–a shade of yellow that causes the death of the perceiver before he or she can experience it.

In "*De re* Propositional Attitudes on Numbers and Logicist Definitions of Numbers," delivered in May 1990 in the Nature of Knowledge lecture series at the University of Edinburgh; in a Princeton seminar in the fall of 1990; and in "Logicism, Wittgenstein and *de re* Beliefs about Numbers," two Alfred North Whitehead Lectures delivered on 4 and 5 May 1992 at Harvard, Kripke described a new problem in the ontology and epistemology of mathematical objects. His colleague Benacerraf had argued in a 1965 *Philosophical Review* article that any computable progression satisfying certain computable conditions defines natural numbers. One condition is that the successor operation must be computable. If any computable progression will serve, Kripke asked, then why is the decimal system of representing numbers preferred to other representational systems? Is it simply anthropomorphism, based on the number of fingers people have? Kripke argued that it is not, for number representations must satisfy other conditions if one is to have *de re* contact with them. Decimal notation is a natural, perspicuous, and unique representation of a particular type of progression. People learn to identify the natural numbers with the particular progression consisting of finite sequences of ten primitively ordered objects with an initial element. Zero never begins the sequence, except for the single sequence zero. This is an identification; mathematically, any identification will do. People do not identify the natural numbers with von Neumann numbers nor with Zermelo numbers; why not, if each progression is isomorphic to every other progression? According to Kripke, the choice is explained by training and by com-

plexity theory. People's training consists in learning a system of notations, which is the same thing as grasping a structure provided that the notations systematically mirror that structure.

Isomorphism of distinct representations of the natural numbers does not mean that all representations are equally acceptable. Finding the successor to a natural number must not only be computable; it must also be easy. Complexity theory is a mathematical theory of how hard it is to solve a problem by an algorithm. Some notations make it exponentially hard to compute the successor of a natural number, and this situation is unacceptable: no one wants to take ten days to find that 121 is the successor of 120. People are trained to use decimal notation, and that fact provides an explanation of their ability to ascertain which number is which in a certain progression and of how they get the right attitude toward numbers. Training would come to naught if the complexity of arithmetical operations exceeded people's stock of resources for making computations. Kripke thus revealed how complexity theory is needed to answer important questions in the epistemology of mathematics. The two Whitehead lectures and the second Edinburgh lecture have been transcribed in an eighty-six-page manuscript.

As a member of the tenure committee reviewing the work of his colleague Scott Soames in the early 1980s, Kripke had become interested in the "projection problem" in linguistics. He found that adequately formulating the problem invokes a little-noticed connection between presupposition and anaphor. He delivered a paper on the topic for a Princeton conference on presupposition in the fall of 1992.

In a yearlong seminar on descriptions from the fall of 1992 to the spring of 1993 Kripke focused on philosophical/linguistic theories of definite and indefinite descriptions and obtained two notable results. The first is the "problem of hydras": according to Kripke, Russell's procedure for eliminating definite descriptions fails for certain notational variants of classical logic; instead of eliminating descriptions, it produces more of them–with each application of the Russellian elimination procedure, the hydra grows more heads. The second result is that latitudinarianism implies that one believes that the Eiffel Tower is a spy, provided that one entertains one false belief and one true belief. *Latitudinarianism* is Kripke's name for the position of those, like Quine and Daniel C. Dennett, who hold that exportation is universally valid. Exportation is the doctrine that a *de re* statement, such as "There is someone whom Jack believes to be a spy," follows from the *de dicto* statement "Jack believes that there are spies." In his fall 1994 seminar Kripke argued that presuppositional anaphor is analogous to the linguistic phenomenon of pronominal anaphor, that Robert Stalnaker's views impose unnecessary requirements on the acceptance of a speaker's presuppositions by their interlocutors, and that the vexing case of uses of the word *too* illustrates the delicate issues about the anaphoric requirements of presuppositions.

Kripke was unhappy with the view of Dreben, John van Heijenoort, and Warren Goldfarb that Frege and, later, Whitehead and Russell's *Principia Mathematica* (1910–1913) objected in principle to the possibility of metamathematical investigations, from which it would follow that they conducted no such investigations. In his fall 1995 history of logic seminar he announced metatheorems in Frege's work and in *Principia Mathematica* that had been invisible to logicians; indeed, one—a shockingly modern Russellian metatheorem that is a key idea in Boolean-valued models of set theory—had been attributed to Robin Gandy fifty years later. In his unpublished manuscript "The Ordered Pair: A Philosophical Paradigm Revisited" Kripke also entertains a provocative conjecture about the origin of the well-ordering theorem and demonstrated that even a technically trivial logical notion, such as the ordered pair, has a highly complicated history and is seriously misdescribed even in current philosophical literature.

Kripke presented a new interpretation of Gödel's incompleteness theorems in his spring 1996 seminar, "Elementary Recursion Theory and Its Applications to Formal Systems"; a 188-page transcription by Mario Gomez-Torrente has not been published. He asked why the Gödel phenomenon took so long to be discovered, since it is a failure of the unrestricted comprehension axiom in set theory that was well known in the late nineteenth century. The axiom says that any condition defines a set. If the condition is "is not a member of itself," Russell's Paradox arises: the paradox, about a barber who shaves all and only those who do not shave themselves and, therefore, would have to both shave and not shave himself, is, in fact, a popularization of the failure. If the condition is "is not true of itself," the liar paradox results. Kripke contends that all of the paradoxes, syntactic and semantic, are instances of failures of the unrestricted-comprehension axiom. He argues that the Gödel sentence is a version of the "heterological paradox" discovered in the 1920s by Kurt Grelling. According to this paradox, a predicate is autological if it is true of itself, heterological if it is false of itself. The word *English* is autological, since it is English, while *long* is heterological, since *long* is not long. If *heterological* is heterological, it is autological, because it is true of itself; but if it is autological, it cannot be true of itself. Kripke pointed out that Russell's Paradox and Grelling's paradox are one and the same. He also devised the property of "Gödel-heterological," which means "not provable of itself," and reformulated the Gödel sentence as "Gödel-

heterological is Gödel-heterological"—that is, "unprovable of itself is unprovable of itself." This sentence is easier to understand and remember than the original Gödel sentence. Gödel sentences require self-reference, while Gödel-heterological sentences do not use self-reference; they arise even in logical theories in which self-reference is proscribed.

During his spring 1997 seminar Kripke illustrated the power of individual concepts in restoring a Fregean interpretation of logic and in reviving Leibniz's original idea of a derivative. Kripke argued that his revival of the Leibnizian calculus comes closer to Leibniz's original conception of the derivative than does Abraham Robinson's use of nonstandard numbers to represent infinitesimals. In spring 1998 he gave another seminar titled "Elementary Recursion Theory and Its Applications to Formal Systems," lecturing on his new interpretation of Gödel's incompleteness theorem; on how Hilbert's program of using finitistic means to prove the consistency of elementary arithmetic, which had been thought to be undermined by Gödel's second incompleteness theorem, actually collapses from within because of the way its claims are mathematically expressed (a crude analogy would be "All generalizations are false," a sentence that undermines itself); and on fulfillability. He also proved Alonzo Church's thesis that the recursive functions and the intuitively computable functions are one and the same. It was Kripke's last Princeton seminar before he took early retirement.

In spring 1999 Kripke gave a seminar on time and identity at Hebrew University. In June a conference honoring him was held at the University of Haifa. He delivered a talk on his new view of the Gödel theorem and made several remarks on Quine's indeterminacy thesis. Between fall 1999 and spring 2001 he returned to Hebrew University twice and was a visiting professor at UCLA and Utrecht University.

In October 2001 Saul Kripke won the Rolf Schock Award for logic and philosophy. The Schock Award has been given every two years since 1993 in logic and philosophy, mathematics, visual arts, and music, areas in which a Nobel Prize is not awarded; winners of the logic and the philosophy and mathematics awards are selected by the Royal Swedish Academy of Sciences, which also selects the Nobel Prize winners in physics and chemistry (the Schock Award winners in visual arts and music are selected by the Royal Academy of Fine Arts and the Royal Swedish Academy of Music, respectively). The previous recipients of the logic and philosophy award were Quine (1993), Dummett (1995), Dana S. Scott (1997), and John Rawls (1999).

References:

Jon Barwise and John Etchemendy, *The Liar: An Essay on Truth and Circularity* (New York: Oxford University Press, 1987);

Alan Berger, "Language and Science as an Epistemic Foundation of Logic: A Critique," dissertation, Rockefeller University, 1979;

Paul Boghossian, "The Rule-Following Considerations," *Mind,* 98 (1989): 507–549;

Taylor Branch, "New Frontiers in American Philosophy," *New York Times Magazine,* 14 August 1977, pp. 12–68;

Charles Chihara, "On Alleged Refutations of Mechanism Using Gödel's Incompleteness Results," *Journal of Philosophy,* 69 (21 September 1972): 507–526;

Charles Crittenden, *Unreality: The Metaphysics of Fictional Objects* (Ithaca, N.Y.: Cornell University Press, 1991);

Dirk van Dalen, "Intuitionistic Logic," in *Alternatives in Classical Logic,* volume 3 of *Handbook of Philosophical Logic,* edited by Dov M. Gabbay and Franz Guenthner (Dordrecht, Netherlands & Boston: Reidel, 1986), pp. 225–339;

Chandler Davis, "Modal Operators, Equivalence Relations and Projective Algebras," *American Journal of Mathematics,* 76 (1954): 747–762;

Michael Devitt and Kim Sterelny, *Language and Reality,* second edition (Cambridge, Mass.: MIT Press, 1998);

Keith Donnellan, "The Contingent A Priori and Rigid Designation," in *Contemporary Perspectives in the Philosophy of Language,* edited by Peter A. French, Theodore E. Uehling Jr., and Howard K. Wettstein (Minneapolis: University of Minnesota Press, 1979);

Donnellan, "Kripke and Putnam on Natural Kind Terms," in *Knowledge and Mind: Philosophical Essays,* edited by Carl Ginet and Sydney Shoemaker (New York: Oxford University Press, 1983);

Donnellan, "Reference and Definite Descriptions," *Philosophical Review,* 75 (1966): 281–304;

Michael A. E. Dummett, *Elements of Intuitionism,* second edition (Oxford: Clarendon Press / New York: Oxford University Press, 2000);

Dummett, *Frege: Philosophy of Language,* second edition (Cambridge, Mass.: Harvard University Press, 1981);

Dummett, *The Interpretation of Frege* (Cambridge, Mass.: Harvard University Press, 1981);

J. Michael Dunn, "Relevance Logic and Entailment," in *Alternatives in Classical Logic,* volume 3 of *Handbook of Philosophical Logic,* edited by Dov M. Gabbay and Franz Guenthner (Dordrecht, Netherlands & Boston: Reidel, 1986), pp. 117–224;

Melvin Fitting and Richard L. Mendelsohn, *First-Order Modal Logic* (Dordrecht, Netherlands: Kluwer Academic, 1998);

James Garson, "Quantification in Modal Logic," in *Handbook of Philosophical Logic,* volume 3, second edition, edited by Dov M. Gabbay and Franz Guenthner (Dordrecht, Netherlands & Boston: Reidel, 2001), pp. 267–323;

Warren Goldfarb, "Herbrand's Theorem and the Incompleteness of Arithmetic," *Iyyun,* 39 (January 1990): 45–64;

Leo Harrington and Jeff Paris, "A Mathematical Incompleteness in Peano Arithmetic," in *Handbook of Mathematical Logic,* edited by Jon Barwise and H. Jerome Keisler (Amsterdam: North-Holland, 1977), pp. 1133–1142;

Hans Herzberger, "Notes on Naive Semantics," *Journal of Philosophical Logic,* 11 (1982): 61–102;

Jaakko Hintikka, "Modality and Quantification," *Theoria,* 27 (1961): 119–128;

Mark Johnston, "Manifest Kinds," *Journal of Philosophy,* 94, no. 11 (1997): 564–583;

Barni Jonsson and Alfred Tarski, "Boolean Algebras with Operators I," *American Journal of Mathematics,* 23 (1951): 891–939;

David Kaplan, "On the Logic of Demonstratives," *Journal of Philosophical Logic,* 8 (1978): 81–98;

Jerrold Katz, "Has the Description Theory of Names Been Refuted?" in *Meaning and Method: Essays in Honor of Hilary Putnam,* edited by George Boolos (Cambridge & New York: Cambridge University Press, 1990), pp. 31–62;

David K. Lewis, "Naming the Colours," "Individuation by Acquaintance and by Stipulation," and "What Puzzling Pierre Does Not Believe," in his *Papers in Metaphysics and Epistemology* (Cambridge & New York: Cambridge University Press, 1999), pp. 332–358, 373–402, 408–417;

Robert L. Martin, *Recent Essays on Truth and the Liar Paradox* (Oxford: Clarendon Press, 1984);

Vann McGee, *Truth, Vagueness, and Paradox: An Essay on the Logic of Truth* (Indianapolis: Hackett, 1991);

Colin McGinn, *Wittgenstein on Meaning: An Interpretation and Evaluation,* Aristotelian Society Series, volume 1 (Oxford & New York: Blackwell, 1984);

John Myhill, "Notes toward an Axiomatization of Intuitionistic Analysis," *Logique et Analyse,* 35 (1967): 280–297;

Thomas Nagel, *The Last Word* (New York: Oxford University Press, 1997);

Stephen Neale, *Descriptions* (Cambridge, Mass.: MIT Press, 1990);

Neale, "No Plagiarism Here: The Originality of Saul Kripke," *TLS: The Times Literary Supplement,* no. 5106 (9 February 2001): 12–13;

Robert Nozick, *Philosophical Explanations* (Cambridge, Mass.: Harvard University Press, 1981), pp. 74, 120, 237, 341, 539, 655, 656–659, 668, 671, 707, 741, 742;

Charles Parsons, "A Plea for Substitutional Quantification," in his *Mathematics in Philosophy: Selected Essays* (Ithaca, N.Y.: Cornell University Press, 1983), pp. 63–70;

David Pears, *The False Prison: A Study of the Development of Wittgenstein's Philosophy,* volume 2 (Oxford: Clarendon Press / New York: Oxford University Press, 1988);

Consuelo Preti, *Kripke* (Belmont, Cal.: Wadsworth, 2002);

Arthur Prior, "Modality and Quantification in S5," *Journal of Symbolic Logic,* 21 (1956): 60–62;

Hilary Putnam, "Is Water Necessarily H_2O?" in his *Realism with a Human Face* (Cambridge, Mass.: Harvard University Press, 1990), pp. 54–79;

Putnam, "The Meaning of Meaning," in *Mind, Language, and Reality,* volume 2 of his *Philosophical Papers* (Cambridge & New York: Cambridge University Press, 1975), pp. 215–271;

Putnam, "Possibility/Necessity" and "Reference and Truth," in *Realism and Reason,* volume 3 of his *Philosophical Papers* (Cambridge & New York: Cambridge University Press, 1980), pp. 46–86;

Joseph Emerson Quinsey, "Some Problems in Logic," dissertation, University of Oxford, 1980;

Nathan Salmon, "Assertion and Incomplete Descriptions," *Philosophical Studies,* 42 (1982): 37–45;

Salmon, "Existence," in *Philosophical Perspectives,* volume 1, *Metaphysics,* edited by James Tomberlin (Atascadero, Cal.: Ridgeview, 1987), pp. 49–108;

Salmon, "How *Not* to Become a Millian Heir," *Philosophical Studies,* 62 (1991): 165–177;

Salmon, "How to Become a Millian Heir," *Noûs,* 23 (1989): 211–220;

Salmon, "How to Measure the Standard Metre," *Proceedings of the Aristotelian Society,* new series 88 (1987/1988): 193–217;

Salmon, "Nonexistence," *Noûs,* 32 (1978): 277–319;

Salmon, "The Pragmatic Fallacy," *Philosophical Studies,* 63 (1991): 83–97;

Salmon, *Reference and Essence* (Princeton: Princeton University Press, 1980);

Salmon, "Reflections on Reflexivity," *Linguistics and Philosophy,* 15 (1992): 53–63;

Salmon, "Trans-World Identification and Stipulation," *Philosophical Studies,* 84 (1996): 203–223;

Richard Shore, "Alpha-Recursion Theory," in *Handbook of Mathematical Logic,* edited by Jon Barwise and H. Jerome Keisler (Amsterdam: North-Holland, 1977), pp. 653–680;

Scott Soames, *Beyond Rigidity: The Unfinished Semantic Agenda of* Naming and Necessity (Oxford & New York: Oxford University Press, 2002);

David Sosa, "The Import of the Puzzle about Belief," *Philosophical Review,* 105, no. 3 (1996): 373–402;

Allen Stairs, "Quantum Mechanics, Logic and Reality," dissertation, University of Western Ontario, 1978;

Robert Stalnaker, "Pragmatic Presuppositions," in *Context and Content: Essays on Intentionality in Speech and Thought* (Oxford & New York: Oxford University Press, 1999), pp. 47–62;

Jason Stanley, "Names and Rigid Designation," in *A Companion to the Philosophy of Language,* edited by Bob Hale and Crispin Wright (Oxford & Malden, Mass.: Blackwell, 1997), pp. 555–585;

Peter Unger, "The Causal Theory of Reference," *Philosophical Studies,* 43 (1983): 1–45;

Peter van Inwagen, "Creatures of Fiction," *American Philosophical Quarterly,* 14 (1977): 299–308;

Albert Visser, "Semantics and the Liar Paradox," in *Topics in the Philosophy of Language,* volume 4 of *Handbook of Philosophical Logic,* edited by Dov M. Gabbay and Franz Guenthner (Dordrecht, Netherlands & Boston: Reidel, 1989), pp. 617–706;

George Wilson, "On Definite and Indefinite Descriptions," *Philosophical Review,* 86 (1978): 48–76;

Crispin Wright, *Rails to Infinity: Essays on Themes from Wittgenstein's* Philosophical Investigations (Cambridge, Mass.: Harvard University Press, 2001).

Papers:

Saul Kripke's unpublished manuscripts and tape recordings of thirty years of his seminars have been assembled and archived by Jeff Buechner. The manuscripts include more than 110 documents, exceeding 9,000 pages. A large portion of this corpus may eventually be published. Some philosophers are trying to obtain funding for a Kripke Institute, where intensive work on the unpublished corpus, including transcription of the tapes, could go forward.

Thomas S. Kuhn

(18 July 1922 – 17 June 1996)

Alexander Bird
University of Edinburgh

BOOKS: *The Copernican Revolution: Planetary Astronomy in the Development of Western Thought* (Cambridge, Mass.: Harvard University Press, 1957);

The Structure of Scientific Revolutions (Chicago: University of Chicago Press, 1962; enlarged, 1970);

The Essential Tension: Selected Studies in Scientific Tradition and Change (Chicago & London: University of Chicago Press, 1977);

Black-Body Theory and the Quantum Discontinuity, 1894–1912 (Oxford: Clarendon Press / New York: Oxford University Press, 1978; enlarged edition, Chicago & London: University of Chicago Press, 1987);

The Trouble with the Historical Philosophy of Science (Cambridge, Mass.: Department of the History of Science, Harvard University, 1992);

The Road since Structure: *Philosophical Essays, 1970–1993, with an Autobiographical Interview,* edited by James Conant and John Haugeland (Chicago & London: University of Chicago Press, 2000).

OTHER: "The Function of Dogma in Scientific Research," in *Scientific Change: Historical Studies in the Intellectual, Social and Technical Conditions for Scientific Discovery and Technical Invention, from Antiquity to the Present,* edited by A. C. Crombie (London: Heinemann, 1963; New York: Basic Books, 1963), pp. 347–369;

"Dubbing and Redubbing: The Vulnerability of Rigid Designation," in *Scientific Theories,* edited by C. Wade Savage, Minnesota Studies in the Philosophy of Science, volume 14 (Minneapolis: University of Minnesota Press, 1990), pp. 298–318.

SELECTED PERIODICAL PUBLICATION– UNCOLLECTED: "The Halt and the Blind: Philosophy and History of Science," *British Journal for the Philosophy of Science,* 31 (1980): 181–192.

Thomas S. Kuhn (photograph © by Stanley Rowlin)

Thomas S. Kuhn was the most influential philosopher of science of the second half of the twentieth century. His most important work, *The Structure of Scientific Revolutions* (1962), was one of the most widely read academic books of the twentieth century and had an influence far beyond the field of philosophy of science. Kuhn's thesis that the physical sciences develop in a cyclical pattern, with alternating periods of "normal" and "revolutionary" science, upset the consensus that science progresses in a linear fashion by adding to existing knowledge and refining theories to bring them ever closer to the truth. Kuhn's key idea that research during periods of normal science is "puzzle-solving" governed by a "paradigm"–an exemplary piece of research that is overthrown and replaced by a scientific revolution–was applied first to the natural sciences, then to the social sciences, and ultimately to activities outside science altogether. While Kuhn did not endorse all of these applications and extensions of his ideas, they helped to popularize his work and gave his use of the term *paradigm* wide currency.

Prior to *The Structure of Scientific Revolutions* the central question in the philosophy of science was: When does observational evidence confirm or disconfirm a hypothesis? The question was to be answered by logical and conceptual analysis, the methods typical of logical positivism. The assumption was that, given a satisfactory answer to this question, a study of the history of science would demonstrate that later theories are better confirmed than earlier ones and that rejected theories are less well confirmed than those that are accepted. The corollary to this assumption was that science yields a picture of the world that is ever increasing in breadth and in proximity to the truth. Kuhn's work provided both a critique of the premises of this way of doing philosophy of science and a model for a new way of pursuing it. Kuhn questioned the assumption that the relationship between observation and theory is one-way, with the choice of theory depending on the observational evidence but not vice versa, arguing that what one observes may depend on the theories one already holds. He claimed, further, that the meanings of key scientific terms depend on the theories of which they are a part. Thus, disparate theories, such as the physics of Aristotle and of Sir Isaac Newton, cannot be directly compared; they are "incommensurable." *The Structure of Scientific Revolutions* turned attention from the static relationship between evidence and theory to the dynamic question of how a discipline develops over time. Kuhn's emphasis on detailed examples from the history of science gave philosophy of science an historical turn that predominated for the next quarter of a century.

Thomas Samuel Kuhn was born on 18 July 1922 in Cincinnati to Samuel L. Kuhn, an industrial engineer, and Annette Stroock Kuhn. As the family moved from place to place, he attended schools in New York, Pennsylvania, and Connecticut. Graduating summa cum laude from Harvard University with a degree in physics in 1943, he spent the remainder of the World War II years in research related to radar, first with the Radio Research Laboratory at Harvard and later in Europe with the U.S. Office of Scientific Research and Development. Returning to Harvard, he earned a master's degree in physics in 1946.

While studying for his doctorate, Kuhn was asked by Harvard president James Conant, a chemist, to assist in Conant's course in science for undergraduates in the humanities, which was part of the General Education in Science curriculum. The course was Kuhn's first exposure to science texts from earlier historical periods; Aristotle's *Physics,* in particular, struck him as so alien to modern ideas on the subject that it could not possibly be the work of one of the greatest thinkers of all time. Intense study of the text, however, yielded the insight that–understood on its own merits, rather than through the lens of subsequent history of science, and undistorted by changes in the meaning of the scientific terminology–Aristotle's work made a great deal of sense. This insight was the germ of his theory of scientific revolutions.

Sponsored by Conant, Kuhn was elected a junior fellow of the Society of Fellows in 1948. On 27 November 1948 he married Kathryn Louise Muhs; they had three children: Sarah, Elizabeth, and Nathaniel. Kuhn received his Ph.D. in physics in 1949 with the dissertation "The Cohesive Energy of Monovalent Metals as a Function of Their Atomic Quantum Defects." In 1951 he moved from junior fellow to instructor and took over the science course from Conant. In 1952 he became an assistant professor of general education and the history of science. He published a series of papers in the history of science, focusing on eighteenth-century theories of matter and the early history of thermodynamics. He was a Guggenheim fellow in 1954–1955.

In 1956 Kuhn was denied tenure at Harvard because the committee thought that his first book, *The Copernican Revolution: Planetary Astronomy in the Development of Western Thought* (1957), which it reviewed before publication, was too popularly written and not sufficiently scholarly. Kuhn promptly accepted a position as assistant professor of history and philosophy at the University of California at Berkeley. Among his colleagues at Berkeley, Stanley Cavell was particularly influential on his thinking. Cavell directed Kuhn toward the works of Ludwig Wittgenstein, whose notion that words have a meaning in virtue of their role in what he called "language games" shaped Kuhn's later contention that paradigms have a semantic function in fixing the meaning of scientific terms.

The Copernican Revolution reflects its origins in the General Education in Science program at Harvard: in the foreword Conant explains that recounting the history of science is an effective method of getting nonscientists to understand how science works. Kuhn's book is easily accessible to nonexperts. Kuhn hoped that his description of an important historical instance of a revolution in science would show that scientific beliefs can be overthrown–that even long-held theories are not immune from criticism and do not last forever. His intention in the work is not skeptical, however: he demonstrates that a core of beliefs is retained even when many important ones are rejected; rather, it was to promote a realistic attitude toward modern science. As shown by the subtitle of the book, *Planetary Astronomy in the Development of Western Thought,* Kuhn is also concerned to point out that the Copernican revolution was not merely significant in astronomy but had wider ramifications in science. The revolution also had a profound effect on philosophy, leading to a reassessment of humanity's place in the universe, of which it was no longer the center, and its conception of its relationship with God.

For the Copernican revolution to show that scientific beliefs are subject to radical revision, Kuhn has to establish that the geocentric view that preceded the revolution was a genuine scientific one and not a religious doctrine, a traditional myth, or a prescientific speculation. Every society, however ancient or scientifically primitive, has beliefs about the nature of the universe. The ancient Greeks were different from almost all other societies in giving a central place to the study of the planets and stars in forming their cosmology. In so doing they posed questions for which straightforward answers were unavailable, such as: what is the radius of the Earth? How far away is the Moon? Why is the motion of the planets not uniform? Such questions require a theoretical rather than a merely observational approach. This early development culminated in the *Almagest,* written by Claudius Ptolemy in the middle of the second century A.D. The work established a mathematically sophisticated tradition of inquiry that was transmitted to medieval Europe via Islamic scholars.

Having shown that Ptolemaic astronomy was more akin to modern science than has generally been thought, Kuhn goes on to claim that Copernican astronomy is less close to modern astronomy than the history of science has typically portrayed it as being. Although Nicolaus Copernicus's innovation in his *De revolutionibus orbium coelestium libri vi* (Six Books Concerning the Revolutions of the Heavenly Orbs, 1543) of putting the Sun at the center of the solar system had the effect of overthrowing Ptolemy's astronomy and, ultimately, Aristotle's physics, as well, Kuhn argues that Copernicus himself saw his heliocentric hypothesis as merely a modification of those traditions meant to respond to mathematical problems that arose in them–in particular, the failure of Ptolemy's system to give an accurate account of the apparent movements of the Sun and the Moon. Copernicus retained Ptolemy's system, based on the principles of Aristotle's physics, of rotating solid spheres, epicycles, and eccentrics. Copernicus's system failed, however, to provide astronomers with the increased mathematical accuracy for which he had hoped. Instead, according to Kuhn, the experts were attracted to the new system by its aesthetic properties: they appreciated Copernicus's ability to do away with ad hoc elements in Ptolemy's system, such as the equant (an imaginary point in space about which the angular velocity of an orbit is constant, introduced as an ad hoc device to meet the Aristotelian requirement of uniform circular motion in the heavens) and the treatment of the orbits of the Sun, Mercury, and Venus. Furthermore, even though Copernicus retained Ptolemy's explanatory device of epicycles so that he could maintain the Ptolemaic-Aristotelian requirement of circular motion, his explanation of the retrograde motion of the planets was far more aesthetically pleasing than Ptolemy's.

While Copernicus intended his heliocentrism as a reformation of the tradition, those who adopted it saw that its consequences were far more profound. With the removal of Earth from the center of the universe, Aristotle's distinction between the different kinds of laws that apply on Earth, where objects tend to move in straight lines, and to the planets, whose motions are naturally circular, could not be maintained, since Earth itself was now held to be a planet. Hence, in the seventeenth century Galileo was able to challenge Aristotle's terrestrial physics, and Johannes Kepler was able to describe planetary motion as elliptical rather than circular. The culmination of these theories was Newton's unification of the laws of physics in a single universal system. Copernicus's beliefs, Kuhn says, have much more in common with those of Aristotle and Ptolemy than with those of Newton. He concludes that while one may legitimately see Copernicus as initiating modern astronomy, he can equally be seen as the last great figure of the preceding tradition.

In 1958 Kuhn was promoted to associate professor. The following year he delivered a paper, "The Essential Tension: Tradition and Innovation in Scientific Research," at a Salt Lake City conference on the identification of scientific talent; it became the title piece of his collection *The Essential Tension: Selected Studies in Scientific Tradition and Change* (1977). From the 1920s to the 1950s the dominant philosophy of science had been logical positivism, according to which all scientific knowledge must ultimately be based on observation–that is, on sense experience. Positivism, however, faced the problem of fully explicating the theoretical language of science in terms of the language of sense-experience, and it lacked an inductive logic–a set of rules for reasoning from particular observations to general theories–that could account for the inferences that scientists were actually making. In the 1950s an alternative to logical positivism was becoming popular among practicing scientists: the "falsificationism" of Karl Popper, according to which scientific theories are not constructed by inductive inference from observations; instead, a scientist makes a tentative, unjustified theoretical conjecture and puts it to an experimental test. If it fails the test, it is rejected, and a new conjecture is sought; if it passes the test, it is subjected to further testing. A theory is never verified; but as long as experiments fail to disconfirm it, it is provisionally accepted. Many scientists admired Popper's emphasis on rigorous testing; they thought that the picture of scientists subjecting their theories to tests that might well falsify them was a more accurate—or, at least, more flattering—depiction of their activities than the positivist conception of science as concerned with confirming evidence. Such scientists stressed the need for educating young scientists to engage in "divergent thinking"—to question common assumptions and to look at familiar subjects in new ways. Insofar as they regarded educational practices as promoting "convergent thinking," they deplored the situation.

Although Kuhn became known as the philosopher of scientific revolutions, in many ways he is most significant for the emphasis he placed on the role of tradition in scientific thinking. His work on the history of astronomy and cosmology had convinced him that Popper's description of scientific practice was incorrect: evidence often conflicts with a currently accepted theory, but the theory is not regarded as refuted. If Popper were correct, the revolutionary overthrow of theories would be the norm rather than the exception. In "The Essential Tension" he argues that for "ordinary science"—the science in which most scientists engage—convergent thinking is essential. He notes that scientific training relies heavily on textbooks in which the background knowledge required in the field is presented in a standard format. The student is tested with questions that can be solved by established techniques and that have known correct answers. This rigid training in convergent thinking has been immensely productive of important scientific innovations: agreement on accepted theories and methods of inquiry sets the stage on which discovery is possible. The tradition provides the scientist with research problems: it provides a "map" of what the world is like—of what it does and does not contain; but in certain areas the map may be drawn only in outline, and the scientist's task is to help fill in the detail. The tradition, through the scientist's training, supplies the techniques required for this development. Sometimes a phenomenon will be discovered that, at first sight, conflicts with the beliefs and theories embedded in the tradition; the scientist's task then is to try to reconcile the phenomenon with the tradition. This task may be so difficult that it can only be undertaken by those who have a thorough commitment to the tradition in which they are working. Kuhn gives the example of the orbit of Uranus, which was unusual and interesting only against the background of expectations generated by Newtonian dynamics. Belief in Newton's system and its ability to explain all the details of planetary motion inspired researchers such as Urbain Leverrier and John Couch Adams to put considerable effort

Cover for the 1959 paperback edition of Kuhn's first book, originally published in 1957, in which he examines the advent of the heliocentric hypothesis in the sixteenth century (Bruccoli Clark Layman Archives)

into showing that the divergence from expectation, far from being an error in Newtonian dynamics, was, in fact, caused by the existence of an unseen planet behaving perfectly in accordance with that dynamics. Without the tradition, Neptune would not have been discovered—at least, not in the way that it was.

At the same time, Kuhn acknowledges, science is not just the addition of detail to an existing map. Scientific innovations do require the rejection of accepted theories—the common picture of science as the stockpiling of knowledge is a mistake. The scientist who makes such an innovation needs to think both convergently and divergently. Convergent thinking is required for the scientist to be in a position to make the discovery in the first place—the innovator must understand and work within a tradition to see that an anomalous finding cannot be accounted for by the tradition. At the same time, solving these problems requires the ability to generate approaches that conflict with the tradition and require the rejection of entrenched beliefs, techniques, and theories: divergent thinking. This conflict is the "essential tension" that Kuhn identifies at the heart of scientific research and progress. Kuhn rejects the assumption, made both by logical positivism and by Popper, that all theories are subject to empirical testing, whether for confirmation or for falsification.

The ideas advanced in "The Essential Tension" are the kernel of the view that Kuhn sets forth in *The Structure of Scientific Revolutions*. That the book was published in the series "International Encyclopedia of Unified Science," edited by the positivists Otto Neurath and Rudolf Carnap, indicates that it was not a root-and-branch attack on positivism. Kuhn presents a picture of an alternation in science between stable periods, in which the leading theories in a particular field are accepted by virtually everyone working in that field, and briefer revolutionary episodes, in which those theories come under scrutiny and are replaced by others. Kuhn calls the stable periods "normal science," the revolutionary episodes "extraordinary science" or "revolutionary science." Normal science is governed by a "paradigm." Since Kuhn's use of the term in *The Structure of Scientific Revolutions, paradigm* has become a cliché that is almost empty of meaning. The concept does not have an unequivocal application even in Kuhn's hands; in a paper published in *Criticism and the Growth of Knowledge* (1970), edited by Imre Lakatos and Alan Musgrave, Margaret Masterman identifies twenty-one senses of the word in *The Structure of Scientific Revolutions*. Even so, the term has two central and related uses: a broader one that refers to all of the shared commitments of a group of scientists and a narrower one that refers to a seminal scientific achievement that acts as a model for research.

Kuhn characterizes normal science as "puzzle-solving." In normal science the leading theories—those encapsulated in the paradigm in the broader sense—are not tested: they are not subject to confirmation or falsification. Paradigms in the narrower sense are exemplary "puzzle-solutions," and they guide normal science in several related ways. First, they provide examples of what counts as a worthwhile research problem. The puzzles that subsequent researchers set themselves must be similar to the exemplary puzzle if they are to be regarded as worthwhile projects. Newton's *Principia Mathematica* (1687), for example, is the paradigm that governed celestial mechanics and much of the rest of physics for 250 years. It laid out the sorts of problems that would be worth attacking: some were specific, such as describing the details of the motions of the planets and their moons; others were more general, such as

finding other laws that, like Newton's law of gravitation, account for the forces objects exert on each other. Second, the paradigm provides the tools with which the solution may be sought. *Principia Mathematica* developed the techniques of the infinitesimal calculus that were employed by all of Newton's successors in their research. Third, the paradigm offers a standard by which the quality of the solution can be measured: similarity to the paradigm is a sign of scientific worth. For example, the experimental success of Coulomb's law was not the only consideration that recommended it to George A. de Coulomb's contemporaries; just as significant was the fact that it is an exact analogue of Newton's law of gravitation.

In claiming that paradigms as exemplars play a role in the assessment of proposed puzzle-solutions, Kuhn breaks with his empiricist predecessors, who assumed that the rules of theory evaluation are independent of any particular theory. Carnap's inductive logic, Carl G. Hempel's hypothetico-deductive model of confirmation, and Popper's falsificationism were a priori philosophical accounts of theory evaluation; hence, they all held that the assessment of a theory should be unaffected by whether or not the theory resembles some other theory.

According to Kuhn, a state of normal science cannot last indefinitely. Scientists will discover phenomena that, despite their best efforts, cannot be explained using the resources of the paradigm. Kuhn calls such intractable puzzles "anomalies." For example, Newton's treatment of the orbit of the Moon failed to fit with astronomical observations, and his successors found that the orbit of Uranus was not what was predicted by the best application of Newton's laws. Both of these anomalies were eventually resolved within the Newtonian paradigm—the first by improved mathematical techniques, the second by the discovery of Neptune. Kuhn notes that a few isolated anomalies may be accepted as part of normal science, rather than, as Popper contended, as immediate refutations of the theories embedded in the paradigm. During normal science a scientist's inability to solve a particular problem may be attributed to the limited capacities of that individual. An accumulation of unresolved anomalies, however, leads the science into its next phase: that of "crisis." A science is in crisis when its practitioners are no longer convinced that the current paradigm has sufficient resources to provide solutions to the increasing number of serious anomalies. During the stage of crisis the failure to resolve anomalies will be regarded as a failure of the paradigm, and a new paradigm will be required that does not suffer from these anomalies.

Kuhn calls the replacement of one paradigm by another a "scientific revolution." Although the use of

Dust jacket for the 1996 edition of Kuhn's best-known and highly influential book, first published in 1962,
in which he develops his theory of "normal" and "revolutionary" science and scientific "paradigms"
(University of Virginia)

the term *revolution* in connection with science was well established by this time, Kuhn's adoption of it reflects two important aspects of his view. First, it points to the cyclical nature of change in science: the adoption of a new paradigm as the result of a scientific revolution inaugurates a new period of normal science, which will lead to another crisis, another revolution, a new paradigm, and so on. Second, Kuhn draws an analogy between scientific and political revolutions. The political parallel to a paradigm is an established mechanism, such as a constitution or traditional lore and accepted practice, for resolving social and political problems. If a political conflict arises that cannot be resolved in the normal fashion, the constitution or traditional practices may have to be replaced by new ones.

Theories based on different paradigms are, Kuhn says, "incommensurable": they share no common measure. The paradigm of one period of normal science may lead scientists to judge one puzzle-solution more favorably than another solution, while the paradigm

from another period of normal science may lead scientists to make the opposite judgment. Kuhn is especially interested in the relationship between paradigm and language and the incommensurability of meanings that can be generated. He is particularly struck by the difficulty historians of science experience in trying to understand earlier theories. In his own case he had found that at first sight Aristotelian physics seemed absurd and full of obvious errors. A deeper understanding of Aristotle's thought and context, however, gave Kuhn a viewpoint from which the older science no longer appeared straightforwardly wrong. In particular, Aristotelian words and phrases that seem to have modern equivalents actually mean something quite different from their counterparts. But that understanding does not permit a perfect translation between the vocabularies of Aristotelianism and modern physics: according to Kuhn, no translation is both precise and accurate, and no common language can express both theories. The appropriate viewpoint cannot, therefore, be achieved simply by a reinterpretation of ancient texts. Understanding Aristotelian physics means learning to see the world in a different way. This change in perception requires the same kind of psychological leap that occurs when scientists make the transition from one paradigm to another.

Kuhn likens this leap to the sort of change that occurs when one undergoes a "gestalt shift." According to the Gestalt psychologists Max Wertheimer, Wolfgang Köhler, and Kurt Koffka, perceptual phenomena cannot be understood atomistically but only in reference to a whole, or gestalt. The Gestalt theory is commonly illustrated by pictures that can be seen as one image at one moment and as a different image at the next, as in the case of a simple drawing that can be interpreted as a rabbit or as a duck. Kuhn says that gestalt-switching should be regarded not merely as analogous to scientific revolution but also as evidence that common features underlie both the psychology of perception and the psychology of theory acceptance and theory change. A scientist's ability to "see" a proposed puzzle solution as similar to or different from an exemplary one results not from the application of logic to the problem but from the employment of a recognitional capacity similar to that which is used in seeing lines on a page as a picture of a person or thing. Scientists acquire such capacities, which Kuhn calls "learned similarity relations," by repeated exposure as students to exemplary puzzles and their exemplary solutions. The largely uniform education one finds within a scientific discipline allows scientists from different countries and cultures to respond in a similar way to scientific developments.

Kuhn also derives from the Gestalt psychology of perception the concept of "theory-dependence (or theory-ladenness) of observation." The positivists regarded observation as a matter of recording one's perceptual experiences, which they understood to be uninfluenced by either previous experience or theoretical commitment. Kuhn notes that the philosopher Norwood Russell Hanson challenged this assumption, using gestalt figures to argue that perceptual experience is influenced by one's presuppositions and beliefs. Kuhn endorses Hanson's contention and amplifies it by drawing on research carried out at Harvard by the psychologists Jerome Bruner and Leo Postman while Kuhn was there. Bruner and Postman showed that subjects had great difficulty in recognizing playing cards that were anomalous in some way, such as a three of clubs with red instead of black pips, and argued that the nature of perceptual experience depends on the expectations and needs of the subject. Kuhn takes their work to indicate the way immersion in a paradigm influences observation: adherents of different paradigms may not have the same experience when they observe the same scene or experimental apparatus. Neutral observation, then, cannot provide a common measure of theories from different paradigms. Revolutionary change is a transformation not just in theoretical belief but even in what a scientist can observe: "in a sense that I am unable to explicate further," Kuhn says, "the proponents of competing paradigms practice their trades in different worlds."

Toward the end of *The Structure of Scientific Revolutions* Kuhn makes it clear that the cyclical nature of science does not mean that scientific progress does not occur. It does occur, and not only during a period of normal science or relative to a given paradigm but also from revolution to revolution: thus, the long-term history of a science is a progressive one. He defines progress as increasing puzzle-solving power: the major factor in the choice of a new paradigm is its ability to provide a framework for solving puzzles. The new paradigm should retain much of the puzzle-solving power of its predecessor but should also be able to resolve some of the major anomalies that caused the crisis for the predecessor. Astronomy and physics can solve more puzzles today than they could in their earlier stages. But Kuhn denies that this increase in puzzle-solving power is a matter of approaching more and more closely to "the truth." For the traditional empiricist picture of science as progress toward the external goal of truth, Kuhn substitutes an evolutionary model in which science aims at the internal goal of solving its puzzles. In so doing, science progresses in the same sense as a species develops through natural selection: in neither case is there an ultimate perfection toward which each developmental step is a closer approximation.

Kuhn's emphasis on paradigms as arbiters of quality during periods of normal science led critics to regard him as an irrationalist who considers all scientific values, including truth, as relative to a paradigm. The accusation of irrationalism was, however, directed even more strongly at his account of revolutionary science. His analogy of scientific with political revolutions seemed to imply that the outcome of a scientific revolution is determined by highly contingent, nonscientific factors—the equivalent of the revolutionary mob, propaganda, coercion, and the like. This impression was reinforced by Kuhn's remark that "external" causes may play a major part in fixing the content of the new paradigm. Such causes include developments outside the science in question, as well as "idiosyncrasies of autobiography and personality"; "Even the nationality or the prior reputation of the innovator and his teachers can sometimes play a significant role," Kuhn writes. He had to put considerable effort into explaining the ways in which such criticism misrepresents his views. At the same time, this aspect of Kuhn's work was emphasized by many who claimed to be his followers, including sociologists of science who saw in his remarks the seed of a new approach to the explanation of scientific change: change was taken to be explicable not, as the positivists claimed, by reference to a priori rules of theory choice but by appeal to explicitly sociological factors. Others who took Kuhn's account as vindicating their views included feminist and postmodernist theorists who wanted to portray science as the expression of a traditional, male-dominated hierarchy rather than as the product of pure reason. Kuhn was thus faced with an interpretation of his work that he denied but that was shared by his detractors and supporters alike.

Another feature of *The Structure of Scientific Revolutions* that attracted charges of irrationalism was Kuhn's emphasis on incommensurability. The claim that scientists operating in different paradigms observe differently led some critics to accuse Kuhn of idealism, while some of his supporters, reading into the claim a strong kind of social constructivism, took it as further criticism of the alleged objectivity of science. Kuhn repudiated both interpretations, pointing out that his claim is clearly linked to the psychological thesis that experience is theory-dependent.

In 1964 Kuhn moved to Princeton University as professor of philosophy and history of science. The following year a conference on his work was held at the International Colloquium in the Philosophy of Science at Bedford College in London. Papers were presented by Kuhn, Popper, Masterman, John Watkins, Stephen Toulmin, and L. Pearce Williams. The papers were published in 1970, along with later contributions by Lakatos and Paul Feyerabend, as *Criticism and the Growth of Knowledge*. Kuhn's paper, "Logic of Discovery or Psychology of Research?" (republished in *The Essential Tension*), compares his and Popper's approaches to scientific change. He acknowledges their shared emphasis on scientific revolutions and the rejection of old theories, in contrast to the traditional view of science as a steady accretion of knowledge. As opposed to the positivists, he and Popper stress the dependence of observation on theory; they are also realists in that they take theories as attempting to explain phenomena by reference to real entities, whereas the positivists regard theories as instruments of prediction that, when properly understood, do not assert the existence of anything other than phenomena. (Although Kuhn does not mention it, he and Popper also employ evolutionary analogies in explicating their conceptions of scientific progress.)

Nonetheless, Kuhn is more concerned to explore the precise nature of their differences. For Popper, science progresses only when a theory is tested, falsified, and replaced by a new theory; for Kuhn, most scientific advances occur during periods of normal science, when an established tradition, crystallized around a paradigm of good research, provides the puzzles and the stan-

dards for an acceptable solution. Revolutions, by definition, do not occur during normal science. Popper regards falsifiability as a defining feature of a science: a genuine science has theories that make predictions that can be tested in such a way that some possible results would show the theory to be false. Astronomical theories, for example, make detailed quantitative predictions about the observable positions of the planets; the "predictions" made by astrologers, on the other hand, are nonquantifiable and imprecise, so that any outcome can be taken to be in accord with them. Astrological claims are, thus, not falsifiable and so are not scientific. Kuhn cannot accept such a criterion, since paradigm theories and puzzle-solutions are not tested during normal science and are not regarded as falsifiable. According to Kuhn, astronomy has a puzzle-solving tradition of research that astrology lacks; even when it was intellectually respectable, astrology was not a science but a craft. Like medicine and mechanical engineering, it was linked to a science but was not itself a science.

Kuhn's first complaint against Popper, then, is that he fails to recognize the existence of normal science. But Popper's account of revolutions is also inaccurate, according to Kuhn. Popper holds the overthrow of an existing theory to be the logical result of testing the theory and finding that it fails the test, while Kuhn argues that revolutions are produced by crises that result from the accumulation of anomalies; hence, revolutions occur, in Kuhn's view, without the underlying theory being put to the test. Furthermore, crises and the response to them are psychological, rather than logical, in character: no logical criterion determines the number of anomalies sufficient to constitute a crisis, nor does logic require that a crisis be resolved by a revolutionary change in theory. Kuhn notes that Popper himself recognizes that conclusive disproof of a theory is not available, since various ad hoc moves, such as denying the reliability of experimental results, may be made. But this admission represents a threat to Popper's basic position, whereas the lack of a conclusive ground for the rejection of a paradigm is central to Kuhn's view. As a crisis develops, "conservatives" can retain their faith in the existing paradigm, and "radicals" can reject it, with neither side committing a logical error. The very fact that uncertainty exists concerning the paradigm indicates a lack of consensus on what had previously been the shared basis for the interpretation of experiments and observations. Thus, although Popper is right that theories are overthrown in revolutions, he is wrong in thinking that such overthrows are dictated by falsification. Falsification, says Kuhn, takes place only during normal science, when agreement on a paradigm permits the unambiguous reading of data collected in the process of puzzle solving; in such cases the underlying theory of the paradigm is not falsified, for that theory is the basis of the test. Rather, the attempted puzzle-solution is disproved. Popper, says Kuhn, makes the mistake of transferring the process of falsification from normal science to revolutionary science and, thereby, from puzzle-solutions to theories.

A second edition of *The Structure of Scientific Revolutions* was published in 1970; it includes "Postscript 1969," in which Kuhn clarifies some of the ideas presented in the first edition that had been misunderstood and also develops and modifies some of his earlier views. Among the ideas clarified is the notion of paradigms and their function. Kuhn now explicitly distinguishes between the broader conception of paradigm, which he calls a "disciplinary matrix" and defines as "the entire constellation of beliefs, values, techniques, and so on shared by the members of a given community," and the narrower conception, which he calls the "exemplar" and defines as "the concrete puzzle-solutions which, employed as models or examples, can replace explicit rules as a basis for the solution of the remaining puzzles of normal science." A sociological concept, the disciplinary matrix refers to the objects of consensus that bind practitioners of a scientific discipline together. The key components of a disciplinary matrix are symbolic generalizations (formal theories, key equations, laws, definitions, and so forth); metaphysical beliefs; scientific values such as accuracy, consistency, breadth of scope, simplicity, and fruitfulness; heuristic models (analogies that help direct thinking); and exemplary puzzle-solutions. The last element of the disciplinary matrix is its most important feature and constitutes the narrower notion of paradigm, which, Kuhn says, was the most novel and least understood aspect of *The Structure of Scientific Revolutions*. He emphasizes the role of exemplars in forging learned similarity relations—the ability to see one puzzle-solution as similar to another. This ability is acquired through training with examples, Kuhn says, not by learning rules. Exemplars are also used to establish the meanings of scientific terms: the symbols employed in symbolic generalizations such as laws and equations derive their meanings from exemplary scientific puzzle-solutions.

"Postscript 1969" also addresses the accusations of Kuhn's critics that he had advanced a relativistic account of science that left no room for the traditionally accepted value of absolute truth. Kuhn notes that his evolutionary picture of scientific progress holds that later theories are better than their predecessors in making more-accurate predictions and solving more problems and is, therefore, not relativistic. But he repeats his denial of any need for the notion of truth in explaining the development of science, going even further to argue that the idea of science presenting ever better represen-

tations of what nature is really like, or of theories growing closer to the truth, is actually incoherent: scientists have no way of knowing what is "really there" independently of their theories, and this situation deprives the idea of truth—understood as a match between a theory and an independent reality—of any sense.

In the decade and a half following the original publication of *The Structure of Scientific Revolutions* most of Kuhn's work was devoted to developing themes from the book or responding to criticism of it. Then, in 1978, he published *Black-Body Theory and the Quantum Discontinuity, 1894–1912,* his second book dealing with a particular episode in the history of science. Unlike *The Copernican Revolution,* the work is highly technical and not readily accessible to readers without a solid background in physics. Also unlike *The Copernican Revolution,* which had referred to sun worship and Neoplatonism in explaining how the heliocentric viewpoint came to be accepted, the new book ignores factors outside of science. The absence of such factors surprised those who regarded Kuhn as promoting sociological explanations in the history of science. Readers were also surprised by the lack of references to paradigms, disciplinary matrices, incommensurability, normal science, crises, and so on; while many historians and philosophers of science had adopted Kuhn's vocabulary, Kuhn himself seemed to have abandoned it.

Kuhn's aim in *Black-Body Theory and the Quantum Discontinuity, 1894–1912* is to show that the traditional understanding of the origin of the quantum revolution in physics is mistaken. In classical physics, particles change from one energy level to another in a continuous fashion, whereas in quantum physics they "jump" from level to level without passing through intermediate levels: change in energy is discontinuous. The discovery of quantum discontinuity was generally believed to have been made by Max Planck in 1900 or 1901, when he described black-body radiation—the distribution of energy within a cavity—as divided into multiples of the unit $h\nu$, in which ν is the frequency of radiation and h is a constant ($6.6260755 \times 10^{-34}$ joule-second, now known as Planck's constant). Kuhn's contention is that at this time Planck was using a statistical technique, previously employed by Ludwig Boltzmann, of dividing the range of possible continuous energies into "cells" that could be treated together for mathematical purposes. Indeed, Kuhn says, Planck was puzzled that he could get the result he wanted only by fixing the cell size at $h\nu$; the technique should have worked for any way of dividing the cells, as long as they were small enough but not too small. According to Kuhn, Planck did not arrive at the genuine quantum concept until 1908, two years after Albert Einstein and Paul Ehrenfest.

The Essential Tension

Selected Studies
in Scientific Tradition
and Change

Dust jacket for Kuhn's 1977 collection of essays. The title piece, originally delivered at a conference in 1959, presents the germ of the theory that he elaborated in The Structure of Scientific Revolutions *(Bruccoli Clark Layman Archives)*

Kuhn and his wife were divorced in September 1978. The following year he became professor of philosophy and history at the Massachusetts Institute of Technology (MIT). On 25 October 1982 he married Jehane R. Burns. Over the next decade he began to seek a linguistic account of incommensurability. In his essay "Commensurability, Comparability, Communicability," delivered at the biennial meeting of the Philosophy of Science Association in 1982 and republished, with revisions, in *The Road since* Structure: *Philosophical Essays, 1970–1993* (2000), Kuhn says that incommensurability can be understood as a certain kind of untranslatability between the language of a new theory or paradigm and that of the old one or, in some cases, as untranslatability between competing paradigms. He points out that contrary to the interpretation of some critics, he did not intend incommensurability to mean that holders of different paradigms

cannot communicate or that their paradigms cannot be compared. Incommensurability does imply, though, that communication will be imperfect and imprecise, just as it is not possible to translate the English *carpet* exactly into French. Similarly, theories cannot be compared in the point-by-point manner that philosophers such as Popper had envisaged. Kuhn notes that in his contribution to *Criticism and the Growth of Knowledge* he had associated his incommensurability thesis with Quine's "indeterminacy of translation" thesis but has now abandoned this parallel. Quine's claim was that too many translations could be found for any single translation to be determinately correct, while Kuhn's contention is that no translation is possible between the languages of incommensurable paradigms. He did retain from Quine, however, the idea that incommensurable languages divide the world into kinds of things in different ways, and he says that

163

learning kind-terms by means of visual exemplars would make it possible to create different divisions by using different exemplars.

Kuhn goes on to develop a taxonomic account of incommensurability. A scientist uses a taxonomy in categorizing entities–a biologist, for example, will have a taxonomy that divides living beings into species, genera, families, and so on. The terms used to express the taxonomy–its lexicon–are related to one another in a "lexical network." The internal relations among members of the lexical network are constitutive of their meanings; hence, one cannot change part of the network without changing all of it. Kuhn identifies incommensurability with differences in taxonomy brought about by changes to lexical networks or differences between networks. Avoiding incommensurability would require adding to one lexicon new terms to translate the terms of the other, as one might import a French word into English when no exact English equivalent exists. In scientific taxonomies, however, Kuhn claims that such importation is not allowed: a "no-overlap" principle prohibits the kind-categories of a taxonomy from cutting across one another. Either the categories are entirely disjoint, sharing no members, or one category is a subkind of the other category, such that all the members of the first are included in the second.

In 1982 Kuhn was awarded the Sarton Medal by the History of Science Society. Two years later he became professor emeritus at MIT. In 1987 a second edition of *Black-Body Theory and the Quantum Discontinuity, 1894–1912* appeared. It includes an afterword, "Revisiting Planck," that Kuhn had published separately earlier that year, in which he seeks to dispel the misconception that *Black-Body Theory and the Quantum Discontinuity, 1894–1912* represents a change in his views from *The Copernican Revolution* and *The Structure of Scientific Revolutions*. The omission of the influence of factors from outside the realm of science in *Black-Body Theory and the Quantum Discontinuity, 1894–1912* resulted from the greater professionalization and specialization of science in the late nineteenth and early twentieth centuries as compared to the seventeenth century and earlier periods. In regard to the absence of the terminology of *The Structure of Scientific Revolutions,* Kuhn explains that he did not believe it was necessary to employ that vocabulary in examining specific episodes in the history of science. He argues, however, that *Black-Body Theory and the Quantum Discontinuity, 1894–1912* reflects several of the themes of *The Structure of Scientific Revolutions*. One such theme is the rejection of the traditional conception of science as the addition of discrete discoveries to the stockpile of knowledge–a conception that motivates disputes over priority in the sciences–in favor of the view that discovery is a process spread out over time,

the product of which may turn out to be incompatible with the thinking that initiated it. This idea was illustrated in *The Copernican Revolution:* Copernicus viewed his work as a means of reconciling Aristotelianism and much of the Ptolemaic system with the need for greater mathematical accuracy in describing planetary motion; yet, the eventual effect of his innovation was the repudiation of Aristotle's physics and all of the remaining elements of Ptolemaic astronomy. As the initiator of this revolution, Copernicus is typically seen as a modern thinker whose conception of the solar system was largely similar to the current one; but for Kuhn, this view is mistaken. Similarly, Planck's conception of the quantum $h\nu$ was quite different in 1901 from what it was ten years later; yet, the prevailing tendency is to think of Planck's earlier use as being the same as the familiar later one. Both cases, Kuhn says, are instances of incommensurability. Where a modern interpretation is readily available, historians tend to see scientists of the past such as Copernicus and the early Planck as being more like themselves than they really are; where no such interpretation is available, they tend to reject the scientists' thought as irrational, as the young Kuhn did with Aristotle's physics. Kuhn notes that such errors can be made by the scientists themselves: Planck, Otto Stern, and Niels Bohr all misremembered the thinking that led them to important findings because of the incommensurability of their earlier ideas with what they went on to discover.

After spending the academic year 1984–1985 studying Kuhn's philosophy of science at MIT, where he had extended discussions with Kuhn himself, the German scholar Paul Hoyningen-Huene published the first monograph devoted exclusively to Kuhn: *Die Wissenschaftsphilosophie Thomas S. Kuhns: Rekonstruktion und Grundlagenprobleme* (1989; translated as *Reconstructing Scientific Revolutions: Thomas S. Kuhn's Philosophy of Science,* 1993). Hoyningen-Huene interprets Kuhn as employing a Kantian distinction between the "world-in-itself," which is independent of scientific investigations, and the phenomenal world, which is partly constituted by the human mind imposing categories on the phenomena. While Immanuel Kant conceived of the categories as immutable mental structures, however, Kuhn regards them as subject to change. An individual's categories are, in part, the product of his or her immersion in a paradigm-governed tradition; hence, when the paradigm changes, the categories through which the individual views the world are likely to change, too. The phenomenal world thus changes, even if the world-in-itself does not. Kuhn endorsed this understanding of his outlook, describing himself in an interview in *The Road since* Structure as a "Kantian with moveable categories." Thus, the charge of early critics that the views put forward in *The Structure of Scientific Revolutions* are idealistic is vindicated, at least in regard to the Kantian form of idealism.

Kuhn's influence has been immense not only in the philosophy and history of science but also in other disciplines and even beyond academia; *The Structure of Scientific Revolutions* is one of the most frequently cited books of all time. Kuhn was especially influential among sociologists, in part because his ideas improved their image as scientists. According to traditional criteria, physics and biology are exemplary sciences: they have impressive histories with bodies of accumulated knowledge, widely recognized achievements, and persisting research programs that seem to be getting ever closer to the truth; sociology has none of those features. But Kuhn denies that such criteria are definitive of science (and that the approximation to truth is not even possible); to be a science, a discipline requires a paradigm to govern its research, and such can be found in sociology. And the disputes among rival theories in sociology corresponds to Kuhn's description of a science in a young state, before a consensus has formed around a single paradigm.

Kuhn also provided sociologists with a new field of study: science itself. Before Kuhn, the standard explanation of changes in science was that they were demanded by rational assessments of the evidence; and since the study of rationality is within the domain of philosophy, the explanation of scientific change was considered a philosophical task. Only in the rare cases when a change went against the requirements of rationality could there be room for a sociological explanation. But Kuhn shows that the standard development of a science does have sociological determinants. Although he acknowledged such extrascientific factors as the personality or nationality of a key figure, the sociological influences he emphasizes are almost always internal to the practice of science. For example, as a matter of group consensus the disciplinary matrix is a sociological phenomenon; but it is a consensus on a scientific exemplar, on scientific values, and so forth. Similarly, crisis is both sociological—a matter of shared doubt about the capacity of the existing paradigm to generate solutions to anomalies—and scientific, since the doubt is about scientific matters. Some sociologists sought to extend the range of explanations of scientific events to include extrascientific factors such as power relations among scientists and between scientists and the society at large. Proponents of the "Strong Programme" in the sociology of science, founded by David Bloor and Barry Barnes, deny that rationality and irrationality play any explanatory role in the study of science. Kuhn repudiated the Strong Programme in a lecture at Harvard in 1991, though some have objected that he was attacking a caricature of the position.

Kuhn might have tried to distance himself from the Strong Programme because of his sensitivity over his reputation as an irrationalist about science. Lakatos had commented that in Kuhn's view the motor of revolutionary change in science is "mob psychology." By the end of his career, however, Kuhn was no longer seen in this light: having started his professional life as an historian of science, he finished it as a philosopher of science. Some critics regard Kuhn as having moderated his views because of the attacks on him: under fire from professional philosophers, they claim, he gave up his radical but ultimately untenable position and retreated to one that, though more philosophically defensible, was not nearly as interesting. Others claim that while this evaluation may apply to the changes in his treatment of the concepts of paradigm and incommensurability, his philosophical work after *The Structure of Scientific Revolutions* consists largely of explications and reformulations of the ideas advanced there. Whereas in the book he expressed those insights in psychological terms, thus incurring accusations of irrationality from traditionalists who regarded psychological and rational explanations as incompatible, he later recast them in philosophical terms.

Kuhn died on 17 June 1996 of cancer of the throat and bronchial tubes. His failure, despite his wide influence, to leave behind anything like a Kuhnian "school" may be attributed to his shift from an historical, psychological, and sociological approach to a philosophical one. Had he developed his earlier insights, which in *The Structure of Scientific Revolutions* are thought-provoking but sketchy, he might have given more direction to research in the social sciences in which he was so influential. On the other hand, Kuhn's philosophical legacy now seems to have been shorter-lived than might have been expected. In the 1960s and 1970s Kuhn, Feyerabend, and Lakatos showed, in opposition to positivism, that the philosophy of science needed to take the history of science seriously, and departments of the history and philosophy of science were established at many English-speaking universities. Although such departments still thrive, this explicitly historical approach to the philosophy of science now appears to have been a temporary phenomenon. Kuhn's qualms about truth—and so, implicitly, about the notion of knowledge; his skepticism that scientific progress is anything more than improved puzzle-solving; and his view that the meanings of scientific terms are closely tied to the theories with which they are connected are symptomatic of the empiricist tradition to which he was objecting. In part because of Kuhn, philosophers have repudiated much of empiricism; but in doing so they have rejected not only the views Kuhn himself criticized but also other empiricist assumptions that he implicitly endorsed. To many contemporary philosophers, the philosophy of science that is needed is one that is not historically grounded but one that is historically sensitive yet philosophically grounded. In this light one may regard Kuhn not as having provided a new paradigm in the philosophy of science but rather, like Copernicus and Planck, as inaugurating a revolution that went beyond what he himself foresaw.

Interviews:

John Horgan, "Profile: Reluctant Revolutionary: Thomas S. Kuhn Unleashed 'Paradigm' on the World," *Scientific American,* 264 (May 1991): 14–15;

Giovanna Borradori, "Paradigms of Scientific Evolution: Thomas K. Kuhn," in *The American Philosopher: Conversations with Quine, Davidson, Putnam, Nozick, Danto, Rorty, Cavell, MacIntyre, and Kuhn,* translated by Rosanna Crocitto (Chicago: University of Chicago Press, 1994), pp. 153–167;

Christian Delacampagne, "Un Entretien avec Thomas S. Kuhn," *Le Monde,* 5–6 February 1995, p. 13;

Armando Massarenti, "Thomas Kuhn: Le rivoluzioni prese sul serio," *Sole* (Milan), 3 December 1995, p. 27;

Aristides Baltas, Kostas Gavroglu, and Vassiliki Kindi, "A Discussion with Thomas S. Kuhn," in *The Road since* Structure: *Philosophical Essays, 1970–1993, with an Autobiographical Interview,* edited by James Conant and John Haugeland (Chicago & London: University of Chicago Press, 2000), pp. 255–323.

References:

Barry Barnes, *T. S. Kuhn and Social Science* (London: Macmillan, 1982; New York: Columbia University Press, 1982);

Alexander Bird, *Thomas Kuhn* (Chesham, U.K.: Acumen, 2000; Princeton: Princeton University Press, 2000);

Michael Devitt, "Against Incommensurability," *Australasian Journal of Philosophy,* 57 (1979): 29–50;

Gerald Doppelt, "Kuhn's Epistemological Relativism: An Interpretation and Defense," *Inquiry,* 21 (1978): 33–86;

Steve Fuller, *Thomas Kuhn: A Philosophical History for Our Times* (Chicago: University of Chicago Press, 2000);

Garry Gutting, ed., *Paradigms and Revolutions: Appraisals and Applications of Thomas Kuhn's Philosophy of Science* (Notre Dame, Ind.: University of Notre Dame Press, 1980);

Ian Hacking, ed., *Scientific Revolutions* (Oxford & New York: Oxford University Press, 1981);

Paul Horwich, ed., *World Changes: Thomas Kuhn and the Nature of Science* (Cambridge, Mass.: MIT Press, 1993);

Paul Hoyningen-Huene, *Die Wissenschaftsphilosophie Thomas S. Kuhns: Rekonstruktion und Grundlagenprobleme* (Brunswick: Vieweg, 1989); translated by Alexander T. Levine as *Reconstructing Scientific Revolutions: Thomas S. Kuhn's Philosophy of Science* (Chicago: University of Chicago Press, 1993);

Imre Lakatos and Alan Musgrave, eds., *Criticism and the Growth of Knowledge* (London: Cambridge University Press, 1970);

Musgrave, "Kuhn's Second Thoughts," *British Journal for the Philosophy of Science,* 22 (1971): 287–297;

W. H. Newton-Smith, *The Rationality of Science* (Boston & London: Routledge & Kegan Paul, 1981);

Thomas Nickles, ed., *Thomas Kuhn* (Cambridge & New York: Cambridge University Press, 2002);

Howard Sankey, *The Incommensurability Thesis* (Aldershot, U.K.: Avebury / Brookfield, Vt.: Ashgate, 1994);

Sankey, "Kuhn's Changing Concept of Incommensurability," *British Journal for the Philosophy of Science,* 44 (1993): 775–791;

Dudley Shapere, "The Structure of Scientific Revolutions," *Philosophical Review,* 73 (1964): 383–394;

Wes Sharrock and Rupert Read, eds., *Kuhn: Philosopher of Scientific Revolution* (Malden, Mass.: Polity, 2002);

Harvey Siegel, "Objectivity, Rationality, Incommensurability and More," *British Journal for the Philosophy of Science,* 31 (1980): 359–375.

David Lewis

(28 September 1941 – 14 October 2001)

Takashi Yagisawa
California State University, Northridge

BOOKS: *Convention: A Philosophical Study,* foreword by W. V. Quine (Cambridge, Mass.: Harvard University Press, 1969);

Counterfactuals (Cambridge, Mass.: Harvard University Press, 1973; Oxford: Blackwell, 1973; reprinted with corrections, 1986);

Philosophical Papers, 2 volumes (Oxford & New York: Oxford University Press, 1983, 1986);

On the Plurality of Worlds (Oxford & New York: Blackwell, 1986);

Parts of Classes, by Lewis, John P. Burgess, and A. P. Hazen (Oxford & Cambridge, Mass.: Blackwell, 1991);

Papers in Philosophical Logic (Cambridge & New York: Cambridge University Press, 1998);

Papers in Metaphysics and Epistemology (Cambridge & New York: Cambridge University Press, 1999);

Papers in Ethics and Social Philosophy (Cambridge & New York: Cambridge University Press, 2000).

SELECTED PERIODICAL PUBLICATIONS–UNCOLLECTED: "Immodest Inductive Methods," *Philosophy of Science,* 38 (1971): 54–63;

"Completeness and Decidability of Three Logics of Counterfactual Conditionals," *Theoria,* 37 (1971): 74–85;

"Spielman and Lewis on Inductive Immodesty," *Philosophy of Science,* 41 (1974): 84–85;

"Possible-World Semantics for Counterfactual Logics: A Rejoinder," *Journal of Philosophical Logic,* 6 (1977): 359–363;

"Vague Identity: Evans Misunderstood," *Analysis,* 48 (1988): 128–130;

"Counterpart Theory, Quantified Modal Logic, and Extra Argument Places," *Analysis,* 53 (1993): 69–71;

"Zimmerman and the Spinning Sphere," *Australasian Journal of Philosophy,* 77 (1999): 209–212;

"Causation as Influence," *Journal of Philosophy,* 97 (2000): 182–197;

David Lewis

"Sleeping Beauty: Reply to Elga," *Analysis,* 61 (2001): 171–176;

"Forget about the 'Correspondence Theory of Truth,'" *Analysis,* 61 (2001): 275–280;

"Truthmaking and Difference-Making," *Noûs,* 35 (2001): 602–615;

"Marshall and Parsons on 'Intrinsic,'" by Lewis and Rae Langton, *Philosophy and Phenomenological Research,* 63 (2001): 353–355;

"Redefining 'Intrinsic,'" *Philosophy and Phenomenological Research,* 63 (2001): 381–398.

David Lewis was the last notable systematic philosopher of the twentieth century. He is known for many important and lucidly expressed contributions to diverse areas of philosophy, including philosophy of language, theory of mind, and metaphysics. He is remembered, in particular, for his audacious advocacy of the reality of all possible worlds.

David Kellogg Lewis was born in Oberlin, Ohio, on 28 September 1941 to John Donald and Ewart Kellogg Lewis, both of whom were college professors. He majored in chemistry at Swarthmore College, but after spending a term at the University of Oxford and attending lectures by Gilbert Ryle, he switched to philosophy. Following his graduation in 1962, he studied under W. V. Quine at Harvard University. In the fall of 1963 he attended a seminar given by the visiting Australian philosopher J. J. C. Smart, one of the earliest and most influential advocates of the mind-body (or psychophysical) identity theory, which holds that mental states are reducible to physical processes in the brain. Another student in the seminar was Stephanie Robinson; she and Lewis were married on 5 September 1965.

While still in graduate school Lewis wrote "An Argument for the Identity Theory." The article, published in *The Journal of Philosophy* in 1966 and republished in volume one of Lewis's *Philosophical Papers* (1983), improves on Smart's position and is considered a classic in the philosophy of mind. Smart's argument for the mind-body identity theory was that, given the findings of the physical sciences, the most economical way of accounting for mental phenomena is to identify them with physical ones, such as processes in the brain. Lewis sets out to provide a "stronger foundation" than economy for the position, which he defines as "the hypothesis that—not necessarily but as a matter of fact—every experience is identical with some physical state. Specifically, with some neurochemical state." The defining characteristic of any experience, or mental occurrence, he says,

> is its causal role, its . . . most typical causes and effects. We materialists believe that these causal roles which belong by analytic necessity to experiences belong in fact to certain physical states. Since those physical states possess the definitive characteristics of experience, they must be the experiences.

He says that his argument for the identity of mind and body parallels an uncontroversial one concerning cylindrical combination bicycle locks. The defining characteristic of such a lock being unlocked is

> the causal role of that state . . . : namely, that setting the combination typically causes the lock to be unlocked and that being unlocked typically causes the lock to open when gently pulled. That is all we need to know in order to ascribe to the lock the state of being . . .

unlocked. But we may learn that, as a matter of fact, the lock contains a row of slotted discs; setting the combination typically causes the slots to be aligned; and alignment of the slots typically causes the lock to open when gently pulled. So alignment of slots occupies precisely the causal role that we ascribed to being unlocked by analytic necessity, as the definitive characteristic of being unlocked. . . . Therefore alignment of slots is identical with being unlocked. . . . They are one and the same.

Lewis justifies the first premise of his argument, that the causal role of a mental occurrence is its defining characteristic, by pointing out that it is "common to all who believe that experiences are . . . real and . . . efficacious outside their own realm." He distinguishes this commonsense belief from such philosophical positions as epiphenomenalism and parallelist dualism, which deny that mental events have effects outside the mind, and suggests an improvement on behaviorism by reconstruing pure dispositions as states defined by their causal roles. His second premise is the "traditional and definitive working hypothesis of natural science" that physics is able in principle, and will eventually be able in fact, to explain all physical phenomena that can be explained at all. This hypothesis "does not rule out the existence of nonphysical phenomena. . . . It only denies that we need ever explain physical phenomena by nonphysical ones." The conclusion is that "experiences are . . . physical phenomena," and the most likely candidate for the kind of physical phenomena they are is states of the nervous system.

Lewis's first premise, that mental occurrences are to be defined in terms of their typical causal functions, is one of the earliest, and to date most concise, formulations of the functionalist position in the philosophy of mind. His version of functionalism is analytic; it asserts that conceptually necessary connections exist between mental concepts and functional concepts. It is to be distinguished from functionalism as an empirical and, therefore, contingent scientific hypothesis. Lewis's dedication to conceptual analysis as the method of philosophy was, thus, manifest at the earliest stages of his career.

Lewis became an assistant professor of philosophy at the University of California, Los Angeles, in 1966, even though he did not receive his Ph.D. from Harvard until the following year. In 1968 he published "Counterpart Theory and Quantified Modal Logic" in *The Journal of Philosophy;* it is collected in volume one of his *Philosophical Papers.* The article is highly technical and filled with formulas written in the notation of symbolic logic, but the basic theory can be illustrated in ordinary language. To say that Hubert Humphrey might have won the 1968 presidential election over

Richard M. Nixon is to say that some possible but non-actual world contains a counterpart of Humphrey who did win the election. The "counterpart" relation is a type of similarity relation.

The counterpart theory is one of the most controversial aspects of Lewis's metaphysics and has generated an enormous amount of literature. One common objection is that a victory by someone other than Humphrey in some other world is irrelevant to the possibility of Humphrey's victory in this world, since it is Humphrey in this world about whom one is talking when one says that he might have won. Some other man, similar to Humphrey, performing actions similar to Humphrey's, and even bearing the name "Hubert Humphrey," may win the election in some other world; but what, the objection asks, does that have to do with the possibility of a victory by Hubert Humphrey in this world? Lewis responds in "Postscripts to 'Counterpart Theory and Quantified Modal Logic'" in volume one of his *Philosophical Papers* that Humphrey might have won in this world if and only if "according to some world," Humphrey did win; to say that Humphrey won "according to some world" is to say that Humphrey had a counterpart in that world and that that counterpart won in that world. Humphrey's counterpart in that world is not Humphrey but is still a counterpart of Humphrey and of no one else. So it is Humphrey, "that very man," who is said to have won according to a nonactual world. Thus, "possibly won" is analyzed as "has a counterpart who won."

Lewis reworked his dissertation into his first book, *Convention: A Philosophical Study* (1969). The work—which won the Franklin J. Matchette Prize in philosophy, a prestigious award for scholars under the age of forty—is a defense of analyticity. The distinction between analytic and synthetic statements was originally made in the eighteenth century by the German philosopher Immanuel Kant and was generally accepted into the twentieth century. According to this distinction, an analytic statement is one in which the concept of the predicate is "contained" in the concept of the subject: for example, "All bachelors are single." Such statements are necessarily true. A synthetic statement is one in which this relationship of containment is not present: for example, "All bachelors are bald." Such statements are contingent—they can be true or false, depending on whether the facts are in accord with them or not ("All bachelors are bald" is, of course, false). In the early twentieth century, logical positivists such as Rudolf Carnap claimed that analyticity depends on linguistic conventions, such as the meanings of words and the grammatical rules governing their combination. Quine attacked both analyticity and the conventionality of language in "Truth by Convention" (1936), "Two

Library of Philosophy and Logic

Counter-factuals

DAVID LEWIS

Basil Blackwell

Dust jacket for the corrected 1986 British edition of Lewis's 1973 book, in which he deals with subjunctive conditional statements (Bruccoli Clark Layman Archives)

Dogmas of Empiricism" (1951), *Word and Object* (1960), and "Carnap and Logical Truth" (1960). Morton White joined the attack on analyticity with "The Analytic and the Synthetic: An Untenable Dualism" (1950). The Quine-White assault persuaded many philosophers that the analytic/synthetic distinction could not be maintained and that the conventions of language were a myth.

Lewis's aim in *Convention* is to resurrect a Carnapian defense of analyticity as truth guaranteed by the conventions of language. To do so, he provides a general definition of convention that goes far beyond anything Carnap produced and then applies it to language. The book includes extensive and carefully laid-out lines of reasoning, with many examples to help the reader. Lewis borrows two key concepts, "coordination problem" and "coordination equilibrium," from game theory, which deals with the strategic interactions of parties with potentially different interests: a coordination problem exists when two or more agents act, the outcome depends on the actions of all the agents, and the agents' interests more or less coincide; a coordination equilibrium is a combination of the agents' actions in which no agent would be better off if any agent acted otherwise. Lewis argues that a regularity in the behavior of members of a population when they are agents in a recurrent situation is a convention if and only if, in any instance of that situation, everyone conforms to the regularity, everyone expects everyone else to conform to it, and everyone prefers to conform to it on the condition that the others do, also. The recurrent situation constitutes a coordination problem, and uniform conformity to the regularity is a coordination equilibrium in that situation. Lewis's analysis allows a convention to exist without any explicit agreement by the participants and is, therefore, well suited to apply to language: the language of a population, he explains, is a conventional signaling system for that population under a convention of truthfulness sustained by a common interest in communication. Finally, Lewis gives his Carnapian definition of analyticity: a sentence is analytic in a language if and only if it has the same truth-value (is true or false) in every possible world. Quine, who wrote the foreword to Lewis's book, remained unconvinced by his defense of analyticity, but many others found it compelling. Lewis may, therefore, be said to have at least stemmed the tide of the Quine-White assault against analyticity.

In 1970 Lewis became associate professor of philosophy at Princeton University. That same year he published "General Semantics," a major work in possible-worlds semantics, in the journal *Synthese;* it is republished in volume one of *Philosophical Papers.* The article provides a logically rigorous theoretical framework for a wide variety of grammatical constructions. The following year Smart arranged for him to deliver the Gavin David Young Lectures at the University of Adelaide in Australia. The trip marked the beginning of a long and fruitful exchange between Lewis and Australian philosophers such as Smart and David M. Armstrong. For the rest of Lewis's life he and his wife spent two or three months there almost every year during Lewis's summer breaks, which coincided with Australia's winter. Lewis became a fan of Australian football and bush ballads and enjoyed birdwatching there. Most of all he loved to ride Australian trains, although English railways were his favorites. He was a train buff and would ride for hours while reading and writing philosophy. He had an extensive model-train set in the basement of his house in Princeton.

Lewis's second book, *Counterfactuals,* was published in 1973. Counterfactual, or subjunctive, conditionals are statements of the form "If it were the case that *p,* then it would be the case that *q,*" where *p* is, in fact, not the case. They are crucially important in diverse areas of philosophy. The Scottish philosopher David Hume pointed out in the eighteenth century that they are integral to the notion of causation: to say that one event was the cause of another is to say, at least in part, that if the first event had not occurred, then (all other conditions being the same) the second event would not have occurred. Thus, if one does not understand counterfactual conditionals, one does not understand causation. Another application of counterfactuals is the notion of dispositional properties such as fragility and solubility. For a thing to be fragile is for it to be such that if it were impacted with a force of a small yet sufficient magnitude, it would break; for a thing to be soluble in water is for it to be such that if it were placed in water, it would dissolve. Some philosophers have argued that human free will should also be understood as a dispositional state: for one to be free in performing an act is for one to perform it and for it to be the case that if one had chosen to do otherwise, one would have done otherwise.

Conditions under which counterfactual conditionals are true were not well understood until Robert Stalnaker's "A Theory of Conditionals" was published in *Studies in Logical Theory,* edited by Nicholas Rescher, in 1968. Stalnaker used the theoretical apparatus of possible worlds to argue that the statement "If kangaroos had no tails, they would topple over" is true if kangaroos topple over in the closest possible world in which kangaroos have no tails. Lewis opens his book by summarizing the basic idea behind this sort of analysis:

> "*If kangaroos had no tails, they would topple over*" seems to me to mean something like this: in any possible state of affairs in which kangaroos have no tails, and which resembles our actual state of affairs as much as kangaroos having no tails permits it to, the kangaroos topple over. I shall give a general analysis of counterfactual conditionals along these lines.

Lewis goes on to provide a much more general and thorough discussion of counterfactual conditionals than Stalnaker, subsuming Stalnaker's analysis as a special case of his own. He asks the reader to imagine various possible worlds, some of which are more similar to the actual world than others. They are scattered in a three-dimensional space defined by the intersecting axes *x, y,* and *z,* with the actual world occupying the origin of the axes; the more similar a world is to the actual world, the closer it is to the origin. The actual world is the most similar to itself, so its distance from the origin is zero. A "sphere of similarity" surrounds the actual world so that in every possible world within the sphere, kangaroos that lack tails topple over. In other words, any world in which kangaroos lack tails and topple over is more similar to the actual world than is any world in which kangaroos lack tails but do not topple over. In that case, the counterfactual conditional "If kangaroos had no tails, they would topple over" is true.

Like Stalnaker's, Lewis's analysis explains the vagueness of counterfactual conditionals by pointing to the vagueness of the similarity relation. Lewis's analysis, furthermore, accounts for the fallaciousness of the "fallacy of strengthening the antecedent" on the basis of a "shifting similarity sphere": from the statement "If Otto had come to the party, it would have been lively," it does not follow that "If Otto and Anna had come to the party, it would have been lively," because the addition of "and Anna" to the antecedent means that the previously close worlds are no longer close, opening up room for worlds in which the party is not lively. Another well-known fallacy that is explained by Lewis's analysis is the "fallacy of transitivity": it does not follow from the statements "If J. Edgar Hoover had been a Communist, he would have been a traitor" and "If J. Edgar Hoover had been born in Russia, he would have been a Communist" that "If J. Edgar Hoover had been born in Russia, he would have been a traitor." The similarity relations governing the two premises need not carry over to a similarity relation that makes the conclusion true, Lewis points out.

Lewis's analysis, in conjunction with his counterpart theory, also explains how the sentences posed in 1947 by Nelson Goodman in "the Problem of Counterfactual Conditionals" (republished in his *Fact, Fiction, and Forecast,* 1955)–"If New York City were in Georgia, New York City would be in the South" and "If Georgia included New York City, Georgia would not be entirely in the South"–can both be true. According to Lewis, New York City and Georgia both have various counterparts in various worlds, and a less stringent counterpart relation is summoned up by the subject terms *New York City* in the first statement and *Georgia* in the second than by the object terms *Georgia* in the first and *New York City* in the second. An even more dramatic illustration of the strength of Lewis's analysis is seen in statements beginning "If I were you . . .":

> The antecedent-worlds are worlds where you and I are vicariously identical; that is, we share a common counterpart. But we want him to be in *your* predicament with *my* ideas, not the other way around. He should be your counterpart under a counterpart relation that stresses similarity of predicament; mine under a different counterpart relation that stresses similarity of ideas.

In 1973 Lewis was named Class of 1943 Professor of Philosophy at Princeton. Two years later Kit

Fine published "Critical Notice of *Counterfactuals* by D. Lewis" in *Mind,* arguing that since a world without a nuclear holocaust is closer to the actual world than a world with such a holocaust, the counterfactual conditional "If Nixon had pressed the button, there would have been a nuclear holocaust" is false on Lewis's analysis. Lewis responded in "Counterfactual Dependence and Time's Arrow," published in *Noûs* in 1979 and collected in volume two of his *Philosophical Papers* (1986), by giving more-detailed standards of the similarity between worlds that is needed for assessing counterfactual conditionals. In order of decreasing importance, they are the avoidance of widespread and diverse violations of law; the maximization of the spatiotemporal region in which a perfect match of particular facts prevails; the avoidance of simple localized violations of law; and approximate similarity of particular facts. According to these standards of similarity, a world in which Nixon pressed the button and a nuclear holocaust occurred is more similar to the actual world than to any world in which Nixon pressed the button and a nuclear holocaust did not occur.

Among the many philosophical theses that Lewis put forth and defended, the most celebrated–some would say infamous–is that of "modal realism," or the plurality of worlds: that every possible world is as real and concrete as the actual one. He argues for it in many places, but the most important are "Counterpart Theory and Quantified Modal Logic"; "Anselm and Actuality," published in *Noûs* in 1970 and republished in volume one of his *Philosophical Papers;* section 4.1 of *Counterfactuals,* "Possible Worlds"; and *On the Plurality of Worlds* (1986), based in part on the John Locke Lectures he delivered at the University of Oxford in 1984. Lewis defines "our world" as the totality of absolutely everything that bears any spatiotemporal relation to the here and now. According to modal realism, there are many other worlds, and each of them is the same kind of entity as "our world": that is, each is an inclusive totality of spatiotemporally related things. Since anything that bears any spatiotemporal relation to a thing in a world is also a thing in that world, no two worlds stand in any spatiotemporal relation to each other; every world is spatiotemporally completely isolated from every other world. Therefore, no causal interactions occur between any two worlds, which means that traveling from one world to another is impossible: however far one traveled by whatever means, one would never get out of one's own world. Also, no object that exists in any one world exists in any other world; that is, every possible object exists in one world only. Using some technical reasoning, Lewis estimates that more worlds exist than real numbers. An obvious objection to such an extravagant ontology is the principle of parsimony, or "Ockham's Razor": "Do not multiply enti-

*Cover for the 1986 book in which Lewis elaborates his well-known
thesis of "modal realism," according to which every possible
world is as real as the actual one (University of
South Carolina Spartanburg Library)*

ties beyond necessity." Lewis responds by distinguishing two versions of Ockham's Razor. One version holds that the number of *individual* entities postulated in a theory should be kept as low as possible. Lewis finds this version, which he terms "unworthy," implausible. He claims that his theory observes the "worthy" version, which says that the number of *kinds of* entity postulated in a theory should be kept low. Since the other worlds are the same kind of entity as "our world," postulating them does not violate the principle—assuming that it is warranted to believe in the existence of "our world." Lewis also contends that the other-worlds postulate does not go "beyond necessity," since it provides the best overall philosophical outlook. He says in *Counterfactuals:*

> One comes to philosophy already endowed with a stock of opinions. It is not the business of philosophy either to undermine or to justify these preexisting opinions, to any great extent, but only to try to discover ways of expanding them into an orderly system. A

metaphysician's analysis of mind is an attempt at systematizing our opinions about mind. It succeeds to the extent that (1) it is systematic, and (2) it respects those of our pre-philosophical opinions to which we are firmly attached. Insofar as it does both better than any alternative we have thought of, we give it credence. There is some give-and-take, but not too much: some of us sometimes change our minds on some points of common opinion, if they conflict irremediably with a doctrine that commands our belief by its systematic beauty and its agreement with more important common opinions.

So it is throughout metaphysics; and so it is with my doctrine of realism about possible worlds. Among my common opinions that philosophy must respect (if it is to deserve credence) are not only my naive belief in tables and chairs, but also my naive belief that these tables and chairs might have been otherwise arranged. Realism about possible worlds is an attempt, the only successful attempt I know of, to systematize these preexisting modal opinions.

In addition to providing a reason for embracing modal realism, this passage summarizes Lewis's view of philosophy as an adjudicating and systematizing endeavor.

The example of tables and chairs illustrates a core application of Lewis's thesis: it can deal with alethic modalities, the various ways or modes—necessity, contingency, possibility, and impossibility—in which statements such as "The tables and chairs are arranged in a certain way" can be true or false. To say that the tables and chairs might have been arranged in a certain nonactual configuration is to say that some possible world contains counterparts of the tables and chairs in the actual world and that these counterparts are arranged in that other configuration in that world. Alethic modality is distinguished from other types of modality, such as epistemic modality, which deals with such statements as "As far as I know, the tables and chairs might have been positioned differently" or "For all little Davy knows, *pi* could be rational." Alethic modality is independent of epistemic modality, but epistemic modality is definable in terms of alethic modality: to say that such-and-such is epistemically possible is to say that what one knows and such-and-such could be jointly true, and to say that such-and-such is epistemically necessary is to say that what one knows and the negation of such-and-such could not be jointly true. Other types of modality can also be defined in terms of alethic modality, which is, thus, the most basic type of modality.

Further theoretical gains to be derived by modal realism, in addition to the analysis of counterfactual conditionals and alethic modality, Lewis says in *On the Plurality of Worlds,* include the clarification of the notion of a property as a set of all of its possessors. The traditional nominalist position is that properties are nothing above and beyond the particular objects that possess them. A problem arises if this claim is combined with the claim that everything is actual: there will be no way to distinguish two different, yet accidentally coextensional, properties. In other words, one will be forced to say that whenever two properties happen to be possessed by exactly the same particular objects, then they are one and the same property. This situation is unsatisfactory, for even if all purple monsters are people-eaters and all people-eating monsters are purple, being a purple monster and being a people-eating monster are not the same property. Lewis upholds the traditional nominalist position by separating it from the claim that everything is actual: if one identifies a property with the set of its possessors and claims at the same time that the possessors may be either actual or merely possible objects, one escapes the problem. Even if all and only purple monsters are people-eating monsters in this world, there are many other worlds where some purple monsters are not people-eaters and many other worlds where some people-eating monsters are not purple. The set of purple monsters is, therefore, different from the set of people-eating monsters, and the distinctness of the two properties is preserved.

In *On the Plurality of Worlds* Lewis addresses several objections to his system. To the objection that only "our world" and its inhabitants actually exist, Lewis responds that he agrees, but he adds that there are more things than those that "actually exist." He offers an "indexical analysis of actuality": to say that something actually exists is to say that it exists in "our world," which is analogous to saying in everyday speech that something exists "here" or "now." *Here* and *now* are stereotypical examples of "indexical" words. *Here* means the spatial location of the speaker, while *now* refers to his or her temporal location. If Stephanie says, "A donkey is here," she is saying that a donkey is near where she is; no matter where she is, if a donkey is near her, what she says is true. If Stephanie says, "The test starts now," she is saying that the test starts as she speaks; no matter when she speaks, if the test starts at the time of her speaking, what she says is true. Likewise, then, according to the indexical analysis of actuality, when Stephanie says, "A talking donkey actually exists," she is saying that a talking donkey exists in the world in which she speaks; no matter in which world she speaks, if a talking donkey inhabits that world, what she says is true. Of course, if she speaks in "our world," what she says is false. Every place is "here" for anyone who occupies it, and every time is "now" for anyone who persists through it. Analogously, every world is "actual" for anyone who inhabits it. In this sense, *actual* means "this-worldly." Lewis's indexical analysis of actuality offers a straightforward answer to

the age-old conundrum, "Why am I actual rather than merely possible?" Lewis's answer is: "Because that is what 'actual' means." Whenever one says "I am actual," one is bound to be right, just as one is right whenever one says "I am here." "I am actual" is as analytic and as knowable a priori as "I am here."

One might be tempted to identify Lewis's modal realism with the "many-worlds" interpretation of quantum physics, which postulates that reality splits into many alternative "worlds" every time a measurement is made. Lewis did not propose his ontology as an interpretation of quantum mechanics or of any other scientific theory; it is an integral part of a wide-ranging metaphysical theory that provides conceptual analyses of alethic modality and other philosophically important notions. Furthermore, Lewis's possible worlds are fundamentally different from the "worlds" of the "many-worlds" interpretation of quantum mechanics. The latter bear spatiotemporal relationships to one another: different "worlds" split away from a common "world." Lewis's possible worlds, by contrast, bear no spatiotemporal relationships to one another. If something bears any spatiotemporal relationship to a given possible world, then that thing is a part of that possible world; it is not another possible world. No two Lewisian possible worlds overlap in any way; hence, no two Lewisian possible worlds share an initial segment and then split away. The "many-worlds" interpretation of quantum mechanics is often erroneously believed to have been proposed by Hugh Everett III, but Everett's interpretation does not postulate splitting worlds; instead, it takes the superposition of all possible states as actual and prevalent. It thus complicates one's view of what the actual world is like but does not require other worlds. Lewis's theory is, thus, distinct both from the "many-worlds" and from Everett's interpretations of quantum mechanics.

Many modal metaphysicians agree with Lewis that alethic modality and counterfactual conditionals are well analyzed in terms of possible worlds; they strongly disagree with him, however, on the nature of possible worlds. While Lewis regards worlds as concrete spatiotemporal wholes, the others view them as abstract representations. Lewis labels such theories "ersatz modal realism." Ersatz modal realists, he says, help themselves to the conceptual apparatus of possible worlds to clarify and advance philosophical debates, but such worlds and their inhabitants do not, for them, carry serious ontological weight: they wish to have the cake of possible worlds and eat it, too. Lewis has two main objections to ersatz modal realism. First, it assumes the notion of possibility, rather than providing an analysis of it. In a linguistic version of ersatz modal realism, for example, a Lewisian possible world is

Lewis at Princeton University in 1998 (photograph by Robert P. Matthews)

charge and spin are fundamental properties of physical particles, but there might have been more such properties than there actually are; if one confines one's resources to actuality, one will be unable to construct any representations for such additional properties.

Lewis's final book, *Parts of Classes* (1991), is a treatise on the foundations of mathematics. Set theory provides a unified basis for almost all of mathematics; the question of the nature of sets, therefore, lies at the heart of the philosophy of mathematics. The orthodox view takes sets to be abstract objects with no spatiotemporal location, which leaves the relationship between a set and its members obscure. A chessboard, for example, may be seen as eight rows of eight squares each or as eight columns of eight squares each. For any collection of objects, there is a set that has precisely those objects as members; thus, there is a set whose members are the eight rows, and another set whose members are the eight columns. Since no row is a column, and no column is a row, these sets do not have a single member in common. They are, therefore, two entirely distinct sets. At the same time, the whole consisting of the rows as its parts and the whole consisting of the columns as its parts are one and the same object: the chessboard. Therefore, neither set is a whole consisting of its members as parts. Lewis proposes that a set is a whole consisting of its subsets as parts. Since every nonempty set can be partitioned into "singletons," or sets with one member, every set is a whole consisting of the singletons of its members as parts. Lewis identifies the empty set—the set with no members—as a whole consisting of all things that are not sets. *Parts of Classes* is a significant first step toward subsuming mathematics under mereology, a general theory of the part-whole relation. An appendix by Lewis, John P. Burgess, and A. P. Hazen examines the nature of the relationship between a singleton and its sole member.

David Lewis died on 14 October 2001 of complications from diabetes. Although modal realism has not been widely adopted by philosophers—Lewis himself said that his ideas on possible worlds were frequently met with "incredulous stares"—it has produced much fruitful debate and significantly advanced the understanding of modality and a wide variety of related issues. As Lewis said in the introduction to volume one of his *Philosophical Papers*:

> I should have liked to be a piecemeal, unsystematic philosopher, offering independent proposals on a variety of topics. It was not to be. I succumbed too often to the temptation to presuppose my views on one topic when writing on another. Most notably, my realism toward unactualized possibles shows up in nearly every paper in the book.

replaced by a maximal consistent set of sentences. This approach yields an analysis of possibility according to which it is possible that *p* if and only if there is a maximal consistent set of sentences according to which it is true that *p*. Lewis objects that this method is circular: possibility is analyzed in terms of the consistency of a set of sentences, but the consistency of a set of sentences is understood as the possibility of the truth of all sentences in that set; possibility is, thus, ultimately analyzed in terms of possibility. Most ersatz modal realists have found this objection serious enough to retreat to the position that use of ersatz worlds should be regarded as nothing more than a useful heuristic tool in philosophical theorizing. Lewis's second objection to ersatz modal realism is that it lacks sufficient resources to represent all distinct possibilities as genuinely distinct. Many variants of ersatz modal realism exist, but all of them draw on the resources of reality as it actually is for constructing the abstract representations of nonactual possibilities. The expressive power of the resultant representations is thereby unduly limited. For example,

Lewis's work in philosophy of language helped to establish possible-worlds semantics as a major research program not only in philosophy but also in theoretical linguistics. His work in philosophy of mind made functionalism a robust theoretical position to be taken seriously. Responsible research in nearly all core areas of philosophy, including metaphysics, epistemology, philosophy of science, philosophy of mind, philosophy of language, and logic, would not be possible without some acquaintance with Lewis's writings.

Lewis's contributions to metaphysics, philosophy of mind, philosophy of language, epistemology, logic, ethics, and social philosophy are held in high regard. His influence on Australian philosophers has been especially profound.

References:

Hugh Everett, "'Relative State' Formulation of Quantum Mechanics," *Reviews of Modern Physics,* 29 (1957): 454–462;

Kit Fine, "Critical Notice of *Counterfactuals* by D. Lewis," *Mind,* 84 (1975): 451–458;

Peter Forrest and David M. Armstrong, "An Argument against David Lewis' Theory of Possible Worlds," *Australasian Journal of Philosophy,* 62 (1984): 164–168;

Patrick Grim, *The Incomplete Universe: Totality, Knowledge, and Truth* (Cambridge, Mass.: MIT Press, 1991);

A. P. Hazen, "Counterpart-Theoretic Semantics for Modal Logic," *Journal of Philosophy,* 76 (1979): 319–338;

William G. Lycan, "The Trouble with Possible Worlds," in *The Possible and the Actual: Readings in the Metaphysics of Modality,* edited by Michael J. Loux (Ithaca, N.Y.: Cornell University Press, 1979), pp. 274–316;

Brian Skyrms, "Possible Worlds, Physics and Metaphysics," *Philosophical Studies,* 30 (1976): 323–332;

Peter Van Inwagen, "Two Concepts of Possible Worlds," in *Studies in Essentialism,* edited by Peter A. French, Theodore E. Uehling Jr., and Howard K. Wettstein, Midwest Studies in Philosophy, volume 11 (Minneapolis: University of Minnesota Press, 1986), pp. 185–213.

Ernest Nagel

(16 November 1901 – 20 September 1985)

Angelo Juffras
William Paterson University

BOOKS: *An Introduction to Logic and Scientific Method,* by Nagel and Morris Raphael Cohen (New York: Harcourt, Brace, 1934);

Principles of the Theory of Probability, International Encyclopedia of Unified Science, volume 1, no. 6 (Chicago: University of Chicago Press, 1939);

Sovereign Reason and Other Studies in the Philosophy of Science (Glencoe, Ill.: Free Press, 1954);

Logic without Metaphysics and Other Essays in the Philosophy of Science (Glencoe, Ill.: Free Press, 1956);

Liberalism and Intelligence (Bennington, Vt.: Bennington College, 1957);

Gödel's Proof, by Nagel and James R. Newman (New York: New York University Press, 1958);

The Structure of Science: Problems in the Logic of Scientific Explanation (New York: Harcourt, Brace & World, 1961);

Observation and Theory in Science, by Nagel, Sylvain Bromberger, and Adolf Grünbaum, introduction by Stephen F. Barker (Baltimore: Johns Hopkins University Press, 1971);

Teleology Revisited and Other Essays in the Philosophy and History of Science (New York: Columbia University Press, 1979).

Edition: *Gödel's Proof,* edited by Douglas R. Hofstadter (New York: New York University Press, 2001).

OTHER: Justus Buchler, *Charles Peirce's Empiricism,* foreword by Nagel (London: Kegan Paul, Trench, Trübner, 1939; New York: Harcourt, Brace, 1939);

John Stuart Mill's Philosophy of Scientific Method, edited by Nagel (New York: Hafner, 1950);

Freedom and Reason: Studies in Philosophy and Jewish Culture, in Memory of Morris Raphael Cohen, edited by Nagel, Salo W. Baron, and Koppel S. Pinson (Glencoe, Ill.: Free Press, 1951);

Augustus De Morgan, *A Budget of Paradoxes: Reprinted, with the Author's Additions, from the* Athenaeum, edited by David Eugene Smith, introduction by Nagel (New York: Dover, 1954);

Ernest Nagel (photograph by Steve Pyke, London)

Dialogue on John Dewey, edited by Corliss Lamont and Mary Redmer, contributions by Nagel (New York: Horizon, 1959);

Dialogue on George Santayana, edited by Lamont and Redmer, contributions by Nagel (New York: Horizon, 1959);

"Philosophical Concepts of Atheism," in *Basic Beliefs: The Religious Philosophies of Mankind,* edited by Johnson E. Fairchild (New York: Sheridan House, 1959), pp. 167–186;

Logic, Methodology, and Philosophy of Science: Proceedings, edited by Nagel, Patrick Suppes, and Alfred Tarski (Stanford, Cal.: Stanford University Press, 1962);

Induction: Some Current Issues, edited by Nagel and Henry Ely Kyburg (Middletown, Conn.: Wesleyan University Press, 1963);

Meaning and Knowledge: Systematic Readings in Epistemology, edited by Nagel and Richard B. Brandt (New York: Harcourt, Brace & World, 1965);

Scientific Psychology: Principles and Approaches, edited by Nagel and Benjamin B. Wolman (New York: Basic Books, 1965);

Aesthetics and the Theory of Criticism: Selected Essays of Arnold Isenberg, edited by Nagel and others (Chicago: University of Chicago Press, 1973).

SELECTED PERIODICAL PUBLICATION–
UNCOLLECTED: "Naturalism Reconsidered," *Proceedings and Addresses of the American Philosophical Association,* 28 (October 1955): 5–17.

From about 1945 to 1965 Ernest Nagel was generally regarded as one of the two or three foremost philosophers in the United States. Noted primarily as a philosopher of science, he devoted the greater part of his work to an explication of the logic, the rational structure, the objectivity, and the tests of science. Although he avoided the label of "pragmatist," his ideas about science were largely guided by the notions of Charles Sanders Peirce and John Dewey that inquiry begins in response to a specific problem, and its conclusions are fallible and subject to revision in the light of further evidence; science is thus self-corrective. Nagel's defense of empirical procedures and naturalism was steadfast throughout his life.

Nagel was born on 16 November 1901 in Nové Mesto, Bohemia (then part of Austria-Hungary, today part of the Czech Republic), to Isidor Nagel, a shopkeeper, and Frida Weisz Nagel. He told Estelle Gilson in a 1980 interview that his father's family was much more orthodox in its Judaism than his mother's, and that his father's relatives considered the Nagel household "déclassé," refusing even to take tea there. Nagel arrived in the United States with his family in 1911 and became an American citizen in 1919. As an undergraduate he studied philosophy with Morris Raphael Cohen at City College of New York. Cohen's other students included the future philosophers Sidney Hook, Paul Weiss, and Justus Buchler, but Nagel was his favorite. Nagel acquired from Cohen a fondness for logic and rational structure, as well as an interest in the writings of Peirce, George Santayana, and Bertrand Russell.

After graduating in 1923, Nagel began teaching in the New York City school system while studying part-time for a master's degree in mathematics at Columbia

University. He told Gilson that he "was a great admirer of Bertrand Russell, who said if you want to be any kind of philosopher, you ought to know some mathematics." He received his M.A. in 1925 and began working on a doctorate in philosophy. The following year his father died, increasing his family responsibilities and slowing his academic progress. Before beginning their dissertations, philosophy students at Columbia were required to pass a written examination on the history of philosophy and an oral examination on two ancient and two modern philosophers. Asked by the doctoral committee why he had chosen Plato, Plotinus, Baruch Spinoza, and Peirce, Nagel explained that "they were all rationalists in one form or another" and that he had been persuaded by Cohen's rationalist approach. Irwin Edman, a member of the committee, reported this reply to Cohen, who arranged through a private sponsor for a fellowship that enabled Nagel to take a year off from teaching to devote himself to his dissertation, "On the Logic of Measurement." In 1930 he began teaching philosophy at City College. He received his Ph.D. the following year and accepted an instructorship in philosophy at Columbia, even though it paid less than his City College salary. Although Frederick J. E. Woodbridge, a professor of philosophy and, at the time, dean of the graduate school, told Nagel that his status at the university was extremely tenuous and that he should look for a permanent position elsewhere, Nagel managed to remain at Columbia.

Between 1930 and 1934 Nagel published articles on the philosopher Alfred North Whitehead, the physicist Arthur Stanley Eddington, and measurement, as well as a review of Peirce's collected papers; these pieces have been collected in his *Sovereign Reason and Other Studies in the Philosophy of Science* (1954) and *Logic without Metaphysics and Other Essays in the Philosophy of Science* (1956). In 1934 he and Cohen co-authored *An Introduction to Logic and Scientific Method.* The book was significant for its rejection of the then-dominant Baconian view that scientific laws are either shorthand summaries of, or inductions derived from, repeated observations of regularities and that hypotheses are to be eschewed as metaphysical speculation. In the chapter "Science and Hypothesis" Nagel and Cohen argue against the admonition to "study the facts, nothing but the facts" and show that hypotheses are a necessary part of science and that the appropriate use of observation is in testing them. They describe the deductive pattern of scientific explanation, distinguishing it from historical and genetic explanations, and show how scientific explanations function logically. Many of their points are commonplace today, but at the time *An Introduction to Logic and Scientific Method* marked an important advance. Their presentation of logic is restricted to the syllogism and some of its extensions, but this limitation put the book within the competence of instructors at a time when understanding of symbolic logic was not widespread.

In 1934–1935 Nagel traveled in Europe on a Guggenheim Fellowship. He visited the leading figures in the new analytic-philosophy movement in Poland, Austria, and England, all of whom thought that philosophy should emulate the practices of the sciences—a conception of the role of the philosopher that was quite different from the one Nagel had imagined. He had planned to write a comprehensive work modeled after Santayana's *The Life of Reason; or, The Phases of Human Progress* (1905–1906), in which he would survey and comment on the course of mathematical and scientific progress; he was dissuaded from this project by leading members of the logical-positivist Vienna Circle, who convinced him that philosophers should shun grand enterprises and systems and focus on limited and solvable problems. Nagel's essay "'Impossible Numbers': A Chapter in the History of Modern Logic" (1935), collected in *Teleology Revisited and Other Essays in the Philosophy and History of Science* (1979), is a residue of his abandoned project.

In January 1935 Nagel married physicist Edith Alexandria Haggstrom. They had two sons: Alexander Joseph, who became a professor of mathematics at the University of Wisconsin at Madison, and Sidney Robert, who became a professor of physics at the University of Chicago. A result of Nagel's trip to Europe was "Impressions and Appraisals of Analytic Philosophy in Europe," published in *The Journal of Philosophy* in 1936 and collected in *Logic without Metaphysics and Other Essays in the Philosophy of Science*. The article was instrumental in acquainting American philosophers with the new movement. Nagel's sympathetic treatment of the Vienna Circle led some to identify him as a logical positivist, but he had reservations about some of their doctrines. His many discussions with them, as well as his articles such as "Verifiability, Truth, and Verification" (1934) and "Truth and Knowledge of the Truth" (1944) both collected in *Logic without Metaphysics and Other Essays in the Philosophy of Science,* persuaded them to moderate some of their views. Nagel found academic positions for logical positivists who came to the United States to escape Nazi persecution.

Nagel was promoted to assistant professor in 1937. That same year he, Dewey, Hook, and Horace M. Kallen organized the first meeting of the Conference on Methods in Philosophy and the Sciences. The purpose of the organization was to combat the intolerance and intellectual obscurantism fostered by authoritarian governments. It met semiannually for more than half a century, and Nagel served as honorary president during the last fifteen years of his life.

Nagel, who was promoted to associate professor in 1939, was one of the few philosophers who was teaching symbolic logic in the late 1930s. Although Alonzo Church and W. V. Quine had written advanced treatises on the subject, no textbooks were available on it. Nagel was also influenced by Dewey's instrumentalist logic. In "Reflections on Some Logical and Metaphysical Themes in Dewey's Philosophy" (1939), collected in *Sovereign Reason and Other Studies in the Philosophy of Science* (1954), he contends that "the splendid ideal of logic as an organon of inquiry" elaborated in Dewey's *Logic: The Theory of Inquiry* (1938) ranks among the great visions of the day. He accepts Dewey's substitution of "warranted assertibility" for "truth," though he himself prefers the phrase "reliably warranted conclusions." Nagel avoided the term *truth* except when responding to others who used it.

In *Principles of the Theory of Probability* (1939) Nagel defines probability in terms of relative frequencies of occurrence of events; the definition is widely regarded as having clarified the notion of probability. He says that the warrant for a claim to knowledge involves the weight of evidence in favor of the claim, and the weight of evidence is to be construed in terms of probability. In "Probability and the Theory of Knowledge," published the same year and collected in *Sovereign Reason and Other Studies in the Philosophy of Science,* Nagel examines Hans Reichenbach's views on probability. Reichenbach, Nagel says, introduced "the infinitely gradated [*sic*] property weight to characterize propositions," using a multivalued logic of probability or weights. In a lengthy criticism Nagel deplores Reichenbach's "venture into epistemology." Nagel criticized Reichenbach for failing to provide a calculus of probability and for claiming to solve the problem of the external world probabilistically. According to Nagel, not only did Reichenbach fail to solve the problem; it was unintelligible as a problem.

In "Logic without Ontology," first published in *Naturalism and the Human Spirit* (1944), edited by Yervant H. Krikorian, and collected in *Logic without Metaphysics,* Nagel addresses the relationship of logic to reality. Some philosophers, such as Russell, Cohen, and Woodbridge, though nominally empiricists, think that the laws of logic say something about reality; since they cannot specify where these laws exist, Cohen and Woodbridge speak of them as "subsisting." Other empiricists, such as John Stuart Mill, hold that logical laws are merely generalizations from experience. Nagel rejects both positions. If the laws of logic say something about reality, he argues, then they should be subject to empirical test and possible falsification; but they cannot be tested, since the conditions for such a test cannot be specified without assuming the validity of the laws. On the other hand, if the laws are empirical generalizations, then one should be willing to countenance the possibility that they might be refuted by further experience. But even empiricists such as Mill are unable to imagine situations that would show the laws of logic to be false. Hence, the laws are not empirical. Nagel interprets the laws of noncontradiction, excluded middle, and identity according to the principles of propositional logic and demonstrates that they are not three distinct laws but variants of a single tautology: "If any sentence p is true, then the sentence p is true." He concludes that the so-called laws of logic have no metaphysical significance but are rules for intelligibly conducting discourse. If one said, for example, that some statement was both true and not true, at the same time and in the same respect, one would not be understood.

In an aside, Nagel criticizes the positivists' verifiability criterion of meaning, which was designed to expose metaphysical speculation as meaningless. He points out that many useful propositions that are parts of scientific theories would have to be excluded as meaningless if they were to be judged by the criterion. This critique in "Logic without Ontology" came long before the positivists' self-criticism and rejection of the verifiability criterion in Carl Hempel's "Problems and Changes in the Empiricist Criterion of Meaning" (1950) and "The Concept of Cognitive Significance: A Reconsideration" (1951).

Nagel became a full professor at Columbia in 1946. He was a Guggenheim fellow for the second time in 1950–1951 and was elected to the American Academy of Arts and Sciences in 1954. His 1954 presidential address to the Eastern Division of the American Philosophical Association, "Naturalism Reconsidered," which was published the following year, articulates most of the major views that he maintained throughout his career. For Nagel, philosophy at its best is a critical commentary on existence and on human claims to have knowledge thereof. Its mission is to illuminate what is obscure in experience. Philosophers no longer believe that there is some one "big thing" that, if known, would make everything else coherent and unlock the mystery of the universe. In consequence, philosophers have ceased to emulate the great system builders of the past. On the other hand, many philosophers dismiss most of the products of analytic philosophy as trivial. Nagel defends analytic philosophy, but weakly: though he agrees that a large portion of recent analytic literature seems inconsequential, he says that analytic philosophy is the continuation of a major philosophical tradition—he implies that it is part of more than two millennia of criticism going back to Socrates—and can count among its assets substantial feats of clarification and an

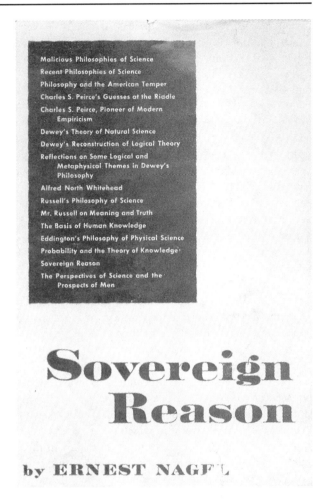

Malicious Philosophies of Science
Recent Philosophies of Science
Philosophy and the American Temper
Charles S. Peirce's Guesses at the Riddle
Charles S. Peirce, Pioneer of Modern
    Empiricism
Dewey's Theory of Natural Science
Dewey's Reconstruction of Logical Theory
Reflections on Some Logical and
    Metaphysical Themes in Dewey's
    Philosophy
Alfred North Whitehead
Russell's Philosophy of Science
Mr. Russell on Meaning and Truth
The Basis of Human Knowledge
Eddington's Philosophy of Physical Science
Probability and the Theory of Knowledge
Sovereign Reason
The Perspectives of Science and the
    Prospects of Men

Sovereign Reason

by ERNEST NAGEL

Dust jacket for the 1954 collection of Nagel's essays in the philosophy of science (Bruccoli Clark Layman Archives)

increased and refreshing sensitivity to the demands of responsible discourse.

Nagel then describes the intellectual commitments of his own position, naturalism. Like Santayana, he says, he refuses to accept anything for the purposes of philosophical debate that he does not believe when he is not arguing, and naturalism formulates what centuries of human experience have repeatedly confirmed. Naturalism is a sound description of the world as encountered both in practice and in critical reflection and is also a just perspective on the human scene. For Nagel, naturalism is set apart from other attempts at a comprehensive philosophy by the inclusive intellectual image of nature and humanity that it supplies. It embraces a generalized account of the cosmic scheme and of humanity's place in it, as well as a logic of inquiry.

Nagel identifies two theses as central to naturalism. The first, the existential and causal primacy of organized matter in the order of nature, is, he believes, one of the best-tested conclusions of experience. He dismisses Platonism and other varieties of idealist meta-physics, because "forms" and "functions" are not agents in their own realization or in that of anything else. The universe has no place for disembodied forces or an immaterial spirit directing the course of events or for the survival of the personality after the death of the body.

The second thesis is that the manifest plurality and variety of things, their qualities, and their functions is a fundamental feature of the cosmos, not a deceptive appearance cloaking some more-homogeneous "ultimate reality." There is no evidence for, and much evidence against, the position that whatever occurs is a phase in a unitary, teleologically (that is, purposefully) organized, and all-inclusive process or system. Irreducible variety and logical contingency are fundamental traits of the world people actually inhabit.

As a naturalist, Nagel also dismisses Cartesian rationalism. Although the orders and connections of things are accessible to rational inquiry, he says, they are not derivable by deductive methods from any set of premises that deductive reason can certify.

Some philosophers, Nagel notes, envisage "possible worlds" and employ the procedures of modal logic (the logic of necessity and possibility) in dealing with them. But philosophy is not mathematics, says Nagel; its concern is with the world in which people live. Contemporary naturalists devote so much attention to the methods of modern empirical science for evaluating evidence because those methods appear to be the most assured way of achieving reliable knowledge.

Naturalism has repeatedly been charged with insensitivity to spiritual values, with a shallow optimism about science as an instrument for ennobling the human estate, and with a philistine blindness toward the ineradicable miseries of human existence. Nagel protests that outstanding exponents of naturalism, both present and past, have exhibited unequaled sensitivity to the aesthetic and moral dimensions of human experience. It is singularly inept, Nagel thinks, to indict naturalism as a philosophy that lacks a sense for the tragic aspects of life: unlike so many other worldviews, naturalism offers no cosmic consolation for the unmerited defeats and undeserved sufferings that all living beings experience. It has never sought to conceal its view of human destiny as "an episode between two oblivions." Neither the pluralism central to naturalism nor its cultivation of scientific reason is compatible with any dogmatic assumption that human beings can be liberated from all the sorrows and evils to which they are heir. Human reason is potent only against evils that are remediable; but only inquiry can show which of the many human ills can, in fact, be mitigated. Naturalism is not a philosophy of general renunciation—even though it recognizes that the better part of wisdom con-sists in being equally resigned to what, in the light of available evidence, cannot be avoided. The actual limitations of rational effort do not warrant a romantic philosophy of general despair, and they do not blind naturalism to possibilities implicit in the exercise of disciplined reason for realizing human excellence.

Nagel was named John Dewey Professor of Philosophy at Columbia in 1955. Four years later he published "Philosophical Concepts of Atheism" (1959), which reveals both his secular humanism and his subtle power of analysis. Nagel distinguishes philosophical atheism from that of the village atheist who baldly denies the existence of God. Philosophical atheism is the denial of theism, which is belief in an omniscient, omnipotent, and benevolent creator. In opposition to theism Nagel reformulates some of the eighteenth-century Scottish empiricist philosopher David Hume's arguments in a Darwinian context. Some thinkers, he notes, take relations in nature that seem to indicate a mathematical order in the universe to imply the existence of a supreme Mathematician, but Nagel points out that any natural assemblage would have some kind of order. His strongest criticism is of theodicies that maintain that evil is necessary, or an illusion, or only the "privation" or absence of good; according to such theodicies, evil is not "really real" but only the product of the failure of a limited intelligence to plumb the true character of God's creative bounty. But facts are not altered or abolished by rebaptizing them. Evil may, indeed, be only an appearance, but this realization does not eliminate the suffering that living beings endure. To be told that one is undergoing only "the absence of good" is little comfort to one suffering a cruel and undeserved misfortune. For Nagel, to be assured that the miseries and agonies people experience are only illusory is a gratuitous insult, a symptom of insensitivity and indifference to suffering.

Nagel's secular humanism comes out most strongly in the final passages of his essay. He says that atheists have made important contributions to the development of a climate of opinion favorable to pursuit of the values of a liberal civilization and that they have played effective roles in rectifying social injustices. Atheism cannot offer the incentives to conduct and the consolations for misfortune that theistic religions supply; it can hold out no hope of personal immortality, no threat of divine chastisement, no promise of eventual recompense for injustices suffered, no blueprint for salvation. For atheism, human excellence and dignity must be achieved within a finite life span or not at all, so that the rewards of moral endeavor must come from the quality of civilized living. Accordingly, atheistic moral reflection at its best is a vigorous call to intelligent activity for the sake of realizing human potentialities and eliminating whatever stands in the way of such realization. Responsible atheists have never pretended that human effort can achieve every legitimate desire a person might have. A tragic view of life is, thus, inherent in atheistic thought. This view does not lead to lamentation, but it does make the philosophical atheist a kindred spirit to those who, within the framework of various religious traditions, have developed a serenely resigned attitude toward the inevitable tragedies of the human estate.

Nagel was a fellow of the Center for Advanced Studies in the Behavioral Sciences in 1959–1960. His best-known work, *The Structure of Science: Problems in the Logic of Scientific Explanation,* appeared in 1961. As the subtitle indicates, the book is a technical treatment of issues in scientific methodology; but the preface is another expression of Nagel's humanism. He describes science as an institutionalized art of inquiry. Among the fruits of this art are generalized theoretical knowledge of the fundamental determining conditions of various types of events and processes; the emancipation of people's minds from ancient superstitions in which barbarous practices and oppressive fears are rooted; the undermining of the intellectual foundations of moral and religious dogmas, with a resultant weakening of the protective cover that unreasoned custom provides for the continuance of social injustices; and, more generally, the gradual development among increasing numbers of people of a questioning attitude toward traditional beliefs, a development that is frequently accompanied by the adoption, in domains previously closed to systematic critical thought, of logical methods for assessing assumptions on the basis of reliable data of observation.

Nagel announces as his objective in the book the analysis of the logic of scientific inquiry and the logical structure of intellectual products. His interest is primarily in examining logical patterns exhibited in the organization of scientific knowledge and the methods whose use, despite changes in special techniques and revolutions in substantive theory, is the enduring feature of modern science. He says that the distinction between scientific laws and theories is not arbitrary but rests on the different function each performs: laws explain facts, while theories explain laws. The distinction has not taken hold in common parlance, and, Nagel notes, one can find indiscriminate use of the term *theory* even among scientists. Nagel goes on to examine the realist and instrumentalist views of theory, concluding that "when the two opposing views . . . are stated with some circumspection, each can assimilate into its formulations not only the facts concerning the primary subject matter explored by experimental inquiry but also all the relevant facts concerning the logic and procedure of science. In brief, the opposition between these views is a

conflict over preferred modes of speech." He discusses four kinds of scientific explanation: the classical deductive model, which he prefers, although he recognizes the problem of avoiding circularity in such explanations; the probabilistic model; the teleological or functional model, which looks for purposes in nature; and the genetic model, which traces the histories of phenomena under investigation. He also analyzes the application of deterministic theories in studying human history and quantum mechanics.

In "Carnap's Theory of Induction," first published in the Library of Living Philosophers volume *The Philosophy of Rudolf Carnap* (1963) and collected in *Teleology Revisited and Other Essays in the Philosophy and History of Science,* Nagel examines the then-unfinished theory that he describes as Carnap's "most ambitious contribution to logical analysis": "the important task of codifying the logic of induction, in a manner analogous to modern systematizations of deductive logic." Nagel concludes, however, that Carnap "has not resolved the outstanding issues in the philosophy of induction, and his general approach to the problems is not a promising one." Among the criticisms is that Carnap set himself the task of codifying the logic of induction in a manner analogous to modern systematizations of deductive logic. Carnap, Nagel says, has not given attention to the methodological problems that are generated when the applicability of the logic to actual scientific procedure is considered. Its worth as a theory of induction—as an explication and refined extension of ideas and principles employed in the search for empirical truth—cannot be judged independently of such reference.

Nagel spent the academic year 1966–1967 at Rockefeller University in New York City. He then returned to Columbia, where he was given the prestigious title university professor. He retired in 1970 but continued to teach. On 28 and 29 March 1977 he delivered the John Dewey Lectures at Columbia; dealing with teleological explanations in biology, they became the two-part title essay of *Teleology Revisited and Other Essays in the Philosophy and History of Science.* Also in 1977 Nagel became one of the few philosophers ever elected to the National Academy of Sciences.

In his introduction to *Teleology Revisited and Other Essays in the Philosophy and History of Science* Nagel states his theme to be "the logic of scientific inquiry and some of its alleged limitations." He explains that during the past quarter century certain philosophers have launched a many-pronged attack on the claim that the logic of scientific inquiry is the paramount instrument for achieving intellectual mastery of nature. Four essays in the volume—"Modern Science in Philosophical Perspective" (originally published in a shorter form as "The Philosopher Looks at Science" [1959]), "The

Page from the first draft of Nagel's best-known work, The Structure of Science: Problems in the Logic of Scientific Explanation, *published in 1961 (Ernest Nagel Papers, Rare Book and Manuscript Library of Butler Library, Columbia University)*

Quest for Uncertainty" (1968), "Theory and Observation" (1971), and "Philosophical Depreciations of Scientific Method" (1976)–carry the brunt of Nagel's response to this attack. According to Nagel, critics have produced a variety of arguments for doubting that "objective" and soundly based knowledge is ever achieved in theoretical science. They deny that scientific theories are ever accepted or rejected purely on the basis of a "rational" evaluation of the evidence. For these critics the belief in an "absolute" distinction between observation and theory is untenable. Statements about empirical observations, they maintain, are not unbiased formulations of supposedly "pure" materials of sensory experience but involve interpretations placed on the sensory data on the basis of theoretical presuppositions. Nagel replies that the distinction is not useless simply because it cannot be made sharply.

Critics have also raised doubts as to whether a "scientific method" can be identified. According to Paul Feyerabend, for example, the growth of knowledge is best served by rejecting definite rules for the conduct of inquiry. Nagel, however, insists that the task of logic is to make explicit the structures of methods and the assumptions employed in the search for reliable knowledge in all fields of inquiry. Logic articulates the principles implicit in critiques of claims to knowledge, assesses the authority of such principles, and weighs the merits of special postulates and intellectual tools (such as "instantaneous velocity" and idealized conditions) used in particular sciences.

The fallible character of scientific inquiry has become a commonplace in postpositivist philosophy, Nagel notes. The notion was taken even further by Sir Karl R. Popper, for whom the proper task of research is to try to refute proposed answers to the problem that initiated the research. Popper denies that science achieves genuine knowledge, claiming, on the contrary, that a scientific theory is "merely a guess" or "conjecture." According to Popper, science is "not interested" in establishing its conjectures, theories, or "anticipations" as certain or even as probable but only in criticizing and testing them with a view to falsifying them. Nagel dubs this growing tendency–which he observes among scientists as well as philosophers–to argue from the fallibility of scientific inquiry to a denial that claims to knowledge are ever warranted "the quest for uncer-

tainty." He responds to it by showing that philosophers such as Popper give idiosyncratic meanings to terms such as *hypothesis, observation, theoretical,* and *knowledge* and that their uses of such terms involve undue generalizations. He finds it perverse to inquire into a problem with the intent to refute any proposed solution that might be offered and defends the commonsense view that in many domains of inquiry people can and do attain genuine knowledge.

Nagel died of pneumonia at Columbia-Presbyterian Medical Center in New York City on 20 September 1985. His wife died in 1988.

Ernest Nagel was one of the outstanding philosophers of science in the twentieth century and one to whom other noteworthy philosophers deferred. His careful and subtle analyses of complex scientific issues laid the groundwork and opened the door for further exploration of those issues by a later generation of philosophers. Some of those philosophers have refined his views, while others, ignoring the logic of scientific practice, have used sociology and the history of science to oppose his ideas on scientific procedure.

Interview:
Estelle Gilson, "Ernest Nagel: Philosopher of Science," *Columbia,* 6 (Winter 1980): 22–24.

References:
Giuliano Di Bernardo and Maurizio Abeni, *La logica dell'analisi funzionale e la psicoanalisi* (Trento: Unicoop, 1975);
Sidney Morgenbesser, Patrick Suppes, and Morton White, eds., *Philosophy, Science, and Method: Essays in Honor of Ernest Nagel* (New York: St. Martin's Press, 1969);
Suppes, "Ernest Nagel," in *Biographical Memoirs,* volume 65 (Washington, D.C.: National Academy of Sciences, 1994), pp. 256–272;
Sandra Tugnoli Pattaro, *Sviluppi critici del pensiero scientifico moderno nella ricostruzione metodologica di Ernest Nagel* (Bologna: CLUEB, 1991).

Papers:
Ernest Nagel's letters, manuscripts, and some of his course outlines are in the Butler Library at Columbia University.

Seyyed Hossein Nasr

(7 April 1933 –   )

Michael Allen

BOOKS IN ENGLISH: *An Introduction to Islamic Cosmological Doctrines: Conceptions of Nature and Methods Used for Its Study by the Ikhwan al-Safa', al-Biruni, and Ibn Sina* (Cambridge, Mass.: Belknap Press of Harvard University Press, 1964; revised edition, Albany: State University of New York Press, 1993);

Three Muslim Sages: Avicenna, Suhrawardi, Ibn 'Arabi (Cambridge, Mass.: Harvard University Press, 1964);

Ideals and Realities of Islam (London: Allen & Unwin, 1966; New York: Praeger, 1967);

Islamic Studies: Essays on Law and Society, the Sciences, and Philosophy and Sufism (Beirut: Librairie du Liban, 1967); revised and enlarged as *Islamic Life and Thought* (London: Allen & Unwin, 1981; Albany: State University of New York Press, 1981);

Science and Civilization in Islam (Cambridge, Mass.: Harvard University Press, 1968; republished with new foreword, Cambridge: Islamic Texts Society, 1987; New York: Barnes & Noble, 1992);

The Encounter of Man and Nature: The Spiritual Crisis of Modern Man (London: Allen & Unwin, 1968); republished with new preface as *Man and Nature: The Spiritual Crisis of Modern Man* (London: Unwin, 1976);

Sufi Essays (London: Allen & Unwin, 1972; Albany: State University of New York Press, 1973; enlarged edition, Chicago: Kazi, 1999); republished as *Living Sufism* (London: Unwin, 1980);

Al-Biruni: An Annotated Bibliography (Tehran: High Council of Culture and the Arts, 1973);

Jalal al-Din Rumi, Supreme Persian Poet and Sage (Tehran: High Council of Culture and the Arts, 1974);

Persia, Bridge of Turquoise, photographs by Roloff Beny, notes by Mitchell Crites (Boston: New York Graphic Society, 1975);

An Annotated Bibliography of Islamic Science, 3 volumes, by Nasr and William Chittick (volumes 1–2, Tehran: Imperial Iranian Academy of Philosophy, 1975,

1978; volume 3, Tehran: Cultural Studies and Research Institute, 1991);

Islam and the Plight of Modern Man (London & New York: Longman, 1975; revised and enlarged edition, Cambridge: Islamic Texts Society, 2002);

Islamic Science: An Illustrated Study, photographs by Roland Michaud (London: World of Islam Festival Publishing, 1976; Chicago: Kazi, 1998);

Western Science and Asian Cultures (New Delhi: Indian Council for Cultural Relations, 1976);

Sadr al-Din Shirazi and His Transcendent Theosophy: Background, Life, and Works (Tehran: Imperial Iranian Academy of Philosophy, 1978; enlarged edition, Tehran: Institute for Humanities and Cultural Studies, 1997);

Knowledge and the Sacred: The Gifford Lectures, 1981 (Edinburgh: Edinburgh University Press, 1981; New York: Crossroad, 1981);

Muhammad: Man of Allah (London: Muhammadi Trust of Great Britain and Northern Ireland, 1982); republished as *Muhammad: Man of God* (Chicago: Kazi, 1995);

Islamic Art and Spirituality (Ipswich, U.K.: Golgonooza Press, 1986; Albany: State University of New York Press, 1987);

Traditional Islam in the Modern World (London & New York: KPI, 1987);

Religion and Religions: The Challenge of Living in a Multi-Religious World (Charlotte: University of North Carolina at Charlotte, 1991);

The Need for a Sacred Science (Albany: State University of New York Press, 1993);

A Young Muslim's Guide to the Modern World (Cambridge: Islamic Texts Society, 1993; Des Plaines, Ill.: Library of Islam, 1993);

The Islamic Intellectual Tradition in Persia, edited by Mehdi Aminrazavi (Richmond, U.K.: Curzon, 1996);

Religion and the Order of Nature: The 1994 Cadbury Lectures at the University of Birmingham (New York & Oxford: Oxford University Press, 1996);

Mecca the Blessed, Medina the Radiant: The Holiest Cities of Islam, photographs by Ali Kazuyoshi Nomachi (New York: Aperture, 1997);

Islamic-Christian Dialogue: Problems and Obstacles to Be Pondered and Overcome (Washington, D.C.: Georgetown University, 1998);

Poems of the Way (Oakton, Va.: Foundation for Traditional Studies, 1999);

The Spiritual and Religious Dimensions of the Environmental Crisis (London: Temenos Academy, 1999);

A Journey through Persian History and Culture (Lahore: Iqbal Academy Pakistan, 2000);

The Heart of Islam: Enduring Values for Humanity (San Francisco: HarperSanFrancisco, 2002);

Islam: Religion, History, and Civilization (San Francisco: HarperSanFrancisco, 2003).

Edition: *Ideals and Realities of Islam*, preface by Huston Smith (Boston: Beacon, 1972).

OTHER: *Mulla Sadra Commemoration Volume: On the Occasion of the Four Hundredth Anniversary of the Birth of Sadr al-Din Shirazi*, edited by Nasr (Tehran: Tehran University Press, 1961);

Henry Corbin, *Histoire de la philosophie islamique*, volume 1, contributions by Nasr (Paris: Gallimard, 1964); translated by Liadain Sherrard and Philip Sherrard as *History of Islamic Philosophy* (London & New York: Kegan Paul, 1993);

"The Unity of the Intellectual and Philosophical Tradition of Iran, Turkey, and Pakistan," in *Papers Read at the RCD Seminar on Common Cultural Heritage* (Tehran: RCD Cultural Institute, 1965), pp. 135–137;

"Mulla Sadra," in *The Encyclopedia of Philosophy*, volume 5, edited by Paul Edwards (New York: Macmillan, 1966), pp. 411–413;

"Les Arts libéraux dans le monde non-Latin," in *Arts libéraux et philosophie au Moyen Age: Actes du quatrième congrès international de philosophie médiévale* (Montreal: Institut d'études médiévales / Paris: Vrin, 1969), pp. 73–77;

Frithjof Schuon, *Dimensions of Islam*, translated by P. N. Townsend, preface by Nasr (London: Allen & Unwin, 1970);

"Islam," in *The Middle East: A Handbook,* edited by Michael Adams (London: Blond, 1971), pp. 179–184;

Historical Atlas of Iran, edited by Nasr and others (Tehran: Tehran University Press, 1971);

"Avicenna," in *Encyclopaedia Britannica*, fifteenth edition (Chicago: Encyclopaedia Britannica, 1974), pp. 540–541;

"Who Is Man? The Perennial Answer of Islam," in *The Sword of Gnosis: Metaphysics, Cosmology, Tradition, Symbolism,* edited by Jacob Needleman (Baltimore: Penguin, 1974), pp. 203–217;

'Allamah Sayyid Muhammad Husayn Tabataba'i, *Shi'ite Islam*, edited and translated by Nasr (Albany: State University of New York Press, 1975);

"Life Sciences, Alchemy, and Medicine," "Philosophy and Cosmology," and "Sufism," in *The Cambridge History of Iran*, volume 4, edited by Richard N. Frye (Cambridge: Cambridge University Press, 1975), pp. 396–463;

"The Religious Sciences," by Nasr and M. Mutahhari, in *The Cambridge History of Iran*, volume 4, edited by Frye (Cambridge: Cambridge University Press, 1975), pp. 464–480;

Schuon, *Islam and the Perennial Philosophy*, translated by J. Peter Hobson, preface by Nasr (London: World of Islam Festival Publishing, 1976);

"Philosophy," in *The Study of the Middle East: Research and Scholarship in the Humanities and the Social Sciences,* edited by Leonard Binder (New York: Wiley, 1976), pp. 327–345;

Mélanges offerts à Henry Corbin, edited by Nasr (Tehran: Institute of Islamic Studies, McGill University, Tehran Branch, 1977);

Isma'ili Contributions to Islamic Culture, edited by Nasr (Tehran: Imperial Iranian Academy of Philosophy, 1977);

"The Writings of Sadr al-Din Shirazi," in *Recherches d'islamologie: Recueil d'articles offerts à Georges C. Anawati et Louis Gardet par leurs collègues et amis* (Louvain: Peeters, 1978), pp. 261–271;

"Some Observations on the Place of 'Attar within the Sufi Tradition," in *Colloquio italo-iraniano sul poeta mistico Fariduddin 'Attar* (Rome: Accademia nazionale dei Lincei, 1978), pp. 5–20;

"In Quest of the Eternal Sophia," in *Philosophes critiques d'eux-mêmes/Philosophische Selbstbetrachtungen,* volume 6, edited by André Mercier and Maja Svilar (Bern: Peter Lang, 1980), pp. 113–121;

A Shi'ite Anthology, edited and translated by William Chittick, introduction by Nasr (London: Muhammadi Trust of Great Britain and Northern Ireland, 1980);

"Islamic Countries," in *Handbook of World Philosophy: Contemporary Developments since 1945,* edited by John R. Burr (Westport, Conn.: Greenwood, 1980), pp. 421–433;

"Islam in the Islamic World: An Overview," in *Islam in the Contemporary World,* edited by Cyriac K. Pullapilly (Notre Dame, Ind.: Cross Roads, 1980), pp. 1–20;

Philosophy, Literature, and Fine Arts, edited by Nasr, Islamic Education Series (Sevenoaks, U.K.: Hodder & Stoughton, 1982);

"Islam and Modern Science," in *Islam and Contemporary Society,* edited by Salem Azzam (London & New York: Longman, 1982), pp. 177–190;

"Post-Avicennan Islamic Philosophy and the Study of Being," in *Philosophies of Existence, Ancient and Medieval,* edited by Parviz Morewedge (New York: Fordham University Press, 1982), pp. 337–344;

"The Metaphysics of Sadr al-Din Shirazi and Islamic Philosophy in Qajar Persia," in *Qajar Iran: Political, Social, and Cultural Change, 1800–1925,* edited by Edmund Bosworth and Carole Hillenbrand (Edinburgh: Edinburgh University Press, 1983), pp. 177–198;

"Islamic Education and Science: A Summary Appraisal," in *The Islamic Impact,* edited by Yvonne Yazbeck Haddad, Byron Haines, and Ellison Findly (Syracuse: University of Syracuse Press, 1984), pp. 47–68;

"Message," in *Quest for New Science,* edited by Rais Ahmad and Syed Naseem Ahmad (Aligarh, India: Centre for Studies on Science, 1984), pp. 15–16;

The Essential Writings of Frithjof Schuon, edited by Nasr (Amity, N.Y.: Amity House, 1986);

"Spiritual Movements, Philosophy, and Theology in the Safavid Period," in *The Cambridge History of Iran,* volume 6, edited by Peter Jackson and Laurence Lockhart (Cambridge: Cambridge University Press, 1986), pp. 656–697;

"The Prayer of the Heart in Hesychasm and Sufism," in *Orthodox Christians and Muslims,* edited by N. M. Vaporis (Brookline, Mass.: Holy Cross Orthodox Press, 1986), pp. 195–203;

"Darwish," "René Guénon," "Nasir-i Khusraw," and "Shi'ism: Ithna 'Ashariyah," in *The Encyclopedia of Religion,* 16 volumes (New York: Macmillan, 1987), IV: 240–241, VI: 136–138, X: 312–313, XIII: 260–270;

Islamic Spirituality: Foundations, edited by Nasr, World Spirituality: An Encyclopedic History of the Religious Quest, volume 19 (New York: Crossroad, 1987; London: Routledge & Kegan Paul, 1987);

"Islamic Science and Western Science: Common Heritage, Diverse Destinies," in *The Revenge of Athena: Science, Exploitation, and the Third World,* edited by Ziauddin Sardar (London: Mansell, 1988), pp. 239–248;

Shi'ism: Doctrines, Thought, and Spirituality, edited by Nasr, Hamid Dabashi, and Seyyed Vali Reza Nasr (Albany: State University of New York Press, 1988);

Expectations of the Millenium: Shi'ism in History, edited by Nasr, Dabashi, and Seyyed Vali Reza Nasr (Albany: State University of New York Press, 1989);

"Islam and the Problem of Modern Science," in *An Early Crescent: The Future of Knowledge and the Environment in Islam,* edited by Sardar (London: Mansell, 1989), pp. 127–139;

"The Islamic View of Christianity," in *Christianity through Non-Christian Eyes,* edited by Paul J. Griffiths (Maryknoll, N.Y.: Orbis, 1990), pp. 126–134;

"Islamic Studies in America," in *Fragments of Infinity: Essays in Religion and Philosophy. A Festschrift in Honour of Professor Huston Smith,* edited by Arvind Sharma (Bridport, U.K.: Prism, 1991), pp. 153–167;

Islamic Spirituality: Manifestations, edited by Nasr, World Spirituality: An Encyclopedic History of the Religious Quest, volume 20 (New York: Crossroad, 1991; London: SCM, 1991);

Religion of the Heart: Essays Presented to Frithjof Schuon on His Eightieth Birthday, edited by Nasr and William Stoddart (Washington, D.C.: Foundation for Traditional Studies, 1991);

"What Is the Meaning of Life?" in *The Meaning of Life: Reflections in Words and Pictures on Why We Are Here,* edited by David Friend (Boston: Little, Brown, 1991), p. 62;

"Le *Mawjud* et le *wujud* dans la tradition orientale" and "Les Commentateurs arabes," in *Penser avec Aristotle: Etudes,* edited by M. A. Sinaceur (Toulouse: Erès, 1991), pp. 525, 757–760;

"The Harmony of Man and Nature," in *Families for Tomorrow,* edited by Joanna Bogle (Leominster, U.K.: Gracewing, 1991), pp. 12–20;

"Persian Sufi Literature: Its Spiritual and Cultural Significance," in *The Legacy of Mediaeval Persian Sufism,* edited by Leonard Lewisohn (London: Khaniqahi Nimatullahi, 1992), pp. 1–10;

"The Significance of Islamic Manuscripts," in *The Significance of Islamic Manuscripts,* edited by John Cooper (London: Al-Furqan Islamic Heritage Foundation, 1992), pp. 7–17;

"The Islamic View of the Environment," in *Human Values and the Environment* (Madison: Wisconsin Academy of Sciences, Arts, and Letters, 1992), pp. 47–49;

"Islam," in *Our Religions,* edited by Sharma (San Francisco: HarperSanFrancisco, 1993), pp. 425–532;

"The Rise and Development of Persian Sufism," in *Classical Persian Sufism: From Its Origins to Rumi* (London & New York: Khaniqahi Nimatullahi, 1993), pp. 1–18;

In Quest of the Sacred: The Modern World in the Light of Tradition, edited by Nasr and Katherine O'Brien (Oakton, Va.: Foundation for Traditional Studies, 1994);

"Oral Transmission and the Book in Islamic Education: The Spoken and the Written Word," in *The Book in the Islamic World: The Written Word and Communication in the Middle East,* edited by George N. Atiyeh (Albany: State University of New York Press, 1995), pp. 57–70;

"Comments on a Few Theological Issues in Islamic-Christian Dialogue," in *Christian-Muslim Encounters,* edited by Yvonne Yazbeck Haddad and Wadi Zaidan Haddad (Gainesville: University of Florida Press, 1995), pp. 457–467;

The History of Islamic Philosophy, 2 volumes, edited by Nasr and Oliver Leaman (London & New York: Routledge, 1996);

"Divine Beauty: The Qur'anic Story of Joseph and Zulaykha," in *Talking about Genesis: A Resource Guide* (New York: Main Street Books/Doubleday, 1996), pp. 149–154;

"Metaphysical Roots of Intolerance: An Islamic Interpretation," in *Philosophy, Religion, and the Question of Intolerance,* edited by Aminrazavi and David Ambuel (Albany: State University of New York Press, 1997), pp. 43–56;

"Islam and Music: The Legal and Spiritual Dimensions," in *Enchanting Powers: Music in the World's Religions,* edited by Lawrence E. Sullivan (Cambridge, Mass.: Harvard University Press, 1997), pp. 219–235;

"Islamic Aesthetics," in *A Companion to World Philosophies,* edited by Eliot Deutsch and Ron Bontekoe (Cambridge, Mass.: Blackwell, 1997), pp. 448–459;

"Sacred Science and the Environmental Crisis: An Islamic Perspective," in *Islam and the Environment,* edited by Harfiyah Abdel Haleem (London: Ta-Ha Publishers, 1998), pp. 118–137;

"Mystical Philosophy in Islam," in *The Routledge Encyclopedia of Philosophy,* volume 6, edited by Edward Craig (London & New York: Routledge, 1998), pp. 616–620;

"What Does It Mean to Be Human?" in *What Does It Mean to Be Human? Reverence for Life Reaffirmed by Responses from around the World,* edited by Frederick Franck, Janis Roze, and Richard Connolly (Nyack, N.Y.: Circumstantial Productions, 1998), pp. 96–103;

"Can Science Dispense with Religion?" in *Can Science Dispense with Religion?* edited by Mehdi Golshani (Tehran: Institute for Humanities and Cultural Studies, 1998), pp. 157–174;

"Preface: What Attracted Merton to Sufism?" in *Merton and Sufism, the Untold Story: A Complete Compendium,* edited by Rob Baker and Gray Henry (Louisville, Ky.: Fons Vitae, 1999), pp. 9–13;

"Prayer," in *Prayers for a Thousand Years: Blessings and Expressions of Hope for the New Millennium,* edited by Elizabeth Roberts and Elias Amidon (San Francisco: HarperSanFrancisco, 1999), p. 129;

"Our Religions in a Religiously Plural World" and "Religion, Globality, and Universality," in *A Dome of Many Colors: Studies in Religious Pluralism, Identity, and Unity,* edited by Sharma and Kathleen M. Dugan (Harrisburg, Pa.: Trinity Press International, 1999), pp. 57–65, 152–178;

An Anthology of Philosophy in Persia, 2 volumes, edited by Nasr and Aminrazavi (New York & Oxford: Oxford University Press, 1999, 2001);

"The Place of the School of Isfahan in Islamic Philosophy and Sufism," in *The Heritage of Sufism,* volume 3, edited by Lewisohn and David Morgan (Oxford: Oneworld, 1999), pp. 3–15;

"Intellectual Autobiography of Seyyed Hossein Nasr" and replies to critics, in *The Philosophy of Seyyed Hossein Nasr,* edited by Lewis Edwin Hahn, Randall E. Auxier, and Lucian W. Stone Jr., The Library of Living Philosophers, volume 28 (Chicago & La Salle, Ill.: Open Court, 2001), pp. 3–85, 132–138, 159–167, 190–201, 221–231, 248–252, 270–276, 304–312, 327–333, 358–370, 381–392, 420–427, 440–444, 463–468, 486–492, 512–518, 542–550, 563–570, 581–587, 612–617, 632–638, 658–668, 679–683, 710–715, 728–734, 753–762, 775–780, 792–797, 809–812, 827–830;

"The Heart of the Faithful Is the Throne of the All-Merciful," in *Paths to the Heart: Sufism and the Christian East,* edited by James S. Cutsinger (Bloomington, Ind.: World Wisdom/Fons Vitae, 2002), pp. 32–45.

SELECTED PERIODICAL PUBLICATIONS–UNCOLLECTED: "Introduction à la mystique musulmane: Le Soufisme," *Cahiers de l'Oronte* (July–August 1965): 8–12;

"Al-Tariqah: The Spiritual Path of Islam," *Middle East Forum* (Winter 1965): 32–33;

"The Death of Thomas Merton," *Monchanin-Information,* 2 (April 1969): 12–13;

"Homage to Jagad Guru Shankaracharya of Kanchi," *Kalki* (5 June 1971): 10–11;

"The Role of Women: A Muslim View," *PHP* (August 1971): 16–17;

"Islam and Music: The Views of Ruzbahan Baqli," *Studies in Comparative Religion,* 10 (Winter 1976): 37–45;

"Islam in the World: Cultural Diversity within Spiritual Unity," *Cultures* (Paris), 4, no. 1 (1977): 15–34;

"Ananda Coomaraswamy and the Metaphysics of Art: A Review Essay of His Selected Papers on Traditional Art and Symbolism," *Temenos,* 2 (1982): 252–259;

"The Relation between Sufism and Philosophy in Persian Culture," *Hamdard Islamicus,* 6 (Winter 1983): 33–47;

"Prayer on the Occasion of the End of Ramadan, 'Idal-Fitr," *Studies in Comparative Religion,* 16 (Winter-Spring 1984): 97–98;

"Response to Thomas Dean's Review of *Knowledge and the Sacred," Philosophy East and West,* 35 (January 1985): 87–90;

"The Role of the Traditional Sciences in the Encounter of Religion and Science: An Oriental Perspective," *MAAS Journal of Islamic Science,* 1 (January 1985): 9–30;

"The Principles of Islamic Architecture and Contemporary Urban Problems," *Arts and the Islamic World,* 3 (Summer 1985): 33–40, 96;

"Islam and the Question of Violence," *Faith* (Cambridge, Mass.), 1 (May 1987): 8–10;

"The Teaching of Art in the Islamic World," *Muslim Educational Quarterly,* 6, no. 2 (1989): 4–10;

"Penultimate Judgements," *Temenos,* 10 (1989): 257–264;

"Studies in Islamic Philosophy after Ibn Rushd: 1955–1970," *Al-Serat,* 15 (1989): 39–45;

"Studies in Sufism in the 1950s and '60s," *Hamdard Islamicus,* 12 (Summer 1989): 3–9;

"Being Muslim in America," *Islamic Horizons* (September 1989): 32–35;

"Existence (*wujud*) and Quiddity (*mahiyyah*) in Islamic Philosophy," *International Philosophical Quarterly,* 29 (December 1989): 409–428;

"Islam and Modern Science," *Journal of the Pakistan Study Group* (Fall 1991): 5–19;

"Religion and the Environment: A Crisis," *Studies in Tradition* (Spring 1992): 30–42;

"Reflection on Man and the Future of Civilization," *Islamic Studies* (Islamabad), 32 (Fall 1993): 253–259;

"Islam, Islamic Science, and the Environmental Crisis," *Eco-Justice,* 13 (Fall 1993): 8–9, 22;

"The Rise and Development of Persian Sufism," *Sufi,* no. 16 (Winter 1993): 5–12;

"What Is Islamic Science?" *MAAS Journal of Islamic Science,* 10 (January–June 1994): 9–20;

"Seyyed Hossein Nasr on 'Islam and Music,'" *Harvard University Center for the Study of World Religions News,* 1 (Spring 1994): 1, 3–5, 10–11;

"The One in the Many," *Parabola,* 19, no. 1 (1994): 12–19;

"To Live as a Young Muslim in America," *Islamic Horizons* (September 1994): 6–8;

"The Islamic World-View and Modern Science," *Islamic Quarterly,* 39, no. 2 (1995): 73–89;

"Spirituality and Science: Convergence or Divergence?" *Sophia,* 1 (Winter 1995): 23–40;

"The Relation between Religions in the Shadow of the Environmental Crisis," *World Faiths Encounter,* no. 13 (March 1996): 3–18;

"To Live in a World with No Center and Many," *Cross Currents,* 46 (Fall 1996): 318–325;

"Revival of Islamic Medical Tradition," *Journal of IMA,* 28 (October 1996): 153–159;

"Islam and the West: Yesterday and Today," *American Journal of Islamic Sciences,* 13 (Winter 1996): 551–562;

"Religious Art, Traditional Art, Sacred Art: Some Reflections and Definitions," *Sophia,* 2 (Winter 1996): 13–30;

"Perennial Ontology and Quantum Mechanics: A Review Essay of *The Quantum Enigma* by Wolfgang Smith," *Sophia,* 3 (Summer 1997): 135–159;

"Incantation of the Griffin (Simurgh) and the Cry of the Eagle: Islam and the Native American Tradition," *Sophia,* 3 (Winter 1997): 35–44;

"Islamic Unity: The Ideal and Obstacles in the Way of Its Realization," *Islamic Studies* (Islamabad), 36 (1997): 657–662;

"Dr. Seyyed Hossein Nasr on Spirituality in Islam," *Muslim Magazine,* 1 (January 1998): 12, 68–69;

"Frithjof Schuon (1907–1998)," *Sacred Web,* no. 1 (1998): 15–17;

"In Memoriam: Frithjof Schuon–a Prelude," *Sophia,* 4 (1998): 7–13;

"Hakim Muhammad Said," *Islamic Studies* (Islamabad), 37 (Winter 1998): 565–566;

"The Spiritual Significance of Jerusalem: The Islamic Vision," *Islamic Quarterly,* 42, no. 4 (1999): 233–242;

"Recollections of Henry Corbin and Reflections upon His Intellectual Significance," *Temenos Academy Review,* 2 (Spring 1999): 34–45;

"Homage to Huston Smith" and "Frithjof Schuon and the Islamic Tradition," *Sophia,* 5 (Summer 1999): 5–8, 27–48;

"The Influence of René Guénon in the Islamic World," *Sophia,* 8 (Winter 2002): 7–26.

Nasr as a Ph.D. candidate at Harvard University in 1958

Seyyed Hossein Nasr is a renowned scholar of Islamic science, philosophy, and religion and one of the leading contemporary representatives of traditional or "perennial" philosophy. The work of the traditionalists is not widely known, in part because the early and chief expositors of the movement, René Guénon and Frithjof Schuon, were not academics–indeed, they were highly critical of academic approaches to philosophy and religion. But their work also tends to receive less attention because their assumptions about the nature of reality and about the ability of human beings to know that reality are fundamentally opposed to modern reductionism and rationalism. Nasr's work has played a central role in bringing traditionalist ideas into the realm of academic debate. His works tend to focus on Persian and Islamic topics, but even in these specialized writings Nasr's concern for certain key ideas that he believes underlie every premodern philosophical and religious tradition is evident. His work is centered on the notion of an absolute truth that is at once transcendent and immanent in the world and that is accessible both through intelligence and divine revelation. He draws out the implications of this idea for metaphysics, epistemology, religion, ethics, and art.

Nasr–the name, which is Persian for "victory," is pronounced as a single syllable–was born in Tehran, Iran, on 7 April 1933 to Seyyed Valiallah and Ashraf Kia Nasr. His parents were traditional Shi'ite Muslims but were well acquainted with Western culture. His mother had been one of the first graduates of what was at the time the only institution of higher education for women in Iran; his father was a physician, scholar, and educator who was fluent in Persian, Arabic, and French, knew some Latin and English, and wrote a philosophical work in Persian, *Danish wa akhlaq* (Knowledge and Ethics, 1959). In his intellectual autobiography in the Library of Living Philosophers volume *The Philosophy of Seyyed Hossein Nasr* (2001) Nasr recalls that the greatest influence on his early development was his extended conversations with his father on philosophy and theology. By age ten Nasr had met many of the greatest Iranian scholars of the day and been exposed to both Western and Persian philosophy. In addition to the traditional curriculum at local schools, he was tutored at home in French, the Qur'an, and Persian poetry.

In late 1945 Nasr traveled to the United States; for the next four and a half years he attended the Peddie School, a Baptist preparatory school in Hightstown, New Jersey. He had learned little English previously but quickly mastered the language and earned honors grades in his second year. He especially excelled in mathematics and graduated as valedictorian.

Wanting, as he says in his intellectual autobiography, to "understand the nature of things," Nasr decided to study physics, and in 1950 he enrolled at the Massachusetts Institute of Technology in Cambridge, Massachusetts, on a scholarship; he was the first Iranian student ever admitted as a freshman to MIT. Although he was at the top of his class, by the end of his first year he was disillusioned by the "overbearingly scientific" environment of the institution and had come to doubt that physics could provide a real understanding of the universe. During his sophomore year the visiting British philosopher Bertrand Russell remarked to a group of students after a lecture that physics reveals nothing about the nature of reality; it only provides mathematical structures that help to explain experimental findings. From that point onward Nasr approached his courses, he says in his intellectual autobiography, "not as a potential physicist but as a potential philosopher who wanted to know modern science well before dealing with it philosophically."

The teacher who most influenced Nasr was the historian of science Giorgio de Santillana, an outspoken critic of positivism who was well versed not only in Western philosophy and science but also in Hindu and Islamic thought. He directed Nasr to two of Guénon's earliest works, *Introduction générale à l'étude des doctrines hindoues* (1921; translated as *Introduction to the Study of Hindu Doctrines,* 1945) and *L'Homme et son devenir selon le Vêdânta* (1925; translated as *Man and His Becoming according to the Vedanta,* 1928), which introduced Nasr to the idea of a metaphysics that is accessible through intellectual intuition. Nasr was also persuaded by Guénon's argument that all traditional civilizations were founded on a recognition of metaphysical principles and that these principles shaped every aspect of these societies. Tradition can take many forms, just as metaphysical truth can be expressed in many ways; but one may speak of an underlying "traditional spirit" in contrast to the modern spirit, which, according to Guénon, is based on the denial of metaphysical principles.

Nasr went on to read the works of Guénon's chief intellectual ally in the United States, the philosopher and art historian Ananda K. Coomaraswamy. Coomaraswamy had died in 1947, but his widow, Dona Luisa Coomaraswamy, lived in Cambridge. Over the next few years Nasr spent many hours in the Coomaraswamy library in her home, digesting the rest of Guénon's works and those of the other most important early spokesmen for "traditionalism" or "perennialism": Schuon, Titus Burckhardt, Marco Pallis, and Martin Lings. In his intellectual autobiography Nasr recalls:

> The discovery of traditional metaphysics and the *philosophia perennis* through the works of these figures settled the crisis that had caused such a deep upheaval in my inner life. I gained an intellectual certitude which has never left me since then and which has only grown stronger. One can speak symbolically of journeying from the vision of certainty to its existential experience or to use the Islamic terminology based upon the Quran from the science of certainty (*'ilm al-yaqin*) to the vision of certainty (*'ayn al-yaqin*) to the truth of certainty (*haqq al-yaqin*), from gaining a theoretical knowledge of fire, to seeing fire, to being consumed by fire, a journey which characterizes the trajectory of my life.

Nasr earned a B.S. with honors in physics and mathematics in 1954 and went on to Harvard University to study geology and geophysics, but he soon found himself frustrated once more by what he considered the dogmatic narrowness and reductionism of modern science—especially in his paleontology courses, where, despite obvious gaps in the fossil record, students were not allowed to question Darwinian theory. After receiving his M.S. in 1956 he decided to devote the rest of his postgraduate studies entirely to philosophy and the history of science.

The Harvard philosophy department in the late 1950s was strongly influenced by logical positivism; in his intellectual autobiography Nasr reports that "Several professors in fact would say openly that philosophy began with Kant and that there was nothing of interest in philosophy before him." Nasr, however, had been persuaded by his reading of the traditionalists that the reverse was nearer the truth: that premodern philosophy offered genuine insights into universal questions of meaning and existence, whereas philosophy since the time of René Descartes in the seventeenth century severed knowledge from its transcendent source and thereby represented less a love of wisdom—the literal meaning of the word *philosophy*—than a "misosophy," or hatred of wisdom. Nasr studied some modern European thinkers, but most of his courses were on Plato and Aristotle. His study of the history of science under George Sarton, I. Bernard Cohen, Harry A. Wolfson, and Hamilton A. R. Gibb focused on Islamic science.

In 1957 Nasr took the first of many trips to Europe to meet with Schuon, Burckhardt, and other representatives of traditionalism. He maintained close ties to Schuon for the next forty years. Schuon stressed the need for spiritual method alongside metaphysical doctrine: since truth is essentially objective, he taught, one's method of realization must be dictated by the traditional norms of an orthodox religion. Nasr accordingly embraced Sufism, the mystical path within Islam, receiving initiation in the line of the Algerian sage Shaykh Ahmad al-'Alawi (1869–1934).

During Nasr's last year at Harvard, de Santillana asked him to write the section on Islamic science for a volume on medieval science de Santillana was editing for the New American Library. De Santillana later decided to devote an entire volume to Islamic science; Nasr added several chapters while teaching in Iran, and the book finally appeared in 1968 as *Science and Civilization in Islam* (1968). In 1958 Nasr completed his dissertation, "Conceptions of Nature in Islamic Thought," and became the first Iranian to receive a Ph.D. from Harvard. He returned to Iran that year and became associate professor of philosophy and the history of science at Tehran University. On 21 November 1958 he married Soussan Daneshvary, who had studied in England and the United States. They have two children: their son, Seyyed Vali Reza, became a political scientist and their daughter, Laili, an art historian.

When Nasr arrived at Tehran University, only an introductory course on Islamic philosophy was offered in the faculty of letters; Nasr arranged for additional courses to be offered, making them a required part of the curriculum in the philosophy department, and sought in other ways to assert the importance of Islamic philosophy in its own right and not merely as peripheral to Western philosophy. At the same time, he helped to expand the Western philosophy curriculum to include contemporary movements such as logical positivism, analytical philosophy, and Continental philosophy. At that time Tehran was the only university in Iran that offered a doctorate in philosophy, and its restructuring provided a model for other departments throughout the country.

In 1963 Nasr's Persian adaptation of his dissertation won the royal book award. He was promoted to full professor that same year. The following year he published a revised version of the dissertation as *An Introduction to Islamic Cosmological Doctrines: Conceptions of Nature and Methods Used for Its Study by the Ikhwan al-Safa', al-Biruni, and Ibn Sina*. His first book in English, it presents Muslim cosmology as it would appear to one living within the tradition instead of through the categories of modern Western thought. Nasr's description in the book of the approach of the eleventh-century scientist al-Biruni might be applied to his own scholarship: "There is for al-Biruni no separation between 'sacred' and 'profane' learning. Whatever he studies, whether it be historical or physical sciences, takes on a religious character."

Nasr at Tehran University in 1968

Opening his work with the traditional Muslim invocation, "In the Name of God Most Merciful and Compassionate," Nasr describes three cosmologies developed during the tenth and eleventh centuries, the "golden age" of Islamic art and science. He then argues that "Despite the differences in perspective and emphasis . . . the general accounts of the sciences of Nature given by most Muslim writers . . . seem like so many exegeses of the same cosmic text" and goes further to claim that this Islamic cosmology is essentially—and not merely through historical accident or borrowing—akin to the cosmology of Greece, India, and China: "Despite the difference in the forms of the ancient and medieval cosmological sciences, there is an element which they shared in common, this element being the unicity of Nature. . . . This unicity is the natural consequence of the Unity of the Divine Principle which formed the basis of all the ancient 'Greater Mysteries' and which, either veiled in a mythological dress or expressed directly as a metaphysical truth, is to be found as the central Idea in all traditional civilizations." The universe, in spite of its seemingly infinite variety, is a manifestation of a divine, transcendent, infinite, and unified source that gives order to all things. This order is expressed in the hierarchy of the universe into levels of being. Human beings stand in a special relation to this universal hierarchy: the individual is a microcosm that recapitulates, through a system of symbolic correspondences, the whole of the universe, or macrocosm. Nasr is clearly sympathetic to the metaphysics of unity that underlies the thought of the cosmologists whose work he examines, and between this reworking of his dissertation and his most recent works little difference in point of view is discernible.

Nasr's next book, *Three Muslim Sages: Avicenna, Suhrawardi, Ibn 'Arabi* (1964), grew out of lectures he delivered at the Center for the Study of World Religions at the Harvard Divinity School in 1962. It is an introduction to the lived philosophies of men who were not "philosophers" in the modern sense of the word but "sages."

In 1964–1965 Nasr occupied the newly established Aga Khan Chair of Islamic Studies at the American University of Beirut. In 1966 he published some of his lectures as *Ideals and Realities of Islam,* which became one of his most widely translated works. Ali H. Abdel Kader, director of the Islamic Center in Washington, D.C., lauded the work in a review in *The Middle East Journal* (Spring 1968) as "valuable reading material for Muslims and non-Muslims alike" but noted that a "preoccupation with philosophy and mysticism . . . dominated the writer's approach throughout the book. Though sophisticated and highly intellectual, the philosophical and sufi coloration of the subject matter covered in the book may tend to confine its use and limit its readability." This observation, which implies a separation between Islamic philosophy and Islam as a religion or between Sufism and "mainstream" Islam, was later raised frequently by Nasr's critics. On the other hand, the scholar of comparative religion Huston Smith writes in his preface to the 1972 edition of the book: "To claim that anyone speaks for Islam as a whole world would be presumptuous, but Professor Nasr may come as close to doing so as anyone today."

In 1967 Nasr published *Islamic Studies: Essays on Law and Society, the Sciences, and Philosophy and Sufism,* a collection of pieces written between 1959 and 1966. The following year he published *Science and Civilization in Islam,* the first scholarly work in English to deal with Islamic science as a whole. Previous treatments had tended to focus on the role Islamic science played in shaping later Western science, particularly in conveying Greek knowledge to the Latin West. This approach, Nasr says, fails to acknowledge the integral role that traditional science plays in Islamic life and thought and overlooks the fundamental differences between it and modern Western science. In his foreword to the 1987 edition of *Science and Civilization in Islam* Nasr writes of the traditional Muslim scientists: "Their thoughts and words are precious because they transmit to us a science which is always rooted in God while studying His creation; a science which reflects systematic knowledge of nature without ever forgetting the Author of Nature Who has inscribed His Wisdom upon every leaf and stone and who has created the world of nature in such a way that every phenomenon is a sign (*ayah*) singing in silent music the glory of His Oneness."

In the introduction to the book Nasr notes that in the West the history of science is often regarded as "the progressive accumulation of techniques and the refinement of quantitative methods in the study of Nature." To Westerners who hold this model of progress or evolution, the stability inherent in the Islamic perspective appears as stagnation; the chief goal of Islamic science is, precisely, the knowledge of immutable principles that underlie the natural world. According to Nasr, the highest form of "science," which comes from the Latin *scientia,* or "knowledge," is that of the contemplative or "gnostic" who has surrendered his whole being to God. The gnostic participates, actively and consciously and not in the manner of a passive mysticism, in the divine Intellect, which knows all of nature from within.

In Nasr's view, intelligence cannot be reduced to reason, the analytical function of the human mind. Reason is the "passive aspect" and "reflection in the human domain" of intellect, which is capable of perceiving spiritual or metaphysical truth directly. The modern confusion of the words *intellect* (*intellectus* in the Scholastic vocabulary) and *reason* (*ratio*) is, for him, a symptom of the reductionist epistemology characteristic of modern philosophy and science. According to Nasr, when the natural link between reason and intellect is not severed, the former receives illumination from the latter, which is a reflection of the divine Intellect: "That is why Muslim metaphysicians say that rational knowledge leads naturally to the affirmation of the Divine Unity." The Muslim scientist is not concerned with isolated facts, viewed apart from their metaphysical principle, and does not wish to analyze, conquer, or control nature; the goal is to know God through nature. The branches of traditional science, from medicine to astronomy to alchemy, are integral applications of a divinely rooted, sacred science.

Science and Civilization in Islam has been widely debated. In his preface to the 1968 edition de Santillana claims that several of the best medieval Muslim scientists were not so different from their Western counterparts; but he also writes that the issues Nasr raises "are so rewarding as to force our gratitude even when we disagree totally." F. E. Peters noted in *The American Historical Review* (1974) that Nasr's emphasis on gnosis and the connection he draws between *scientia* and *sapientia* (wisdom) "colors everything he has written here." In his 1987 foreword Nasr acknowledges receiving heavy criti-

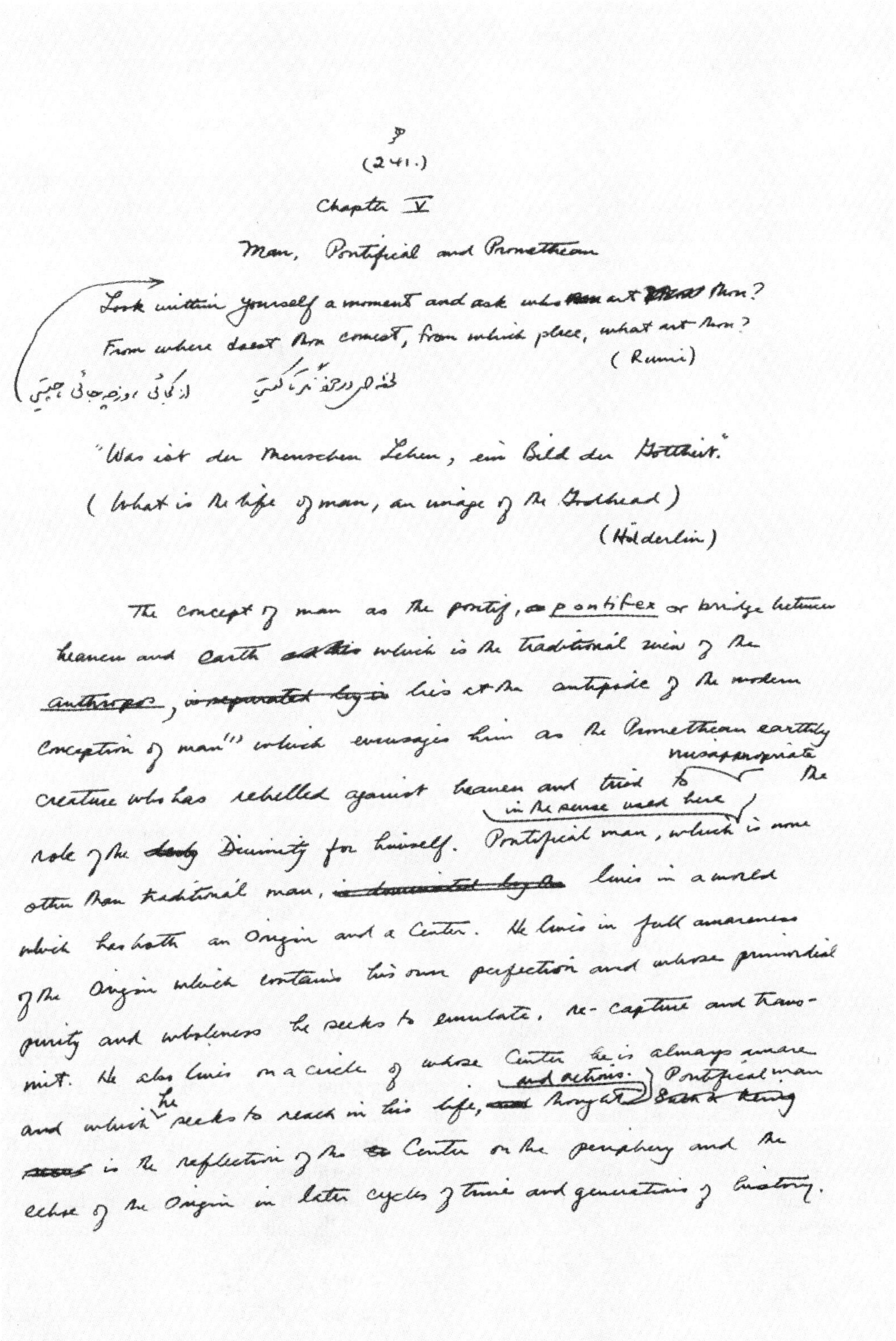

p
(241.)

Chapter V

Man, Pontifical and Promethean

Look within yourself a moment and ask who art thou?
From where doest thou comest, from which place, what art thou?
(Rumi)

قل لي بربك من انا من اين جئت وما انا

"Was ist der Menschen Leben, ein Bild der Gottheit."
(What is the life of man, an image of the Godhead)
(Hölderlin)

The concept of man as the pontif, or *pontifex* or bridge between heaven and earth which is the traditional view of the *anthropos*, lies at the antipode of the modern conception of man" which envisages him as the Promethean earthly creature who has rebelled against heaven and tried to misappropriate the role of the Divinity for himself. Pontifical man, which is none other than traditional man, lives in a world which has both an Origin and a Center. He lives in full awareness of the Origin which contains his own perfection and whose primordial purity and wholeness he seeks to emulate, re-capture and transmit. He also lives on a circle of whose Center he is always aware and which he seeks to reach in his life, thought and actions. Pontifical man is the reflection of the Center on the periphery and the echo of the Origin in later cycles of time and generations of history.

Corrected manuscript page for Nasr's 1981 Gifford Lectures, published as Knowledge and the Sacred
(from Lewis Edwin Hahn, Randall E. Auxier, and Lucian W. Stone Jr., eds.,
The Philosophy of Seyyed Hossein Nasr, *2001)*

cism both from Western scholars "imbued with the positivistic philosophy which has dominated the history of science in the West since Ernst Mach" and from Muslim thinkers influenced by what Nasr calls "scientism."

Nasr's first work of general philosophy was *The Encounter of Man and Nature: The Spiritual Crisis of Modern Man* (1968), which was republished in 1976 as *Man and Nature*. Based on lectures he delivered at the University of Chicago in 1966, the book analyzes the environmental crisis as a symptom of a greater and too often unmentioned problem: humanity's separation from God and from nature, which is created by God and manifests him. He particularly faults "scientism," which he describes in the preface to the 1976 edition as the perspective that presents "modern science not as a particular way of knowing nature, but as a complete and totalitarian philosophy which reduces all reality to the physical domain." The modern disdain for the natural world is not an accidental result of increased technological capabilities but a consequence of the point of view that regards nature as an object to be tamed or controlled. An anonymous reviewer in *The Times Literary Supplement* (3 October 1968) acknowledged that Nasr's "knowledge of western scientific writing is profound and his criticisms well documented" but predicted that "he may not find many sympathetic readers in the West."

After serving as dean of the Faculty of Letters at Tehran University from 1968 to 1972, Nasr became president of Aryamehr University, the leading technical school in Iran; he had been asked by the shah, Mohammad Reza Pahlavi, to reform its curriculum by rooting it more in Persian culture. Also in 1972 he published *Sufi Essays,* in which he shows how Sufism offers, within a distinctly Islamic framework, a path that is founded on universal principles of what it means to be human. Sufism is a way of "reminding man of who he really is, which means that man is awakened from this dream which he calls his ordinary life and that his soul is freed from the confines of that illusory prison of the ego which has its objective counterpart in what is called 'the world' in religious parlance." Beneath the illusion of the ego within and beyond the illusion of the world without is the Divine Nature, which alone is ultimately real and is the ground of all being. The final goal of the Sufi is the same as that of Christian, Hindu, and Buddhist mystics, but the Sufi's path is firmly grounded in the symbolic language and revelatory world of the Qur'an and the prophet Muhammad.

In 1973, at the request of the *shahbanou* (empress), Farah Pahlavi, Nasr founded the Imperial Iranian Academy of Philosophy, of which he served as the first president. Two years later he published *Islam and the Plight of Modern Man;* it includes the chapter "Metaphysics and

Philosophy East and West: Necessary Conditions for Meaningful Comparative Study," which was originally published in the journal *Philosophy East and West* in 1972. Here Nasr insists that one must begin by defining *philosophy*. If one takes the term to refer exclusively to a logical or rational discipline of the mind, of which metaphysics is merely one branch among many rather than the root, one will not be in a position to understand oriental philosophy, which comprises "the doctrinal part of a total spiritual way, tied to a method of realization and inseparable from the revelation or tradition which has given birth to the way in question." One must further understand that for non-Western philosophy, and even for much of premodern philosophy in the West, human faculties are ordered hierarchically, and knowledge is not limited to sensory perception and ratiocination. Because traditional philosophy shares these first principles, comparison of, say, Indian and Persian philosophy is quite possible. But comparative studies of modern and traditional philosophy must focus on dissimilarities; to compare Georg Wilhelm Friedrich Hegel's thought with the Upanishads or David Hume's with the early Buddhist philosopher Nagarjuna "is to fall into the worst form of error, one which prevents any type of profound understanding from being achieved, either for Westerners wanting to understand the East or *vice-versa*." Nasr's own sympathies lie with the traditional side: "the whole movement of thought in the West from the period after Nicolas of Cusa to Hegel, not to speak of twentieth century philosophy, is a movement toward 'anti-metaphysics' and an ever greater alienation from all that constitutes the very basis of all true 'philosophy,' namely the twin sources of truth, which for traditional or perennial philosophy are none other than revelation and intellectual intuition or spiritual vision."

In 1978, at the request of the shahbanou, Nasr became head of a special bureau concerned with, among other things, Iranian cultural affairs. Around this time the country began to undergo political turmoil, largely as a result of reforms the shah had implemented during the preceding two decades. The leading critic of the shah's government was the fundamentalist Islamic leader Ruholla Mussaui Khomeini–later known as the Ayatollah Khomeini–who had been exiled from Iran in 1964. On 6 January 1979 Nasr left Tehran to represent the shahbanou at the opening of an exhibition of Persian art in Tokyo; when he reached London, the shahbanou called to warn him not to return. On 16 January she and the shah left Iran, and by February the revolution was completed.

Nasr was stranded in London with his wife and two children and virtually no money or possessions. He writes in his intellectual autobiography: "It was the best time to remember Plato's definition of philosophy as the practice of death. I had to rebuild my external life from the beginning, at a time when my friends among the religious classes in Iran did nothing to prevent the confiscation of all my belongings and assets, and the vast majority of my Western friends . . . decided to ignore my plight for political expediency." Because of his connection with the shah's government, Nasr's house was ransacked, and the several thousand volumes in his personal library were confiscated or destroyed. Several manuscripts and sets of notes were lost, including his preparation for the prestigious 1981 Gifford Lectures at the University of Edinburgh.

In March 1979 Nasr and his family moved to Salt Lake City, where Nasr had been given a visiting professorship at the University of Utah by his friend David Gardner, the president of the university. At the end of the summer they moved to Boston for the children's schooling, though Nasr had accepted a professorship of Islamic studies at Temple University in Philadelphia. For the next five years he commuted between the two cities.

In 1981 Nasr delivered the Gifford Lectures, the first Muslim and the first non-Westerner to do so since their inception in 1889. Despite the loss of his notes he prepared the ten lectures in two and a half months; in his intellectual autobiography he describes the writing as "a gift from Heaven. The text would in a sense 'descend' upon me and crystallize clearly in my mind and I was able to write each chapter in a continuous flow." Nasr published the lectures in book form the same year, adding copious footnotes, as *Knowledge and the Sacred*. It is his most important work and one of the best introductions in English to the central doctrines of the *sophia perennis* (Latin for "perennial wisdom") and its revival in the twentieth century. Nasr analyzes the modern desacralization of knowledge and the consequent eclipse of human intelligence, urging its restoration through the recovery of traditional wisdom. His central thesis is that true knowledge is profoundly and by its very essence related to the sacred. This idea, he argues, underlies the basic teachings of every traditional religion, whether Hinduism, Buddhism, Taoism, Zoroastrianism, Judaism, Islam, or Christianity. Only in the modern world, which Nasr dates from the Renaissance, has the connection between knowledge and the sacred been lost. The roots of the crisis, he says, go back as far as the rationalists and skeptics of ancient Greece, but more immediate and grave in effect were the humanism of the Renaissance, which shifted the focus of knowledge from God to human beings and from the sacred cosmos to the secular order, and the full-blown rationalism of the Enlightenment, which reduced human knowledge to reason alone. Nasr contends that epistemology since Descartes has taken an increasingly

Dust jacket for the American edition of Nasr's 1981 Gifford Lectures (Collection of Michael Allen)

reductionistic trajectory in which the traditional doctrine of knowledge rooted in intellection and revelation was replaced by an idolatry of reason. Rationalism gave way to empiricism, with its tendency to reject metaphysics altogether; and empiricism has been followed by various forms of irrationalism, including existentialism and deconstructionism. For Nasr, then, the modern notion of progress is tragically flawed. The general course of modern history has been one of desacralization and decay, robbing humanity of its intelligence and stripping the cosmos of beauty and meaning.

The only possible solution, Nasr argues, is a return to tradition, which he defines as "truths or principles of a divine origin revealed or unveiled to mankind and, in fact, a whole cosmic sector through various figures envisaged as messengers, prophets, *avataras,* the Logos or other transmitting agencies, along with all the ramifications and applications of these principles in different realms including law and social structure, symbolism, the sciences, and

Cover for Nasr's 1993 collection of essays, in which he urges the need for a recovery of traditional science rooted in knowledge of the sacred (Thomas Cooper Library, University of South Carolina)

The knowledge of the Principle which is at once the absolute and infinite Reality is the heart of metaphysics. . . . The Principle is Reality in contrast to all that appears as real but which is not reality in the ultimate sense. The Principle is the Absolute compared to which all is relative. It is Infinite while all else is finite. The Principle is One and Unique while manifestation is multiplicity. . . . These are all manners of speaking of the Ultimate Reality which can be known but not by man as such.

Ultimately, Reality cannot be known qua individual being, but it can be known insofar as one participates, in one's inmost being, in that supraindividual reality. Knowledge at the highest or most inward level is "Self-Knowledge"; the individual shares in this knowledge "through the sun of the Divine Self residing at the center of the human soul." But the language of "Selfhood," or immanence, does not exhaust Reality, which is "not only the Inward but also the Outward, not only the One but also the essential reality of the many which is but the reflection of the One." That is, Ultimate Reality is not only a simple, exclusive unity in contrast to multiplicity but also a unity that embraces and, in a sense, even affirms multiplicity. Failure to grasp this point, Nasr believes, leads to misunderstandings of traditional metaphysics. In the Library of Living Philosophers volume, for example, Archie J. Bahm objects that "Nasr's view of the Absolute as an eternal, formless, pure unity sterilizes existence of all genuine activity. For him, actual existences are debased unities in which all plurality is by nature exteriorization of the supposed inner unity of the Absolute immanent within each thing." Nasr responds:

To speak of the integration of the levels of the cosmos into the Divine Principle is certainly not to deprive cosmic realities of their vitality, beauty, and reality on their own level. On the contrary, it is to bring out the deepest significance of all cosmic qualities. Metaphysical knowledge means not only to fix one's gaze upon the Absolute and to realize that there is nothing *ultimately* but the One. It also means to realize that to the extent that anything exists, it reflects metaphysical realities.

Being infinite, Ultimate Reality must realize all possibilities; not to do so would mark a limitation. The Principle, therefore, actualizes the possibility of multiplicity both on the level of discrete archetypes and at the various levels of cosmic existence. From another perspective, one can say that Ultimate Reality is supremely good or perfect and that the world is its joyful and effusive creation. The levels of creation are relative and, therefore, not ultimately real; it is in this sense that Hindu metaphysics describes the world as *maya,* or cosmic "illusion." But it also reflects Ultimate Reality in

embracing of course Supreme Knowledge along with the means for its attainment." Readers will recognize at once the gulf between Nasr's definition and the common understanding of tradition as mere custom, or the passing on from generation to generation of particular beliefs and practices. For Nasr, "Tradition implies truths of a supraindividual character rooted in the nature of reality as such for as it has been said"–here he quotes from Schuon–"'Tradition is not a childish and outmoded mythology but a science that is terribly real.'"

The chapter "Scientia Sacra" offers one of the clearest and most concise expressions of the fundamental metaphysical principles that inform Nasr's view of tradition. *Scientia sacra,* or sacred knowledge, is equivalent to *sophia perennis.* The root of this knowledge or wisdom is discernment of "the Real":

its own way, Nasr explains: absoluteness is reflected in the distinct existence of things; infinity is reflected in the indefinite extension of space and the duration of time; and goodness is reflected in quality itself.

The remaining chapters of *Knowledge and the Sacred* are applications or extensions of these principles. "Man, Pontifical and Promethean" examines the central role of humanity in the world, both what it is meant to be and the state to which it falls when it forsakes knowledge. "The Cosmos as Theophany" returns to some of the ideas presented in *An Introduction to Islamic Cosmological Doctrines*. "Eternity and the Temporal Order" examines time. "Traditional Art as Fountain of Knowledge and Grace" looks at the vital role played by art in the spiritual life. "Principial Knowledge and the Multiplicity of Sacred Forms" explains the seeming exclusivity of various religions at the outer, formal level in light of their inner, metaphysical unity. The final chapter, "Knowledge of the Sacred as Deliverance," concludes: "Through this sacred knowledge man becomes aware of the purpose for which he was created and gains that illimitable spiritual freedom and liberation which alone is worthy of man if only he were to realize who he is."

Nasr's Gifford Lectures signaled one of the first recognitions of traditional philosophy by mainstream academia. Wolfgang Smith, a traditionalist mathematician, physicist, and philosopher of science, writes in his contribution to the Library of Living Philosophers volume: "For the first time in modern history, I would venture to say, the undistorted and unadulterated voice of the perennial and universal tradition could be heard within the prestigious halls of academe." The response to that voice by other academics has not always been positive. In a review of the book in *Philosophy East and West* (April 1984) Thomas Dean brings up one of the most common objections when he comments that traditionalism presents a "methodological impasse," inasmuch as it appeals to an inner, firsthand "taste" of reality that the modern critic will be accused of lacking. In his contribution to the Library of Living Philosophers volume Mehdi Aminrazavi makes the same point more sharply: "The question which Nasr's opponents pose is how a serious philosophical debate is possible when one encounters non-verifiable and esoteric truth claims. . . . Nasr's system becomes self-referential, its truth value depending upon the system itself." In his response to Aminrazavi, Nasr replies that such a critique "could be and in fact has been leveled against Plato and Plotinus as well and is nothing new. . . . What Aminrazavi considers as 'truth claims,' . . . are in fact not claims at all but truths reached by means of the eye of the intellect and based on certainty that is not available to the unaided reason. But that does not make these truths non-verifiable." The average person cannot verify the "truth claims" of quantum mechanics, either, he argues, but accepts their authority nonetheless. Yet, he concludes, modernists seem adamantly opposed to accepting the authority of sacred science.

In 1984 Nasr became University Professor of Islamic Studies at The George Washington University in Washington, D.C. Despite the ostensibly Islamic focus of this position, over the next two decades Nasr offered many classes on comparative religion and philosophy, as well as on the relationship of religion to science and of humankind to the environment. In 1984 he helped establish the Foundation for Traditional Studies. He has since served as the presiding member on a board of some of the foremost representatives of perennial philosophy in the United States. The original membership included Joseph Epes Brown, an authority on Native American tradition best known for his friendship and work with the Lakota Sioux Black Elk, and Rama Coomaraswamy, the son of Ananda Coomaraswamy. The mission statement of the foundation provides a summary of traditionalist goals: "to make known the principles and philosophies at the heart of various traditions and to provide access in a variety of ways to their religious practices, arts, sciences, and social structures" and "to preserve and make available in a contemporary language the extremely rich treasury of traditional wisdom and to apply these millennial teachings to the contemporary situation." Since 1995 the foundation has published *Sophia*, the leading journal for traditional studies in English.

In 1986 Nasr edited *The Essential Writings of Frithjof Schuon*, which includes a valuable introduction to the work of the foremost contemporary authority on the *sophia perennis*. That same year Nasr published his only work devoted solely to aesthetics, *Islamic Art and Spirituality*. Nasr shows how Islamic calligraphy, architecture, poetry, and music are united by the defining characteristics of Islamic spirituality just as traditional arts in general are united as expressions of the sacred. He concludes, "The sacred art of Islam is, like all veritable sacred art, a descent of heavenly reality upon the earth. . . . It is an echo of the other world (*al-akhirah*) in the matrix of the temporal existence in which men live (*al-dunya*)." Art, for Nasr, is not sentimental or subintellectual but the manifestation of truth in a nondiscursive mode; he agrees with Plato that "Beauty is the splendor of the True." (According to the traditionalists' interpretation of Plato, the critique of art in the *Republic* is directed not at sacred art, which is based directly on a vision of the Forms, but "realist" art, which is based on imperfect earthly instantiations of the Forms.) Indeed, Nasr claims that Islamic art is capable of expressing the inward reality of Islam much more directly than "many a purportedly scholarly exposition."

Nasr in 2001

A consequence of Nasr's acceptance of tradition is his critique of modernity. In "Reflections on Islam and Modern Thought," an essay collected in his *Traditional Islam in the Modern World* (1987), Nasr defines the "modern"–which is not to be confused with such neutral terms as *contemporary* or *up-to-date*–as "that which is cut off from the Transcendent, from the immutable principles which in reality govern all things and which are made known to man through revelation in its most universal sense." He points out that the period in which the modern, secular perspective has held sway, compared to the long history "during which man has continuously celebrated the Divine and performed his function as God's vice-regent (*khalifah*) on earth . . . appears as no more than the blinking of an eye." He goes on to critique what he considers common modern illusions of evolution, progress, and social utopianism.

Many of these themes are developed in *A Young Muslim's Guide to the Modern World* (1993), which includes a chapter with half-page accounts of major modern philosophers from Francis Bacon to Jean-Paul Sartre. After these descriptions Nasr provides a general critique: "The various figures and schools of modern thought have followed upon the wake of one another starting with the rebellion of reason against both the intellect and revelation." He details the forms of this rebellion from early rationalist philosophy through the nineteenth-century system builders to twentieth-century phenomenology, existentialism, and positivism, then notes that "meanwhile also in the West, so strongly in the grip of highly anti-metaphysical and anti-religious philosophies, there began at the beginning of the century a restatement of perennial philosophy which is completely opposed to modern European philosophy." Nasr believes that perennial philosophy is poised to answer a newly felt need since "postmodernist" currents have caused the erosion of many modern philosophical schools and led Westerners to an even deeper state of intellectual confusion. Nasr concludes the chapter "Modern Western Philosophy and Schools of Thought" by stating that one cannot ignore modern philosophy but must study it carefully so as to be able

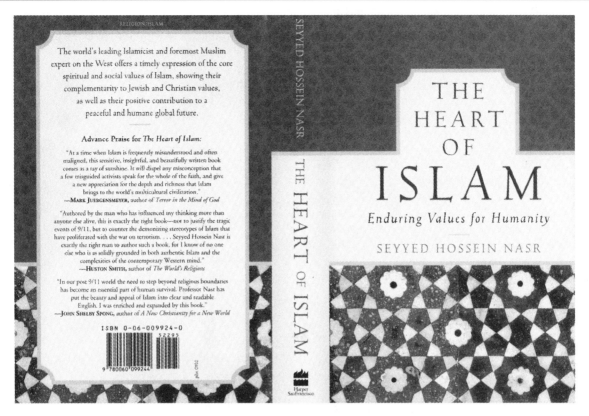

Dust jacket for Nasr's 2002 book, written to provide Westerners with a balanced view of Islam following the terrorist attacks of 11 September 2001 (Collection of Adrian C. Polit)

to understand the causes of the modern world. Nasr is a traditionalist but not a "fundamentalist," and his writings have nothing of the anti-intellectual; indeed, he most often criticizes modern thinkers for their "anti-intellectualism," where intellect is taken to refer to the highest faculty of knowledge and not merely to isolated, profane reason.

In 1993 Nasr also published *The Need for a Sacred Science,* a collection of essays organized around several of the themes of *Knowledge and the Sacred.* The following year he delivered the Edward Cadbury Lectures at the University of Birmingham in England. Published in 1996 as *Religion and the Order of Nature,* the lectures offer a broader treatment of the ideas presented in *The Encounter of Man and Nature.* Nasr reexamines the lack of harmony between modern human beings and the environment that, he contends, results from the loss of a sense of the sacred and argues that this crisis has consequences for both religion and philosophy. He proposes the "resacralization of nature" through a return to the traditional religious understanding of humanity's relationship to God and the world and a recovery of traditional, nonreductionistic sciences.

Nasr elaborated on this theme in his 1999 book *The Spiritual and Religious Dimensions of the Environmental Crisis.* That same year he published *Poems of the Way,* a collection of original spiritual poems in English. In the Library of Living Philosophers volume Luce López-Baralt, a scholar of comparative literature, claims that the poems are ecstatic verse equivalents of Nasr's *Knowledge and the Sacred:* "Philosophy is put into practice, *logos* dissolves into experience, theoretical knowledge (*'aql*) becomes realized knowledge (*'ishq*) before our startled eyes." In 2002 Nasr published *The Heart of Islam: Enduring Values for Humanity,* which was followed in 2003 by *Islam: Religion, History, and Civilization;* both seek to present Islam to a Western audience and to correct misunderstandings following the terrorist attacks of 11 September 2001.

Seyyed Hossein Nasr's significance as a philosopher lies not in the invention of a new system of thought but in his restatement in contemporary language of traditional doctrines that have been almost completely neglected in the modern world. This restatement constitutes a forceful and articulate challenge to contemporary Western philosophy. In his reply to López-Baralt in the Library of Living Philosophers volume Nasr writes, "'The philosophical challenge' based on traditional sapiential knowledge and the perennial philosophy was presented long before me by Guénon, Coomaraswamy, and Schuon. My role has been to carry this challenge to the heart of the Western academic community and centers of mainstream Western philosophy, which until recently had chosen to neglect and even overlook the very existence of traditional teachings." Nasr's philosophical work is, therefore, not "original" in the typical sense of the word; but he and other traditionalists criticize the modern idolization of "originality" and "creativity" and point out that their work is "original" in the sense of harking back to the divine origin that they believe to be the eternal heart of all philosophy. In "In Quest of the Eternal Sophia," an autobiographical sketch contributed to volume six of the series *Philosophes critiques d'eux-mêmes/Philosophische Selbstbetrachtungen* (Philosophers on Their Own Work, 1980), Nasr writes: "I have found the greatest joy of creativity not in fabricating a 'truth' from my own mind and experience, . . . but in trying to become transparent before the ray of Truth which shines whenever and wherever the veil before it is lifted or rent asunder."

Interviews:

Philip and Carol Zaleski, "Traditional Cosmology and Modern Science: An Interview with Seyyed Hossein Nasr," *Parabola,* 8, no. 4 (1983): 20–31;

"The Long Journey," *Parabola,* 10, no. 1 (1985): 28–41;

Jeffrey P. Zaleski, "Echoes of Infinity: An Interview with Seyyed Hossein Nasr," *Parabola,* 13, no. 1 (1988): 24–35;

Jay Kinney, "Islam, Tradition, and the West," *Gnosis,* no. 37 (Fall 1995): 50–55;

Gray Henry, "The First Prophet: An Interview with Seyyed Hossein Nasr," *Parabola,* 21, no. 1 (1996): 13–19;

Hugh Hewitt, "A Conversation with Seyyed Hossein Nasr," in his *Searching for God in America* (Dallas: Word, 1996), pp. 75–96;

Amira El-Zein, "Sufism, Creativity, and Exile: An Interview with Seyyed Hossein Nasr," *Jusoor* (1996): 131–158;

Bill Moyers, "Conversations," in his *Genesis: A Living Conversation* (New York: Doubleday, 1996), pp. 219–247, 319–347;

Adnan Aslan, "Religions and the Concept of the Ultimate," in his *Religious Pluralism in Christian and Islamic Philosophy: The Thought of John Hick and Seyyed Hossein Nasr* (Richmond, U.K.: Curzon, 1998), pp. 257–273;

Henry, "Separation from God: An Interview with Seyyed Hossein Nasr," *Parabola,* 24, no. 4 (1999): 59–66;

Lucian W. Stone Jr., "The Perennial Voice of Islam: An Interview with Seyyed Hossein Nasr," *Kinesis,* 25 (Fall 1999): 5–26.

Bibliographies:

William Chittick, *The Works of Seyyed Hossein Nasr through His Fortieth Birthday* (Salt Lake City: Middle East Center, University of Utah, 1977);

Mehdi Aminrazavi and Zailan Moris, *The Complete Bibliography of the Works of Seyyed Hossein Nasr from 1958 through April 1993* (Kuala Lumpur: Islamic Academy of Science of Malaysia, 1994);

Aminrazavi, Moris, and Ibrahim Kalin, "Bibliography of the Writings of Seyyed Hossein Nasr," in *The Philosophy of Seyyed Hossein Nasr,* edited by Lewis Edwin Hahn, Randall E. Auxier, and Lucian W. Stone Jr., The Library of Living Philosophers, volume 28 (Chicago & La Salle, Ill.: Open Court, 2001), pp. 835–964.

Biography:

Zailan Moris, "The Biography of Seyyed Hossein Nasr," in her *Knowledge Is Light: Essays in Honor of Seyyed Hossein Nasr* (Chicago: ABC International Group, 1999), pp. 9–32.

References:

Amy Aldrich, "The Soul and Science of Islam," *George Washington University Magazine* (Spring 1992): 15–17;

Mehdi Aminrazavi, "The Intellectual Contributions of Seyyed Hossein Nasr," in *The Complete Bibliography of the Works of Seyyed Hossein Nasr from 1958 through April 1993,* by Aminrazavi and Zailan Moris (Kuala Lumpur: Islamic Academy of Science of Malaysia, 1994), pp. xix–xxv;

Adnan Aslan, *Religious Pluralism in Christian and Islamic Philosophy: The Thought of John Hick and Seyyed Hossein Nasr* (Richmond, U.K.: Curzon, 1998);

William Chittick, "Preface," in his *The Works of Seyyed Hossein Nasr through His Fortieth Birthday* (Salt Lake City: Middle East Center, University of Utah, 1977), pp. 7–12;

Lewis Edwin Hahn, Randall E. Auxier, and Lucian W. Stone Jr., eds., *The Philosophy of Seyyed Hossein Nasr,* The Library of Living Philosophers, volume 28 (Chicago & La Salle, Ill.: Open Court, 2001);

Moris, *Knowledge Is Light: Essays in Honor of Seyyed Hossein Nasr* (Chicago: ABC International Group, 1999);

Jane I. Smith, "Seyyed Hossein Nasr: Defender of the Sacred and Islamic Traditionalism," in *The Muslims of America,* edited by Yvonne Yazbeck Haddad (New York: Oxford University Press, 1991), pp. 80–95.

Robert Nozick

(16 November 1938 – 23 January 2002)

Philip B. Dematteis
Saint Leo University

BOOKS: *Anarchy, State, and Utopia* (New York: Basic Books, 1974; Oxford: Blackwell, 1975);

Philosophical Explanations (Cambridge, Mass.: Harvard University Press, 1981; Oxford: Clarendon Press, 1981);

The Examined Life: Philosophical Meditations (New York: Simon & Schuster, 1989);

The Normative Theory of Individual Choice (New York: Garland, 1990);

The Nature of Rationality (Princeton: Princeton University Press, 1993);

Socratic Puzzles (Cambridge, Mass.: Harvard University Press, 1997);

Invariances: The Structure of the Objective World (Cambridge, Mass.: Belknap Press, 2001).

OTHER: "Man as an Ethical Being," in *Medicine, Science, and Society: Symposia Celebrating the Harvard Medical School Bicentennial*, edited by Kurt J. Isselbacher (New York: Wiley, 1984), pp. 35–48;

"Knowledge and Skepticism," in *The Possibility of Knowledge: Nozick and His Critics*, edited by Steven Luper-Foy (Totowa, N.J.: Rowman & Littlefield, 1987), pp. 19–115;

"Bedingungen für Wissen" and "Skeptizismus," in *Analytische Philosophie der Erkenntnis*, edited by Peter Bieri (Frankfurt am Main: Athenäum, 1987), pp. 167–176, 332–349.

SELECTED PERIODICAL PUBLICATIONS–
UNCOLLECTED: "Escaping the Good Samaritan Paradox," by Nozick and Richard Routley, *Mind*, 71 (1962): 377–382;

"Distributive Justice," *Philosophy and Public Affairs*, 3 (1973): 45–126;

"Invariance and Objectivity," *Proceedings and Addresses of the American Philosophical Association*, 72, no. 2 (1998): 21–48.

Robert Nozick, who spent most of his career at Harvard University, did original work in metaphysics, epistemology, and decision theory and was interested in topics such as animal rights and Eastern philosophy and religion. But he became one of the most influential thinkers of the late twentieth century with, and will apparently be mainly remembered for, his first book: *Anarchy, State, and Utopia* (1974), in which he uses the techniques of analytic philosophy, including counterexamples and bizarre thought experiments, to argue for the libertarian viewpoint in political philosophy.

Nozick was born on 16 November 1938 in Brooklyn, New York, to Russian Jewish immigrants Max Nozick, a manufacturer, and Sophie Cohen Nozick. He attended public grade and high schools in Brooklyn. A leftist like many Jewish New Yorkers, in high school he joined the youth branch of the Socialist Party. His interest in philosophy began around the same time. In the half-page chapter "Portrait of the Philosopher as a Young Man" that concludes *The Examined Life: Philosophical Meditations* (1989) he recalls: "When I was fifteen years old or sixteen I carried around in the streets of Brooklyn a paperback copy of Plato's *Republic*, front cover facing outward. I had read only some of it and understood less, but I was excited by it and knew it was something wonderful."

Nozick went to Columbia University, where, still a leftist, he founded a chapter of the Student League for Industrial Democracy (in 1962 it became Students for a Democratic Society). He received his B.A. in 1959. On 15 August of that year he married Barbara Claire Fierer, a teacher. They had two children: Emily Sarah and David Joshua.

Nozick began graduate school at Princeton University in the fall. Bruce Goldberg, a graduate of the City College of New York, also entered the Princeton philosophy program in 1959, and he and Nozick became friends. Goldberg–an analytic philosopher who went on to teach at the University of Illinois, Cornell University, and the University of Maryland, Baltimore County, and died in 1999–had recently been converted to libertarianism by followers of Ayn Rand and was an enthusiastic proselytizer for that point of view. In the

Robert Nozick (photograph by Gjertrud Schnackenberg; from the dust jacket for
Invariances: The Structure of the Objective World, *2001)*

acknowledgments to *Anarchy, State, and Utopia* Nozick says that "arguments with Bruce Goldberg led me to take libertarian views seriously enough to want to refute them, and so to pursue the subject further." In a *Forbes Magazine* interview in 1975 he said, "At first, I thought: 'No, those arguments aren't good ones.' The more I explored the arguments, the more convincing they looked. For a while I thought: 'Well, yes, the arguments are right, capitalism is the best system, but only bad people would think so.'" He read works by free-market economists such as Ludwig von Mises, Friedrich Hayek, Henry Hazlitt, and Milton Friedman and then confronted his old friends at the socialist *Dissent* magazine: if the minimum wage is such a good idea, he asked, why not set it at, say, $10 an hour? These respected and widely published writers could not answer the question.

Nozick earned his M.A. in 1961 and was hired as an assistant professor of philosophy at Princeton. He received his Ph.D. in 1963 with a dissertation on theories of rational decision.

Around that time Goldberg took Nozick to a meeting of the Circle Bastiat, a group of free-market economists, at the apartment of Murray N. Rothbard

on West Eighty-eighth Street in New York City. There, apparently, he had the "long conversation" with Rothbard that, he says in the acknowledgments to *Anarchy, State, and Utopia,* "stimulated my interest in individualist anarchist theory." Soon after, as he told *Forbes,* "my mind and heart were in unison."

In 1965 Nozick moved to Harvard University as an assistant professor. After a stint as an associate professor at Rockefeller University in New York City from 1967 to 1969, he returned to Harvard as a full professor. In a 2001 interview with *Laissez Faire Books.com* Nozick recalled that soon after his return he announced a course titled "Capitalism" that the catalogue described as "a moral examination of capitalism." The students, some of whom had occupied the administration building the previous year, no doubt expected a moral condemnation of capitalism, but

Somehow a rumor had spread, or maybe they saw what books were there in the textbook section of the bookstore, where in addition to something by Marx and some socialist book were Hayek and Mises and Friedman. So one graduate student came up to me at the beginning of the term and said, "We don't know if you're going to be able to give this course." This was a graduate student in philosophy. And I said, "What do you mean?" He said: "Well, you're going to be saying things . . ." and he mumbled something, "there may be interruptions or demonstrations in class." And I said–I was then, you have to remember, 30 years old–I said, "If you disrupt my course, I'm going to kick the shit out of you." He said, "You're taking this very personally!"

I said, "It's my course. If you want to pass out leaflets outside the classroom door, and tell people that they shouldn't come in and take the course, that's fine. I won't allow you to do things inside the classroom." He said, "Yes, well, we may pass out leaflets." Time went by and nothing happened during the first week, the second week. So I saw him in the hallway and asked, "Where are the leaflets?" He said, "Well, you know, we're very busy, we have a lot of things to do these days." I said, "I called my mother living in Florida and told her that I was going to be leafleted, now come on!" But nothing ever happened.

Nozick established his reputation with such densely argued and highly technical articles in decision theory as "Moral Complications and Moral Structures" (1968), "Weighted Voting and 'One-Man, One-Vote,'" (1968), "Coercion" (1969), and "Newcomb's Problem and Two Principles of Choice" (1969), all of which are collected in his *Socratic Puzzles* (1997). He became a member of the editorial board of *Philosophy and Public Affairs* in 1971. In 1971–1972 he was a fellow of the Center for Advanced Study in the Behavioral Sciences in Palo Alto, California, where he wrote the first nine chapters of *Anarchy, State, and Utopia;* the final chapter was delivered as a talk in a symposium at a meeting of the Eastern Division of the American Philosophical Association in 1969. Nozick rewrote the entire manuscript in the summer of 1973, and the book was published in 1974.

The preface to *Anarchy, State, and Utopia* opens with the words: "Individuals have rights, and there are things no person or group may do to them (without violating their rights). So strong and far-reaching that they raise the question of what, if anything, the state and its officials may do. How much room do individual rights leave for the state?" Nozick answers the question in the next paragraph:

> Our main conclusions about the state are that a minimal state, limited to the narrow functions of protection against force, theft, fraud, enforcement of contracts, and so on, is justified; that any more extensive state will violate persons' rights not to be forced to do certain things, and is unjustified; and that the minimal state is inspiring as well as right. Two noteworthy implications are that the state may not use its coercive apparatus for the purpose of getting some citizens to aid others, or in order to prohibit activities to people for their *own* good or protection.

The strong emphasis on rights shows that Nozick's position rests on a deontological, or nonconsequentialist, ethical theory, which holds that certain actions are morally right or wrong in themselves. It is opposed to teleological, or consequentialist, ethical theories, which maintain that actions are made right or wrong by their effects or results, so that the same type of action, such as lying, can be the right thing to do in some situations and wrong in others. The leading teleological ethical theory, utilitarianism, holds that those actions are right–and, therefore, morally obligatory– that maximize the amount of aggregate pleasure and minimize the aggregate amount of suffering experienced by sentient beings. Nozick criticizes utilitarianism by invoking the science-fiction hypothesis of the sort of "experience machine" that was later depicted in the motion picture *The Matrix* (1999): if what is good is simply the greatest amount of subjective states of happiness, people would want to be plugged into machines that gave them the same experiences they would enjoy in real life, while they were actually floating in tanks with electrodes attached to their brains; they could be detached from the machines every two years, choose to continue the same experiences or opt for a new set, and be hooked up again. Nozick thinks that most people would reject such an existence, no matter how blissful, for three reasons: "First, we want to *do* certain things, and not just have the experiences of doing them. . . . A second reason for not plugging in is that we want to *be* a certain way, to be a certain sort of person. A person floating in a tank is an indeterminate blob. . . . Thirdly, plugging into an experience machine limits us to a manmade reality, to a world no deeper than that which people can construct."

It is noteworthy that, unlike many other libertarian thinkers, Nozick–a vegetarian in his personal life– gives serious consideration to extending rights to nonhuman animals. He points out that

> *eating* animals is not necessary for *health* and is not less expensive than alternate equally healthy diets available to people in the United States. The gain, then, from the eating of animals is pleasures of the palate, gustatory delights, varied tastes. . . . The question is: do they, or rather does the marginal addition in them gained by eating animals rather than only nonanimals, *outweigh* the moral weight to be given to animals' lives and pain?

To approach the issue, typically, he sets up a thought experiment:

> Suppose then that I enjoy swinging a baseball bat. It happens that in front of the only place to swing it stands a cow. Swinging the bat unfortunately would involve smashing the cow's head. But I wouldn't get

Dust jacket for the much acclaimed—and much attacked—1974 book in which Nozick argues that only a minimal or "night-watchman" state, restricted to protecting individuals against force, theft, and fraud and to enforcing contracts, is justified (Bruccoli Clark Layman Archives)

fun from doing *that;* the pleasure comes from exercising my muscles, swinging well, and so on. It's unfortunate that as a side effect (not a means) of my doing this, the animal's skull gets smashed. To be sure, I could forego swinging the bat, and instead bend down and touch my toes or do some other exercise. But this wouldn't be as enjoyable as swinging the bat; I won't get as much fun, pleasure, or delight out of it. So the question is: would it be all right for me to swing the bat in order to get the *extra* pleasure of swinging it as compared to the best alternative available activity that does not involve harming the animal? . . . Is there some principle that would allow killing and eating animals for the additional pleasure this brings, yet would not allow swinging the bat for the extra pleasure it brings?

In the first six chapters of *Anarchy, State, and Utopia* Nozick argues that government could arise from the anarchic "state of nature" in John Locke's *Second Treatise*

of Government (1690), "even though no one intended this or tried to bring it about, by a process which need not violate anyone's rights." In Locke's theory, most people in the state of nature would be able to reason out for themselves the dictates of morality and would conclude that each person has natural rights to life, liberty, and "estate," or property. Nevertheless, certain "inconveniences" would arise: each person would be the judge in his or her own case and would think that justice required punishing transgressions against himself or herself more severely than those against others, and individuals might lack the strength to defend themselves against violations of their rights. To remedy these inconveniences, people would enter into a social contract to establish a state to act as an impartial referee and to protect their rights more effectively than they could do as individuals.

Nozick asks whether these inconveniences could be remedied within the state of nature, without establishing a state. Locke says that in the state of nature an individual who is attacked may call on others for help; thus, Nozick suggests, mutual protection associations would arise: "some entrepreneurs will go into the business of selling protected services." The contracts offered by the protection agencies would require their clients to renounce private retaliation, which would "lead to counter-retaliation by another agency or individual, and a protective agency would not wish . . . to get drawn into the affair by having to defend its client against the counter-retaliation." If several agencies were operating in the same area, and their clients came into conflict, and each agency backed its own client, the agencies would have to battle each other. Such a situation would be bad for business; therefore, the agencies would either enter into agreements to confine their services to particular territories; or, in a series of conflicts one would eventually dominate, and clients of the other agencies would transfer to it; or the agencies would set up a superagency to adjudicate conflicts and enforce its decisions; or the agencies would merge. In one way or another, a dominant protection agency would be formed. Thus, "Out of anarchy, pressed by spontaneous groupings, mutual-protection associations, division of labor, market pressures, economies of scale, and rational self-interest there arises something very much resembling a minimal state or a group of geographically distinct minimal states." Furthermore, the clients of the dominant protection agency would be exposed to unjustified injuries by nonclients if the nonclients were allowed to exercise their right of self-defense; therefore, the agency will prohibit them from exercising that right, and it will compensate them for this prohibition by undertaking their defense itself. It is entitled to charge them for doing so; thus, the distinction between clients and nonclients disappears, and the dominant protection agency has become a state: it protects everyone in a given territory, possesses a monopoly on the use of force in that territory, and imposes taxes. It is, however, a minimal or "night-watchman" state that functions only to protect individuals' natural and negative rights to life, liberty, and property; in practical terms, it is "limited to the functions of protecting all its citizens against violence, theft, and fraud, and to the enforcement of contracts, and so on."

In the second part of the book Nozick argues that a state that goes beyond those minimal functions violates individuals' natural rights and is, therefore, unjustified. The major area in which governments go beyond their rightful boundaries in this way is the attempt to establish "social" or "economic justice" by redistributing wealth from the haves to the have-nots. This part is primarily a critique of *A Theory of Justice* (1971), in which Nozick's Harvard colleague John Rawls argued that the state should redistribute wealth to benefit the disadvantaged. Nozick points out that the very notion of distributive justice wrongly implies that things fall from heaven like manna and that "society" then must decide how to distribute them; but, in fact,

we are not in the position of children who have been given portions of pie by someone who now makes last minute adjustments to rectify careless cutting. There is no *central* distribution, no person or group entitled to control all the resources, jointly deciding how they are to be doled out. What each person gets, he gets from others who give it to him in exchange for something, or as a gift. . . . There is no more a distributing or distribution of shares than there is a distribution of mates in a society in which persons choose whom they shall marry.

Thus, "In the non-manna-from-heaven world in which things have to be made or produced or transformed by people, there is no separate process of distribution for a theory of distributions to be a theory of."

According to Nozick, theories of distributive justice such as Rawls's are "patterned" or "end-state" theories: they specify some pattern that should be realized, such as distribution according to equality, need, effort, social usefulness, and so on; if that pattern is not realized, goods should be redistributed so that, in the end, the pattern is realized. Nozick calls his own position the "historical entitlement" theory: any distribution, regardless of any pattern that it may or may not exhibit, is just, provided that it came about in accordance with just rules of acquisition, transfer, and rectification. In regard to acquisition, Nozick again follows Locke, who held that a person has a right to own what he or she makes and to appropriate anything that is not

already owned, provided that he or she leaves "enough and as good" for others–that is, that the appropriation leaves them no worse off. The overall distribution of goods results from exchanges between individuals, each of whom is entitled to bestow his or her "holdings" as he or she chooses. Ownership includes the right to give things to others–the principle of transfer. The principle of rectification deals with goods that have been taken unjustly–by theft or fraud–and holds that, if possible, they must be restored to their rightful owners. Nozick does not work out the rules of rectification in detail; he leaves open the possibility that some tax-financed welfare program, or even Rawls's rule of favoring the worst-off group, may be justified as a means of rectification if it can be shown that the better-off are the beneficiaries, and the worse-off the victims, of past injustices.

But if justice consisted in the pattern according to which goods are distributed, then giving, which changes the pattern, would be unjust. "The view that holding *must* be patterned perhaps will seem less plausible when it is seen to have the consequence that people may not choose to do acts that upset the patterning, even with things they legitimately hold." Nozick illustrates this point with what has become the best-known passage in *Anarchy, State, and Utopia,* the Wilt Chamberlain story:

suppose a distribution favored by one of these nonentitlement conceptions is realized. Let us suppose it is your favorite one and let us call this distribution D_1. Perhaps everyone has an equal share, perhaps shares vary in accordance with some dimension you treasure. Now suppose that Wilt Chamberlain is greatly in demand by basketball teams, being a great gate attraction. . . . He signs the following sort of contract with a team: In each home game, twenty-five cents from the price of each ticket of admission goes to him. (We ignore the question of whether he is "gouging" the owners, letting them look out for themselves.) The season starts, and people cheerfully attend his team's games; they buy their tickets, each time dropping a separate twenty-five cents of their admission price into a special box with Chamberlain's name on it. They are excited about seeing him play; it is worth the total admission price to them. Let us suppose that in one season one million persons attend his home games, and Wilt Chamberlain winds up with $250,000, a much larger sum than the average income and larger even than anyone else has. Is he entitled to this income? Is this new distribution, D_2, unjust? If so, why? There is *no* question about whether each of the people was entitled to the control over the resources they had in D_1; because that was the distribution (your favorite) that (for the purposes of argument) we assumed was acceptable. Each of those persons *chose* to give twenty-five cents of their money to Chamberlain. They could have spent it on going to the movies, or on candy bars, or on

Nozick in 1974 (from the dust jacket for
Anarchy, State, and Utopia*)*

copies of *Dissent* magazine. But they all, at least one million of them, converged on giving it to Wilt Chamberlain in exchange for watching him play basketball. If D_1 was a just distribution, and people voluntarily moved from it to D_2, transferring parts of their shares they were given under D_1 (what was it for if not to do something with?), isn't D_2 also just? If the people were entitled to dispose of the resources to which they were entitled (under D_1), didn't this include their being entitled to give it to, or exchange it with, Wilt Chamberlain? Can anyone else complain on grounds of justice? Each other person already has his legitimate share under D_1. Under D_1, there is nothing that anyone has that anyone else has a claim of justice against. After someone transfers something to Wilt Chamberlain, third parties *still* have their legitimate shares; *their* shares are not changed. By what process could such a transfer among two persons give rise to a legitimate claim of distributive justice on a portion of what was transferred, by a third party who had no claim of justice on any holding of the others *before* the transfer?

Nozick further demonstrates the absurdity of redistributionist schemes by proposing that sex appeal be redistributed by plastic surgery. He concludes that "no

end-state principle or distributional patterned principle of justice can be continuously realized without continuous interference with people's lives" and that "The socialist society would have to forbid capitalist acts between consenting adults." Instead of trying to fill in the blanks in "from each according to his _____" and "to each according to his _____," Nozick prefers to say "*From each as they choose, to each as they are chosen.*" Taxation to provide welfare benefits is literally theft and is tantamount to forced labor, since taking a portion of a person's earnings is to make him or her work that proportion of his or her time for another's benefit.

Not only should the state not confiscate people's holdings, Nozick argues, it also has no right to interfere with "victimless crimes" such as pornography, prostitution, gambling, or drugs. The minimal state is, he says, "inspiring as well as right," because it allows room for many visions of utopia: "The idea that there is . . . one best society for *everyone* to live in . . . seems to me to be incredible." How, he asks, could one design a single society that would be best for "Wittgenstein, Elizabeth Taylor, Bertrand Russell, Thomas Merton, Yogi Berra, Allen Ginsburg [*sic*], Harry Wolfson, Thoreau, Casey Stengel, The Lubavicher Rebbe, Picasso, Moses, Einstein, Hugh Heffner [*sic*], Socrates, Henry Ford, Lenny Bruce, Baba Ram Dass, Gandhi, Sir Edmund Hillary, Raymond Lubitz, Buddha, Frank Sinatra, Columbus, Freud, Norman Mailer, Ayn Rand, Baron Rothschild, Ted Williams, Thomas Edison, H. L. Mencken, Thomas Jefferson, Ralph Ellison, Bobby Fischer, Emma Goldman, Peter Kropotkin, you, and your parents?" The minimal state would not try to impose any such single vision; it would allow like-minded people voluntarily to form diverse communities that could be religious, communistic, laissez-faire capitalist, and so on, as long as they did not try to impose their particular visions on others.

Anarchy, State, and Utopia won the 1975 National Book Award—an unusual achievement for a work of philosophy. In *The New York Review of Books* (6 March 1975) the Australian utilitarian philosopher Peter Singer, who disagrees with most of Nozick's positions (except for his concern for animal welfare), called *Anarchy, State, and Utopia* "a major event in contemporary political philosophy," after which the right of the state to bring about redistribution through such "coercive means" as progressive taxation "will need to be defended and argued for instead of being taken for granted."

The book ignited a firestorm in the philosophical community. Many of those who were acquainted with Nozick through his early work in decision theory respected his ability and no doubt assumed that his political views, like theirs, would be of the Left. This impression would have been reinforced by his critique of the much-despised libertarian novelist/philosopher Rand in his 1971 article "On the Randian Argument" (collected in *Socratic Puzzles*). They were shocked and appalled to discover that an obviously intelligent person could believe such things, but they were forced to acknowledge that he had presented powerful arguments for them. Refuting Nozick became something of a cottage industry. Among the criticisms were that he failed to justify his theory of rights, that positive rights are at least as valid as negative ones, that the state-of-nature hypothesis is outdated and unhistorical, that his conception of human nature is unrealistically atomistic, that his view of liberty is inadequate, that the dominant protection agency lacks the moral legitimacy that characterizes an actual state, that the minimal state would leave the poor and helpless at the mercy of the rich and powerful, that the costs of insurance and security measures the rich would have to buy to protect themselves in the minimal state would be even higher than taxes in a welfare state.

Although some of the more radical libertarians–the so-called no-government libertarians or anarcho-capitalists–also criticized Nozick, holding that even a minimal state is unjustifiable, *Anarchy, State, and Utopia* made Nozick a hero to the nascent libertarian movement. The Libertarian Party had run its first presidential candidate, the philosopher John Hospers, two years earlier, and Nozick was sought out as a spokesman for the ideology. He declined, however. He was even less comfortable being regarded as a proponent of conservatism. In a 1978 article by Jonathan Lieberson in *The New York Times Magazine* he was quoted as saying that "right-wing people like the pro-free-market argument, but don't like the arguments for individual liberty in cases like gay rights–although I view them as an interconnecting whole." Nozick did not bother to reply to his critics and soon abandoned political philosophy altogether, since, as he later said in *Socratic Puzzles,* he "did not want to spend my life writing 'The Son of Anarchy, State, and Utopia,' 'The Return of the Son of . . . ,' etc." Many of his critics hoped that his silence meant that he had returned to his senses and abandoned libertarianism, and they were on the alert for evidence that he had done so.

In 1981 Nozick's marriage ended in divorce; he began a three-year term as chairman of the Harvard philosophy department; and he published his second book, *Philosophical Explanations,* which he had completed in 1979. In this work he explores such traditional philosophical issues as the identity of the self, why there is something rather than nothing, knowledge and skepticism, free will and determinism and their implications for the retributive theory of punishment, the founda-

tions of ethics, and the meaning of life. In dealing with these questions Nozick advances a libertarian conception of philosophical argument that rejects the notion of strict proof in favor of the less coercive procedure of philosophical explanation. As early as the preface to *Anarchy, State, and Utopia* he had expressed his puzzlement that "Works of philosophy are written as though their authors believe them to be the absolutely final word on their subject. But it's not, surely, that each philosopher thinks that he finally, thank God, has found the truth and built an impregnable fortress around it." In Lieberson's *New York Times Magazine* article he pointed out that "It is as though what philosophers want is a way of saying something that will leave the person they're talking to no escape. Well, why should they be bludgeoning people like that? It's not a nice way to behave." In *Philosophical Explanations* he says:

> The terminology of philosophical art is coercive: arguments are *powerful* and best when they are *knockdown,* arguments *force* you to a conclusion, if you believe the premises you *have to* or *must* believe the conclusion, and so forth. A philosophical argument is an attempt to get someone to believe something, whether he wants to or not. . . .
>
> Perhaps philosophers need arguments so powerful they set up reverberations in the brain; if the person refuses to accept the conclusion, he *dies.* How's that for a powerful argument?

Whereas philosophical proofs start from premises that one knows, or at least strongly believes, to be true and argue for the truth of conclusions that one does not yet believe, philosophical explanations start with things that one believes to be true and proposes hypotheses–perhaps several incompatible hypotheses–to account for them. It does not insist on the truth of the hypotheses, merely their plausibility. The goal is "increased understanding," which "can be produced even by an explanation known to be wrong." The attempt to produce a single unassailable philosophical position is misguided, Nozick thinks: "There are various philosophical views, mutually incompatible, which cannot be dismissed or simply rejected. Philosophy's output is the basketful of these admissible views, all together." He suggests that this basketful of views can be ordered according to criteria of coherence and adequacy and that even second- and third-ranked views might offer valuable insights. He develops a "closest continuer" theory of personal identity; asks why one should assume that nonexistence is a natural state and that existence requires explanation; holds that for a belief to count as knowledge, it must "track the truth"; explains free will in terms of "reflexive self-subsuming acts"; and develops an

Dust jacket for Nozick's second book, published in 1981, in which he explores such traditional philosophical issues as the identity of the self, why there is something rather than nothing, knowledge and skepticism, and free will versus determinism (Richland County Public Library)

organic theory of value. *Philosophical Explanations* won the Ralph Waldo Emerson Award of Phi Beta Kappa.

Nozick was an adviser to the United States delegation to the United Nations Educational, Scientific, and Cultural Organization Conference on World Cultural Policy in 1982. Throughout his career he taught courses jointly with members of the government, psychology, and economics departments and at the divinity and law schools. Speaking without notes, Nozick paced back and forth with a can of soda in his hand while drawing his students into free-ranging discussions of various topics. He believed that this "thinking out loud" approach, as opposed to the traditional method of presenting completely worked-out philosophical views, enabled students to see what it is like to do original work in philosophy. He actually used his teaching to work out the ideas that he later presented in book form; he said that anyone who wanted to know what he was going to do next should keep an eye on the Harvard course catalogue. The only course he ever presented

more than once was "The Best Things in Life," which he offered in 1982 and 1983; the description in the course catalogue said it was an exploration of "the nature and value of those things deemed best, such as friendship, love, intellectual understanding, sexual pleasure, achievement, adventure, play, luxury, fame, power, enlightenment, and ice cream."

Nozick was named Arthur Kingsley Porter Professor of Philosophy in 1985. In 1986 he showed that he had not abandoned the free-market ideas he expressed in *Anarchy, State, and Utopia* by contributing the article "Why Do Intellectuals Oppose Capitalism?" to an anthology, *The Future of Private Enterprise,* edited by Craig E. Aronoff, Randall B. Goodwin, and John L. Ward; a revised version was republished in *Socratic Puzzles.* By "intellectuals," Nozick says, he means "wordsmiths": people such as poets, novelists, literary critics, journalists, and professors who make their livings dealing with ideas expressed in words. Wordsmiths are concentrated in academia, the media, and government, and they shape the public's ideas and lay out the policy alternatives that bureaucrats consider. They tend to do well under capitalism: they have the freedom to express their ideas, and their incomes are above average. But, says Nozick, intellectuals feel that they are the most valuable people in society and, therefore, that they are entitled to have the most prestige and power and the highest rewards, and they are resentful because capitalist society does not honor them in these ways. Nozick theorizes that the intellectuals' feelings of superior value have been produced in school, where they were praised and rewarded: "The schools told them, and showed them, they were better. . . . The intellectual wants the whole society to be a school writ large, to be like the environment where he did so well and was so well appreciated." In the market society, however, the greatest rewards do not necessarily go to those who are the verbally brightest. Furthermore, the official rewards in school are distributed by a central authority: the teacher. But "schools contain another informal social system within classrooms, hallways, and schoolyards, wherein rewards are distributed not by central direction but spontaneously at the pleasure and whim of schoolmates. Here the intellectuals do less well. It is not surprising, therefore, that distribution of goods and rewards via a centrally organized distributional mechanism later strikes intellectuals as more appropriate than the 'anarchy and chaos' of the marketplace." The animus against capitalism is reinforced in pupils by teachers and textbook writers who, being intellectual wordsmiths themselves, present these anticapitalist attitudes. As opposed to a communist or a feudal society, "The ethos of the wider society is close enough to that of the schools so that the nearness creates resentment.

Capitalist societies reward individual accomplishment or announce they do, and so they leave the intellectual, who considers himself most accomplished, particularly bitter." Also, "the intellectuals later will resentfully remember how superior they were academically to their peers who advanced more richly and powerfully."

On 5 October 1987 Nozick married the poet Gjertrud Schnackenberg. His next book, *The Examined Life: Philosophical Meditations,* appeared in 1989. It is aimed at a general audience and comprises twenty-seven nontechnical essays, including "Dying," "Parents and Children," "Creating," "The Holiness of Everyday Life," "Sexuality," "Love's Bond," "Happiness," "The Holocaust," and "What Is Wisdom and Why Do Philosophers Love It So?" Some critics considered the work disappointingly schmaltzy, and less attention was paid to it than to his other books; one suggestion that did attract some comment was his contention in the chapter "Love's Bond" that love should not depend on the beloved's specific characteristics, because this perspective reduces the beloved to a mere "placeholder" for some set of desired qualities. Many of those who hoped that Nozick had returned to the leftist fold seized on his remark in the chapter "The Zigzag of Politics" that the libertarian position he had advanced in *Anarchy, State, and Utopia* now seemed "seriously inadequate" to him, "in part because it did not fully knit the humane considerations and joint cooperative activities it left room for more closely into its fabric. It neglected the symbolic importance of an official political concern with issues or problems, as a way of marking their importance or urgency, and hence of expressing, intensifying, channeling, encouraging, and validating our private actions and concerns toward them." Even in this essay, however, he remains consistent with his former view in pointing out that no single political scheme can satisfy the vast diversity of values that people hold: "The electorate wants the zigzag. Sensible folk, they realize that *no* political position will adequately include all of the values and goals one wants pursued in the political realm, so these will have to take turns. The electorate as a whole behaves in this sensible fashion, even if significant numbers of people stay committed to their previous goals and favorite programs come what may."

In 1994 Nozick was diagnosed with stomach cancer and given six months to live. He refused to allow the illness to interfere with his projects, depending on his wife to keep track of his treatment regimen, and the doctors' six months became more than seven years.

In his next book, *The Nature of Rationality* (1993), Nozick asks what function principles serve in daily life and why people do not simply act on whims or out of self-interest. He explores the rationality of decision and the rationality of belief. In regard to the former he proposes a rule of rational decision making that he calls "maximizing decision-value" and applies it to such classic issues in decision theory as Newcomb's Problem and the Prisoner's Dilemma. Rationality of belief involves the reasons that make a belief credible, the practical consequences of believing it, and the discovery of a process that reliably produces true beliefs. Evolution, he says, has instilled some factual connections in human beings as seemingly self-evident. He introduces the notion of the "symbolic utility" of an act to explain why people support public policies in the name of principles that would be frustrated if those policies were enacted and deals with the essential role that imagination plays in rationality, the characteristic that is thought to make humanity "special."

In the spring of 1997 Nozick was a Christensen visiting fellow at St. Catherine's College of the University of Oxford and delivered the six John Locke Lectures at the university. That year he and his colleague and friendly rival Rawls were among six leading political philosophers who submitted a brief urging the United States Supreme Court to uphold two federal appeals court rulings that mentally competent, terminally ill patients have a constitutional right to assisted suicide. Also in 1997 Nozick published *Socratic Puzzles,* a collection of his articles, book reviews, and the philosophical short stories "Testament" (1971), "Teleology" (1971), "R.S.V.P.–A Story" (1972), and "Fiction" (1980). He served as president of the Eastern Division of the American Philosophical Association in 1997–1998. In 1998 he was named Joseph Pellegrino University Professor, Harvard's highest academic position. Also in 1998 he received the American Psychological Association Presidential Citation as "one of the most brilliant and original living philosophers."

Nozick's final book, *Invariances: The Structure of the Objective World,* was published in October 2001. Nozick observes that people's belief that truth is relative or absolute tends to reflect the way they want it to be. He argues that truth is not relative among human beings in regard to cultural and social factors such as race, sex, or sexual preference but that certain aspects of quantum mechanics and special relativity theory indicate that it is relative to space and time; Martians, for example, might not have the same "truth property" that human beings do. He defines an objective fact as one that is invariant under various transformations and says that a belief or judgment is objective when it is arrived at by a process in which biasing factors do not play a significant role. He says that various human capacities, including that of apprehending truth, have been created by evolution. He views consciousness as a process of streams of information merging in the brain, which has evolved to put human beings in closer touch with reality so that they

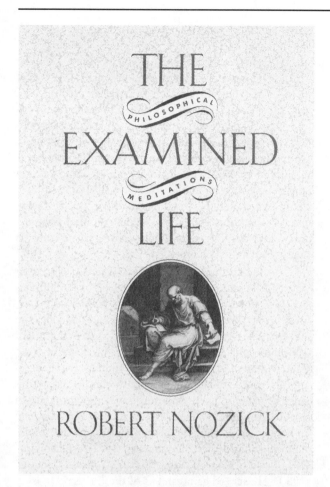

Dust jacket for Nozick's 1989 book, his nontechnical musings on such topics as death, parenting, creation, God, love, and sexuality (Richland County Public Library)

can more accurately conform their behavior to it. He proposes a "Zoom-Lens" theory of how consciousness brings various aspects of the world to "center stage." Nozick critiques Sir Karl R. Popper's anti-inductivist philosophy of science as incoherent; he also critiques Thomas S. Kuhn's theory of scientific revolutions as unduly relativistic and as giving comfort to academic leftists who wish to ignore the overwhelming empirical evidence in favor of capitalism by allowing them to say, "You have your paradigm, I have mine." He contends that past events, to be true, must make some difference in the present, whether one is in a position to know of that difference or not. He outlines a series of levels of ethics that have been produced by evolution; the most basic is peaceful, voluntary cooperation for mutual benefit, while the higher levels involve positive aid for others. Government, he argues, should only enforce the most basic requirement of peaceful cooperation.

In the *Laissez Faire Books.com* interview, one of the last of his life, Nozick responded to those who thought that his remark about the inadequacy of his former lib-

ertarian position in *The Examined Life* and a similar one in *The Nature of Rationality* meant that he had abandoned that standpoint. Asked whether, in view of some libertarian tendencies in *Invariances* in regard to coordination of behavior and cooperation to mutual benefit, he would again apply the "L-word" to himself, he replied:

> Yes. But I never stopped self-applying it. What I was really saying in *The Examined Life* was that I was no longer as hardcore a libertarian as I had been before. But the rumors of my deviation (or apostasy!) from libertarianism were much exaggerated. I think this book makes clear the extent to which I still am within the general framework of libertarianism, especially the ethics chapter and its section on the "Core Principle of Ethics." One thing that I think reinforced the view that I had rejected libertarianism was a story about an apartment of [*Love Story* author] Erich Segal's that I had been renting. . . . In the rent he was charging me, Erich Segal was violating a Cambridge rent control statute. I knew at the time that when I let my intense irritation with representatives of Erich Segal lead me to invoke against him rent control laws that I opposed and disapproved of, that I would later come to regret it, but sometimes you have to do what you have to do.

He also said, "Of my six books, I think that the three that are intellectually most exciting are *Anarchy, State, and Utopia, Philosophical Explanations . . .*, and *Invariances*."

Nozick was a fellow of the American Academy of Arts and Sciences, a corresponding fellow of the British Academy, and a senior fellow of the Society of Fellows at Harvard. He was a member of the Council of Scholars of the Library of Congress, the American Association of University Professors, the American Civil Liberties Union, the American Philosophical Association, the Society for Ethical and Legal Philosophy, the Jewish Vegetarian Society, and Phi Beta Kappa. He held fellowships from the Guggenheim Foundation, the Rockefeller Foundation, the National Endowment for the Humanities, and the Center for Advanced Study in the Behavioral Sciences. One of the last courses he taught was the interdisciplinary "Thinking about Thinking," with paleontologist and evolutionary biologist Stephen Jay Gould and law professor Alan Dershowitz. He taught a course on the Russian Revolution during the fall 2001 semester jointly with a professor of history and was planning to teach a course in the spring jointly with a Slavic Languages professor on Fyodor Dostoevsky's philosophical ideas and the difference that is made when such ideas are presented in fiction rather than in discursive prose. He continued talking with his colleagues and critiquing their work until a week before his death of complications from stomach cancer on 23 January 2002.

Dust jacket for Nozick's 1993 book, in which he inquires into the function rational principles serve in daily life (Richland County Public Library)

Nozick's work in decision theory, metaphysics, epistemology, ethics, and philosophy of science continues to be studied and critiqued, but he will apparently be remembered mainly for *Anarchy, State, and Utopia*. The book has been translated into eleven languages and was included by *TLS: The Times Literary Supplement* in its 1995 list of the hundred most influential books published since World War II. It is commonly cited in philosophy textbooks as exemplifying the libertarian viewpoint on distributive justice—a viewpoint that until its publication was generally ignored in such books as unworthy of consideration. In these textbooks, which frequently paraphrase or excerpt the Wilt Chamberlain story, it is usually contrasted with Rawls's *A Theory of Justice*. The work has entered popular culture sufficiently to have appeared in an episode from the second season of the Home Box Office television series *The Sopranos* that was originally broadcast on 19 March 2000: in an ironic comment on the state's inability to protect its citizens, a witness to a murder is seen reading the book, which is immediately recognizable to those who are familiar with it from the four bands of yellow

and brown on the white dust jacket, when his wife tells him that a newscaster has just reported that the person he saw was mob boss Tony Soprano; terrified, he quickly calls the prosecutor and recants his testimony.

In an obituary in *National Review Online* the University of Chicago and Hoover Institution legal theorist Richard A. Epstein sums up Nozick's legacy:

> the frequency and severity of the attacks on *Anarchy, State, and Utopia* only provide further evidence of his richness and profundity. If the book had been refuted but once, it would have counted for little. That it has been "refuted" countless times proves that he is the author of one of the enduring classics of the political philosophy. To be a Nozickian stands for something. His influence on his own profession, on collateral social disciplines, and on the law has been enormous. In his later years he refused to go back in print to the issues raised in *Anarchy, State, and Utopia* but instead directed his endless energy to more purely philosophical inquiries. Doubtless under Harvard's influence, he even expressed some communitarian doubts about some of the sharp individualist conclusions that he articulated and defended so ably in *Anarchy, State, and Utopia*.

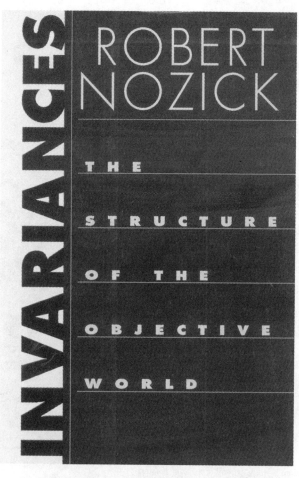

Dust jacket for Nozick's final book, in which he argues that the human capacity of apprehending truth has been created by evolution (Richland County Public Library)

It seems fair to say that he will not be remembered or praised for these latter recantations, nor even his later work in other disciplines. But he will long be remembered for what he did best when he was young: To take up arms against the conventional wisdom in favor of big government and extensive political power, and in so doing to secure for himself a place as one of the great political philosophers of the twentieth century.

Interviews:

"How Is Business Different from Sex?" *Forbes,* 115 (15 March 1975): 22–24;

Giovanna Borradori, "Anarchy at Harvard: *Robert Nozick,*" in *The American Philosopher: Conversations with Quine, Davidson, Putnam, Nozick, Danto, Rorty, Cavell, MacIntyre, and Kuhn,* translated by Rosanna Crocitto (Chicago: University of Chicago Press, 1994), pp. 70–85;

"Interview with Robert Nozick," *Laissez Faire Books.com* (24 January 2002) part 1: <http://www.laissezfairebooks.com/index.cfm?eid=358>; part 2: <http://www.laissezfairebooks.com/index. cfm?eid=359>.

References:

Robert B. Baker, "A Theory of International Bioethics: The Negotiable and the Non-Negotiable," *Kennedy Institute of Ethics Journal,* 8, no. 3 (1998): 233–274;

Randy E. Barnett, "Whither Anarchy: Has Robert Nozick Justified the State?" *Journal of Libertarian Studies,* 1 (1977): 15–21;

Norman P. Barry, *On Classical Liberalism and Libertarianism* (New York: St. Martin's Press, 1987);

Nora K. Bell, "Nozick and the Principle of Fairness," *Social Theory and Practice,* 5 (1978): 65–73;

Fred R. Berger, "Mill's Substantive Principles of Justice: A Comparison with Nozick," *American Philosophical Quarterly,* 19 (1982): 373–380;

Walter Block, "On Robert Nozick's 'On Austrian Methodology,'" *Inquiry,* 23 (1980): 397–444;

Anthony Brueckner, "Unfair to Nozick," *Analysis,* 51 (1991): 61–64;

Nicholas Capaldi, "Exploring the Limits of Analytic Philosophy: A Critique of Nozick's *Philosophical Explanations,*" *Interpretation,* 12 (1984): 107–125;

Kenneth Cauthen, *The Passion for Equality* (Totowa, N.J.: Rowman & Littlefield, 1987);

Timothy Chappell, "The Implications of Incommensurability," *Philosophy,* 76 (January 2001): 137–148;

G. A. Cohen, "Robert Nozick and Wilt Chamberlain: How Patterns Preserve Liberty," *Erkenntnis,* 11 (1977): 5–23;

Cohen, *Self-ownership, Freedom, and Equality* (New York: Cambridge University Press, 1995);

John R. Danley, "Contracts, Conquerors, and Conquests," *Southwestern Journal of Philosophy,* 10 (1979): 171–177;

Danley, "Robert Nozick and the Libertarian Paradox," *Mind,* 88 (1979): 419–423;

Douglas Den Uyl and Douglas B. Rasmussen, "Nozick on the Randian Argument," *Personalist,* 59 (1978): 184–205;

B. J. Diggs, "Liberty without Fraternity," *Ethics,* 87 (January 1977): 97–112;

Richard A. Epstein, "Life of Liberty: Robert Nozick, R.I.P.," *National Review Online* (24 January 2002) <http://www.nationalreview.com/comment/comment-epstein012402.shtml>;

John Exdell, "Distributive Justice: Nozick on Property Rights," *Ethics,* 87 (January 1977): 142–149;

Exdell, "Liberty, Equality and Capitalism," *Canadian Journal of Philosophy,* 11 (1981): 457–472;

Tatiana Facio, "La explicacion filosofica de Robert Nozick y la etica," *Revista de filosofia de la Universidad de Costa Rica,* 25 (1987): 31–39;

Evan Fox-Decent, "Why Self-Ownership Is Prescriptively Impotent," *Journal of Value Inquiry,* 32, no. 4 (1998): 489–506;

Brian J. Garrett, "A Sceptical Tension," *Analysis,* 59 (1999): 205–206;

Emily R. Gill, "Responsibility and Choice in Robert Nozick: Sins of Commission and of Omission," *Personalist,* 59 (1978): 344–357;

Jeffrey D. Goldworthy, "Nozick's Libertarianism and the Justification of the State," *Ratio,* 29 (1987): 180–189;

Michael Gorr, "Nozick's Argument against Blackmail," *Personalist,* 58 (1977): 187–191;

Simon A. Hailwood, "Why 'Business's Nastier Friends' Should Not Be Libertarians," *Journal of Business Ethics,* 24 (March 2000): 77–86;

Steven Hales, "The Impossibility of Unconditional Love," *Public Affairs Quarterly,* 9, no. 4 (1995): 317–320;

Virginia Held, "John Locke on Robert Nozick," *Social Research,* 43 (1976): 169–195;

Stephen Cade Hetherington, "Nozick and Sceptical Realism," *Philosophical Papers,* 21, no. 1 (1992): 33–44;

Richard P. Hiskes, *Community without Coercion* (Newark: University of Delaware Press, 1982);

Christopher Hughes, "Giving the Skeptic Her Due?" *Epistemologia,* 19, no. 2 (1996): 309–326;

"The Hundred Most Influential Books since the War," *TLS: The Times Literary Supplement,* no. 4827 (6 October 1995): 95;

Bredo C. Johnsen, "Nozick on Skepticism," *Philosophia,* 16 (1986): 65–69;

Simon Keller, "How Do I Love Thee? Let Me Count the Properties," *American Philosophical Quarterly,* 37 (2000): 163–173;

D. R. Knowles, "Autonomy, Side Constraints and Property," *Mind,* 88 (1979): 263–265;

R. Lacey, *Robert Nozick* (Princeton: Princeton University Press, 2001);

Hugh LaFollette, "Why Libertarianism Is Mistaken," in *Justice and Economic Distribution,* edited by John Arthur and William H. Shaw (Englewood Cliffs, N.J.: Prentice Hall, 1991), pp. 194–206;

Jonathan Lieberson, "Harvard's Nozick: Philosopher of the Right," *New York Times Magazine,* 17 December 1978, pp. 39, 68–84;

Morris Lipson, "Nozick and the Sceptic," *Australasian Journal of Philosophy,* 65 (1987): 327–334;

Steven Luper-Foy, "The Epistemic Predicament: Knowledge, Nozickian Tracking, and Scepticism," *Australasian Journal of Philosophy,* 62 (1984): 26–49;

Luper-Foy, ed., *The Possibility of Knowledge: Nozick and His Critics* (Totowa, N.J.: Rowman & Littlefield, 1987);

Tibor R. Machan, "Fishkin on Nozick's Absolute Rights," *Journal of Libertarian Studies,* 6 (1982): 317–320;

Machan, "Nozick and Rand on Property Rights," *Personalist,* 58 (1977): 192–195;

Eric Mack, "Nozick's Anarchism," in *Anarchism,* edited by J. Roland Pennock and John W. Chapman (New York: New York University Press, 1978), pp. 43–62;

Mack, "The Self-Ownership Proviso: A New and Improved Lockean Proviso," *Social Philosophy and Policy,* 12 (1995): 186–218;

Raymond Martin, "Tracking Nozick's Sceptic: A Better Method," *Analysis,* 43 (1983): 28–33;

James G. Mazoue, "Self-Synthesis, Self-Knowledge, and Skepticism," *Logos* (1990): 111–125;

Christopher Megone, "Reasoning about Rationality: Robert Nozick, *The Nature of Rationality,*" *Utilitas,* 11 (November 1999): 359–374;

Gregory Mellema, "Symbolic Value, Virtue Ethics, and the Morality of Groups," *Philosophy Today,* 43 (Fall 1999): 302–308;

Thaddeus Metz, "Arbitrariness, Justice, and Respect," *Social Theory and Practice,* 26 (Spring 2000): 25–45;

Leroy N. Meyer, "Wisdom and the Well-Being of Humanity," *Contemporary Philosophy,* 20, nos. 1–2 (1998): 15–18;

Diana T. Meyers, "The Inevitability of the State," *Analysis,* 41 (1981): 46–49;

Justyna Miklaszewska, "The Libertarian Utopia: Robert Nozick and Aleksander Swietochowski," *Reports on Philosophy,* 13 (1989): 51–60;

Fred D. Miller, "The Natural Right to Private Property," in *The Libertarian Reader,* edited by Machan (Totowa, N.J.: Rowman & Littlefield, 1982), pp. 275–287;

Tim Mulgan, "Teaching Future Generations," *Teaching Philosophy,* 22, no. 3 (1999): 259–273;

Thomas Nagel, "Libertarianism without Foundations," *Yale Law Journal,* 85 (1975): 136–149;

Jan Narveson, *The Libertarian Idea* (Philadelphia: Temple University Press, 1988);

Narveson, "Libertarianism vs. Marxism: Reflections on G. A. Cohen's 'Self-Ownership, Freedom and Equality,'" *Journal of Ethics,* 2, no. 1 (1998): 1–26;

Narveson, "Property Rights: Original Acquisition and Lockean Provisos," *Public Affairs Quarterly,* 13 (1999): 205–207;

Michael Neumann, "Entitlements: A Sheep in Wolf's Clothing," *Journal of Value Inquiry,* 14 (1980): 149–156;

Harold W. Noonan, "The Closest Continuer Theory of Identity," *Inquiry,* 28 (1985): 195–230;

David L. Norton, "Individualism and Productive Justice," *Ethics,* 87 (January 1977): 113–125;

Jeffrey Obler, "Fear, Prohibition, and Liberty," *Political Theory,* 9 (1981): 65–80;

D. E. Over, "Knowledge and Non-Constructive Reasoning," *Philosophical Quarterly,* 36 (1986): 29–36;

Ellen Frankel Paul, "The Just Takings Issue," *Environmental Ethics,* 3 (1981): 309–328;

Jeffrey Paul, "Property, Entitlement, and Remedy," *Monist,* 73 (1990): 564–577;

Paul, ed., *Reading Nozick: Essays on* Anarchy, State, and Utopia (Totowa, N.J.: Rowman & Littlefield, 1981; Oxford: Blackwell, 1982);

Philip Pettit, "Rights, Constraints and Trumps," *Analysis,* 47 (1987): 8–14;

William S. Robinson, "Evolution and Self Evidence," *Philosophica* (Belgium), 57, no. 1 (1996): 33–51;

Kenneth F. Rogerson, "Rights at Risk," *Southwest Philosophy Review,* 1 (1984): 119–130;

Murray N. Rothbard, "Robert Nozick and the Immaculate Conception of the State," *Journal of Libertarian Studies,* 1 (1977): 45–57;

Geoffrey Sampson, "Liberalism and Nozick's 'Minimal State,'" *Mind,* 88 (1978): 93–97;

John T. Sanders, "The Free Market Model versus Government: A Reply to Nozick," *Journal of Libertarian Studies,* 1 (1977): 35–44;

Husain Sarkar, "Something, Nothing and Explanation," *Southwest Philosophy Review,* 9 (1993): 151–161;

Charles Sayward, "Should Persons Be Sacrificed for the General Welfare?" *Journal of Value Inquiry,* 16 (1982): 149–152;

David Schmidtz, ed., *Robert Nozick* (Cambridge: Cambridge University Press, 2002);

Adina Schwartz, "Against Universality," *Journal of Philosophy,* 78 (1981): 127–143;

Robert K. Shope, "Cognitive Abilities, Conditionals, and Knowledge: A Response to Nozick," *Journal of Philosophy,* 81 (1984): 29–48;

John Skorupski, "In a Socratic Way," *Dialogue,* 38 (Fall 1999): 871–875;

Tara Smith, "Look-Say Ethics," *Journal of Value Inquiry,* 32 (1998): 539–553;

Smith, "Why Do I Love Thee? A Response to Nozick's Account of Romantic Love," *Southwest Philosophy Review,* 7 (1991): 47–57;

Ernest Sosa, "Beyond Scepticism, to the Best of Our Knowledge," *Mind,* 97 (1988): 153–188;

Horacio Spector, *Autonomy and Rights: The Moral Foundations of Liberalism* (New York: Oxford University Press, 1992);

Hillel Steiner, "Nozick on Hart on the Right to Enforce," *Analysis,* 41 (1981): 50;

James P. Sterba, "In Defense of Rawls against Arrow and Nozick," *Philosophia,* 7 (1978): 293–303;

William Sweet, "Les 'droits naturels' et les 'titres' selon Robert Nozick," *Lekton* (1991): 81–98;

Adam James Tebble, "The Tables Turned: Wilt Chamberlain versus Robert Nozick on Rectification," *Economics and Philosophy,* 17 (April 2001): 89–108;

Fernando R. Teson, "Self-Defeating Symbolism in Politics," *Journal of Philosophy,* 98 (December 2001): 636–652;

Robert B. Thigpen, "Two Approaches to the Principles of Justice in Recent American Political Philosophy: An Essay Review," *Journal of Thought,* 21 (1986): 118–126;

Paul Torek, "Liberties, Not Rights: Gauthier and Nozick on Property," *Social Theory and Practice,* 20, no. 3 (1994): 343–361;

Candace Vogler, "Sex and Talk," *Critical Inquiry,* 24 (Winter 1998): 328–365;

Paul Warren, "Self-Ownership, Reciprocity, and Exploitation, or Why Marxists Shouldn't Be Afraid of Robert Nozick," *Canadian Journal of Philosophy,* 24 (1994): 33–56;

Jonathan Wolff, *Robert Nozick: Property, Justice, and the Minimal State* (Stanford, Cal.: Stanford University Press, 1991);

David Zimmerman, "Coercive Wage Offers," *Philosophy and Public Affairs,* 10 (1981): 121–145.

Alvin Plantinga

(15 November 1932 –   )

George W. Shields
Kentucky State University

BOOKS: *God and Other Minds: A Study of the Rational Justification of Belief in God* (Ithaca, N.Y.: Cornell University Press, 1967);

The Nature of Necessity (Oxford: Clarendon Press, 1974);

God, Freedom, and Evil (New York: Harper & Row, 1974; London: Allen & Unwin, 1975);

Does God Have a Nature? The Aquinas Lecture, 1980 (Milwaukee: Marquette University Press, 1980);

Warrant: The Current Debate (New York & Oxford: Oxford University Press, 1993);

Warrant and Proper Function (New York & Oxford: Oxford University Press, 1993);

Essays in Ontology (New York & Oxford: Oxford University Press, 1996);

The Analytic Theist: An Alvin Plantinga Reader, edited by James F. Sennett (Grand Rapids, Mich.: Eerdmans, 1998);

Warranted Christian Belief (New York & Oxford: Oxford University Press, 2000);

Essays in the Metaphysics of Modality, edited by Matthew Davidson (New York: Oxford University Press, 2003).

OTHER: "Necessary Being," in *Faith and Philosophy: Philosophical Studies in Religion and Ethics,* edited by Plantinga (Grand Rapids, Mich.: Eerdmans, 1964), pp. 97–110;

The Ontological Argument: From St. Anselm to Contemporary Philosophers, edited by Plantinga (Garden City, N.Y.: Doubleday Anchor, 1965; London: Macmillan, 1968);

"Comments [on Hilary Putnam's 'The Mental Life of Some Machines']," in *Intentionality, Minds, and Perception,* edited by Hector-Neri Castañeda (Detroit: Wayne State University Press, 1966), pp. 201–205;

"Malcolm, Norman," in *The Encyclopedia of Philosophy,* volume 5, edited by Paul Edwards (New York: Macmillan, 1967), pp. 139–140;

"Aquinas on Anselm," in *God and the Good: Essays in Honor of Henry Stob,* edited by Clifton Orlebeke

Alvin Plantinga

and Lewis Smedes (Grand Rapids, Mich.: Eerdmans, 1975);

"Hector-Neri Castañeda: A Personal Statement," in *Agent, Language, and the Structure of the World: Essays Presented to Hector-Neri Castañeda, with His Replies,* edited by James E. Tomberlin (Indianapolis: Hackett, 1983), pp. 7–13;

"Reason and Belief in God," in *Faith and Rationality: Reason and Belief in God,* edited by Plantinga and Nicholas Wolterstorff (Notre Dame, Ind.: Notre Dame University Press, 1983), pp. 16–93;

"Self-Profile," in *Alvin Plantinga,* edited by Tomberlin and Peter van Inwagen, Profiles, volume 5 (Dordrecht, Netherlands & Boston: Reidel, 1985), pp. 3–97;

"Religion and Groundless Believing," in *Religious Experience and Religious Belief: Essays in the Epistemology of Religion,* edited by Joseph Runzo and Craig K. Ihara (Lanham, Md.: University Press of America, 1986);

"Prologue: Advice to Christian Philosophers," in *Christian Theism and the Problems of Philosophy,* edited by Michael D. Beaty, Library of Religious Philosophy, volume 5 (Notre Dame, Ind.: University of Notre Dame Press, 1990), pp. 14–37;

"An Evolutionary Argument against Naturalism," in *Faith in Theory and Practice: Essays on Justifying Religious Belief,* edited by Carol White and Elizabeth Radcliff (Chicago: Open Court, 1993), pp. 35–65;

"On Christian Scholarship," in *The Challenge and Promise of a Catholic University,* edited by Theodore Hesburgh (Notre Dame, Ind.: University of Notre Dame Press, 1994), pp. 267–295;

"Pluralism: A Defense of Religious Exclusivism," in *The Rationality of Belief and the Plurality of Faith: Essays in Honor of William P. Alston,* edited by Thomas D. Senor (Ithaca, N.Y.: Cornell University Press, 1995), pp. 191–215;

"Respondeo," in *Warrant in Contemporary Epistemology: Essays in Honor of Plantinga's Theory of Knowledge,* edited by Jonathan Kvanvig (Lanham, Md.: Rowman & Littlefield, 1996), pp. 307–378;

"Methodological Naturalism?" in *Facets of Faith and Science,* edited by Jitse M. van der Meer (Lanham, Md.: Pascal Centre for Advanced Studies in Faith and Science/University Press of America, 1996), pp. 177–221;

"Essence and Essentialism," "Haecceity," "Natural Theology," and "Pantheism," in *A Companion to Metaphysics,* edited by Ernest Sosa and Jaegwon Kim (Oxford & Cambridge, Mass.: Blackwell, 1999), pp. 138–140, 199, 346–349, 376;

Michael J. Murray, ed., *Reason for the Hope Within,* foreword by Plantinga (Grand Rapids, Mich.: Eerdmans, 1999);

Fransisco Conesa, *Dios y el mal: La defensa del teismo frente al problema del mal según Alvin Plantinga,* prologue by Plantinga (Pamplona: EUNSA, 2000).

SELECTED PERIODICAL PUBLICATIONS–
UNCOLLECTED: "An Existentialist's Ethics," *Review of Metaphysics,* 12 (1958): 235–256;

"Things and Persons," *Review of Metaphysics,* 14 (1960): 493–519;

"A Valid Ontological Argument?" *Philosophical Review,* 70 (1961): 93–101;

"The Perfect Goodness of God," *Australasian Journal of Philosophy,* 40 (1962): 70–75;

"Analytic Philosophy and Christianity," *Christianity Today,* 8, no. 2 (1963): 17–20;

"Comment on Paul Ziff's 'The Simplicity of Other Minds,'" *Journal of Philosophy,* 62 (1965): 585–586;

"Pike and Possible Persons," *Journal of Philosophy,* 63 (1966): 104–108;

"The Incompatibility of Freedom with Determinism: A Reply," *Philosophical Forum,* 2 (1970): 141–148;

"The Boethian Compromise," *American Philosophical Quarterly,* 15 (1978): 129–138;

"Reply to the Basingers on Divine Omnipotence," *Process Studies,* 11 (1981): 25–29;

"How to Be an Anti-Realist," *Proceedings of the American Philosophical Association,* 56, no. 1 (1982): 47–70;

"Is Theism Really a Miracle?" *Faith and Philosophy,* 3 (1986): 109–134;

"Science, Neutrality, and Biblical Scholarship: A Reply to McMullin, Pun, and Van Till," *Christian Scholar's Review,* 21 (1991): 80–109;

"Augustinian Christian Philosophy," *Monist,* 75, no. 3 (1992): 291–320;

"Truth, Omniscience, and Cantorian Arguments: An Exchange," by Plantinga and Patrick Grim, *Philosophical Studies,* 71 (1993): 267–306;

"Précis of *Warrant: The Current Debate* and *Warrant and Proper Function,*" *Philosophy and Phenomenological Research,* 55 (1995): 393–396;

"Ad Hick," *Faith and Philosophy,* 14 (1997): 295–298;

"Internalism, Externalism, Defeaters and Arguments for Christian Belief," *Philosophia Christi,* series 2, 3, no. 2 (2001): 377–398.

Alvin Plantinga has made wide-ranging, vigorously discussed contributions to many topics in the philosophy of religion, the metaphysics of modality and associated issues in the philosophy of logic, and epistemology. In his "Plantinga on the Problem of Evil" in *Alvin Plantinga* (1985), edited by James E. Tomberlin and Peter van Inwagen, Robert Merrihew Adams of Yale University says that "*No one* has contributed more to the development of an analytical philosophy of religion than has Alvin Plantinga." Known for his technical expertise and high standards of precision, Plantinga's overarching career interest has been the defense of classical Christian belief in the light of contemporary intellectual concerns. He has offered a justification of the rationality of theistic belief on the basis of its isomorphism with the rationality of belief in other minds; a "Free Will Defense" meant to show that the existence of God is logically compatible with the existence of moral and natural evil; and a modal version of the ontological argument for God's existence that attempts to escape the weaknesses of other versions of the argument. More recently, he has argued that belief in God is rationally acceptable and warranted and requires no evidence or "foundations," because, like certain perceptual beliefs, it is "properly basic" and has no successful "defeaters."

Alvin Carl Plantinga was born in Ann Arbor, Michigan, on 15 November 1932 to Cornelius A. and Lettie Bossenbroeck Plantinga. Both parents were of Dutch ancestry; the father had immigrated to the United States in 1913. At the time of Alvin Plantinga's birth, Cornelius was studying for an M.A. in philosophy at the University of Michigan. The family then moved to Durham, North Carolina, where they lived for a time on the mother's $50 per month salary at the Typing Bureau while Cornelius Plantinga studied for his Ph.D. at Duke University. In 1941 Cornelius got his first teaching job at Huron College in South Dakota, which was followed in 1943 by a post at Jamestown College in North Dakota. Alvin Plantinga attended Jamestown High School but, at his father's insistence, went straight to Jamestown College in 1949 instead of finishing his senior year. In January 1950 his father took a new position at his alma mater, Calvin College in Grand Rapids, Michigan, and Plantinga transferred there.

Like his father, Plantinga majored in philosophy at Calvin College and, as his father had been, was greatly inspired by the charismatic professor William Harry Jellema. Plantinga spent the academic year 1950–1951 on a scholarship at Harvard University, but hearing Jellema's lectures at Calvin during a visit home on spring break led him to return to Calvin in the fall of 1951. Plantinga says in his "Self-Profile" in the Tomberlin and van Inwagen volume that Jellema was "by all odds, I think, the most gifted teacher of philosophy I have ever encountered." Under the tutelage of Jellema and Henry Stob, Plantinga concentrated on the history of philosophy from Plato to Immanuel Kant and also spent a good deal of time—rather reluctantly—studying languages, especially Greek, French, and German. He received his B.A. in 1953.

In January 1954 Plantinga began graduate study in philosophy at the University of Michigan. In the spring term he took a seminar in the philosophy of Alfred North Whitehead from William P. Alston. While many of his fellow students discoursed learnedly in the language of Whitehead's *Process and Reality* (1929), Plantinga found the work difficult to grasp and began to wonder if philosophy were his true calling. He soon realized that the other students were only pretending to understand Whitehead's concepts. Nevertheless, Alston's teaching methods set a standard of clarity that Plantinga emulated in his own career. He was also greatly inspired by the moral philosopher William K. Frankena, who had also attended Calvin College.

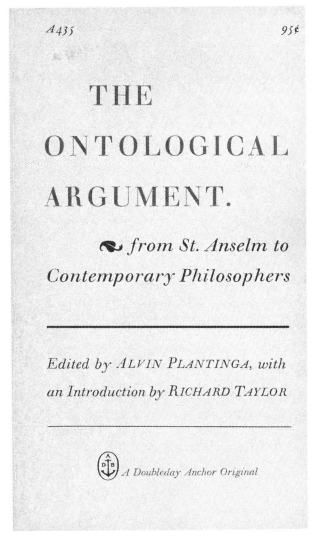

A435   95¢

THE ONTOLOGICAL ARGUMENT.

❧ *from St. Anselm to Contemporary Philosophers*

Edited by ALVIN PLANTINGA, *with an Introduction by* RICHARD TAYLOR

A Doubleday Anchor Original

Cover for the anthology of articles for and against the classical proof of the existence of God that Plantinga edited in 1965 (Collection of Philip B. Dematteis)

In the summer of 1954 Plantinga traveled with his fiancée, Kathleen De Boer, whom he had met in the fall of 1953 when she was a senior at Calvin College, to her hometown of Lynden, Washington. Joining her family on hiking expeditions, Plantinga became an outdoors enthusiast. He later took up mountaineering, with climbs ranging from the Tetons and Devil's Tower in Wyoming to the Matterhorn in Switzerland.

Plantinga received his M.A. in philosophy in the spring of 1955. While he had learned much at Michigan, he thought, as he says in his "Self-Profile," that philosophy there was "too piecemeal and too remote from the big questions." He asked Frankena where he might find philosophy done in the grand manner; without hesitation Frankena replied "Yale" but warned Plantinga that it might not be his best choice. Plantinga nonetheless applied to Yale and was admitted to the Ph.D. program. He married De Boer on 16 June 1955; they eventually had four children: Carl, Jane, William Harry, and Ann.

At Yale, Plantinga received training in modal logic (the logic of necessity and possibility) from Fredric Fitch and was exposed to the "grand style" of philosophy he desired by Brand Blanshard and Paul Weiss. While he was particularly impressed by Weiss's dialectical skill and energy, after a year and a half he gave up trying to make sense of Weiss's thought; he could find in it, he says in his "Self-Profile," only a set of "puzzling propositions." Plantinga was ultimately frustrated by two features of Yale's philosophy program: first, many of the courses were surveys with little sustained in-depth examination of arguments, leaving the apprentice philosopher without guidance as to how to do original work; second, the students tended to be distant and ironic and unwilling to commit themselves to any philosophical conviction, as if the philosopher's task were simply to answer any question with a panoply of possible answers—"this is the Thomistic view" or "the existentialist view" or "the Wittgensteinian view," and so forth. This attitude ran strongly against the grain of the serious quest for "sober metaphysical truth" that Plantinga had relished during his undergraduate Calvin days. In retrospect, Plantinga understood Frankena's warning about Yale.

In the fall of 1957 Plantinga began teaching undergraduate philosophy courses in Yale's Directed Studies Program. He also began receiving telephone calls from George Nakhnikian, chairman of the philosophy department at Wayne State University in Detroit, inviting him to come there. In the spring of 1958 Plantinga was awarded the Ph.D. in philosophy from Yale, and in the fall, worn down by Nakhnikian's persistence, he began teaching at Wayne State.

Nakhnikian had assembled one of the most dynamic departments in the country, with an array of prominent and future prominent names in Anglo-American analytic philosophy: Richard Cartwright, Edmund Gettier of "Gettier's Paradox" fame, Keith Lehrer, Hector-Neri Castañeda, and Robert C. Sleigh. Plantinga particularly enjoyed the outstanding philosophy conferences held there and the constant faculty discussions, usually lasting most of the working day, with participants drifting in and out as teaching schedules demanded. At Wayne State, Plantinga was part of a circle of philosophers who were willing to think through problems in a fresh, painstaking, and meticulous way—who were willing and able to do philosophy, rather than, as had been the main preoccupation at Yale, just talk about it. This meticulous manner of philosophizing was expressed in the attention paid to the modal structure of arguments and to careful expositions of logical confusions.

One such confusion was what the Wayne State philosophers came to call "Sleigh's Fallacy." Sleigh noticed that an argument in the prominent British philosophy journal *Mind* had the modal structure "In all possible worlds, either A is true or B is true; A is not true; therefore, in all possible worlds B is true." Since by the standard rules of the propositional calculus "not-A or B" is equivalent to "if A, then B," the argument can be restated as "In all possible worlds, if A is true, then B is true; A is true; therefore, in all possible worlds B is true." This argument says that from the supposition that in all possible worlds, if A is true, then B is true, it follows that if A is true as a matter of fact, then B is true in all possible worlds. But, Sleigh pointed out, B is not true in all possible worlds on that supposition: the first premise states only a condition for possible worlds, a condition that may not be satisfied in some possible worlds where the consequent of the conditional, B, may not be true. Plantinga began to search the philosophical literature for instances of Sleigh's Fallacy and discovered that it was rampant; he also discovered that some previous philosophers had been well aware of it. He showed convincingly that recognition of the fallacy was a commonplace among scholastic philosophers of the thirteenth century, who referred to it as "the fallacy of conflating the necessity of the consequent with the necessity of the consequence." This recovery of analytical and logical insights from medieval philosophers became an important thread running throughout Plantinga's career; he is well known for his quip that contemporary thinkers "need to catch up with the thirteenth century!" Plantinga sees this kind of modal error not as trivial but as lying at the heart of much confused discourse by prestigious philosophers on such central issues as determinism, the supposed conflict between divine foreknowledge and human freedom, and the logic of relations.

In 1963 Jellema retired from Calvin College, and Plantinga was invited to replace him. Despite his love for the Wayne State department in its "golden era," he saw his own mission as that of a Christian scholar and moved back to Calvin in the fall.

In 1967 Plantinga presented a highly original strategy in defense of the rationality of theism in *God and Other Minds,* the work that made his international reputation as an analytic philosopher of religion. He begins by examining the classic arguments for the existence of God: the ontological argument, according to which the definition of God as a perfect being necessarily entails his existence; the cosmological argument, which holds that the universe requires God as its ultimate cause; and the teleological argument, which claims that the evidence of design in the universe implies an intelligent creator. He finds each of these arguments defective. On the other hand, he finds the various atheistic arguments—the strongest of which is the argument from the existence of evil–to be defective also. Rather than concluding that agnosticism is the most reasonable position, Plantinga turns the inquiry in an unexpected direction by examining the analogical argument for the existence of other minds. This argument holds that because one's own pain is usually accompanied by certain behavior, similar behavior observed in others supports the proposition that they are also in pain; hence, other minds probably exist. Plantinga then points to a certain similarity between this argument and the teleological argument for the existence of God: some propositions essential to the analogical argument, such as "Sometimes certain areas of my body are free from pain," are supported by evidence, but others, such as "There are some pains not in my body," are not; by the same token, some propositions essential to the teleological argument, such as "The universe exhibits behavioral regularity," are supported by evidence, but others, such as "the universe was designed by exactly one person," are not. The analogical argument for the existence of other minds is, then, no more probable than the teleological argument for the existence of God. But the fact that the analogical argument cannot conclusively prove that other minds exist does not make belief in the existence of other minds irrational; Plantinga concludes that "if my belief in other minds is rational, so is my belief in God."

In *God and Other Minds* Plantinga calls his critique of the atheistic argument from evil "The Free Will Defense." He had encountered that phrase not in the work of theistic apologists but in the British atheistic philosopher Antony Flew's "Divine Omnipotence and Human Freedom" (1964). Plantinga refined and improved his version of the argument and restated it–in a less technical form than in *God and Other Minds*–in *God, Freedom, and Evil* (1974).

Flew had argued that the existence of a morally perfect, omnipotent, and omniscient God is logically incompatible with the existence of evil in a world supposedly created by God. He had raised the Free Will Defense as an objection to his argument: perhaps the evil in the world is entirely the result of the wickedness of free human beings. Flew responded to this defense by observing that one form of evil, animal pain, cannot be explained away in this manner, since animals predated the emergence of human beings. Plantinga replies that Flew's observation is irrelevant to the issue of the logical consistency of the existence of God and the existence of evil. To rebut Flew, he contends, all that is needed is to show that at least one possible state of affairs is consistent with the proposition "God is omnipotent, omniscient, and wholly good" and that this state of affairs and that proposition, taken together, logically entail the proposition "Evil exists." Plantinga stresses that the state of

GOD AND OTHER MINDS

A Study of the Rational Justification of Belief in God

By Alvin Plantinga

CORNELL UNIVERSITY PRESS

Dust jacket for Plantinga's 1967 book, in which he argues that belief in the existence of God is justified by reasons analogous to those that justify one's belief that other people have minds (Bruccoli Clark Layman Archives)

affairs need not actually exist and need not even be plausible: it only needs to be logically possible.

Plantinga's own Free Will Defense focuses on the suggestion of the atheist philosopher J. L. Mackie in his "Evil and Omnipotence" (1955) that God, as an omnipotent being, could have created a world containing free agents who always choose rightly. Mackie, according to Plantinga, is assuming that omnipotence means that God could have created any world he pleased. But Plantinga argues that this crucial assumption–which he calls "Leibniz's Lapse," since Mackie shares it with the German rationalist philosopher Gottfried Wilhelm Leibniz (1646–1716)–is false. Employing the example of a fictitious "Curley" who suffers from "Transworld Depravity," Plantinga argues that a possible world cannot be actualized by God if it contains the possibility of Curley's choosing morally wrongly with respect to a given action and yet, at the same time, one assumes with Mackie that Curley will always choose rightly. Such a world cannot be actualized by definition, since it is self-contradictory. But it also cannot be actualized, Plantinga says, if God "*causes* Curley to go right with respect to [action] A or *brings it about that* he does so," for then Curley would not be significantly free in this possible world. This result can be generalized: God could not actualize any possible world with significantly free creatures who always choose rightly.

Plantinga moves from moral evil to consider so-called natural evils, such as earthquakes, volcanic eruptions, diseases, and so forth. The Free Will Defense would seem to be inapplicable to such cases, but Plantinga takes up St. Augustine's suggestion that "Satan and his cohorts"–nonhuman but free spirits created before the creation of humans–rebelled against God and have been bringing destruction in their wake ever since: "So the natural evil we find is due to free actions of nonhuman spirits." Plantinga does not claim that this hypothesis is true or even plausible but merely that it is logically possible; but that is enough, he says, to defeat all those who would argue, like Flew, that the existence of God is logically incompatible with the existence of natural evil.

George Mavrodes has objected that Plantinga's stress on mere logical possibility puts the epistemic bar too low; normally, one thinks of rational beliefs as those for which one can show at least plausibility. Mavrodes complains that Plantinga's "minimal ambition" for his beliefs is analogous in the ethical realm to someone who is not concerned to do what is morally right but is satisfied if his or her actions conform to the letter of the law. Such a criterion of rationality seemingly makes it impossible for anyone to offer an argument against theism or for a theist to engage in a meaningful philosophical dialectic with someone who holds a nontheistic position. Plantinga has replied that he was only refuting a particular objection–that God's existence is incompatible with that of evil–and was, therefore, only arguing that God and evil are compatible, not that belief in God is rational. He contends that Mavrodes's objection is, thus, beside the point.

Plantinga had long taken a particular interest in St. Anselm of Canterbury's so-called ontological argument for the existence of God in his *Proslogion* (An Address of the Mind to God, written 1077–1078) and the debates on the argument in the subsequent history of philosophy; his second book, published in 1965, was an anthology of classical and contemporary readings on the argument. In *God and Other Minds* Plantinga had rejected what he then regarded as the best version of the argument, but in *God, Freedom, and Evil* he reexamines it and declares that one version is sound. Rejecting the traditional objections of the eleventh-century monk

Gaunilo of Tours and the eighteenth-century German philosopher Kant, Plantinga examines twentieth-century "modal" versions of the argument developed by Charles Hartshorne and Norman Malcolm. According to Plantinga, the modal version shows that if the notion of a greatest possible being (that is, God) is coherent and, thus, God possibly exists, and if that notion entails the idea of necessary existence, then it follows logically that such a being exists in every possible world. It also, however, entails the logically weaker thesis that God's degree of greatness is unexcelled only in some possible worlds. This possibility allows for the notion that God exists in the actual world but that, relative to this world, his greatness is on a rather low level. Plantinga points out that such a result is religiously inadequate: the concept of God required by monotheistic worship is one in which the attributes that make God great do not exist accidentally. He quotes the philosopher J. N. Findlay: "an adequate object of our worship must possess its various excellences *in some necessary manner.*"

To meet this objection, Plantinga distinguishes between "greatness" and "excellence." A being has excellence in a possible world if its properties in that particular world make it excellent; but a being has greatness in a possible world depending on the properties it has in that world and in all other possible worlds in which it exists. A being, then, has maximal greatness if it has maximal excellence in every possible world. But to so define such a being is, in effect, to say that it must be omniscient, omnipotent, and morally perfect. On the basis of these distinctions, Plantinga restates the ontological argument: a being that has maximal greatness is possible; so there is a possible being that has maximal greatness in some world; a being has maximal greatness in a given world only if it has maximal excellence in every world; a being has maximal excellence in a given world only if it has omniscience, omnipotence, and moral perfection in that world; since the actual world is included in the set of possible worlds, these premises entail that there is a being with maximal excellence in the actual world. This argument remedies the difficulty of the previous modal version and also has the advantage that it nowhere refers to necessary existence as a distinctive perfection, which meets Kant's objection to the ontological argument that existence is not a predicate or attribute. For a being with maximal greatness in at least one possible world has maximal excellence in every world, and a being obviously cannot have an excellence in any world unless it exists in that world.

Plantinga raises an objection to his own argument: the first two premises raise the prospect of merely possible beings that do not actually exist. He rejects the supposition of merely possible but nonexistent beings as "either unintelligible or necessarily false," but he revises those premises so that this supposition is not entailed. Instead of speaking of possible beings that do or do not exist in various possible worlds, he says, one may speak of properties and the worlds in which they are or are not instantiated:

Instead of speaking of the possible fat man in the corner, noting that he doesn't exist, we may speak of the property *being a fat man in the corner,* noting that it isn't instantiated (although it could have been). So, rather than speak of a possible being that has greatness or excellence in a possible world, we can speak of the property of maximal greatness as being *instantiated* in a possible world.

The two premises can, thus, be revised as three premises: there is a possible world in which maximal greatness is instantiated; necessarily, a being is maximally great only if it has maximal excellence in every world; necessarily, a being has maximal excellence in every world only if it has omniscience, omnipotence, and moral perfection in every world. These premises entail that the proposition "There is no omnipotent, omniscient, morally perfect being" is logically impossible in some world; and what is logically impossible in one world is, of course, impossible in every world. But if such a proposition is impossible, then an omnipotent, omniscient, and morally perfect being actually exists; this being, furthermore, has these qualities essentially and exists in every possible world.

Plantinga does not hold that what he calls this "triumphant" version of the ontological argument proves the existence of God. No one who is not already convinced by the main premise of the argument, that maximal greatness is instantiated in at least one possible world, will accept the conclusion that a greatest possible being actually exists. While Plantinga believes that the main premise is true, and that the argument is, thus, sound, he admits that he has shown only that accepting the main premise is not irrational. The argument, therefore, establishes "not the *truth* of theism, but its rational acceptability." In 1974, the same year as *God, Freedom, and Evil,* Plantinga published a more technical version of his ontological argument in *The Nature of Necessity.*

In 1982 Plantinga was appointed to the prestigious John A. O'Brien Professorship in Philosophy and made director of the Center for Philosophy of Religion at the University of Notre Dame. In his inaugural address, "Advice to Christian Philosophers," he called for more intellectual autonomy on the part of Christian philosophers, who should be wary of pursuing every passing intellectual fad. Such philosophers, he said, should exhibit an integrity based on the courage of their Christian convictions.

Cover for Plantinga's 1974 book, in which he states his "Free Will Defense" of the rationality of belief in God in the face of the existence of evil in the world (Bruccoli Clark Layman Archives)

An example of such autonomy and courage of convictions can be found in Plantinga's "Reason and Belief in God," a monograph-length article published in the anthology *Faith and Rationality: Reason and Belief in God* (1983), edited by Plantinga and his former fellow Calvin College undergraduate Nicholas Wolterstorff. In this essay Plantinga introduces and defends the concept of a "Reformed epistemology" of religious belief. He calls it "Reformed" because it is inspired by the writings of Reformed Christian theologians such as John Calvin, Karl Barth, and Herman Bavnick. According to these thinkers, belief in God need not and ought not be based on conclusions derived from either the allegedly self-evident or the allegedly empirically warranted premises of "natural theology." Plantinga argues that this Reformed attitude coalesces with two major developments in contemporary epistemology of which he wholeheartedly approves: the collapse of evidentialism, the view that rational beliefs must be based on sufficient evidence, and the related collapse of classical foundational-

Plantinga in Amsterdam, 1995 (photograph © by Sijmen Hendriks)

ism, the view that rational beliefs that are not themselves nonderivative or self-standing—"properly basic," in Plantinga's terminology—must be based on arguments that terminate in "foundations," that is, in properly basic propositions. Both proponents of theistic metaphysical programs such as St. Thomas Aquinas, René Descartes, and John Locke and such atheistic critics as Flew and W. K. Clifford assume evidentialism and foundationalism; but both views, Plantinga says, are riddled with difficulties. For instance, for many beliefs that most people take to be rational and entirely uncontroversial the provision of evidence is simply inappropriate; most beliefs based on perception and on memory of the recent past fall into this category. One of the most important difficulties besetting foundationalism is the problem of self-referential incoherence. A foundationalist can be regarded as believing that something is properly basic only if it is self-evident or incorrigible or evident to the senses. But, Plantinga asks, how is a foundationalist justified in holding that criterion? If the criterion is believed on the grounds of nonbasic propositions, what could these propositions be? On the other hand, a criterion for

"proper basicality" cannot legitimately appeal to itself as a properly basic proposition. Now, either the criterion is properly basic or it is inferred from nonbasic propositions; since neither is the case, the criterion incoherently requires its own denial.

Plantinga argues that belief in God is as properly basic as perceptual beliefs that are acquired under normal conditions—that is, in the absence of optical illusions, hallucinations, and so forth. He declares with Calvin that God has created human beings with a "*sensus divinitatis*," a disposition to believe, which, although suppressed in varying degrees in various people, is "universally present" and capable of being "triggered" under the right circumstances. The theist who beholds "a starry night or the beauty of a snow-capped mountain" may experience the presence of God as part of this beholding. In such a triggering circumstance the theist is perfectly within his or her epistemic rights to hold that God exists. In this situation belief in God is properly basic in that no argument or appeal to special propositions is involved; the presence of God is simply experienced. In light of the collapse of evidentialism and foundationalism, the theist is within his or her rights to make belief in God its own foundation.

Plantinga defends his notion of theism as properly basic against several objections. He points out that he is not asserting that argument no longer has any purpose in theology or that basic beliefs are groundless. Rational argument still has an important defensive role to play in theology. That is, just as other properly basic beliefs have "defeaters"—for example, one may find that a laser-radiation device has been hidden in one's room, thus giving one's otherwise clear soda bottle a red hue—belief in God may also have purported defeaters, such as Sigmund Freud's doctrine that the experience of God originates in wish fulfillment, and rational defensive argument may appropriately be employed to defeat these defeaters. Moreover, while properly basic beliefs are not derived from other beliefs, they are not groundless:

> Suppose we consider perceptual beliefs, memory beliefs, and beliefs ascribing mental states to other persons, such beliefs as:
>
> I see a tree,
>
> I had breakfast this morning, and
>
> That person is in pain.
>
> Although beliefs of this sort are typically taken as basic, it would be a mistake to describe them as *groundless*. Upon having experience of a certain sort, I believe that I am perceiving a tree. In the typical case I do not hold this belief on the basis of other beliefs; it is nonetheless not groundless. . . . We could say, if we wish, that this experience is what justifies me in holding [the belief]; this is the *ground* of my justification, and, by extension, the ground of the belief itself.

Now similar things may be said about belief in God. When the Reformers claim that this belief is properly basic, they do not mean to say, of course, that there are no justifying circumstances for it, or that it is in that sense groundless or gratuitous.

Finally, and perhaps most important, Plantinga envisions the objection that if belief in God is properly basic, why can just any belief not be so regarded? Why should voodoo or astrology or the belief that the Great Pumpkin appears in a field every Halloween not be similarly privileged? Plantinga specifies that properly basic beliefs are beliefs held as such under the right circumstances and with the proper functioning of one's faculties. The difference between belief in the Great Pumpkin and belief in God is that no natural tendency or disposition to believe in the Great Pumpkin exists. Also, certain experiences count as grounds for the proper basicality of theistic belief; no such experiences "ground" belief in the Great Pumpkin.

Plantinga's thesis of Reformed epistemology has been extremely controversial, eliciting critical comment from believers and unbelievers alike. The Christian philosopher Stephen J. Wykstra, for example, argues that Plantinga's account of evidentialism misses an important distinction between derivational and discriminational evidence. The idea of God is not something to be derived through inferential evidence; on this score, Wykstra says, Plantinga is correct. While a *sensus divinitatis* may steel and maintain belief, however, only discriminational evidence of an inferential sort can provide a "direction" for belief. Which beliefs about God are properly basic and which are cultural constructs are important questions. Wykstra notes that religious experience in a wide variety of cultures "ostensibly" authenticates "innumerable beliefs many of which are in contradiction with one another." Inferential natural theology may well be the only way available for cutting through the ambiguity of multiple conceptualizations of God.

Moreover, critics such as D. R. Griffin have pointed out that Plantinga's reply to the Great Pumpkin objection is evasive. The Great Pumpkin is not a good candidate for considerations of proper basicality, because, as Plantinga himself points out, no social community has a natural disposition for belief in the Great Pumpkin. But what about religious beliefs held by substantial social communities? Plantinga's Reformed epistemology would allow Hindus to argue—as, in fact, they have—that, contrary to orthodox Christianity, belief in reincarnation is a natural and universal disposition: newspapers in Sri Lanka regularly report past lives vividly remembered by thousands of adults and children; such experiences also occur in the West in dreams and in memories recovered through regression under hypnosis,

but the cultural opposition to belief in reincarnation leads to such occurrences being repressed and underreported. The question then is how these differing claims can be adjudicated, given Plantinga's epistemic criteria.

Terence Penelhum says that Plantinga's invitation to each community of belief to be "responsible to *its* set of examples" of proper basicality will lead to "a Balkanized world." In Penelhum's view, the implications of Reformed epistemology are dangerous, especially in religious-political contexts such as the conflict between Jews and Muslims in the Middle East. "Balkanization" would only exacerbate this intractable, seemingly never-ending strife.

Undaunted by such criticisms, Plantinga has extended the program of Reformed epistemology in a three-volume project: *Warrant: The Current Debate* (1993), *Warrant and Proper Function* (1993), and *Warranted Christian Belief* (2000). In the first two volumes he argues that modern epistemology got off on the wrong track by buying into the Cartesian and Lockean notions that knowledge is fundamentally about answering to "epistemic obligations" that provide justification for beliefs. Knowledge is to be equated neither with justification, since one can believe a proposition on good grounds but find out that it is, in fact, false, nor with true belief: one may believe that one's favorite team will win the championship in some future year, and it may in fact win in that year; but one still cannot say that one knew that the team would win. Warrant is the missing key element in the analysis of knowledge.

A warranted belief is one that is produced by reliable cognitive faculties; an example would be a belief produced by short-term memory as opposed to one produced by wishful thinking. In addition, a warranted belief must be produced by reliable faculties under the right circumstances that fit the basic design of those faculties. For example, one's faculties will not be reliable in environments for which they were not designed, such as extreme heat or cold or sensory deprivation. Moreover, the faculties must be functioning properly. If one is suffering from a lesion on the neocortex that affects one's judgment, one's beliefs cannot be warranted—not even the true belief that one has a lesion on one's neocortex. Also, such faculties must be aimed at getting the truth and must be reliable in the sense that they provide true beliefs at least most of the time. Plantinga sums up his position in a formal definition: "A belief has warrant for a person S only if that belief is produced in S by cognitive faculties functioning properly (subject to no dysfunction) in a cognitive environment that is appropriate for S's kind of cognitive faculties, according to a design plan that is successfully aimed at truth."

The final volume in the trilogy, *Warranted Christian Belief*, argues that one has every reason to think that

could have that feature. But isn't it doubtful that a belief could be like that? If one of my beliefs is such that it is irrational for me to accept it, then that belief, even if true, does not constitute knowledge for me. At any rate this is a consequence of my accounts of warrant and rationality. That is because I explain both in terms of proper function. The basic idea here is that a belief is irrational for a human being in circumstances C, just if it couldn't be produced in those circumstances by (human) cognitive faculties that are functioning properly. A belief is irrational for human beings, in circumstances C, just if the human design plan precludes the production of that belief in those circumstances. Thus the beliefs of Descartes' madmen, who thought their heads were made of glass and that they themselves were gourds, would be paradigm cases of irrational beliefs. But the notion of warrant, as I understand it, includes rationality: a belief has warrant only if it is produced by cognitive faculties functioning properly in a favorable environment according to a design plan successfully aimed at the production of true beliefs. Since (as I see it) a belief constitutes knowledge for S only if it has a good deal of warrant for S, it follows that if a belief is irrational for me (in my circumstances) then that belief does not constitute knowledge for me. Hence it is not possible to know a proposition (N&E, for example) for which you have a rationality defeater of this sort.

If the devotee of N&E has a defeater for N&E, therefore, he can't rationally accept N&E. But just how bad is this? How bad is this condition in which, if I am right, the canny naturalist finds himself, the condition of believing something such that it is irrational for him to believe it? Is it like a dented fender, asks Yandell, or is it more like your car's engine overheating and the pistons getting fused to the cylinder walls? Well, I'm not sure I know the answer to that question. Those atheologians who object to Christian belief on the grounds that, as they think, such belief is irrational seem to think that a serious criticism. (They sometimes seem also to think that people who accept irrational beliefs ought to be ashamed of themselves.) Here I think they are right. No doubt there are worse things than holding irrational beliefs; no doubt this isn't in quite the same league as, say, robbing a bank or making ~~politically insensitive comments~~. Still, a position that can't be rationally ~~accepted~~ displays a serious defect. Perhaps it is an even more serious defect in a self-consciously adopted philosophical position, such as N&E. And surely one who sees that he holds an irrational belief should do what he can to give it up.

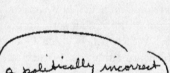

a politically incorrect remark.

Ad Moser

I turn finally to Paul Moser's paper; first, I'll mention a couple of places where it seems to me there is misunderstanding (which I'm perfectly pre-

Corrected proof page for Plantinga's article "Internalism, Externalism, Defeaters and Arguments for Christian Belief," published in 2001 (Collection of Alvin Plantinga)

classical Judeo-Christian-Islamic monotheism and the whole edifice of orthodox Christian belief–Christology, Trinity, Resurrection, and so forth–conform to the definition of warranted belief. Plantinga subjects the purported defeaters of such views, inspired by the thought of Freud, Karl Marx, Charles Darwin, and so on, to detailed critical examination and rejects them. Plantinga's attack on the naturalistic metaphysical interpretation of evolutionary theory has drawn special attention; *Naturalism Defeated? Essays on Plantinga's Evolutionary Argument against Naturalism* (2002), edited by James Beilby, is devoted to a discussion of his critique. The problem with coupling naturalism and evolution, Plantinga argues, is that unguided natural selection cannot adequately account for the cognitive reliability of human faculties in choosing successful, high-order scientific theories. Consequently, the acceptance of both naturalism and evolution entails the acceptance of at least one undefeatable defeater of those theories; that is, the theories together entail that they cannot be reliably believed, and their acceptance is, therefore, "pragmatically circular." On the other hand, evolution coupled with a theistic metaphysics, which assumes that human cognitive faculties were designed by a divinely guided evolutionary process to aim at truth, has no difficulty in accounting for cognitive reliability. Hence, evolutionary theory fits a theistic metaphysics but not a naturalistic one.

Whatever one thinks of the soundness of Alvin Plantinga's philosophical views, there can be no question that he has been a leading force in keeping the traditional Christian worldview intellectually alive in the late twentieth and early twenty-first centuries. Constructive theistic philosophy of religion has experienced a renaissance in good measure because of his influence.

References:

David Basinger and Ransdell Basinger, "Divine Omnipotence: Plantinga vs. Griffin," *Process Studies,* 11 (Spring 1981): 11–24;

Michael D. Beaty, ed., *Christian Theism and the Problems of Philosophy,* Library of Religious Philosophy, volume 5 (Notre Dame, Ind.: University of Notre Dame Press, 1990);

James Beilby, ed., *Naturalism Defeated? Essays on Plantinga's Evolutionary Argument against Naturalism* (Ithaca, N.Y.: Cornell University Press, 2002);

Kelly James Clark, *Return to Reason: A Critique of Enlightenment Evidentialism, and a Defense of Reason and Belief in God* (Grand Rapids, Mich.: Eerdmans, 1990);

Fransisco Conesa, *Dios y el mal: La defensa del teismo frente al problema del mal según Alvin Plantinga* (Pamplona: EUNSA, 2000);

D. R. Griffin, *Reenchantment without Supernaturalism* (Ithaca, N.Y.: Cornell University Press, 2001);

Dewey J. Hoitenga, *From Plato to Plantinga: An Introduction to Reformed Epistemology* (Albany: State University of New York Press, 1991);

Jonathan Kvanvig, ed., *Warrant in Contemporary Epistemology: Essays in Honor of Plantinga's Theory of Knowledge* (Lanham, Md.: Rowman & Littlefield, 1996);

George Mavrodes, "Jerusalem and Athens Revisited," in *Faith and Rationality: Reason and Belief in God,* edited by Plantinga and Nicholas Wolterstorff (Notre Dame, Ind.: University of Notre Dame Press, 1983), pp. 192–218;

Mark S. McLeod, *Rationality and Theistic Belief: An Essay on Reformed Epistemology* (Ithaca, N.Y.: Cornell University Press, 1993);

Enrique R. Moros, *El argumento ontológico modal de Alvin Plantinga* (Pamplona: EUNSA, 1997);

Moros, *Modalidad y esencia: La metaphysica de Alvin Plantinga* (Pamplona: University of Navarre Press, 1996);

Keith M. Parsons, *God and the Burden of Proof: Plantinga, Swinburne, and the Analytic Defense of Theism* (Buffalo, N.Y.: Prometheus, 1989);

Terence Penelhum, "Parity Is Not Enough," in *Faith, Reason, and Skepticism: Essays,* edited by Marcus Hester (Philadelphia: Temple University Press, 1992), pp. 98–120;

James F. Sennett, *Modality, Probability, and Rationality: A Critical Examination of Alvin Plantinga's Philosophy* (New York: Peter Lang, 1992);

James E. Tomberlin and Peter van Inwagen, eds., *Alvin Plantinga,* Profiles, volume 5 (Dordrecht, Netherlands & Boston: Reidel, 1985);

van Inwagen, "Plantinga on Trans-World Identity," in his *Ontology, Identity, and Modality: Essays in Metaphysics* (Cambridge & New York: Cambridge University Press, 2001), pp. 186–205;

Bartosz Wieckowski, *Gott in möglichen Welten: Eine Analyse des modalen ontologischen Arguments für die Existenz Gottes von Alvin Plantinga* (Münster: Lit, 1999);

Stephen J. Wykstra, "Toward a Sensible Evidentialism: On the Notion of 'Needing Evidence,'" in *Philosophy of Religion: Selected Readings,* second edition, edited by William L. Rowe and William J. Wainwright (Fort Worth: Harcourt Brace Jovanovich, 1989), pp. 426–437.

Hilary Putnam
(31 July 1926 –   )

Lance P. Hickey
Rose-Hulman Institute of Technology

BOOKS: *Philosophy of Logic* (New York: Harper & Row, 1971);

Philosophical Papers, volume 1: *Mathematics, Matter, and Method* (London & New York: Cambridge University Press, 1975);

Philosophical Papers, volume 2: *Mind, Language, and Reality* (Cambridge & New York: Cambridge University Press, 1975);

Meaning and the Moral Sciences (London & Boston: Routledge & Kegan Paul, 1978);

Reason, Truth and History (Cambridge & New York: Cambridge University Press, 1981);

Philosophical Papers, volume 3: *Realism and Reason* (Cambridge & New York: Cambridge University Press, 1983);

The Many Faces of Realism (La Salle, Ill.: Open Court, 1987);

Representation and Reality (Cambridge, Mass.: MIT Press, 1988);

Realism with a Human Face, edited by James Conant (Cambridge, Mass.: Harvard University Press, 1990);

The Meaning of the Concept of Probability in Application to Finite Sequences (New York: Garland, 1990);

Renewing Philosophy (Cambridge, Mass.: Harvard University Press, 1992);

Words and Life, edited by Conant (Cambridge, Mass.: Harvard University Press, 1994);

Pragmatism: An Open Question (Oxford & Cambridge, Mass.: Blackwell, 1995);

The Threefold Cord: Mind, Body and World (New York: Columbia University Press, 1999);

The Collapse of the Fact/Value Dichotomy, and Other Essays (Cambridge, Mass.: Harvard University Press, 2002).

OTHER: "Information and the Mental," in *Truth and Interpretation: Perspectives on the Philosophy of Donald Davidson,* edited by Ernest LePore (Oxford & New York: Blackwell, 1986), pp. 262–271;

Hilary Putnam (photograph by Bachrach)

"Comments and Replies," in *Reading Putnam,* edited by Peter Clark and Bob Hale (Oxford & Cambridge, Mass.: Blackwell, 1994), pp. 242–295;

"Putnam, Hilary," in *A Companion to the Philosophy of Mind,* edited by Samuel Guttenplan (Oxford & Cambridge, Mass.: Blackwell, 1994), pp. 507–513.

SELECTED PERIODICAL PUBLICATIONS– UNCOLLECTED: "Synonymity and the Analysis of Belief Sentences," *Analysis,* 14 (1954): 114–122;

"A Definition of Degree of Confirmation for Very Rich Languages," *Philosophy of Science,* 23 (1956): 58–62;
"Mathematics and the Existence of Abstract Entities," *Philosophical Studies,* 7 (1956): 81–88;
"Reds, Greens, and Logical Analysis," *Philosophical Review,* 65 (1956): 206–217;
"Psychological Concepts, Explication, and Ordinary Language," *Journal of Philosophy,* 54 (1957): 94–99;
"Red and Green All Over Again: A Rejoinder to Arthur Pap," *Philosophical Review,* 66 (1957): 100–103;
"Comments on the Paper of David Sharp," *Philosophy of Science,* 28 (1961): 234–239;
"More about 'About,'" by Putnam and J. S. Ullian, *Journal of Philosophy,* 62 (1965): 305–310;
"Replies," *Philosophical Topics,* 20 (Spring 1992): 347–408;
"Pragmatism," *Proceedings of the Aristotelian Society,* 95, part 3 (1995): 291–306;
"On Wittgenstein's Philosophy of Mathematics," *Proceedings of the Aristotelian Society,* supplementary volume, 70 (1996): 243–264;
"Pragmatism and Realism," *Cardozo Law Review,* 18 (September 1996): 153–170;
"On Negative Theology," *Faith and Philosophy,* 4 (October 1997): 407–422;
"Thoughts Addressed to an Analytical Thomist," *Monist,* 80 (October 1997): 487–499;
"A Half Century of Philosophy, Viewed from Within," *Daedalus,* 126 (Winter 1997): 175–208;
"God and the Philosophers," *Midwest Studies in Philosophy,* 21 (1997): 175–187;
"A Note on Wittgenstein's 'Notorious Paragraph' about the Gödel theorem," by Putnam and Juliet Floyd, *Journal of Philosophy,* 97 (November 2000): 624–632;
"Nonstandard Models and Kripke's Proof of the Gödel Theorem," *Notre Dame Journal of Formal Logic,* 41, no. 1 (2000): 53–58;
"Skepticism, Stroud and the Contextuality of Knowledge," *Philosophical Explorations,* 4, no. 1 (2001): 2–16;
"Travis on Meaning, Thought, and the Ways the World Is," *Philosophical Quarterly,* 52 (2002): 96–106.

One of the most influential American philosophers of the post–World War II generation, Hilary Putnam has also been one of the most prolific. His corpus includes fifteen books and more than two hundred articles ranging over philosophy of science, philosophy of language, philosophy of mind, philosophy of logic and mathematics, metaphysics, ethics, and political philosophy. His original contributions include one of the first attempts to compare the mind to a computer, the development of a "quantum logic," a comprehensive theory of meaning for natural languages, arguments for and against various kinds of realism, and a thoroughgoing critique of the materialistic outlook that was characteristic of most American philosophers during the latter half of the twentieth century. Richard Rorty, another influential philosopher of Putnam's generation, compared him in *Philosophy and the Mirror of Nature* (1979) to the British philosopher Bertrand Russell, "not just in intellectual curiosity and willingness to change his mind, but in the breadth of his interests and in the extent of his social and moral concerns." The historian of philosophy John Passmore has remarked that trying to catch Putnam's philosophy is like trying to "capture the wind with a fishing net," since, in addition to addressing a wide range of topics, Putnam has shifted his position several times on some key philosophical issues. Throughout his career, however, Putnam has been consistent in his opposition to all forms of what he calls "philosophical imperialism"–views that insist that "one and only one" way exists to describe the world or to approach philosophical problems. Positivism, reductionism, conventionalism, behaviorism, materialism, scientism, and metaphysical realism have all borne the brunt of his attacks. Following loose threads wherever they take him, drawing from the latest discoveries in the sciences without uncritically accepting them, and even taking inspiration from science fiction, Putnam has constantly followed the experimental route in the hope that real progress can be made in philosophy.

Hilary Whitehall Putnam was born in Chicago on 31 July 1926 to the writer and translator Samuel Putnam and Riva Sampson Putnam. In early 1927 the family moved to France, where Putnam's father was a member of the American literary expatriate community; they lived briefly in Paris and then in the suburbs of Suresnes, Seaux, and Fortenay-aux-Roses, and finally in the artists' colony of Mirmande in the south. Concerned about the rise of fascism in Europe and about the fact that their son was growing up speaking a French patois that could not be understood in a village four miles away, the Putnams returned to the United States in 1933. They soon settled in Philadelphia.

After receiving a B.A. in mathematics and philosophy from the University of Pennsylvania in 1948, Putnam studied the philosophy of mathematics, logic, and the philosophy of science under the logical positivist Hans Reichenbach at the University of California at Los Angeles. On 1 November 1948 he married Erna Diesendruck; they had a daughter, Erika. He

Putnam, circa 1981 (from the dust jacket for Reason, Truth and History, *1981)*

received his Ph.D. in philosophy in 1951; his dissertation, *The Meaning of the Concept of Probability in Application to Finite Sequences,* was published in 1990. He was an instructor at Northwestern University in 1952–1953, moving to Princeton University as an assistant professor in 1953.

Logical positivism was the dominant outlook in American philosophy in the mid twentieth century; but as a result of dialogues with the positivists Reichenbach and Rudolf Carnap, and the influence of W. V. Quine, Putnam became disillusioned with positivism and initiated attacks on some of its most important theses. His articles of the late 1950s and early 1960s, which are collected in *Mathematics, Matter, and Method* (1975) and *Mind, Language, and Reality* (1975)–the first two volumes of his *Philosophical Papers*–did much to break the hold of positivism on Anglo-American philosophy. Even as one of the most trenchant critics of the movement, however, he retained from it the idea that philosophy should be modeled on the methods of the natural sciences, the use of linguistic and logical analysis to solve philosophical puzzles, and the rejection of a priori approaches and other remnants of "metaphysical" ways of thinking.

Putnam's philosophical style has always been to try to strike a balance between extreme positions, and he took this approach toward positivism. An example is his adjudication of the debate between Quine and the positivists concerning the concept of analyticity. According to the positivists' verifiability criterion, every meaningful declarative sentence either states a "rule of language" and so is "analytic"–in Ludwig Wittgenstein's phrase, a "mere tautology"–in that the concept of the predicate is "contained in" the concept of the subject; or it states a "matter of fact" known by experience and so is "synthetic," in that the predicate adds information that is not already presented by the subject. In "Two Dogmas of Empiricism" (1951) Quine argued that the positivists could not give a noncircular account of analyticity and that because individual sentences cannot be verified in isolation from a body of theory, the idea that the meaning of a sentence could be tested against experience in a one-to-one fashion is part of a naive "museum myth" of meaning. He advised philosophers to give up on the concept of analyticity and even on the concept of "meaning" itself, for no further progress could be made in those areas.

In 1957, while he was a visiting research professor at the Minnesota Center for Philosophy of Science, Putnam wrote "The Analytic and the Synthetic" in response to Quine; it was published in 1962 in volume three of the Minnesota Studies in the Philosophy of Science series, *Scientific Explanation, Space, and Time,* edited by Herbert Feigl and Grover Maxwell. It is collected in *Mind, Language, and Reality.* Putnam agrees with Quine that the positivist distinction is untenable: many statements are neither purely analytic nor purely synthetic but shift back and forth as new knowledge is acquired. But Quine was wrong, Putnam argues, in claiming that no sentences are analytic. "All bachelors are unmarried males" and "Oculists are eye-doctors" are examples of statements that are analytic, since they cannot be rephrased without changing the meanings of the terms. Putnam calls terms such as *bachelor* "one-criterion" terms; he contrasts them with scientific terms such as *energy* and mathematical terms such as *straight line,* which he calls "law-cluster terms" because their meanings depend on a cluster of laws and not on a criterion. Statements such as "$E=1/2mv^2$" (the Newtonian formula for kinetic energy) and "The shortest distance between two points is a straight line" were analytically true relative to the theoretical systems in which they were couched–Newtonian physics and Euclidean geometry, respectively–but they are not analytically true, or even true at all, in the contexts of relativity theory and non-Euclidean geometry. The lesson to be learned from this history is that one should be suspicious of claims that statements of a certain class are "immune to revision." A few such statements may exist, but they are trivial; the "weighty" definitions and laws of mathematics, logic, and science are, Putnam says, "statements with respect to which it is not *happy* to ask the question 'analytic or synthetic?'"

Putnam also criticized the positivists' rigid distinction between the statements of mathematics and those of empirical science. According to logical positivism, the principles of mathematics are mere conventions that say nothing about reality—as opposed to being empirical truths, as the nineteenth-century British philosopher John Stuart Mill thought, or referring to Platonic objects of which one can have a priori knowledge, as traditional metaphysics holds. Putnam argues that what one considers "a priori" is relative to a particular theory; even if the principles of mathematics are "more a priori" than those of physics, they are not a collection of analytic truths but are as subject to revision as any other kind of statement. One cannot even say that basic logical laws such as the principle of noncontradiction are true a priori, for cases can be envisioned where they break down: in quantum physics, for example, any physical system can be found in a "superposition"—that is, in two places, two energy levels, or two frequencies at the same time. If the world is so bizarre, logic may have to be modified to account for it. In short, there are no privileged truths: there may be a difference in how well entrenched a given statement is in relation to another, but the difference is one of degree rather than of kind.

Putnam was promoted to associate professor at Princeton in 1960; the following year he moved to the Massachusetts Institute of Technology (MIT) as a full professor. He and his wife were divorced in 1962, and Putnam married Ruth Anna Hall on 11 August of that year. They had three children: Samuel, Joshua, and Polly. In 1963 Putnam organized one of the first faculty and student committees against the Vietnam War. He was particularly outraged by David Halberstam's report that the United States claimed to be "defending" the peasants of South Vietnam from the Viet Cong by poisoning their rice crop.

In 1965 Putnam moved to Harvard University; his wife took a position teaching philosophy at MIT. Putnam quickly became one of the most popular teachers at Harvard, as well as one of the most politically active. He organized campus protests against the Vietnam War and was the faculty adviser to Students for a Democratic Society, the main antiwar organization on campus. In 1968 he became a member of the Progressive Labor Party, which espoused what he

Dust jacket for the book in which Putnam presents his "brains in a vat" thought experiment (Richland County Public Library)

called an "idiosyncratic version of Marxism-Leninism." In 1972 he became disillusioned with the party for practicing what he perceived as the same manipulative and exploitative measures for which it was criticizing the United States government, and he severed his ties with it.

Putnam was a pioneer in the field that has come to be known as "artificial intelligence." In the early 1960s the two leading philosophical positions on the nature of the mind were logical behaviorism, which reduces statements about the mind to statements about the behavior of the organism and patterns of stimulus and response, and type-identity theory, which identifies a given type of mental state with a particular type of brain state. Putnam rejected both positions and developed his own theory, which has come to be known as functionalism. He did not bother to argue against dualism (the claim that the mind and the body are separate entities), which was not considered scientifically respectable; but his attacks on behaviorism and type-identity theory are frequently anthologized as classics in the philosophy of mind. In "Brains and Behavior," published in *Analytical Philosophy: Second Series* (1965), edited by R. J. Butler, and collected in *Mind, Language, and Reality,* he argues that behaviorism is based on a faulty theory of meaning. According to this theory, being in a certain mental state, such as pain, simply means that one is in a certain behavioral state. According to Putnam, this position ignores the fact that *pain* is often used as a name for a sensation that is private to the individual and has no conceptually or logically necessary behavioral manifestations.

In the even more widely cited "The Nature of Mental States," originally published as "Psychological Predicates" in *Art, Mind, and Religion* (1967), edited by William H. Capitan and Daniel Davy Merrill, and collected in *Mind, Language, and Reality,* Putnam attacks type-identity theory, according to which all organisms that are in the same mental state must be in exactly the same physical brain state. Putnam objects that a mammal and an octopus could be in the same state of "being hungry," but since their neural structures are dissimilar, they could not be in the same physical state. The issue, he says, is one of "multiple realizability": the same mental-state type can be realized in a variety of types of physical structure.

Putnam's proposal is that mental states be described not as behavioral dispositions nor as physical-chemical states but as those states that are causally responsible for the production of behavior in a computationally defined system of inputs and outputs. Just as a computer program can be realized in a variety of kinds of hardware, so a shared mental-state type or belief can be registered in a variety of organisms or functional systems—including robots or silicon-based space aliens.

For a long time, Putnam's functionalism seemed to carry the day: it was widely seen as an improvement over behaviorism, since it defines mental states in terms of intrinsic properties rather than of overt behavior; it also overcomes the demand of type-identity theory of too strict a connection between mental and physical states; it appears to allow for talk of intrinsic properties while preserving the important connections to behavior; and it falls in line with most commonsense beliefs about the nature of mental activity. In the late twentieth century, however, functionalism came under attack from many quarters—even from Putnam himself, who in *Representation and Reality* (1988) launches a battery of argu-

ments against his own theory. Even so, functionalism continued to be the most respected theory available.

In his first book, *Philosophy of Logic* (1971), Putnam proposes that nothing is wrong with countenancing the existence of "abstract" entities such as numbers, which were deemed too "metaphysical" by the positivists, so long as numbers are indispensable in the formulation of physical theories. This claim—now called "the Quine-Putnam 'indispensability' argument"—is still a topic of much debate, particularly among naturalist philosophers trying to account for the role mathematics and logic play in the "hard" sciences. In his later work Putnam goes even further, holding that statements about numbers, the cruelty or justice of certain actions, ice cubes, baseball games, electrons, and flowers are equally examples of cognitively meaningful discourse and equally governed by norms of truth and falsity. Furthermore, he says, when one points at three baseballs and asks how many objects there are, the answer might vary depending on one's background "theory" about what it means to be an object. To a Polish logician, for example, there may be nine objects, since an object can be defined as any mereological (whole-part) sum of two or more individuals. In short, although there are many wrong answers to such questions—Putnam is not saying that it is all relative, or a matter of arbitrary convention—there does not necessarily have to be one right answer.

Putnam was critical of the use, by some of Noam Chomsky's more zealous followers, of linguistic methods in answering questions of meaning. For Putnam, this approach ignores the way the world itself contributes to determining the meanings of terms. He developed this idea into a comprehensive theory in what many consider his most influential philosophical work: "The Meaning of 'Meaning,'" published in volume seven of the Minnesota Studies in the Philosophy of Science series, *Language, Mind, and Knowledge* (1975), edited by Keith Gunderson, and collected in *Mind, Language, and Reality.* Putnam's semantics begins as an attempt to solve a problem in regard to "natural-kind terms" that was largely ignored before he drew attention to it: how to account for the meaning of mass terms such as *water* and *gold* and sortals (terms that tell what kind of an object something is and provide a criterion for counting such objects) such as *lemon* and *cat.* The traditional conception held that the meanings of these terms can be captured by analytic definitions such as "*cat* means 'feline animal'" and "*lemon* means 'yellow, tart-tasting, thick-peeled fruit.'" The natural-kind term is synonymous with the description, and a speaker of the language must "grasp" the linguistic information associated with the term if he or she is to use the term competently. Although this view of meaning had been called into question by Wittgenstein and Quine, no clear alternative emerged prior to Putnam's work.

Putnam points out that a typical speaker need not have a grasp of any specific linguistic or conceptual information to use a term; terms are not synonymous with any description or cluster of descriptions. Language is more flexible than is implied by such a conception: a term can continue to have the same meaning, even though theories change, because the meaning is anchored in the referential use of the term–that is, in the things to which the term applies. This reasoning leads to Putnam's thesis of "semantic externalism," according to which the meanings of certain terms–proper names, natural-kind terms, and "indexicals" such as *here* and *now*–cannot be determined merely by an examination of what is in the mind of a speaker using the term; one has to look at the causal relationships between these terms and objects in the world to know what the speaker means. To illustrate, Putnam asks the reader to imagine a planet, Twin-Earth, somewhere in the universe that is identical molecule-for-molecule with Earth, except that what is called "water" on that planet is the chemical compound XYZ, not H_2O. When Oscar on Earth and Twin-Oscar on Twin-Earth say "Water is wet," they are in the same psychological state, but they mean different things. Oscar means that water is wet, whereas Twin-Oscar means that twin-water is wet. The meanings of terms change with differences in the environment. Putnam concludes his discussion with the adage: "Cut the pie any way you like it, 'meanings' just ain't in the head!"

Putnam's externalism, together with some of Saul Kripke's arguments in *Naming and Necessity* (1980) that were originally presented in a series of lectures at Princeton in 1970, inaugurated a revolution in the philosophy of language and the philosophy of mind. Putnam and Kripke radically subverted the "internalist" conception of meaning held by nearly every philosopher since Plato. On the internalist view, knowing what a word means is a matter of associating it with the proper conceptual information, whether or not this information is true of anything in the world. One can understand what a word means and, therefore, possess one's concepts, regardless of the way the world is–indeed, regardless of whether an independent world exists at all. This conception of meaning in the philosophy of language leads to the epistemological thesis that concepts–thoughts and beliefs–are "mental objects" that the mind perceives in an immediate and noninferential fashion. Thus, a fundamental asymmetry exists between one's knowledge of one's mind and one's knowledge of the world. This epistemological thesis, in turn, leads to the metaphysical one, most clearly enunciated by the seventeenth-century French philosopher René Descartes, that the mind and the world form two ontologically distinct domains. Putnam and Kripke upset this view, for their thesis about the meanings of terms leads to an equivalent thesis about concepts: the possession of concepts is not a matter of introspection but of connections between words and the world; thus, to know what a person's thoughts and beliefs are, one has to know what objects and properties those thoughts and beliefs are about. The result is an inversion of the Cartesian view of the mind: the fundamental asymmetry between knowledge of the mind and knowledge of the world exists because knowledge of thoughts and beliefs depends on the world, not vice versa. This view, now known as "psychological externalism," is at the center of contemporary discussion in the philosophy of mind. It presents a particular challenge to materialistic conceptions of the mind, which hold that thoughts and beliefs depend on internal states of an organism, such as neurophysiological patterns. This consequence of his semantic views led Putnam to question his own earlier views in the philosophy of mind.

Putnam's most significant change of view, the one that earned him the epithet "renegade Putnam," was his renunciation of metaphysical realism. Prior to his presidential address to the Eastern Division of the American Philosophical Association in 1976 Putnam had held a strongly "realist" position with respect to the independence from the mind of theoretical entities such as electrons; he was the leading spokesperson for "scientific realism," the view that theoretical entities exist even if they have not been proved to exist within any particular theory. In his address, "Realism and Reason," collected in *Meaning and the Moral Sciences* (1978), Putnam distinguishes "metaphysical realism," which holds on to the "radically non-epistemic" nature of truth, from his own modified version of scientific realism, "internal realism," which takes science at face value and contends that truth is nothing more than what would be rationally accepted at the end of scientific inquiry.

In 1976 Putnam was named Walter Beverly Pearson Professor of Modern Mathematics and Mathematical Logic at Harvard. During the next ten years he continued to attack metaphysical realism and to develop his own views of truth and rationality. He had come to regard philosophy as a total view of the human condition, rather than as a series of piecemeal arguments and refutations of authors and texts. The

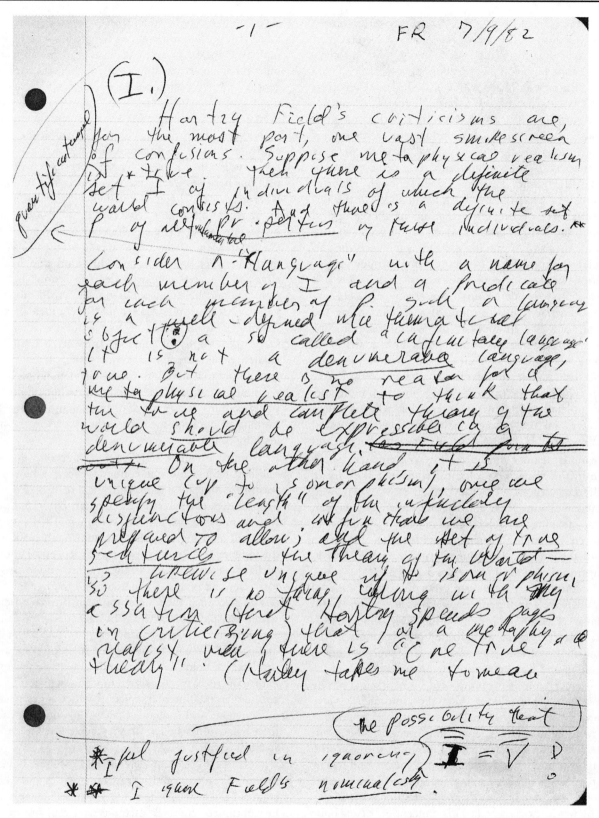

Pages from Putnam's notebook in which he deals with criticism of Reason, Truth and History *(Collection of Hilary Putnam)*

-2-

that this is so in an
ordinary language, with ~~the~~
not only denumerability, but
even with vagueness. But
this is totally unreasonable:
Metaphysical realists have always
thought in terms of an ideal
language, one whose structure
corresponds to "the" "true nature of
the world".

II : The most substantive — but
also the most amazing — idea
in Halsey's paper is the suggestion
that a realist of any kind, can
also be a disquotationalist.

This ~~idea~~ is totally wrong. to
see why, assume that there are no
objective epistemic — norms. (this is fair, because Field's
whole claim is that a realist can consistently
be a relativist about these,) in particular
what we say is it "right" or
"wrong" in the sense of being
"warrantedly assertible" or "justified"
in any objective sense or is it what
seems as what are seen more
than mere noise (or subvocalization)
with a certain causal history and
certain effects, perhaps, but

↓ is he going back on his
own correspondence theory?

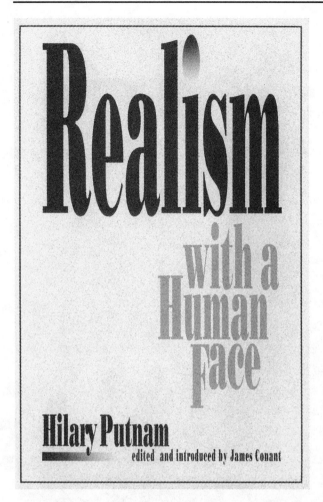

Dust jacket for a 1990 collection of Putnam's essays on metaphysics, ethics, aesthetics, and various American philosophers (Richland County Public Library)

titles of two of his ensuing books, *The Many Faces of Realism* (1987) and *Realism with a Human Face* (1990), reflect his attempt to point to the human context within which all philosophical discussion takes place and to advocate tolerance of norm-governed discourse that is not susceptible to materialistic or "scientistic" reductions.

Putnam's best-known challenge to the metaphysical realist outlook is the chapter "Brains in a Vat" in his *Reason, Truth and History* (1981). Here he says that the realist who is committed to the thesis that there are no epistemic constraints on concepts of reality or truth must also accept the possibility of a gap between what reality is and what it is taken to be. This skeptical possibility is dramatized by a thought experiment in which all human beings are disembodied brains in a vat hooked up to a sophisticated computer that simulates their experience of the world.

Putnam attacks metaphysical realism indirectly by advancing the claim that it is impossible that all people are brains in a vat: on the hypothesis that all people were brains in a vat, they could not really refer to external objects, since they would have no information-carrying causal connection with real trees or real stones or real vats; at best, they would have such a causal connection with events in the computer. Thus, when a brain in a vat says, "There is an apple," the sentence does not mean that there is an apple, since its word *apple* does not refer to apples; and when it says, "I am a brain in a vat," the sentence does not mean that it is a brain in a vat, since its word *vat* does not refer to vats. It follows that if one is oneself a brain in a vat, then the sentence "There is an apple" in one's own language does not mean that there is an apple, and so forth. But–and this is the step in Putnam's argument that has proved most controversial–any view that implies that a sentence *S* does not mean that S, for the great majority of sentences S in a language, is self-refuting. Putnam calls the argument a "transcendental" one in a loosely Kantian sense: it follows from the conditions of reference–which are also the conditions of thought, according to Putnam–that all people cannot be brains in a vat.

Many philosophers believe that Putnam's argument involves some semantic sleight of hand, but no consensus as to its validity has emerged. In a discussion Putnam remarked that the real point of the argument is to illustrate the "alienated" nature of metaphysical realists' ways of looking at the world. Notions such as the brains in a vat, or Descartes's suggestion that one is continually being deceived by an "evil demon," have traditionally been taken to pose deep epistemological and metaphysical problems. These notions, Putnam says, are based on the idea that one can "step outside of" one's skin and see oneself and one's situation from an objective "God's-eye view"; but people are not God. Philosophers cannot step outside the human situation any more than other human beings can. Even if Putnam's argument is not foolproof, it serves to make clear the worldview that is entailed by realism.

Putnam has argued that the collapse of the absolutist perspective in epistemology and metaphysics makes it possible to affirm the genuineness of norm-governed moral and political discourse. If the concepts of truth and objectivity are not defined in terms of some relationship to objects independent of the mind but are linked to human evaluation and deliberation, then the way is open to construe moral and political claims as "objective" and "truthful" in their own right. Analytic philosophers have historically looked down on ethics and politics as areas where conjecture and speculation abound but no solid "results" are to be had; without denying the differences between the sciences and subjects such as ethics and politics, Putnam points out that the absolute distinction with respect to claims to truth and objectivity is no longer tenable. The "hard" sciences themselves are normative through and through, he points out: the conclusions that are reached as to what theories to adopt or even what questions to pose are influenced by the values and belief systems of scientists, and this process is not much different from what goes on in moral and political discourse. Putnam has turned to Jürgen Habermas's theory of "ideal communication" as a way to show how moral objectivity might be attained in a modern society that is admittedly subjectivist in character. Giovanna Borradori's *The American Philosopher: Conversations with Quine, Davidson, Putnam, Nozick, Danto, Rorty, Cavell, MacIntyre, and Kuhn* (1994) includes an account by Putnam of his encounters with Habermas's work and Continental thought in general.

In the discussion with Borradori, Putnam explains that his abandonment of the absolutist approach to epistemology and metaphysics led him to a newfound appreciation for American pragmatists such as Charles Sanders Peirce, John Dewey, and, especially, William James. Putnam has written several articles and a book, *Pragmatism: An Open Question* (1995), on the pragmatists. While he is critical of them—he clearly disagrees with their theories of truth, for example—he thinks that they represent a worldview to which returning would be worthwhile now that materialistic and scientistic views such as naturalized epistemology and functionalism are no longer widely accepted. In particular, he finds James's views on perception useful in dismantling what he calls an "interface conception of the mind," which holds that people do not perceive the world directly but only through the filter of sense-impressions or mental representations. Putnam uses James and more-recent "direct" realist theories of perception such as John McDowell's to illustrate a return to what he calls a "philosophy of the common man," a conception of philosophy that does justice to how ordinary people experience the world. Putnam quotes approvingly from John Wisdom that such a return would mark a "journey from the familiar to the familiar," a goal to which he believes modern philosophy should aspire.

Putnam has connected the idea of the return of philosophy to common experience with an interest in religious experience as depicted by James, Wittgenstein, and Søren Kierkegaard and with the recovery of his own Judaism. Borradori notes in the introduction to her interview with Putnam that he traces the moral image of "equality among human beings" back through Immanuel Kant and Jean-Jacques Rousseau to the biblical tradition. This Judaic contribution to Western civilization is indicative of a commitment to one's fellow human beings and belies the relativistic tendencies of much French poststructuralism and even "postanalytical" thinkers in the United States such as Rorty. Putnam believes that his new religious outlook accords with his idea that reality can be "taken" in more than one way, as well as with his belief–similar to Dewey's–that pluralism and experimentalism can only be beneficial to humanity.

Since the publication of his "Comments and Replies" in *Reading Putnam* (1994), edited by Peter Clark and Bob Hale, Putnam has renounced the idea that truth can be identified with "idealized rational acceptability." He explains this change in his position in detail in his papers "Pragmatism" (1995) and "Pragmatism and Realism" (1996) and his book *The Threefold Cord: Mind, Body and World* (1999). But his arguments that truth is sometimes verification-transcendent do not amount to a return to "metaphysical realism," because he retains what he considers two important insights of pragmatism: that reality cannot be completely described in any one "language game," not even the mythical language game of "completed science" (antimonism); and that the existence of some "verification-transcendent" truths does not mean that all truth is verification-transcendent.

Hilary Putnam retired in June 2000. Throughout his fifty-year career he embodied the principle of "realism with a human face." He is known by colleagues and students for his unaffected approach to all, regardless of academic rank, and for his enthusiasm for real philosophical discussion. The quotation from Rainer Maria Rilke's *Briefe an einen jungen Dichter* (1929; translated as *Letters to a Young Poet*, 1934) that he selected to preface *Realism with a Human Face* captures the spirit of Putnam's legacy to philosophy: "Be patient toward all that is unsolved in your heart and try to love the *questions themselves* like locked rooms and like books that are written in a very foreign tongue. . . . *Live* the questions now. Perhaps you will then gradually, without noticing it, live along some distant day into the answer."

Interview:

Giovanna Borradori, "Between the New Left and Judaism: Hilary Putnam," in her *The American Philosopher: Conversations with Quine, Davidson, Putnam, Nozick, Danto, Rorty, Cavell, MacIntyre, and Kuhn,* translated by Rosanna Crocitto (Chicago & London: University of Chicago Press, 1994), pp. 55–69.

References:

David L. Anderson, "What Is the Model-Theoretic Argument?" *Journal of Philosophy,* 90 (1993): 311–322;

George Bailey, "Putnam and Metaphysical Realism," *International Studies in Philosophy,* 15 (1983): 11–14;

Ann Michelle Baker, "Putnam on Truth: Metaphysical Realism vs. Kantian Constructivism," dissertation, University of Washington, 1990;

George Boolos, ed., *Meaning and Method: Essays in Honor of Hilary Putnam* (Cambridge & New York: Cambridge University Press, 1990);

Anthony Brueckner, "Brains in a Vat," *Journal of Philosophy,* 83 (1986): 148–167;

Brueckner, "Knowledge of Content and Knowledge of the World," *Philosophical Review,* 103 (1994): 327–343;

Brueckner, "Putnam's Model-Theoretic Argument against Metaphysical Realism," *Analysis,* 44 (1984): 134–141;

Peter Clark and Bob Hale, eds., *Reading Putnam* (Oxford & Cambridge, Mass.: Blackwell, 1994);

Tim Crane, "All the Difference in the World," *Philosophical Quarterly,* 41 (January 1991): 1–25;

John Koethe, "Putnam's Argument against Realism," *Philosophical Review,* 88 (1979): 92–99;

Alan Malachowski, "Metaphysical Realist Semantics: Some Moral Desiderata," *Philosophia,* 16 (1986): 167–174;

John Passmore, *Recent Philosophers* (La Salle, Ill.: Open Court, 1985), pp. 10, 75, 92–101, 104–107, 114–116, 127, 133, 144, 146, 153, 155, 157–158, 160, 163;

Andrew Pessin and Sanford Goldberg, eds., *The Twin Earth Chronicles: Twenty Years of Reflection on Hilary Putnam's "The Meaning of 'Meaning'"* (Armonk, N.Y.: M. E. Sharpe, 1996);

Philosophical Topics, special Putnam issue, 20 (Spring 1992);

W. V. Quine, *From a Logical Point of View: Nine Logico-Philosophical Essays,* revised edition (Cambridge, Mass.: Harvard University Press, 1980);

Michael Resnick, "You Can't Trust an Ideal Theory to Tell the Truth," *Philosophical Studies,* 52 (1987): 151–160;

Richard Rorty, *Philosophy and the Mirror of Nature* (Princeton: Princeton University Press, 1979);

Edward Shirley, "Putnam on Analyticity," *Philosophical Studies,* 24 (1972): 268–271;

James Stephens and Lilly-Marlene Russow, "Brains in Vats and the Internalist Perspective," *Australasian Journal of Philosophy,* 63 (1985): 205–212;

Edward Zemach, "Putnam's Theory on the Reference of Substance Terms," *Journal of Philosophy,* 73 (1976): 116–127.

W. V. Quine

(25 June 1908 – 25 December 2000)

Roger F. Gibson Jr.
Washington University, St. Louis

BOOKS: *A System of Logistic* (Cambridge, Mass.: Harvard University Press, 1934);

Mathematical Logic (New York: Norton, 1940; revised edition, Cambridge, Mass.: Harvard University Press, 1951);

Elementary Logic (Boston & New York: Ginn, 1941; revised edition, New York: Harper & Row, 1965);

O sentido da nova lógica (São Paulo: Martins, 1944);

Methods of Logic (New York: Holt, 1950; revised, 1959; revised and enlarged edition, New York: Holt, Rinehart & Winston, 1972; revised and enlarged again, Cambridge, Mass.: Harvard University Press, 1982);

From a Logical Point of View: Nine Logico-Philosophical Essays (Cambridge, Mass.: Harvard University Press, 1953; revised, 1961);

Word and Object (Cambridge, Mass.: Technology Press of the Massachusetts Institute of Technology, 1960);

Set Theory and Its Logic (Cambridge, Mass.: Belknap Press of Harvard University Press, 1963; revised, 1969);

The Ways of Paradox, and Other Essays (New York: Random House, 1966; revised and enlarged edition, Cambridge, Mass.: Harvard University Press, 1976);

Selected Logic Papers (New York: Random House, 1966; enlarged edition, Cambridge, Mass.: Harvard University Press, 1995);

Ontological Relativity, and Other Essays (New York: Columbia University Press, 1969);

The Web of Belief, by Quine and J. S. Ullian (New York: Random House, 1970; revised, 1978);

Philosophy of Logic (Englewood Cliffs, N.J.: Prentice-Hall, 1970; revised edition, Cambridge, Mass.: Harvard University Press, 1986);

The Roots of Reference (La Salle, Ill.: Open Court, 1974);

Theories and Things (Cambridge, Mass.: Harvard University Press, 1981);

Saggi Filosofici, 1970–1981, edited and translated by Michele Leonelli (Rome: Armando, 1982);

The Time of My Life: An Autobiography (Cambridge, Mass.: MIT Press, 1985);

Quiddities: An Intermittently Philosophical Dictionary (Cambridge, Mass.: Belknap Press of Harvard University Press, 1987);

La scienza e i dati di senso, edited and translated by Leonelli (Rome: Armando, 1987);

The Logic of Sequences: A Generalization of "Principia Mathematica" (New York: Garland, 1990);

Pursuit of Truth (Cambridge, Mass.: Harvard University Press, 1990; revised, 1992);

From Stimulus to Science (Cambridge, Mass.: Harvard University Press, 1995).

OTHER: "Os Estados Unidos e o ressurgimento da Logica," in *Vida intellectual nos Estados Unidos,* volume 2, edited by A. C. Pacheco e Silva (São Paulo: Union Cultural Brasil–Estados Unidos, 1946), pp. 267–286;

"The Ordered Pair in Number Theory," in *Structure, Method, and Meaning: Essays in Honor of Henry M. Sheffer,* edited by Paul Henle, Horace M. Kallen, and Susanne K. Langer (New York: Liberal Arts Press, 1951), pp. 84–87;

Joseph T. Clark, *Conventional Logic and Modern Logic: A Prelude to Transition,* preface by Quine (Woodstock, Md.: Woodstock College Press, 1952);

"Logical Truth," in *American Philosophers at Work: The Philosophic Scene in the United States,* edited by Sidney Hook (New York: Criterion, 1956), pp. 121–134;

"The Philosophical Bearing of Modern Logic," in *Philosophy in the Mid-Century: A Survey,* volume 1: *Logic and Philosophy of Science,* edited by Raymond Klibansky (Florence: La Nuova Italia, 1958), pp. 3–4;

"Le Mythe de la signification," in *La Philosophie Analytique,* Cahiers de Royaumont, no. 4 (Paris: Minuit, 1962), pp. 139–169;

W. V. Quine (photograph © by K. Kelly Wise)

"Thoughts on Reading Father Owens," in *Proceedings of the VII Inter-American Congress of Philosophy,* volume 1 (Quebec: Presses de l'Université Laval, 1967), pp. 60–63;

"Introductory Notes to Bertrand Russell's 'Mathematical Logic as Based on the Theory of Types,'" "Introductory Notes to Alfred North Whitehead's and Bertrand Russell's 'Incomplete Symbols: Description,'" and "Introductory Notes to Moses Schonfinkel's 'On the Building Blocks of Mathematical Logic,'" in *From Frege to Gödel: A Source Book in Mathematical Logic, 1879–1931,* edited by Jean van Heijenoort (Cambridge, Mass.: Harvard University Press, 1967), pp. 150–152, 216–217, 355–357;

"Comments on Fred Sommers' 'On a Fregean Dogma'" and "Three Remarks," in *Problems in the Philosophy of Mathematics,* edited by Imre Lakatos, International Colloquium in the Philosophy of Science, Bedford College, 1965, Proceedings, 1: Studies in Logic and the Foundations of Mathematics (Amsterdam: North-Holland, 1967), pp. 47–62, 70–71;

"Discussion-Comments on Grover Maxwell's 'Scientific Methodology and the Causal Theory of Perception,'" "Discussion-Comments on Wolfgang Yourgrau's 'A Budget of Paradoxes in Physics,'" and "Discussion-Comments on Roman Suszko's 'Formal Logic and the Development of Knowledge,'" in *Problems in the Philosophy of Science,* edited by Lakatos and Alan Musgrave, International Colloquium in the Philosophy of Science, Bedford College, 1965, Proceedings, 3: Studies in Logic and the Foundations of Mathematics (Amsterdam: North-Holland, 1968), pp. 161–163, 200–210, 223;

David Lewis, *Convention: A Philosophical Study,* foreword by Quine (Cambridge, Mass.: Harvard University Press, 1969);

"Stimulus and Meaning," in *The Isenberg Memorial Lecture Series, 1965–1966,* edited by Ronald Suter (East Lansing: Michigan State University Press, 1969), pp. 39–61;

"Grades of Theoreticity," in *Experience and Theory,* edited by Lawrence Foster and J. W. Swanson (Amherst: University of Massachusetts Press / London: Duckworth, 1970), pp. 1–17;

"Predicate-Functor Logic," in *Proceedings of the Second Scandinavian Logic Symposium,* edited by J. E. Fenstad (Amsterdam: North-Holland, 1971), pp. 309–315;

"Remarks for a Memorial Symposium," in *Bertrand Russell,* edited by David Pears (New York: Doubleday, 1972), pp. 1–5;

"On Popper's Negative Methodology," in *The Philosophy of Karl Popper,* edited by Paul Arthur Schilpp, The Library of Living Philosophers, volume 14 (La Salle, Ill.: Open Court, 1974), pp. 218–220;

"The Nature of Natural Knowledge" and "Mind and Verbal Dispositions," in *Mind and Language,* edited by Samuel Guttenplan (Oxford: Clarendon Press / New York: Oxford University Press, 1975), pp. 67–81, 83–95;

"A Letter to Mr. Ostermann," in *The Owl of Minerva: Philosophers on Philosophy,* edited by Charles J. Bontempo and S. Jack Odell (New York: McGraw-Hill, 1975), pp. 227–230;

"Comments," in Norbert Wiener, *Collected Works, with Commentaries,* volume 1, edited by P. Masani (Cambridge, Mass.: MIT Press, 1976), pp. 225, 233;

"Whither Physical Objects?" in *Essays in Memory of Imre Lakatos,* edited by R. S. Cohen, Paul K. Feyerabend, and Marx W. Wartofsky, Boston Studies in the Philosophy of Science, volume 39 (Dordrecht, Netherlands & Boston: Reidel, 1976), pp. 497–504;

"Homage to Yehoshua Bar-Hillel," by Quine, Noam Chomsky, Carl G. Hempel, Sidney Morgenbesser, and Ernest Nagel, in *Language in Focus: Foundations, Methods and Systems. Essays in Memory of Yehoshua Bar-Hillel,* edited by Asa Kasher, Boston Studies in the Philosophy of Science, volume 43 (Dordrecht, Netherlands & Boston: Reidel, 1976), pp. xiii–xviii;

"Facts of the Matter," in *American Philosophy from Edwards to Quine,* edited by Robert W. Shahan and Kenneth R. Merrill (Norman: University of Oklahoma Press, 1977), pp. 176–196;

"Comments," in *Meaning and Use: Papers Presented at the Second Jerusalem Philosophical Encounter, April 1976,* edited by Avishai Margalit (Dordrecht, Netherlands & Boston: Reidel / Jerusalem: Magnes, 1979), pp. 21–22;

"The Variable and Its Place in Reference," in *Philosophical Subjects: Essays Presented to P. F. Strawson,* edited by Zak van Straaten (Oxford: Clarendon Press, 1980), pp. 164–173;

"Grammar, Truth, and Logic," in *Philosophy and Grammar: Papers on the Occasion of the Quincentennial of Uppsala University,* edited by Stig Kanger and Sven Öhman (Dordrecht, Netherlands & Boston: Reidel, 1981), pp. 17–28;

"Reply to Chihara's 'Quine and the Confirmational Paradoxes'" and "Reply to Stroud's 'The Significance of Naturalized Epistemology,'" in *The Foundations of Analytic Philosophy,* edited by Peter A. French, Theodore E. Uehling Jr., and Howard K. Wettstein, Midwest Studies in Philosophy, volume 6 (Morris: University of Minnesota Press, 1981), pp. 453–454, 473–475;

"The Pragmatist's Place in Empiricism," in *Pragmatism: Its Sources and Prospects,* edited by Robert J. Mulvaney and Philip M. Zeltner (Columbia: University of South Carolina Press, 1981), pp. 21–39;

"Gegenstand und Beobachtung," in *Kant oder Hegel? Über Formen der Begründung in der Philosophie,* edited by Dieter Henrich (Stuttgart: Klein-Cotta, 1983), pp. 412–422;

"What I Believe," in *What I Believe: Thirteen Eminent People of Our Time Argue for Their Philosophy of Life,* edited by Mark Booth (London: Firethorn Press, 1984; New York: Crossroad, 1984), pp. 69–75;

"Sticks and Stones; or, The Ins and Outs of Existence," in *On Nature,* edited by Leroy S. Rouner (Notre Dame, Ind.: University of Notre Dame Press, 1984), pp. 13–26;

"Events and Reification," in *Actions and Events: Perspectives on the Philosophy of Donald Davidson,* edited by Ernest Lepore and Brian P. McLaughlin (Oxford & New York: Blackwell, 1985), pp. 162–171;

"Autobiography of W. V. Quine" and replies to critics, in *The Philosophy of W. V. Quine,* edited by Lewis Edwin Hahn and Paul Arthur Schilpp, The Library of Living Philosophers, volume 18 (La Salle, Ill.: Open Court, 1986; revised and enlarged edition, Chicago: Open Court, 1998);

"Peano as Logician," in *Celebrazione in memoria di Giuseppe Peano,* edited by Alberto Conte (Turin: Universita, 1986), pp. 33–43;

"Books That Mattered," in *Harvard Guide to Influential Books,* edited by C. Maury Devine, Claudia M.

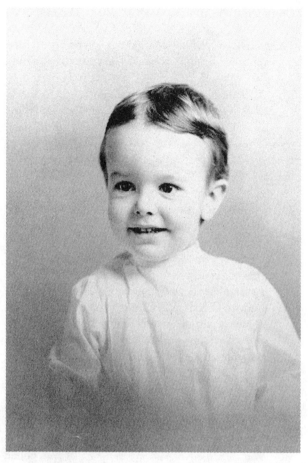

Quine aged two years, nine months (photograph courtesy of Margaret Quine McGovern and Douglas Quine)

Dissel, and Kim D. Parrish (New York: Harper & Row, 1986), pp. 204–205;

"Symbols," in *The Oxford Companion to the Mind,* edited by Richard L. Gregory (Oxford & New York: Oxford University Press, 1987), pp. 763–765;

"Respuesta a Garcia," "Respuesta a Villanueva," "Respuesta a Calvo," "Respuesta a Julián Garrido," "Respuesta a Moulines," "Respuesta a Manuel Garrido," "Respuesta a Pérez," "Respuesta a Orayen," "Respuesta a Quesada," "Respuesta a Acero," and "Respuesta a Mosterin," in *Symposium Quine,* edited by Juan José Acero and Tomás Calvo Martinez (Granada: Universidad de Granada, 1987), pp. 35–36, 49, 68–70, 83, 102–103, 115, 131–132, 153–155, 175–176, 205–207, 223;

"Mind, Brain, and Behavior," in *Progress in Behavioral Studies,* edited by Aaron J. Brownstein, volume 1 (Hillsdale, N.J.: Erlbaum, 1989), pp. 1–6;

"Frege, Gottlob," in *Collier's Encyclopedia,* volume 10 (New York: Macmillan / London & New York: Collier, 1990), pp. 362–363;

"Three Indeterminacies," "Comment on Berger," "Comment on Bergstrom," "Comment on Creath," "Comment on Haack," "Comment on Hacking," "Comment on Koppelberg," "Comment on Lauener," "Comment on Marcus," "Comment on Orenstein," "Comment on Parsons," "Comment on Quinton," "Comment on Strawson," "Comment on Stroud," and "Comment on Ullian," in *Perspectives on Quine,* edited by Robert B. Barrett and Roger F. Gibson Jr. (Oxford: Blackwell, 1990), pp. 1–16, 36–37, 53–54, 67, 80, 96–97, 110, 128, 142–143, 158, 176, 198–199, 212, 229, 244, 271–272, 291–293, 309, 319–320, 334–335, 347;

"Let Me Accentuate the Positive," in *Reading Rorty: Critical Responses to "Philosophy and the Mirror of Nature" (and Beyond),* edited by Alan R. Malachowski (Oxford & Cambridge, Mass.: Blackwell, 1990), pp. 117–119;

"The Phoneme's Long Shadow," in *Emics and Etics: The Insider/Outsider Debate,* edited by Thomas N. Headland, Kenneth L. Pike, and Marvin Harris, Frontiers of Anthropology, volume 7 (Newbury Park, Cal.: Sage, 1990), pp. 164–167;

"The Elusiveness of Reference," in *Sprache, Theorie und Wirklichkeit,* edited by Michael Sukale (Frankfurt am Main: Peter Lang, 1990), pp. 13–24;

"Truth," in *Philosophical Problems Today / Problèmes philosophiques d'aujourd'hui,* edited by Guttorm Fløistad, volume 1 (Dordrecht, Netherlands & Boston: Kluwer, 1994), pp. 1–20;

"Comment," in *Logic, Language, and the Structure of Scientific Theories,* edited by Wesley C. Salmon and Gereon Wolters (Pittsburgh: University of Pittsburgh / Constance: Universitätsverlag Konstanz, 1994), pp. 345–351;

"The Flowering of Thought in Language," in *Thought and Language,* edited by John Preston (Cambridge & New York: Cambridge University Press, 1997), pp. 171–176;

"I, You and It: An Epistemological Triangle," in *Knowledge, Language, and Logic: Questions for Quine,* edited by Alex Orenstein and Petr Kotatko, Boston Studies in the Philosophy of Science, volume 210 (Dordrecht, Netherlands & Boston: Kluwer, 2000), pp. 1–6.

SELECTED PERIODICAL PUBLICATIONS–
UNCOLLECTED: "A Note on Nicod's Postulate," *Mind,* 41 (1932): 345–350;

"A Theorem in the Calculus of Classes," *Journal of the London Mathematical Society,* 8 (April 1933): 89–95;

"Concepts of Negative Degree," *Proceedings of the National Academy of Sciences,* 22 (1936): 40–45;

"On the Axiom of Reducibility," *Mind,* 45 (October 1936): 498–500;

"A Theory of Classes Presupposing No Canons of Type," *Proceedings of the National Academy of Sciences,* 22 (1936): 320–326;

"A Reinterpretation of Schönfinkel's Logical Operators," *Bulletin of the American Mathematical Society,* 42 (1936): 87–89;

"Toward a Calculus of Concepts," *Journal of Symbolic Logic,* 1 (1936): 2–25;

"On Derivability" and "On Cantor's Theorem," *Journal of Symbolic Logic,* 2 (1937): 113–119, 120–124;

"Relations and Reason," *Technology Review,* 41 (1939): 299–301, 324–332;

"Russell's Paradox and Others," *Technology Review,* 44 (1941–1942): 16–17;

"Reply to Professor Ushenko," *Journal of Philosophy,* 39 (25 January 1942): 68–71;

"On Existence Conditions for Elements and Classes," *Journal of Symbolic Logic,* 7 (1942): 157–159;

"On Decidability and Completeness," *Synthese,* 7 (1948–1949): 441–446;

"On Natural Deduction," *Journal of Symbolic Logic,* 15 (1950): 93–102;

"A Simplification of Games in Extensive Form," by Quine, J. C. C. McKinsey, and W. D. Krcntcl, *Duke Mathematical Journal,* 18 (1951): 885–900;

"On the Consistency of 'New Foundations,'" *Proceedings of the National Academy of Sciences,* 37 (1951): 538–540;

"Some Theorems of Definability and Decidability," by Quine and Alonzo Church, *Journal of Symbolic Logic,* 17 (September 1952): 179–187;

"On Reduction to a Symmetric Relation," by Quine and William Craig, *Journal of Symbolic Logic,* 17 (September 1952): 188;

"The Problem of Simplifying Truth Functions," *American Mathematical Monthly,* 59 (October 1952): 521–531;

"A Way to Simplify Truth Functions," *American Mathematical Monthly,* 62 (November 1955): 627–631;

"On Formulas with Valid Cases," *Journal of Symbolic Logic,* 21 (June 1956): 148;

"Unification of Universes in Set Theory," *Journal of Symbolic Logic,* 21 (September 1956): 267–279;

"A Basis for Number Theory in Finite Classes," *Bulletin of the American Mathematical Society,* 67 (July 1961): 391–392;

"On Ordinals," by Quine and Hao Wang, *Bulletin of the American Mathematical Society,* 70 (March 1964): 297–298;

"Les Frontières de la théorie logique," translated by Jacques Derrida and Roger Martin, *Etudes Philosophiques,* 19 (April–June 1964): 191–208;

"On the Reasons for Indeterminacy of Translation," *Journal of Philosophy,* 67 (26 March 1970): 178–183;

"Reply to D. A. Martin," *Journal of Philosophy,* 67 (23 April 1970): 247–248;

"Comments on Donald Davidson," *Synthese,* 27 (July–August 1974): 325–329;

"Comments on Michael Dummett," *Synthese,* 27 (July–August 1974): 399;

"On Empirically Equivalent Systems of the World," *Erkenntnis,* 9 (1975): 313–328;

"A Closer Look," *Journal of Philosophy,* 74 (July 1977): 415–416;

"Reply to Lycan and Pappas," *Philosophia,* 7 (July 1978): 637–638;

"Comments on W. Newton-Smith," *Analysis,* 39 (1979): 66–67;

"On Not Learning to Quantify," *Journal of Philosophy,* 76 (August 1979): 429–430;

"Cognitive Meaning," *Monist,* 62 (1979): 129–142;

"Clauses and Classes," *Bulletin d'Information, Société Française de Logique, Methodologie et Philosophie des Sciences,* 6 (1979): 23–39;

"Sellars on Behaviorism, Language, and Meaning," *Pacific Philosophical Quarterly,* 61 (January–April 1980): 26–30;

"Burdick's Attitudes," *Synthese,* 52 (1982): 231–232;

"Respuestas," *Analisis Filosófico* (Buenos Aires), 2 (1982): 159–173;

"Donald Cary Williams," *Proceedings and Addresses of the American Philosophical Association,* 57 (1983): 245–248;

"Ontology and Ideology Revisited," *Journal of Philosophy,* 80 (1983): 499–502;

"Relativism and Absolutism," *Monist,* 67 (1984): 293–296;

"Carnap's Positivistic Travail," *Fundamenta Scientiae,* 5 (1985): 325–333;

"Carnap," *Yale Review,* 76 (Winter 1987): 226–230;

"Indeterminacy of Translation Again," *Journal of Philosophy,* 84 (1987): 5–10;

"A Comment on Agassi's Remarks," *Zeitschrift für Allgemeine Wissenschaftstheories / Journal for General Philosophy of Science,* 19 (1988): 117–118;

"To a Graduate Student in Philosophy," *Proceedings and Addresses of the American Philosophical Association,* supplement, 62 (September 1988): 258–259;

"Elementary Proof That Some Angles Cannot Be Trisected by Ruler and Compass," *Mathematics Magazine,* 63 (April 1990): 95–105;

"Two Dogmas in Retrospect," *Canadian Journal of Philosophy,* 21 (1991): 265–274;

"Structure and Nature," *Journal of Philosophy,* 89 (January 1992): 5–9;

Quine (seated) with his parents, Cloyd Robert and Harriet Ellis Van Orman Quine, and his older brother, Robert
(photograph courtesy of Margaret Quine McGovern and Douglas Quine)

"Hobbling the Hawkers," *Common Knowledge*, 1 (Spring 1992): 17–18;

"Words Are All We Have to Go On," *TLS: Times Literary Supplement*, no. 4657 (3 July 1992): 8;

"Commensurability and the Alien Mind," *Common Knowledge*, 1 (Winter 1992): 1–2;

"Replies to Professor Riska's Eight Questions," *Filozofia*, 47 (1992): 501–503;

"In Praise of Observation Sentences: With Appendix on Neural Intake," *Journal of Philosophy*, 90 (1993): 107–116;

"Promoting Extensionality," *Synthese*, 98 (1994): 143–151;

"Indeterminacy without Tears," *Cannocchiale*, 1–2 (1994): 57–58;

"Responses," *Inquiry*, 37 (December 1994): 495–505;

"Assuming Objects," *Theoria*, 60 (1994): 226–231;

"Exchange between Donald Davidson and W. V. Quine Following Davidson's Lecture," *Theoria*, 60 (1994): 226–231;

"Naturalism; or, Living within One's Means," *Dialectica*, 49 (1995): 251–261;

"Progress on Two Fronts," *Journal of Philosophy*, 93 (1996): 159–163;

"Response to Leemon McHenry," *Process Studies*, 26 (Spring–Summer 1997): 13–14;

"Free Logic, Description, and Virtual Classes," *Dialogue*, 36 (Winter 1997): 101–108;

"Response to Hintikka," "Response to Smart," "Response to Haack," "Response to Orenstein," "Response to Lewis and Holdcroft," "Response to Laugier," and "Response to Lauener," *Revue Internationale de Philosophie*, 51 (December 1997): 567–582.

W. V. Quine was one of the most important analytic philosophers of the twentieth century, with contributions rivaling those of Bertrand Russell, Ludwig Wittgenstein, and Rudolf Carnap. His early work was strongly influenced by Russell and Carnap, but by 1950 he had begun to develop a distinct philosophy based on his long-term commitments to naturalism and extensionalism. As a naturalist, Quine believed that science is common sense become self-conscious, and philosophy is science become self-conscious. Philosophy, therefore, has no special knowledge with which to justify science; if science needs a justification it will have to come from within. As an extensionalist, Quine held that

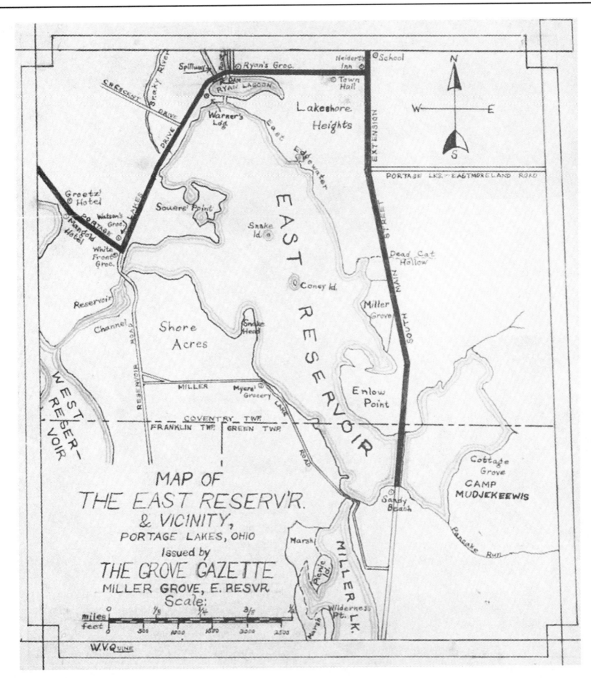

Map drawn and blueprinted by Quine in 1923 for sale to his neighbors (from W. V. Quine,
The Time of My Life: An Autobiography, *1985)*

to state a theory or explanation in intensional idiom is to block the road to inquiry; to state it in extensional idiom is necessary, though not sufficient for understanding. Quine's naturalism is the view that it is up to natural science to determine what exists and how one knows what exists. His extensionalism is the view that a necessary condition for understanding a theory is that the theory be stated in an extensional language, that is, a language in which terms that refer to the same objects can be substituted for one another without altering the truth or falsity of the containing sentence. For example, the true sentence "Mark Twain was from Missouri" is extensional, since *Mark Twain* can be replaced by *Samuel Clemens* to yield another true sentence, "Samuel Clemens was from Missouri." On the other hand, "Huck believes that Mark Twain was a writer" is intensional, since, if Huck does not know that Mark Twain and Samuel Clemens were the same person, that sentence could be true but "Huck believes that Samuel Clemens is a writer" could be false. Quine asserted that the bulk

Quine with his first wife, Naomi Clayton Quine, in 1932

of his mature philosophy consists of corollaries to naturalism and extensionalism; in this sense his philosophy is systematic.

Willard Van Orman Quine was born in Akron, Ohio, on 25 June 1908, the second of two children of Cloyd Robert Quine, who ran a small machine shop, and Harriet Ellis Van Orman Quine, an elementary-school teacher; Quine's brother, Robert, was seventeen months older than he. As a child Quine displayed a keen interest in maps, geography, and faraway places. By the time he graduated from West High School in 1926, he had also acquired an interest in English word origins and languages. These early interests proved lifelong: during the next seventy-four years Quine traveled to six continents and more than 110 countries, published reviews of atlases and dictionaries, and lectured in English, French, German, Italian, Spanish, and Portuguese.

Quine entered Oberlin College in the fall of 1926, majoring in mathematics. His real interest was in the new mathematical philosophy then being developed by philosophers such as Russell and Alfred North Whitehead; no one on the faculty at Oberlin knew modern logic, but the head of the mathematics department arranged for Quine to do his honors reading on the subject. The reading list included John Venn's *Symbolic Logic* (1881), Giuseppe Peano's *Formulaire de mathématiques* (Mathematical Formulary, 1894–1908), Louis Couturat's *L'Algèbre de la logique* (1905; translated as *The Algebra of Logic,* 1914), Cassius Jackson Keyser's *Mathematical Philosophy, a Study of Fate and Freedom: Lectures for Educated Laymen* (1922), Russell's *The Principles of Mathematics* (1903), Whitehead's *An Introduction to Mathematics* (1911), and Whitehead and Russell's seminal *Principia Mathematica* (1910–1913). In a psychology course Quine read John B. Watson's *Psychology from the Standpoint of a Behaviorist* (1919); he later developed a behaviorist theory of language acquisition.

Quine graduated summa cum laude in 1930. He wanted to study under Whitehead, who had moved from England to teach at Harvard University. Admitted to graduate study in philosophy and granted a $400 tuition scholarship, Quine hitchhiked with his fiancée, Naomi Clayton, to Cambridge, Massachusetts. The couple were married after Quine successfully petitioned the university for permission to do so without losing his scholarship.

As a newly married graduate student in the midst of the Great Depression, Quine, who had studied little philosophy at Oberlin, pushed himself to complete his doctorate in two years. He received his M.A. in the spring of 1931; in the summer he began his dissertation, "The Logic of Sequences: A Generalization of 'Principia Mathematica,'" under the direction of Whitehead. He delivered the completed dissertation to Whitehead's apartment at 9:00 P.M. on 1 April 1932—three hours before the deadline. A few weeks later he received his Ph.D.

On his graduation the university awarded Quine a Frederick Sheldon Traveling Fellowship. During the summer he reworked his dissertation; when he and his wife departed for Europe in August, he left the manuscript with one of his professors, C. I. Lewis, who had agreed to oversee its publication by the Harvard University Press. The Quines spent five months in Vienna, where Quine attended Moritz Schlick's lectures and some meetings of Schlick's discussion group, the logical positivist Vienna Circle; he met A. J. Ayer, Kurt Gödel, Karl Menger, Hans Hahn, and Hans Reichenbach. While in Vienna, he learned from Lewis that publication of his book had been delayed because of typographical difficulties; Lewis thought that Quine should resolve

Quine in the mid 1930s

the notation questions himself. In Prague, where he attended lectures by Carnap, Quine received a cable from Whitehead informing him that he had been elected to the newly established Society of Fellows at Harvard; as a junior fellow he would have three years of financial support with no duties. In Warsaw, Quine attended lectures by the logicians Alfred Tarski, Stanisław Leśniewski, and Jan Łukasiewicz; he also met the logicians Tadeusz Kotarbiński, Kazimierz Ajdukiewicz, Kazimierz Kuratowski, and Bolesław Sobociński.

The delayed publication of his first book allowed Quine to incorporate the latest developments in logic that he learned about in Warsaw. *A System of Logistic* appeared in March 1934, after his return to Harvard (the original dissertation was published in 1990). The Quines' first child, Elizabeth, was born on 28 August 1935. At the end of his term as a junior fellow in 1936

Quine began a three-year instructorship. A second daughter, Norma, was born on 25 May 1937.

Quine's next book, *Mathematical Logic,* was published in 1940. Like *A System of Logistic,* the work aimed to improve on the symbolic and mathematical logic developed in *Principia Mathematica.* In addition to clarifying and systematizing Whitehead and Russell's pioneering efforts, *Mathematical Logic* included more-recent advances in logic and set theory; among them was Gödel's incompleteness theorems, first published in 1931, which demonstrate that any system of formal logic rich enough to express arithmetic will include statements that are true but unprovable within that system. Quine proves the theorems again in the last chapter of his book.

In the summer of 1941 Quine was promoted to associate professor. That fall the logician J. Barkley

Quine (right) with his brother, Robert, during Quine's service in the navy during World War II (photograph courtesy of Margaret Quine McGovern and Douglas Quine)

Rosser telephoned Quine with the news that he had derived Cesare Burali-Forti's "paradox of ordinals" from Quine's *Mathematical Logic*. According to this paradox, no greatest ordinal number can exist, but the ordinal number of the series of ordinal numbers must be the greatest. Quine devised a way to block the paradox from arising, and a correction slip was inserted into the unsold copies of the book.

From May to September 1942 Quine was a visiting professor at the University of São Paulo in Brazil; he adapted his lectures, given in Portuguese, as *O sentido da nova lógica* (The Sense of the New Logic, 1944). The book covers the same ground as *Mathematical Logic* but includes the ad hoc emendations that block the derivation of the Burali-Forti paradox.

Quine entered the navy in October 1942 as a lieutenant. During most of his service he was engaged in radio intelligence work in Washington, D.C., as part of the Atlantic antisubmarine campaign. He was discharged in late 1945 with the rank of lieutenant commander and resumed teaching at Harvard in February 1946. He and his wife were divorced in 1947; on 2 September 1948 he married Marjorie Boynton, a teacher and former member of the Women Appointed for Voluntary Emergency Services (WAVES)–the naval

women's auxiliary–who had served under his command in Washington. Also in 1948 he was promoted to full professor and appointed a senior fellow of the Society of Fellows. A son, Douglas, was born on 20 December 1950.

Quine's next book, *Methods of Logic* (1950), is a sophisticated and frequently witty introductory textbook. A revised edition of *Mathematical Logic* appeared in 1951; it includes a more elegant solution to the problem of the Burali-Forti paradox that was discovered in 1949 by Hao Wang, who was then a student of Quine's.

In 1950 Quine had begun to contemplate writing a book of a more broadly philosophical character than any of his previous ones; but by 1952 he realized that such a work would take some years to complete. To make some of his ideas more widely accessible he published *From a Logical Point of View* (1953); the book is a collection of nine "logico-philosophical" essays, all but one of which had been published previously. Quine claimed that the title was suggested by his Harvard colleague Henry D. Aiken after they heard Harry Belafonte perform the calypso song "From a Logical Point of View" while they were out with their wives in a Greenwich Village nightclub. "On What There Is" (1948), "Two Dogmas of Empiricism" (1951), and

Quine and his second wife, Marjorie Boynton, on 2 September 1948, the day of their wedding in Meriden, Connecticut.
At left is her father, Augustus Boynton (photograph courtesy of Margaret Quine McGovern and Douglas Quine).

"New Foundations for Mathematical Logic" (1937) are considered classics of analytic philosophy; the first two essays have been anthologized in more than a dozen languages. *From a Logical Point of View* has sold more than forty thousand copies in English.

"Two Dogmas of Empiricism," originally published in *The Philosophical Review,* is particularly important. The "dogmas" are the analytic-synthetic distinction and epistemological reductionism. According to the former, declarative sentences can be divided into analytic sentences, which are true or false solely in virtue of the meanings of the words in them, and synthetic sentences, which are true or false in virtue of both the meanings of their words and how the world is. "No bachelor is married" is an example of a true analytic sentence; "No bachelor is happy" is an example of a false synthetic sentence. Epistemological reductionism holds that each synthetic sentence is associated with unique confirming and disconfirming experiential conditions. Thus, in principle, any synthetic statement about unobservable theoretical entities should be reducible to statements about observable entities. Logical positivists accepted both of these doctrines, along with the principle of verifiability; according to the latter, a sentence is

cognitively meaningful if, and only if, it is either empirically verifiable or analytic. They hoped to vindicate empiricism by showing that all meaningful synthetic sentences either possess precise experiential content or are reducible to sentences with such content. On the other hand, the sentences of logic and mathematics are analytic: they are necessarily true solely by virtue of the meanings of their terms. Quine rejects both "dogmas of empiricism." He rejects the analytic-synthetic distinction on the ground that it has never been clearly stated, and he rejects epistemological reductionism on the ground of "holism"—the view that not every sentence of a scientific theory has its own confirming and disconfirming experiential conditions. He does not, however, reject empiricism itself. A large part of his accomplishment is his systematic articulation and defense of an empiricism pruned of these two doctrines—an empiricism capable of accounting for knowledge not only of the external world but also of logic and mathematics.

Quine's final child, Margaret, was born on 1 February 1954. In 1956 Quine was appointed Edgar Pierce Professor of Philosophy. In 1960 he published the book for which he is best known: *Word and Object* virtually set the agendas for analytic metaphysics, epistemology,

Quine's daughters Elizabeth and Norma in 1949

and philosophy of language for decades after its publication. The problems Quine addresses in this 276-page book became the problems of the profession.

The opening paragraphs of the preface to *Word and Object* summarize Quine's concerns in the book:

> Language is a social art. In acquiring it we have to depend entirely on intersubjectively available cues as to what to say and when. Hence there is no justification for collating linguistic meanings, unless in terms of men's dispositions to respond overtly to socially observable stimulations. An effect of recognizing this limitation is that the enterprise of translation is found to be involved in a certain systematic indeterminacy; and this is the main theme of Chapter II.
>
> The indeterminacy of translation invests even the question what objects to construe a term true of. Studies of the semantics of reference consequently turn out to make sense only when directed upon substantially our language, from within. But we do remain free to reflect, thus parochially, on the development and structure of our own referential apparatus; and this I do in ensuing chapters. In so doing one encounters various anomalies and conflicts that are implicit in this apparatus (Chapter IV), and is moved to adopt remedies in the spirit of modern logic (Chapters V and VI). Clarity

also is perhaps gained on what we do when we impute existence, and what considerations may best guide such decisions; thus Chapter VII.

Quine asks the reader to imagine a field linguist faced with the task of translating, for the first time, the language of a remote tribe; he refers to this situation as "radical translation." A rabbit scurries by, and a native utters "Gavagai." Since the English-speaking linguist would utter "Lo, a rabbit" or, at least, would assent to the query "Rabbit?" under these circumstances, the linguist tentatively translates the native's "Gavagai" as "Lo, a rabbit." The linguist's hypothesis that the native's "Gavagai" and his own "Lo, a rabbit" are cognitively equivalent is an induction that can be tested in future settings where the native volunteers "Gavagai"—or, assuming that the linguist has caught on to the native expressions for assent and dissent, where the linguist can query the native with "Gavagai?" under various stimulus conditions. If the linguist discovers that the native would assent to and dissent from the query in just those circumstances where the linguist would do likewise for "Rabbit?" the linguist has good inductive evidence for the correctness of the translation.

Most sentences of a language such as English, however, are not tied directly to concurrent nonverbal stimuli, as "Gavagai" and "Lo, a rabbit" were assumed to be. Translating sentences that are remote from sensory stimuli requires the use of what Quine calls "analytical hypotheses," which, unlike "real" hypotheses, are not testable inductive generalizations. But analytical hypotheses are not arbitrary: they are chosen because they are believed to facilitate communication between users of the natives' tongue and the linguist. Quine maintains that nonequivalent analytical hypotheses might yield different translations of some native's sentence and that both translations might equally facilitate communication with the native. Quine's controversial thesis of the "indeterminacy of translation of sentences" claims that no one and only correct translation exists. A native's utterance might be translated on one hypothesis as "Pelicans are our half-brothers" and on another as "Pelicans are supernatural"; if both translations facilitate communication, they are equally correct. Quine does not think that the indeterminacy of translation of sentences presents a problem for translation; that is, he is arguing not that translation is impossible but that multiple translations are possible.

Quine maintains that radical translation reveals an "indeterminacy of translation of terms" or "inscrutability of reference." On the basis of his translation of "Gavagai" as "Lo, a rabbit," Quine says, the linguist cannot conclude that since *rabbit* is a concrete general term for rabbits in English, *gavagai* must be a concrete general term for rabbits in the native's language: the circumstances under which *gavagai* is warranted may include the presence of rabbits, undetached rabbit parts, and so on. Thus, depending on which analytical hypotheses the linguist adopts, *gavagai* can be equated to "rabbit," "undetached rabbit part," "instantiation of rabbithood," and so on. No one analytical hypothesis can be singled out as the correct one as long as all can be interwoven to effect smooth communication with the natives.

Quine's indeterminacy-of-translation thesis continues to generate philosophical debate, but it is by no means the only issue he treats in *Word and Object*. He also theorizes about the learning of sentences and the genesis of reference, explaining that for a language such as English, a child must learn to use a cluster of interrelated grammatical particles and constructions, such as plural endings, pronouns, numerals, the *is* of identity, *same* and *other,* and so on: "the contextual learning of these various particles goes on simultaneously, we may suppose, so that they are gradually adjusted to one another and a coherent pattern of usage is evolved matching that of society. The child scrambles up an intellectual chimney, supporting himself against each side by pressure against the others." Quine also argues for physicalism over phenomenalism and for extensionality over intensionality; he offers a behaviorist classification of sentences and a behaviorist conception of sentence meaning, which he calls "stimulus meaning"; he recommends measures for regimenting language so as to eliminate vagueness and ambiguity; he argues against assuming the existence of propositions and attributes; he rejects quantified modal logic and the essentialism it presupposes; and he argues for scientific realism over instrumentalism. One can make the case that no book published since 1960 has exerted more influence on analytic philosophy than has *Word and Object,* which went into its fifteenth printing in 1988.

In 1963 Quine published *Set Theory and Its Logic.* Three years later he brought out two collections, *Selected Logic Papers* and *The Ways of Paradox, and Other Essays.* Another collection, *Ontological Relativity, and Other Essays,* appeared in 1969. In 1970 he and J. S. Ullian coauthored *The Web of Belief,* a brief treatise on scientific method, and Quine published *Philosophy of Logic,* a revised version of lectures he had given at the Collège de France in May and June 1969.

Quine's dissatisfaction with having given "so brief and metaphorical an account" of the learning of language in *Word and Object* prompted him to write *The Roots of Reference* (1974), in which he provides a speculative account of how a child might acquire the referential apparatus of English by means of a series of grammatical transformations and irreducible leaps of analogy.

*Quine and the philosopher Rudolf Carnap
in New Mexico, 1949*

Quine's account is an idealization of this process. He understands quantification to be an encapsulation of this referential apparatus; thus he speculates on how a child might acquire the idiom of quantification. "By considering what steps could lead the small child or primitive man to quantification, rather than to the less tidy referential apparatus of actual English, we arrive at a psychogenetic reconstruction in skeletal outline. We approximate the essentials of the real psychogenesis of reference while avoiding inessential complications." Quantification theory construes the variable x in the expression "There is an x such that" to function as the pronoun *it,* insofar as the variable refers to an object for the rest of the sentence to say something about—for example, "There is an x such that x is a cat." In learning the use of quantifier expressions and of variable, one masters reference.

While Quine's early philosophical interests focused on the foundations of logic and mathematics, by the mid 1970s those interests represented only part of a larger philosophical concern: laying the groundwork for scientific answers to the central epistemological questions of how scientific knowledge is acquired and why such knowledge works so well. Quine dubbed this larger

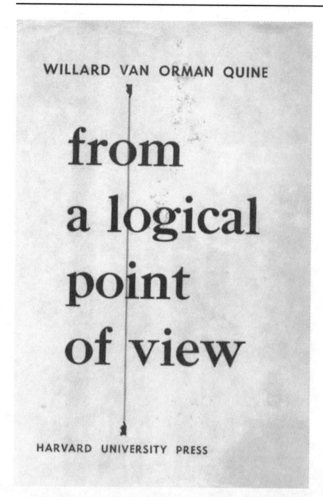

Dust jacket for Quine's 1953 collection of nine essays on logic and philosophy, including "Two Dogmas of Empiricism," in which he attacks the distinction between analytic and synthetic statements and the notion that statements about theoretical entities should be reducible to statements about observable ones (Reason Alone Books)

philosophical concern "naturalized epistemology," and his position might be called "naturalized empiricism."

For Quine, naturalism has both negative and affirmative aspects. Its negative aspect is the rejection of "first philosophy," the view that scientific knowledge must be justified on grounds that lie outside of science itself. Naturalized epistemology gives up the Cartesian dream of trying to ground science on something firmer than science, such as innate ideas or sense-data. Naturalism's affirmative aspect is that first philosophy ought to be replaced by science itself. Naturalized epistemology is, thus, the scientific investigation of the acquisition of science, and it is partly descriptive and partly normative.

In *The Roots of Reference* Quine argues for naturalism on the grounds of "holism" and "unregenerate realism." Holism is the view that Quine opposed to the empiricist "dogmas" of analyticity and epistemological reductionism: it holds that not every sentence of a scientific theory is associated with a unique set of confirm-

ing and disconfirming experiences; therefore, to try to distinguish absolutely between sentences that are true in virtue of how the world is from those that are true solely by virtue of their meanings is futile, and to try to reduce theoretical sentences to observational sentences that do have such experiences associated with them is equally futile. Unregenerate realism is the view that scientific knowledge is continuous with commonsense knowledge and that to raise global doubts about such knowledge is senseless. The unregenerate realist recognizes that the skeptical challenge to science arises from within science itself; that is, reasons for doubting scientific claims are themselves further scientific claims. Thus, Quine's naturalism emerges from limiting the excessive optimism of radical empiricism—analyticity and epistemological reductionism—and the excessive pessimism of radical skepticism.

Empiricism, for Quine, is the view that both the scientific evidence and the meanings of words rest ultimately on the senses: "*nihil in mente quod non prius in sensu*" (nothing in the mind that is not first in the senses), as he puts it in *Pursuit of Truth* (1990). Quine's is not the old introspective empiricism of John Locke, George Berkeley, and David Hume, however, nor even that of the early Carnap; Quine's empiricism is externalized. Since he thinks that scientific theories are either sets of sentences or statable as such sets and that the evidence for, and the meanings of, scientific claims are ultimately sensory, he concludes that the evidential basis for science can best be accessed by studying language acquisition: in learning the meaning of a sentence, one is learning what evidence exists for the truth of the sentence.

Since, as Quine said at the beginning of *Word and Object,* "Language is a social art. In acquiring it we have to depend entirely on intersubjectively available cues as to what to say and when," language acquisition must be studied behavioristically. The advantage of this form of empiricism over the old introspective one is that the learning of language is out in the open and amenable to study by the intersubjective techniques of science. Quine calls this approach "externalized empiricism."

Quine's answer to the central epistemological questions—how scientific knowledge is acquired and why it works so well—begins with an acceptance of naturalism, that is, of the best theories of contemporary science and, in particular, of a learning theory according to which children are innately endowed with the ability to notice and group together recurrent salient sensory stimuli. Because children are also innately disposed to babble and to mimic adult speech, and because they are susceptible to conditioning, reinforcement emanating largely from their elders soon has them responding to various concurrent nonverbal stimulus conditions by emitting appropriate strings of phonemes. For example, a rabbit scurries by, and the child utters the holophrastic string "Theregoesarabbit"; or an adult says "There goes a rabbit" while pointing out the presence of the rabbit, thereby eliciting the child's assent. Observation sentences can be learned by the relatively simple method of ostension: a rabbit is present; the parent sees the rabbit and sees that the child sees it. While pointing to the rabbit, the parent utters "Rabbit." Taking notice, the child mimics the parent's utterance with his or her own "Rabbit." The parent then positively reinforces the child's utterance. Occasionally, the child will venture "Rabbit" when no rabbit is present; the parent will negatively reinforce such utterances. In the latter circumstances the child's tendency to utter "Rabbit" when no rabbits are present withers. The psychological mechanism underlying these simple instances of language learning–inductive generalization over observed similarities–is simple conditioning.

Once the child has mastered several such observation sentences, which are directly keyed to concurrent nonverbal stimuli, he or she goes on to learn "nonobservation sentences," which are not so keyed and which comprise the bulk of language. To learn nonobservation sentences the child has to be able to segment holophrastically learned observation sentences into conveniently short recurrent patterns–that is, into words: "Theregoesarabbit" becomes "There goes a rabbit." Eventually, the child catches on to the whole referential apparatus of English–the *is* of identity, plural endings, *same, other,* and so on–and therewith catches on to a great deal of commonsense knowledge about the world around him or her. *Rabbit,* for example, can now find its way into nonobservation sentences such as "A rabbit is an animal." Talk of ordinary objects is close at hand, and science is not far behind. For example, through what Quine calls the "interanimation of sentences," the child who goes on to acquire a bit of chemical theory will assent to "There is copper in it" on witnessing the mixture of the contents of two test tubes turn green. Such theoretical sentences acquire their empirical content via the multifarious connections they have with observation sentences: for example, *rabbit* of "Theregoesarabbit" eventually occurs in countless nonobservation sentences.

In time the child surpasses behavioristic conditioning and induction to acquire that greater part of language that goes beyond observation sentences. *The Roots of Reference* includes speculations on the nature of the methods and psychological mechanisms that could account for the learning of such language. Whatever these methods and mechanisms turn out to be, Quine says, they will not be traceable backward to reveal a smooth derivation of theoretical, nonobservational lan-

Quine in his Harvard University office in 1971 (photograph courtesy of Margaret Quine McGovern and Douglas Quine and courtesy of Harvard University)

guage on the basis of observational language–the dream of the early empiricists.

Transcending low-level inductions from observed similarities, theoretical language makes it possible to talk of objects–both observable and unobservable. Furthermore, predictive power now outstrips simple inductions such as "Where there is smoke, there is fire." This development is a great boon to science, but it comes at a price: if several instances of smoke without fire were observed, the habit of assenting to "Where there is smoke, there is fire" would wither. But with the hypothetico-deductive method in full force, things are not so simple if some expected prediction fails to materialize. Because theoretical sentences derive their empirical content from the multifarious connections they have with observation sentences, if a predicted observation implied by some hypothesis together with relevant background assumptions fails to materialize, all sorts of steps can be taken to explain the discrepancy. For example, if the hypothesis that pure water boils at one hundred degrees Celsius at sea level, together with var-

Dust jacket for Quine's 1974 book, in which he presents an idealized account of how a child might learn the referential apparatus of English (Reason Alone Books)

ious background assumptions, entails that if this liquid is pure water, then it will boil at one hundred degrees Celsius, and this prediction fails to materialize, one might say that the hypothesis is refuted; but one might equally suppose that the water is not pure, that the experiment is not being conducted at sea level, that the thermometer is faulty or misread by the experimenter, that the laws of physics do not hold at the site of the experiment, that the laws of logic or of mathematics are inapplicable, and so on. Quine maintains that no recipe exists for deciding what to do in such cases. Here the norms of what is vaguely known as "scientific method" come into play.

According to Quine's holistic account of natural knowledge, the apparent necessity of logic and mathematics is explained by their centrality to one's web of belief and not by their being analytic (true by definition). Their centrality is demonstrated by the great degree of disruption to one's web of belief that would

ensue if some logical or mathematical truth were given up as false. In the example of the water that fails to boil, adopting the hypothesis that the laws of logic or mathematics are inapplicable to save the hypothesis that water boils at one hundred degrees Celsius would wreak more havoc on one's web of belief—would require changing the truth-values of far more sentences in the web—than would adopting any of the other hypotheses suggested. Quine calls the desideratum that the least possible modification be done to one's web of belief the "maxim of minimum mutilation." Still, sometimes the drastic step of denying some general principle, or even some logical or mathematical "law," must be taken. For example, quantum mechanics can be accommodated to one's web of belief by denying the law of excluded middle, which states that every proposition is either true or false.

Quine argues for his empiricism naturalistically, that is, on the grounds of natural science: science says that its only evidence is, ultimately, the activation of one's nerve endings. Thus, in Quine's view, natural science and empiricism reciprocally support each other: natural science says that empiricism is true, and empiricism says that natural science is warranted. Of course, Quine says, science is fallible, so its present-day commitments to a physicalist ontology and an empiricist epistemology might someday lapse. For example, science might someday come to admit disembodied spirits in addition to physical objects into its ontology and extrasensory perception in addition to the sensory into its epistemology.

Quine retired from Harvard a few months before his seventieth birthday. In 1981 he published a collection of philosophical and popular essays, *Theories and Things.* Four years later appeared *The Time of My Life: An Autobiography. Quiddities: An Intermittently Philosophical Dictionary* was published in 1987. In 1990 Quine published *Pursuit of Truth,* a serious philosophical work in which he undertakes, he says, "to update, sum up, and clarify . . . my variously intersecting views on cognitive meaning, objective reference, and the grounds of knowledge." In November of that year Quine delivered a series of ten lectures at the Universitat Autònoma de Barcelona in Girona, Spain; they formed the basis of his final book, *From Stimulus to Science* (1995). A startling inconsistency obtains between these last two books, as Quine acknowledged in his "Reply to Roger F. Gibson, Jr." in the enlarged edition of the Library of Living Philosophers volume *The Philosophy of W. V. Quine* (1998): "Gibson has found, to my chagrin but gratitude, a disagreement between my consecutive little books *Pursuit of Truth* and *From Stimulus to Science* regarding empirical content of mathematics. I rest with the later position, namely, that mathematics lacks empirical content."

Prior to *From Stimulus to Science* Quine had steadfastly maintained, in opposition to the logical positivists and, in particular, to Carnap, that applied mathematics acquires empirical content by being associated with a cluster of sentences having such content. Carnap believed mathematics to be without empirical content yet necessarily true; Quine, on the other hand, believed that applied mathematics has empirical content and is only contingently true. Both of these properties, he held, are explicable in terms of holism. For example, "7 + 5 = 12" derives empirical content from being associated in various ways with a multiplicity of statements that do possess empirical content, and its apparent necessity is merely a measure of its centrality to one's conceptual scheme and its remoteness from sensory experience. Thus, where Carnap saw analyticity, Quine saw only holism. (Carnap also advocated holism but refused to apply it to mathematics.) In *From Stimulus to Science,* however, Quine agrees with Carnap that mathematics is without empirical content, though he presumably still believes its apparent necessity to be explicable in terms of holism and not analyticity. The Quine-Carnap debate, which began in Prague during Quine's Sheldon Traveling Fellowship year, outlived its principals: the issue continues to be argued in philosophical journals.

Quine received honorary Litt.D.s from Oberlin College in 1955, the University of Akron in 1965, Washington University in 1966, Temple University in 1970, the University of Oxford in 1970, the University of Cambridge in 1978, and Ripon College in 1983; honorary Ph.D.s from the University of Lille in 1956, the University of Uppsala in 1980, the University of Bern in 1982, and the University of Granada in 1986; honorary L.L.D.s from Ohio State University in 1957 and Harvard University in 1979; and honorary L.H.D.s from the University of Chicago in 1967, Syracuse University in 1981, and Adelphi University in 1988. He was a fellow of the Center for Advanced Study in the Behavioral Sciences in 1958–1959 and of the Center for Advanced Studies at Wesleyan University in 1965 and a Sir Henry Saville Fellow of Merton College, Oxford, in 1973–1974. He received the Nicholas Murray Butler Gold Medal from Columbia University in 1970. He was a member of the American Philosophical Society, the British Academy, the American Academy of Arts and Sciences, the National Academy of the Sciences, the Institut de France, and the Norwegian Academy of Sciences.

In 1996 W. V. Quine received the Kyoto Prize in Creative Arts and Moral Sciences, a prestigious award worth nearly half a million dollars. His wife died on 14 April 1998; Quine died on Christmas Day 2000. He was, borrowing a term he once used to describe Carnap, a "towering figure" of the twentieth century. It is too soon to predict what Quine's legacy for the twenty-

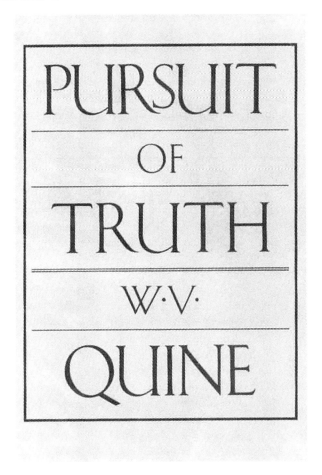

Dust jacket for Quine's 1990 book, in which he updates and clarifies his views on cognitive meaning, objective reference, and the grounds of knowledge (Reason Alone Books)

first century will be, but one might hazard a guess that naturalism will be a large part of that legacy.

Letters:

Dear Carnap, Dear Van: The Quine-Carnap Correspondence and Related Work, edited by Richard Creath (Berkeley: University of California Press, 1991);

"Selected Correspondence with Geach," in *Peter Geach: Philosophical Encounters,* edited by Harry A. Lewis, Synthese Library, volume 213 (Dordrecht, Netherlands & Boston: Kluwer, 1991), pp. 27–43.

Interviews:

Bryan Magee, "The Ideas of Quine," in *Men of Ideas: Some Creators of Contemporary Philosophy* (London: British Broadcasting Corporation, 1978), pp. 168–179;

Edo Pivčević, "Quine Speaks His Mind," *Cogito,* 2, no. 2 (1988): 1–5;

Lars Bergström and Dagfinn Føllesdal, *Theoria*, 60 (1994): 193–206;

Giovanna Borradori, "Twentieth-Century Logic: Willard Van Orman Quine," in her *The American Philosopher: Conversations with Quine, Davidson, Putnam, Nozick, Danto, Rorty, Cavell, MacIntyre, and Kuhn*, translated by Rosanna Crocitto (Chicago & London: University of Chicago Press, 1994), pp. 27–39;

Rudolf Fara and others, *In Conversation: W. V. Quine*, video, 7 parts, Philosophy International, 1994.

Bibliography:
Rita Bruschi, *Willard Van Orman Quine: A Bibliographic Guide* (Florence: La Nouva Italia, 1985).

References:
Análisis filosófico, special Quine issue, 2, nos. 1–2 (1982);

Robert B. Barrett and Roger F. Gibson Jr., eds., *Perspectives on Quine* (Oxford: Blackwell, 1990);

Donald Davidson and Jaakko Hintikka, eds., *Words and Objections: Essays on the Work of W. V. Quine* (Dordrecht, Netherlands: Reidel, 1969);

Ilham Dilman, *Quine on Ontology, Necessity, and Experience: A Philosophical Critique* (Albany: State University of New York Press, 1984);

Robert Feleppa, *Convention, Translation, and Understanding: Philosophical Problems in the Comparative Study of Culture* (Albany: State University of New York Press, 1988);

Manuel Garrido, ed., *Aspectos de la filosofía de W. V. Quine: Actas del V simposio de lógica y filosofía de la ciencia: Cullera, 28 y 29 de junio de 1974* (Valencia: Departamento de Lógica y Filosofía de la Ciencia, Universidad de Valencia, 1976);

Roger F. Gibson Jr., *Enlightened Empiricism: An Examination of W. V. Quine's Theory of Knowledge* (Gainesville: University Presses of South Florida / Tampa: University of South Florida Press, 1988);

Gibson, *The Philosophy of W. V. Quine: An Expository Essay* (Tampa: University Presses of Florida, 1982);

Paul Gochet, *Ascent to Truth: A Critical Examination of Quine's Philosophy* (Munich: Philosophia, 1986);

Gochet, *Quine en perspective: Essai de philosophie comparée* (Paris: Flammarion, 1978);

Lewis Edwin Hahn and Paul Arthur Schilpp, eds., *The Philosophy of W. V. Quine*, The Library of Living Philosophers, volume 18 (La Salle, Ill.: Open Court, 1986; revised and enlarged edition, Chicago: Open Court, 1998);

Sandra G. Harding, ed., *Can Theories Be Refuted? Essays on the Duhem-Quine Thesis* (Dordrecht, Netherlands & Boston: Reidel, 1976);

Jane Heal, *Fact and Meaning: Quine and Wittgenstein on Philosophy of Language* (Oxford & New York: Blackwell, 1989);

Christopher Hookway, *Quine: Language, Experience, and Reality* (Stanford, Cal.: Stanford University Press, 1988);

Robert Kirk, *Translation Determined* (Oxford: Clarendon Press / New York: Oxford University Press, 1986);

Dirk Koppelberg, *Die Aufhebung der analytischen Philosophie: Quine als Synthese von Carnap und Neurath* (Frankfurt am Main: Suhrkamp, 1987);

Henri Lauener, *Willard Van Orman Quine* (Munich: Beck, 1982);

Paolo Leonardi and Mario Santambrogio, eds., *On Quine: New Essays* (Cambridge: Cambridge University Press, 1995);

Alex Orenstein, *Willard Van Orman Quine*, Twayne's World Leaders Series, no. 65 (Boston: Twayne, 1977);

Orenstein and Petr Kotatko, eds., *Knowledge, Language, and Logic: Questions for Quine*, Boston Studies in the Philosophy of Science, volume 210 (Dordrecht, Netherlands & Boston: Kluwer, 2000);

George D. Romanos, *Quine and Analytic Philosophy* (Cambridge, Mass.: MIT Press, 1983);

Richard Rorty, *Philosophy and the Mirror of Nature* (Princeton: Princeton University Press, 1979), pp. 169–175, 177–182, 192–204, 207–209, 217–230, 268–270, 275–276;

Robert W. Shahan and Chris Swoyer, eds., *Essays on the Philosophy of W. V. Quine* (Norman: University of Oklahoma Press, 1978);

Barry Stroud, *The Significance of Philosophical Scepticism* (Oxford: Clarendon Press / New York: Oxford University Press, 1984);

Hao Wang, *Beyond Analytic Philosophy: Doing Justice to What We Know* (Cambridge, Mass.: MIT Press, 1986);

Willard Van Orman Quine 1908-2000 <http://www.wvquine.org>.

Papers:
W. V. Quine's manuscripts, correspondence, and other papers are in the Houghton Library of Harvard University.

Ayn Rand

(2 February 1905 – 6 March 1982)

Stephen Cox

University of California, San Diego

See also the Rand entry in *DLB 227: American Novelists Since World War II, Sixth Series.*

BOOKS: *We the Living* (New York: Macmillan, 1936; London: Cassell, 1937; revised edition, New York: Random House, 1959);

Night of January 16th: A Comedy-Drama in Three Acts, edited by Nathaniel Edward Reeid (New York & Chicago: Longmans, Green, 1936; revised and restored edition, New York: World, 1968);

Anthem (London: Cassell, 1938; revised edition, Los Angeles: Pamphleteers, 1946);

The Fountainhead (Indianapolis & New York: Bobbs-Merrill, 1943; London: Cassell, 1947);

Atlas Shrugged (New York: Random House, 1957);

For the New Intellectual: The Philosophy of Ayn Rand (New York: Random House, 1961);

America's Persecuted Minority: Big Business (New York: Nathaniel Branden Institute, 1962);

The Virtue of Selfishness: A New Concept of Egoism, by Rand and Nathaniel Branden (New York: New American Library, 1964);

Capitalism: The Unknown Ideal, by Rand, Branden, Alan Greenspan, and Robert Hessen (New York: New American Library, 1966);

Introduction to Objectivist Epistemology (New York: Objectivist, 1967; enlarged edition, edited by Harry Binswanger and Leonard Peikoff, New York: New American Library, 1990);

The Romantic Manifesto: A Philosophy of Literature (New York: World, 1969; enlarged edition, New York: New American Library, 1975);

The New Left: The Anti-Industrial Revolution (New York: New American Library, 1971); enlarged as *Return of the Primitive: The Anti-Industrial Revolution,* edited, with contributions, by Peter Schwartz (New York: Meridian, 1999);

Philosophy: Who Needs It, edited by Peikoff (Indianapolis & New York: Bobbs-Merrill, 1982);

Ayn Rand (photograph © by the Ayn Rand Estate)

The Early Ayn Rand: A Selection from Her Unpublished Fiction, edited by Peikoff (New York: New American Library, 1984);

The Voice of Reason: Essays in Objectivist Thought, by Rand, Peikoff, and Schwartz, edited by Peikoff (New York: New American Library, 1989);

The Ayn Rand Column: A Collection of Her Weekly Newspaper Articles, Written for the Los Angeles Times; *with Additional, Little-Known Essays,* edited by Schwartz (Oceanside, Cal.: Second Renaissance, 1991); revised as *The Ayn Rand Column: Written for the* Los

Angeles Times (New Milford, Conn.: Second Renaissance, 1998);

Ayn Rand's Marginalia: Her Critical Comments on the Writings of over 20 Authors, edited by Robert Mayhew (New Milford, Conn.: Second Renaissance, 1995);

Journals of Ayn Rand, edited by David Harriman (New York: Dutton, 1997);

Russian Writings on Hollywood, edited by Michael S. Berliner (Marina del Rey, Cal.: Ayn Rand Institute Press, 1999);

Why Businessmen Need Philosophy, by Rand, Peikoff, Binswanger, Richard Salsman, Edwin A. Locke, Jaana Woiceshyn, and John B. Ridpath, edited by Richard E. Ralston (Marina del Ray, Cal.: Ayn Rand Institute Press, 1999);

The Art of Fiction: A Guide for Writers and Readers, edited by Tore Boeckmann (New York: Plume, 2000);

The Art of Nonfiction: A Guide for Writers and Readers, edited by Mayhew (New York: Plume, 2001).

Collections and Editions: *The Fountainhead: 25th Anniversary Edition, with a Special Introduction by the Author* (Indianapolis: Bobbs-Merrill, 1968);

The Ayn Rand Lexicon: Objectivism from A to Z, edited by Harry Binswanger (New York: New American Library, 1986);

Atlas Shrugged: 35th Anniversary Edition, introduction by Leonard Peikoff (New York: Dutton, 1992);

The Fountainhead: With a Special Introduction by the Author, afterword by Peikoff (New York: Plume, 1994);

Anthem: 50th Anniversary Edition, introduction by Peikoff (New York: Dutton, 1995);

We the Living: 60th Anniversary Edition, introduction by Peikoff (New York: Dutton, 1995);

The Ayn Rand Reader, edited by Peikoff and Gary Hull (New York: Plume, 1999).

PLAY PRODUCTIONS: *Woman on Trial,* Los Angeles, Hollywood Playhouse, 22 October 1934; revised as *Night of January 16th,* New York, Ambassador Theater, 16 September 1935;

The Unconquered, New York, Biltmore Theatre, 14 February 1940.

PRODUCED SCRIPTS: *Love Letters,* motion picture, Paramount, 1945;

You Came Along, motion picture, screenplay by Rand and Robert Smith, Paramount, 1945;

The Fountainhead, motion picture, Warner Bros., 1949.

RECORDINGS: *The New Fascism–Rule by Consensus: A Lecture Given at the Ford Hall Forum, Boston, April 18, 1965,* New York, NBI Communications, 1965;

Ethics in Education: A Lecture Given at Rutgers University, March 18, 1966, New York, NBI Communications, 1966;

Day at Night with James Day: Ayn Rand in New York, video, New York, Jeffrey Norton Publisher, 1976.

OTHER: Victor Hugo, *Ninety-Three,* translated by Lowell Bair, introduction by Rand (New York: Bantam, 1962);

Objectivist Newsletter, 1–4, edited by Rand and Nathaniel Branden (January 1962–December 1965); republished in one volume as *The Objectivist Newsletter* (New York: Objectivist, 1967);

Objectivist, 5–10, edited by Rand and Branden until the April 1968 issue, thereafter by Rand (January 1966–September 1971); republished in one volume as *The Objectivist* (Palo Alto, Cal.: Palo Alto Book Service, 1982);

Samuel Merwin and Henry Kitchell Webster, *Calumet "K,"* introduction by Rand (New York: NBI Press, 1967);

Ayn Rand Letter, 1–4, edited and almost wholly written by Rand (11 October 1971–January/February 1976); republished in one volume as *The Ayn Rand Letter* (Palo Alto, Cal.: Palo Alto Book Service, 1979).

Ayn Rand, one of the few systematic philosophers who have used imaginative literature to develop their ideas, was a novelist and the founder of the Objectivist school of philosophy. She was an advocate of realism in epistemology, rational self-interest in ethics, limited government in politics, and laissez-faire capitalism in economics. Although Rand rejected ordinary political labels, preferring to call herself a "radical for capitalism," her work strongly influenced the conservative, classical-liberal, and libertarian movements in the United States.

Rand was born Alissa (Russian for Alice) Zinovievna Rosenbaum in St. Petersburg, Russia, on 2 February 1905 to Zinovy "Fronz" Zakharovich Rosenbaum and Anna Borisovna Rosenbaum. Her parents were Jewish but were little concerned with religion. Fronz Rosenbaum, a self-made businessman, owned a pharmacy. Alissa was raised in a comfortable middle-class environment in which her intelligence was recognized and encouraged. She learned French and German, and she discovered an early interest in writing.

Alissa Rosenbaum was a young partisan of the February Revolution of 1917 and of the revolutionary leader Alexander Kerensky. It "was the only time," she later said, when she "was synchronized with history." After the Bolshevik revolution of October 1917 she began her long career of opposition to the expansive political state. Her father's business was nationalized, and the family fled to the Crimea in a futile attempt to escape from communism. There they lived as if "on a battlefield" from 1918 to 1921, when they returned to metropolitan Russia. Alissa attended Leningrad University; most of her course work was in history, but she received instruction in philosophy, as well. She was graduated in 1924.

Wanting to write, but knowing that she would be unable to survive in Soviet society as an articulate opponent of communism, Rosenbaum escaped to the United States in 1926. She changed her name to Ayn Rand, choosing those syllables because she liked their sound ("Ayn" is pronounced to rhyme with *mine*).

Rand traveled to Hollywood, where, failing to support herself by writing for the motion-picture industry, she worked as a waitress, envelope stuffer, wardrobe clerk, and movie extra. On the set of Cecil B. DeMille's *The King of Kings* (1927) she met an actor, Charles Francis (Frank) O'Connor; they were married on 15 April 1929. The gentle, unassuming O'Connor was easily dominated by his strong-willed wife. His acting career came to nothing, and although he later pursued a variety of other vocations and avocations–including ranching, flower arranging, and painting–his principal job was always that of consort to Ayn Rand.

Her marriage enabled Rand to become an American citizen, and she was naturalized on 13 March 1931. In November 1934 she and O'Connor moved to New York City in anticipation of the Broadway production the following year of her play *Night of January 16th*. The play, which had premiered in Los Angeles in 1934 under the title *Woman on Trial*, was a commercially successful courtroom drama in which a jury drawn from the audience at each performance revealed its moral character by pronouncing Rand's heroine guilty or innocent.

Rand's novel *We the Living*, which she had begun in 1930 and completed in 1933, appeared in 1936. It is an attack on the Soviet system and, by extension, on all systems in which individuals are forced to "live for the state." Rand uses the characters of the novel to explore the ways in which individual lives are affected by state-imposed collectivism. The heroine, Kira Argounova, an ambitious would-be engineer, is prevented by her middle-class background from doing any meaningful work in "proletarian" society; she attempts to escape from Russia and is killed. One of her two lovers, Leo Kovalensky, an aristocrat, is psychologically ruined by the demoralizing effects of the Soviet dictatorship; the other, Andrei Taganov, a proletarian idealist, kills himself because of his disillusionment with the collectivist regime that he fought to establish.

Alissa Rosenbaum in Russia, circa 1924. She changed her name to Ayn Rand two years later, after immigrating to the United States (photograph © by the Ayn Rand Estate).

We the Living presents Rand's ideas at an early stage of development. Her novels are not a series of attempts to express a preexisting philosophical system but stages in the growth of a system. Opposed–on what she regarded as more than sufficient evidence–to the theory and practice of collectivism, she proposed an ethic of individualism and then tested, refined, corrected, and extended this ethic until it developed into an analysis of human action supported by political, cultural, psychological, and epistemological theories. In her foreword to the 1959 revision of *We the Living* she observes that when she wrote the novel, she intended to assert the supreme value of the individual human life but did not yet understand how to solve many of the philosophical and psychological problems associated with that claim. The 1936 version of *We the Living* is egalitarian in its contempt for what collectivism does to weak, as well as to strong, individuals; but its individualism becomes confused at times with an elitism that reflects Rand's early emotional attachment to the work of Friedrich Nietzsche. For example, Andrei, speaking

*Rand and Frank O'Connor in Hollywood, circa 1928. They were married in 1929
(photograph © by the Ayn Rand Estate).*

as a collectivist, asks Kira, "Don't you know . . . that we can't sacrifice millions for the sake of the few?" and Kira responds, "You can! You must. When those few are the best. Deny the best its right to the top–and you have no best left. . . . men are not born equal and I don't see why one should want to make them equal." Rand could not rest content with this position: if individual human life is the supreme value, and if, as Andrei discovers, no one ought to "tell men what they must live for," then how can certain individuals be "sacrificed" for the sake of others–even if the latter are, in some sense, "the best"? The original version of *We the Living* does not define what "sacrifice" could possibly mean in this context. In the 1959 revision Rand retains her protest against the idea of people's equality of worth but eliminates the suggestion that inequality entails sacrifice. In this version Kira asks, "Can you sacrifice the few? When those few are the best? . . . men are not equal in ability and one can't treat them as if they were." In the title essay of *For the New Intellectual: The Philosophy of Ayn Rand* (1961) Rand expresses regret that "Nietzsche's rebellion against altruism consisted of replacing the sacrifice of oneself to others by the sacrifice of others to oneself." If this is what it means to be "beyond good and evil," she concludes, then Nietzsche has surrendered any attempt to base an ethic on reason and general principles–such principles as Rand expounded in the decades following *We the Living*.

We the Living was little noticed on its first appearance; still less noticed was Rand's next novel, the clever and engaging *Anthem*. Written in 1937, it appeared in England in 1938 but did not achieve American publication until 1946. *Anthem* contrasts two imaginary utopias: a collectivist state and a community founded on the principle of self-seeking individualism. Utopian literature has traditionally idealized the first kind of society and satirized the second. *Anthem* inverts the genre's traditional values. It represents the moral consequences of collectivism and egoism as precisely opposite to those generally anticipated by utopian writers. The effects of collectivism are shown to be a worse-than-medieval stagnation and cruelty, while the effects of egoism are material progress and the conditions of freedom, responsibility, and voluntary cooperation that are appropriate to a humane social order.

Rand's fame began with her third novel, *The Fountainhead* (1943), which she had started writing in 1935. The novel sold more than four million copies during its first four decades of publication. In late 1943 Rand sold the movie rights for the then-considerable sum of $50,000, the first substantial money she had ever had. She and her husband returned to California, where she wrote screenplays for *The Fountainhead* and other motion pictures. The book with which Rand rose to prominence as an advocate of individualist political ideas is, however, concerned much less with politics

Rand (seated, center) on the set of the 1949 motion picture The Fountainhead, *for which she wrote the screenplay based on her 1943 novel. To the left of Rand is the producer, Henry Blanke; to the right the director, King Vidor. Standing, left to right, are the actors Robert Douglas (Ellsworth Toohey), Kent Smith (Peter Keating), Patricia Neal (Dominique Francon), Gary Cooper (Howard Roark), and Raymond Massey (Gail Wynand) (photograph © by the Ayn Rand Estate).*

than with the cultural and psychological aspects of individualism and collectivism. The protagonist, Howard Roark, is an architect of genius who believes that every building must have an individual form to match its individual purpose; anything less reveals a lack of "integrity." Roark's modernist ideas put him at odds with the institutionalized beaux-arts taste of the early twentieth century. His ability to create is matched by his ability to negate—to refuse to grant legitimacy to collectively sanctioned values and practices. The most dramatic episode of negation in the novel begins when he agrees to design a housing project, Cortlandt Homes, for no reward other than the pleasure of seeing it built according to his plans. After his design is wantonly disfigured, he dynamites the project—taking care not to kill or injure anyone but making sure that no one benefits from his work without paying the stipulated price.

Brought to trial for his action, Roark defends himself with a philosophical account of property rights, especially the right to one's own time, talent, energy, and labor. He argues that only when this right is respected, as it was not in regard to his design for Cortlandt Homes, can society expect to enrich itself from the creative work of the individual mind—the fountainhead of human progress. The jury acquits him, confirming his claim that the American system is founded on respect for the absolute rights of individuals. The Cortlandt site is then purchased by a private investor, who commissions Roark to build on it in accordance with his own design.

The other major characters in *The Fountainhead* are defined by varying degrees of contrast to Roark; they exemplify a variety of erroneous ethical, psychological, and cultural positions. Peter Keating is an architect who achieves material success by conforming to the accepted taste, sometimes borrowing Roark's ideas and compromising them. He represents the common form of parasite and "second-hander." Architectural critic Ellsworth Toohey is a "social thinker" and activist; correctly perceiving Roark's aesthetic individualism as a threat to collectivist ideals, he attempts to destroy Roark's career. He is the epitome of the intellectually corrupted cultural leader. Gail Wynand is a newspaper tycoon who admires Roark's genius and independence but has spent his own life seeking power over the public mind by feeding it the nonsense it seems to require. He is the superior man who betrays himself to the mob. Dominique Francon is a talented writer who loves Roark but believes that genius has no chance in a world that devotes itself to rewarding careerists such as Keating and power-crazed intellectuals such as Toohey. She is the individualist who sacrifices herself to her own anxieties.

Rand intends these characters to illuminate different aspects and effects of the conflict between selflessness and egoism and to support her special understanding of those concepts. Roark, who is anything but greedy for wealth and fame, is egoistic or selfish in his refusal to accept other people's views or standards as his own—or even to waste his consciousness on them: when Toohey asks what Roark thinks of him, Roark replies, "But I don't think of you." Toohey, however, thinks about Roark a great deal, because Toohey lives his life "unselfishly": not only does he preach a collectivist ethic of unselfishness, but his attempt to dominate others means that his chief concern lies outside himself, in the people whom he wishes to control. A similarly inappropriate concern about others appears in Wynand's pursuit of power, Keating's hunger for popularity, and Dominique's neurotic conviction that genius is always at the mercy of mediocrity.

Roark's vindication by the jury illustrates the falseness of Dominique's view, which Rand later called the belief in a "malevolent universe." In the novel, sound ethical principles ultimately result in real-world success—on the job, as well as in court. Roark's triumphs in architecture, which is simultaneously an artistic and a practical enterprise, illustrate the connection between integrity of thought and proficiency of workmanship. Roark is understood as winning a victory on behalf of all good thinkers and workers, not simply on behalf of an intellectual elite. The exponent of an unhealthy elitism is Toohey, the apostle of collectivism. Anticipating the anticollectivist arguments of Friedrich Hayek's classical-liberal work *The Road to Serfdom* (1944), Toohey recognizes that a collectivist society can exist only if a "humanitarian" elite imposes it on the masses; Toohey is eager to accomplish what Hayek

hopes to prevent. Roark, by contrast, insists on making his own way in a system in which everyone has an equal right to compete. Free exchange "is the only possible form of relationship between equals," he says. "Anything else is a relation of slave to master." Rand's case for individualism extends to an opposition not just to exploitation but also to "altruism." Like the decision to exploit, altruism implies to her a choice to sacrifice one self to other selves. It is an ethic favorable to collectivism and opposed to human dignity.

Resolving some of the philosophical conflicts of *We the Living, The Fountainhead* clearly grounds the rights of "the best" on a principle applicable to all, whatever their variations in talent or intelligence. Roark declares that "in all proper relationships there is no sacrifice of anyone to anyone." When, therefore, he goes on to announce that "the first right on earth is the right of the ego," he is expounding an essentially liberal ethic based on the principle, handed down from the Enlightenment, of the equal right of all individuals to be left alone. The economic expression of this right is a laissez-faire or "hands off" policy; its political expression is the traditional American ideal of limited government.

Rand's understanding of Enlightenment liberalism was shaped, during the period when she was completing *The Fountainhead,* by her close association with the novelist and critic Isabel Paterson. Paterson, who was much better informed about history and politics than Rand, was a vigorous exponent of a minimal-government, free-enterprise system that she called "classical Americanism." Paterson's theoretical work, *The God of the Machine* (1943), describes history as the effect of individual creative energy "circuited" through social institutions and practices that are more or less favorable to freedom—an idea that had a marked effect on Rand's later work. Insofar as Rand is concerned with individual liberty as a solution to practical, as well as ideological, problems, she also resembles such rehabilitators of classical, limited government liberalism as Hayek and Ludwig von Mises, a major figure in the free-market Austrian school of economics who became her friend after the publication of *The Fountainhead*. She was troubled, however, by the tendency of some classical liberals to ground an individualist ethic on what she regarded as merely utilitarian considerations or to reduce it to the "negative" principle of disapproval of coercion. Although she came to detest conservatism, viewing it as an appeal to faith and fear, she shared with conservatives a conviction of the insufficiency of a negative morality, or one that offers itself solely as a way of resolving social problems. She believed that ethics must offer positive guidance for all significant actions, including those of solitary individuals.

Rand (seated, right) and some members of her circle in the mid 1950s: Joan Mitchell, Alan Greenspan, Nathaniel Branden, Barbara Branden, Leonard Peikoff, Elayne Kalberman, Harry Kalberman, O'Connor, and Allan Blumenthal. The occasion was the wedding of Nathaniel Branden's sister, Elayne, to Harry Kalberman (photograph by A. Levine).

Rand's need for an expansive and positive ethical system was increased by her emphasis on the importance of choice. "The choice," Roark says, "is independence or dependence," and his formulation is far from accidental. If individuals had no capacity for effective choice, if they were merely controlled or conditioned by the outside world, then it would be pointless to debate the rival claims of individualism and collectivism. In Rand's view, the maintenance of any individual human life requires a long sequence of successful choices. But the necessity of choice implies, for her, the necessity of standards for choice, and she sees no reason to believe that the choices of private life have any less need for such standards than the choices of social life. Furthermore, the standards must ultimately be moral, not utilitarian. It is not enough to say, for instance, that a laissez-faire economic system should be chosen because it "works better" than any other system—although, in Rand's terms, it does work better. One must also determine what ought to be regarded as "good" or "better" in the first place, and this determination is a moral one. The moral conflicts that are central to the plot of *The Fountainhead* demonstrate that Randian

individualism has nothing to do with relativism: individuals should be free to choose; but some individual choices are right, and others are wrong.

The works that Rand published after *The Fountainhead* respond to the threat of relativism by insisting on the need for an ethical system that is both universally applicable and objectively ascertainable. Her next novel, *Atlas Shrugged*, begun in 1943 and published in 1957, describes such an ethical system and embeds it in a comprehensive philosophy that she called Objectivism, which is based on the idea that reality is objectively existent and can be objectively known.

Rand regarded *Atlas Shrugged* as her greatest artistic accomplishment and the major, though not the complete or final, statement of her philosophy. The novel began as a fairly simple project. The premise of *The Fountainhead* was the idea that the independent, creative mind is the source of everything valuable in civilization. *Atlas Shrugged* offers a corollary of that premise: civilization will collapse if independent, creative minds decide to stop supporting it. The novel, which Rand originally thought of naming "The Strike," is the story of people who refuse, in Rand's words, to continue giving an

September 20, 1955

(1)

Consciousness, Purpose & Happiness

Just as man's actions require values to determine choices among alternative possibilities, so does the action of thinking require values, for the mind is constantly confronted with an infinitely greater variety of subjects than it can focus on at any given time. It is, therefore, in the nature of a human consciousness that thought must be purposeful, must move toward the attainment of specific goals or values.

Page from the manuscript for an essay that Rand used to organize her ideas for John Galt's speech in her 1957 novel, Atlas Shrugged
(Butterfield, Butterfield, and Dunning, The Papers of Ayn Rand, *sale number 5893, 18 November 1998)*

unjust social order "the sanction of the victim." Scientists, industrialists, artists, and financiers abandon an increasingly collectivist American society and withdraw to an individualist community hidden in the Rocky Mountains, where the Atlases of the world shrug off the weight of economic, political, and psychological exploitation. It is a utopia like that of *Anthem,* though much more imbued with political theory. Citizens of this utopia renounce the initiation of force and declare that they will neither live for others nor expect others to live for them; and they are free to compete with one another. The result of their strike is the collapse of the economic and social order, after which they emerge from hiding to reconstruct the world on the principles of limited-government, laissez-faire capitalism.

The central drama of the story, however, is not the social conflict between individualists and collectivists; it is the moral and philosophical conflict within the minds of the individualists themselves. The leader of the strike, physicist John Galt, must persuade such productive individuals as railroad executive Dagny Taggart that they are acting in a self-contradictory and reprehensible manner when they dutifully produce wealth for collectivists to consume. Essentializing vigorously, Rand traces the origin of evil, as well as good, to the individual's defining attribute of "volitional consciousness." Virtue is the effect of deciding to engage in focused, noncontradictory thinking; evil is the effect of refusing to think in this way. Galt's Gulch, Rand's individualist utopia, exists because a few people have made the choice to stop "faking reality *in any manner whatever.*" Its ethic is the only rule compatible with reason. Rand had named the major parts of *The Fountainhead* after the characters in that novel; she names the major parts of *Atlas Shrugged* after principles of Aristotelian logic: "Non-Contradiction," "Either-Or," and "A Is A."

Atlas Shrugged did not remain a simple story. The emphasis on a fully conscious and rational assessment of reality challenged Rand to identify all her major philosophical premises, develop all their significant implications, and purge them of any apparent contradictions. In doing so, she expanded and codified her views on ethics, politics, history, economics, psychology, epistemology, and metaphysics. She included many speeches in which characters expound her views, demonstrate their consistency, and refute predictable objections. In one of the longest speeches in world literature, Galt's radio address to the American public, Rand attempts to outline the most important branches of her philosophy and to ground them in one simple, self-evident, and apparently unobjectionable axiom: *"existence exists."*

Inquiring into the significance of this axiom, she finds that the act of grasping it implies the existence both of consciousness and of an object of which consciousness is aware. To exist is to exist as a specific something, and a rational consciousness works to identify the somethings that exist: "Existence is Identity, Consciousness is Identification." Correct identifications are not guaranteed; there are no "automatic" values or achievements. But the work of consciousness can avoid absurdity if it is directed by Aristotelian logic, "the art of *non-contradictory identification.*"

Use of reason is voluntary; one can decide to think in an irrational, contradictory fashion or not to think at all. But to make such decisions would be absurd: it would be objectively contrary to the requirements of human life. Rand's standard of value is "man's life," the survival of the human being as the kind of being "man" is: "a thinking being." No other values can exist without life, and human life cannot be preserved without the exercise of reason. "If existence on earth is your goal," Galt says, "you must choose your actions and values by the standard of that which is proper to man—for the purpose of preserving, fulfilling and enjoying the irreplaceable value which is your life." This assertion is followed in fairly short order by an enumeration of the moral virtues that Rand regards as appropriate to the purpose, such as the independence, integrity, honesty, and justice implied by a noncontradictory exercise of volitional consciousness. The surrender of these virtues, she argues, is necessarily involved in the antilife ethics of subjectivism, altruism, collectivism, and all their personal, social, and institutional expressions—expressions of which *Atlas Shrugged* presents a nearly exhaustive catalogue.

Rand's philosophic project is remarkable for its ambition and ingenuity. Indeed, most commentators—even those such as Robert Nozick, J. Charles King, and Eric Mack who are sympathetic to individualism—suggest that some of its claims outrun the arguments given for them. The various connections that *Atlas Shrugged* and Rand's succeeding books of essays develop between "life" and "value" have seemed especially vulnerable to criticism. Granted, critics say, a person must be alive to have values; but why must one regard life itself as a "standard of value," even if one understands "life" as the life of a rational being? And what, precisely, allows Rand to make her seemingly facile transitions from the standard of value for the species to the moral principles that ought to govern individual lives? For Rand, of course, "man's life" is always a matter of the lives of individuals. Nevertheless, it is not self-evident that her assertion of human life as the standard of value has sufficient force to govern the whole realm of ethics, as she wishes it to do, or even to justify the ethical distinctions that she wants to make between dependence and independence. One may accept the

vary. In the essay "What Is Capitalism?"—originally published in *The Objectivist Newsletter* in November and December 1965 and collected in *Capitalism: The Unknown Ideal* (1966)—Rand tries to deal with this issue by arguing, ingeniously, that market values are not subjective but "*socially objective.*" This claim did not resolve the issue. Some advocates of capitalism who embrace Mises's "subjective" theory of economic values have regarded Rand as repeating the mistake of socialist economists—trying to derive a theory of economics from a theory of ethics.

Atlas Shrugged was published, however, when intellectual advocates of anything similar to Rand's ideas were rare, and judicious criticism of laissez-faire and minimal-government conceptions, supposedly long discredited by "history," was rarer still. In most intellectual circles the novel was greeted with faint comprehension and strong hostility. Of course, *Atlas Shrugged* itself is full of hostility, especially in its attribution of intellectual errors to a voluntary rebellion against rationality, a refusal to think—in Galt's memorable phrase, "There is no honest revolt against reason." This attitude was not conducive to intellectual fairness and tolerance, either on Rand's part or on that of her critics. *Atlas Shrugged* elicited reactions that would have killed a hundred other books. Leftists and modern liberals were predictably averse; but even Whittaker Chambers, one of the foremost American opponents of collectivism, accused Rand of advocating philosophical materialism and, implicitly, the dictatorship of a technocratic elite.

The effect of Chambers's article—which appeared in William F. Buckley Jr.'s *National Review,* the leading organ of American conservatism—was to separate Rand and her followers from the mainstream of the conservative movement. Rand counterattacked in "Conservatism: An Obituary," a lecture delivered at Princeton University on 7 December 1960 and published in revised form in *Capitalism: The Unknown Ideal.* She accused conservatives of committing ideological suicide by defending conformity and tradition, rather than independent thought and progressive capitalism. Political events later proved the obituary premature. One reason for American conservatism's rise to political dominance in the 1980s, however, was its gradual assimilation of the ideas advocated by Rand and other friends of laissez-faire capitalism. Although many conservatives were repelled by her uncompromising atheism and rationalism and by her defense of extramarital sex, many others continued to be attracted by her strongly moral arguments for individual responsibility and limited government. Despite the animosity that *Atlas Shrugged* engendered on both left and right, it still enjoys tremendously large sales, thus demonstrating

Photograph of Rand that appeared on the dust jacket of Atlas Shrugged (*photograph © by the Ayn Rand Estate/photograph by Phyllis Cerf*)

idea that the individual human life is the standard of value but still not discern a clear logical relationship between this idea and Rand's exhaustive ethical dualism—the claim that, as Roark puts it, "All that which proceeds from man's independent ego is good. All that which proceeds from man's dependence upon men is evil. . . . Independence is the only gauge of human virtue and value."

Atlas Shrugged distinguishes itself from many other defenses of capitalism by its determined effort to show that "selfish" economic behavior is not a "private vice" that just happens to produce "public virtues" but is itself virtuous. The book is much stronger, however, in its critical analysis of the economic and social practice of collectivism—an analysis that has received striking confirmation from events in Eastern Europe, Latin America, and elsewhere—than in its contributions to the economic theory of capitalism. It does not fully clarify the relationship between the objective ethical values on which capitalist society is supposed to be based and the subjective preferences that govern its economic life. Rand asserts that "when men live by trade—with reason, not force, as their final arbiter—it is the best product that wins." But just as consumers—even rational ones—vary in their wants, so economic determinations of the products "best" able to satisfy those wants also

Georgia billboard with the mysterious question that appears as graffiti in
Atlas Shrugged *(photograph © by the Ayn Rand Estate)*

the width of the gulf that separates general from official culture in the United States.

Although the success of *Atlas Shrugged* provided Rand with a sizable income, she and her husband continued to live in modest circumstances in an apartment in New York, the city she loved and to which she and O'Connor had returned in 1951. She wrote no more novels, but she found new ways of disseminating her views. In this effort she was assisted by two young admirers, Nathaniel Branden and his wife, Barbara Weidman Branden. Rand regarded Nathaniel Branden, who became an influential psychotherapist and writer on psychological subjects, as her "intellectual heir." In 1958, with Rand's cooperation, he established an organization, the Nathaniel Branden Lectures–the name was soon changed to the Nathaniel Branden Institute– to publicize her philosophy. The institute offered live and recorded lecture courses on Objectivism. Rand and Branden started *The Objectivist Newsletter* in 1962–it became *The Objectivist* in 1966–in which essays by Rand were regularly featured. These projects found a large audience.

Although Rand wanted her philosophy to exert an influence on American culture, and the success of the Nathaniel Branden Institute helped her to realize this ambition, she had no interest in founding a party or ideological cult and little desire for personal power. But

her commanding presence, the ambitious claims of her philosophy, and the dogmatic moralism that pervaded her movement promoted a spirit of conformity that was quite at odds with her explicit teaching. In Rand's circle, ideas were constantly analyzed and debated, but the judgments of the leadership tended to be respected as authoritative on all important–and many unimportant– subjects. Talented disciples were frequently purged because of intellectual disputes or disputes about matters of taste that were interpreted as intellectual disputes. Rand was embattled against the world and psychologically isolated among her followers, and she suffered severely from anxiety and depression. Nevertheless, she continued to develop her philosophy and to apply it more concretely to contemporary problems than she had permitted herself to do in *Atlas Shrugged*.

Rand had attempted to give *Atlas Shrugged* a timeless quality by keeping it free from all strictly topical concerns, going so far as to eliminate virtually all direct references to actual people, institutions, and events. In *Atlas Shrugged* Congress is "the Legislature," and the president is "Mr. Thompson, the Head of the State." By contrast, the essays that she wrote for the Objectivist periodicals–many of which were republished in collections such as *The Virtue of Selfishness: A New Concept of Egoism* (1964), *Capitalism: The Unknown Ideal, The New Left: The Anti-Industrial Revolution* (1971), and the posthu-

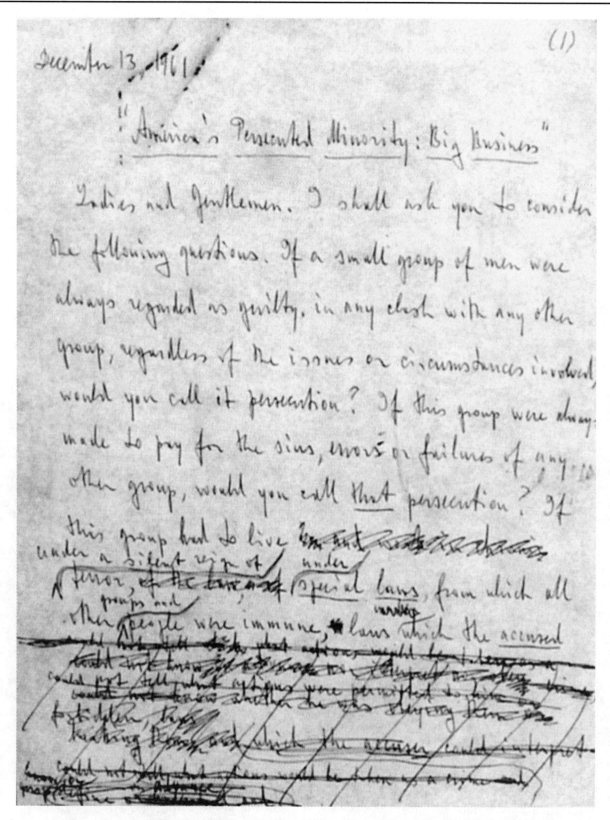

First page of the manuscript for a 1961 lecture by Rand that was published as a pamphlet in 1962 and collected in her
Capitalism: The Unknown Ideal *in 1966 (Butterfield, Butterfield, and Dunning, The Papers*
of Ayn Rand, sale number 5893, 18 November 1998)

mous *Philosophy: Who Needs It* (1982)–often include specific analyses of contemporary political and cultural phenomena. Rand's essays also expand her theories, particularly in the areas of politics, epistemology, and aesthetics.

Rand's political philosophy–as developed especially in *The Virtue of Selfishness*–is grounded in the natural right to life, which, she argues, implies a natural right to property. As she understands it, "The right to life means the right to engage in self-sustaining and self-generated action–which means: the freedom to take all the actions required by the nature of a rational being for the support, the furtherance, the fulfillment and the enjoyment of his own life." Human life cannot be supported without property, and "without property rights, no other rights are possible." Rights, however, concern actions, not objects: rights do not guarantee that people will actually acquire property, although they do sanction people's freedom to act so as to acquire and keep it. No one's right to action imposes any duty of action on anyone else, except the "negative" obligation to abstain from violating that right.

Rand opposes the modern liberal "inflation" of positive "rights" as intellectually incoherent. To claim, for example, that some person has a right to a house or a job and cannot be "free" if he or she does not possess it is to impose on some other person the duty of providing a house or a job if one is lacking, thereby violating the latter person's freedom of action. No such incoherent views of freedom appear in a theory that simply obliges everyone not to coerce anyone else, thus leaving all free to acquire whatever goods they are able to acquire on their own. Government's role is to defend individual rights against those who would initiate coercion against others. Although everyone has a natural right to self-defense, a civilized society requires an agency that can exert effective defensive force in accordance with objectively defined laws: this agency is a government. Legitimate government is minimal government, the kind of government that exists to defend the individual's right to be left alone.

For much of her conception of government Rand is indebted to the seventeenth-century English philosopher John Locke and to the American Founding Fathers–at least as such sources were interpreted by Paterson and other classical liberals. Rand's deductions, definitions, and tests of governmental legitimacy are often clearer and warier than Locke's. She seeks to avert plausible criticism, as does Locke, but she also seeks to avoid saying more than she needs to say; thus, unlike Locke, she demonstrates that she can reason about natural rights without encumbering herself with arguments about a hypothetical "state of nature." She does, however, agree with Locke in viewing government as properly resulting from "the consent of the governed," which she understands to imply the Lockean principle that government is the "*agent* of the citizens." As such, she indicates in *The Virtue of Selfishness,* government "has no rights except the rights *delegated* to it by the citizens." She also appropriates–or reinvents–Thomas Paine's distinction between government and society: "If a society is to be free," she says, "its government has to be controlled." It is not "society" that Randian egoism opposes, but collectivism and its patron, expansive government.

Rand permits government three functions. It should provide an army and a police force (antidotes to aggression), and it should provide law courts "to settle disputes among men according to objective laws." Because she opposes the initiation of force, she distinguishes herself from mainstream Lockeans by also opposing coercive taxation. She believes that a properly limited government would require only the minimal funding achievable through "voluntary" taxation. One source of funds, she speculates, might be a small fee on the millions of credit transactions that take place daily in a capitalist society; this "insurance" fee would be paid by people who wanted the government to enforce their contracts.

In her discussions of government Rand characteristically attempts to remove any seeds of statism from classical liberalism, converting the classical-liberal idea of limited government into her own ideal of minimal government. Like her mentor Paterson, however, she also tries to remove the seeds of anarchism from her theory. On the one hand, she wants to prevent government from expanding its functions so as to provide an inflated list of "rights"; on the other hand, she wants to protect the legitimate functions of government from criticism by "some of the younger advocates of freedom"–that is, some of her own readers–who suggest that government can be replaced by private, competing rights-protection organizations. This "anarcho-capitalist" idea, which came to be associated with Rand's acquaintance Murray N. Rothbard and his followers, gained prominence in certain circles of libertarians and encouraged Rand to dissociate herself completely from the libertarian movement–a movement on which she was the strongest contemporary influence.

Although Rand disapproved of attempts to defend capitalism on exclusively practical grounds, her essays on social and political issues sometimes appeal more to practical than to moral considerations or fail to show that the two types of considerations are complementary. For example, in the essay "Patents and Copyrights," published in *The Objectivist Newsletter* in May 1964 and collected in *Capitalism: The Unknown Ideal,* she defends patents and copyrights as "the legal implemen-

Dust jacket for Rand's 1964 collection of articles extolling the ethics of egoism (Butterfield, Butterfield, and Dunning, The Papers of Ayn Rand, sale number 5893, 18 November 1998)

tation of the base of all property rights: a man's right to the product of his mind"; but she denies that intellectual property should be protected for more than a limited time. It would be too difficult, she argues, for distant generations to continue paying royalties to the heirs of inventors. She even refers to "the unreality of [the heirs'] unearned claims"—language that she would never allow in regard to the more easily satisfied claims of the heirs of other forms of property. Likewise, Rand's argument against anarchism is concerned mainly with practical considerations: competing rights-protection institutions would be incapable of enforcing objective law; they just would not work. Continuing debates about Rand's political ideas tend to focus on the perceived tension between the practical and the moral imperatives in her work.

Rand's major effort in epistemology is a series of essays published in *The Objectivist* in 1966 and 1967 and collected in 1967 as *Introduction to Objectivist Epistemology*—a "preview" of a "future book on Objectivism" that was

never written. In these essays Rand discusses the differences between her view of knowledge and the views of Plato, Immanuel Kant, the logical positivists, and the linguistic analysts. She seeks to establish an epistemological basis for both the individualism and the objectivism of her philosophical system. Her analysis characterizes thinking as the source of a more-than-subjective knowledge of the world and yet as an active process that is responsive to the individual will.

To support this view she focuses not on percepts, "sensations automatically retained and integrated by the brain," but on concepts, which are products of "volitional consciousness." She defines a concept as "a mental integration of two or more units which are isolated according to a specific characteristic(s) and united by a specific definition." A "unit" is an "existent" that is regarded as a member of a group of similar existents. The units possess "the same distinguishing characteristic(s)," but in the process of concept formation their "particular measurements" are "omitted." To generate a concept from one's awareness of several existents requires an active process of thought that involves the abstraction of similar characteristics and then the integration or uniting of the existents, now seen as units, into a "new *mental* entity which is used thereafter as a single unit of thought." This mental entity is not merely an artifact of some arbitrary subjective process; it responds to "attributes which a consciousness observes in reality." To put this point in another way, concepts are "*objective* . . . neither revealed nor invented, but . . . produced by man's consciousness in accordance with the facts of reality, . . . mental integrations of factual data computed by man."

Rand assumes the general validity of the senses; as she maintains in *Atlas Shrugged*, one cannot argue against their validity without relying in some way on the evidence of the senses themselves. But definitions—which, according to *Introduction to Objectivist Epistemology*, identify "the nature of the units subsumed under a concept"—may be invalid, and they may be false: they may fail to specify "known relationships among existents (in terms of the known *essential* characteristics)," or they may contradict available knowledge. True definitions are "not changelessly absolute, but they are *contextually absolute*"; they may be expanded, but not contradicted, by increased knowledge. Given the fundamental significance of properly defined concepts, the significance of logic as "the art of non-contradictory identification" is manifest. Logic, not subjectivity, makes every mind an "ultimate authority" on truth. Logical, objective thought does not require omniscience, but it does require acceptance of "the responsibility of cognitive precision."

Rand gives this responsibility its full moral weight as a requirement for leading a properly human life.

Rand's literary aesthetic is the subject of her essay collection *The Romantic Manifesto: A Philosophy of Literature* (1969). Her aesthetic ideas are not as well organized as those on politics and epistemology, but they display many suggestive features–among them, her definition of art as "a selective re-creation of reality according to an artist's metaphysical value-judgments." Her approach may be called Aristotelian, though not for the major reason she considers it such. In the *Poetics* Aristotle argues that poetry is concerned not with historical accuracy but with imaginative probability–with the way in which certain kinds of people "probably or inevitably" act. Rand interpreted this Aristotelian principle as an argument for the heroic, morally idealizing literature that she enjoyed writing, literature that represents things "as they might be and ought to be." Her real points of agreement with Aristotle, however, lie in their mutual emphasis on plot or meaningful action in literature and their tendency to assess works of art as made objects, the results of their creators' purposeful actions. Rand's concern with conscious choice allows her to construct a theory that combines the Aristotelian with the "Romantic." She regards Romanticism as the kind of art that assumes the centrality of value judgments, choices of what "ought to be"; Romanticism thus implies not a flight from human reality but an emphasis on its volitional aspect. Rand labels herself a "Romantic Realist."

Rand contrasts her idea of Romanticism with "naturalism," which she understands as an artistic movement that proceeds from a deterministic philosophy and often manifests itself in a narrowly mimetic practice. In modern literature, however, she finds few "romanticists," little of interest among the many "naturalists," and an "eclectic shambles" that has taken the place of both great schools of literature. She is interested, however, in what happens to elements of high culture that maintain their artistic usefulness but are no longer associated with vital and prestigious intellectual movements. She argues that Romantic assumptions and methods are still current but are allowed to express themselves only in peripheral genres or as disguised by self-reflexive comedy or "camp" effects. This, in her pungent phrase, is "bootleg romanticism." She concludes that the "last remnants of Romanticism are flickering only in the field of popular art, like bright spots in a stagnant gray fog."

By the time *The Romantic Manifesto* appeared in print, Rand had sustained a disaster to her personal life and also, to a degree, to her intellectual and public life. In 1968 she quarreled with Nathaniel and Barbara Branden, her chief disciples and closest friends, over

O'Connor in his studio in New York City in 1966
(photograph © by the Ayn Rand Estate)

the consequences of her romantic involvement with Nathaniel. Her break with them, which Rand never forthrightly explained to her followers, fractured the Objectivist movement. The Nathaniel Branden Institute ceased to exist, and although Rand continued to address the public through a new periodical, *The Ayn Rand Letter,* and occasional lectures, she wrote neither a fifth novel nor her promised book on Objectivism. Her health deteriorated in 1974; she lost part of a lung to cancer, and she soon ceased publication of her periodical. Her husband, O'Connor, died on 9 November 1979. Disputes with close followers recurred, and by the early 1980s few remained in her formerly large and lively "inner circle." Rand died in her apartment on East Thirty-fourth Street in New York City on 6 March 1982.

A conclusive assessment of Ayn Rand's achievement and influence cannot yet be made. Both her fiction and her works of philosophy remain highly popular with general readers, and her ideas continue to exert a political effect, especially on the American libertarian movement. The fact that intellectuals initially

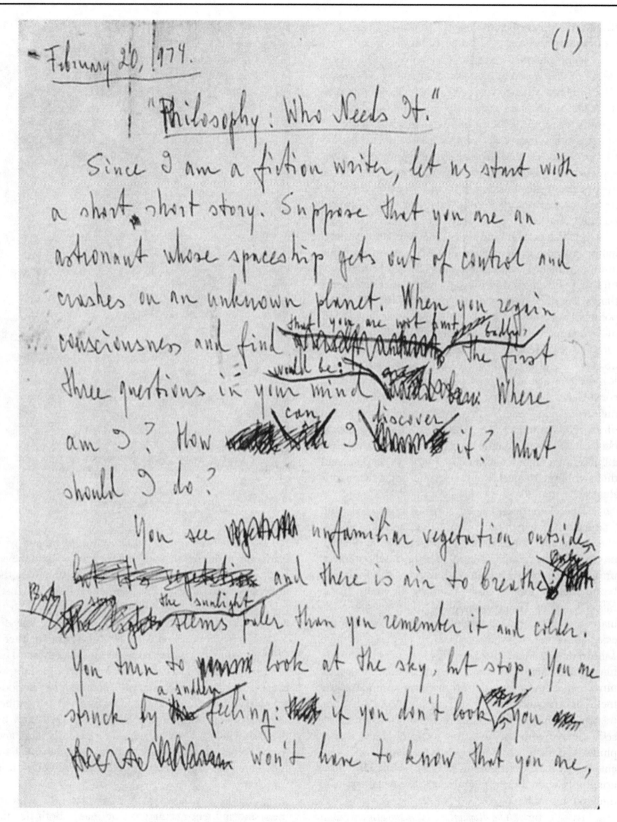

(1)

February 20, 1974.

"Philosophy : Who Needs It."

Since I am a fiction writer, let us start with a short, short story. Suppose that you are an astronaut whose spaceship gets out of control and crashes on an unknown planet. When you regain consciousness and find ~~that you are not hurt badly~~ the first three questions in your mind ~~would be:~~ Where am I? How ~~can~~ I ~~discover~~ it? What should I do?

You see ~~~~ unfamiliar vegetation outside ~~~~ and there is air to breathe ~~~~ the sunlight ~~seems~~ paler than you remember it and colder. You turn to ~~~~ look at the sky, but stop. You are struck by ~~the~~ a sudden feeling: ~~~~ if you don't look ~~~~ you ~~~~ won't have to know that you are,

Page from the manuscript for the essay that became the title piece in Rand's posthumous 1982 collection
(Butterfield, Butterfield, and Dunning, The Papers of Ayn Rand,
sale number 5893, 18 November 1998)

tended either to detest or to idolize her, however, meant that judicious scholarly and critical evaluation was slow to appear. Professional philosophers showed little interest in appraising the ideas of a novelist and political heretic who refused to practice or even to interest herself in established modes of academic discourse. Since her death, however, a substantial scholarly industry has grown up around her. Two organizations—the Ayn Rand Institute in Irvine, California, and the Objectivist Center in Poughkeepsie, New York—are devoted to the investigation of her thought. Selections from her letters, her literary notebooks or "journals," and her lectures on writing have been published. A new edition (1990) of *Introduction to Objectivist Epistemology* includes a long transcription of Rand's "workshops," conversations in which she demonstrates impressive philosophical agility and ingenuity. A biography by Barbara Branden, a memoir by Nathaniel Branden, and briefer accounts by other persons have made substantial information about her life available. In *Ayn Rand: The Russian Radical* (1995) Chris Matthew Sciabarra has investigated her early intellectual training and her relationship to Continental traditions of thought.

Rand's political and moral philosophy is a frequent subject of analysis in libertarian and classical-liberal journals, especially *Liberty,* which began publication in 1987. The *Journal of Ayn Rand Studies,* founded in 1999, publishes scholarly papers on all areas of her thought. Several aspects of her work have elicited substantial studies, beginning with a series of papers on egoism, theories of value, property rights, and related topics in *The Personalist* between 1969 and 1979. Valuable essays by scholars such as King, Mack, and Wallace Matson are collected in *The Philosophic Thought of Ayn Rand* (1984). Especially worthy of note among recent works are *What Art Is* (2000), by Michelle Marder Kamhi and Louis Torres, a groundbreaking inquiry into the principles and applications of Rand's aesthetic theory, and Sciabarra's *Total Freedom: Toward a Dialectical Libertarianism* (2000), which makes provocative connections between Rand's approach to philosophy and a broadly defined "dialectical" tradition or traditions.

Scholarly interest in Rand shows every sign of continued growth. People once inclined to dismiss her philosophy now find it more substantial than they had anticipated, while those inclined to sympathize with it now find her views more complex and challenging than they once believed. Among the barriers to objective assessment that still exist, the chief is undoubtedly political: scholars are often so strongly attracted or repelled by Rand's politics as to be incapable of providing a fair account of that or any other aspect of her thought. Other barriers result from her characteristic modes of

discourse. Her use of fiction as a medium for philosophical expression presents obvious problems. Additional problems arise from the peculiarly direct approach she adopted in her nonfiction works. She took a justifiable pride in her ability to formulate ideas in concise, everyday language, avoiding arcane terms, complex qualifications and exemplifications, and commentaries on the history of her ideas. The major features of her arguments often emerge with brilliant clarity, but secondary features that may be important to their persuasiveness or applicability sometimes remain ill defined.

Difficulties also result from Rand's alienation from other thinkers. Like her great enemy Karl Marx, she indulged a taste for vitriolic expression that has made less polemical thinkers reluctant to entertain, or admit that they entertain, ideas so vituperatively advanced. After reaching adulthood, Rand was a largely self-taught thinker, with Paterson her only crucial outside influence. She worked primarily by answering the questions raised by her own writing. Operating in this way, she frequently reinvented (or remodeled) the philosophic wheel or discovered ways of repairing wheels that had been discarded by other philosophers. This method of developing her ideas gave them a vitality and unpredictability that they would not otherwise have acquired, but it can make precise judgments about the significance of her particular contributions somewhat difficult to render.

What does seem clear is that Ayn Rand was a leading figure in the restoration of intellectual confidence in individualism, which at the beginning of her career was often regarded more as the distinguishing problem than as the distinguishing achievement of American thought. Denying the apparent affinity between the individual and the purely subjective, she mounted a broad challenge to the subjectivist and "antifoundationalist" tendencies of post-Enlightenment philosophy, tendencies she identified as threats to the authority of the individual and rational mind. Her advocacy of individual choice and action inspired both intellectual and nonintellectual readers, and her moral defense of economic individualism exerted a substantial influence on contemporary political ideology. It is likely that as her ideas become better known and assimilated within American intellectual culture, she will be increasingly viewed as a formidable participant in the discourse of America's defining tradition of individualism.

Letters:

Letters of Ayn Rand, edited by Michael S. Berliner (New York: Dutton, 1995).

Interview:

Alvin Toffler, "The *Playboy* Interview: Ayn Rand," *Playboy,* 11 (March 1964): 35–43.

Bibliographies:

Vincent L. Perinn, *Ayn Rand–First Descriptive Bibliography* (Rockville, Md.: Quill & Brush, 1990);

Mimi Reisel Gladstein, *The New Ayn Rand Companion* (Westport, Conn.: Greenwood Press, 1999), pp. 127–152.

Biographies:

Barbara Branden, *The Passion of Ayn Rand* (Garden City, N.Y.: Doubleday, 1986);

Nathaniel Branden, *Judgment Day: My Years with Ayn Rand* (Boston: Houghton Mifflin, 1989); revised as *My Years with Ayn Rand* (San Francisco: Jossey-Bass, 1999).

References:

Nathaniel Branden, *The Moral Revolution in* Atlas Shrugged (Poughkeepsie, N.Y.: Atlas Society, 2000);

Whittaker Chambers, "Big Sister Is Watching You," *National Review,* 4 (28 December 1957): 594–596;

John Cody, "Ayn Rand's Promethean Heroes," *Reason,* 5 (November 1973): 30–35;

Stephen Cox, "Ayn Rand: Theory versus Creative Life," *Journal of Libertarian Studies,* 8 (Winter 1986): 19–29;

Cox, "The Evolution of Ayn Rand," *Liberty,* 11 (July 1998): 49–57;

Douglas J. Den Uyl, *The Fountainhead: An American Novel* (New York: Twayne, 1999);

Den Uyl and Douglas Rasmussen, "Nozick on the Randian Argument," *Personalist,* 59 (April 1978): 184–201;

Den Uyl and Rasmussen, eds., *The Philosophic Thought of Ayn Rand* (Urbana: University of Illinois Press, 1984);

William Dwyer, "The Argument against 'an Objective Standard of Value,'" *Personalist,* 55 (Spring 1974): 165–181;

Peter F. Erickson, *The Stance of Atlas: An Examination of the Philosophy of Ayn Rand* (Portland, Ore.: Herakles Press, 1997);

Mimi Reisel Gladstein, *Atlas Shrugged: Manifesto of the Mind* (New York: Twayne, 2000);

Gladstein, *The New Ayn Rand Companion* (Westport, Conn.: Greenwood Press, 1999);

Gladstein and Chris Matthew Sciabarra, eds., *Feminist Interpretations of Ayn Rand* (University Park: Pennsylvania State University Press, 1999);

Sidney Hook, "Each Man for Himself," *New York Times Book Review,* 66 (9 April 1961): 3, 28;

John Hospers, "Conversations with Ayn Rand," *Liberty,* 3 (July 1990): 23–36; 4 (September 1990): 42–52;

Journal of Ayn Rand Studies, 1– (Fall 1999–   );

Michelle Marder Kamhi and Louis Torres, *What Art Is: The Esthetic Theory of Ayn Rand* (Chicago: Open Court, 2000);

David Kelley, *The Contested Legacy of Ayn Rand: Truth and Toleration in Objectivism* (Poughkeepsie, N.Y.: Objectivist Center / New Brunswick, N.J.: Transaction, 2000);

Dale Lugenbehl, "The Argument for an Objective Standard of Value," *Personalist,* 55 (Spring 1974): 155–164;

Tibor R. Machan, *Ayn Rand* (New York: Peter Lang, 1999);

Machan, "Recent Work in Ethical Egoism," *American Philosophical Quarterly,* 16 (January 1979): 1–15;

Machan, "Some Recent Work in Human Rights Theory," *American Philosophical Quarterly,* 17 (April 1980): 103–115;

George I. Mavrodes, "Property," *Personalist,* 53 (Summer 1972): 245–262;

Ronald E. Merrill, *The Ideas of Ayn Rand* (La Salle, Ill.: Open Court, 1991);

Robert Nozick, "On the Randian Argument," *Personalist,* 52 (Spring 1971): 282–304;

William F. O'Neill, *With Charity toward None: An Analysis of Ayn Rand's Philosophy* (New York: Philosophical Library, 1971);

Michael Paxton, *Ayn Rand: A Sense of Life. The Companion Book* (Layton, Utah: Gibbs Smith, 1998);

Leonard Peikoff, *Objectivism: The Philosophy of Ayn Rand* (New York: Dutton, 1991);

Chris Matthew Sciabarra, *Ayn Rand: The Russian Radical* (University Park: Pennsylvania State University Press, 1995);

Sciabarra, *Total Freedom: Toward a Dialectical Libertarianism* (University Park: Pennsylvania State University Press, 2000);

Judith Wilt, "On *Atlas Shrugged,*" *College English,* 40 (November 1978): 333–336.

Papers:

The Papers of Ayn Rand in the Library of Congress include drafts, typescripts, and galley proofs for *We the Living, Anthem, The Fountainhead,* and *Atlas Shrugged;* material pertaining to Rand's newsletter; photographs; and a letter. The Ayn Rand Archives at the Ayn Rand Institute in Irvine, California, include manuscripts, notes, journals, clipping files, correspondence, photographs, audio and video recordings, and microfilm of the papers at the Library of Congress.

John Herman Randall Jr.

(14 February 1899 – 1 December 1980)

Angelo Juffras
William Paterson University

BOOKS: *An Introduction to Reflective Thinking,* by Randall, Herbert W. Schneider, and James Gutmann (Boston: Houghton Mifflin, 1923);

The Western Mind: Its Origins and Development, 2 volumes (New York: Columbia University Press, 1924); revised and enlarged as *The Making of the Modern Mind: A Survey of the Intellectual Background of the Present Age* (Boston & New York: Houghton Mifflin, 1926; revised and enlarged, 1940);

Introduction to Contemporary Civilization: A Syllabus (New York: Columbia University Press, 1925);

Reading List of Current Books on World Unity (New York: World Unity Publishing Corporation, 1927);

Our Changing Civilization: How Science and Machines Are Reconstructing Modern Life (London: Allen & Unwin, 1929; New York: Stokes, 1929);

Religion and the Modern World, by Randall and John Herman Randall Sr. (New York: Stokes, 1929; London: Williams & Norgate, 1929);

Philosophy: An Introduction, by Randall and Justus Buchler, College Outline Series, no. 41 (New York: Barnes & Noble, 1942; revised, 1971);

Emily Greene Balch of New England, Citizen of the World (Washington, D.C.: Women's International League for Peace and Freedom, 1946);

Nature and Historical Experience: Essays in Naturalism and in the Theory of History (New York: Columbia University Press, 1958);

The Role of Knowledge in Western Religion (Boston: Starr King Press, 1958);

The Ethical Challenge of a Pluralistic Society (New York: New York Society for Ethical Culture, 1959);

Aristotle (New York: Columbia University Press, 1960);

The School of Padua and the Emergence of Modern Science, Series Saggi e Testi of Il Centro per La Storia della Tradizione Aristotelica nel Veneto of the University of Padua and Columbia University Seminar on the Renaissance, volume 1 (Padua: Editrice Antenore, 1961);

John Herman Randall Jr.

From the Middle Ages to the Enlightenment, in *The Career of Philosophy,* volume 1 (New York: Columbia University Press, 1962);

How Philosophy Uses Its Past, Matchette Foundation Lecture Series, no. 14 (New York & London: Columbia University Press, 1963);

From the German Enlightenment to the Age of Darwin, in *The Career of Philosophy,* volume 2 (New York: Columbia University Press, 1965);

Hellenistic Ways of Deliverance and the Making of the Christian Synthesis (New York & London: Columbia University Press, 1970);

Plato: Dramatist of the Life of Reason (New York: Columbia University Press, 1972);

Philosophy after Darwin: Chapters for The Career of Philosophy, *Volume III, and Other Essays,* edited by Beth J. Singer (New York: Columbia University Press, 1977).

OTHER: "Religio Mathematici: The Geometrical World of Malebranche," in *Studies in the History of Ideas,* volume 2, edited by the Department of Philosophy of Columbia University (New York: Columbia University Press, 1925), pp. 183–218;

"Education as Propaganda," in *Adult Education vs. Worker's Education,* edited by a Committee of Local 189, American Federation of Teachers, Fourth Annual Conference, 18–20 February 1927 (Brookwood, Katonah, N.Y.: American Federation of Teachers, 1927), pp. 77–83;

"Dualism in Metaphysics and Practical Philosophy," in *Essays in Honor of John Dewey on the Occasion of His Seventieth Birthday,* edited by John J. Coss (New York: Holt, 1929), pp. 306–323;

"Copernicus," in *Encyclopedia of the Social Sciences,* edited by Edwin R. A. Seligman, volume 4 (New York: Macmillan, 1930), pp. 400–401;

"The Forces That Are Destroying Traditional Beliefs," in *Readings in Contemporary Problems in the United States,* edited by Horace Taylor and Joseph McGolddrick, volume 11 (New York: Columbia University Press, 1930), pp. 690–700;

"Deism," in *Encyclopedia of the Social Sciences,* edited by Seligman, volume 5 (New York: Macmillan, 1931), pp. 61–63;

"Dewey's Interpretation of the History of Philosophy," in *The Philosophy of John Dewey,* edited by Paul Arthur Schilpp, The Library of Living Philosophers, volume 1 (Evanston, Ill.: Northwestern University Press, 1939), pp. 77–102;

"Unifying Factors in the Development of Modern Ideas," in *Studies in Civilization* (Philadelphia: University of Pennsylvania Press, 1941), pp. 105–118;

"Newton's Natural Philosophy: Its Problems and Consequences," in *Philosophical Essays in Honor of Edgar Arthur Singer, Jr.,* edited by Francis P. Clarke and Milton C. Nahm (Philadelphia: University of Pennsylvania Press, 1942), pp. 335–357;

"The Nature of Naturalism," in *Naturalism and the Human Spirit,* edited by Yervant H. Krikorian (New York: Columbia University Press, 1944), pp. 354–382;

Ernst Cassirer, *Rousseau, Kant, Goethe: Two Essays,* translated by Randall, James Gutmann, and Paul Oskar Kristeller (Princeton: Princeton University Press, 1945);

"Part 4: The Meaning of Religion for Man," in *Preface to Philosophy,* by Randall, Brand Blanshard, Charles Hendel, and William Ernest Hocking, edited by William Pearson Tolley (New York: Macmillan, 1946), pp. 297–410; revised as *The Meaning of Religion for Man* (New York: Harper & Row, 1968);

Readings in Philosophy, edited by Randall, Justus Buchler, and Evelyn Urban Shirk, College Outline Series, no. 59 (New York: Barnes & Noble, 1946; revised, 1950);

"David Hume: Radical Empiricist and Pragmatist," in *Freedom and Experience: Essays Presented to Horace M. Kallen,* edited by Sidney Hook and Milton R. Konvitz (Ithaca, N.Y.: Cornell University Press, 1947), pp. 289–312;

"The Spirit of American Philosophy," in *Wellsprings of the American Spirit,* edited by F. Ernest Johnson (New York: Institute for Religious and Social Studies, 1948), pp. 117–133;

The Renaissance Philosophy of Man, edited by Randall, Cassirer, and Kristeller (Chicago: University of Chicago Press, 1948);

"Cassirer's Theory of History as Illustrated in His Treatment of Renaissance Thought," in *The Philosophy of Ernst Cassirer,* edited by Schilpp, The Library of Living Philosophers, volume 6 (Evanston, Ill.: Northwestern University Press, 1949), pp. 689–728;

"What Isaac Newton Started," in *Sir Isaac Newton, Newton's Philosophy of Nature: Selections from His Writings,* edited by Horace S. Thayer (New York: Hafner, 1953), pp. ix–xvi;

William Peery, ed., *Studies in the Renaissance,* foreword by Randall (Austin: University of Texas Press, 1954);

"Introduction" and "The Department of Philosophy," in *The Faculty of Philosophy: The Bicentennial History of Columbia University* (New York: Columbia University Press, 1957), pp. 3–57, 102–145;

"Naturalistic Humanism," in *Patterns of Faith in America Today,* edited by Johnson (New York: Harper, 1957);

John Dewey, *Dictionary of Education,* edited by Ralph Winn, foreword by Randall (New York: Philosophical Library, 1959);

Aristotle, *Aristotle's Physics,* translated by Richard Hope, foreword by Randall (Lincoln: University of Nebraska Press, 1961);

"Philosophy and Religion," in *The Great Ideas Today*, edited by Robert M. Hutchins and Mortimer J. Adler (Chicago: Encyclopaedia Britannica, 1963), pp. 227–277;

Emmanuel G. Mesthene, *How Language Makes Us Know*, foreword by Randall (The Hague: Nijhoff, 1964);

Frederick J. E. Woodbridge, *Aristotle's Vision of Nature*, edited by Randall, Charles H. Kahn, and Harold A. Larrabee, introduction by Randall (New York: Columbia University Press, 1965);

"The University Seminar as a Source of Spiritual Power," in *A Community of Scholars*, edited by Frank Tennenbaum (New York: Praeger, 1965), pp. 46–52.

SELECTED PERIODICAL PUBLICATIONS–
UNCOLLECTED: "Instrumentalism and Mythology," *Journal of Philosophy*, 16 (5 June 1919): 309–324;

"E. Troilo, *Figuri e Studii di storia della Filosofia*," *Journal of Philosophy*, 16 (28 August 1919): 501–502;

"Henry Taylor, *Prophets, Poets and Philosophers of the Ancient World*," *Journal of Philosophy*, 17 (8 April 1920): 220–222;

"The Really Real," *Journal of Philosophy*, 17 (17 June 1920): 337–345;

"Obituary: Theodore Flournoy," *Journal of Philosophy*, 18 (17 February 1921): 110–112;

"Eugenio Rignano, *Psychologie du Raisonnement*," *Journal of Philosophy*, 18 (9 June 1921): 332–334;

"Obituary: Emile Boutroux," *Journal of Philosophy*, 19 (5 January 1922): 26–28;

"Charles C. Josey, *The Social Philosophy of Instinct*," *Journal of Philosophy*, 20 (30 August 1923): 494–497;

"Nicolas Malebranche, *Dialogues on Metaphysics and Religion*, Translated by Morris Ginsberg," *Journal of Philosophy*, 20 (6 December 1923): 696–697;

"Henri Busson, *Les sources et le développement du rationalisme dans la littérature française de la renaissance (1533–1601)*," *Journal of Philosophy*, 20 (6 December 1923): 697;

"Arthur A. Luce, *Bergson's Doctrine of Intuition*, and Firmin Nicolardot, *Un Pseudonyme Bergsonien?*" and "Edme Tassy, *La Philosophie Constructive*," *Journal of Philosophy*, 20 (20 December 1923): 718–719;

"The 23rd Annual Meeting of the Eastern Division of the American Philosophical Association," *Journal of Philosophy*, 21 (17 January 1924): 40–51;

"J. Maréchal, *Le Point de départ de la métaphysique*, Cahier 1–2," *Journal of Philosophy*, 21 (31 January 1924): 74–76;

"Paul Masson-Oursel, *La Philosophie comparée*," *Journal of Philosophy*, 21 (24 April 1924): 241–244;

"Samuel Gompers–Business Unionist," *Standard*, 11 (January 1925): 140–143;

"American Labor–What of the Future?" *Standard*, 11 (February 1925): 182–186;

"Law and Ethics: Review of Benjamin Cardozo, *The Growth of the Law*," *Standard*, 12 (July 1925): 21–23;

"The 25th Annual Meeting of the Eastern Division of the American Philosophical Association," *Journal of Philosophy*, 23 (21 January 1926): 34–46;

"Gentlemanly Ethics: Review of Stephen Ward, *Ethics: An Historical Introduction*," *Standard*, 12 (March 1926): 229;

"The Public and Its Problems: A Discussion of John Dewey's *The Public and Its Problems*," *World Unity*, 1 (November 1927): 129–133;

"The Science of Man," *World Unity*, 1 (December 1927): 209–215;

"Nationalism and Economic World Unity: A Discussion of François Delaisi's *Political Myths and Economic Realities*," *World Unity*, 1 (January 1928): 281–287;

"The Unification of the Social Sciences," *World Unity*, 1 (February 1928): 354–358;

"Outstanding Books of the Season," *World Unity*, 2 (April 1928): 65–71;

"Peace–the Condition of Survival: A Discussion of Henry N. Brailsford's *Olives of Endless Age*," *World Unity*, 2 (May 1928): 135–140;

"The Rainbow of Human Cultures: A Discussion of Roland Dixon's *The Building of Cultures* and Charles Ellwood's *Cultural Evolution*," *World Unity*, 2 (June 1928): 212–217;

"The Problems of Religion in the Modern World: A Discussion of Reinhold Niebuhr's *Does Civilization Need Religion?*" *World Unity*, 2 (July 1928): 285–291;

"The Cooperation of Europe: A Discussion of John Spencer Bassett's *The League of Nations*," *World Unity*, 2 (August 1928): 359–361;

"Toward Pan-Europeanism: A Discussion of Count Herman Keyserling's *Europe*," *World Unity*, 2 (September 1928): 422–425;

"The Future of Christianity: A Discussion of Charles Guignebert's *Christianity Past and Present*," *World Unity*, 3 (October 1928): 67–73;

"Realpolitik and the Realistic Mind: A Discussion of Herman Stegemann's *The Mirage of Versailles* and Alfred Fabre-Luce's *Locarno: The Reality*," *World Unity*, 3 (November 1928): 132–139;

"Philosophy for an Industrial Civilization: A Discussion of Charles A. Beard (ed.), *Whither Mankind?*" *World Unity*, 3 (December 1928): 201–209;

"Martha Ornstein, *The Role of Scientific Societies in the Seventeenth Century*," *American Historical Review*, 34 (January 1929): 386;

"Books on the New Civilization," *World Unity*, 3 (January 1929): 274–276;

"The Reconstruction of Religious Thought: A Discussion of Gerald Smith's *Religious Thought in the Last Quarter-Century*, Harry Barnes's *Living in the Twentieth Century*, William Wallace's *The Scientific World View*, and Roy Sellars's *Religion Coming of Age*," *World Unity*, 3 (February 1929): 347–356;

"The Meaning of the Pact of Paris: A Discussion of James T. Shotwell's *War as an Instrument of National Policy*," *World Unity*, 4 (May 1929): 150–155;

"John Dewey, *Characters and Events: Popular Essays in Social and Political Philosophy*, Edited by Joseph Ratner," *New York Evening Post*, 18 May 1929;

"Religion's Peril from the Machine Age," *Current History*, 30 (June 1929): 355–362;

"Harry Barnes, *Living in the Twentieth Century*, and Thomas Jones, *Essentials of Civilization*," *Political Science Quarterly*, 44 (September 1929): 435–438;

"Science and the Educated Man," *World Unity*, 5 (November 1929): 120–125;

"The Ordeal of Liberalism: A Discussion of Gilbert Murray's *The Ordeal of This Generation*," *World Unity*, 5 (December 1929): 200–207;

"Pacifism in the Modern World: A Discussion of Devere Allen, ed., *Pacifism in the Modern World*," *World Unity*, 5 (January 1930): 276–283;

"The Role of Science in Modern Life: What Must Religion Learn from It?" *Religious Education*, 25 (February 1930): 107–115;

"A Budget of Books: A Discussion of Alfred Zimmern's *America and Europe*, Bernard Joseph's *Nationality, Its Nature and Problems*, Jackson Ralston's *International Arbitration from Athens to Locarno*, and John Donaldson's *International Economic Relations: A Treatise on World Economy and World Politics*," *World Unity*, 5 (March 1930): 419–423;

"Some Major Characteristics of Our Changing Civilization," *Religious Education*, 25 (June 1930): 507–515;

"Victor Francis Calverton and Samuel D. Schmalhausen, Eds., *The New Generation*," *Current History*, 32 (August 1930): 1028;

"Personal Liberty and Social Control," *Federal Council Bulletin* (September 1930): 9–10;

"Science and Human Imagination: A Discussion of John Langdon-Davies's *Man and His Universe*," *World Unity*, 7 (November 1930): 133–139;

"Individuality through Social Unity: A Discussion of John Dewey's *Individualism Old and New*," *World Unity*, 7 (December 1930): 193–201;

"The United States of Europe: A Discussion of Edouard Herriot's *The United States of Europe*," *World Unity*, 7 (January 1931): 293–299;

"Humanized Religion: A Discussion of Nathaniel Schmidt's *The Coming Religion* and Abby Hillel Silver's *Religion in a Changing World*," *World Unity*, 7 (March 1931): 428–438;

"Elements of a World Culture," *World Unity*, 8 (April 1931): 38–49;

"Religions of the World: A Discussion of Carl Clemen, ed., *Religions of the World*," *World Unity*, 8 (May 1931): 137–140;

"Equality as Equalizing: A Discussion of R. H. Tawney's *Equality*," *World Unity*, 8 (June 1931): 209–215;

"The Stages of Nationalism," *World Unity*, 8 (August 1931): 353–360;

"Humanism and Humility," *New Humanist*, 4 (September–October 1931): 1–9;

"The Living God–a Power or an Ideal?" *Christian Century*, 48 (11 November 1931): 1418–1421;

"The Latent Idealism of a Materialist: A Review of Santayana's *Realm of Matter*," *Journal of Philosophy*, 28 (19 November 1931): 645–660;

"The Value of Science: A Discussion of Bertrand Russell's *The Scientific Outlook* and John Dewey's *Philosophy and Civilization*," *World Unity*, 9 (December 1931): 187–197;

"Cecil Burns, *Modern Civilization on Trial*," *International Journal of Ethics*, 42 (January 1932): 213–215;

"The Stupidity of the Sword: A Discussion of Esme Wingfield Stratford's *They That Take the Sword*," *World Unity*, 9 (February 1932): 324–331;

"Nationalism and Reason: A Discussion of Norman Angell's *The Unseen Assassins*," *World Unity*, 9 (March 1932): 414–421;

"On the Humanity of Scientists: A Discussion of T. Swann Harding's *The Degradation of Science*," *World Unity*, 10 (April 1932): 56–63;

"Liberalism as Faith in Intelligence," *Journal of Philosophy*, 32 (9 May 1935): 253–264;

"Lane Cooper, *Aristotle, Galileo, and the Tower of Pisa*," *Journal of Philosophy*, 32 (10 October 1935): 583–584;

"Art and Religion as Education," *Social Frontier*, 2 (January 1936): 109–113;

"William Heidel, *The Heroic Age of Science*," *Philosophical Review*, 45 (March 1936): 215–217;

"Bertrand Russell, *Religion and Science*," *Christendom* (Spring 1936): 551–555;

"This So-Called Revolt against Reason," *American Scholar*, 5 (Summer 1936): 347–360;

"*Science and Society: A Marxian Quarterly*, Spring 1937," *New York Teacher*, 2 (June 1937): 31–32;

"The Perfection of Rottenness: Review of George Santayana, *The Philosophy of Santayana: Selections from the Works of George Santayana*, Edited by Irwin Edman," *Social Frontier*, 4 (October 1937): 33;

"Joyce Hertzler, *The Social Thought of the Ancient Civilizations*," *American Historical Review*, 43 (October 1937): 81–82;

"Walter Lippmann, *Inquiry into the Principles of the Good Society*," *New York Teacher*, 3 (November 1937): 26;

"Charles Hartshorne, *Beyond Humanism: Essays in the New Philosophy of Nature*," *Journal of Philosophy*, 34 (9 December 1937): 691–693;

"Irwin Edman, *Four Ways of Philosophy*," *New York Herald Tribune Books*, 26 December 1937, p. 2;

"Lancelot Hogben, *Retreat from Reason*," *Journal of Philosophy*, 35 (20 January 1938): 51–53;

"Michael Roberts, *The Modern Mind*," *Journal of Philosophy*, 35 (17 February 1938): 104–106;

"Arthur O. Lovejoy, *The Great Chain of Being*," *Philosophical Review*, 47 (March 1938): 214–218;

"Arthur O. Lovejoy, *The Great Chain of Being*," *Review of Religion*, 2 (March 1938): 343–353;

"On Professor Hartshorne's Reply to J. H. Randall's Review of Hartshorne's *Beyond Humanism*," *Journal of Philosophy*, 35 (3 March 1938): 132–133;

"On the Importance of Being Unprincipled," *American Scholar*, 7 (Spring 1938): 131–143;

"Richard Honigswald, *Denker der italienischen Renaissance: Gestalten und Probleme*," *Journal of Philosophy*, 35 (12 May 1938): 378;

"St. Augustine, *Concerning the Teacher* (*De Magistro*) and *On the Immortality of the Soul* (*De Immortalitae animae*), Translated by G. G. Leckie," *Journal of Philosophy*, 35 (26 May 1938): 302–303;

"Friedrich Oesterle, *Die Anthropologie des Paracelsus*," *Journal of Philosophy*, 35 (1 September 1938): 488;

"Folke Leander, *Humanism and Naturalism: A Comparative Study of Ernest Seilliere, Irving Babbitt and Paul Elmer More*," *Journal of Philosophy*, 35 (1 September 1938): 490–491;

"Joseph K. Hart, *Mind in Transition*," *Journal of Philosophy*, 35 (1 September 1938): 497;

"On Understanding the History of Philosophy: Abstract of a Paper Presented in December 1938," *Journal of Philosophy*, 35 (8 December 1938): 681–683;

"Tommaso Campanella, *The Defense of Galileo*, Edited and Translated by Grant McColley," *Journal of Philosophy*, 35 (22 December 1938): 720;

"Emile Durkheim, *L'Evolution pedagogique en France*, volumes 1–2," *Journal of Philosophy*, 36 (2 March 1939): 135–136;

"Reply to G. McColley's Note on the Review of His Edition of Campanella's *Defense of Galileo*," *Journal of Philosophy*, 36 (16 March 1939): 158;

"Maurice Mandlebaum, *The Problem of Historical Knowledge*," *Journal of Philosophy*, 36 (3 August 1939): 442–446;

"Etienne Gilson, *Reason and Revelation in the Middle Ages*," *Journal of Philosophy*, 36 (31 August 1939): 495–496;

"The Paradox of Intellectual Freedom," *American Scholar*, 11 (Winter 1939–1940): 5–18;

"Dean Woodbridge," *Columbia University Quarterly*, 32 (December 1940): 324–331;

"Karl Mannheim, *Man and Society in an Age of Reconstruction*," *Journal of the History of Ideas*, 2 (June 1941): 372–381;

"The Study of the Philosophies of the Renaissance," by Randall and Paul O. Kristeller, *Journal of the History of Ideas*, 2 (October 1941): 449–496;

"Joseph Gittler, *Social Thought among the Early Greeks*," *American Historical Review*, 48 (October 1942): 170–171;

"John Nef, *The United States and Civilization*," *American Historical Review*, 48 (January 1943): 346–348;

"Human Destiny–Reinhold Niebuhr, a Symposium," by Randall, Paul Lehmann, Edwin E. Aubrey, and John C. Bennett, *Union Review*, 4 (March 1943): 18–26;

"Friedrich Solmsen, *Plato's Theology*," *Review of Religion*, 7 (May 1943): 384–389;

"Sidney Hook, *The Hero in History*," *Journal of Philosophy*, 40 (14 October 1943): 575–580;

"Jacques Maritain, *Education at the Crossroads*," *Journal of Philosophy*, 40 (28 October 1943): 609–614;

"Jacques Barzun, *Romanticism and the Modern Ego*," *Journal of Philosophy*, 40 (11 November 1943): 635–639;

"The Ethics of Good Usage: Review of Paul A. Schilpp, ed., *The Philosophy of G. E. Moore*," *Standard*, 30 (March 1944): 172–173;

"Which Are the Liberating Arts?" *American Scholar*, 13 (April 1944): 135–148;

"To Win Out, Must Humanists Embrace Sin?" *Humanist*, 4 (1946): 20–27;

"Metaphysics, Its Function, Consequences, and Criteria: Abstract of a Symposium with William E. Hocking and Sterling P. Lamprecht," *Journal of Philosophy*, 43 (31 January 1946): 62–67;

"Morris R. Cohen, *The Meaning of Human History*," *Journal of the History of Ideas*, 10 (April 1949): 305–312;

"Leo Strauss, *On Tyranny*," *New York Times Book Review*, 1 May 1949, p. 14;

"Fulton Anderson, *The Philosophy of Francis Bacon*," *University of Toronto Quarterly*, 19 (October 1949): 99–103;

"Salute to John Dewey," *Survey*, 85 (October 1949): 508–510;

"Hiram Haydn, *The Counter-Renaissance*," *Saturday Review of Literature*, 33 (24 June 1950): 21;

"*Nicolas von Cues: Texte seiner philosophischen schriften nach der Ausgabe von Paris 1514, sowie nach der Druckle-gung von Basel 1565*, Volume 1," *Journal of Philosophy*, 47 (3 August 1950): 472–473;

"Ernst Cassirer, *The Problem of Knowledge*, Translated by W. H. Woglom and C. W. Hendel," *New York Times Book Review*, 10 September 1950, p. 27;

"Kathleen Freeman, *Greek City-States*," *New York Times Book Review*, 17 December 1950, p. 6;

"Arthur O. Lovejoy, *Essays on the History of Ideas*," *Kenyon Review*, 12 (Winter 1950): 156–161;

"Some Observations on Contemporary Historical Theory," by Randall, Merle Curti, Bert J. Lowenberg, and Harold Taylor, *American Historical Review*, 56 (January 1951): 450–452;

"Crane Brinton, *Ideas and Men*," *American Historical Review*, 57 (October 1951): 91–94;

"Philosophy: Seminal Thoughts," *Saturday Review*, 35 (20 September 1952): 19–20;

"William Walsh, *An Introduction to Philosophy of History*," *American Historical Review*, 58 (January 1953): 328–329;

"John Dewey, 1859–1952," *Journal of Philosophy*, 50 (1 January 1953): 5–13;

"Statement Commenting on the Humanist Manifesto," *Humanist*, 13 (1953): 68;

"Frederick Artz, *The Mind of the Middle Ages A.D. 200–1500: A Historical Survey*," *New York Times Book Review*, 31 May 1953, p. 16;

"On Being Rejected," *Journal of Philosophy*, 50 (17 December 1953): 797–805;

"George Santayana–Naturalizing the Imagination," *Journal of Philosophy*, 51 (21 January 1954): 50–52;

"Plato, *The Dialogues of Plato*, 4 Volumes, Translated, with Analyses and Introductions, by B. Jowett," *Journal of Philosophy*, 51 (21 January 1954): 64–69;

"Symposium: Are Religious Dogmas Cognitive and Meaningful?" *Journal of Philosophy*, 51 (4 March 1954): 158–163;

"Patrick Romanell, *Verso un Naturalismo Critico: Riflessioni Sulla Recente Filosofia Americana*," *Journal of Philosophy*, 51 (24 June 1954): 389–390;

"Morris R. Cohen, *Reason and Nature*, Revised Edition, and George Santayana, *The Life of Reason*, Revised in Collaboration with Daniel Cory," *Journal of Philosophy*, 51 (24 June 1954): 391–393;

"J. J. Rousseau, *Political Writings*, Translated and Edited by Frederick Watkins, and Plato, *Socratic Dialogues*, Translated and Edited by W. D. Woodhead," *Journal of Philosophy*, 51 (24 June 1954): 393;

"The Wrong and the Bad," *Journal of Philosophy*, 51 (25 November 1954): 764–775;

"Morris R. Cohen, *American Thought: A Critical Sketch*, Edited with a Critical Foreword by Felix S. Cohen," *Jewish Social Studies*, 17 (January 1955): 76–78;

"George Berkeley, *Philosophical Writings*, Edited by T. E. Jessop, David Hume, *Theory of Knowledge*, Edited by D. C. Yalden-Thomson, and David Hume, *Theory of Politics*, Edited by F. Watkins," *Journal of Philosophy*, 52 (28 April 1955): 248–249;

"*Alfred North Whitehead: An Anthology*, Selected by F. S. C. Northrop and M. W. Gross," *Journal of Philosophy*, 52 (9 June 1955): 333–334;

"*The Works of Aristotle*, Volume 12: *Select Fragments*, Translated by W. D. Ross, and D. J. Allen, *The Philosophy of Aristotle*," *Journal of Philosophy*, 52 (23 June 1955): 358–360;

"*The Ethics of Aristotle*, Translated by J. A. K. Thompson, and Aristotle, *Ethics for English Readers*, Translated by H. Rackham," *Journal of Philosophy*, 52 (23 June 1955): 360–364;

"Talking and Looking: Presidential Address Delivered before the Fifty-third Annual Meeting of the Eastern Division of the American Philosophical Association, University of Pennsylvania, December 1956," *Proceedings and Addresses of the American Philosophical Association*, 30 (1956–1957): 5–24;

"Sterling P. Lamprecht, *Our Philosophical Traditions: A Brief History of Philosophy in Western Civilization*," *Journal of Philosophy*, 53 (16 February 1956): 168–174;

"Norman DeWitt, *Epicurus and His Philosophy*," *Journal of Philosophy*, 53 (1 March 1956): 201–202;

"George Boas, *Dominant Themes of Modern Philosophy: A History*," *American Historical Review*, 63 (January 1958): 371–372;

"The Mirror of USSR Philosophizing: Review of *Reports and Papers of Representatives of Soviet Philosophical Science at the XII International Congress of Philosophy*," *Journal of Philosophy*, 55 (6 November 1958): 1019–1028;

"A Humanist Symposium on Metaphysics: No. 6, Epilogue," *Journal of Philosophy*, 56 (15 January 1959): 55–62;

"John Dewey's Contribution to Scientific Humanism," *Humanist*, 19 (June 1959): 134–138;

"The Future of John Dewey's Philosophy," *Journal of Philosophy*, 56 (17 December 1959): 1005–1010;

"Dagobert Runes, *Pictorial History of Philosophy*, and Bertrand Russell, *Wisdom of the West*, Edited by Paul Foulkes," *Journal of Philosophy*, 57 (26 May 1960): 365–368;

"The Changing Impact of Darwin on Philosophy," *Journal of the History of Ideas*, 22 (October–December 1961): 435–462;

"Ernst Cassirer, *The Logic of the Humanities*, Translated by Clarence S. Howe," *History and Theory*, 2 (1962): 66–74;

"Friedrich Solmscn, *Aristotle's System of the Physical World*," *Philosophical Review*, 71 (October 1962): 520–523;

"Religious Language," *Humanist*, 22 (November–December 1962): 186;

"Justice, Mercy, Love, Ethics: Review of Paul Ramsey, *Nine Modern Moralists*," *New York Herald Tribune Book Section*, 11 December 1962;

"The Art of Language and the Linguistic Situation: A Naturalistic Analysis," *Journal of Philosophy*, 60 (17 January 1963): 29–56;

"Arthur O. Lovejoy and the History of Ideas," *Philosophy and Phenomenological Research*, 23 (June 1963): 475–479;

"John H. Randall's Shelf," *New York Herald Tribune Book Week*, 12 January 1964, p. 32;

"*The Philosophy of Aristotle*, Edited by Renford Bambrough; Marjorie Grene, *A Portrait of Aristotle*: Whitney Oates, *Aristotle and the Problem of Value*; Sir David Ross, *Aristotle*; James Walsh, *Aristotle's Conception of Moral Weakness*," *Humanist*, 24 (November–December 1964): 196–197;

"*Aristote et les problemes de methode*, Papers Presented at the Symposium Aristotelicum, Louvain, 1960," *Philosophical Review*, 74 (April 1965): 244–251;

"Reinhold Niebuhr, *Man's Nature and His Communities*," *Journal of Philosophy*, 63 (20 January 1966): 46–53;

"Robert Paul Wolff et al., *A Critique of Pure Tolerance*," *Journal of Philosophy*, 63 (1 September 1966): 457–465;

"Melvin Richter, *The Politics of Conscience: T. H. Green and His Age*," *Journal of Philosophy*, 63 (1 September 1966): 476–478;

"The Manifold Experience of Augustine," *American Scholar*, 38 (Winter 1968): 127–134.

Best known for his monumental work in the history of ideas, *The Making of the Modern Mind: A Survey of the Intellectual Background of the Present Age* (1926; revised and enlarged, 1940), John Herman Randall Jr. also did original work in metaphysics and was widely considered one of the greatest teachers of phi-

losophy in the United States. He served with Ernest Nagel as co-editor of the prestigious *Journal of Philosophy* from 1937 until 1980 and was chairman of the editorial committee of the *Journal of the History of Ideas* from 1941 to 1955. John P. Anton, the editor of the festschrift *Naturalism and Historical Understanding: Essays on the Philosophy of John Herman Randall, Jr.* (1967), says that Randall never touched a subject matter without making it luminous and intelligible.

Randall was born on 14 February 1899 in Grand Rapids, Michigan, to John Herman Randall, a liberal Protestant minister, and Minerva I. Ballard Randall. His father later became pastor of a church on Convent Avenue in New York City near Columbia University, which Randall attended. In *Naturalism and Historical Understanding* the historian and sociologist Harry Elmer Barnes recalls that as a graduate student at Columbia in 1917–1918 he was assigned to grade the examinations in Carlton J. H. Hayes's modern social politics course; he used Hayes's lecture notes to help him in the task. Among the first group of tests he found one perfect paper that stood out for thoroughness of information, logical organization, clarity of expression, and maturity of perspective: it was Randall's. When Randall repeated this performance on the next examination, Barnes sent a note inviting the young man to his office. At Barnes's request, Randall showed him the notes he had taken in the Hayes course; Barnes found them to be clearer than Hayes's own notes.

Randall graduated Phi Beta Kappa in 1918 and received a master of arts degree from Columbia in 1919. The following year, while working on his Ph.D. at Columbia, he was hired by the university as a philosophy instructor. In 1922 he submitted the dissertation "The Problem of Group Responsibility to Society: An Interpretation of the History of American Labor" and was awarded the doctorate. That year he married Mercedes Irene Moritz, a teacher of English and history in the New York City schools and a peace activist. They had two sons, John Herman Randall III and Francis Ballard Randall, both of whom became college professors.

Randall had come to adulthood during the period of optimism just before World War I. That conflict, with its seemingly senseless loss of millions of lives, disillusioned his generation. The problem of securing international peace occupied Randall from the early 1920s to the mid 1930s; during this period he wrote more than thirty essays for the periodical *World Unity*.

In 1924 Randall published the ambitious two-volume survey *The Western Mind: Its Origins and Development*. The following year he was promoted to assis-

Nature
and
Historical
Experience

ESSAYS IN NATURALISM
AND IN THE
THEORY OF HISTORY

John Herman Randall, Jr.

Dust jacket for the 1958 book in which Randall develops a metaphysics that combines ideas
from Aristotle and John Dewey (Reason Alone Books)

tant professor. In 1926 a revised and enlarged edition of *The Western Mind* appeared as *The Making of the Modern Mind: A Survey of the Intellectual Background of the Present Age*. The 650-page work is amazing for the number of sources cited or quoted by a man in his mid twenties. In 1929 Randall published *Our Changing Civilization: How Science and Machines Are Reconstructing Modern Life*. In 1931 he was promoted to associate professor, and in 1935 he became a full professor.

In 1938 Randall published in *The American Scholar* an essay with the provocative title "On the Importance of Being Unprincipled." He points out that anyone who has ever had a friend or a spouse knows that the only way to do anything together is by compromise. People who "stand on principle" never accomplish anything.

In 1940 Randall revised *The Making of the Modern Mind* once again, adding forty pages to keep up with major new developments. In 1947 he was awarded the Butler Medal by Columbia for distin-

guished work in his field. In 1951 he became Frederick J. E. Woodbridge Professor of Philosophy. In 1956 he served as president of the Eastern Division of the American Philosophical Association and was also elected to a two-year term as president of the Renaissance Society of America.

In *The Role of Knowledge in Western Religion* (1958) Randall denies that a conflict exists between religion and science; the conflict, he says, is between older scientific beliefs that have become enshrined as religious doctrines and new scientific discoveries. Since the function of science is to change people's beliefs, such conflicts will always occur. Most religions celebrate the important secular activities of their society. Randall follows the German philosopher and theologian Friedrich Schleiermacher and the American philosopher George Santayana in holding that religion is neither true nor false; it is either adequate or inadequate to its function. For Randall, religion, considered worldwide and historically, can be seen to have the three distinctive functions of consecration, celebration, and clarification. Like Santayana, Randall finds that people such as the seventeenth-century Dutch philosopher Baruch Spinoza and the physicist and mathematician Albert Einstein worship nature's power. Randall and Santayana, however, believe that whatever makes for each individual's perfection is good. Although there are not resources nor time enough for each person to realize his or her perfection, Randall follows Santayana in choosing to consecrate himself to realizing as much of it as he can. Randall himself belonged to three religions: Universalist, Ethical Culture, and the Quakers. Each had ideals to which he consecrated himself. He particularly liked the pacifism of the Quakers, and he refused to condone war even against Adolf Hitler.

In *Nature and Historical Experience: Essays in Naturalism and in the Theory of History* (1958) Randall says that history is an explanation of how something came to be. Once one knows the outcome one wants to explain, then one holds only those factors that contribute to that outcome to be relevant. Which outcome one chooses to explain is relative to the historian's interests; but the causes of that outcome can be objectively investigated and a publicly verifiable history made available. As more is learned in the future about the consequences of that outcome, histories will be revised. Randall notes that histories are always written with present-day problems and solutions in mind.

Randall's metaphysics, as elaborated in this volume, combines ideas from Aristotle and John Dewey. For Aristotle, to be is to operate, to be a "this" (something to which one can point), and—ruling out the ineffable—to be a subject of discourse (something about which one can talk). This sort of thing is what Aristotle means by *substance*. Cartesian substance, by contrast, is what endures unchanged through a process of change; since it underlies perceivable qualities, it is nothing to which one could point; and it is ineffable. For Randall, as for Aristotle, a thing is its powers, not its actual operations; but powers are known only through the operations they make possible. Powers, however, are never completely or exhaustively known; thus, knowledge can never be final and complete. The "scientific attitude," the "experimental temper" with its never-ending inquiry and discovery, is grounded in the inexhaustible powers of things that new contexts and new situations can bring to light. Randall identifies substance with Dewey's "situation" as the universal trait of anything that exists. The situation, like a soup, has many factors as ingredients; the factors operate jointly to produce an outcome, and a variation in any one factor can produce a different outcome. The factors have potentialities or pow-

Dust jacket for the 1958 book in which Randall denies the existence of a conflict between religion and science (Richland County Public Library)

ers that are realized under appropriate circumstances; the extent of these powers cannot be determined except by experience. For Randall, the purpose of science is to find out what things can do.

In Randall's metaphysics "fundamental ways of functioning" or "ways of being" are expressed by various parts of speech: operations by verbs, powers by nouns, ways of operating by adverbs, and kinds of power by adjectives and connectives. "To be" any particular thing means to function in one of these ways. Verbs, or operations, are not objects of inquiry; objects of inquiry are adverbs, or ways of operating: how operations take place, how something is or can be done. The "ultimate object" of inquiry, however, is not "how" something can be done but "how best" to do it. Evaluation—the determination of the "better" and the "worse" ways of acting—is fundamental. Translating adverbs into nouns results in "hypostatizing" processes or operations into "things," "means," or "mechanisms." The noun language is in constant need of clarification through an operational analysis. The rule, Randall says, is "*Cherchez le verb*": translate

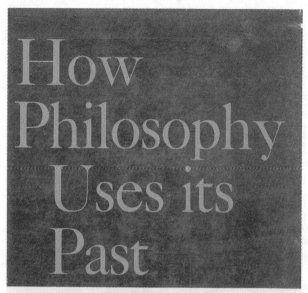

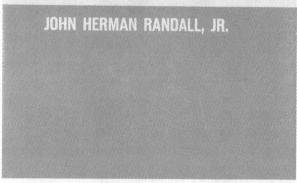

JOHN HERMAN RANDALL, JR.

*Dust jacket for the 1963 published version of Randall's
1961 Matchette Lectures, in which he shows how the
historical treatment of philosophy illuminates all
other aspects of cultural history (Bruccoli
Clark Layman Archives)*

nouns into verbs. Randall often does so in his own work, particularly when writing on Greek philosophy; as a consequence, his writing is refreshingly intelligible and free of substantives and reifications. English translations of Aristotle derived from Latin sources have nominalized operations and adverbs, and those brought up on such translations have looked at Randall's interpretations of Greek philosophy with suspicion: they just "do not seem right."

Randall notes that nature exhibits a thoroughgoing diversity and plurality: it is a fundamental metaphysical fact that nature is radically and ineradicably manifold. But it is also a fundamental metaphysical fact that nature can become unified in human vision, Randall says. In the beginning, people saw the world whole through the great creation myths of primitive cultures. More recently, some have tried to see it through knowledge and science.

In the chapter "Ways of Construing Mind and Intelligibility" Randall says that he is not sure that *mind* is satisfactory as a metaphysical term: "*mind* is bound up with the very insular thought of the British and also with the varied meanings *mind* has in French, German, Latin, and Greek." The various cognates of *mind* in other languages, influenced by differing cultures, are not intertranslatable.

In *Aristotle* (1960) Randall accepts Werner Jaeger's thesis that Aristotle's philosophy underwent a change over the years that he taught in his school, the Lyceum. In putting together the *Metaphysics* five hundred years later the Alexandrian editors of his treatises patched together much that was repetitive, much that might have been part of his early thinking, and much that was logically incoherent. Randall finds that only two of the fourteen books of the *Metaphysics* form a consistent unity. Discussing the medieval Christian and Arabic interpretations of the passive intellect and the active intellect—the nous that makes all things—in Aristotle's *Peri Psyche* (*De Anima,* or *On the Soul*), Randall disagrees with the Christian interpreters' attempts to reconcile Aristotle with Christian theology.

Randall received a Litt.D. from Ohio Wesleyan University in 1961. The following year he published *From the Middle Ages to the Enlightenment,* the first volume of *The Career of Philosophy*. In the foreword Randall calls the work an "attempt to write a history of modern philosophy from a perspective of American philosophizing in mid-century." He describes Augustinian Platonism, Thomistic Aristotelianism, and the nominalistic Aristotelianism of William of Occam as the medieval roots of modern philosophy, which developed through the advent of humanism, the rediscovery of the classics of ancient philosophy, the Reformation, and the rise of science. While nineteenth-century German historians of philosophy, such as Wilhelm Windelband, had ignored the defects of British empiricism and treated it as a necessary historical step to Immanuel Kant's critical philosophy, Randall has a devastating criticism of the British empiricist tradition from John Locke to David Hume. In Locke and Hume "experience" consists of the data of the senses; Randall considers this construal rather narrow. One would be more apt to consider experience to be something undergone, as in "Boy! Did I have an experience!" or "I had *some* [an unusual] experience!" Another fault is that experience is taken to be both the origin and the test of knowledge; but, Randall says, if it is the former, it cannot very well be the latter, as well.

In *How Philosophy Uses Its Past* (1963), the published version of his Franklin J. Matchette Foundation Lectures, given at Wesleyan University in the spring of 1961, Randall says that the historical treatment of philosophy illuminates all other strands of cultural history. Philosophy is the intellectual reaction of outstanding minds to culturally significant events; it displays not merely ideas in the process of being worked out but ideas in action as they intervene in the other activities of human beings and influence the course of institutional development.

In *From the German Enlightenment to the Age of Darwin* (1965), volume two of *The Career of Philosophy,* Randall follows German, French, and British philosophy from the eighteenth to the middle of the nineteenth century. He shows how the German Enlightenment grew into a penetrating criticism of the Newtonian scientific ideal and sought a broader and deeper intellectual method that would do greater justice to the manifold areas of cultural experience. In the Romantic era, he says, the main impulses to philosophizing came from nonscientific areas; the central thread of science ran underground until it reemerged with Karl Marx, Auguste Comte, and John Stuart Mill. Randall received the Ralph Waldo Emerson Award from the Phi Beta Kappa senate for *The Career of Philosophy* in 1966. He was awarded an honorary Ph.D. by the University of Padua in 1967; the following year he received an L.H.D. from Columbia University and an LL.D. from Temple University.

In *Hellenistic Ways of Deliverance and the Making of the Christian Synthesis* (1970) Randall says that he owes much to Arthur Cushman McGiffert, the professor of church history at the Union Theological Seminary who had died in 1933, who enabled him to understand the Pauline version of the Christian message that the tutelage of his father, who had been trained at the Chicago Divinity School in the 1890s, had led him to underestimate. Randall describes the fortunes of Greek philosophy in Rome, emphasizing the importance of Cicero for subsequent philosophizing in the West. He also includes several chapters on St. Augustine.

Randall was honored with an L.H.D. from Bard College in 1972. In *Plato: Dramatist of the Life of Reason,* published that year, he largely agrees with Gilbert Ryle's interpretation of Plato, according to which dialogues such as the *Parmenides* cast doubt on the notion that Plato seriously entertained the Theory of Forms or Ideas. Plato's nephew Speusippus, who succeeded Plato as the head of the Academy, might have been the originator of the doctrines that have come to be known as Platonism, Randall says; such views are not to be found in Plato's works, unless one takes literally notions that are explicitly stated, in dialogues such as the *Phaedo,* to be myths.

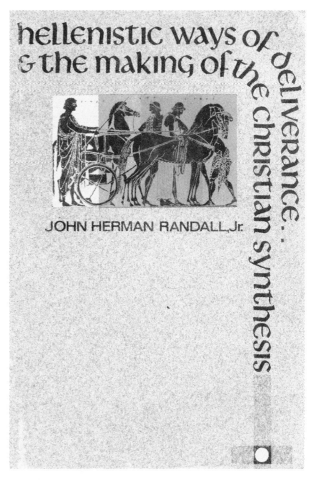

Dust jacket for Randall's 1970 book, in which he traces the influence of ancient Greek philosophy on the early development of Christianity by such church fathers as St. Augustine (Bruccoli Clark Layman Archives)

Randall suffered the ultimate indignity for one who had written eloquently about the power of *logos* (Greek for speech, word, or reason): a cerebral hemorrhage that left him without the power of speech. His writing ceased, and the third volume of *The Career of Philosophy* was left unfinished. The foreword to the previous volume reveals that he would have said that with Charles Darwin, science returned to serve as a central thread; but Romanticism remained a force, and science was no longer taken as offering a satisfactory philosophy of life. In 1977 Beth J. Singer published *Philosophy after Darwin: Chapters for* The Career of Philosophy, *Volume III, and Other Essays.* As might be expected, it is disjointed and contains many gaps. An important but frequently overlooked contribution, however, is Randall's notion of what constitutes modern philosophy. At the beginning of the first chapter of *Philosophy after Darwin* he says that "the problem of knowledge" has been central in modern philosophy. "Knowledge" will always present a number of particular problems. But they will normally be either psychological problems dealing with the origin and growth of knowledge, or logical problems dealing with the structure and tests of knowledge. . . . But "knowledge in general" presents a central "metaphysical" or—as it came to be called—"epistemological problem," only when two conflicting types of knowledge are struggling for men's allegiance. . . . The struggle has lasted until the present-day acceptance of an enlarged and deepened "science" and "scientific method" as the one type of *knowledge* . . . *"the* problem of knowledge," as such, has vanished. . . . "Modern philosophy" can be defined, in other than chronological terms, as the conflict between two types of knowledge. Such "modern philosophy" has ended when one type has won out, as science now has.

"Modern philosophy" can be revived, Randall concludes, whenever the problem of knowledge reasserts itself as a central one.

Mercedes Randall died on 9 March 1977. John Herman Randall Jr. died in his apartment on Claremont Avenue in New York City on 1 December 1980.

References:
John P. Anton, ed., *Naturalism and Historical Understanding: Essays on the Philosophy of John Herman Randall, Jr.* (Albany: State University of New York Press, 1967);

Sister M. Sharon Burns, "The Philosophy of Religion of John Herman Randall, Jr.: A Challenge to Christian Theologians," dissertation, Catholic University of America, 1972;

William Osborn Kerr, "An Examination of John Herman Randall, Jr.'s Philosophy of Religion," dissertation, State University of New York at Buffalo, 1969;

Po-wen Kuo, "Naturalism and the Interpretation of History," dissertation, Yale University, 1966;

Roy Dennis Morrison, "Ontology and Naturalism in the Philosophies of John Herman Randall, Jr. and Paul Tillich," dissertation, University of Chicago, 1972;

William Michael Shea, "Intelligence, Intelligibility and God: An Horizon Analysis of the American Naturalist Philosophies of Frederick J. E. Woodbridge and John Herman Randall, Jr.," dissertation, Columbia University, 1973.

Papers:
John Herman Randall Jr.'s papers are in Butler Library of Columbia University.

John Rawls

(21 February 1921 – 24 November 2002)

Robert B. Talisse
Vanderbilt University

BOOKS: *A Theory of Justice* (Cambridge, Mass.: Belknap Press of Harvard University Press, 1971; Oxford: Clarendon Press, 1972; revised edition, Cambridge, Mass.: Belknap Press of Harvard University Press, 1999; Oxford: Oxford University Press, 1999);

Political Liberalism, The John Dewey Essays in Philosophy, no. 4 (New York & Chichester, U.K.: Columbia University Press, 1993; enlarged, 1996);

The Law of Peoples; with The Idea of Public Reason Revisited (Cambridge, Mass.: Harvard University Press, 1999);

Collected Papers, edited by Samuel Freeman (Cambridge, Mass.: Harvard University Press, 1999);

Lectures on the History of Moral Philosophy, edited by Barbara Herman (Cambridge, Mass.: Harvard University Press, 2000);

Justice as Fairness: A Restatement, edited by Erin Kelly (Cambridge, Mass.: Harvard University Press, 2001).

OTHER: "Punishment as a Practice," in *Punishment and Rehabilitation,* edited by Jeffrie G. Murphy (Belmont, Cal.: Wadsworth, 1973), pp. 83–91;

"The Basic Structure as Subject," in *Values and Morals: Essays in Honor of William Frankena, Charles Stevenson, and Richard B. Brandt,* edited by Alvin I. Goldman and Jaegwon Kim (Dordrecht, Netherlands & Boston: Reidel, 1978), pp. 47–71;

Henry Sidgwick, *The Methods of Ethics,* foreword by Rawls (Indianapolis: Hackett, 1981);

"The Basic Liberties and Their Priority," in *The Tanner Lectures on Human Values,* edited by Sterling M. McMurrin (Salt Lake City: University of Utah Press / Cambridge: Cambridge University Press, 1982), pp. 1–87;

"Social Unity and Primary Goods," in *Utilitarianism and Beyond,* edited by Amartya Sen and Bernard Williams (Cambridge: Cambridge University Press /

John Rawls (photograph © by Paula Lerner; from the dust jacket for The Law of Peoples; with The Idea of Public Reason Revisited, *1999)*

Paris: Editions de la Maison des Sciences de l'Homme, 1982), pp. 159–185;

"Themes in Kant's Moral Philosophy," in *Kant's Transcendental Deductions: The Three Critiques and the "Opus Postumum,"* edited by Eckhart Forster (Stanford, Cal.: Stanford University Press, 1989), pp. 81–113, 253–256.

SELECTED PERIODICAL PUBLICATIONS– UNCOLLECTED: "Reply to Lyons and Teitelman," *Journal of Philosophy,* 69 (5 October 1972): 556–557;

"Roderick Firth: His Life and Work," *Philosophy and Phenomenological Research,* 51 (March 1991): 109–118;

"The Law of Peoples," *Critical Inquiry,* 20 (Fall 1993): 36–68;

"Reconciliation through the Public Use of Reason," *Journal of Philosophy,* 92 (March 1995): 132–180.

John Rawls was, by any reasonable standard, the most influential political theorist of the twentieth century. Despite this status, he maintained an uncommon humility, as his sole autobiographical statement, quoted in Steve Pyke's *Philosophers* (1995), demonstrates:

> From the beginning of my study of philosophy in my late teens I have been concerned with moral questions and the religious and philosophical basis on which they might be answered. Three years spent in the U.S. Army in World War II led me to be concerned with political questions. Around 1950 I started to write a book on justice, which I eventually completed.

The "book on justice" is his seminal *A Theory of Justice* (1971), which Robert Nozick–who disagreed strongly with its conclusions–called "a powerful, deep, subtle, wide-ranging, systematic work in political and moral philosophy which has not seen its like since the writings of John Stuart Mill, if then." Jonathan Wolff has said that "Contemporary English-language political philosophy began in 1971 with the publication of John Rawls's *A Theory of Justice.*"

The second of five sons, John Bordley Rawls was born on 21 February 1921 in Baltimore, Maryland, to William Lee Rawls, a self-taught attorney who argued cases before the United States Supreme Court, and Anna Abel Stump Rawls. He attended the Kent School in Connecticut and received his bachelor of arts from Princeton University in 1943. He served in New Guinea, the Philippines, and Japan with the Thirty-second Infantry Division of the United States Army from 1943 to 1945. In 1946 he returned to Princeton to do graduate study in philosophy. He married Margaret Warfield Fox on 28 June 1949; they had four children: Anne Warfield, Robert Lee, Alexander Emory, and Elizabeth Fox. Rawls earned his Ph.D. in 1950 with the dissertation "A Study in the Grounds of Ethical Knowledge: Considered with Reference to Judgments on the Moral Worth of Character." That year he took a position as an instructor in philosophy at Cornell University. He was a Fulbright fellow at Christchurch College of the University of Oxford in 1952–1953 and was promoted to assistant professor at Cornell in 1953 and to associate professor in 1956. He was a co-editor of the journal *Philosophical Review* from 1956 to 1959. In 1959–1960 he was a visiting professor at Harvard University; he then

moved to the Massachusetts Institute of Technology as a professor of philosophy. In 1962 he took a similar position at Harvard, where he remained for the rest of his career. He served on the executive committee of the Eastern Division of the American Philosophical Association from 1959 to 1962.

For most of the twentieth century prior to Rawls's work, systematic political philosophy was in a nearly moribund condition. The reigning conception of social justice derived from utilitarianism, which maintains that "pleasure" or "satisfaction" is the only intrinsic good and, consequently, that individual actions and social policies are morally right only to the degree to which they maximize satisfaction across an entire population. The appeal of utilitarianism is that it makes normative questions of social policy answerable in terms of descriptive social-scientific data; a question concerning whether a proposed policy should be adopted is simply a matter of whether the policy reasonably can be expected to generate a greater amount of satisfaction across the population than any of its realizable rivals; this question is, surely, one for social scientists, not philosophers. Thus, utilitarianism removes philosophy from the political realm; with utilitarianism in place, there is no need for philosophical theorizing about social questions. Consequently, moral and social philosophers confined themselves to the analysis of normative language. Two main schools developed from these efforts: emotivism and intuitionism. On the former view, terms of normative evaluation are simply disguised forms of emotional exclamations such as "boo!" and "hooray!"; according to the latter view, normative judgments express the percepts of a mysterious faculty of direct moral intuition. Despite important differences, both schools agreed that deep philosophical conflicts of value could not be settled by any rational process; philosophers had theorized themselves into impotence. Hence, as Wolff says, "before Rawls there were only two options in political philosophy: utilitarianism, or no theory at all."

In his essay "Distributive Justice," first published in *Philosophy, Politics, and Society,* Third Series (1967), edited by Peter Laslett and W. G. Runciman, and included in his *Collected Papers* (1999), Rawls criticizes utilitarianism because it cannot adequately account for justice. Since on the utilitarian view "the precepts of justice are derivative from the one end of attaining the greatest net balance of satisfactions," no reason exists "in principle" why "the greater gains of some should not compensate for the lesser losses of others; or why the violation of the liberty of a few may not be made right by a greater good shared by many." That is, utilitarianism cannot countenance a sufficiently robust set of individual rights; it cannot acknowledge that "each member of society has an inviolability founded on justice which even the welfare of society cannot override" and that a "loss of freedom for some is not made right by a greater sum of satisfactions enjoyed by many." Putting the point more generally, he says that utilitarianism "is incapable of explaining the fact that in a just society the liberties of equal citizenship are taken for granted, and the rights secured by justice are not subject to political bargaining."

A second line of criticism Rawls deploys concerns the role of distribution in justice. Utilitarianism requires one to maximize the total sum of satisfactions in society; therefore, it can make no distinction between different distributions of the same amount of satisfaction among individuals. The only thing that matters is how much satisfaction is produced, not how it is distributed. Accordingly, a state of affairs in which great satisfaction is enjoyed by a relatively small sector of the population is morally equivalent to one in which the same degree of satisfaction is distributed more broadly. Rawls insists, however, that there are cases in which distributions matter for justice, especially in cases in which certain distributions of satisfaction will be unfair or will grant undeserved benefits or burdens to some. The utilitarians must define concepts such as *desert* and *fairness* in terms of satisfaction, whereas Rawls contends that these are values independent of satisfaction. That is, on Rawls's view, an unfair distribution of goods is unjust even if it is indistinguishable from the point of view of the sum of satisfactions from a fair distribution. Given these failings of utilitarianism, "We shall have to look for another account of the principles of justice," Rawls says in "Distributive Justice."

Rawls held a fellowship at the Center for Advanced Study in the Behavioral Sciences at Stanford University in 1969–1970. From 1970 to 1972 he was president of the American Association of Political and Legal Philosophy. In 1971 he published *A Theory of Justice,* in which he presents an original view of social justice that he calls "justice as fairness." *A Theory of Justice* marks a return to grand-scale normative theorizing about politics and morality; within its pages is developed a systematic account of distributive justice, individual rights, and political legitimacy that is not only philosophically rigorous but also attentive to important developments in related disciplines such as rational-choice theory, sociology, and economics. Rawls thus brought philosophy back into the conversation of contemporary social theory. The defense and further development of justice as fairness was his sole philosophical occupation for the rest of his career.

In the preface to *A Theory of Justice* Rawls says, "What I have attempted to do is to generalize and carry to a higher order of abstraction the traditional theory of

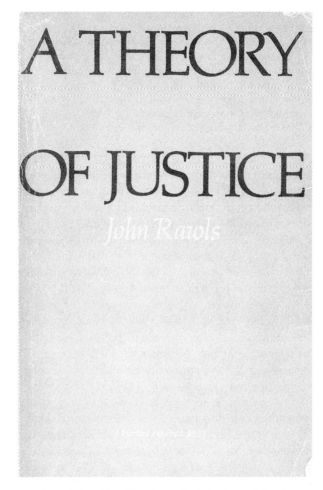

Cover for Rawls's acclaimed 1971 book of political philosophy, in which he works out two basic principles of justice by which societies ought to be judged (Collection of Philip B. Dematteis)

the social contract as represented by Locke, Rousseau, and Kant. . . . Indeed, I must disclaim any originality for the views I put forward. The leading ideas are classical and well known." Thus, justice as fairness begins with a recognizably contractarian device. The reader is to imagine "parties" in a hypothetical "original position" who are "free and rational" and "concerned to further their own interests." These parties are given the task of choosing "in one joint act" a conception of justice that will "assign basic rights and duties," "determine the division of social benefits," "regulate all further agreements," and "specify the kinds of social cooperation that can be entered into and the forms of government that can be established." Unlike traditional social-contract theories, which employ the idea of an agreement in a "state of nature" to explain the origin of government and its authority, Rawls's parties deliberate not about whether to form a state but about the nature of justice itself. Rawls explains,

>   Justice as fairness begins . . . with one of the most general of all choices which persons might make together, namely, with the choice of the first principles of a conception of justice which is to regulate all subsequent criticism and reform of institutions. Then, having chosen a conception of justice, we can suppose that they are to choose a constitution and a legislature to enact laws, and so on, all in accordance with the principles of justice initially agreed upon.

The agreement made in the original position establishes, "once and for all," the first principles of justice. Consequently, the deliberations are monumental: the agreement reached in the original position will affect all persons in society, including the descendants of the parties to the original agreement. A classic objection to social contractarianism contends that the original agreement will simply reflect the will of the most powerful, or the most clever and persuasive, or the best informed; hence, it is charged, the original agreement cannot be rightly said to be free–the weak will be subjected to the strong.

Rawls meets this traditional challenge by introducing into his original position the "veil of ignorance," which deprives the parties of information about their personal interests, desires, and capacities. Hence, in the original position no one knows his or her social status or fortune in the distribution of natural assets and abilities such as intelligence, strength, and the like. The veil of ignorance corrects "the arbitrariness of the world" insofar as it guarantees that "no one is advantaged or disadvantaged in the choice of principles by the outcome of natural chance or the contingency of social circumstances." Although Rawls stipulates that the parties in the original position are rational and self-interested, the veil nullifies "the effects of specific contingencies which put men at odds and tempt them to exploit social and natural circumstances to their own advantage." Thus, in the original position none of the parties is "in a position to tailor principles to his advantage." Consequently, whatever conception of justice is chosen will be "the result of a fair agreement."

Justice as fairness is based on the fundamental intuition that the connection between social justice and fairness is so essential that justice simply is that which would emerge from an agreement reached by rational and self-interested agents from behind the veil of ignorance. Thus, Rawls's contractarianism differs greatly from traditional versions. He is not offering an historical or anthropological explanation of how justice comes to be; rather, he is proposing a "thought experiment" about justice. The original position provides a theoretical vantage point from which to evaluate competing conceptions of justice. The veil of ignorance represents the kinds of constraints on thinking about justice that seem reasonable to impose: someone who proposes

principles of social justice that are intentionally designed to favor his or her own preferences and talents is not properly thinking about justice; such thinking requires one to take the kind of impartial or objective standpoint represented by the veil of ignorance. In short, the original position "best expresses the conditions that are widely thought reasonable to impose on the choice of principles"; it collects together "into one conception a number of conditions on principles that we are ready upon due consideration to recognize as reasonable." Consequently, "one or more persons can at any time enter the position, or perhaps better, simulate the deliberations of this hypothetical situation, simply by reasoning in accordance with the appropriate restrictions."

Rawls notes that a problem with his description of the original position is that it is difficult to imagine how rational choice is possible from behind a veil of ignorance. If the veil blocks all information pertaining to one's preferences, goals, talents, desires, and projects, then how is one to rank the various proposals for principles of justice? Certainly, such a ranking, and the eventual choice, must involve some standard by which the proposals can be evaluated. Yet, any relevant standards would seem to involve knowledge of the kind of information that the veil is supposed to block. Hence, the choice in the original position must come to nothing but an arbitrary selection or a guess.

Rawls meets this difficulty by stipulating that the parties in the original position are motivated by what he calls a "thin" theory of the good. He supposes that the parties recognize that there is a set of "primary goods" that "normally have a use whatever a person's rational plan of life." Primary goods are things "that every rational man is presumed to want," Rawls says, "no matter what else he wants." Among the primary goods are "rights, liberties, and opportunities, and income, and wealth," and "self-respect." Any rational agent in the original position can be assumed to "prefer more primary goods rather than less," because "With more of these goods men can generally be assured of greater success in carrying out their intentions and in advancing their ends, whatever these ends may be."

Thus, rational deliberation and choice are, after all, possible in the original position–the veil of ignorance blocks information about one's personal desires, objectives, and talents but not about the kinds of preferences one must have qua rational agent:

>   Thus even though the parties are deprived of information about their particular ends, they have enough knowledge to rank the alternatives. They know that in general they must try to protect their liberties, widen their opportunities, and enlarge their means for pro-

moting their aims whatever these are. Guided by the theory of the good and the general facts of moral psychology, their deliberations are no longer guesswork. They can make a rational decision in the ordinary sense.

Rawls imagines that his parties are presented with a list of traditional conceptions of justice, including several versions of utilitarianism and egoism and Rawls's own justice-as-fairness theory. They are "required to agree unanimously that one conception is best among those enumerated." Each party will, of course, seek to maximize his or her share of the primary goods, but the question of how the parties will compare the various proposals is still open. If on one conception of justice an extremely small minority enjoys an enormous share of the primary goods, and on another the primary goods are distributed roughly equally, Rawls argues that rational parties in the original position, concerned to maximize their share of the primary goods, would not assume a "winner take all" strategy and choose the conception in which the best off are better off than in any alternative option; nor would they adopt a strategy in which the average person is better off than he or she would be in any other scheme. Instead, rational parties would adopt the strategy known among decision theorists as "maximin": one is to *maxi*mize the *min*imum outcome for oneself. The maximin strategy calls for one to "rank alternatives by their *worst* possible outcome: we are to adopt the alternative the worst outcome of which is superior to the worst outcomes of the others." The parties in the original position would imagine themselves in the worst possible situation and select the conception of justice in which the worst off are as well-off as possible.

On Rawls's view, then, the question of social justice is simply the question of what conception of justice would be chosen by rational and self-interested parties in the original position. Any conception of justice that would, for obvious reasons, not be chosen may be dismissed as unjust. The bulk of *A Theory of Justice* is devoted to demonstrating the worthiness for choice in the original position of a conception of justice that consists of two principles prioritized in a certain way. These principles are formulated in various ways in *A Theory of Justice;* in Rawls's final formulations the first principle of justice is "Each person is to have an equal right to the most extensive total system of equal basic liberties with a similar system of liberty for all," and the second principle is "Social and economic inequalities are to be arranged so that they are both: (a) to the greatest benefit of the least advantaged . . . , and (b) attached to offices and positions open to all under conditions of fair equality of opportunity." In the literature Rawls's

Dust jacket for Rawls's collection of two of his essays on political philosophy. "The Law of Peoples" is a major reworking of a much shorter 1993 piece; "The Idea of Public Reason Revisited" was first published in 1997 (Richland County Public Library).

first principle is known as the "equal liberty principle," and the second is broken down into its two parts: part (a) is called the "difference principle" and part (b) the "equal opportunity principle."

In addition to agreeing on the principles themselves, Rawls contends, the parties in the original position would unanimously agree that the equal liberty principle has priority over the second principle and that within the second principle the equal opportunity principle has priority over the difference principle. Accordingly, liberty cannot be sacrificed for social and economic gains, and equality of opportunity cannot be sacrificed for distributions that benefit the least advantaged.

Though they are stated simply, the principles are actually quite complicated; and considerable dispute has arisen about how they are to be interpreted and what kind of social arrangements they recommend. This uncertainty has struck many as a crucial weakness of Rawls's theory. An early critic, Robert Paul Wolff, went so far as to say that Rawls had raised the question of justice "to so high a level of abstraction that the empirical specificity needed to lend any plausibility to" justice as fairness is "drained away. . . . What remains, it seems to me, is ideology." Others have been more sympathetic to Rawls in this regard; some, such as Thomas W. Pogge, have even argued for specific global and local economic policies on Rawlsian principles.

The main controversy concerns the difference principle. The principle stipulates that certain kinds of social and economic inequalities are consistent with, and perhaps required by, justice; hence, Rawls is not a strict egalitarian. Nor, however, is he a typical laissez-faire capitalist—the difference principle calls for distributive efforts that go beyond the standard free-market mechanisms. The hand of Rawlsian distribution is not "invisible," like that of Adam Smith's free market in *An Inquiry into the Nature and Causes of the Wealth of Nations* (1776): the difference principle calls for government intervention to eliminate any inequality that is not to the advantage of the worst off. In "A Critical Introduction to Rawls' Theory of Justice," collected in *John Rawls' Theory of Social Justice: An Introduction* (1980), edited by H. Gene Blocker and Elizabeth H. Smith, Allen Buchanan provides an example of how the difference principle might be applied:

> Suppose that large-scale capital investment in a certain industry is required to raise employment and to produce new goods and services. Suppose that by raising employment and producing these new goods and services such capital investment will ultimately be of great benefit to the least advantaged members of the society. Suppose in particular that such capital investment, if it can be achieved, will greatly increase the income prospects of the least advantaged through employing many who are not now employed and by raising the wages of those who are already employed. Suppose, however, that individuals will not be willing to undertake the risks of this large-scale capital investment unless they have the opportunity to reap large profits from the enterprise, should it succeed. In such a case, tax advantages for capital investment and lowered taxes on profits might provide the needed incentives for investment.

Under such conditions, the difference principle would require the tax policies Buchanan suggests. These policies would involve an unequal distribution of the tax burden, but it has been stipulated that this inequality works to the advantage of the worst off. Hence, it is required by justice.

A Theory of Justice was nominated for a National Book Award and won the Ralph Waldo Emerson Award of Phi Beta Kappa in 1972. Rawls served as vice president of the American Philosophical Association in 1973 and as president in 1974. He became John Cowles Pro-

fessor of Philosophy at Harvard in 1974. He was a visiting fellow at the Institute for Advanced Study at Princeton University in the fall of 1977. In 1979 he was named James Bryant Conant University Professor at Harvard, the highest rank the university can bestow. He received the Ames Prize for outstanding work on legal subjects from the Harvard Law School in 1985 for *A Theory of Justice*. In the spring of 1986 he was a visiting fellow of All Souls College, Oxford. He received the Brandeis University Award for *A Theory of Justice* in 1990.

In addition to widespread praise, *A Theory of Justice* has generated a mountain of critical work from across the spectrum of political theory. Philosophers generally sympathetic to Rawls's two principles have criticized his contractarian methodology. Chief among these critics is Thomas Nagel. In "Rawls on Justice," collected in *Reading Rawls: Critical Studies on Rawls' A Theory of Justice* (1989), edited by Norman Daniels, Nagel questions the value of framing the question of justice in terms of choice in the original position:

> The egalitarian liberalism which he develops and the conception of the good on which it depends are extremely persuasive, but the original position serves to model, rather than to justify them. . . . I believe Rawls's conclusions can be more persuasively defended by direct moral arguments for liberty and equality.

Nagel is suggesting that Rawls has described the original position so as to ensure that his favored principles would be chosen there; Nagel accepts Rawls's principles but wants a "direct" argument for their justice. Ronald Dworkin makes a similar argument in "The Original Position," also included in *Reading Rawls*.

Another line of criticism, often characterized as "communitarian," comes from those who not only question Rawls's methodology but also reject his principles of justice. Chief among these critics is Michael J. Sandel, who attacks the fundamental assumptions of Rawls's theory in his *Liberalism and the Limits of Justice* (1982). Sandel charges that justice as fairness presupposes a philosophical conception of the self that is demonstrably false. According to Sandel, the construct of the original position commits Rawls to the view that the self is essentially an asocial chooser of its ends and purposes—that "what is most essential to our personhood is not the ends we choose but our capacity to choose them." Such a conception disallows the view that certain commitments, projects, traditions, and relationships are constitutive of people's identities, not detachable baggage that may be peeled away by the veil of ignorance. The image of the asocial individual unencumbered by and independent of social relatedness has long been a target of republican and feminist political theory, and critics from these camps such as Benjamin Barber (in "Justifying Justice: Problems of Psychology, Politics, and Measurement in Rawls," collected in *Reading Rawls*), Seyla Benhabib, Virginia Held, Alasdair MacIntyre, Charles Taylor, and Michael Walzer join Sandel in raising this criticism.

The criticisms of his first book led Rawls to recast his justice-as-fairness theory in his second book, *Political Liberalism* (1993). Here he does not so much answer the objections occasioned by *A Theory of Justice* as subvert them. The criticisms share the common premise that one's political theory must derive from deeper philosophical premises concerning the nature of the self or the normative value of liberty. Rawls characterizes political theories of liberal democracy that rely on such premises as "comprehensive" theories. The traditional theories of John Locke, Immanuel Kant, Thomas Jefferson, and John Stuart Mill fit neatly into this category, since those thinkers attempt to derive the principles of their political philosophies from more-basic philosophical claims about human nature, God, natural right, and so on. Rawls, however, refuses to provide a comprehensive political theory. Instead, he proposes what he calls a "political" theory of liberal democracy, or a "political liberalism." A political theory does not seek support in philosophical premises but "deliberately stays on the surface, philosophically speaking," and tries "to avoid philosophy's longstanding problems." Instead of defending his notion of the self against Sandel's objections or providing Nagel with direct arguments for his principles, then, Rawls introduces a new conception of the architecture of political theory. A political liberalism begins with the "tradition of democratic thought" and the "public culture" of society; it draws not on philosophical theories but on the "shared fund of implicitly recognized basic ideas and principles of contemporary democratic states." Whereas justice as fairness had been cast in *A Theory of Justice* as a comprehensive liberal theory, it is presented in *Political Liberalism* as a strictly "political" theory.

Rawls's "political" reformulation of justice as fairness retains much of the substance of his original theory; the original position, the veil of ignorance, and the two principles of justice remain as before. The difference—which is considerable—is the justification offered for these concepts. Sandel had claimed that a metaphysical conception of the human self appeared to be lurking in Rawls's conception of the original position; the pivotal 1985 essay in the journal *Philosophy and Public Affairs* that launched Rawls's reformulation is titled "Justice as Fairness: Political not Metaphysical" (it is included in his *Collected Papers*). The fundamental idea behind Rawls's shift to political liberalism is, he says in *Political Liberalism*, "the fact of reasonable pluralism."

Rawls in his office at Harvard University (from the dust jacket for Lectures on the History of Moral Philosophy, *2000)*

Rawls notes that in any free society a plurality of comprehensive philosophical, religious, and moral views will be held by the citizens. Moreover, many of these comprehensive doctrines will be equally reasonable, though mutually incompatible: "Under political and social conditions secured by the basic rights and liberties of free institutions, a diversity of conflicting and irreconcilable—and what's more, reasonable—comprehensive doctrines will come about and persist if such diversity does not already obtain." This pluralism is, thus, "not an unfortunate condition of human life" but the "long-run outcome of the work of human reason under enduring free institutions"; reasonable pluralism is a "permanent feature" of a free society.

Reasonable pluralism entails what Rawls calls the "fact of oppression," which means that

a continuing shared understanding on one comprehensive religious, philosophical, or moral doctrine can be maintained only by the oppressive use of state power. If we think of political society as a community united in affirming one and the same comprehensive doctrine, then the oppressive use of state power is necessary for political community. In the society of the Middle Ages, more or less united in affirming the Catholic faith, the

Inquisition was not an accident; its suppression of heresy was needed to preserve that shared religious belief. . . . The same holds, I believe, for any reasonable comprehensive philosophical and moral doctrine, whether religious or nonreligious. A society united on a reasonable form of utilitarianism, or on the reasonable liberalisms of Kant and Mill, would likewise require the sanctions of state power to remain so.

Given the facts of reasonable pluralism and oppression, Rawls rejects the project of formulating a comprehensive liberal theory. Such a theory attempts to derive the fundamental principles of liberal political philosophy from some set of more-basic philosophical premises. These foundational premises traditionally invoke specific religious, metaphysical, and moral conceptions. Because of reasonable pluralism, however, one cannot expect all citizens to agree freely on any basic premises of this sort. As a fundamental principle of any liberal democratic political theory is that state power is legitimate only when it is exercised with the consent of the people, no state based on a comprehensive philosophical, religious, or moral doctrine can be fully liberal. Any such state will require coercion and oppression to hold its grounding doctrine in place among the citizenry. Hence, only a political liberalism can be a consistent liberal theory.

Rawls is being quite radical here: political liberalism overturns the tradition of political philosophy by reconstructing the task of political theory. Traditional theorists sought the proper philosophical, religious, or moral foundation for the fundamental commitments of liberal democracy; Rawls, by contrast, contends that "the question the dominant tradition has tried to answer has no answer: no comprehensive doctrine is appropriate as a political conception for a constitutional regime." The alternative task Rawls sets for political theory is to answer the question "how is it possible for there to exist over time a just and stable society of free and equal citizens, who remain profoundly divided by reasonable religious, philosophical, and moral doctrines?"

One way to answer the question that Rawls rejects is to imagine proponents of the divided doctrines coming, in what Rawls calls a "modus vivendi" agreement, to endorse the liberal state as a matter of power-balancing compromise. Where the liberal state is endorsed as a modus vivendi, each citizen sees it as a livable compromise between what he or she sees as the best possible arrangement (a state based solely on his or her own comprehensive doctrine) and the worst possible arrangement (a state based solely on a comprehensive doctrine opposed to his or her own). Hence, under a modus vivendi agreement each citizen sees the liberal state as no more than a second-best political order; for this reason, Rawls argues, a modus vivendi liberal

democracy will be unstable. He illustrates this claim with an example from the sixteenth-century contest between Catholicism and Protestantism:

> Both faiths held that it was the duty of the ruler to uphold the true religion and to repress the spread of heresy and false doctrine. In such a case the acceptance of the principle of toleration would indeed be a mere modus vivendi, because if either faith becomes dominant, the principle of toleration would no longer be followed.

Rawls insists that the stability of a liberal democracy requires a deeper commitment on the part of the citizens than exists in a modus vivendi. If a liberal democracy is to be stable, its political conception of justice and its principal institutions must be endorsed by an "overlapping consensus." Each citizen will then see the conception of justice and major political institutions as an appropriate expression of his or her own comprehensive doctrine in the political sphere. Rawls sees his political liberalism as a "module" that "fits into and can be supported by various reasonable comprehensive doctrines that endure in a society regulated by it":

> An overlapping consensus, therefore, is not merely a consensus on accepting certain authorities, or on complying with certain institutional arrangements, founded on a convergence of self- or group-interests. All those who affirm the political conception start from within their own comprehensive view and draw on the religious, philosophical, and moral grounds it provides.

Hence, a politically liberal conception of justice that is the focus of an overlapping consensus is stable, because it is endorsed by citizens in a way that gives them reason to uphold its principles regardless of the balance of power among their respective doctrines; citizens endorse the political conception of justice "for its own sake" and "on its own merits." The stability of a politically liberal democratic state does not, therefore, rely on compromise and bargaining or on a deep agreement across society on a single philosophical doctrine; instead, stability comes from the fact that the political conception of justice and the basic political institutions can be endorsed from within the plurality of reasonable comprehensive doctrines the citizens endorse. Consequently, in a politically liberal democracy each citizen endorses the state for a different reason—a reason that is internal to his or her own comprehensive religious, philosophical, or moral doctrine.

A fundamental feature of any liberal democratic theory, Rawls says, is that the state is answerable to the citizens it governs; that is, the state must justify its actions and policies to the citizens affected by them.

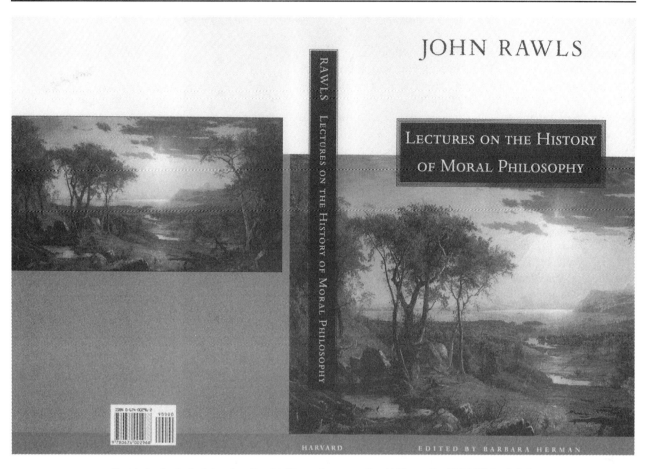

*Dust jacket for the book based on Rawls's Harvard course on David Hume, Gottfried Wilhelm Leibniz,
Immanuel Kant, and Georg Wilhelm Friedrich Hegel (Richland County Public Library)*

The idea of an overlapping consensus places strict constraints on the kind of justification the state can offer. Given the fact of reasonable pluralism, the state cannot justify its policies via appeals to specific theological or philosophical principles. Similarly, Rawls maintains that discourse among citizens concerning essential issues of basic justice must be conducted in terms that do not favor or presuppose any particular comprehensive view. Rawls advocates the establishment of a "public domain" in which "public reason" operates–that is, reasoning that makes no appeal to the comprehensive doctrines over which reasonable citizens will disagree:

> This means that in discussing constitutional essentials and matters of basic justice we are not to appeal to comprehensive religious and philosophical doctrines–to what we as individuals or members of associations see as the whole truth–nor to elaborate economic theories of general equilibrium. As far as possible, the knowledge and ways of reasoning that ground our affirming the principles of justice and their application to constitutional essentials and basic justice are to rest

on plain truths now widely accepted, or available to citizens generally.

The idea of public reason establishes an ideal of politically liberal citizenship. In a politically liberal society, citizens try "to explain to one another . . . how the principles and policies they advocate and vote for can be supported by the political values of public reason"; hence, citizens are "ready to listen to others" and "meet others halfway" when disagreements arise. Thus, political liberalism, and the consequent idea of public reason, entail a conception of civic duty and civility in political discussion. This feature of political liberalism places Rawls at the core of a growing literature concerning deliberative democracy, ensuring the centrality of his ideas to political theorizing for decades to come. He received the Spitz Book Prize of the Conference for the Study of Political Thought for *Political Liberalism* in 1995.

Rawls was an avid sailor in his younger years and later took up mountain climbing. He suffered a stroke in 1995 that left him partially incapacitated and unable to continue teaching. In 1999 he published *The Law of Peoples; with The Idea of Public Reason Revisited,* two essays in which he further explicates the idea of public reason. His *Collected Papers,* edited by Samuel Freeman, were also published in 1999. That same year Rawls received the National Humanities Medal of the National Endowment for the Humanities from President Bill Clinton for helping women enter the male-dominated field of philosophy; he was also honored by the Royal Swedish Academy with the "Nobel Prize for philosophers," the Rolf Schock Award for Logic and Philosophy. *Lectures on the History of Moral Philosophy* (2000), edited by Barbara Herman, is based on Rawls's course on David Hume, Gottfried Wilhelm Leibniz, Kant, and Georg Wilhelm Friedrich Hegel. *Justice as Fairness: A Restatement* (2001), edited by Erin Kelly, is an attempt "to rectify the more serious faults in *A Theory of Justice* that have obscured the main ideas of justice as fairness—and to connect into one unified statement the conception of justice presented in *Theory* and the main ideas in my essays beginning in 1974."

Rawls refused hundreds of honorary doctorates, accepting them only from institutions at which he had taught: from Oxford in 1983, Princeton in 1987, and Harvard in 1997. John Rawls died of heart failure on 24 November 2002 at his home in Lexington, Massachusetts.

References:

Brian Barry, *The Liberal Theory of Justice: A Critical Examination of the Principal Doctrines in* A Theory of Justice *by John Rawls* (Oxford: Clarendon Press, 1973);

Seyla Benhabib, *Situating the Self: Gender, Community, and Postmodernism in Contemporary Ethics* (New York: Routledge, 1992);

H. Gene Blocker and Elizabeth H. Smith, eds., *John Rawls' Theory of Social Justice: An Introduction* (Athens: Ohio University Press, 1980);

Norman Daniels, ed., *Reading Rawls: Critical Studies on Rawls'* A Theory of Justice (Stanford, Cal.: Stanford University Press, 1989);

Virginia Held, *Feminist Morality* (Chicago: University of Chicago Press, 1993);

Hans-Jürgen Kühn, *Soziale Gerechtigkeit als moralphilosophische Forderung: Zur Theorie der Gerechtigkeit von John Rawls* (Bonn: Bouvier, 1984);

Alasdair MacIntyre, *After Virtue: A Study in Moral Theory* (Notre Dame, Ind.: University of Notre Dame Press, 1981);

Robert Nozick, *Anarchy, State, and Utopia* (New York: Basic Books, 1974), pp. 90, 93, 183–231;

Philosophischen Gesellschaft Bad Homburg and Wilfried Hinsch, eds., *Zur Idee des politischen Liberalismus: John Rawls in der Diskussion* (Frankfurt am Main: Suhrkamp, 1997);

Thomas W. Pogge, *Realizing Rawls* (Ithaca, N.Y.: Cornell University Press, 1989);

Steve Pyke, *Philosophers* (New York: Distributed Arts, 1995; London: Zelda Cheatle Press, 1995);

Andrews Reath, Barbara Herman, and Christine M. Korsgaard, eds., *Reclaiming the History of Ethics: Essays for John Rawls* (Cambridge & New York: Cambridge University Press, 1997);

Henry S. Richardson, ed., *Development and Main Outlines in Rawls's Theory of Justice,* The Philosophy of Rawls: A Collection of Essays, no. 1 (New York: Garland, 1999);

Richardson, ed., *Opponents and Implications of* A Theory of Justice, The Philosophy of Rawls: A Collection of Essays, no. 3 (New York: Garland, 1999);

Richardson, ed., *The Two Principles and Their Justifications,* The Philosophy of Rawls: A Collection of Essays, no. 2 (New York & London: Garland, 1999);

Michael J. Sandel, *Liberalism and the Limits of Justice* (Cambridge & New York: Cambridge University Press, 1982);

Charles Taylor, "Atomism," in *Philosophy and the Human Sciences,* volume 2 of his *Philosophical Papers* (Cambridge: Cambridge University Press, 1985), pp. 187–210;

Michael Walzer, *Spheres of Justice: A Defense of Pluralism and Equality* (New York: Basic Books, 1983);

Paul J. Weithman, ed., *Moral Psychology and Community,* The Philosophy of Rawls: A Collection of Essays, no. 4 (New York & London: Garland, 1999);

Weithman, ed., *Reasonable Pluralism,* The Philosophy of Rawls: A Collection of Essays, no. 5 (New York & London: Garland, 1999);

Jonathan Wolff, "John Rawls: Liberal Democracy Restated," in *Liberal Democracy and Its Critics: Perspectives in Contemporary Political Thought,* edited by April Carter and Geoffrey Stokes (Cambridge: Polity Press / Malden, Mass.: Blackwell, 1998), pp. 118–134;

Robert Paul Wolff, *Understanding Rawls: A Reconstruction and Critique of* A Theory of Justice (Princeton: Princeton University Press, 1977).

Richard Rorty

(4 October 1931 –   )

William G. Weaver
University of Texas at El Paso

See also the Rorty entry in *DLB 246: Twentieth-Century American Cultural Theorists.*

BOOKS: *Philosophy and the Mirror of Nature* (Princeton: Princeton University Press, 1979; revised edition, Princeton: Princeton University Press, 1980; Oxford: Blackwell, 1980);

Consequences of Pragmatism: Essays, 1972–1980 (Minneapolis: University of Minnesota Press, 1982; Brighton, U.K.: Harvester, 1982);

The Contingency of Selfhood: The Seventh Tykociner Memorial Lecture, University of Illinois at Urbana-Champaign, Foellinger Auditorium, April 3, 1986, 8:00 p.m. (Urbana: University of Illinois at Urbana-Champaign, 1986);

The Barber of Kasbeam: Nabokov on Cruelty, Bennington Chapbooks in Literature: Ben Belitt Lectureship Series, no. 11 (Bennington, Vt.: Bennington College, 1989);

Contingency, Irony, and Solidarity (Cambridge & New York: Cambridge University Press, 1989);

Anti-Essentialism in General: The Number Seventeen as a Model for Reality, Legal Theory Workshop Series 1989–90, no. 8 (Toronto: Faculty of Law, University of Toronto, 1990);

Philosophical Papers, 3 volumes (Cambridge & New York: Cambridge University Press, 1991–1998)—comprises volume 1, *Objectivity, Relativism, and Truth* (1991); volume 2, *Essays on Heidegger and Others* (1991); and volume 3, *Truth and Progress* (1998);

Hoffnung statt Erkenntnis: Eine Einführung in die pragmatische Philosophie, translated by Joachim Schulte (Vienna: Passagen, 1994);

Truth, Politics, and "Post-Modernism": Spinoza Lectures (Assen, Netherlands: Van Gorcum, 1997)—comprises "Is it Desirable to Love Truth?" and "Is 'Post-Modernism' Relevant to Politics?";

Achieving Our Country: Leftist Thought in Twentieth-Century America, The William E. Massey Sr. Lectures in the History of American Civilization, 1997 (Cambridge, Mass.: Harvard University Press, 1998);

Richard Rorty

Philosophy and Social Hope (New York: Penguin, 1999).

RECORDINGS: *The Contemporary Status of Philosophy: Jürgen Habermas and Richard Rorty on the Present and Future of Philosophical Endeavor. A Debate at the Institute of Philosophy and Sociology of the Polish Academy of Sciences, Warsaw 8–9 May 1995,* video, IFIS, 1995;

Donald Davidson in Conversation: The Rorty Discussion, video, Philosophy International, 1997.

OTHER: "The Limits of Reductionism," in *Experience, Existence and the Good: Essays in Honor of Paul Weiss,* edited by Irwin C. Lieb (Carbondale: Southern Illinois University Press, 1961), pp. 100–116;

"Matter and Event," in *The Concept of Matter,* edited by Ernan McMullin (Notre Dame, Ind.: Notre Dame University Press, 1963), pp. 497–524; revised in *Explorations in Whitehead's Philosophy,* edited by Lewis S. Ford and George L. Kline (New York: Fordham University Press, 1983), pp. 68–103;

"The Subjectivist Principle and the Linguistic Turn," in *Alfred North Whitehead: Essays on His Philosophy,* edited by Kline (Englewood Cliffs, N.J.: Prentice-Hall, 1963), pp. 134–157;

"Mind-Body Identity, Privacy, and Categories," in *Philosophy of Mind,* edited by Stuart Hampshire (New York: Harper & Row, 1966), pp. 30–62;

"Aristotle," in *The American Peoples Encyclopedia: A Modern Reference Work,* volume 2, edited by Walter D. Scott (New York: Grolier, 1966), pp. 399–400;

The Linguistic Turn: Recent Essays in Philosophical Method, edited by Rorty (Chicago: University of Chicago Press, 1967); enlarged as *The Linguistic Turn: Essays in Philosophical Method, with Two Retrospective Essays* (Chicago: University of Chicago Press, 1992);

"Intuition" and "Relations, Internal and External," in *The Encyclopedia of Philosophy,* 8 volumes, edited by Paul Edwards (New York: Macmillan & Free Press / London: Collier-Macmillan, 1967), IV: 204–212; VII: 125–133;

"Cartesian Epistemology and Changes in Ontology," in *Contemporary American Philosophy,* edited by John E. Smith (London: Allen & Unwin / New York: Humanities Press, 1970), pp. 273–292;

"In Defense of Eliminative Materialism," in *Materialism and the Mind-Body Problem,* edited by David M. Rosenthal (Englewood Cliffs, N.J.: Prentice-Hall, 1971), pp. 223–231;

"Genus as Matter: A Reading of Metaphysics Z-H," in *Exegesis and Argument: Studies in Greek Philosophy Presented to Gregory Vlastos,* edited by Rorty, Edward N. Lee, and Alexander P. D. Mourelatos (Assen, Netherlands: Van Gorcum, 1973), pp. 393–420;

"Transcendental Argument, Self-reference, and Pragmatism," in *Transcendental Arguments and Science,* edited by Peter Bieri, Rolf-Peter Horstmann, and Lorenz Krüger (Dordrecht, Netherlands & Boston: Reidel, 1979), pp. 77–103;

"Genteel Syntheses, Professional Analyses, Transcendentalist Culture," in *Two Centuries of Philosophy in America,* edited by Peter Caws (Oxford: Blackwell, 1980; Totowa, N.J.: Rowman & Littlefield, 1980), pp. 228–239;

"Idealism, Holism, and the 'Paradox of Knowledge,'" in *The Philosophy of Brand Blanshard,* edited by Paul Arthur Schilpp, The Library of Living Philosophers, volume 15 (La Salle, Ill.: Open Court, 1980), pp. 719–738;

"Mind as Ineffable," in *Mind in Nature: Nobel Conference XVII Gustavus Adolphus College, St. Peter, Minnesota,* edited by Richard Elvee (San Francisco: Harper & Row, 1982), pp. 60–95;

"The Historiography of Philosophy: Four Genres," in *Philosophy in History: Essays on the Historiography of Philosophy,* edited by Rorty, J. B. Schneewind, and Quentin Skinner (Cambridge & New York: Cambridge University Press, 1984), pp. 49–75;

"Philosophy without Principles," in *Against Theory: Literary Studies and the New Pragmatism,* edited by W. J. T. Mitchell (Chicago: University of Chicago Press, 1985), pp. 132–138;

"Epistemological Behaviorism and the De-Transcendentalization of Analytic Philosophy," in *Hermeneutics and Praxis,* edited by Robert Hollinger (Notre Dame, Ind.: University of Notre Dame Press, 1985), pp. 89–121;

"Beyond Realism and Anti-Realism," in *Wo Steht die Analytische Philosophie heute?* edited by Ludwig Nagl and Richard Heinrich (Vienna: Oldenbourg, 1986), pp. 103–115;

"Foucault and Epistemology," in *Foucault: A Critical Reader,* edited by D. C. Hoy (Oxford: Blackwell, 1986), pp. 41–49;

John Dewey, *1933: Essays and How We Think,* edited by Bridget A. Walsh and Harriet Furst Simon, introduction by Rorty, volume 8 of *The Later Works of John Dewey, 1925–1953,* edited by Jo Ann Boydston and others (Carbondale: Southern Illinois University Press / London: Feffer & Simons, 1986);

"Should Hume be Answered or Bypassed?" in *Human Nature and Natural Knowledge: Essays Presented to Marjorie Grene on the Occasion of Her Seventy-fifth Birthday,* edited by Alan Donegan, Anthony N. Perovich Jr., and Michael V. Wedin (Dordrecht, Netherlands & Boston: Reidel, 1986), pp. 341–352;

John P. Murphy, *Pragmatism: From Peirce to Davidson,* introduction by Rorty (Boulder, Colo.: Westview Press, 1990);

"Comments on Taylor's 'Paralectics,'" in *On the Other: Dialogue and/or Dialectics. Mark Taylor's "Paralectics,"* edited by Robert P. Scharlemann, Working Paper no. 5 of the University of Virginia Committee on the Comparative Study of the Individual and Society (Lanham, Md.: University Press of America, 1991), pp. 71–78;

Vladimir Nabokov, *Pale Fire,* introduction by Rorty (New York: Knopf, 1992);

"Reponses de Richard Rorty," in *Lire Rorty,* edited by Jean-Pierre Cometti (Paris: Editions de l'Eclat, 1992), pp. 147–250;

"Robustness: A Reply to Jean Bethke Elshtain," in *The Politics of Irony: Essays in Self-betrayal,* edited by David W. Conway and John E. Seery (New York: St. Martin's Press, 1992), pp. 219–223;

"An Antirepresentationalist View: Comments on Richard Miller, van Fraassen/Sigman, and Churchland" and "A Comment on Robert Scholes' 'Tlon and Truth,'" in *Realism and Representation: Essays on the Problem of Realism in Relation to Science, Literature, and Culture,* edited by George Levine (Madison: University of Wisconsin Press, 1993), pp. 125–133, 186–189;

"Does Democracy Need Foundations?" in *Politisches Denken: Jahrbuch 1993,* edited by Volker Gerhardt and others (Stuttgart & Weimar: Metzler, 1994), pp. 21–23;

"Dewey between Hegel and Darwin," "Response to Hartshorne," "Response to Lavine," "Response to Bernstein," "Response to Gouinlock," "Response to Hance," "Response to Haack," "Response to Farrell," and "Philosophy and the Future," in *Rorty and Pragmatism: The Philosopher Responds to His Critics,* edited by Herman J. Saatkamp Jr. (Nashville: Vanderbilt University Press, 1995), pp. 1–15, 29–36, 50–53, 68–71, 91–99, 122–125, 148–153, 189–206;

Sidney Hook, *John Dewey: An Intellectual Portrait,* introduction by Rorty (Amherst, N.Y.: Prometheus, 1995);

"Emancipating our Culture: A Response to Habermas," "Relativism: Finding and Making," "On Moral Obligation, Truth and Common Sense," "Response to Kołakowski," and "The Notion of Rationality," in *Debating the State of Philosophy: Habermas, Rorty, and Kołakowski,* edited by Józef Niżnik and John T. Sanders (Westport, Conn.: Praeger, 1996), pp. 24–30, 31–47, 48–52, 58–66, 84–88;

"Remarks on Deconstruction and Pragmatism," "Response to Simon Critchley," and "Response to Ernesto Laclau," in *Deconstruction and Pragmatism,* edited by Chantal Mouffe (London & New York: Routledge, 1996), pp. 13–18, 41–46, 69–76;

"Tales of Two Disciplines," in *Beauty and the Critic: Aesthetics in an Age of Cultural Studies,* edited by James Soderholm (Tuscaloosa: University of Alabama Press, 1997), pp. 208–224;

"The People's Flag Is Deepest Red," in *Audacious Democracy: Labor, Intellectuals, and the Social Reconstruction of America,* edited by Steven Fraser and Joshua B. Freeman (Boston: Houghton Mifflin, 1997), pp. 57–63;

Wilfrid Sellars, *Empiricism and the Philosophy of Mind,* introduction by Rorty (Cambridge, Mass.: Harvard University Press, 1997);

"Justice as a Larger Loyalty," in *Justice and Democracy: Cross-Cultural Perspectives,* edited by Ron Bontekoe and Marietta Stepaniants (Honolulu: University of Hawaii Press, 1997), pp. 9–22;

"Realism, Antirealism and Pragmatism: Comments on Alston, Chisholm, Davidson, Harman and Searle," in *Realism/Antirealism and Epistemology,* edited by Christopher Kulp (Lanham, Md.: Rowman & Littlefield, 1997), pp. 149–171;

"Relativismus: Finden und Machen," in *Die Wiederentdeckung der Zeit: Reflexionen-Analysen-Konzept,* edited by Antje Gimmler, Mike Sandbothe, and Walters Zimmerli, translated by Sandbothe and Andrew Inkpin (Darmstadt: Wissenschaftliche Buchgesellschaft, 1997), pp. 9–26;

"A Defense of Minimalist Liberalism," in *Debating Democracy's Discontent: Essays on American Politics, Law and Public Philosophy,* edited by Anita L. Allen and Milton C. Regan Jr. (New York: Oxford University Press, 1998), pp. 117–125;

"Pragmatism," in *Routledge International Encyclopedia of Philosophy,* volume 7 (New York: Routledge, 1998), pp. 632–640;

"Davidson's Mental-Physical Distinction," in *The Philosophy of Donald Davidson,* edited by Lewis Edwin Hahn, The Library of Living Philosophers, volume 27 (La Salle, Ill.: Open Court, 1999), pp. 575–594;

Nancy Fraser, *Adding Insult to Injury: Social Justice and the Politics of Recognition,* edited by Kevin Olson, introduction by Rorty (London: Verso, 1999);

"Keine Zukunft ohne Träume," in *Die Gegenwart der Zukunft: Die Serie der "Süddeutschen Zeitung" über unsere Welt im neuen Jahrhundert* (Berlin: Wagenbach, 2000), pp. 182–190;

"Kuhn," in *A Companion to the Philosophy of Science,* edited by W. H. Newton-Smith (Oxford & Malden, Mass.: Blackwell, 2000), pp. 203–206;

Essays in Honor of Hubert L. Dreyfus, volume 1: *Heidegger, Authenticity, and Modernity,* edited by Mark A. Wrathall and Jeff Malpas, foreword by Rorty (Cambridge, Mass.: MIT Press, 2000).

SELECTED PERIODICAL PUBLICATIONS–
UNCOLLECTED: "Pragmatism, Categories and Language," *Philosophical Review,* 70 (April 1961): 197–223;

"Recent Metaphilosophy," *Review of Metaphysics,* 15 (December 1961): 299–318;

"Realism, Categories, and the 'Linguistic Turn,'" *International Philosophical Quarterly,* 2 (May 1962): 307–322;

"Empiricism, Extensionalism and Reductionism," *Mind,* 72 (April 1963): 176–186;

"Comments on Prof. Hartshorne's Paper," *Journal of Philosophy,* 60 (10 October 1963): 606–608;

"Do Analysts and Metaphysicians Disagree?" *Proceedings of the Catholic Philosophical Association,* 41 (1967): 39–53;

"Incorrigibility as the Mark of the Mental," *Journal of Philosophy,* 67 (25 June 1970): 399–429;

"Wittgenstein, Privileged Access, and Incommunicability," *American Philosophical Quarterly,* 7 (July 1970): 192–205;

"Strawson's Objectivity Argument," *Review of Metaphysics,* 24 (December 1970): 207–244;

"Verificationism and Transcendental Arguments," *Noûs,* 5 (February 1971): 3–14;

"Indeterminacy of Translation and of Truth," *Synthese,* 23 (March 1972): 443–462;

"Dennett on Awareness," *Philosophical Studies,* 23 (April 1972): 153–162;

"Functionalism, Machines, and Incorrigibility," *Journal of Philosophy,* 69 (20 April 1972): 203–220;

"Criteria and Necessity," *Noûs,* 7 (November 1973): 313–329;

"Matter as Goo: Comments on Marjorie Grene's Paper," *Synthese,* 28 (September 1974): 71–77;

"More on Incorrigibility," *Canadian Journal of Philosophy,* 4 (September 1974): 195–197;

"Realism and Reference," *Monist,* 59 (July 1976): 321–340;

"Derrida on Language, Being and Abnormal Philosophy," *Journal of Philosophy,* 74 (November 1977): 673–681;

"A Middle Ground between Neurons and Holograms?" *Behavioral and Brain Sciences,* 1 (1978): 248;

"Freud, Morality, and Hermeneutics," *New Literary History,* 12 (Autumn 1980): 177–185;

"Searle and the Special Powers of the Brain," *Behavioral and Brain Sciences,* 3 (1980): 445–446;

"Reply to Professor Yolton," *Philosophical Books,* 22 (1981): 134–135;

"Comments on Dennett's 'How to Study Human Consciousness Empirically,'" *Synthese,* 53 (November 1982): 181–187;

"What Are Philosophers For?" *Center Magazine,* 16 (September/October 1983): 40–51;

"A Reply to Six Critics," *Analyse & Kritik,* 6 (June 1984): 78–98;

"Comments on Sleeper and Edel," *Transactions of the Charles S. Peirce Society,* 21 (Winter 1985): 40–48;

"Pragmatism and Literary Theory," *Critical Inquiry,* 11 (1985): 459–465;

"The Higher Nominalism in a Nutshell: A Reply to Henry Staten," *Critical Inquiry,* 12 (Winter 1986): 462–466;

"From Logic to Language to Play," *Proceedings and Addresses of the American Philosophical Association,* 59 (1986): 747–753;

"Nominalismo e Contestualismo," *Alfabeta,* 9 (September 1987): 11–12;

"Thugs and Theorists: A Reply to Bernstein's 'One Step Forward, Two Steps Backward,'" *Political Theory,* 15 (November 1987): 564–580;

"That Old-Time Philosophy," *New Republic* (4 April 1988): 28–33;

"Comments on Castoriadis' 'The End of Philosophy,'" *Salmagundi,* 82–83 (Spring–Summer 1989): 24–30;

"Philosophy and Post-Modernism," *Cambridge Review,* 110 (June 1989): 51–53;

"Truth and Freedom: A Reply to Thomas McCarthy," *Critical Inquiry,* 16 (Spring 1990): 633–643;

"Two Cheers for the Cultural Left," *South Atlantic Review,* 89 (Winter 1990): 227–234;

"The Dangers of Over-Philosophication–Reply to Arcilla and Nicholson," *Educational Theory,* 40 (1990): 41–44;

"Nietzsche, Socrates and Pragmatism," *South African Journal of Philosophy,* 10 (August 1991): 61–63;

"Intellectuals in Politics: Too Far In? Too Far Out?" *Dissent,* 38 (Autumn 1991): 483–490;

"Reply to Andrew Ross' 'On "Intellectuals in Politics,"'" *Dissent,* 39 (Spring 1992): 265–267;

"What Can You Expect from Anti-Foundationalist Philosophers? A Reply to Lynn Baker," *Virginia Law Review,* 78 (April 1992): 719–727;

"Centers of Moral Gravity: Comments on Donald Spence's 'The Hermeneutic Turn,'" *Psychoanalytic Dialogues,* 3 (Winter 1993): 21–28;

"Feminism, Ideology and Deconstruction: A Pragmatist View," *Hypatia,* 8 (Spring 1993): 96–103;

"Taylor on Self-Celebration and Gratitude," *Philosophy and Phenomenological Research,* 54 (March 1994): 197–201;

"Half a Million Blue Helmets?" *Common Knowledge,* 4 (Winter 1995): 10–13;

"Remembering John Dewey and Sidney Hook," *Free Inquiry,* 16 (Winter 1995): 40–42;

"Only Connect: Response to Steven Lukes," *Dissent,* 42 (Spring 1995): 264–265;

"The Necessity of Inspired Reading," *Chronicle of Higher Education,* 9 February 1996, p. A48;

"The Ambiguity of 'Rationality,'" *Constellations,* 3 (April 1996): 73–82;

"What's Wrong with 'Rights'?" *Harper's,* 292 (June 1996): 15–18;

"Duties to the Self and Others: Comments on a Paper by Alexander Nehamas," *Salmagundi,* 111 (Summer 1996): 59–67;

"Intellectuals and the Millenium," *New Leader,* 80 (24 February 1997): 10–11;

"Can Philosophers Help Their Clients?" *New Leader,* 80 (7 April 1997): 11–12;

"Nietzsche and the Pragmatists," *New Leader,* 80 (19 May 1997): 9;

Introduction to "Symposium: Science Out of Context: The Misestimate and Misuse of Natural Sciences," *Common Knowledge,* 6 (Fall 1997): 20–103;

"First Projects, Then Principles," *Nation,* 265 (22 December 1997): 18–21;

"Comments on Michael Williams' 'Unnatural Doubts,'" *Journal of Philosophical Research,* 22 (1997): 1–10;

"What Do You Do When They Call You a 'Relativist'?" *Philosophy and Phenomenological Research,* 57 (1997): 173–177;

"Against Unity," *Woodrow Wilson Quarterly,* 22 (Winter 1998): 28–38;

"Davidson between Wittgenstein and Tarski," *Critica: revista hispanoamericana de filosofia,* 30 (April 1998): 49–71;

"The Dark Side of the Academic Left," *Chronicle of Higher Education,* 3 April 1998, pp. B4–B6;

"The American Road to Fascism," *New Statesman,* 127 (8 May 1998): 28–29;

"McDowell, Davidson, and Spontaneity," *Philosophy and Phenomenological Research,* 58 (June 1998): 389–394;

"Response to Stuart Rennie's 'Elegant Variations,'" *South African Journal of Philosophy,* 17 (November 1998): 343–345;

"Vive la Différence," *2B: A Journal of Ideas,* 13 (1998): 79–80;

"Can American Egalitarianism Survive a Globalized Economy?" *Business Ethics Quarterly: Journal of the Society for Business Ethics,* Ruffin Series, special issue no. 1 (1998): 1–6;

"Saved from Hypocrisy," *Dissent,* 46 (Spring 1999): 16–17;

"Not all *That* Strange: A Response to Dreyfus and Spinosa," *Inquiry,* 42 (March 1999): 125–128;

"Mein Jahrhundertbuch: Freud's Vorlesungen zur Einführung in die Psychoanalyse," *Die Zeit,* 20 May 1999, p. 61;

"Rorty v. Searle, at Last: A Debate," by Rorty and John Searle, *Logos,* 2 (Summer 1999): 20–67;

"Comment on Robert Pippin's 'Naturalness and Mindedness: Hegel's Compatibilism,'" *European Journal of Philosophy,* 7 (August 1999): 213–216;

"The Communitarian Impulse," *Colorado College Studies,* 32 (1999): 55–61;

"Corragio, Europa!" *Iride,* 12 (1999): 241–243;

"Pragmatism as Anti-authoritarianism," *Revue Internationale de Philosophie,* 53 (1999): 7–20;

"Darwin versus 'Erkenntnistheorie'–Reply to Janos Boros," *Deutsche Zeitschrift für Philosophie,* 48 (Winter 2000): 149–152;

"Response to Randall Peerenbloom," *Philosophy East and West,* 50 (Winter 2000): 90–91;

"The Overphilosophization of Politics," *Constellations,* 7 (March 2000): 128–132;

"Is 'Cultural Recognition' a Useful Concept for Leftist Politics?" *Critical Horizons,* 1 (2000): 7–20;

"The Moral Purposes of the University: An Exchange," by Rorty, Julie A. Reuben, and George Marsden, *Hedgehog Review,* 2 (Fall 2000): 106–120;

"Pragmatism," *International Journal of Psycho-Analysis,* 81 (2000): 819–825.

Richard Rorty is one of the most widely read living philosophers; yet, few people would want to call themselves "Rortians" or to be considered to be in too much accord with his positions. The foremost contemporary pragmatist thinker, Rorty sees his thought as a continuation of the tradition set by William James and John Dewey. He rekindled widespread interest in pragmatist thought by merging traditional pragmatist ideas with the views of contemporary thinkers such as Donald Davidson, Wilfrid Sellars, and W. V. Quine. His progression from philosopher to social commentator and political theorist has provoked a great deal of interest and admiration but also much criticism. He has been called everything from "the most interesting philosopher in the world" (on the dust jacket for his *Contingency, Irony, and Solidarity,* 1989) to a "pseudodeviant" (by David Brooks), and virtually no one familiar with his work remains neutral as to its scholarly or social value. Figures ranging from the singer David Bowie to the political pundit George F. Will have commented on his work, and his notoriety is unlikely to wane soon.

Rorty has published hundreds of articles in journals as varied as *The New Republic, Dissent, Mind, New Literary History,* and *The Journal of Philosophy.* He is the rare academic who has a multitude of audiences: there is a Rorty for philosophers, English professors, political scientists, law-school faculty members, historians, and the lay public; he even has a fair readership among architects, biologists, and physicists. Few scholars are taken so seriously in so many fields. He is, perhaps, even bet-

Political philosopher Leo Strauss, under whose influence Rorty came as a student at the University of Chicago. Later, Rorty read Strauss's Natural Right and History *(1950) and said that he was unable to find a single clear argument in it.*

ter known in Europe and Asia than in the United States. His works have been translated into two dozen languages, and he receives requests to present lectures all over the world. But this interest in Rorty belies virtually unanimous disagreement with much of what he has to say. In the academy he really has no safe haven, and this situation is reflected in his two most recent academic positions: in one he was "departmentless," and he is presently employed in a comparative literature program instead of a philosophy department. The roots of Rorty's controversial views can be traced to his childhood.

Richard McKay Rorty was born in New York City on 4 October 1931 to prominent disaffected Marxists, James and Winifred Raushenbush Rorty, and grew up on a steady diet of revolutionary political philosophy. James Rorty was a well-known poet widely credited with bringing Robinson Jeffers to public attention. A decorated World War I veteran, he had returned from Europe disgusted with the capitalists he believed to be responsible for the war. He became a communist,

though he was never an official member of the Communist Party; Earl Browder, the head of the party in the United States, told him that he could be more effective if he were not on the official lists. In 1926–1927 he served as an editor of the communist journal *New Masses,* which published the work of such notable writers and artists as John Dos Passos, Meridel Le Sueur, Upton Sinclair, and Ezra Pound. His political sentiments ran counter to those of the rest of his family: his brothers were successful businessmen, and one, Malcolm, who was vice president of the International Telephone and Telegraph Corporation and, later, president of the Academy of Management Association, wrote many articles and books attacking communists and New Deal initiatives. Rorty's mother was a writer and an expert on race relations. Her father, Walter Rauschenbusch (she dropped the two *c*s from her last name), a well-known theologian and popular writer, was the most notable figure in the Social Gospel movement. Despite his best efforts to lead his five children to the church, they all became atheists. All three of his sons became economists and worked in President Franklin D. Roosevelt's New Deal government in the 1930s. After graduating from Oberlin College, Winifred spent 1917 canvassing Ohio in support of women's suffrage. She then entered the graduate school of the University of Chicago and, though she never completed her doctorate, worked as a graduate assistant for sociologist Robert Park for five years. She met James Rorty at a party in San Francisco in 1927; they were married the following year, after he divorced his first wife. Winifred Rorty was also a communist, though she was more ambivalent about the party than her husband was.

In 1932 the Rortys and some of their friends broke with the American Communist Party when they realized the extent to which it was controlled by Soviet dictator Joseph Stalin. At first they became Trotskyites and, finally, anticommunists. In 1935 FBI (Federal Bureau of Investigation) director J. Edgar Hoover warned the Federal Emergency Relief Administration about James Rorty, saying that "it appears possible that Rorty has been instrumental in organizing strikes among workers" employed by the agency. That same year the sheriff in El Centro, California, arrested him for reporting on efforts to organize agricultural workers. At the top of his booking sheet, in large red print, is the word "RED." Even after he became stridently anticommunist, the FBI investigated him on several occasions and subjected him to varying degrees of surveillance for many years.

Soon after Rorty's birth his parents, inspired by the Romantic vision of writers living close to nature, moved from New York City to Westport, Connecticut; when he was seven, they moved to Flatbrookville, New

Jersey. When he was five, Rorty marched down the main street of Westport to protest the treatment of the "Scottsboro Boys," nine black teenagers convicted of raping two white girls in Alabama in 1931; he bribed a classmate with a nickel's worth of chocolate to protest with him. He then wrote United States senator Homer T. Bone, "I want you to sign a bill about the Scottsboro case. I want the Supreme Court . . . to be able to say that the boys are guilty or are not guilty." In "Trotsky and the Wild Orchids," published in the journal *Common Knowledge* in 1992 and collected in *Philosophy and Social Hope* (1999), Rorty says that when he was twelve the "most salient books on my parents' shelves were two red-bound volumes: *The Case of Leon Trotsky* [1937] and *Not Guilty* [1938]," the Dewey Commission reports of the investigation into the Moscow trials under Stalin. The leftist journalist Carlo Tresca, gunned down on a New York City street in 1943, was a family friend; the Rortys believed—incorrectly—that Stalin had ordered Tresca's killing (the case has never been solved, but the gunman is known to have been a member of the Mafia). After the murder of Trotsky in Mexico—which *was* ordered by Stalin—Trotsky's secretary John Frank hid out in the Rorty home to escape assassination by the Russian GRU (Glavnoe Razvedyvatel'noe Upravlenic [Chief Intelligence Directorate]). In this atmosphere Rorty grew up, he says, "knowing that all decent people were, if not Trotskyites, at least socialists." By early adolescence he was convinced that "the point of being human was to spend one's life fighting social injustice."

Although they made a strong political impression on their son, James and Winifred Rorty were inattentive parents. In an unpublished April 1996 interview he said, "I was something of a neglected child; my parents didn't really have much time for me." Having no siblings, he "lived in books all the time." He learned to read at a young age and especially enjoyed the writings of family friends such as Jeffers, Lionel Trilling, James T. Farrell, Edmund Wilson, Hildegarde Flanner, Allen Tate, and Caroline Gordon.

Rorty felt out of place in the one-room school he attended in Flatbrookville. The other students regarded Rorty as an eggheaded city boy, and he was often ridiculed and bullied. Nevertheless, he helped start a student newspaper, *The Minisink Valley News,* for which he wrote editorials on subjects ranging from Jesus to food shortages caused by World War II. Mainly, however, he substituted communion with nature for the companionship of people. He became fixated on wild orchids, vowing to find all of the forty-odd species alleged to exist in the New Jersey hills. He never lost the Romantic love of nature he developed in Flatbrookville and is still an avid bird-watcher. In an unpublished 15 June

1997 interview the Marxist philosopher and activist Milton Fisk recalled that he and Rorty were driving on a rural road in the 1960s when Rorty "yelled out" for Fisk to "stop the car!" Fisk "came to a screeching halt," and Rorty leaped from the car and ran back to a clump of bushes they had just passed on the side of the road. As Fisk tried to regain his composure, Rorty urged him to get out of the car and come over to the bushes. Rorty was "very disappointed" to find that the insect cocoons on the bushes were from the previous season and so were empty. According to Fisk, Rorty is happiest when he is in the woods looking for rare flowers and birds.

Rorty's parents often spent the winters in New York City, where they worked for the black labor leader A. Phillip Randolph, the American Civil Liberties Union, and other leftist causes. Sometimes they left their son in the care of neighbors in Flatbrookville; at other times they took him with them. In New York they usually lived in the Hotel Chelsea on West Twenty-third Street and Seventh Avenue; in an unpublished 24 November 1993 interview Rorty recalled it as a "cheap, dirty, and nasty" haven for the avant-garde of politics, "filled with communists, various shades of leftists, Stalinists on one floor, Trotskyites on another floor. . . . A lot of intellectuals lived there because it was fashionable." Rorty said in the 1996 interview that his parents "didn't have the guts to make me go" to school, "so rather than have me sit around the hotel room all day" when the family was in New York City "they let me hang around the office and do odd jobs and run the mimeograph machine." He sometimes served as a runner, carrying "drafts of press releases from the Worker's Defense League office in Grammercy Park" or "long petitions to Congress, and I went to get Pearl Buck's signature and Randolph's and Norman Thomas's." On the subway he read the materials he was carrying, absorbing the various political positions.

By the end of 1945, Rorty said in the 1996 interview, his mother was looking for a way to get him out of the house: "she didn't much like the idea of having a teenager around." She decided to send him to Hutchins College at the University of Chicago, which allowed students who made outstanding scores on a standardized examination developed by the college to enroll immediately after their sophomore year in high school. As the son of a wounded World War I veteran, Rorty won a special scholarship and entered the college in August 1946.

All new students were evaluated through a comprehensive battery of tests. Rorty scored lowest in "Skill in Analyzing Scientific Writing" and in "Knowledge of Physics and Chemistry," managing to make only the ninth percentile on those examinations. But he ranked

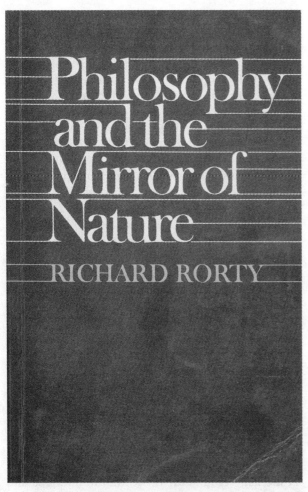

*Cover for the revised edition (1980) of Rorty's first book,
originally published in 1979, in which he says
that philosophers should abandon the search
for absolute truth (Bruccoli Clark
Layman Archives)*

Strauss's other students would "sit at his feet drinking . . . tea, listening to the great man," Rorty said in the 1996 interview, but his awe was "combined with complete bafflement. I hadn't the slightest idea what he was going on about." Rorty also took classes with Rudolf Carnap and Charles Hartshorne.

In letters home Rorty often complained about loneliness, as well as a mysterious "sickness" that seemed to be a euphemism for major depression. By the beginning of his third year his problems were affecting his studies. In a 25 October 1948 letter he told his father: "I have just sort of stopped caring about my work, the future. . . . The most obvious consequence is that I, who participated actively in discussions, and was always well ahead in my work last year, haven't said a word in class all year and am far behind in everything." Nevertheless, he received his B.A. in 1949.

As a child, Rorty had often turned to God for solace in his loneliness. He thought that if he prayed hard enough and was perfectly sincere, God would be revealed to him. He labored with his faith until he was around nineteen, when he concluded that belief in God was infantile.

To move from a Hutchins College degree to a major graduate program without completing an M.A. at Chicago was virtually impossible; Rorty's was thus, in effect, a six-year program. His talent only began to stand out markedly during his work on his master's degree. Part of his renewed interest in academics came through his acquaintance of Amélie Oksenberg, who was one year behind Rorty. Oksenberg came from a family of Jewish diamond cutters who had fled Poland, foreseeing Adolf Hitler's rise to power. The Oksenbergs, like the Rortys, followed a Thoreauvian vision and lived on Southern farms, while Amélie's father, Israel, maintained his trade as a master diamond cutter. In Oksenberg, Rorty found an intellectual equal and someone to help him through his depression and loneliness. Around this time his impression of his former idol Strauss's obscurantism was confirmed when he read Strauss's *Natural Right and History* (1950) and could not find a single clear argument in the entire book.

Rorty received his M.A. in 1952. He had applied to four doctoral programs: the University of Wisconsin, Harvard University, New York University, and Yale University. He had no intention of going to Wisconsin but applied to make his uncle Paul Raushenbush happy (like Rorty's mother, the uncle had also changed the spelling of his name). He also had little desire to attend New York University, applying only because Sidney Hook chaired the philosophy department there. Harvard admitted Rorty without financial aid, which in his case was tantamount to a rejection. Yale, however, offered him a fellowship, and in the fall of 1952 he left

in the ninetieth percentile on "Skill in the Fundamentals of Verbal Logic" and made a perfect score on the "Ability to Apply Stated Mathematical Rules to Verbal Statements and Mathematical Equations."

At Chicago, Rorty gravitated toward the philosophers Leo Strauss, Mortimer J. Adler, and Richard McKeon. Believing that the purpose of philosophy was to reveal, clarify, and support just social arrangements, he writes in "Trotsky and the Wild Orchids," he sought a means to "hold reality and justice in a single vision." The quest for social justice seemed to him to presuppose a fully worked-out metaphysics and epistemology (theory of knowledge). In a 1999 interview with Michael Shelden he recalled: "I wanted a way to be both an intellectual and spiritual snob and a friend of humanity—a nerdy recluse and a fighter for justice." For a time he fell under the spell of the charismatic political philosopher Strauss. Every afternoon Rorty and

for New Haven, Connecticut. Oksenberg soon joined him there. Rorty ranked first of all the doctoral candidates in his preliminary examinations, and his professors were impressed by his knowledge of the history of philosophy.

Oksenberg forced Rorty out of his introspection and shyness. On 19 February 1953 he wrote his parents that he needed some money, because a "more-than-usually active social life has left me broke again." While Rorty had asked his parents for money previously, he had never before cited social activities as a reason. That spring he and Oksenberg announced their engagement to his parents, which thrilled them; fearing disapproval, however, Rorty and Oksenberg delayed notifying her parents of their plans. When they did break the news, the Oksenbergs wrote to Rorty's parents in April 1954, "After spending ten days with Amélie and Dick in our home we feel that we cannot approve of their marriage." After a trying few weeks for the young couple, Israel and Clara Oksenberg relented and sanctioned the marriage. The wedding took place on 15 June 1954.

As a married man, Rorty felt pressured to finish his Ph.D. as soon as possible. His somewhat hurried dissertation was "The Concept of Potentiality"; his dissertation committee was made up of Paul Weiss, Brand Blanshard, and Frederick Fitch. He later regretted not delaying the completion of the degree until after his twenty-sixth birthday, so that he could have retained his student deferment until he was no longer subject to military conscription. Instead, acting on what he considered in retrospect to have been bad advice, he joined the army reserve just as he was finishing his degree in October 1956. The following January the army–thinking, he said in the 1996 interview, that "one Ph.D. is as good as another"–called him to active duty and assigned him to a fledgling department charged with developing battlefield computers. The other Ph.D. in the department was an electrical engineer. Rorty did make one notable contribution: he persuaded the army to use Polish notation for computer programming, abandoning the notation developed by Bertrand Russell and Alfred North Whitehead in *Principia Mathematica* (1910–1913). This change made computer instructions much easier to write and faster to execute.

During his service Rorty met people who worked for the major computer manufacturers; as he approached the end of his enlistment, these companies, thinking that his connections could help them win army contracts, competed with one another to hire him. Rorty has joked that he may have been the most sought-after private first class in the history of the army. Instead, he received an early discharge in October 1958 to accept a job as a philosophy instructor at Wellesley College. The chairperson, Virginia Onderdonk, almost

RICHARD RORTY

Contingency, irony, and solidarity

Cover for Rorty's 1989 book, in which he continues the attack on the quest for truth that he began in Philosophy and the Mirror of Nature (Bruccoli Clark Layman Archives)

did not hire him, thinking that he was too shy to be an effective teacher. These fears were not borne out: he was popular with his students but was considered "heretical" by some of his colleagues. In his classes he used unauthorized translations by Hubert L. Dreyfus and other students of John Wild of the first hundred-odd pages of Martin Heidegger's *Sein und Zeit* (1927; translated as *Being and Time*, 1962). He was promoted to assistant professor of philosophy in 1960.

Meanwhile, at Princeton the Plato scholar Gregory Vlastos was looking for someone to relieve him of the duty of teaching Aristotle; Blanshard recommended Rorty. Rorty had little interest in becoming an Aristotle scholar, but he accepted a one-year post at Princeton beginning in the fall of 1961. After a few months Princeton offered him a three-year contract; later it was changed to a tenure-track position. Around this time Amélie Rorty began to feel that their marriage was hindering her career as a philosopher. The couple had a son, Jay, in 1961; but the relationship continued to deteriorate, and Rorty's depression returned. Furthermore, in 1962 Rorty's father suffered a mental breakdown; he "would insist he was a key figure in a system of international intrigue. He had all kinds of psychotic delusions connected with the Cuban Missile Crisis," Rorty said in the 1996 interview. His mother was helpless in the face of her husband's illness, and Rorty was forced to commit him to an institution. His father spent the last ten years of his life on the antipsychotic drug Thorazine, which allowed him to live at home but "left him only sort of half human," Rorty recalled in the 1996 interview. He never forgave Rorty for committing him. The shock of his father's breakdown led Rorty himself to seek psychiatric treatment, and between 1962 and 1968 he saw a psychotherapist who had trained under one of Sigmund Freud's students. She put him on medication in addition to therapy, but the treatment did little to relieve his depression. The turmoil in his personal life interfered with his scholarship; between 1962 and 1968 he published fewer than half a dozen articles of any substance or length; and in 1968–1969, when his marriage was at its lowest point, he had no publications at all. Nevertheless, he was granted tenure. He explained in the 1996 interview that in those days receiving tenure was "just damned easy . . . Ivy League places" were "very reluctant to admit they made a mistake. Once you are in the club they don't want to say we should never have let you in." Vlastos also protected Rorty against potential enemies in the department; and, in view of the strong reactions his ideas aroused later, Rorty might have benefited from not publishing too much at this stage in his career.

In 1971 Amélie Rorty went to England to take up a research fellowship at King's College of the University of Cambridge. On 1 September 1972 the Rortys were divorced; on 4 November Richard Rorty married Mary Varney, who taught ancient philosophy at the State University of New York in Buffalo. Rorty's productivity increased, but many of his colleagues at Princeton were friends of Amélie's, making the atmosphere uncomfortable for him. He said in the 1996 interview:

> The first ten years I very much enjoyed life in the department, but life was miserable at home. And then after the divorce and remarriage life was fine at home, but everything had somehow changed in the department. I was no longer Gregory's fair-haired boy, and I was sort of edgy in my relations with my colleagues. It was very unpleasant.

Nevertheless, his new marriage reinvigorated Rorty: in 1972 he published one of his best-known essays, "The World Well Lost," in *The Journal of Philos-*

ophy; it is collected in his *Consequences of Pragmatism: Essays, 1972–1980* (1982). In an unpublished April 2001 interview Rorty identified it as the "first paper, period, that I got a kick out of writing." The Rortys had two children, Patricia and Kevin, and as stability returned to Rorty's life his interest in his work dramatically increased. Between 1972 and the publication of his first book in 1979 he wrote several dozen articles. During this time his pragmatism began to take on its distinctive style, though he claimed the humanist pragmatism of Dewey, with its breadth and power, its broad historical sweep, and its social relevance, as his model.

Dewey had been the hero of Rorty's parents and their circle; Rorty had met Dewey in 1938 at a party given by his parents that also included the Hooks, the Trillings, Farrell, Tresca, and a host of other literati. He said in the 1996 interview that Hook "had convinced my parents and everybody else in the neighborhood that if you had Dewey you didn't really need Marx." He went on to say that early in his academic career he had liked the work of James and Dewey "but couldn't figure out how to make use of them."

What Rorty took from Dewey has less to do with philosophy than with Dewey's "Americanism." The roots of Rorty's general philosophical disposition lead more clearly back to Quine, Sellars, and Ludwig Wittgenstein than to Dewey's pragmatism; but Dewey represents a time when Americans were not self-conscious about their Americanism. His work is an expression of a naive, Walt Whitmanesque belief in the power of America to transform its imaginings into truth. This sort of patriotism, which is unapologetic and grounded in a people's power to envision justice and act on it, is the patriotism of Oliver Wendell Holmes Jr., Eleanor Roosevelt, and Martin Luther King Jr. Dewey's embrace of Romantic possibilities for American culture attracted Rorty; he said in the 1993 interview that "if I was going to be a pragmatist, then you can only be a pragmatist in America. . . . I'm very sentimental about being an American–I'm very patriotic."

After "The World Well Lost" Rorty constantly referred to Dewey. Dewey appears on nearly every page of *Consequences of Pragmatism,* and Rorty plainly sees his own work as a continuation of Dewey's. For example, both Rorty and Dewey view the ancients' belief that nonnatural objects support the sensible realm, on the one hand, and modern philosophers' commitment to epistemology, on the other hand, as arising from the same impulse to have something outside of human beings, something beyond contingency, tell people what is true and how they should behave. "The best thing about Dewey," Rorty says in "Dewey's Metaphysics," a 1975 lecture collected in *Consequences of Pragmatism,* "is that he did not, like Plato, pretend to be a 'spectator of all time and eternity,' but used philosophy . . . as an instrument of social change." Rorty agrees with Dewey that philosophers need to live up to the demands of culture, rather than the other way around, for nothing greater than culture exists to guide people.

Both Rorty and Dewey are deeply skeptical of academic intellectuals, and this skepticism is a reflection of a broader distrust of academics by Americans. It is also one of the primary sources of pragmatist antiprofessionalism and its occasional tendency to trivialize scholarly work. Rorty told Shelden, "I am very glad that I have spent all those years reading philosophy books, for I learnt something that still seems very important: to distrust the intellectual snobbery which originally led me to read them." From James and Charles Sanders Peirce through Dewey and C. Wright Mills, pragmatists not only have attacked the revered traditions of theory but also have viewed their starting points for such attacks as lying outside of philosophy—as beginning with the mundane, rather than with the "grand." The lofty aspirations of the philosophical tradition are anathema to pragmatists; effectiveness and "what works" are the watchwords of pragmatism, which regards philosophy that does not directly connect to issues important to the community as useless.

Deweyan pragmatism led Rorty to lionize the novelist over the philosopher, the Romantic over the cold analytic. He said in the 2001 interview that "novelists and poets are more heroic figures than philosophers." He had originally wanted to become a poet, but at thirteen he had shown his father some poetry he had written, and his father had termed it "doggerel." Rorty never again wrote poetry; he abandoned what he considered the heroic paths of poetry and fiction for the "inferior" profession of academic philosophy. He was attracted to thinkers such as Jacques Derrida, Cornelius Castoriadis, and Michel Foucault, who blend philosophy with poetic sentiment and make it possible for academic writing to escape its normal bounds and range of influence. Rorty had been assigning Foucault to his classes since the late 1960s, and in the 1970s he began to write about the work of European thinkers. The move was hardly a professionally astute one at that time: American philosophers concerned with their reputation and influence in the profession would never have touched contemporaneous Continental thinkers, and respected Anglo-American philosophical journals would not have considered publishing analyses of these thinkers' work or even the work of the thinkers themselves. Between 1970 and 1985 the name Foucault appears only twice—both times in the same article—in *Mind,* one of the most highly regarded philosophy journals, and the name Derrida appears only once; in *The Journal of Philosophy* Derrida again gets but one mention

Dust jacket for Rorty's 1998 book, in which he criticizes "spectatorial, disgusted, mocking" left-wing academics (Richland County Public Library)

during the period, and Foucault does not appear in a single article. Rorty said in the 1996 interview that being "one of the few American philosophers who said something nice about Derrida . . . in itself was enough" to engender scorn. Despite the risk of professional isolation, however, Rorty found Derrida's language play and Castoriadis's psychological investigations liberating and invigorating. While Rorty finds many of the ideas of Continental thinkers agreeable, those thinkers have little influenced his style: his writing is clear, mostly free of jargon, tinged with humor and the absurd, and characterized by sweeping analyses of the landscape of social history and thought.

Rorty has frequently been attacked for consorting with Continental thinkers. Predictably, analytic philosophers are the most critical, but even his philosophical allies and defenders have joined in the attacks. In "The Quest for Uncertainty: Richard Rorty's Pragmatic Pilgrimage" (2001) James Ryerson quotes the philosopher

Daniel Dennett as saying that Rorty's philosophy of mind is "just about perfect" but that Rorty "has failed to discourage a lot of nonsense that I wish he had discouraged. It's an obligation of us in the field to grit our teeth and discourage the people who do the things that give philosophy a bad name. I don't think he does that enough." On the other hand, the literary critic Harold Bloom told Rorty in a 24 October 1988 letter that he regards Rorty "as not only the most interesting philosopher in the world today, but as the antidote to Derrida & Co." and that "no critic or thinker living has influenced my work from 1980 on" as has Rorty. Thus, while Dennett sees Rorty as opening up the doors of philosophy to undesirables such as Derrida, Bloom views him as helping to protect English departments from European obscurantist mysticism. Such conflicting views are the norm in commentary on Rorty's work.

Rorty's departures from the usual professional fare during the 1970s were but precursors to a more severe rift between him and academic philosophy. His break with his analytic colleagues began in earnest in 1979 with the publication of *Philosophy and the Mirror of Nature*, in which he sets out to add a capstone to the anti-Enlightenment writings of Wittgenstein, Heidegger, and Dewey by marrying the work of two of his other heroes: Sellars and Quine. All of these philosophers, he says, helped to "set aside" the epistemology of the seventeenth century. Rorty wants to block access to a position to which all epistemology aspires: a position beyond time and chance, where competing theories are sorted out by their proximity to the real. He invites his readers to envision what a philosophy without epistemology—"philosophy without mirrors," as he terms it—might look like. He proposes a philosophy that gives up the idea that "man's essence is to be a knower of essences"; philosophers, he says, should be concerned with edification rather than with discovering truth. Philosophy should carry on the "conversation of mankind" rather than "putting itself forward as the final commensurating vocabulary for all possible rational discourse." In Rorty's view, epistemology pretentiously perpetuates the myth of philosophy as the caretaker of culture, the discipline that orders all other disciplines within a matrix of reality.

According to Rorty, seventeenth- and eighteenth-century philosophers tried to manufacture problems that could not be explained by the new science of the Enlightenment as a means of preserving philosophy's superiority over other disciplines. The philosophers' "reality" was meant to hold both science and religion at bay. But after Sir Isaac Newton threatened to make philosophy irrelevant by opening the door to completely causal accounts of everything, philosophers, according to Rorty, did the only thing they could: they

invented modern epistemology. This move had the advantage of keeping science subject to philosophy—especially in the formulations of Immanuel Kant, who put "outer space inside inner space" and made "outdoor" events items of the "transcendental ego." Kant thus put philosophy "on the secure path of science" by "claiming Cartesian certainty about" this "inner" space "for the laws of what had previously been thought to be outer" space. But if "rational certainty" is thought of "as a matter of victory in argument rather than of relation to an object known, we shall look toward our interlocutors rather than to our faculties for the explanation of" phenomena. In that case, "Our certainty will be a matter of conversation between persons, rather than a matter of interaction with nonhuman reality," and "we shall not see a difference in kind between 'necessary' and 'contingent' truths."

Because philosophers saw language as a "public" mirror of nature, just as thought is a "private" one, they believed that they could reformulate many Cartesian and Kantian questions and answers in linguistic terms and thereby rehabilitate many standard philosophical issues. This "linguistic turn" began as an "attempt to produce a nonpsychologistic empiricism by rephrasing philosophical questions as questions of 'logic'"; philosophers eventually came to see that claims about the "nature and extent of human knowledge" could be "stated as remarks about language." For Rorty, however, this modern shift is just as pointless as the epistemology of the seventeenth and eighteenth centuries. The overarching theme of *Philosophy and the Mirror of Nature* is that philosophy has created problems whose solutions—if they could be found—would have no social consequences. The main shifts in philosophical debate, Rorty says, are the result of a discipline trying to save itself, rather than a progression toward a world of "truth."

Except for a thoughtful and careful review by Quentin Skinner in *The New York Review of Books* (19 March 1981), *Philosophy and the Mirror of Nature* initially received little favorable attention from philosophers. If philosophers did not like *Philosophy and the Mirror of Nature*, however, historians, anthropologists, sociologists, law professors, and literary critics loved it. The work has never been out of print—no small feat for a philosophy book. (Indeed, as of 2003 all of Rorty's books and collected essays were still in print.)

Philosophy and the Mirror of Nature marks the denouement of a decade of increasing dissatisfaction on Rorty's part with his colleagues at Princeton and with the sort of research that was valued by the community of analytic philosophers. What he perceived as the iciness and complete disregard for intellectual history of analytic philosophers had finally become too much for him. In his view their work had little connection with the vibrancy of the community of Americans or the passions of life. In return, though many philosophers admired the persuasiveness of *Philosophy and the Mirror of Nature,* they thought that the aims of the book were dangerous and destabilizing of the rational processes that underlie knowledge. John Searle, a well-known philosopher of mind and longtime opponent of Rorty, argued in an unpublished May 2001 interview that the work is "a bad book" because it is pernicious to the foundations of morality. Richard Schmitt, who was a friend of Rorty's during the 1950s and 1960s, said in an unpublished 21 May 2001 interview that the concern that bad philosophy can undermine morals is evidence of "the hubris of professional philosophers who think they are maintaining a tradition which keeps children from shooting their schoolmates." Searle went on to say that Rorty's threat to the culture is the result of his being "educated at the two worst places in the world: Chicago and Yale," where the focus was on the history of philosophy rather than the advancement of philosophical method. Searle claimed that Rorty "thinks of philosophy as the history of thought since Plato, and that's a disaster." Searle and other analytic philosophers see philosophy as an experimental science that can find new ways of discovering or validating truth, while Rorty regards truth as an ever-shifting reflection of the communal will. For Rorty, truth is not an interesting philosophical subject and does not require any deep analysis; philosophers, he thinks, should free themselves from the "truth industry" and set out in new directions.

The conservative Intercollegiate Studies Institute's Internet site lists *Philosophy and the Mirror of Nature* among the fifty worst books of the twentieth century, describing it as "The best, and therefore worst, exposition of American philosophical pragmatism. Had devastating effects on the study not only of philosophy but also of literature." (Rorty's grandfather Walter Rauschenbusch's *Christianity and the Social Crisis* [1907] is also on the list for maintaining that "'[The Church] should therefore strengthen the existing communistic institutions and aid the evolution of society from the present temporary stage of individualism to a higher form of communism.' Eek!") Curiously, the institute puts Wittgenstein's *Philosophical Investigations* (1953) on the fifty best books list, even though little or no difference exists between Wittgenstein's and Rorty's epistemological beliefs.

In 1979 a war was raging in the American Philosophical Association (APA) between analytic philosophers and "pluralists"; the pluralists included Thomists, phenomenologists, Whiteheadians, Continentalists, and "fuzzies" who did not hold the hardheaded analytic

Cover for a 1999 collection of Rorty's articles that includes his memoir "Trotsky and the Wild Orchids" (Bruccoli Clark Layman Archives)

approach in high regard. Analytic philosophers at a few elite schools held most of the power in the APA, and the pluralists believed that this minority was tyrannizing an organization that was supposed to represent the entire profession of philosophy in the United States. In those days, Rorty said in the 1996 interview, the selection of presidents was an "inside job": the "nominating committee met and submitted one name to the meeting as the next president, which was always ratified." The outgoing president of the Eastern Division of the APA, Hilary Putnam, put Rorty's name forward to be his successor. The nomination and election took place before the publication of *Philosophy and the Mirror of Nature;* Rorty probably would not have been considered had his book come out a year earlier. In the event, he was the youngest person ever to become president. Until this time the analytic philosophers had not taken the threat from the pluralists seriously. "But then," Rorty said in the 1996 interview, "the office began getting all these membership applications from people they'd never heard of. During the Vietnam War we had, in a spirit of Sixties openness, said that anybody could be a member of the APA who wanted to be." The rumor was that "hundreds and hundreds and hundreds of nuns teaching philosophy courses at Catholic institutions, not to mention priests," were sending in applications for membership in the APA. When Rorty "tried to be the person who could speak to both sides, the result was that both sides figured I had betrayed them. The establishment decided I had sold out to the pluralists, the pluralists never believed a word of my conciliatory rhetoric; they thought I was maneuvering for a position in the philosophy establishment." Rorty parried several procedural maneuvers by the analytic philosophers, with the result that the pluralist candidate, John Smith of Yale, succeeded Rorty as president of the Eastern Division. Branded a traitor by the analytic philosophers, some of whom have still never forgiven him, Rorty knew that the discomfort he already felt in the department at Princeton would only intensify: "Being a marginal member in the department means never having any influence, never getting anything you want, never getting any friends appointed, never getting your students good jobs," he said in the 1996 interview. "I should have left around '75 instead of going it until '82." On the other hand, pluralists thought that he was still too closely aligned with the APA establishment.

After the 1979 APA meeting Rorty made it known that he wanted to take another position, but few departments were interested in having him. He received offers from the University of California at Santa Cruz, the University of Michigan, and the University of Virginia. He accepted a position as University Professor of Humanities and Kenan Professor of Humanities at the University of Virginia, to begin in 1982. The offer came at the instigation of the chairman of the English department, E. D. Hirsch Jr., an acquaintance of Rorty's from graduate-school days.

Just before leaving for Virginia, Rorty was given a fellowship from the John D. and Catherine T. MacArthur Foundation for the period 1981 to 1986. The so-called genius award, which provided several hundred thousand dollars, allowed him to distance himself further from professional philosophy. After the award was announced, institutions besieged him with requests for visits and offered him prestigious lectureships. He fulfilled as many of these requests as he could, prompting Bloom to tell him in a 28 January 1994 letter, "I remain in awe (not in envy) of your travels. Someday I will read of Rorty atop a sacred mountain in Tannu Tuva, instructing the Mongol shamans on the ecstasies of Rortean pragmatism."

At the University of Virginia, Rorty was not affiliated with a particular department, though his mailbox was in the philosophy department. His office was separated from other offices on the fourth floor of Cabell Hall. His relations with the philosophy department were cordial, but graduate students usually could not apply courses they took with Rorty toward graduation requirements in philosophy. Rorty's position had all the earmarks of professional exile, but to Rorty it was freedom. Asked in the 2001 interview what it was like spending the last twenty years outside of philosophy departments, Rorty responded, "Wonderful."

As a speaker, Rorty is known for his ability to hold rapt an audience of people with widely diverse training and backgrounds. In the classroom and in public presentations he is gregarious, humorous, and witty, though the British philosopher Jonathan Rée told Ryerson that his mode of presentation has "a tremendous kind of melancholy about it. He tries to be a gay Nietzschean, but it's an effort for him." Dennett told Ryerson that Rorty's lectures are "sort of striking—these firebrand views delivered in the manner of Eeyore," the donkey in the Winnie-the-Pooh stories. He is a devastating critic in his written work, but his opponents can fare even worse in direct confrontation. While he never personalizes his attacks, sometimes his use of humor goes awry. Responding to a paper presented at the University of Virginia by a well-known young scholar in the late 1980s, Rorty burlesqued the man's arguments and literally brought him to tears. (Rorty later told a friend that he felt "awful" about the incident.) In private life, however, Rorty is often shy and reserved. In the 1996 interview he explained: "I'm much better in class than I am in the office. I don't know how to handle office hours, but in class I sort of rev myself up to put on a performance." Schmitt said in the 2001 interview that Rorty is a "kind-hearted, morally serious person," and Fisk said in the 1996 interview that Rorty's persona in class and during presentations obscures a deep and broad compassion for people. In 1967, Fisk recalled, he and Rorty, in Pittsburgh for a conference, saw a bus strike an elderly man who was selling newspapers. Fisk's response was to dash into the nearest store to call the police and an ambulance; Rorty's was to kneel, embrace the man, and comfort him with the promise he would be all right. In what would no doubt be shocking to many of Rorty's opponents, the most prominent features of Rorty's personality seem to be kindness and humility. He told Shelden,

I don't consider myself a great thinker, and I never intended to create so much controversy. . . . I don't think I'm doing much more than creating a more receptive audience for truly original thinkers. Originality may be scarce, but not intelligence; so maybe a little of my intelligence can help to improve the climate for greater minds than mine.

When a suggestion was made that he share the dais at an event at the University of Virginia with Jesse Jackson, Rorty immediately rejected the idea. He believes that people such as Jackson are vital to society in a way philosophers could never be.

In the 1980s Rorty's work was seized on by some members of the intellectual Left who thought that *Philosophy and the Mirror of Nature* and Rorty's actions in the APA indicated that he shared their radical politics and anti-American bias. They thought that Rorty would agree with them that if claims to neutrality and objectivity are untenable, as he argued, then political systems that rely on such claims for justification are unjust and that the undercutting of Enlightenment epistemology and its later mutations leads directly to a radical politics. They saw *Philosophy and the Mirror of Nature* and much of Rorty's other writing as tools for attacking liberalism. Rorty does not, however, share the view that to knock out a political regime's philosophical supports ipso facto discredits the regime. He distrusts the academic Left because he does not think that any useful connection exists between theory and justice. The rhetoric from the Left revived his revulsion for anti-Americanism, communism, and communist tactics. He develops his position on theory and politics in his article "The Priority of Democracy to Philosophy" and his controversial 1989 book *Contingency, Irony, and Solidarity.*

Rorty's main aim in "The Priority of Democracy to Philosophy"—originally published in *The Virginia Statute for Religious Freedom: Its Evolution and Consequences in American History* (1988) and collected in *Objectivity, Relativism, and Truth* (1991), volume one of Rorty's *Philosophical Papers*—is to show that no unifying principle links private self-forming activity and the needs of public policy. Rorty says that the search for such a principle has been discredited by thinkers such as Heidegger and Hans-Georg Gadamer, who "have given us ways of seeing human beings as historical all the way through," as well as by Quine and Davidson, who have "blurred the distinction between permanent truths of reason and temporary truths of fact." The result is to "erase the picture of the self common to Greek metaphysics, Christian theology, and Enlightenment rationalism: the picture of an ahistorical nature center, the locus of human dignity, surrounded by an adventitious and inessential periphery." The destruction of this picture causes liberal social theory to become polarized between an absolutist side, which insists on talking about inalienable rights and "one right answer" to moral and political dilemmas "without trying to back

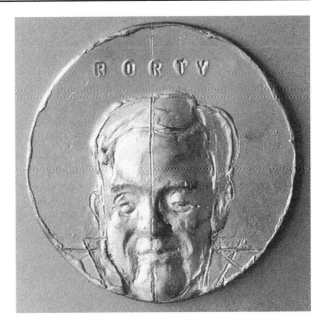

Bronze coin of Rorty cast by Eric Claus for an exhibition on twentieth-century philosophers at Erasmus University in Rotterdam in January and February 2000
(Erasmus University)

up such talk with a theory of human nature," and a "pragmatist side," which regards the talk of "rights" as "an attempt to enjoy the benefits of metaphysics without assuming the appropriate responsibilities." Nevertheless, the pragmatist will "still need something to distinguish the sort of individual conscience we respect from the sort we condemn as 'fanatical.'" This distinguishing feature "can only be something relatively local and ethnocentric—the tradition of a particular community, the consensus of a particular culture." For Rorty, "what counts as rational or as fanatical is relative to the group to which we think it necessary to justify ourselves—to the body of shared belief that determines the reference of the word 'we.'" He concludes:

It is no more evident that democratic institutions are to be measured by the sort of person they create than they are to be measured against divine commands. It is not evident that they are to be measured by anything more specific than the moral intuitions of the particular historical community that has created those institutions. . . . truth, viewed in the Platonic way . . . is simply not relevant to democratic politics. . . . So philosophy as the explanation of the relation between such an order and human nature, is not relevant either. . . . When the two come into conflict, democracy takes precedence over philosophy.

Contingency, Irony, and Solidarity fleshes out many of the ideas expressed in "The Priority of Democracy to Philosophy"; Rorty says in the introduction, "This book tries to show how things look if we drop the demand for a theory" that will unify private self-creation and public responsibility "and are content to treat the demands of self-creation and of human solidarity as equally valid, yet forever incommensurable." His first and most important aim is to undercut the notion that the world makes some statements true and others false. "The world does not speak," Rorty says, but it can, "once we have programmed ourselves with a language, cause us to hold beliefs," though "it cannot propose a language for us to speak." The world is "out there," but the truth is not. A proposition is true not because it corresponds to some reality outside the mind but because it comports with many other propositions that are also true. Rorty readily admits that this criterion is circular; the search for noncircular justification is precisely the bad habit displayed by ancient and Enlightenment thinkers. His goal in *Contingency, Irony, and Solidarity* is, thus, the same as in *Philosophy and the Mirror of Nature,* but it is now cast in terms more conducive to political theory and to reaching a broader audience. Language and culture, Rorty says, are "as much a contingency, as much a result of thousands of small mutations finding niches (and millions of others finding no niches), as are the orchids and the anthropoids." Once Rorty dispenses with representational theories, it is a short step to turning selfhood and community over to the vagaries of contingency. When language is cut free from the universe, nothing is left for selfhood or community to hang onto that is any more sure or fundamental than linguistically caused solidarity.

In *Contingency, Irony, and Solidarity* Rorty introduces his notion of the "liberal ironist." Ironists are people who understand that their final vocabularies have no noncircular justification and that who they are and what they believe are the results of events that are contingent through and through: "All human beings carry about a set of words which they employ to justify their actions, their beliefs, their lives. . . . These are the words in which we formulate praise of our friends and contempt for our enemies, our long-term projects, our deepest self-doubts and our highest hopes." This set of words is a person's "final vocabulary." It is "final" in that if those words are put into doubt, "their user has no noncircular argumentative recourse. . . . Those words are as far as he can go with language; beyond them there is only helpless passivity or a resort to force." For an ironist acculturated to liberalism, the perfect society would be one in which "no trace of divinity remained, either in the form of a divinized world or a divinized self"; for "To see one's language, one's conscience, one's morality, and one's highest hopes as contingent products, as literalizations of what once were accidentally produced metaphors, is to adopt a self-identity which suits one for citizenship in . . . an ideally

liberal state." Liberal ironists find it "impossible to think that there is something which stands to my community as my community stands to me, some larger community called 'humanity' which has an intrinsic nature."

Political theorists generally responded to Rorty with displeasure. For Rorty, the optimal society should be both liberal and devoid of cruelty, and many on the Left consider such a combination impossible. Ian Shapiro criticized what he termed Rorty's uncritical acceptance of the status quo, and Allan C. Hutchinson, reviewing *Contingency, Irony, and Solidarity* in the *Harvard Law Review* (December 1989) accused Rorty of having "a lack of democratic nerve" for "putting democratic politics in the service of liberal ideology." One commentator on the Right claimed that Rorty, "postmodernism's most gifted defender . . . may ultimately do more to destroy the movement than to defend it." Analytic philosophers accused Rorty of blinding society by undercutting reason, and a reviewer for *The American Spectator* (August 1997) called Rorty's book the "masterwork of Yuppie Enlightenment." Nonphilosophers, though, tended to enjoy the book, and it was embraced by people in many disciplines. The self-actualization guru Werner Erhard read the first three chapters to participants in his "est" seminars. The record producer and avant-garde musician Brian Eno keeps crates of the book in his offices and hands out copies to visitors. This popularity disgusts Rorty's former analytic colleagues, who see him as poisoning not only public perceptions of philosophy but also the cultural tradition of the United States. Shelden cites a writer for the German magazine *Der Spiegel* who said that Rorty made "yuppie regression look good," and Searle lamented in the unpublished 2001 interview that the worst thing a philosopher can do "is give people the impression they understand something when they don't . . . and I think Richard somehow gives people the idea that they've understood philosophy." Rorty sent a copy of *Contingency, Irony, and Solidarity* to the logical positivist Carl Hempel, an old friend at Princeton; after reading as much of the book as he could tolerate, Hempel concluded that Rorty had repudiated much of what Hempel had spent his life defending. Relations between the two men cooled but remained cordial. Among other philosophers the popular success of Rorty's book engendered both revulsion and jealousy. Many complained that the always marginal interest of the general public in philosophy should not be squandered on such a heretical book.

During the 1990s Rorty began to write more social commentary, but his production of scholarly work did not diminish: in 1992 alone he published a dozen articles in academic journals. He also became more directly involved in political activity. Democratic

Rorty in 2000 (photograph © 2003 by Heather Conley)

New Jersey senator Bill Bradley made Rorty part of a small, unofficial group of advisers in his formulation of policy and issues, and at a "Big Think" dinner on 14 January 1998 President Bill Clinton and his adviser Sidney Blumenthal solicited suggestions from Rorty and thirteen other guests for ideas for the upcoming state of the union address. Rorty told the reporter of a 19 January 1998 article in *The Guardian* that the latter experience "caused an upswelling of sentimental patriotism within me. As I left the White House I looked back and saw the flag flying on the top of the building, illuminated against the night sky, and I have to say that my eyes misted over."

In the fall of 1997 Rorty accepted a position in the Department of Comparative Literature at Stanford University, to begin the following year. (His appointment was approved by university provost Condoleeza Rice, who later became President George W. Bush's national security adviser.) In 1998 Rorty's first book of purely political analysis appeared. In *Achieving Our Country: Leftist Thought in Twentieth-Century America* he attacks the Left for fleeing from politics and the Right

for greediness and moral hypocrisy. But he is mainly concerned with exploring the events that caused leftist energies to shift away from labor unions and other practically oriented organizations to universities. After the Vietnam War, the "spectatorial, disgusted, mocking left," sheltered within colleges of arts and sciences, withdrew into their own fabricated visions of cultural politics. Theory fetishism, leftist cabalism, and loathing for the United States, he says, replaced the social activism of an earlier era.

The book seems to have annoyed almost everyone who reviewed it. Leftist academics felt betrayed, and intellectuals on the Right such as *Salon* reviewer David Horowitz sneered at Rorty's "hand-wringing" and "whimpering." In *Newsweek* (25 May 1998) Will called *Achieving Our Country* a "remarkably bad book" that "radiates contempt for the country." Once again, Rorty found himself the shy, reserved academic at the center of a crowd of furious critics.

At this point in his life, two features of Rorty's thought stand out as particularly important. First, one can hardly overemphasize his patriotism and its effects on his ideas. For Rorty, philosophy can be of service to politics; but tinkering, innovations in practice, and persuasion with limited goals have been the hallmarks of progress in the United States. In this light, his detour into analytic philosophy in the 1950s and 1960s appears to be a short-lived distraction from the lessons he learned as a child. One who did not know Rorty's background would think that he was an analytic philosopher who—lamentably or fortunately, depending on one's point of view—gave himself over to social and political criticism, irrationalism, and relativism. But the political seeds in Rorty's writing were sown long before he contemplated becoming a philosopher, and his increasing concern with social justice over the course of his career is a return to his upbringing. Rorty thinks that people can have better lives in the United States than they can anywhere else. This belief is a chauvinism not of superiority but of possibility, and this Romanticism is another prominent feature of Rorty's thought. He admires figures such as Whitman, Holmes, and Jane Addams, who combine a street-smart cynicism with the belief in the power of a single person to transform his or her community. Philosophy, he thinks, is generally of no use in this kind of work, except in the supporting role of refuting opponents of justice who propagate claims that the desires of a community must accord with the wishes of some greater power. Rorty sees his purpose as that of a worker clearing the underbrush of philosophy that stands in the way of achieving social justice.

Richard Rorty's work elicits strong feelings and misunderstandings from virtually every quarter. Mainstream philosophers and critics on the Right tend to see his program as a threat to the stability of the Western rationalist tradition, while some of his supporters read into it a radical political position that he does not hold. David L. Hall's *Richard Rorty: Prophet and Poet of the New Pragmatism* (1994) and John Patrick Diggins's *The Promise of Pragmatism: Modernism and the Crisis of Knowledge and Authority* (1994) stand out as balanced treatments of Rorty's political and philosophical positions. Rorty's engaging prose style and his wiliness in escaping easy categorization ensure that his works will be widely read for many years to come.

Letters:

Anindita Niyogi Balslev, *Cultural Otherness: Correspondence with Richard Rorty,* second edition (Atlanta: Scholars Press, 1999).

Interviews:

Irene Klaver, Pieter Pekelharing, and Jan Flameling, "Interview with Richard Rorty," *Krisis: Tijdschrift voor Filosofie,* 8 (September 1988): 68–83;

Gary A. Olson, "Social Construction and Composition Theory: A Conversation with Richard Rorty," *Journal of Advanced Composition,* 9 (1989): 1–9;

Richard Marino, "Shattering Philosophy's Mirror: A Conversation with Richard Rorty," *Commonweal,* 121 (6 May 1994): 11–14;

Martyn Oliver, "Towards a Liberal Utopia: An Interview with Richard Rorty," *TLS: Times Literary Supplement,* no. 4760 (24 June 1994): 14;

Giovanna Borradori, "After Philosophy, Democracy: Richard Rorty," in her *The American Philosopher: Conversations with Quine, Davidson, Putnam, Nozick, Danto, Rorty, Cavell, MacIntyre, and Kuhn,* translated by Rosanna Crocitto (Chicago & London: University of Chicago Press, 1994), pp. 103–117;

Joshua Knobe, "A Talent for Bricolage: An Interview with Richard Rorty," *Dualist: A National Journal of Undergraduate Work in Philosophy,* 2 (Spring 1995): 56–71;

Michael O'Shea, "Richard Rorty: Toward a Post-Metaphysical Culture," *Harvard Review of Philosophy,* 5 (Spring 1995): 58–66;

Sean Sayers, "Is the Truth out There?" *Times Higher Education Supplement* (London), no. 1283 (6 June 1997): 18;

Pragmatism, Neo-Pragmatism, and Religion: Conversations with Richard Rorty, edited by Charley D. Hardwick and Donald A. Crosby (New York: Peter Lang, 1997);

Derek Nystrom and Kent Puckett, *Against Bosses, against Oligarchies: A Conversation with Richard Rorty* (Charlottesville, Va.: Prickly Pear Pamphlets, 1998);

Michael Shelden, "Thinker with No Belief in Truth," *Daily Telegraph,* 8 May 1999, Arts and Books Features, p. 5.

Bibliographies:

René Görtzen, "Auswahlbibliographie Rorty," in *Richard Rorty zur Einführung,* by Detlef Horster (Hamburg: Junius, 1991), pp. 142–159;

"A Bibliography of Publications by Richard Rorty," in *Rorty and Pragmatism: The Philosopher Responds to His Critics,* edited by Herman J. Saatkamp Jr. (Nashville: Vanderbilt University Press, 1995), pp. 231–244;

"Richard Rorty: Selected Publications," in *Rorty and His Critics,* edited by Robert B. Brandom (Malden, Mass.: Blackwell, 2000), pp. 378–392.

References:

René Vincente Arcilla, *For the Love of Perfection: Richard Rorty and Liberal Education* (New York & London: Routledge, 1995);

Bruce Aune, "Rorty on Language and the World," *Journal of Philosophy,* 69 (1972): 665–667;

Roy Bhaskar, *Philosophy and the Idea of Freedom* (Oxford & Cambridge, Mass.: Blackwell, 1991);

Robert B. Brandom, ed., *Rorty and His Critics* (Malden, Mass.: Blackwell, 2000);

David Brooks, "Achieving Richard Rorty: Leftist Thought in Middle-Class America," *Weekly Standard,* 1 June 1998, p. 31;

Anthony Brueckner, "Transcendental Arguments I," *Noûs,* 17 (1983): 551–575;

Jean-Pierre Cometti, ed., *Lire Rorty* (Paris: Editions de l'Eclat, 1992);

John Patrick Diggins, "Pragmatism: A Philosophy for Adults Only," *Partisan Review,* 67 (1999): 255–262;

Diggins, *The Promise of Pragmatism: Modernism and the Crisis of Knowledge and Authority* (Chicago: University of Chicago Press, 1994), pp. 407–473;

Robert J. Dostal, "The World Never Lost: The Hermeneutics of Trust," *Philosophy and Phenomenological Research,* 47 (1987): 413–434;

Frank B. Farrell, *Subjectivity, Realism, and Postmodernism: The Recovery of the World* (Cambridge & New York: Cambridge University Press, 1994);

Matthew Festenstein, *Pragmatism and Political Theory: From Dewey to Rorty* (Chicago: University of Chicago Press, 1997);

Festenstein and Simon Thompson, eds., *Richard Rorty: Critical Dialogues* (Cambridge: Polity Press / Malden, Mass.: Blackwell, 2001);

Paul D. Forster, "What Is at Stake between Putnam and Rorty?" *Philosophy and Phenomenological Research,* 52 (1992): 585–603;

Nancy Fraser, "From Irony to Prophecy to Politics," *Michigan Quarterly Review,* 30 (1991): 259–266;

John Furlong, "Scientific Psychology as Hermeneutics? Rorty's Philosophy of Mind," *Philosophy and Phenomenological Research,* 48 (1988): 489–503;

Kenneth T. Gallagher, "Rorty's Antipodeans: An Impossible Illustration?" *Philosophy and Phenomenological Research,* 45 (1985): 449–455;

Eric M. Gander, *The Last Conceptual Revolution: A Critique of Richard Rorty's Political Philosophy* (Albany: State University of New York Press, 1999);

Norman Geras, *Solidarity in the Conversation of Humankind: The Ungroundable Liberalism of Richard Rorty* (London & New York: Verso, 1995);

Eugene Goodheart, "The Postmodern Liberalism of Richard Rorty," *Partisan Review,* 63 (1996): 223–235;

Charles B. Guignon, "On Saving Heidegger from Rorty," *Philosophy and Phenomenological Research,* 46 (1986): 401–417;

Guignon and David Hiley, eds., *Richard Rorty* (Cambridge: Cambridge University Press, 2003);

Gary Gutting, *Pragmatic Liberalism and the Critique of Modernity* (Cambridge & New York: Cambridge University Press, 1999);

Honi Fern Haber, *Beyond Postmodern Politics: Lyotard, Rorty, Foucault* (New York: Routledge, 1994);

David L. Hall, *Richard Rorty: Prophet and Poet of the New Pragmatism* (Albany: State University of New York Press, 1994);

Detlef Horster, *Richard Rorty zur Einführung* (Hamburg: Junius, 1991);

D. Vaden House, *Without God or His Doubles: Realism, Relativism, and Rorty* (Leiden & New York: Brill, 1994);

Monika Kilian, *Modern and Postmodern Strategies: Gaming and the Question of Morality. Adorno, Rorty, Lyotard, and Enzensberger* (New York: Peter Lang, 1998);

Konstantin Kolenda, *Rorty's Humanistic Pragmatism: Philosophy Democratized* (Tampa: University of South Florida Press, 1990);

Robert Kraut, "Varieties of Pragmatism," *Mind,* 99 (1990): 157–183;

Ronald Alexander Kuipers, *Solidarity and the Stranger: Themes in the Social Philosophy of Richard Rorty* (Toronto: Institute for Christian Studies / Lanham, Md.: University Press of America, 1997);

Marek Kwiek, *Rorty's Elective Affinities: The New Pragmatism and Postmodern Thought* (Poznań: Wydawnictwo Naukowe Instytutu Filozofii, Uniwersytet im. Adama Mickiewicza w Poznaniu, 1996);

Lenore Langsdorf and Andrew R. Smith, eds., *Recovering Pragmatism's Voice: The Classical Tradition, Rorty, and the Philosophy of Communication* (Albany: State University of New York Press, 1995);

Ben H. Letson, *Davidson's Theory of Truth and Its Implications for Rorty's Pragmatism* (New York: Peter Lang, 1997);

Arnold B. Levinson, "Rorty, Materialism, and Privileged Access," *Noûs,* 21 (1987): 381–393;

Mark J. Lutz, "Socratic Virtue in Post-Modernity: The Importance of Philosophy for Liberalism," *American Journal of Political Science,* 41 (1997): 1128–1149;

Danielle MacBeth, "Pragmatism and the Philosophy of Language," *Philosophy and Phenomenological Research,* 55 (1995): 501–523;

Tibor Machan, "Indefatigable Alchemist: Richard Rorty's Radical Pragmatism," *American Scholar,* 65 (1996): 417–424;

Alan Malachowski, *Richard Rorty* (Princeton: Princeton University Press, 2002);

Malachowski and Jo Burrows, eds., *Reading Rorty: Critical Responses to* Philosophy and the Mirror of Nature *(and Beyond)* (Oxford & Cambridge, Mass.: Blackwell, 1990);

Gerald M. Mara and Suzanne L. Dovi, "Mill, Nietzsche, and the Identity of Postmodern Liberalism," *Journal of Politics,* 57 (1995): 1–23;

Brian May, *The Modernist as Pragmatist: E. M. Forster and the Fate of Liberalism* (Columbia: University of Missouri Press, 1997);

John McCumber, *Philosophy and Freedom: Derrida, Rorty, Habermas, Foucault* (Bloomington: Indiana University Press, 2000);

Markar Melkonian, *Richard Rorty's Politics: Liberalism at the End of the American Century* (Amherst, N.Y.: Humanity Books, 1999);

H. O. Mounce, *The Two Pragmatisms: From Peirce to Rorty* (London & New York: Routledge, 1997), pp. 175–228;

Walter G. Neumann, *Wider den Pragmatismus: Zur Philosophie von Richard Rorty* (Würzburg: Königshausen & Neumann, 1992);

Kai Nielsen, *After the Demise of the Tradition: Rorty, Critical Theory, and the Fate of Philosophy* (Boulder, Colo.: Westview Press, 1991);

J. Judd Owen, *Religion and the Demise of Liberal Rationalism: The Foundational Crisis of the Separation of Church and State* (Chicago: University of Chicago Press, 2001);

Michael A. Peters and Paulo Ghiraldelli Jr., eds., *Richard Rorty: Education, Philosophy, and Politics* (Lanham, Md.: Rowman & Littlefield, 2001);

John Pettegrew, ed., *A Pragmatist's Progress? Richard Rorty and American Intellectual History* (Lanham, Md.: Rowman & Littlefield, 2000);

Walter Reese-Schäfer, *Richard Rorty* (Frankfurt am Main & New York: Campus, 1991);

Franco Restaino, *Filosofia e post-filosofia in America: Rorty, Bernstein, MacIntyre* (Milan: Angeli, 1990);

David M. Rosenthal, "Mentality and Neutrality," *Journal of Philosophy,* 73 (1976): 386–415;

Dianne Rothleder, *The Work of Friendship: Rorty, His Critics, and the Project of Solidarity* (Albany: State University of New York Press, 1999);

Richard Rumana, *On Rorty* (Belmont, Cal.: Wadsworth/ Thomson Learning, 2000);

James Ryerson, "The Quest for Uncertainty: Richard Rorty's Pragmatic Pilgrimage," *Lingua Franca,* 10 (2001): 42–52;

Herman J. Saatkaap Jr., ed., *Rorty and Pragmatism: The Philosopher Responds to His Critics* (Nashville: Vanderbilt University Press, 1995);

Anders Tolland, *Epistemological Relativism and Relativistic Epistemology: Richard Rorty and the Possibility of a Philosophical Theory of Knowledge* (Göteborg, Sweden: Acta Universitatis Gothoburgensis, 1991);

Keith Topper, "Richard Rorty, Liberalism, and the Politics of Redescription," *American Political Science Review,* 89 (1995): 954–965.

John R. Searle
(31 July 1932 -   )

Jennifer Hudin
University of California, Berkeley

BOOKS: *Speech Acts: An Essay in the Philosophy of Language* (London: Cambridge University Press, 1969);

The Campus War: A Sympathetic Look at the University in Agony (New York: World, 1971; Harmondsworth, U.K.: Penguin, 1972);

Expression and Meaning: Studies in the Theory of Speech Acts (Cambridge & New York: Cambridge University Press, 1979);

Intentionality: An Essay in the Philosophy of Mind (Cambridge & New York: Cambridge University Press, 1983);

Minds, Brains, and Science, The 1984 Reith Lectures (London: British Broadcasting Corporation, 1984; Cambridge, Mass.: Harvard University Press, 1984);

Foundations of Illocutionary Logic, by Searle and Daniel Vanderveken (Cambridge & New York: Cambridge University Press, 1985);

The Rediscovery of the Mind (Cambridge, Mass.: MIT Press, 1992);

Is There a Crisis in American Higher Education? Founder's Day Pamphlets, no. 1 (Cheney: Eastern Washington University Press, 1995);

The Construction of Social Reality (New York: Free Press, 1995; London: Allen Lane, 1995);

The Mystery of Consciousness, by Searle, Daniel C. Dennett, and David J. Chalmers (New York: New York Review of Books, 1997; London: Granta, 1997);

Mind, Language, and Society: Philosophy in the Real World (New York: BasicBooks, 1998); republished as *Mind, Language, and Society: Doing Philosophy in the Real World* (London: Weidenfeld & Nicolson, 1998);

Rationality in Action (Cambridge, Mass.: MIT Press, 2001);

Consciousness and Language (New York: Cambridge University Press, 2002).

OTHER: "The Lessons of Black Friday," in *The Bridge: Youth in Revolt* (Stanford, Cal.: Institute of International Relations, Stanford University, 1961);

John R. Searle

"Meaning and Speech Acts," in *Knowledge and Experience: Proceedings of the Third Oberlin Colloquium in Philosophy, Oberlin College, 1962,* edited by C. D. Rollins (Pittsburgh: University of Pittsburgh Press, 1962), pp. 28–37;

"Proper Names," in *Philosophy and Ordinary Language,* edited by Charles E. Caton (Urbana: University of Illinois Press, 1963), pp. 154–161;

"What Is a Speech Act?" in *Philosophy in America: Essays,* edited by Max Black (Ithaca, N.Y.: Cornell University Press, 1965), pp. 221–239;

"The Faculty Resolution," in *Revolution at Berkeley: The Crisis in American Education,* edited by Michael V. Miller and Susan Gilmore (New York: Dial, 1965), pp. 92–104;

"Assertions and Aberrations," in *British Analytical Philosophy,* edited by Bernard Williams and Alan Montefiore (London: Routledge & Kegan Paul, 1966; New York: Humanities Press, 1966), pp. 41–54;

"Human Communication Theory and the Philosophy of Language," in *Human Communication Theory: Original Essays,* edited by Frank E. X. Dance (New York: Holt, Rinehart & Winston, 1967), pp. 116–129;

"Essay," in *Freedom and Order in the University,* edited by Samuel Gorovitz (Cleveland: Press of Western Reserve University, 1967), pp. 89–103;

"How to Derive 'Ought' from 'Is,'" in *Theories of Ethics,* edited by Philippa Foot (Oxford: Oxford University Press, 1967), pp. 101–114;

"Russell's Objections to Frege's Theory of Sense and Reference," in *Essays on Frege,* edited by E. D. Klemke (Urbana: University of Illinois Press, 1968), pp. 337–345;

"A Foolproof Scenario for Student Revolts," in *Starting Over: A College Reader,* edited by Frederick Crews and Orville Schell (New York: Random House, 1970);

"Reply to 'The Promising Game,'" in *Readings in Contemporary Ethical Theory,* edited by Kenneth Pahel and Marvin Schiller (Englewood Cliffs, N.J.: Prentice-Hall, 1970);

The Philosophy of Language, edited by Searle (London: Oxford University Press, 1971);

"Austin on Locutionary and Illocutionary Acts," in *Readings in the Philosophy of Language,* edited by Jay F. Rosenberg and Charles Travis (Englewood Cliffs, N.J.: Prentice-Hall, 1971), pp. 262–275;

"Chomsky's Revolution in Linguistics," in *On Noam Chomsky: Critical Essays,* edited by Gilbert Harman (Garden City, N.Y.: Anchor, 1974), pp. 2–33;

"The Role of the Faculty" and "Agenda for the Future," in *The Idea of a Modern University,* edited by Sidney Hook, Paul Kurtz, and Miro Todorovich (Buffalo, N.Y.: Prometheus, 1974), pp. 147–156;

"Linguistics and the Philosophy of Language," in *Linguistics and Neighboring Disciplines,* edited by Renate Bartsch and Theo Venneman (Amsterdam: North-Holland / New York: American Elsevier, 1975), pp. 89–100;

"Sociobiology and the Explanation of Behavior," in *Sociobiology and Human Nature: An Interdisciplinary Critique and Defense,* edited by Michael S. Gregory, Anita Silvers, and Diane Sutch (San Francisco: Jossey-Bass, 1978), pp. 164–182;

"Prima Facie Obligations," in *Practical Reasoning,* edited by Joseph Raz (Oxford & New York: Oxford University Press, 1978), pp. 81–90;

"The Philosophy of Language," in *Men of Ideas: Some Creators of Contemporary Philosophy,* edited by Bryan Magee (London: British Broadcasting Corporation, 1978; New York: Viking, 1979), pp. 180–200;

"Mind and Language," in *Prospects for Man: Communication,* edited by W. J. Megaw (Toronto: Centre for Research on Environmental Quality, Faculty of Science, York University, 1978);

"A More Balanced View," in *The University and the State: What Role for Government in Higher Education?* edited by Hook, Kurtz, and Todorovich (Buffalo, N.Y.: Prometheus, 1978), pp. 205–213;

"Intentionality and the Use of Language," in *Meaning and Use: Papers Presented at the Second Jerusalem Philosophical Encounter, April 1976,* edited by Avishai Margalit (Dordrecht, Netherlands & Boston: Reidel, 1979), pp. 181–197;

"Chairman's Opening Address and Concluding Remarks," in *Brain and Mind: Proceedings of the CIBA Conference on Brain and Mind* (Amsterdam: Excerpta medica / New York: Elsevier/North-Holland, 1979);

"The Intentionality of Intention and Action," in *Sprache, Logik und Philosophie: Akten des vierten internationalen Wittgenstein Symposiums, 28. August bis 2. September 1979, Kirchberg am Wechsel (Österreich) / Language, Logic, and Philosophy: Proceedings of the Fourth International Wittgenstein Symposium, 28th August to 2nd September 1979, Kirchberg Am Wechsel (Austria),* edited by Rudolf Haller and Wolfgang Grassl (Vienna: Hölder-Pichler-Tempsky / Hingham, Mass.: Reidel, 1980), pp. 83–99;

"Psychology Group Report," by Searle and others, in *Morality as a Biological Phenomenon: The Pre-suppositions of Sociobiological Research* (Berkeley: University of California Press, 1980), pp. 231–252;

"The Background of Meaning," in *Speech Act Theory and Pragmatics,* edited by Searle, Ferenc Kiefer, and Manfred Bierwisch (Dordrecht, Netherlands & Boston: Reidel, 1980), pp. 221–232;

"*Las Meninas* and the Paradoxes of Pictorial Representation," in *The Language of Images,* edited by W. J. T. Mitchell (Chicago: University of Chicago Press, 1980), pp. 247–258;

"Minds, Brains and Programs," in *Mind Design: Philosophy, Psychology, Artificial Intelligence,* edited by John Haugeland (Montgomery, Vt.: Bradford, 1980), pp. 282–306;

"Meaning," in *Meaning: Protocol of the Forty Fourth Colloquy, 3 October 1982,* edited by Julian Boyd (Berkeley,

Cal.: Center for Hermeneutical Studies in Hellenistic and Modern Culture, 1983);

"Meaning Communication and Representation," in *Philosophical Grounds of Rationality: Intentions, Categories, Ends,* edited by Richard E. Grandy and Richard Warner (Oxford: Clarendon Press / New York: Oxford University Press, 1986);

"Notes on Conversation," in *Contemporary Issues in Language and Discourse Processes,* edited by Donald G. Ellis and William A. Donohuc (Hillsdale, N.J.: Lawrence Erlbaum Associates, 1986), pp. 7–19;

"Wittgenstein," in *The Great Philosophers: An Introduction to Western Philosophy,* edited by Magee (Oxford & New York: Oxford University Press, 1987), pp. 330–347;

"Minds and Brains without Programs," in *Mindwaves: Thoughts on Intelligence, Identity and Consciousness,* edited by Colin Blakemore and Susan Greenfield (London: Blackwell, 1987);

"Turing the Chinese Room," in *Synthesis of Science and Religion: Critical Essays and Dialogues,* edited by T. D. Singh and Ravi Gomatam (San Francisco: Bhaktivedanta Institute, 1988);

"Cognitive Science and the Computer Metaphor," in *Artificial Intelligence, Culture, and Language: On Education and Work,* edited by Bo Göranzon and Magnus Florin (London & New York: Springer, 1990);

"Epilogue to the Taxonomy of Illocutionary Acts," in *Cultural Communication and Intercultural Contact,* edited by Donal Carbaugh (Hillsdale, N.J.: Lawrence Erlbaum Associates, 1990), pp. 409–417;

"Consciousness, Unconsciousness and Intentionality," in *Propositional Attitudes: The Role of Content in Logic, Language, and Mind,* edited by C. Anthony Anderson and Joseph Owens (Stanford, Cal.: Center for the Study of Language and Information, 1990);

"Yin and Yang Strike Out," in *The Nature of Mind,* edited by David M. Rosenthal (New York: Oxford University Press, 1991), pp. 525–526;

"Response: Meaning, Intentionality, and Speech Acts," "Response: The Mind-Body Problem," "Response: Perception and the Satisfactions of Intentionality," "Response: Reference and Intentionality," "Response: The Background of Intentionality and Action," "Response: Explanation in the Social Sciences," and "Response: Applications of the Theory," in *John Searle and His Critics,* edited by Ernest Lepore and Robert Van Gulick (Cambridge, Mass.: Blackwell, 1991), pp. 81–102, 141–146, 181–192, 227–241, 289–299, 335–342, 385–391;

"Contemporary Philosophy in the United States," in *Divided Knowledge: Across Disciplines, across Cultures,* edited by David Easton and Corinne S. Schelling (Newbury Park, Cal.: SagePublications, 1991);

"Is the Brain's Mind a Computer Program?" in *Annual Editions: Psychology 1991/92,* edited by Michael G. Walreven and Hiram E. Fitzgerald (Guilford, Conn.: Dushkin, 1991);

"Individual Intentionality and Social Phenomena in the Theory of Speech Acts," in *Bologna: La Cultura Italiana e le Letterature Straniere Moderne* (Bologna: Università di Bologna / Ravenna: Longo, 1992);

"The Word Turned Upside Down" and "Reply to Mackey," in *Working through Derrida,* edited by Gary B. Madison (Evanston, Ill.: Northwestern University Press, 1993), pp. 170–183;

"Rationality and Realism: What Is at Stake?" in *The Research University in a Time of Discontent,* edited by Jonathan R. Cole, Elinor G. Barber, and Stephen R. Graubard (Baltimore & London: Johns Hopkins University Press, 1994), pp. 55–83;

"Some Relations between Mind and Brain," in *Neuroscience, Memory, and Language: Papers Presented at a Symposium Series Cosponsored by the National Institute of Mental Health and the Library of Congress,* edited by Richard D. Broadwell, Decade of the Brain, volume 1 (Washington, D.C.: Library of Congress, 1995), pp. 25–34;

"The Mind and Computation," in *Revolutionary Changes in Understanding Man and Society: Scopes and Limits,* edited by Johann Götschl (Dordrecht, Netherlands & Boston: Kluwer Academic, 1995), pp. 93–105;

"Literary Theory and Its Discontents," in *The Emperor Redressed: Critiquing Critical Theory,* edited by Dwight Eddins (Tuscaloosa: University of Alabama Press, 1995), pp. 166–198;

"A Philosophical Self-Portrait," in *A Dictionary of Philosophy,* edited by Thomas Mautner (Oxford & Cambridge, Mass.: Blackwell, 1996), pp. 388–390.

SELECTED PERIODICAL PUBLICATIONS–
UNCOLLECTED: "Does It Make Sense to Suppose That All Events, Including Personal Experiences, Could Occur in Reverse?" by Searle, J. N. Findlay, J. E. McGechie, and Richard Taylor, *Analysis,* 16 (June 1956): 121–125;

"Symposium: On Determinables and Resemblance," by Searle and Stephán Körner, *Proceedings of the Aristotelian Society, Supplement,* 33 (1959): 125–158;

"*Logical Positivism,* edited by A. J. Ayer," *Philosophical Review,* 70 (July 1961): 411–413;

"*The Coherence Theory of Truth: A Critical Evaluation,* by Haig Khatchadourian," *Philosophical Review,* 74 (1965): 392–394;

"*Locutionary and Illocutionary Acts: A Main Theme in J. L. Austin's Philosophy,* by Mats Furberg," *Philosophical Review,* 75 (1966): 389–391;

"The Grammar of Dissent," *TLS: The Times Literary Supplement,* no. 3845 (21 November 1975): 1377;

"The Rules of the Language Game," *TLS: The Times Literary Supplement,* no. 3887 (10 September 1976): 1118–1120;

"*Toward a Linguistic Theory of Speech Acts,* by Jerrold M. Saddock," *Language,* 52 (December 1976): 966–971;

"Reiterating the Differences: A Reply to Derrida," *Glyph,* 1, no. 1 (1977): 198–208;

"Rules and Representation" and "Two Objections to Methodological Solipsism," *Behavioral and Brain Sciences,* 3 (March 1980): 37–38, 92–94;

"Minds, Brains, and Programs," *Behavioral and Brain Sciences,* 3 (September 1980): 417–424;

"Intentionality and Method," *Journal of Philosophy,* 78 (November 1981): 720–733;

"The Myth of the Computer," *New York Review of Books,* 29 (29 April 1982): 3–6;

"The Chinese Room Revisited," *Behavioral and Brain Sciences,* 5 (June 1982): 345–348;

"The Myth of the Computer: An Exchange," *New York Review of Books,* 29 (24 June 1982): 56–57;

"Reply to Jacquette," *Philosophy and Phenomenological Research,* 49 (June 1989): 701–708;

"Consciousness, Explanatory Inversion, and Cognitive Science," *Behavioral and Brain Sciences,* 13 (December 1990): 585–596;

"The Storm over the University," *New York Review of Books* (6 December 1990): 34–42;

"The Storm over the University: An Exchange," *New York Review of Books* (14 February 1991): 48–49;

"Intentionalistic Explanations in the Social Sciences," *Philosophy of the Social Sciences,* 21 (September 1991): 332–344;

"Is There a Problem about Realism?" *Filisoficky Casopis* (Prague), 40, no. 3 (1992): 413–433;

"The Failures of Computationalism," *Think,* 2 (June 1993): 68–71;

"The Mission of the University: Intellectual Discovery or Social Transformation?" *Academic Questions,* 7 (Winter 1993/1994): 80–85;

"Structure and Intention in Language: A Reply to Knapp and Michaels," *New Literary History,* 25 (Summer 1994): 677–681;

"The Connection Principle and the Ontology of the Unconscious," *Philosophy and Phenomenological Research,* 54 (December 1994): 847–855;

"Consciousness, the Brain and the Connection Principle: A Reply," *Philosophy and Phenomenological Research,* 55, (March 1995): 217–232;

"How Artificial Intelligence Fails," *World and I* (July 1995): 285–295;

"Précis of *The Construction of Social Reality*" and "Responses to Critics of *The Construction of Social Reality,*" *Philosophy and Phenomenological Research,* 57 (June 1997): 427–434, 449–458.

John R. Searle is noted for contributing to the philosophy of language a theory of speech acts and a theory of intentionality. He has also written extensively on the philosophy of mind; here he is particularly noted for his "Chinese Room Argument," a much-debated attack on the view that the mind is a computer program. In social philosophy he has developed a theory of human institutions that employs the ideas he developed earlier for his theories of speech acts and intentionality.

John Rogers Searle was born on 31 July 1932 in Denver, Colorado, to George W. Searle, an electrical engineer employed by the Mountain States Telephone and Telegraph Company, and Hester Beck Searle, a physician in general practice. Both parents came from families that had been in the United States for several generations; Searle is named after an ancestor on his father's side, John Rogers, who came to America on the *Mayflower*. He is also, on his father's side, part Cherokee.

Searle attended public schools in Denver until 1944, when, because of wartime needs, his father was transferred to the head office of the American Telephone and Telegraph Corporation in New York City. His mother took a position at a New York hospital. The family lived in the New York suburb of Short Hills, New Jersey, where Searle attended Milburn High School. His mother died on 6 August 1945.

In 1945–1946 Searle attended the Horace Mann–Lincoln School, an experimental school run by Columbia University Teachers' College in New York. In 1946 his father, who had remarried, was transferred to Wisconsin, and Searle graduated from high school in the Milwaukee suburb of Shorewood. In the fall of 1949 he enrolled in the Integrated Liberal Studies program at the University of Wisconsin, Madison, which gave him a good background in natural sciences, social sciences, and humanities. He was a member of the ski team and was elected student body president in 1951. He received an Alumni Scholarship for 1951–1952.

Even as a child Searle had been interested in philosophical problems; his formal study of philosophy began, however, when he took a course in the history of philosophy taught by Julius Weinberg at the University of Wisconsin. In his junior year he was awarded a Rhodes Scholarship to the University of Oxford, where he studied philosophy, politics, and economics at Christ Church. He had distinguished tutors in all three subjects: in philosophy, J. O. Urmson and P. F. Strawson; in politics, Robert, Lord Blake, and Frank, Lord Packenham (who became Earl Longford in 1961); and in economics, Sir Roy Harrod. Searle arranged to be tutored by Strawson, even though Strawson was officially a tutor not at Christ Church but at University College. This period was decisive in forming Searle's philosophical outlook, and no other philosopher has had as strong an influence on him as Strawson. He began to consider a career in philosophy at this time.

During his early terms at Oxford, Searle began attending J. L. Austin's lecture series "Words and Deeds"; but he was so bored that he dropped out after two or three sessions. The lectures, however, formed a principal inspiration for Searle's first book, *Speech Acts: An Essay in the Philosophy of Language* (1969).

Searle's serious professional interest in philosophy began in his second and third years at Oxford, 1953 to 1955; he received a Boulter Exhibition (scholarship) to Christ Church for 1954–1955. At this time Oxford was the philosophical capital of the world, and an enormous amount of discussion was carried on in meetings of philosophy societies, where both undergraduates and faculty members read papers. Searle attended lectures by, or had philosophical conversations with, such eminent philosophers as Gilbert Ryle, H. H. Price, Isaiah Berlin, Stuart Hampshire, Michael Dummett, Oscar Wood, Bernard Williams, Patrick Gardiner, David Pears, W. V. Quine, G. E. M. Anscombe, Geoffrey Warnock and Mary Warnock, Iris Murdoch, Paul Grice, Anthony Quinton, G. D. H. Cole, Brian McGuinness, Friedrich Waismann, H. L. A. Hart, Philippa Foot, Patrick Nowell-Smith, and Stephen Toulmin. Among his fellow undergraduates were Charles Taylor, Ronald Dworkin, Frank Cioffi, David Wiggins, and Nigel Lawson.

Searle graduated with first-class honors in 1955. He had been accepted by various American graduate schools but at the last minute received a senior scholarship at St. Antony's College that enabled him to stay at Oxford. He was also appointed a research lecturer at Christ Church. On Christmas Eve 1958 he married Dagmar Carboch, a research student at Nuffield College who had just completed a B.Phil. in philosophy.

Searle received his M.A. from Oxford in 1959. Working with Strawson, Austin, and Peter Geach, who served as his supervisor, Searle wrote a D.Phil. thesis, "Problems Arising in the Theory of Meaning out of the Notions of Sense and Reference." He was awarded the degree in 1959. In the fall of that year he began his

Searle circa 1995 (photograph by Anne Selders; from the dust jacket for The Construction of Social Reality, *1995)*

teaching career as an assistant professor at the University of California at Berkeley.

The dominant mode of philosophizing in the United States and England at that time was ordinary-language philosophy. Ordinary-language philosophers distinguish between the philosophy of language and linguistic philosophy. Linguistic philosophy is the attempt to solve philosophical problems by examining the use of ordinary language. For example, in discussing skepticism, an ordinary-language philosopher would pay close attention to the criteria that one uses in ordinary speech to apply words such as *know*, *evidence*, and *certain*. The philosophy of language, on the other hand, is concerned with analyzing the relationship of language to the world; it describes that relationship in terms of truth, reference, and meaning. Searle is much more a philosopher of language than a linguistic philosopher: he has never accepted the view that all, or even most, philosophical problems can be solved simply by examining the use of words, but he does think that the use of linguistic methods is essential to achieve clarity about the nature of the problems being investigated.

Before the publication of his first book Searle wrote several influential articles, including "Proper Names," which originally appeared in the journal *Mind* in 1958; "Meaning and Speech Acts" in *Philosophical*

Review in 1962; "How to Derive 'Ought' from 'Is'" in the same journal in 1964; and "What Is a Speech Act?" in *Philosophy in America* (1965), edited by Max Black. The most controversial was "How to Derive 'Ought' from 'Is.'" A long philosophical tradition going back at least to David Hume in the eighteenth century holds that statements about what ought to be done cannot be derived from factual statements that describe what is the case. Searle points out, however, that a certain class of "is" statements exists such that a person who makes such a statement is already committed to the existence of certain reasons for action and, hence, to certain "ought" statements. For example, the factual statement that a person has made a promise implies that the person has undertaken an obligation; the fact that the person has undertaken an obligation implies that the person has a good reason to perform a certain action; and because *ought* expresses reasons for action, the fact that the person has a good reason to perform the action implies that the person ought to perform the action. Searle grants that in real-life situations all sorts of reasons may be advanced why one ought not to do something that one has promised to do, but he maintains that the fact that promises create reasons for actions is already built into the notion of promising.

The article provoked a storm of opposition, but Searle has always believed that the standard criticisms of the article were based on misunderstandings of its main contention. One common misconception is the idea that unless one endorsed the institution of promising or thought that promising was a good thing, one would not have undertaken an obligation when one made a promise. Searle points out in the last chapter of *Speech Acts* that this notion rests on an error: the institution of promising is a vehicle whereby one creates desire-independent reasons for oneself to do something; one's stance toward the institution of promising is irrelevant. The debate about these issues continues, and the article has been widely anthologized and translated.

In 1961–1962 Searle was a visiting professor at the University of Michigan in Ann Arbor. He found the Michigan philosophy department highly congenial but, though he was offered a tenured position there, he chose to return to Berkeley for the fall 1962 term. He was a visiting professor at the University of Washington in Seattle in the summer of 1963. He received an American Council of Learned Societies Study Fellowship for the academic year 1963–1964 and took a sabbatical leave, spending the first semester studying generative linguistics with Noam Chomsky at the Massachusetts Institute of Technology and the second semester in Oxford working on *Speech Acts*. In the summer he and his family–which by then included two children, Thomas and Mark–went to Greece, where he

completed the draft of *Speech Acts* while staying on Tolon Beach in the Peloponnesus.

Returning to Berkeley in the fall of 1964, Searle was promoted to associate professor and resumed teaching full-time. His philosophical work was soon interrupted, however, by the explosion of student unrest that took place in Berkeley at that time. Searle was at the center of the conflict. He made many speeches defending the students' right to free speech and was active in faculty committees and in the many debates and discussions that were held on campus. In the summer of 1965 the new chancellor, Roger Heyns, asked Searle to accept the position of special assistant for student affairs; he served in the post during the chaotic years 1965 to 1967, at the end of which he was promoted to full professor. He was unable to complete the final version of *Speech Acts* until he received a University of California Humanities Research Institute Fellowship and took a leave of absence for the academic year 1967–1968. He and his family went back to Oxford, where Searle was a visiting fellow of Brasenose College. While in England he took the typescript for his book to Cambridge University Press, which published it in 1969.

Speech Acts brought Searle's philosophy to world attention. In the book he combines Ludwig Wittgenstein's idea that to understand meaning one should look at the use that human beings make of language in actual communication with Austin's notion that the basic unit of communication in language is not the word or the sentence but a type of "speech act" that Austin called an "illocutionary act." To these two ideas he adds Grice's claim that to know what a person means by an utterance one needs to know the intention with which the utterance has been made. He then goes further to suggest that language is behavior governed by "constitutive rules," that is, rules that constitute the activity in question, just as playing chess is constituted by acting in accordance with the rules of chess. These constitutive rules, according to Searle, typically are of the form "X counts as Y" or "X counts as Y in context C." He works out rules as to how, for example, making a certain sort of utterance could count as making a promise, making a statement, or asking a question.

Speech Acts went through several editions in Britain and the United States and was translated into more than a dozen languages. It became a basic text in the developing discipline of linguistic pragmatics.

Though Searle was no longer a member of the Berkeley administration, he continued to be active in the academic senate and in the various conflicts that took place in the late 1960s and early 1970s. He served on the Special Committee on Campus Tensions of the American Council on Education from 1968 to 1970. He then spent the summer of 1970 at the White House as a member of the Presidential Advisory Group on Student Unrest, informally known as the "Heard Commission," an independent organization, financed by a private foundation, that advised President Richard M. Nixon on how national policy related to university affairs. He also served as an adviser to the Presidential Commission on Student Unrest, or "Scranton Commission." In the summer of 1971, while he was a visiting professor at the Summer Linguistics Institute of the Linguistics Society of America at the State University of New York at Buffalo, he completed a book about student conflicts, *The Campus War: A Sympathetic Look at the University in Agony* (1971). In the fall he was a visiting professor at the University of Oslo in Norway. Also in 1971 he edited an anthology, *The Philosophy of Language*. He was a member of the board of directors of the Northern California branch of the American Civil Liberties Union from 1969 to 1972. He served on the American Philosophical Association's Committee on the Status and Future of the Profession from 1971 to 1973. From 1972 to 1974 he was the moderator of the *World Press* television program on the Public Broadcasting System; he had been a panelist on the show from time to time since 1960 and continued to do so from 1974 to 1977. He was on the Massachusetts Institute of Technology Visiting Committee from 1972 to 1978. He served as chairman of the Berkeley philosophy department from 1973 to 1975 and held both a Guggenheim Fellowship and another University of California Humanities Institute Research Fellowship for 1975–1976. He was a member of the Council of Philosophical Studies from 1975 to 1980. In the summer of 1976 he was a Rockefeller Scholar at the Aspen Institute for Humanistic Studies. He was a member of the American Academy of Arts and Sciences Committee to Establish a National Humanities Center from 1974 to 1976 and then a member of the board of directors of the center from 1976 to 1990. He became a member of the Academy of Arts and Sciences in 1977.

In the late 1970s Searle published a series of articles in which he dealt with issues left untreated in *Speech Acts*: "The Logical Status of Fictional Discourse" (1975), "Indirect Speech Acts" (1975), "A Taxonomy of Illocutionary Acts" (1975), "Speech Acts and Recent Linguistics" (1975), "Literal Meaning" (1978), "Metaphor" (1979), and "Referential and Attributive" (1979). These articles were assembled in 1979 as his third book, *Expression and Meaning: Studies in the Theory of Speech Acts*.

During the late 1970s Searle had become active in the developing field of cognitive science. He welcomed the rejection that cognitive science promised of behaviorist models of psychological explanation, but he was skeptical about the possibility of treating the mind as a computer program. In the autumn of 1980 he was Distinguished Visiting Professor at the University of Colo-

Dust jacket for the book in which Searle endeavors to create a new branch of philosophy: the philosophy of society (Richland County Public Library)

rado at Boulder; that year he published in the journal *The Behavioral and Brain Sciences* the article "Minds, Brains and Programs," in which he first stated the Chinese Room Argument. The argument is that the mind cannot be a computer program because minds have an essential feature that computer programs do not have: minds have semantic, or symbolic, content–content that has meaning–whereas the computer program is defined entirely in terms of formal or syntactical processes–manipulations of zeros and ones. The Chinese Room Argument asks the reader to imagine that he or she is locked in a room, shuffling symbols according to a computer program that enables him or her to produce answers to questions that are indistinguishable from the answers that would be given by a native speaker of Chinese; the person does not thereby understand Chinese. And if the person in the Chinese room does not understand Chinese on the basis of implementing a computer program, then neither does any other computational system, because no computational system has anything that the person in the Chinese room does not have.

Searle was a visiting professor at the University of Campinas in Brazil in the summer of 1981 and at the International Semiotics Institute at the University of Toronto in the summer of 1982. He lectured at many American universities in 1982–1983 as a Phi Beta Kappa Visiting Scholar. He received a Fulbright Award in 1983 but was unable to accept it because of scheduling conflicts.

In *Intentionality: An Essay in the Philosophy of Mind* (1983), his most comprehensive treatment of the relationship between mind and language, Searle analyzes the property of the mind whereby it is directed at things other than itself. He deals with the intentionality of perception and the intentionality of action; proposes a theory, "the Background," of a nonintentional ground for intentionality; and treats meaning and the mind-body problem. The book was in part motivated by Searle's need to analyze the basic notions on which the theory of speech acts rests, such as belief, desire, and intention. If speech acts are a form of human action and are motivated, as are other forms of human action, by belief and desire, then a complete theory of speech acts must include a theory of intentions, beliefs, and desires, as well as of other intentional states. Thus, the project of analyzing intentionality was important both in its own right and also to provide a foundation for the theory that Searle had expounded in *Speech Acts* and *Expression and Meaning*.

The debate that ensued on the publication of "Minds, Brains, and Programs" led to an invitation for Searle to give the 1984 Reith Lectures on BBC Radio in England; the lectures were published that year as *Minds, Brains, and Science,* Searle's first philosophical book addressed to the general public. The book has gone through many printings in the United States and Britain and has been translated into French, Spanish, German, Portuguese, Italian, Hebrew, Chinese, Russian, Czech, Greek, Polish, and Turkish.

One of the questions a theory of speech acts has to face is the extent to which it can be formalized using the techniques of modern mathematical logic. Searle undertook such a formalization, in collaboration with the Belgian-born Canadian logician Daniel Vanderveken, in *Foundations of Illocutionary Logic* (1985). The book has proved useful for logical investigation of speech acts and in programming speech acts into computers. Vanderveken has carried the work further in a series of publications.

In 1985 Searle once again was forced to turn down a Fulbright Award because of schedule conflicts. He was a visiting professor at the Johann Wolfgang Goethe-Universität in Frankfurt am Main, Germany, in the summer of 1985; Distinguished Visiting Professor at Rutgers University in the spring of 1986; a visiting professor at the University of Venice in the summer of 1986; and Jeanette K. Watson Distinguished Visiting Professor in the Humanities at Syracuse University in the winter of 1986. He was Patrick Romanell-Phi Beta Kappa Professor and University of California Faculty Research Lecturer for 1986–1987. A conference on his ideas was held at the Australian Philosophical Association meetings at the University of Queensland in Brisbane in 1987. He was a delegate from the American Academy of Arts and Sciences to the Chinese Academy of Social Sciences in the summer of 1988, a visiting professor of psychology at the University of Florence in Italy in the summer of 1989, and a visiting professor at the Free University of Berlin in the summer of 1990. He served as president of the Pacific Division of the American Philosophical Association in 1990 and was a fellow of the Rockefeller Center in Bellagio, Italy, in 1991. In the summer of 1991 he was a visiting professor at both the College Internationale de Philosophie in Paris and the Charles University in Prague; in the summer of 1992 he was a visiting professor at the Collège de France in Paris. He delivered the Immanuel Kant Lectures at Stanford University and the Thalheimer Lectures at Johns Hopkins University in 1992, and a conference on his work was held at the University of Notre Dame that same year.

In *The Rediscovery of the Mind* (1992) Searle expounds in detail his thesis, which he had introduced in *Intentionality,* of biological naturalism: that mental states and processes are essential parts of the human biological makeup. What is ordinarily thought of as "the mind" is a set of higher-level states and processes of a system composed of lower-level elements—specifically, of neurons. Biological naturalism solves the traditional mind-body problem by holding, first, that all mental states are caused by lower-level microbiological processes in the brain, presumably at the level of neurons and synapses, and second, that mental states and processes are themselves higher-level features of the system composed of these lower-level elements.

Searle also discusses in the book two controversial theses that are consequences of biological naturalism. The first is anticomputationalism. Searle had taken a strong anticomputational stance on the mind-body relation in 1980 with the Chinese Room Argument. His anticomputational thesis is augmented in *The Rediscovery of the Mind* by considering the nature of syntax itself: he asks whether it is an intrinsic feature of a physical entity independent of any observer, or whether it is observer-dependent, that is, something that is created by and requires an observer. Searle argues that the ontology of syntax requires symbols, systems, and rules, all of which are constructs of human observation and dependent on the human ability to impose and create such things. Syntax is, then, observer-dependent and not an intrinsic feature of any entity. This position leads to the conclusion that computation cannot be intrinsic to any physical system or entity and, thus, is not intrinsic to the brain. Something is a digital computer only relative to the assignment of a certain function and a certain interpretation of the process. The notion of computation is like the notions of word, symbol, or sentence: many such entities exist, but the concepts of them are not concepts of physics; something is a word, symbol, sentence, or computation only relative to an interpretation. Mental states, on the other hand, are intrinsically mental states. If a person is hungry or thirsty, that is a brute fact about that person and does not depend on outside interpretation. Since computation is observer-relative, the computational thesis is not so much false as ill defined. If it is the claim that the brain is intrinsically a digital computer, the answer is that nothing is intrinsically a digital computer; something is a computer only relative to a computational interpretation. On the other hand, if the thesis is the claim that a computational interpretation can be attached to mental processes, it is trivial because any process can be arbitrarily assigned a sequence of zeros and ones. Thus, the computational theory of the mind turns out to be much worse off than Searle had proposed in his 1980 article.

The second controversial thesis in *The Rediscovery of the Mind* is the conceptual connection between consciousness and mental states. This thesis, which Searle calls "The Connection Principle," is that the only sense in which a mental state can exist is in virtue of its potential accessibility to consciousness. Mental states may be repressed or inaccessible to consciousness because of brain pathologies or psychological factors; but in principle, mental states only exist in virtue of being potentially conscious. The thesis has wide implications for cognitive science, which postulates the existence of mental processes that are unconscious in principle. Such processes are not even the sort of thing that could be brought to consciousness because they consist of the manipulation of huge numbers of binary symbols. Searle argues that these forms of explanation are conceptually inadequate and proposes an alternative Darwinian model of explaining the apparent goal-directed behavior of brain processes.

Searle was a member of the Neurosciences Research Program of the Neurosciences Research Institute from 1989 to 1996 and of the National Council of the National Endowment for the Humanities from 1992 to 1996. He was the Carl Gustav Hempel Lecturer at Princeton University and the Gordon Tomkins Lecturer in the Department of Biochemistry and Biophysics at the University of California at San Francisco in 1993.

Cover for Searle's 1997 book, which comprises expanded versions of a series of articles for The New York Review of Books and includes exchanges with the philosophers Daniel C. Dennett and David J. Chalmers (Richland County Public Library)

He received the Homer Smith Award from New York University Medical School in 1993 and honorary degrees from Adelphi University in 1993 and from the University of Wisconsin in 1994. He was the Founder's Day Lecturer at Eastern Washington University and the M. H. Wood Memorial Lecturer at the University of the South in Sewanee, Tennessee, in 1994. In the spring of 1994 he was a visiting professor at the Universität Graz in Austria, and in the spring of 1995 he was a visiting professor at the University of Rome, Italy.

Searle's 1995 book, *The Construction of Social Reality,* is a pioneering effort to create a new branch of philosophy. Just as the philosophy of language and the philosophy of mind emerged in the past century or two, so, Searle urges, "the philosophy of society" should now be recognized as a legitimate branch of philosophy. Prior to the publication of *The Construction of Social Reality,* "social philosophy" was either a subdiscipline within political

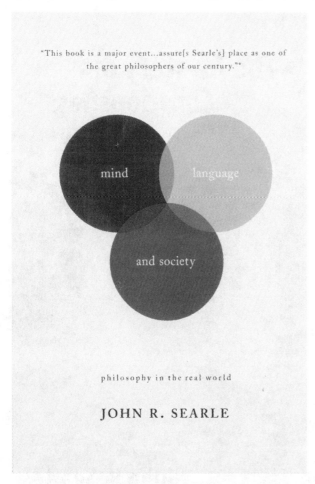

"This book is a major event...assure[s] Searle's] place as one of the great philosophers of our century."*

mind   language

and society

philosophy in the real world

JOHN R. SEARLE

Cover for Searle's 1998 book, in which he integrates many of the ideas from his earlier works (Richland County Public Library)

philosophy or a discussion of the methodology of the social sciences. Searle argues that political philosophy and the methodology of the social sciences should be regarded as branches of a wider subject, the philosophy of society. The basic subject matter of the philosophy of society is the question of the ontology of—the kind of existence possessed by—social and institutional facts. Specifically, the question is how there can be a class of objective facts, such as money, property, government, and marriage, that are facts only because people recognize them as such. It is not just a matter of opinion or a subjective feeling that the pieces of paper in one's wallet are dollars and function as money in the United States; these are objective facts, though they are so only because people believe that they are. To remove the apparent paradoxical feature of saying both that the existence of money depends on subjective attitudes and that it is a matter of objective fact, Searle distinguishes between the epistemic and the ontological senses of the objective-subjective distinction. In the epistemic sense, a statement is subjective if its truth cannot be established

objectively—that is, independently of the attitudes of the investigators and observers. Thus, the statement "Rembrandt was a better painter than Rubens" is epistemically subjective, while the statement "Rembrandt was born in 1606" is epistemically objective. But the distinction between epistemic subjectivity and objectivity should not be confused with ontology: a phenomenon is ontologically subjective if its mode of existence involves mental entities; pains, for example, have an ontologically subjective mode of existence. Searle's point is that epistemic objectivity does not preclude ontological subjectivity. One can have an objective science of pain, for example, even though the mode of existence of pain is ontologically subjective. Less obvious, but more important, is the fact the ontologies of money, property, marriage, and government contain both objective and subjective elements; but that fact does not prevent one from having objective knowledge of such things.

The central thesis of *The Construction of Social Reality* is that in spite of the enormous complexity of human society, the underlying logical structure of the ontology of human social institutions is quite simple: it is a matter of combining three primitive elements—collective intentionality, or the human capacity to act and think in cooperation with others; the assignment of function, which is the human ability to assign functions to objects that are not intrinsic to the objects but rest on outside assignment; and constitutive rules of the sort that Searle discussed in his theory of speech acts. The central concept that results from these three elements is that of a "status function," which is a function that cannot be performed in virtue of physical structure but only in virtue of the collective acceptance or recognition of a status. This simple apparatus enables Searle to give a powerful analysis of the structure of social and institutional reality.

Searle became Mills Professor of Mind and Language at Berkeley in 1996. In 1997 he published *The Mystery of Consciousness,* consisting of expanded versions of a series of articles that he wrote for *The New York Review of Books* between 1995 and 1997 in which Searle appraises books by the neuroscientists Francis Crick, Gerald Edelman, and Israel Rosenfeld and the philosophers Daniel C. Dennett and David J. Chalmers; the book includes his exchanges in the periodical with Dennett and Chalmers. It is an overview of the curious current state of the study of consciousness.

Searle was a visiting professor at the University of Aarhus, Denmark, in the spring of 1997 and Distinguished Austin J. Fogethey, S.J., Professor of Philosophy at Santa Clara University in Santa Clara, California, in the summer of 1998. In *Mind, Language and Society: Philosophy in the Real World* (1998) he integrates much of the work from his earlier books to show how they form a coherent account of human beings and their relation to the rest of the universe, including the social universe. His work was the subject of conferences of the Spanish Philosophical Association at the Universitá de Laguna in Tenerife, Canary Islands, in 1997; of the Argentine Philosophical Society in Buenos Aires in 1998; and at the Zentrum für interdisziplinäre Forschung in Bielefeld, Germany, and the University of Leipzig, Germany, in 1999. He received the Distinguished Teaching Award at the University of California at Berkeley in 1999. In 2000 he ended ten years of service on the steering committee of the Library of Congress's Decade of the Brain and received honorary degrees from the University of Turin and the University of Bucharest; the Jovanellos Prize from Spain; the Jean Nicod Prize from France; and the Tasan Award from South Korea. He was a fellow of and lecturer at the World Economic Forum in Davos, Switzerland, in 2001, as he had been in 1991, 1995, and 1998.

In *Rationality in Action* (2001) Searle criticizes the "classical model" of rationality, which assumes that human beings' rational actions are always caused by beliefs and desires, and shows that, in fact, beliefs and desires form causally sufficient conditions for irrational actions. The normal rational action, he argues, has a gap between the causes, in the form of one's reasons for action, and the effect, in the form of one's decisions and actions. This gap raises the traditional problem of free will, and Searle devotes considerable space to discussing such questions as how it is possible for humans to create and act on desire-independent reasons for action, the scientific status of the hypothesis that humans have free will, and, perhaps most substantial of all, the logical structure of the explanation of human behavior in terms of rational reasons for action. *Consciousness and Language* (2002) is a collection of Searle's previously published articles on the philosophy of language and the the problem of consciousness. One of the most influential pieces in the volume is "Consciousness," originally published in *Annual Review of Neuroscience* in 2000. Searle points out that most neurobiologists adopt what he calls "the building block model of consciousness," according to which the aim of a science of consciousness is to find the neuronal correlate of each element in conscious experience, such as the experience of red. Searle thinks that this method is likely to fail and advocates the adoption of "the unified field theory." According to this theory, perception does not so much create consciousness as modify the pre-existing field.

John R. Searle has been a member of the Cognitive Science Group at the University of California at Berkeley since 1981, of the European Academy of Science and Art since 1993, and of the Scientific Board of the Vilem Methsius Centre of the Charles University, Prague, since 1994. He serves on the editorial boards of the *Journal of Psycholinguistic Research, Linguistics and Philosophy, Philosophy and Artificial Intelligence,* the *Journal of Consciousness Studies,* and the Harvard University Press Cognitive Science Series.

Interviews:

Bill D. Moyers, "John Searle: Philosopher," in his *A World of Ideas: Conversations with Thoughtful Men and Women about American Life Today and the Ideas Shaping Our Future* (New York: Doubleday, 1989), pp. 203–211;

"Ontology Is the Question," in *Speaking Minds: Interviews with Twenty Eminent Cognitive Scientists,* edited by Peter Baumgartner and Sabine Payr (Princeton: Princeton University Press, 1995), pp. 203–214.

References:

Francesca Di Lorenzo Ajello, *Mente, azione, e linguaggio nel pensiero di John R. Searle* (Milan: FrancoAngeli, 1998);

Eric Dietrich, ed., *Thinking Computers and Virtual Persons: Essays on the Intentionality of Machines* (San Diego: Academic Press, 1994);

Nick Fotion, *John Searle* (Princeton: Princeton University Press, 2000);

William Garnett, *The Springs of Consciousness: The 1984 Reith Lectures of Professor Searle, Crictically Examined* (Padstow, U.K.: Tabb House, 1987);

William Hirstein, *On Searle* (Belmont, Cal.: Wadsworth/ Thomson Learning, 2001);

Ernest Lepore and Robert van Gulick, eds., *John Searle and His Critics* (Oxford & Cambridge, Mass.: Blackwell, 1991);

Wallace Matson, *From Descartes to Searle,* volume 2 of his *A New History of Philosophy* (Fort Worth: Harcourt College, 2000);

E. B. Nolte, *Einführug in die Sprechaktheorie John R. Searles* (Freiburg & Munich: Alber, 1978);

Herman Parret and Jef Versheuren, eds., *(On) Searle on Conversation* (Amsterdam & Philadelphia: Benjamins, 1992);

Erich Schäfer, *Grenzen der künstlichen Intelligenz: John R. Searles Philosophie des Geistes* (Stuttgart: Kohlhammer, 1994);

"Searle—with His Replies," special issue of *Révue Internationale de Philosophy,* 55 (June 2001);

"Speech Act Theory: Ten Years Later," special issue of *Versus* (Milan), 26/27 (1980).

Wilfrid Sellars

(20 May 1912 – 2 July 1989)

Willem A. deVries
University of New Hampshire

BOOKS: *Science, Perception and Reality* (London: Routledge & Kegan Paul, 1963; New York: Humanities Press, 1963);

Form and Content in Ethical Theory, The Lindley Lecture for 1967 (Lawrence: Department of Philosophy, University of Kansas, 1967);

Philosophical Perspectives, American Lecture Series, no. 667 (Springfield, Ill.: Charles C. Thomas, 1967); republished in two volumes as *Philosophical Perspectives: History of Philosophy* (Reseda, Cal.: Ridgeview, 1967) and *Philosophical Perspectives: Metaphysics and Epistemology* (Reseda, Cal.: Ridgeview, 1977);

Science and Metaphysics: Variations on Kantian Themes, The John Locke Lectures for 1965–1966 (London: Routledge & Kegan Paul / New York: Humanities Press, 1968);

Essays in Philosophy and Its History (Dordrecht, Netherlands & Boston: Reidel, 1974);

Naturalism and Ontology (Reseda, Cal.: Ridgeview, 1980);

Pure Pragmatics and Possible Worlds: The Early Essays of Wilfrid Sellars, edited by Jeffrey F. Sicha (Reseda, Cal.: Ridgeview, 1980);

The Metaphysics of Epistemology: Lectures, edited by Pedro V. Amaral (Atascadero, Cal.: Ridgeview, 1989);

Kant and Pre-Kantian Themes: Lectures, edited by Amaral (Atascadero, Cal.: Ridgeview, 2002);

Kant's Transcendental Metaphysics: Sellars' Cassirer Lectures and Other Essays, edited by Sicha (Atascadero, Cal.: Ridgeview, 2002).

Edition: *Empiricism and the Philosophy of Mind,* introduction by Richard Rorty, study guide by Robert Brandom (Cambridge, Mass.: Harvard University Press, 1997).

OTHER: *Readings in Philosophical Analysis,* edited by Sellars and Herbert Feigl (New York: Appleton-Century-Crofts, 1949);

"Aristotelian Philosophies of Mind," in *Philosophy for the Future: The Quest of Modern Materialism,* edited by Roy Wood Sellars, V. J. McGill, and Marvin Farber (New York: Macmillan, 1949), pp. 544–570;

Wilfrid Sellars

Readings in Ethical Theory, edited by Sellars and John Hospers (New York: Appleton-Century-Crofts, 1952)–includes Sellars's "Obligation and Motivation," pp. 511–517;

"The Concept of Emergence," by Sellars and Paul Meehl, and "Empiricism and the Philosophy of Mind," by Sellars, in *The Foundations of Science and the Concepts of Psychology and Psychoanalysis,* edited by Feigl and Michael Scriven, Minnesota Studies in the Philosophy of Science, volume 1 (Minneapolis: University of Minnesota Press, 1956), pp. 239–252, 253–329;

"Counterfactuals, Dispositions, and the Causal Modalities," by Sellars, and "Intentionality and the Mental," by Sellars and Roderick Chisholm, in *Concepts, Theories, and the Mind-Body Problem,* edited by Feigl, Scriven, and Grover Maxwell, Minnesota Studies in the Philosophy of Science, volume 2 (Minneapolis: University of Minnesota Press, 1957), pp. 225–308, 507–539;

"Time and the World Order," in *Scientific Explanation, Space, and Time,* edited by Feigl and Maxwell, Minnesota Studies in the Philosophy of Science, volume 3 (Minneapolis: University of Minnesota Press, 1962), pp. 527–616;

"Imperatives, Intentions, and the Logic of 'Ought'," in *Morality and the Language of Conduct,* edited by Hector-Neri Castañeda and George Nakhnikian (Detroit: Wayne State University Press, 1963), pp. 159–214;

"Thought and Action" and "Fatalism and Determinism," in *Freedom and Determinism,* edited by Keith Lehrer (New York: Random House, 1966), pp. 105–139, 141–174;

"Some Problems about Belief," in *Philosophical Logic,* edited by J. W. Davis, D. T. Hockney, and W. K. Wilson (Dordrecht, Netherlands: Reidel, 1969), pp. 46–65;

"Belief and the Expression of Belief," in *Language, Belief, and Metaphysics,* edited by Howard E. Kiefer and Milton K. Munitz (Albany: State University of New York Press, 1970), pp. 146–158;

Basic Issues in the Philosophy of Time, edited by Sellars and Eugene Freeman (La Salle, Ill.: Open Court, 1971);

New Readings in Philosophical Analysis, edited by Sellars, Feigl, and Lehrer (New York: Appleton-Century-Crofts, 1972);

"Ontology and the Philosophy of Mind in Russell," in *Bertrand Russell's Philosophy,* edited by Nakhnikian (New York: Barnes & Noble, 1974), pp. 57–100;

"Autobiographical Reflections" and "The Structure of Knowledge," in *Action, Knowledge, and Reality: Studies in Honor of Wilfrid Sellars,* edited by Castañeda (Indianapolis: Bobbs-Merrill, 1975), pp. 277–293, 295–347;

"Volitions Re-affirmed," in *Action Theory: Proceedings of the Winnipeg Conference on Human Action, Held at Winnipeg, Manitoba, Canada, 9–11 May 1975,* edited by Myles Brand and Douglas Walton (Dordrecht, Netherlands & Boston: Reidel, 1976), pp. 47–66;

"Berkeley and Descartes: Reflections on the 'New Way of Ideas'," in *Studies in Perception: Interpretations in the History of Philosophy and Science,* edited by Peter K. Machamer and Robert G. Turnbull (Columbus: Ohio State University Press, 1977), pp. 259–311;

"Some Reflections on Perceptual Consciousness," in *Crosscurrents in Phenomenology,* Selected Studies in Phenomenology and Existential Philosophy, volume 7, edited by Ronald Bruzina and Bruce Wilshire (The Hague & Boston: Nijhoff, 1978), pp. 169–185;

"The Role of Imagination in Kant's Theory of Experience," in *Categories: A Colloquium,* edited by Henry W. Johnstone Jr. (University Park: Pennsylvania State University, Department of Philosophy, 1978), pp. 231–245;

"More on Givenness and Explanatory Coherence," in *Justification and Knowledge: New Studies in Epistemology,* edited by George S. Pappas (Dordrecht, Netherlands & Boston: Reidel, 1979), pp. 169–182;

"Towards a Theory of Predication," in *How Things Are: Studies in Predication and the History of Philosophy and Science,* edited by James Bogen and James E. McGuire (Dordrecht, Netherlands & Boston: Reidel, 1983), pp. 281–318.

SELECTED PERIODICAL PUBLICATIONS–
UNCOLLECTED: "Acquaintance and Description Again," *Journal of Philosophy,* 46 (1949): 496–505;

"The Identity of Linguistic Expressions and the Paradox of Analysis," *Philosophical Studies,* 1 (1950): 24–31;

"Gestalt Qualities and the Paradox of Analysis," *Philosophical Studies,* 1 (1950): 92–94;

"Mind, Meaning, and Behavior," *Philosophical Studies,* 3 (1952): 83–95;

"Presupposing," *Philosophical Review,* 63 (1954): 197–215;

"Logical Subjects and Physical Objects," *Philosophy and Phenomenological Research,* 17 (1957): 458–472;

"Reflections on Contrary to Duty Imperatives," *Noûs,* 1 (1967): 303–344;

"Science, Sense Impressions, and Sensa: A Reply to Cornman," *Review of Metaphysics,* 25 (1971): 391–447;

"The Double-Knowledge Approach to the Mind-Body Problem," *New Scholasticism,* 45 (1971): 269–289;

"Givenness and Explanatory Coherence," *Journal of Philosophy,* 70 (1973): 612–664;

"Meaning as Functional Classification," *Synthèse,* 27 (1974): 417–437;

"The Adverbial Theory of the Objects of Sensation," *Metaphilosophy,* 6 (1975): 144–160;

"Is Scientific Realism Tenable?" *Proceedings of PSA,* 2 (1976): 307–334;

"Behaviorism, Language and Meaning," *Pacific Philosophical Quarterly,* 61 (1980): 3–30;

Science, Perception and Reality

International Library of Philosophy and Scientific Method

EDITOR: TED HONDERICH

W. F. SELLARS

Dust jacket for Sellars's first book (1963), a collection of eleven of his most important essays (Bruccoli Clark Layman Archives)

"On Reasoning about Values," *American Philosophical Quarterly,* 17 (1980): 81–101;

"Foundations for a Metaphysics of Pure Process," *Monist,* 64 (1981): 3–90;

"Mental Events," *Philosophical Studies,* 39 (1981): 325–345;

"Sensa or Sensings: Reflections on the Ontology of Perception," *Philosophical Studies,* 41 (1982): 83–111;

"On Accepting First Principles," *Philosophical Perspectives,* 2 (1988): 301–314.

Wilfrid Sellars was an original and profound systematic philosopher who exercised a huge, though often indirect, influence on late-twentieth-century Anglo-American philosophy. A founding editor of the first American journal of analytic philosophy and the editor of two seminal collections of essays, Sellars is known principally for his development of an antifoundationalist epistemology in response to what he attacked as the "myth of the given," his distinction between the "mani-

fest image" and the "scientific image," his proposal that psychological concepts are like theoretical ones, his tough-minded scientific realism, and his rich interpretations of historical figures in philosophy. He can also lay claim to the first explicit formulation of a functionalist treatment of intentional states; an early recognition of the "hard problem" of sensory consciousness, as well as a distinctive solution to it; and a thoroughgoing nominalism. Sellars is, however, a "philosopher's philosopher": his essays are complex and difficult, each revealing only a part of the system from which they draw their power and motivation. Because he never wrote a major work summarizing his system, readers must piece it together from his articles. Consequently, many of his ideas have entered broad circulation not directly from his own work but through the more easily accessible writings of his students and colleagues. Sellars was a captivating lecturer and teacher, and many of his early advocates were students or colleagues who had a significant opportunity to listen and talk to him. After a lull around the time of his death in 1989, interest in his work has been renewed owing to a better understanding of the importance of his philosophical contributions.

Wilfrid Stalker Sellars was born on 20 May 1912 in Ann Arbor, Michigan, the first child of the University of Michigan philosopher Roy Wood Sellars, a leader of the Critical Realists, and Helen Maud Stalker Sellars; both parents were Canadian immigrants. Sellars's sister, Cecily, was born in 1913. Sellars discusses his father's work in only one essay, but he employed the idiom of analytic philosophy to argue positions that his father would, in most cases, have found congenial.

As a boy, Sellars established a lifelong pattern of keeping to himself and not making friends easily. When he was nine and ten, the family spent a year in Providence, Rhode Island, and Boston; a summer in Oxford; and then a year in Paris, where Sellars attended the Lycée Montaigne. His mother helped him to master the new language: in 1926 she published a translation of Célestin Bouglé's *The Evolution of Values: Studies in Sociology with Special Applications to Teaching.*

After two years in a public school Sellars graduated in 1929 from the high school operated by the University of Michigan School of Education. After taking a summer course in algebra at the university, he returned to Paris with his mother and sister and enrolled in a science-oriented program at the Lycée Louis le Grand. He claimed in his "Autobiographical Reflections," published in *Action, Knowledge, and Reality: Studies in Honor of Wilfrid Sellars* (1975), edited by Hector-Neri Castañeda, that he first encountered philosophy at the lycée, for he and his father had not previously discussed it. Outside of his classes he studied Marxist political thought; his principal ideological influences were the anti-Stalinist Russian expatriate Boris Souvarine and Leon Trotsky. In "Autobiographical Reflections" he remarks that his first philosophical reading was "Marx, Engels, Lenin, and, in general, the philosophical and quasi-philosophical polemical literature which is the life blood of French intellectuals." He also took a survey course in philosophy at the lyceé. Sellars was finally aware of what his father did, and when Roy Wood Sellars arrived in Paris in the spring of 1930, a philosophical dialogue commenced that lasted until the elder Sellars's death in 1973. Under his father's influence Sellars quickly abandoned what he calls "the pseudo-Hegelian jargon of Marxist *Naturphilosophie*," though he retained sympathies with Hegelian and Marxist approaches to social and historical interpretation. After the school year in Paris was over, Sellars audited courses at the University of Munich for six months.

In January 1931 Sellars returned to the University of Michigan, where he studied mathematics, economics, and philosophy and campaigned for the Socialist Party candidate for president, Norman Thomas, in 1932. His serious work in philosophy began with Cooper Harold Langford's course on the seventeenth- and eighteenth-century British empiricists John Locke, George Berkeley, and David Hume, which he says "was at least as much on G. E. Moore and Cambridge Analysis as it was on the Empiricists." Sellars was impressed by the methods, though not the results, of Cambridge analytic philosophy. He was also, as were many at the time, convinced of the power of the new logic developed by Bertrand Russell and Alfred North Whitehead in *Principia Mathematica* (1910–1913) and extended by others, such as Langford and C. I. Lewis in their *Symbolic Logic* (1932). He recalls in "Autobiographical Reflections" that although most attempts to capture philosophically interesting concepts and principles in the logical forms then available seemed "wildly implausible" to him, he "regarded the strategy as a sound one and believed that the crucial question concerned the manner in which the technical apparatus of *Principia* would have to be fleshed out in order to do justice to the conceptual forms of human knowledge." That early conviction shaped much of his later philosophical method.

Sellars received his B.A. in 1933 and began graduate work at the State University of New York at Buffalo, where he studied Immanuel Kant and Edmund Husserl with Marvin Farber. Farber's naturalistic interpretation of Husserl convinced Sellars that important structural insights usually stated in nonnaturalistic terms could be reconciled with naturalism. He earned his M.A. in 1934 with the thesis "Substance, Change and Event," which concerned the nature of time.

Awarded a Rhodes scholarship, Sellars enrolled in the philosophy, politics, and economics program at Oriel College of the University of Oxford in the fall of 1934. His official tutor was W. G. Maclagan, but he soon fell under the influence of H. A. Prichard and John Cook Wilson. Kant also became a central influence as Sellars read his works under the tutelage of H. H. Price. Sellars took a first-class degree in 1936 (it turned into an M.A. in 1940) and undertook a D.Phil. degree. He tried to write a dissertation on Kant under T. D. Weldon, but though he believed that he knew what was wrong with other interpretations of Kant, he could not yet spell out his own interpretation clearly enough. Abandoning the dissertation, he enrolled at Harvard University in the fall of 1937 to study for a Ph.D. He took courses with Lewis, D. W. Prall, Ralph Barton Perry, Charles L. Stevenson, and W. V. Quine and passed his doctoral preliminary examinations in the spring of 1938. That summer he married Mary Sharp, from Yorkshire, whom he had met when she was studying English literature at Oxford.

In the fall, Sellars, who had still not written his dissertation, was hired by Herbert Feigl to teach the history of philosophy at the University of Iowa. In his courses Sellars developed sophisticated interpretations of the major and many minor figures in philosophy, as well as of the relationships among philosophical movements and tendencies.

In 1943 Sellars was commissioned an ensign in the Naval Reserves and assigned to Air Intelligence; he spent the rest of the World War II years working in antisubmarine warfare in Rhode Island. Returning to Iowa after the war, Sellars realized that he could not keep his job unless he began to publish. He and his wife, a short-story writer, resolved to spend ten hours a day writing. After seventeen drafts, Sellars completed his first paper, "Realism and the New Way of Words"; it was published in *Philosophy and Phenomenological Research* in June 1948 and is collected in *Pure Pragmatics and Possible Worlds: The Early Essays of Wilfrid Sellars* (1980). (Two other papers, written after "Realism and the New Way of Words," had already appeared in print by the time it was published.) Sellars had found a procedure for writing; as if a dam had burst, he became highly prolific.

In 1946 Sellars moved to the University of Minnesota as an assistant professor; he was promoted to associate professor the following year. In 1949 Sellars and Feigl, who had moved to the University of Minnesota in 1941, published *Readings in Philosophical Analysis,* a collection of essays that defined the canon of analytic philosophy for many years. In 1950 they founded *Philosophical Studies,* the first journal devoted exclusively to analytic philosophy. Sellars became a full professor in

1951 and department chairman in 1952. In the latter year he and his colleague John Hospers edited the anthology *Readings in Ethical Theory,* which also became a widely used textbook.

Sellars's publishing career can be divided into three periods, according to the mode of expression and emphases he employed; the fundamental themes, however, remain constant: naturalism, the thesis that everything that exists is an element in a unitary causal nexus in space-time; realism, the claim that human knowledge extends to those elements; nominalism, the contention that abstract entities do not exist but are artifacts of language; and a commitment to the rationality and authority of scientific methods that is sometimes characterized—usually by its detractors—as "scientism." Also present from his first works are his opposition to abstractionist theories of concept acquisition; his belief that—as he puts it in "Epistemology and the New Way of Words," published in the *Journal of Philosophy* (1947) and collected in *Pure Pragmatics and Possible Worlds*—"classical rationalism . . . made explicit the grammar of epistemological and metaphysical predicates," which classical empiricism confused with psychological predicates; and his contention that these epistemological and metaphysical notions are not factual but practical ones that express the normative commitments constitutive of one's conceptual framework or language.

Except for the death of his sister in an automobile accident in 1954, little is known about Sellars's personal life during the early period, which extends from 1946 to about 1955. Philosophically, during this period Sellars is still finding his voice; his articles are characterized by shifting terminology as he struggles to discover the best way to express his positions. In "Realism and the New Way of Words," as well as in "Pure Pragmatics and Epistemology" (1947) and "Epistemology and the New Way of Words" (1947), which are also collected in *Pure Pragmatics and Possible Worlds,* he characterizes his project as a "pure pragmatics." He contends that analytic philosophy, which first saw itself—for example, in Carnap's work—as an analysis of the syntax of an ideal language and then as an analysis of the semantics of such a language, needs to move further and recast itself as pure pragmatics, which analyzes the structures necessary to a language that is about the world in which it is used and, thus, includes a formal analysis of concepts such as "meaningful" and "verification." This analysis is a formal, in contrast to an empirical psychological, one, and it explicitly recognizes the normative character of these concepts.

This approach leads to one of Sellars's distinctive claims: that meaning is not a relation. He admits that meaning statements seem to be relational: "'*Rot*' means *red* in German" seems to express a relationship between

"*rot*" and *red,* but Sellars asks what the *red* is to which "*rot*" is supposed to be related. According to his analysis, semantic talk classifies expressions by their roles in a language system. "'*Rot*' means *red* in German" conveys the information that a certain visual sign or sound plays among German speakers a role similar to that played by a certain sign or sound among speakers of English. What an expression means is a matter of its function in the language; that it and the language to which it belongs are meaningful at all is a matter of the use of the language.

The contribution of an expression to good inferences is the functional role Sellars emphasizes most. This doctrine is a familiar one as applied to the logical constants, such as *and, either-or,* and *if-then,* the meaning of which is determined by the formally valid inferences in which they occur. Sellars contends in "Inference and Meaning" (1953), collected in *Pure Pragmatics and Possible Worlds,* that "material transformation rules determine the descriptive meaning of the expressions of a language within the framework established by its logical transformation rules." The inference from "X is red" to "X is colored" is formally invalid, but it is clearly a good inference. Sellars holds that it is not an enthymeme in which the premise "For all X, if X is red, then X is colored" is left out; rather, an extralogical or material rule of inference in English is partially constitutive of the meanings of *red* and *color* and licenses this inference. This aspect of Sellars's philosophy has been worked out in great detail by Robert Brandom in his *Making It Explicit: Reasoning, Representing, and Discursive Commitment* (1994).

Sellars also develops a naturalistic treatment of the logical, causal, and deontological modalities, that is, the forms of necessity and possibility expressed in logical principles such as "If both p and q, then, necessarily, q," causal statements such as "If the temperature of water exceeds 100 degrees Celsius in standard conditions at sea level, then, necessarily, it will boil," and moral prescriptions and permissions such as "You should not plagiarize your ethics paper." Such modal discourse, according to Sellars, is implicitly metalinguistic. In his view, modal assertions such as "If I drop the chalk, then, *necessarily,* it will fall" or "The journal *ought* to review submissions blindly" express, in the "material mode," a commitment that the basic claim—"If I drop the chalk, it will fall" or "The journal reviews submissions blindly"—is made in accordance with, or is endorsed by, a rule of an ideal language. In the case of a logical modality it will be a formal rule of the language; in the causal and deontic cases it will be a material rule of inference. This complex of doctrines, which constitutes Sellars's attempt to avoid the traps of empiricist skepticism and rationalist Platonism while preserving the most important insights of each, is worked out in

"Concepts as Involving Laws and Inconceivable with Them" (1948), "Language, Rules, and Behavior" (1949), and "Inference and Meaning" (1953), all of which are collected in *Pure Pragmatics and Possible Worlds*.

The middle period of Sellars's career extends from around 1956 to 1977; in this period he elaborates what has become, for all intents and purposes, a philosophical system. In 1956 he delivered three lectures at the University of London; they were published the same year as "Empiricism and the Philosophy of Mind" in the first volume of the Minnesota Studies in the Philosophy of Science series, *The Foundations of Science and the Concepts of Psychology and Psychoanalysis,* edited by Feigl and Michael Scriven. Though abstruse, it became his best-known article and a classic of twentieth-century philosophy. Sellars states that his goal is to attack the "entire framework of givenness"–that is, the belief that there must be some fundamental epistemological states, collectively referred to as "the given," that serve as a foundation for all other such states. Since the most attractive candidate for "the given" is knowledge of one's own present mental state, to demolish the "myth of the given" Sellars has to dismantle the traditional Cartesian conception of the mind as a realm separable from the physical with direct, privileged, and incorrigible access to its own states. He begins the essay with a critique of accounts according to which knowledge of physical objects is based on more-direct knowledge of appearances or "sense-data." He argues that observational knowledge is directly about physical objects but is not epistemically independent of other empirical, even general, knowledge.

All such Cartesian theories, he says, commit mistakes: sense-datum theories conflate two different notions, that of an nonpropositionally structured inner episode, such as a sensation of red, that is a causally necessary condition of a perception that something is red, on the one hand, and that of a propositionally structured inner episode that is noninferential knowledge that something is red and provides evidence for other kinds of empirical knowledge, on the other hand; and appearance theories misconstrue the semantics of words such as *appears* or *looks.* Sellars's argument against the given is: knowledge is epistemically independent if it does not derive its epistemic status from any other knowledge and is epistemically efficacious if it enhances the epistemic status of (or supports) other knowledge; the doctrine of the given requires that for any empirical knowledge *p,* some epistemically independent knowledge *g* is epistemically efficacious with respect to *p; g* can be epistemically efficacious with respect to *p* only if *g* can serve as a premise in an argument for *p; g* can serve as a premise in an argument only if *g* has propositional form; therefore, the nonpropositional (for example, sense-data) is epistemically

Form and Content in Ethical Theory

The Lindley Lecture, University of Kansas, April 17, 1967 by Wilfrid Sellars, University Professor of Philosophy and Research Professor of the Philosophy of Science University of Pittsburgh

Cover for Sellars's second book, published in 1967 (Thomas Cooper Library, University of South Carolina)

inefficacious; if *g* is propositionally structured (a belief), it is acquired either by inference or noninferentially; no inferential belief of a subject is epistemically independent; noninferential empirical beliefs are justified for *S* only if they are reliable responses to the empirical condition reported, and subject *S* knows that they are reliable; therefore, no noninferential belief is epistemically independent; therefore, if *g* is nonpropositional, it cannot be epistemically efficacious, and if it is propositional, it cannot be epistemically independent; therefore, nothing can be given.

Sellars then proposes that psychological concepts are like theoretical concepts in important ways. He relates a philosophical myth in which a tribe of protohumans, called Ryleans in honor of the Oxford analytic philosopher Gilbert Ryle, speaks a language that contains terms for physical objects and the properties of such objects and for humans and their behaviors and dispositions to behave but no terms for inner states such as thoughts or sense impressions. A genius named Jones develops theories of unobservable inner states of humans that enable him to explain otherwise anomalous phenomena such as complex, intelligent behaviors without accompanying speech and pink-elephant-avoidance behavior after a hard night of drinking, even though there are no pink elephants around. Jones calls these states "thoughts" and "sense impressions," and his companions soon learn to employ the theoretical vocabulary of thoughts and impressions in direct, noninferential, observation-like reports of their own states. Mentalistic vocabulary is, thus, reconstructed on a physicalistic, though nonreductive, basis, showing that knowledge of the mental cannot be assumed to be simply given.

"Empiricism and the Philosophy of Mind" is one of the earliest functionalist treatments of the mind; several later research programs in philosophy and psychology picked up its idea that mentalistic concepts are like theoretical ones. Together with Quine's "Two Dogmas of Empiricism" (1951), the essay initiated a sea change in twentieth-century epistemology, putting foundationalism—the view that there must be some instances of knowledge that are both epistemically independent and epistemically efficacious and that provide the "foundation" from which all other empirical knowledge is derived by inference—on the defensive.

In 1958–1959 Sellars was a visiting professor at Yale University; in 1959 he accepted a tenured position there. He did not remain long, however: the Yale philosophy department had split into factions that were vying for Sellars's allegiance, and he felt that the departmental politics was getting in the way of his work. He mentioned his dissatisfaction to Adolf Grünbaum while giving a talk at the University of Pittsburgh. Pittsburgh pursued him, and Sellars moved there in 1963 as University Professor of Philosophy and Research Professor of the Philosophy of Science; he brought Alan Ross Anderson and Nuel Belnap from Yale with him, and Jerome Schneewind followed a year later. With a few other hires, Pittsburgh became one of the best philosophy departments in the United States.

In "Philosophy and the Scientific Image of Man," first published in *Frontiers of Science and Philosophy* (1962), edited by Robert Colodny, and republished in his first book, *Science, Perception and Reality* (1963), Sellars gives an overview of his philosophical project. He draws a contrast, which has become familiar since then, between the "manifest image" and the "scientific image" of the world. Both images are idealized categorical frameworks, schemes of concept families in terms of which human beings confront the world and organize their activities. The manifest image begins as the "original image," the conceptual framework in which persons first become aware of themselves as persons and, thus,

first become persons, but it is revised and supplemented on the basis of experience. Its fundamental categories—persons and things—remain central, however. One aspect of the manifest image—controlled empirical inquiry—starts to take on a life of its own when it reaches beyond the resources of the manifest image by positing the existence of new categories of unobservable entities to explain observable phenomena. This creative extension of the conceptual framework does more than supplement the manifest image; ultimately, it coalesces into a new categorical framework that also claims to provide a complete picture of the world and, thus, challenges the manifest image. In the manifest image persons are unitary, basic entities with physical, psychological, and moral properties; in the scientific image they appear as congeries of microparticles, and moral properties are not present at all. Paraphrasing the ancient Greek Sophist Protagoras, Sellars says in "Empiricism and the Philosophy of Mind" that "in the dimension of describing and explaining the world, science is the measure of all things, of what is that it is, and of what is not that it is not." But describing and explaining are not the only tasks that face human beings. They also, for instance, prescribe and justify actions. Thus, they must develop a "synoptic vision" in which the normative categories that are the distinctive ingredient of the manifest image are united with the ontological framework developed by science.

Science, Perception and Reality brought together eleven of Sellars's most important essays so that his readers could begin to see the outlines of his system. In "Being and Being Known" (1960) and "Truth and Correspondence" (1962) Sellars argues that a causal "picturing" relationship must exist between symbols and reality. "Naming and Saying" (1962), "Grammar and Existence: A Preface to Ontology" (1960), and "Particulars" (1952) expound and defend Sellars's nominalism. "Is There a Synthetic A Priori?" (1953; revised, 1957) and "Some Reflections on Language Games" (1951) deal with meaning as a functional classification.

Among the important articles Sellars published at this time are two technical pieces in which he analyzes away the apparent Platonic commitments of assertions about properties, propositions, and other abstractions: "Abstract Entities" and "Classes as Abstract Entities and the Russell Paradox" appeared in *The Review of Metaphysics* in 1963 and were collected in *Philosophical Perspectives* (1967). Sellars argues that a statement such as "Triangularity is a universal" is really a disguised statement about language, roughly equivalent to "*Triangular* is a predicate."

In 1965–1966 Sellars delivered the John Locke Lectures at the University of Oxford; they were published as *Science and Metaphysics: Variations on Kantian*

Themes (1968). Having long believed that his own relationship to idealism and logical empiricism was similar to that of Kant to Kant's predecessors, Sellars presents his own views on perception, meaning, truth, reality, and ethics as what Kant should have said. *Science and Metaphysics* is as close to a unified and complete exposition of his system as Sellars ever wrote, filling out especially his treatment of the foundations of ethics. In 1967 he published the collection of essays *Philosophical Perspectives*. The first part comprises interpretations of Plato, Aristotle, and Gottfried Wilhelm Leibniz; the second part is devoted mostly to metaphysics and the philosophy of science.

Sellars's wife committed suicide in 1970 after a long illness. He remained at the University of Pittsburgh for the rest of his career, although he spent the winter terms from 1976 to 1982 teaching at the University of Arizona and was also a visiting professor at the Universities of Illinois, Indiana, and Massachusetts and at Princeton and Rockefeller Universities. He was generally revered in the department: his undergraduate courses on epistemology and Kant were always full, and graduate students often sat through them two or three times; his graduate seminars were also filled; and he supervised many dissertations. A sense of his lectures can be gleaned from *The Metaphysics of Epistemology* (1989), a transcription by Pedro V. Amaral of his fall 1975 epistemology course. He was also increasingly recognized elsewhere as a major philosopher. In 1970 he served as president of the Eastern Division of the American Philosophical Association. His Matchette Foundation Lectures at the University of Texas in 1971 were published as "The Structure of Knowledge" in *Action, Knowledge, and Reality;* his John Dewey Lectures at the University of Chicago in 1973 were published as *Naturalism and Ontology* (1980); and his Paul Carus Lectures at the Eastern Division meetings of the American Philosophical Association in 1977 were published as "Foundations for a Metaphysics of Pure Process," a special issue of the journal *The Monist* (1981).

Despite the many honors, Sellars seemed to be increasingly frustrated that he could not persuade more philosophers of the correctness of his views. He seemed to encounter the same objections again and again, despite his best efforts to rebut or disarm them. His position was complex; increasingly tightly woven, albeit dispersed across many essays; and grounded in a comprehensive vision of the history of philosophy. Convincing others always seemed to require going back to basic assumptions, which made widespread acceptance a far-off prospect at best. By the late 1970s Sellars, always fairly awkward with people except in the context of a philosophical discussion, grew more defensive about his views and, sometimes, too rote in responding to questions or objections that he thought he had dealt with too many times before.

Still, Sellars was highly productive in the late 1960s and early 1970s. He devoted several articles–"Metaphysics and the Concept of a Person" (1969; collected in his *Essays in Philosophy and Its History,* 1974), "Science, Sense Impressions, and Sensa: A Reply to Cornman," and "The Double-Knowledge Approach to the Mind-Body Problem"–to the mind-body problem, on which his position is more complex than those of most other philosophers who have dealt with the issue. He defends his functionalist treatment of mental states as compatible with materialism, though not reducible to it. He also argues against a reductive account of sensations that identifies them with complexes of microphysical or neurophysiological entities. Sellars takes it to be a principle of ordinary talk about colors that every part of a colored object is colored. He admits that a pink object need not be pink everywhere–it could be covered in a pattern of fine red and white dots; but red and white are also colors. He denies that colors are actually "out there" in physical objects, since physical objects are congeries of microparticles, none of which is itself colored. Classical tradition relocated color "in the mind," but if minds and brains are identified with each other, the problem returns: brains are also congeries of microparticles. Sellars argues that to accommodate sensations in a satisfactory scientific theory, science would have to enrich its stock of fundamental entities to include those that occur only in the context of sensing organisms. In their 1956 paper "The Concept of Emergence" Sellars and Paul Meehl had distinguished two senses of *physical:* "Physical$_1$: an event or entity is physical$_1$ if it belongs in the space-time network. Physical$_2$: an event or entity is physical$_2$ if it is definable in terms of theoretical primitives adequate to describe completely the actual states though not necessarily the potentialities of the universe before the appearance of life." Sensa would be physical$_1$ but not physical$_2$. Further, such entities would differ from classical microparticles: Sellars predicts that physics will have to expand to countenance nonparticulate entities (pure processes) that embody sensory qualities. Sellars's argument has puzzled many. He conducted a public exchange with James Cornman about it in *The Review of Metaphysics* in 1970–1971 and revisited the issue in "The Structure of Knowledge" and "Foundations for a Metaphysics of Pure Process," but few have been convinced.

In *Naturalism and Ontology* Sellars spells out his nominalism, particularly by refining his theory of predication. He had argued in "Abstract Entities" that sentences that Platonists believe commit one to realism about properties and relations, such as "Redness is a

Science and Metaphysics

Variations on Kantian Themes

International Library of Philosophy and Scientific Method

EDITOR: TED HONDERICH   ADVISORY EDITOR: BERNARD WILLIAMS

WILFRID SELLARS

Dust jacket for the 1968 published version of Sellars's 1965–1966 John Locke Lectures at the University of Oxford, in which he presents his own views on perception, meaning, truth, reality, and ethics as what the German philosopher Immanuel Kant should have said (Reason Alone Books)

about that referring expressions stand in certain relations." The result is that one is ontologically committed only to the kinds of entities named in the most basic scientific laws. *Naturalism and Ontology* is Sellars's final and most complete statement of his nominalism.

Several of Sellars's later pieces, especially "The Structure of Knowledge" and "Foundations for a Metaphysics of Pure Process," revisit the concept of the given, but with differences from "Empiricism and the Philosophy of Mind." Sellars no longer equates thought and language but tries to make room for other modes of thought. For instance, in "The Structure of Knowledge" he is willing to say that a musician is "thinking in sound" and that visual imagination involves "thinking in color." He also seems to relax his opposition to the given, claiming in "Foundations for a Metaphysics of Pure Process" only that the categorical status of sensations is not given—apparently leaving open the possibility that the descriptive content of sensible predicates is in some way "given." Whether these developments are conservative improvements or revolutionary rejections of his earlier views has been debated by scholars.

Sellars had given up editing *Philosophical Studies* in 1974; after "Foundations for a Metaphysics of Pure Process" he entered his late period, in which his pace of production slowed. Still, he produced some high-quality work, such as "Mental Events" (1981), the last and most concise statement of his position on the nature of the mental and on the mentality of languageless organisms. In 1984 he suffered a stroke that made walking difficult. His alcohol consumption also seems to have become significant enough to have disrupted his ability to produce, although testimony on that score varies. In 1987 the University of Pittsburgh hosted a conference on Sellars's philosophy in celebration of his seventy-fifth birthday. A relationship with Susanna Felder Downie begun in the early 1970s culminated in their marriage shortly before his death of liver failure on 2 July 1989. His widow scattered his ashes from a canoe on Chautauqua Lake in New York.

Sellars left behind a dauntingly complex but extraordinarily rich body of work. He also left behind many students, colleagues, and others who take inspiration from that work. In his *Mind and World* (1994), particularly, John McDowell has elaborated on Sellars's conception of the intentional realm as "the logical space of reasons." Robert Brandom has developed an inferentialist theory of meaning inspired by Sellars. Richard Rorty portrays Sellars as one of the heroes of postpositivist thought. Daniel C. Dennett, Ruth Millikan, Paul M. Churchland, and Patricia Churchland have all developed Sellars's philosophy of mind, though in different directions. Even those students who reject central portions of his thought, such as Castañeda and Bas C.

quality" or "Triangularity is an abstract individual," can be given a nominalistic interpretation as material-mode judgments about the semantic characteristics of linguistic expressions. In *Naturalism and Ontology* Sellars argues further that no Platonistic commitments are inherent in the notion of predication. Ontological commitment, he claims, is carried by a language's most primitive referential devices. Drawing on his analysis of Ludwig Wittgenstein's treatment of predication in the *Tractatus Logico-Philosophicus* (1922) in his 1962 article "Naming and Saying" (collected in *Science, Perception and Reality*), Sellars argues that "The Tractarian analysis of predication is the heart of views on ontology. The essential point is to treat predicates as auxiliary symbols which don't have the full-blooded semantic role of referring expressions but rather are used to bring it

van Fraassen, who disavow his antiphenomenalism and his scientific realism, respectively, remain deeply influenced by him in the ways in which they interpret the history of philosophy and set up and endeavor to solve their philosophical problems. Sellars's writings have been widely read in Germany, where the systematic nature of his thought and his work on Kant make him stand out among analytic philosophers. Most philosophers in the Anglo-American tradition acknowledge Sellars's importance and recognize an obligation to be familiar with his thought, but many find his work too difficult and time-consuming to master. Sellars was a seminal, profound, and comprehensive thinker, but his long-term influence on philosophy has yet to be seen.

Bibliography:

Andrew Chrucky, ed., "Problems from Wilfrid Sellars," *University of Chicago Philosophy Project* <http://www.ditext.com/sellars/>.

References:

William Alston, "What's Wrong with Immediate Knowledge?" in his *Epistemic Justification: Essays in the Theory of Knowledge* (Ithaca, N.Y.: Cornell University Press, 1989), pp. 57–78;

Bruce Aune, *Knowledge, Mind and Nature: An Introduction to Theory of Knowledge and the Philosophy of Mind* (New York: Random House, 1967);

Aune, "Sellars's Two Images of the World," *Journal of Philosophy,* 87 (1990): 537–545;

Richard J. Bernstein, "Sellars's Vision of Man-in-the-Universe," *Review of Metaphysics,* 20 (1966): 113–143, 290–312;

Laurence BonJour, "Sellars on Truth and Picturing," *International Philosophical Quarterly,* 13 (1973): 243–265;

Robert Brandom, *Making It Explicit: Reasoning, Representing, and Discursive Commitment* (Cambridge, Mass.: Harvard University Press, 1994);

Harold I. Brown, "Sellars, Concepts and Conceptual Change," *Synthèse,* 68 (1986): 275–307;

Richard Burian, "Sellarsian Realism and Conceptual Change in Science," in *Transcendental Arguments and Science: Essays in Epistemology,* edited by Peter Bieri, Rolf-Peter Horstmann, and Lorenz Krüger (Dordrecht, Netherlands & Boston: Reidel, 1979), pp. 97–225;

Hector-Neri Castañeda, ed., *Action, Knowledge, and Reality: Critical Studies in Honor of Wilfrid Sellars* (Indianapolis: Bobbs-Merrill, 1975);

Paul M. Churchland, *Scientific Realism and the Plasticity of Mind* (Cambridge & New York: Cambridge University Press, 1979);

Churchland and Patricia S. Churchland, "Functionalism, Qualia, and Intentionality," *Philosophical Topics,* 12 (1981): 121–145;

Patricia S. Churchland, *Neurophysiology: Toward a Unified Science of the Mind/Brain* (Cambridge, Mass.: MIT Press, 1986);

Romane Clark, "Sensibility and Understanding: The Given of Wilfrid Sellars," *Monist,* 65 (1983): 350–364;

James Cornman, "Sellars, Scientific Realism and Sensa," *Review of Metaphysics,* 23 (1970): 417–451;

C. F. Delaney, Michael Loux, Gary Gutting, and W. David Solomon, *The Synoptic Vision: Essays on the Philosophy of Wilfrid Sellars* (Notre Dame, Ind.: University of Notre Dame Press, 1977);

Daniel C. Dennett, "Mid-term Examination: Compare and Contrast," in *The Intentional Stance* (Cambridge, Mass.: MIT Press, 1987), pp. 339–350;

Willem A. deVries and Timm Triplett, *Knowledge, Mind, and the Given: A Reading of Sellars's "Empiricism and the Philosophy of Mind," Including the Complete Text of Sellars's Essay* (Indianapolis: Hackett, 2000);

Charles G. Echelbarger, "Sellars on Thinking and the Myth of the Given," *Philosophical Studies,* 25 (1974): 231–246;

Joseph Claude Evans Jr., *The Metaphysics of Transcendental Subjectivity: Descartes, Kant, and W. Sellars* (Amsterdam: Grüner, 1984), pp. 85–105;

Evan Fales, *A Defense of the Given* (Lanham, Md.: Rowman & Littlefield, 1996);

Jay F. Garfield, "The Myth of Jones and the Mirror of Nature: Reflections on Introspection," *Philosophy and Phenomenological Research,* 50 (1989): 1–26;

Gilbert Harman, "Sellars' Semantics," *Philosophical Review,* 79 (1970): 404–419;

C. A. Hooker, "Sellars' Argument for the Inevitability of the Secondary Qualities," *Philosophical Studies,* 32 (1977): 335–348;

Murray Kiteley, "Sellars' Ontology of Categories," *Noûs,* 7 (1973): 103–120;

Anton Friedrich Koch, *Vernunft und Sinnlichkeit im praktischen Denken: Eine sprachbehavioristische Rekonstruktion Kantischer Theoreme gegen Sellars* (Würzburg: Königshausen & Neumann, 1980);

David Kolb, "Sellars and the Measure of All Things," *Philosophical Studies,* 34 (1978): 381–400;

Rebecca Kukla, "Myth, Memory, and Misrecognition in Sellars' 'Empiricism and the Philosophy of Mind,'" *Philosophical Studies,* 101 (2000): 161–211;

Mark Norris Lance and John O'Leary-Hawthorne, *The Grammar of Meaning: Normativity and Semantic Discourse* (Cambridge & New York: Cambridge University Press, 1997);

Stephen Leeds, "Qualia, Awareness, Sellars," *Noûs,* 27 (1993): 303–330;

Vicki Choy Levine, "Sellars's Argument for Extreme Scientific Realism," *Pacific Philosophical Quarterly,* 61 (1980): 463–468;

Ausonio Marras, "The Behaviorist Foundation of Sellars's Semantics," *Dialogue,* 16 (1977): 664–675;

Marras, *Intentionality, Mind, and Language* (Urbana: University of Illinois Press, 1972);

Marras, "On Sellars's Linguistic Theory of Conceptual Activity," *Canadian Journal of Philosophy,* 2 (1973): 471–483;

John McDowell, "Having the World in View: Sellars, Kant, and Intentionality," *Journal of Philosophy,* 95 (1998): 431–490;

McDowell, *Mind and World* (Cambridge, Mass.: Harvard University Press, 1994);

Robert G. Meyers, "Sellars' Rejection of Foundations," *Philosophical Studies,* 39 (1981): 61–78;

Ruth Millikan, *Language, Thought, and Other Biological Categories: New Foundations for Realism* (Cambridge, Mass.: MIT Press, 1984);

Millikan, *White Queen Psychology and Other Essays for Alice* (Cambridge, Mass.: MIT Press, 1993);

Noûs, special Sellars issue, 7 (1973);

Philosophical Studies, special Sellars issue, 101 (2000);

Joseph C. Pitt, *Pictures, Images and Conceptual Change: An Analysis of Wilfrid Sellars' Philosophy of Science,* Synthèse Library, volume 151 (Dordrecht, Netherlands & Boston: Reidel, 1981);

Pitt, ed., *The Philosophy of Wilfrid Sellars: Queries and Extensions. Papers Deriving from and Related to a Workshop on the Philosophy of Wilfrid Sellars Held at Virginia Polytechnic Institute and State University, 1976* (Dordrecht, Netherlands & Boston: Reidel, 1978);

Robert C. Richardson and G. Muilenberg, "Sellars and Sense Impressions," *Erkenntnis,* 17 (1982): 171–212;

William S. Robinson, "Sellarsian Materialism," *Philosophy of Science,* 49 (1982): 212–227;

Richard Rorty, *Consequences of Pragmatism: Essays, 1972–1980* (Minneapolis: University of Minnesota Press, 1982), pp. xviii, xx, xxiii, xxxvi, 4, 16, 18n, 29, 75, 84, 88n, 211, 226;

Rorty, "Epistemological Behaviorism and the De-Transcendentalization of Analytic Philosophy," *Neue Hefte für Philosophie,* 14 (1978): 115–142;

Rorty, *Philosophy and the Mirror of Nature* (Princeton: Princeton University Press, 1979), pp. 141–143, 167–188, 218–220, 275–276, 296–299, 381–382, 389–390;

Rorty, "Representation, Social Practice, and Truth," *Philosophical Studies,* 54 (1988): 215–228;

Jay F. Rosenberg, "Fusing the Images: Nachruf for Wilfrid Sellars," *Journal for General Philosophy of Science / Zeitschrift für allgemeine Wissenschaftstheorie,* 21 (1990): 3–25;

Rosenberg, *Linguistic Representation* (Dordrecht, Netherlands & Boston: Reidel, 1974);

Rosenberg, "The Place of Color in the Scheme of Things: A Roadmap to Sellars's Carus Lectures," *Monist,* 65 (1982): 315–335;

Eric M. Rubenstein, "Absolute Processes: A Nominalist Alternative," *Southern Journal of Philosophy,* 35 (1997): 539–555;

Rubenstein, "Sellars without Homogeneity," *International Journal of Philosophical Studies,* 8 (2000): 47–72;

Johanna Seibt, *Properties as Processes: A Synoptic Study of Wilfrid Sellars' Nominalism* (Atascadero, Cal.: Ridgeview, 1990);

Seibt, "Wilfrid Sellars' systematischer Nominalismus," *Information Philosophie,* 3 (1995): 22–26;

Jeffrey Sicha, *A Metaphysics of Elementary Mathematics* (Amherst: University of Massachusetts Press, 1974);

Sicha, "Sellarsian Realism," *Philosophical Studies,* 54 (1988): 229–256;

Ernest Sosa, "Mythology of the Given," *History of Philosophy Quarterly,* 14 (1997): 275–286;

Michael Tye, "The Adverbial Theory: A Defence of Sellars against Jackson," *Metaphilosophy,* 6 (1975): 136–143;

Bas C. van Fraassen, *The Scientific Image* (Oxford: Clarendon Press / New York: Oxford University Press, 1980);

van Fraassen, "Wilfrid Sellars on Scientific Realism," *Dialogue* (Canada), 14 (1975): 606–616;

Edmond Wright, "Defence of Sellars," *Philosophy and Phenomenological Research,* 46 (1985): 73–90.

Papers:

Most of Wilfrid Sellars's papers are in the Archive for Scientific Philosophy, Hillman Library, University of Pittsburgh. As of 2003 they were not yet available to the public, pending cataloguing. A few items are with Roy Wood Sellars's papers in the Bentley Historical Library at the University of Michigan.

Paul Weiss

(19 May 1901 – 5 July 2002)

Thomas Krettek
Marquette University

BOOKS: *Reality* (Princeton: Princeton University Press / London: H. Milford, Oxford University Press, 1938);

Nature and Man (New York: Holt, 1947);

Man's Freedom (New Haven: Yale University Press, 1950);

Modes of Being, 2 volumes (Carbondale: Southern Illinois University Press, 1958);

Our Public Life (Bloomington: Indiana University Press, 1959);

The World of Art (Carbondale: Southern Illinois University Press, 1961);

Nine Basic Arts (Carbondale: Southern Illinois University Press, 1961);

History: Written and Lived (Carbondale: Southern Illinois University Press, 1962);

Religion and Art, The Aquinas Lecture, 1963 (Milwaukee: Marquette University Press, 1963);

The God We Seek (Carbondale: Southern Illinois University Press, 1964);

Philosophy in Process, 11 volumes in 12 (volumes 1–7, part 1, Carbondale: Southern Illinois University Press, 1966–1978; volumes 7, part 2, and 8–11, Albany: State University of New York Press, 1983–1988);

Right and Wrong: A Philosophical Dialogue between Father and Son, by Weiss and Jonathan Weiss (New York: Basic Books, 1967);

The Making of Men (Carbondale: Southern Illinois University Press, 1967);

Sport: A Philosophic Inquiry (Carbondale: Southern Illinois University Press, 1969);

Philosophical Interrogations (New York: Holt, Rinehart & Winston, 1970);

Beyond All Appearances (Carbondale: Southern Illinois University Press, 1974);

Cinematics (Carbondale: Southern Illinois University Press, 1975);

First Considerations: An Examination of Philosophical Evidence, by Weiss and Abner Shimony (Carbondale: Southern Illinois University Press, 1977);

Paul Weiss

You, I, and the Others (Carbondale: Southern Illinois University Press, 1980);

Privacy (Carbondale: Southern Illinois University Press, 1983);

Toward a Perfected State (Albany: State University of New York Press, 1986);

Creative Ventures (Carbondale: Southern Illinois University Press, 1992);

Being and Other Realities (Chicago: Open Court, 1995);

Emphatics (Nashville: Vanderbilt University Press, 2000);

Surrogates (Bloomington: Indiana University Press, 2002).

OTHER: "Entailment and the Future of Logic," in *Proceedings of the Seventh International Congress of Philosophy, Held at Oxford, England, September 1–6, 1930,* edited by Gilbert Ryle (London: H. Milford, Oxford University Press, 1931), pp. 143–150;

Collected Papers of Charles Sanders Peirce, 6 volumes, edited by Weiss and Charles Hartshorne (Cambridge, Mass.: Harvard University Press, 1931–1935);

"A Memorandum for a System of Philosophy," in *American Philosophy Today and Tomorrow,* edited by Sidney Hook and Horace M. Kallen (New York: Furman, 1935);

"The Nature and Status of Time and Passage," in *Philosophical Essays for Alfred North Whitehead, February Fifteenth, Nineteen Hundred and Thirty-six* (London & New York: Longmans, Green, 1936), pp. 153–173;

"God and the World," in *Science, Philosophy and Religion: A Symposium* (New York: Conference on Science, Philosophy and Religion in Their Relation to the Democratic Way of Life, 1941), pp. 379–436;

"Democracy and the Rights of Man," in *Science, Philosophy, and Religion: Second Symposium* (New York: Conference on Science, Philosophy and Religion in Their Relation to the Democratic Way of Life, 1942), pp. 273–296;

"Art and Henry Miller," in *The Happy Rock,* edited by Bern Porter (Big Sur, Cal.: Porter Press, 1944);

"Freedom and Rights," in *Perspectives on a Troubled Decade: Science, Philosophy, and Religion, 1939–1949. Tenth Symposium,* edited by Lyman Bryson, Louis Finkelstein, and Robert M. MacIver (New York: Harper, 1950), pp. 507–530;

"The Logic of the Creative Process," in *Studies in the Philosophy of Charles Sanders Peirce,* edited by Philip P. Wiener and F. H. Young (Cambridge, Mass.: Harvard University Press, 1952), pp. 166–182;

"Some Neglected Ethical Questions," in *Moral Principles of Action: Man's Ethical Imperative,* edited by Ruth Nanda Anshen (New York: Harper, 1952), pp. 207–220;

"Persons, Places and Things," in *Moments of Personal Discovery,* edited by MacIver (New York: Institute for Religious and Social Studies, 1953), pp. 47–60;

"The New Outlook," in *American Philosophers at Work: The Philosophic Scene in the United States,* edited by Hook (New York: Criterion, 1956), pp. 301–314;

"Common Sense and Beyond," in *Determinism and Freedom in the Age of Modern Science: A Philosophical Symposium,* edited by Hook (New York: New York University Press, 1958), pp. 218–224;

"Love in a Machine Age," in *Dimensions of Mind: A Symposium,* edited by Hook (New York: New York University Press, 1960), pp. 193–197;

"Thank God, God's Not Impossible," in *Religious Experience and Truth: A Symposium,* edited by Hook (New York: New York University Press, 1961), pp. 83–89;

"History and Objective Immortality," in *The Relevance of Whitehead: Philosophical Essays in Commemoration of the Centenary of the Birth of Alfred North Whitehead,* edited by Ivor Leclerc (London: Allen & Unwin / New York: Macmillan, 1961), pp. 319–332;

"It's about Time," in *Philosophy and History: A Symposium,* edited by Hook (New York: New York University Press, 1963), pp. 367–371 ;

"The Right to Disobey," in *Law and Philosophy: A Symposium,* edited by Hook (New York: New York University Press, 1964);

"C. S. Peirce, Philosopher," in *Perspectives on Peirce: Critical Essays on Charles Sanders Peirce,* edited by Richard J. Bernstein (New Haven: Yale University Press, 1965);

"The Economics of Economists," in *Human Values and Economic Policy: A Symposium,* edited by Hook (New York: New York University Press, 1967);

"Some Paradoxes Relating to Order," in *The Concept of Order,* edited by Paul G. Kuntz (Seattle: Published for Grinnell College by Washington University Press, 1968), pp. 14–20;

"Introduction to Metaphysics," in *The Future of Metaphysics,* edited by Robert E. Wood (Chicago: Quadrangle, 1970);

"On What There Is beyond the Things There Are," in *Contemporary American Philosophy,* second series, edited by John Edwin Smith (London: Allen & Unwin / New York: Humanities Press, 1970), pp. 82–92;

"Science and Religion," in *Evolution in Perspective: Commentaries in Honor of Pierre Lecomte du Noüy,* edited by George N. Schuster and Ralph E. Thorson (Notre Dame, Ind.: University of Notre Dame Press, 1971), pp. 146–154;

"Wood in Aesthetics and Art," in *Design and Aesthetics in Wood,* edited by Erica A. Anderson and George F. Earle (Syracuse: State University of New York, College of Environmental Science and Forestry, 1972), pp. 19–25;

"The Philosophic Quest," in *Mid-Twentieth Century American Philosophy: Personal Statements,* edited by Peter Anthony Bertocci (New York: Humanities Press, 1974), pp. 240–245;

"Some Pivotal Issues in Spinoza," in *The Philosophy of Baruch Spinoza,* edited by Richard Kennington

(Washington, D.C.: Catholic University of America Press, 1980), pp. 3–13;

"Nature, God and Man," in *Existence and Actuality: Conversations with Charles Hartshorne,* edited by John B. Cobb Jr. and Franklin I. Gamwell (Chicago: University of Chicago Press, 1984), pp. 113–121;

"Lost in Thought: Alone with Others," "Reply to Hans Lenk," "Reply to John Lachs," "Reply to Daniel O. Dahlstrom," "Reply to Paul G. Kuntz," "Reply to Andrew J. Reck," "Reply to George R. Lucas," "Reply to Thomas R. Flynn," "Reply to Nathan Rotenstreich," "Reply to Sandra Rosenthal," "Reply to Kevin Kennedy," "Reply to Jay Schulkin," "Reply to Eric Walther," "Reply to David Weissman," "Reply to Abner Shimony," "Reply to Jacqueline Ann K. Kegley," "Reply to Eugene Thomas Long," "Reply to Robert Cummings Neville," "Reply to Robert L. Castiglione," "Reply to Eugenio Benitez," "Reply to Richard L. Barber," "Reply to Antonio S. Cua," "Reply to Thomas Krettek," "Reply to William Desmond," "Reply to George Kimball Plochmann," "Reply to Carl R. Hausman," "Reply to Robert E. Wood," "Reply to Daniel A. Dombrowski," and "Reply to S. K. Wertz," in *The Philosophy of Paul Weiss,* edited by Lewis Edwin Hahn, The Library of Living Philosophers, volume 23 (Chicago: Open Court, 1995), pp. 3–45, 64–71, 84–91, 110–116, 133–138, 153–158, 177–182, 201–209, 224–228, 244–251, 269–274, 289–294, 307–311, 324–329, 349–353, 368–372, 384–388, 415–425, 453–457, 472–477, 489–493, 515–521, 538–542, 558–564, 585–590, 608–613, 630–635, 655–660, 675–679.

SELECTED PERIODICAL PUBLICATIONS–
UNCOLLECTED: "Relativity in Logic," *Monist,* 38 (October 1928): 536–548;

"The Theory of Types," *Mind,* 37 (1928): 338–348;

"The Nature of Systems," *Monist,* 39 (April 1929): 281–319; (July 1929): 440–472;

"Two-Valued Logic–Another Approach," *Erkenntnis,* 2 (1931): 242–261;

"The Metaphysics and Logic of Classes," *Monist,* 42 (January 1932): 112–154;

"The Metaphysical and the Logical Individual," *Journal of Philosophy,* 30 (25 May 1933): 288–293;

"On Alternative Logics," *Philosophical Review,* 42 (September 1933): 520–525;

"Metaphysics: The Domain of Ignorance," *Philosophical Review,* 43 (July 1934): 402–406;

"Time and Absolute," *Journal of Philosophy,* 32 (23 May 1935): 286–290;

"Toward a Cosmological Ethics," *Journal of Philosophy,* 35 (24 November 1938): 645–651;

"The Self Contradictory," *Philosophical Review,* 48 (1938): 531–533;

"The Locus of Responsibility," *Ethics,* 49 (April 1939): 349–355;

"The Meaning of Existence," *Philosophy and Phenomenological Research,* 1 (1940): 191–198;

"The Essence of Peirce's System," *Journal of Philosophy,* 37 (9 May 1940): 253–264;

"Adventurous Humility," *Ethics,* 51 (April 1941): 337–348;

"An Introduction to a Study of Instruments," *Philosophy of Science,* 8 (July 1941): 287–296;

"The Golden Rule," *Journal of Philosophy,* 38 (31 July 1941): 421–430;

"Midway between Traditionalism and Progressivism," *School and Society,* 53 (1941): 651–763;

"Freedom of Choice," *Ethics,* 3 (January 1942): 186–199;

"The Logic of Semantics," *Journal of Philosophy,* 39 (26 March 1942): 169–177;

"The Purpose of Purposes," *Philosophy of Science,* 9 (April 1942): 162–165;

"Morality and Ethics," *Journal of Philosophy,* 39 (2 July 1942): 381–385;

"Cosmic Behaviorism," *Philosophical Review,* 51 (July 1942): 345–356;

"Habits, Instincts and Reflexes," *Philosophy of Science,* 9 (July 1942): 268–274;

"The Ethics of Pacifism," *Philosophical Review,* 51 (September 1942): 476–496;

"Charles Sanders Peirce," *Sewanee Review,* 50 (1942): 184–192;

"Beauty, Individuality and Personality," *Personalist,* 23 (1942): 34–43;

"Pain and Pleasure," *Philosophy and Phenomenological Research,* 3 (1942): 137–144;

"Sources of the Idea of God," *Journal of Religion,* 22 (1942): 156–172;

"The Social Character of Gestures," *Philosophical Review,* 53 (March 1943): 182–186;

"Determinism in Will and Nature," *Journal of Liberal Religion,* 4, no. 4 (1943): 206–211;

"Issues in Ethical Theory: Some Presuppositions of an Aristotelian Ethics," *American Journal of Economics and Sociology,* 2 (1943): 245–254;

"History and the Historian," *Journal of Philosophy,* 42 (29 March 1945): 169–179;

"Peirce's Sixty-Six Signs," by Weiss and Arthur Burks, *Journal of Philosophy,* 42 (5 July 1945): 383–388;

"The Universal Ethical Standard," *Ethics,* 56 (October 1945): 38–48;

"The Quest for Certainty," *Philosophical Review,* 55 (March 1946): 132–151;

"The True, the Good, and the New," *Commentary,* 2 (October 1946): 310–316;

"Philosophy and Faith," *Journal of Religion,* 26 (October 1946): 278–282;

"Social, Legal and Ethical Responsibility," *Ethics,* 57 (July 1947): 259–273;

"Being, Essence and Existence," *Review of Metaphysics,* 1 (September 1947): 69–92;

"Existenz and Hegel," *Philosophy and Phenomenological Research,* 8 (December 1947): 206–216;

"Immortality," *Review of Metaphysics,* 1 (June 1948): 87–103;

"Job, God and Evil," *Commentary,* 6 (August 1948): 144–151;

"Sacrifice and Self-Sacrifice," *Review of Metaphysics,* 2 (March 1949): 76–98;

"Otis H. Lee" and "Alfred North Whitehead," *Philosophical Review,* 58 (September 1949): 465–466, 468–469;

"Good and Evil," *Review of Metaphysics,* 3 (September 1949): 81–94;

"Some Epochs of Western Civilization," *Et Veritas,* 4 (December 1949): 8–18;

"Law and Other Matters," *Review of Metaphysics,* 4 (December 1950): 131–135;

"Cosmic Necessities," *Review of Metaphysics,* 4 (March 1951): 359–375;

"The Prediction Paradox," *Mind,* 51 (April 1952): 265–269;

"The Nature and Status of the Past" and "Some Theses of Empirical Certainty," *Review of Metaphysics,* 5 (June 1952): 507–522, 627;

"The Perception of Stars," *Review of Metaphysics,* 6 (December 1952): 233–238;

"On the Responsibility of the Architect," *Perspecta: The Yale Architectural Journal,* 2 (1953): 51–55;

"The Contemporary World," *Review of Metaphysics,* 6 (June 1953): 525–538;

"Grünbaum's Relativity and Ontology," *Review of Metaphysics,* 7 (September 1953): 124–125;

"The Past: Some Recent Discussions," *Review of Metaphysics,* 7 (December 1953): 299–306;

"Man's Inalienable Rights," *Ixyun,* 5 (January 1954): 129–130;

"The Four Dimensions of Reality," *Review of Metaphysics,* 7 (June 1954): 558–562;

"Guilt, God and Perfection, I," *Review of Metaphysics,* 7 (September 1954): 30–48;

"The Gita, East and West," *Philosophy East and West,* 5 (October 1954): 253–258;

"Guilt, God and Perfection, II," *Review of Metaphysics,* 8 (December 1954): 246–263;

"Real Possibility," *Review of Metaphysics,* 9 (June 1955): 669–670;

"Greek, Hebrew and Christian," *Judaism,* 4, no. 2 (1955): 116–123;

"The Paradox of Necessary Truth Once More," *Philosophical Studies,* 7, no. 6 (1956): 88–89;

"On Being Together," *Review of Metaphysics,* 9 (March 1956): 391–403;

"The Fortunate Philosophers," *Yale Alumni Journal* (June 1956): 20;

"On the Difference between Actuality and Possibility," *Review of Metaphysics,* 10 (September 1956): 165–171;

"The Nature and Locus of Natural Law," *Journal of Philosophy,* 53 (8 November 1956): 713–721;

"The Real Art Object," *Philosophy and Phenomenological Research,* 16, no. 3 (1956): 341–352;

"A Reconciliation of the Religions: A Non-Ironic Proposal," *Journal of Religion,* 26, no. 1 (1956): 36–44;

"Ten Theses Relating to Existence," *Review of Metaphysics,* 10 (March 1957): 401–411;

"Eighteen Theses in Logic," *Review of Metaphysics,* 11 (September 1957): 12–27;

"Philosophy and the Curriculum of a University," *Journal of General Education,* 11, no. 3 (1958): 141–145;

"The Semantics of Truth Today and Tomorrow," *Philosophical Studies,* 9 (January–February 1958): 21–23;

"The Paradox of Obligation," *Journal of Philosophy,* 55 (27 March 1958): 291–292;

"Art, Substance and Reality," *Review of Metaphysics,* 12, no. 3 (1960): 365–382;

"Man's Existence," *International Philosophy Quarterly,* 1 (1961): 547–568;

"Historic Time," *Review of Metaphysics,* 15 (June 1962): 578–585;

"Weiss Asks Coffins: 'Is Christianity Necessary?'" *Yale News and Review,* 1 (September 1962): 8–9;

"Twenty-Two Reasons for Continuing as Before," *Philosophical Studies,* 13 (October 1962): 65–68;

"Religious Experience," *Review of Metaphysics,* 17 (September 1963): 3–17;

"The Use of Ideas," *Review of Metaphysics,* 17 (December 1963): 200–204;

"The Religious Turn," *Judaism,* 13 (Winter 1963): 3–27;

"Our Knowledge of What Is Real," *Review of Metaphysics,* 18 (September 1964): 3–22;

"Types of Finality," *Journal of Philosophy,* 64 (5 October 1967): 584–593;

"Equal and Separate but Integrated," *Proceedings of the American Catholic Philosophical Association,* 29 (1967): 5–17;

"Sport and Its Participants," *Science*, 161 (September 1968): 1161–1162;

"Paul Weiss' Recollections of Editing the Peirce Papers," *Transactions of the Charles S. Peirce Society*, 6, nos. 3–4 (1970): 161–187;

"The Distinctive Nature of Man," *Idealistic Studies*, 1, no. 2 (1971): 89–101;

"Bestowed, Acquired, and Native Rights," *Proceedings of the American Catholic Philosophical Association*, 49 (1975): 138–149;

"Reason, Mind, Body and World," *Review of Metaphysics*, 30 (December 1976): 325–334;

"The God of Religion, Theology and Mysticism," *Logos: Philosophical Issues in Christian Perspective*, 1 (1980);

"Second Thoughts on First Considerations," *Process Studies*, 10 (Spring–Summer 1980): 34–38;

"Truth and Reality," *Review of Metaphysics*, 34 (September 1980): 57–69;

"The Game as a Solution to the Problem of the One and the Many," *Journal of the Philosophy of Sport*, 7 (Fall 1980): 7–14;

"Things in Themselves," *Review of Metaphysics*, 39 (September 1985): 23–46;

"Induction: Its Nature, Justification and Presupposition," *Journal of Speculative Philosophy*, 1, no. 1 (1987): 6–23;

"Dunamis," *Review of Metaphysics*, 40 (June 1987): 657–674;

"On the Impossibility of Artificial Intelligence," *Review of Metaphysics*, 44 (December 1990): 335–342.

Weiss, circa 1937 (Special Collections Research Center, Morris Library, Southern Illinois University, Carbondale)

The Harvard University philosopher C. I. Lewis observed in an 11 January 1946 letter to F. S. C. Northrop of Yale University that had Paul Weiss done nothing else, his co-editing with Charles Hartshorne of the first six volumes of the *Collected Papers of Charles Sanders Peirce* (1931–1935) would have secured him "a fairly high place in the present generation of American scholars in philosophy." Weiss was, however, a singular intellect in his own right, and his place in the history of American philosophy rests not on his editorial work or on his synthetic abilities but on the fact that he is widely acknowledged to be one of America's great creative thinkers and premier philosophers. In the introduction to his unpublished manuscript "The Offense and the Vision: The Life and Work of Paul Weiss" Robert L. Castiglione says that "Weiss is the most creative and visionary philosopher on the American continent since Peirce; he is the most tenaciously logical, imaginative and systematic Western thinker since Hegel; and the most accepting of the truths of ordinary men and women since William James." Weiss is regarded by many as having saved metaphysics for America not only by his founding of the Metaphysical Society of America and the journal *Review of Metaphysics* but also by his own resolute rethinking of such fundamental metaphysical issues as the nature of individuals, the possibility of knowing and using transcendents or ultimates, the acknowledgment of ideal objectives and their realization, the use of intensive moves to get beyond surfaces, and the identification of diverse types of reality.

Weiss's thought challenges the tediousness of much contemporary and American philosophy. Although he is not as widely known as some of his contemporaries, his work is without peer in American philosophical literature. As Mortimer Adler said in 1986 in honoring Weiss on his eighty-fifth birthday (the remark is quoted in the introduction to *Creativity and Common Sense: Essays in Honor of Paul Weiss* [1987], edited by Thomas Krettek), "In the arid desert of academic philosophy, in the twentieth century, there is one lovely flower and one sparkling oasis. The beauty of Paul's mind is that flower. That oasis is in Paul's books. Wisdom can be found there for those who thirst after it."

Weiss (third from right) at Harvard University in 1939 with Raphael Demos,
Cornelius Benjamin, Ernest Nagel, Haskell Curry, and Morris Cohen

Weiss was born on 19 May 1901 on Manhattan's Lower East Side to Samuel Weiss, a laborer, and Emma Rothschild Weiss. He had one older brother and two younger ones. Like many immigrant families (Samuel was from Hungary, Emma from Germany), the Weisses were poor; but they were able to move to the somewhat more upscale Yorkville section of the city when Weiss was eight. Although Weiss was not an observant Jew, his Jewish heritage influenced his thought. Another formative influence was his mother's interest in intellectual matters, art, and culture. As a child Weiss was, as he told Castiglione, "manic" and bombarded with many disorganized thoughts. Something of his philosophic temperament was evident from the age of six or seven in his questioning how all English words could come from so few letters in the alphabet. His mother died in 1915 and his father in 1917.

Weiss graduated from P.S. 77 and went on to the High School of Commerce. After three years of failing grades he became disenchanted with school, and for the next seven years he worked in various offices as a stenographer. At one point he tried to enlist in the military but was turned down. During this period he became an avid but eclectic reader and began to study proverbs as a way of ordering his thinking. In 1923, after a Japanese salesman told him that his reading and questions indi-

cated that he was interested in philosophy, he began studying the subject in the evening division of the City College of New York.

Weiss won the Kenyon Prize in Philosophy in the spring of 1924. A remark by his teacher, John Pickett Turner, led him to enroll as a full-time day student the following term. He began with a course from Morris Raphael Cohen, who stimulated his appetite for logic and aroused in him an interest in Peirce. He published articles in the college's literary magazine, *The Lavender,* of which he became editor, and in *The Open Court* magazine; he also wrote book reviews for *The New Republic* and *The Nation.* Weiss graduated cum laude and Phi Beta Kappa in February 1927 and immediately went on to Harvard University to study with Alfred North Whitehead. On 27 October 1928 he married Victoria Brodkin, whom he had met in 1926. They had two children: Judith, born in 1935, and Jonathan, born in 1939.

Weiss's primary academic interest was in logic, which he studied under Whitehead and Lewis; he published two articles on the subject in 1928. Weiss was inspired and challenged by Whitehead, and over the years the Weisses became good friends of Whitehead and his wife, Evelyn. Weiss also studied with Etienne Gilson, who gave him an appreciation of the history of philosophy and was largely responsible for his later ability to span the secular and Catholic worlds in American philosophy. While still in graduate school he volunteered to help Hartshorne organize Peirce's unpublished manuscripts; he later became co-editor of the first six volumes of the *Collected Papers of Charles Sanders Peirce*.

Weiss received his doctorate in 1929 with the dissertation "The Nature of Systems," in which he examined issues related to the formulation of a general theory of symbolic systems. After a trip to Europe, which included a brief and unsatisfying meeting with the German phenomenologist Martin Heidegger, he became an instructor at Harvard and its women's college, Radcliffe. In 1931 he accepted a position as an associate in philosophy at Bryn Mawr College. A popular lecturer with a stimulating and provocative style, he conveyed to his students a sense of the importance of philosophy and encouraged them to join him in the enterprise by thinking for themselves. He was an active member of Philadelphia's philosophical society, the Fullerton Club. He was promoted to associate professor in 1933.

Weiss's early articles reflected his interest in logical terms, principles, and relations, but "The Metaphysical and the Logical Individual," published in *The Journal of Philosophy* in 1933, heralded a shift from consideration of the "logical" to a study of the concretely real, private individual. In this article he introduces the fundamental commonsense fact that he could never meet himself coming toward himself; he returned often to this existential insight. The article signaled Weiss's rejection of the positivist, process, and pragmatist approaches to philosophical questions and committed him to a method of philosophizing that makes him unique among American philosophers.

Weiss completed his work on the Peirce papers at Bryn Mawr, with volumes two through six being published between 1932 and 1935. In *The Journal of Philosophy* (March 1935) H. G. Townsend praised the work as a vital source for the study not only of Peirce but also of the origins and early development of pragmatism. Weiss's more systematic interpretation of Peirce's thought in terms of logic and metaphysics, however, brought him into conflict with such notable pragmatist interpreters of Peirce as Sidney Hook and Justus Buchler. Weiss's editorial work deepened his perspective on fundamental philosophical issues.

In "The Nature and Status of Time and Passage" (1936) Weiss holds that "to be," for actualities, "is to be incomplete." He carries this idea forward in his first book, *Reality* (1938), which presents the nucleus of the ontological, epistemological, and ethical issues that occupied him for the next sixty years. He upholds common sense as the origin and test of any inquiry and reflection, whether in science, mathematics, or philoso-

Dust jacket for Weiss's 1950 book, in which he identifies the principles of equality, kinship, familial autonomy, and social freedom as essential to a good life (Reason Alone Books)

phy. Ontology and epistemology are presented as providing mutually reciprocating questions and answers. For Weiss, "incompletion-seeking-to-be-complete" is the basic ontological status of an actuality, but human beings can become "self-complete" through knowledge and moral action. Weiss discusses perception, knowledge, reasoning, truth and falsity, mind and body, self-identity, the individual, and virtue; the unique and legitimate claims of science, mathematics, art, and religion, as well as common sense and speculation, to disclose the nature of the real; the nature of time, space, and causation; the private and public aspects of human nature; and the relationship of the one to the many and the part to the whole. Weiss's keen analytic and synthetic powers enable him to separate out from competing philosophical positions insights that are worth retaining and to weave them dialectically into a stronger and more adequate view. Although Harry Ruja, the reviewer for the journal *Ethics* (April 1939), held that Weiss's endeavor to provide "a conceptual analysis of

Dust jacket for the first volume of Weiss's two-volume 1958 work of metaphysics, in which he argues for the acceptance of four primary realities: Actuality, Ideality, Existence, and God (Collection of Philip B. Dematteis)

the most generic and fundamental traits of reality" was significant, *Reality* did not sell well and was not well received by the larger philosophic community, including Whitehead.

Weiss was promoted to full professor in 1940. He became chairman of the philosophy department in 1944.

Weiss translated his philosophical positions into political views with results similar to those that he attained with *Reality*. He came into conflict with fellow liberals and legal theorists with a defense of equality and rights that was based on a common human nature rather than on individual desires. During World War II he challenged both militarists and pacifists pointing out both the merits and the defects of their respective positions. Because of his ability to separate the philosophy from the philosopher, Weiss played an important role in inviting Bertrand Russell to Bryn Mawr for a lecture series when Russell was living in the United States during the war; at that time Russell was regarded

with disfavor by American politicians and philosophers who considered his ideas on sex and marriage immoral.

In 1945 Brand Blanshard, who was facing the prospect of surgery, invited Weiss to replace him at Yale University. Weiss was appointed a visiting professor, and in the fall of 1946 he was the first Jew to become a tenured full professor in Yale's undergraduate school. That same year he was one of the founding members of the Charles Sanders Peirce Society. Weiss challenged the subtle and not so subtle forms of social discrimination at Yale, and he formed lasting friendships with such prominent figures as Northrop, the literary biographer Richard B. Sewall, the psychotherapist Jerome Frank, the future conservative writer and publisher William F. Buckley Jr., the philosopher Irwin C. Lieb, and the philosopher and future chancellor of Boston University John Silber.

Weiss's second book, *Nature and Man,* was published in 1947 as the first volume of a two-volume work on ethics. Attempting to preserve what is worthwhile in both the Aristotelian and the modern traditions and to go beyond them to ground a credible naturalist ethics, Weiss argues that freedom exists even in the transition from cause to effect in nature. Human freedom is only one manifestation of the freedom characteristic of all realities. Hartshorne in *Ethics* (January 1948) and Leo R. Ward in *The Review of Politics* (April 1948) praised the book for its consideration of crucial ethical issues but reacted unfavorably to its metaphysical aspects.

Also in 1947 Weiss—instead of starting a periodical devoted to his own thought, as proposed by a student—began *The Review of Metaphysics* as a journal to deal with neglected thinkers and aspects of philosophy. In 1950 he founded the Metaphysical Society of America.

In *Man's Freedom* (1950), the second volume of his work on ethics, Weiss calls his approach an "epochalism" that takes seriously the occurrence of crisis points that result in radically novel changes. Although "genuine unpredictable becoming" exists and allows for novelty, Weiss holds that an explanatory and predictive science of human beings is possible. Human freedom, which Weiss calls "static" or "native freedom," is "an intelligible process by which the indeterminate, the possible, the future, the good, is made determinate, actual, present; it is an activity by which the general is specified, specialized, delimited, given one of a number of possible concrete shapes." The most important of those manifestations are preference, choice, and will. The will's creative use of freedom to bring about absolute goodness is the way to human self-completion. A basic ethical truth is that it is absolutely wrong to reduce values. Weiss identifies the principles of equality, kinship, familial autonomy, and social freedom, along with the rights that these principles entail, as essential to a good life. Henry Nelson Weiman in the *Annals of the American Academy of Social and Political Science* (November 1950) called the book penetrating, thorough, and innovative.

Weiss was a visiting professor at Hebrew University in Jerusalem in 1951 and lectured at the Aspen Institute and the University of Denver in 1952. His wife died in 1953. Weiss returned to Hebrew University as Orde Wingate Lecturer in 1954. On 24 June 1955 he began the philosophical/autobiographical journal that was published in eleven volumes (one of them a two-part volume) from 1966 to 1988 as *Philosophy in Process;* the final entry in the first volume is for 25 December 1955. The volumes are valuable records of an eminent thinker's daily struggles with philosophical issues.

Weiss delivered the Powell Lectures at Indiana University in 1958. That same year he published his ambitious work of metaphysics, *Modes of Being,* in which he argues for the acceptance of four primary realities: Actuality, Ideality, Existence, and God. Each is an irreducible mode of being with its own integrity and career, but each is incomplete: all are required if the nature of the universe is to be intelligible. Actualities are limited spatiotemporal-dynamic beings, each of which strives to complete itself by realizing indeterminate objectives provided by Ideality, which is a common future Good. Existence is sheer vitality, both immanent in and transcending other realities and enabling actualities to be spatially and temporally copresent and fixated on the Ideal. God, the eternal assessing and unifying ground of all that is, secures the realization of the Ideal and the perfection of actualities. While they are dynamically related to one another, each mode retains its own character: their interplay does not constitute a new entity.

While noting the originality of Weiss's approach and his illuminating observations on art, morals, culture, and religion, George L. Kline in *Ethics* (October 1958) questioned the usefulness of his ontological categories and deemed his attempt to devise a system to make sense of everything a failure. In *The Review of Metaphysics* (June 1958) John Wild called the book provocative and suggestive and judged it to be a metaphysics on the grand scale.

Our Public Life (1959) focuses on the mode of Ideality as it enters into human experience and manifests itself in politics. In the manner of Plato in the *Republic,* Weiss uses a method of "dialectical construction" to "present a likely story of how men might ideally get together and progressively fulfill themselves." He shows how humans move from society, culture, and state to civilization in their effort to become self-complete. Civilization, "a realm which includes all mankind so far as it is engaged in peaceful and liberal activities, among which are the pursuit of the arts and sciences," makes a

Weiss circa 1964 (Special Collections Research Center, Morris Library, Southern Illinois University, Carbondale)

human individual as complete as a public being can be. Weiss elaborates his thinking on the natures of individuals and social groups, natural and civil law, rights, the individual's relation to society, and the Absolute Good. Reviews by social scientists George E. Gordon Catlin in *The American Political Science Review* (June 1960), William W. Hollister in *The American Scholar* (Winter 1959–1960), and Ralph H. Gabriel in *Annals of the American Academy of Social and Political Sciences* (May 1960) discounted *Our Public Life* as a significant contribution to the solution of political problems, but the philosopher Eliseo Vivas in *Ethics* (January 1960) considered it a fresh, bold, and imaginative continuation of the tradition of classical political philosophy. The reviewer particularly commented on Weiss's treatment of natural law.

Weiss was Gates Lecturer at Grinnell College in 1960 and the Matchette Foundation Lecturer at Purdue University in 1961. The second volume (1966) of *Philosophy in Process* covers the years 1960 to 1964. Many of the entries are systematic essays expanding on topics raised in *Modes of Being.* The volume also includes Weiss's thoughts leading to the writing of his works on art, history, and religion. Volumes three (1968) and four (1969) cover a year and a half in 1964–1965 and

THE GOD WE SEEK

Paul Weiss

Dust jacket for Weiss's 1964 book, in which he tries to move beyond the specialized rituals of various religions "to isolate the pure undistorted relation men have to God" (Reason Alone Books)

offer further examination of themes developed in *Modes of Being*. Reviewing the first three volumes in *The Review of Metaphysics* (June 1968), Andrew J. Reck likened *Philosophy in Process* to Gabriel Marcel's *Journal métaphysique* (1927; translated as *Metaphysical Journal,* 1952) and *Être et avoir* (1935; translated as *Being and Having: An Existentialist Diary,* 1965) and Ludwig Wittgenstein's *Notebooks, 1914–1916* (1961).

In *Reality* Weiss had claimed a legitimate role for art in revealing the nature of the real. Two closely related books on art, *The World of Art* and *Nine Basic Arts,* were published in 1961. Rejecting a common interpretation that understands art as producing only semblances, rather than truth and reality, Weiss argues in *The World of Art* that art and artistic creation teach basic truths about human beings and the world. Bringing to bear his own engagement in painting and other forms of artistic activity, Weiss says that art exists in an interplay between structure and creativity. Referring to the categories he developed in *Modes of Being,* he says that art makes Existence concrete and humanly pertinent by

representing the space, time, and dynamics of daily experience and that it embodies the Ideal in a sensuous guise. He examines the relationships between art, on the one hand, and the emotions, science, religion, politics, philosophy, ethics, and natural objects, on the other hand. *Nine Basic Arts* distinguishes arts into kinds on the basis of how they creatively use and transform time, space, and becoming. The human drive for self-completion manifests itself in the restructuring of emotions by art. Reviewers in *Ethics* and *The Review of Metaphysics* commended the books as original, clear, coherent, and informed presentations of the arts, their relation to emotion, and the metaphysical features of the real. Each was reprinted several times.

In 1962 Weiss published *History: Written and Lived,* in which, contrary to most other philosophers of history, he argues that the historian can know the past because of the causal relationship between it and the present. The "historic world" is the outcome of the interaction of nonhistoric items; it makes public rather than private use of Existence. The "historic ought-to-be," as a delimited form of the absolute Good, offers a standard of excellence that is the norm for assessing events and actions. God preserves the freedom of the present by making the past an irreducible objective reality that excludes it. Historical knowledge is uniquely self-completing, while history itself is the "process of civilizing mankind." Leonard Krieger in *The American Historical Review* (July 1963) judged *History: Written and Lived* to be valuable for anyone who was interested in Weiss's metaphysics but as failing to contribute to the contemporary discussion of issues in the philosophy of history. The anonymous reviewer for *Ethics* (January 1963), William Sacksteder in *Ethics* (October 1963), and Charles Frankel in *History and Theory* (1964), on the other hand, deemed it a major work in the philosophy of history that is more open, flexible, and contemporary than the writings of Benedetto Croce and R. G. Collingwood.

Weiss was the Matchette Lecturer at Wesleyan College in 1963. That same year Yale named Weiss Sterling Professor of Philosophy, its highest honor. Weiss returns to the subject of art in *Religion and Art* (1963), the published version of his 1963 Aquinas Lecture at Marquette University. He discusses the way in which art relates humans to God.

Weiss was Rhodes Lecturer at Haverford College in 1964. That year he published the last in his series of books based on *Modes of Being:* in *The God We Seek* Weiss endeavors to move beyond the specialized rituals of various religions "to isolate the pure undistorted relation men have to God." He depicts God as a constant lover who guarantees that the basic needs of humans, to love and to be loved, are fulfilled. *The God We Seek* was praised by the anonymous reviewer in *Ethics* (April 1965) and by James Collins in *The Review of Metaphysics* (December 1965) for its neutrality in regard to religious conflicts and its treatment of the phenomenon of becoming religious and of the religious community; one of the reviews placed it among "the finest analyses of the religious life available in philosophic literature."

Despite strong support from Weiss, Yale in 1965 refused tenure to Richard Bernstein. This situation made Weiss's final four years at Yale unhappy ones. Parts of volumes four and six (1975) and all of volume five (1974) of *Philosophy in Process* cover this period in Weiss's life.

In *Right and Wrong: A Philosophical Dialogue between Father and Son* (1967) Paul and Jonathan Weiss discuss human action and individual, familial, social, and political obligations. *Time* (19 January 1968) compared the book to St. Augustine's *De Magistro* (On the Teacher, written 387; published 1502; translated as *The Philosophy of Teaching: A Study in the Symbolism of Language,* 1924).

Also published in 1967, *The Making of Men* elaborates Weiss's concept of education as "philosophy made practical, philosophy lived through." The purpose of education is the preparation of an individual to live a full life as a self-completed being. Weiss says that schools are society's way of transforming itself, rather than, as John Dewey thought, of preserving itself. Thomas A. Duggan in *America* (11 November 1967) called Weiss's discussion of the place of philosophy in the educational process "articulate, comprehensive, clear and thought-provoking."

In preparation for writing *Sport: A Philosophic Inquiry* (1969) Weiss attended workouts and games and interviewed players, coaches, and spectators in various athletic endeavors. Weiss's understanding of education as perfective of the individual is carried further here to include fulfilling "the promise of the body." Athletics, he holds, enables one to encounter other modes of being and thereby to achieve a kind of self-completion that is not otherwise possible. The book was a best-seller. Joseph Ullian in *The Journal of Philosophy* (24 May 1973) considered Weiss's position inadequate at best; but the book received a laudatory review from Hans Lenk in the German journal *Sportswissenschaft,* was translated into Japanese, and led to the founding of a society and journal for the study of sport. It is now considered a classic.

Weiss retired from Yale in 1969. His former student Robert Cummings Neville, who was teaching at Fordham University, suggested that Weiss be offered the Schweitzer Chair in Humanities there. The offer did not materialize, and Weiss instead accepted the position of visiting Heffer Professor of Philosophy at The Catholic University of America. In 1971 Weiss

Dust jacket for the first volume of Weiss's eleven-volume philosophical/ autobiographical journal, which was published from 1966 to 1988. The first entry is dated 24 June 1954 and the final one 27 May 1987 (Collection of Philip B. Dematteis).

unsuccessfully sued Fordham for $1 million on the grounds of age discrimination and breach of contract. Volume six of *Philosophy in Process,* which begins on 28 August 1968 and ends on 22 May 1971, provides a partial record of this period.

Weiss's new environment led him to modify and make more rigorous his thinking on various fundamental philosophical issues. *Beyond All Appearances* (1974) begins this renewed examination by setting out the way in which one can move beyond appearances to arrive at ultimate realities. Weiss says that the book is a good introduction to *Modes of Being,* were the latter to be revised in the light of *Philosophy in Process.* He characterizes the cosmos as the law-abiding interplay of actualities and five "finalities": Substance, Being, Possibility, Existence, and Unity. Unlike any other beings, humans interact with all of the finalities. A human, Weiss says, is "a substance enriched with a being, nature, existence, and unity" and "an individual with rights, a trued self,

A Philosophical Dialogue
between Father and Son

Right & Wrong

PAUL WEISS and
JONATHAN WEISS

*Dust jacket for Weiss's 1967 book, in which he and his son discuss
human action and individual, familial, social, and political
obligations (Reason Alone Books)*

an identity, and an immortality." "G.F.R." in *The Review of Metaphysics* (March 1975) considered *Beyond All Appearances* an excellent work of speculative philosophy and recommended Weiss's treatment of epistemological issues and theory of symbolization for particular attention.

Weiss's next book, *Cinematics* (1975), extends his empirical and metaphysical analysis of art to motion pictures. It was praised by G.F.R. in *The Review of Metaphysics* (September 1975) and Arnold Berleant in *Philosophy and Phenomenological Research* (December 1977) for relating motion pictures to classical art.

First Considerations: An Examination of Philosophical Evidence (1977) is a short work that presents, Weiss says, "the musculature of a systematic account" of his thought. It supplements *Beyond All Appearances* by setting out the principles by which the interplay of actualities and finalities should be examined. The second part of the book includes invited criticisms of Weiss's ideas by other prominent philosophers and Weiss's replies to them. Volume seven, part one (1978) of *Philosophy in*

Process can be read as a companion volume to *Beyond All Appearances* and *First Considerations,* because it reevaluates and clarifies the theory of actualities and finalities systematically developed in those works. "R.N." in *The Review of Metaphysics* (March 1978), Irwin C. Lieb in *Process Studies* (Spring–Summer 1979), and Jere P. Surber in *The New Scholasticism* (Winter 1983) acknowledged *First Considerations* as an important work for anyone interested in fundamental philosophical questions and as a benchmark in metaphysical speculation.

You, I, and the Others (1980) presents a philosophy of language and a philosophy of the human person. Major themes of the work are "the you," which is the public means of access to the depth of another person; "the me," the public means of access to one's own depth; "the we," which enables individuals to be together in a variety of ways; the self as the private source of action; and the mutually presupposed relationship between oneself and others. Humans are characterized as complex public beings present in a world with others but rooted in privacy. Weiss shows speculative metaphysics to be the goal of the analysis of human language and experience. *You, I, and the Others* was praised by Daniel Dahlstrom in *The Thomist* (October 1981), Neville in the *International Philosophical Quarterly* (June 1981), and "A.B.W." in *The Review of Metaphysics* (December 1982) as brilliantly original in its analysis of personal pronouns and as ranking with St. Augustine's *Confessiones* (written 397–401; published 1465–1460?; translated as *The Confessions of the Incomparable Doctour S. Augustine,* 1620), Baruch Spinoza's *Ethica ordine geometrico demonstrata* (Ethics Demonstrated according to the Order of Geometry, 1677; translated as "Ethics," 1870), and Georg Wilhelm Friedrich Hegel's *Die Phänomenologie des Geistes* (1807; translated as *The Phenomenology of Mind,* 1910) for the way it relates selfhood to the rest of reality.

Privacy (1983) is concerned with Weiss's central ontological notion of humans as privately grounded beings. Here Weiss introduces his concept of the *"dunamis"* as a primal, dynamic continuum, the fragmentation of which is exhibited in the privacies of individual actualities. He deals with the self, responsibility, the inherent rights of humans as private beings, and human excellence. Edward Pols in *The Review of Metaphysics* (June 1984) said the book was as close to a commonsense account as a work by Aristotle and called it a challenge to contemporary philosophical orthodoxy. Volume eight (1984) of *Philosophy in Process* includes the reflections that led to the positions presented in *Privacy;* volume nine (1986) offers a further development of the notion of the *dunamis.*

In *Toward a Perfected State* (1986) Weiss discusses the legitimacy and authority of government and law.

He argues that societies and states can be improved if reasonable people recognize that they are rooted in realities that transcend them. Volume ten (1987) of *Philosophy in Process* presents Weiss's reflections during the writing of *Toward a Perfected State,* as well as a further clarification of the *dunamis.* Weiss's discussion of the Preamble to the United States Constitution is particularly important.

Despite health problems that included two major surgeries, Weiss published volume eleven (1988) of *Philosophy in Progress* and *Creative Ventures* (1992). In 1992 Catholic University declined to renew his contract; once again, Weiss charged age discrimination. This time he was assisted by his son, who was the director of Legal Services for the Elderly in New York. An investigation by the Equal Employment Opportunity Commission supported his claim; the university apologized; and he was reinstated. He retired in 1994. He went on to publish *Being and Other Realities* (1995), *Emphatics* (2000), and *Surrogates* (2002). He died on 5 July 2002 at the age of 101.

Paul Weiss's image of the philosopher as an individual suspended in a prison, shackled hand and foot, who turns to a similarly confined person and says "I have a plan" is a self-characterization. He consistently refused to be bound by philosophical conventions, and his works are a series of attempts to find new ways to deal with basic issues. Creativity always played a vital role, not only as a category in his understanding and interpretation of the real but also as an aspect of his own philosophizing. His more pluralistic, open-ended, nuanced, and multifaceted philosophy prepares the way for a richer philosophic future in the United States and abroad.

Interviews:
Ellen Haring, "Interrogation of Paul Weiss," in *Philosophical Interrogations,* edited by Sydney Rome and Beatrice Rome (New York: Holt, Rinehart & Winston, 1964), pp. 259–317;
S. Coffey, "Paul Weiss: 'Making It' in the Major Leagues," *Potomac Magazine of the Washington Post,* 10 January 1971.

Bibliography:
Thomas Krettek, "Publications of Paul Weiss," in *The Philosophy of Paul Weiss,* edited by Lewis Edwin Hahn, The Library of Living Philosophers, volume 23 (Chicago: Open Court, 1995), pp. 684–694.

References:
Keith Algozin, "Man and Sport," *Philosophy Today,* 20 (Fall 1976): 190–195;
William A. Banner, "Dialectic, Law, and Civilization," *Review of Metaphysics,* 13 (June 1960): 668–677;

Richard Bernstein, "Human Beings: Plurality and Togetherness," *Review of Metaphysics,* 34 (December 1981): 349–366;
Bernstein, "Paul Weiss's Recollections of Editing the Peirce Papers," *Transactions of the Charles S. Peirce Society,* 6 (Summer–Fall 1970): 161–188;
Robert W. Browning, "Weiss's Doctrine of Concern," *Review of Metaphysics,* 9 (December 1955): 328–358;
Robert L. Castiglione, "Paul Weiss' *Privacy:* The Rediscovery of Human Being," *Philosophy Today,* 28 (Spring 1984): 20–35;
Castiglione, "The Reality of the Past: A Comparison of the Philosophies of A. N. Whitehead and P. Weiss," dissertation, Catholic University of America, 1971;
Antonio S. Cua, "The Structure of Social Complexes," *Review of Metaphysics,* 41 (December 1987): 335–354;
Randolph M. Feezell, "Sport: Pursuit of Bodily Excellence of Play. An Examination of Paul Weiss's Account of Sport," *Modern Schoolman,* 58 (May 1981): 257–270;
Max Fisch, "Peirce and Leibnitz," *Journal of the History of Ideas,* 33 (July–September 1972): 485–496;
Warren P. Fraleigh, "On Weiss, on Records, and on the Significance of Athletic Records," *Philosophic Exchange,* 1 (Summer 1974): 105–111;
Adolf Grünbaum, "Relativity, Causality, and Weiss's Theory of Relations," *Review of Metaphysics,* 7 (September 1953): 115–122;
Lewis Edwin Hahn, ed., *The Philosophy of Paul Weiss,* The Library of Living Philosophers, volume 23 (Chicago: Open Court, 1995);
Norwood Russell Hanson, "On Being in Two Places at Once," *Review of Metaphysics,* 12 (September 1958): 3–18;
Leroy T. Howe, "One God, One Proof," *Southern Journal of Philosophy,* 6 (Winter 1968): 235–245;
Irdell Jenkins, "The Being and Meaning of Art," *Review of Metaphysics,* 14 (June 1961): 685–694;
James Keating, "The Ethics of Competition and Its Relation to Some Moral Problems of Athletics," *Philosophic Exchange,* 1 (Summer 1974): 5–20;
D. A. Kelly, "Peirce, Hartshorne, and Weiss," *Indian Philosophical Quarterly,* 4 (October 1976): 41–58;
Kevin Kennedy, "The Self and I: An Investigation of the Metaphysics of Personal Responsibility," dissertation, Catholic University of America, 1990;
Thomas Krettek, "Ontology, Individuals, and Rights in the Thought of Paul Weiss: A Critical Study," dissertation, Catholic University of America, 1987;

Krettek, ed., *Creativity and Common Sense: Essays in Honor of Paul Weiss* (Albany: State University of New York Press, 1987);

Paul G. Kuntz, "Aesthetics Applies to Sports as Well as to the Arts," *Philosophic Exchange,* 1 (Summer 1974): 25–39;

Kuntz, "The God We Find: The God of Abraham, the God of Anselm, and the God of Weiss," *Modern Schoolman,* 47 (May 1976): 433–453;

Kuntz, "Paul Weiss on Sports as Performing Arts," *International Philosophical Quarterly,* 17 (June 1977): 147–165;

Kuntz, "Paul Weiss: What Is a Philosophy of Sport?" *Philosophy Today,* 20 (Fall 1976): 170–189;

Kuntz, "Weiss's Search for Adequacy," *Modern Schoolman,* 46 (March 1969): 251–264;

John Lachs, "Consciousness and Weiss's Mind," *Review of Metaphysics,* 13 (December 1959): 259–270;

Robert Cummings Neville, "Paul Weiss's *Philosophy in Process,*" *Review of Metaphysics,* 24 (December 1970): 276–301;

Charner Perry, "A Metaphysical Ethics," *Review of Metaphysics,* 3 (June 1950): 523–533;

"The Philosophy of Paul Weiss," *Review of Metaphysics,* twenty-fifth anniversary supplement, 25 (June 1972);

Andrew J. Reck, "Paul Weiss–Systematic Metaphysics and Open Thinking," in his *The New American Philosophers* (Baton Rouge: Louisiana State University Press, 1968), pp. 315–344;

Nathan Rotenstreich, "Weiss's Historical Argument for the Existence of God," *Review of Metaphysics,* 8 (March 1955): 520–525;

Richard W. Rousseau, "Secular and Christian Images of Man," *Thought,* 47 (Summer 1972): 165–200;

C. Sanders, "Peirce's Sixty–Six Signs?" *Transactions of the Charles S. Peirce Society,* 6 (Winter 1970): 3–16;

Richard Schacht, "On Weiss, on Records, Athletic Activity, and the Athlete," *Philosophic Exchange,* 1 (Summer 1974): 99–103;

Kenneth L. Schmitz, "The Modes in Process," *Review of Metaphysics,* 21 (December 1964): 310–342;

George Schrader, "Weiss and the Problem of Togetherness," *Review of Metaphysics,* 10 (December 1956): 227–243;

Calvin O. Schrag, "The Meaning of History," *Review of Metaphysics,* 16 (June 1963): 703–717;

Michael J. Seidler, "Problems of Systems Epistemology," *International Philosophical Quarterly,* 19 (March 1979): 29–60;

Carolyn Thomas, "Toward an Experiential Sport Aesthetic," *Philosophic Exchange,* 1 (Summer 1974): 49–62;

Spencer K. Wertz, "Sports: VanderZwaag's View Appraised," *Journal of Thought,* 13 (November 1978): 300–309;

Robert E. Wood, "Weiss on Adumbration," *Philosophy Today,* 28 (Winter 1984): 339–348.

Papers:

The main collection of Paul Weiss's letters and manuscripts is in the Delyte W. Morris Library at Southern Illinois University at Carbondale. The Pusey Library at Harvard University and the library at Yale University also have collections of Weiss's letters.

Checklist of Further Readings

Ames, Van Meter. *Zen and American Thought*. Honolulu: University of Hawaii Press, 1962.

Ayer, A. J. *Philosophy in the Twentieth Century*. London: Weidenfeld & Nicolson, 1982; New York: Random House, 1982.

Bertocci, Peter Anthony, ed. *Mid-Twentieth Century American Philosophy: Personal Statements*. New York: Humanities Press, 1974.

Canfield, John V., ed. *Philosophy of Meaning, Knowledge, and Value in the Twentieth Century*. London & New York: Routledge, 1997.

Caws, Peter, ed. *Two Centuries of Philosophy in America*. Totowa, N.J.: Rowman & Littlefield / New York: Oxford University Press, 1980.

Cotkin, George. *Existential America*. Baltimore: Johns Hopkins University Press, 2002.

Deledalle, Gérard. *La philosophie américaine*. Lausanne: L'Age d'homme, 1983.

Diggins, John P. *The Promise of Pragmatism: Modernism and the Crisis of Knowledge and Authority*. Chicago: University of Chicago Press, 1994.

Donnell, Franklin H., ed. *Aspects of Contemporary American Philosophy*. Würzburg: Physica, 1965.

Edie, James M., ed. *Phenomenology in America: Studies in the Philosophy of Experience*. Chicago: Quadrangle, 1967.

Festenstein, Matthew. *Pragmatism and Political Theory: From Dewey to Rorty*. Chicago: University of Chicago Press, 1997.

Flower, Elizabeth, and Murray G. Murphey. *A History of Philosophy in America*, 2 volumes. New York: Capricorn, 1977.

Fulton, Ann. *Apostles of Sartre: Existentialism in America, 1945–1963*. Evanston, Ill.: Northwestern University Press, 1999.

Goodman, Russell B. *American Philosophy and the Romantic Tradition*. Cambridge: Cambridge University Press, 1990.

Gunn, Giles B. *Thinking across the American Grain: Ideology, Intellect, and the New Pragmatism*. Chicago: University of Chicago Press, 1992.

Hartshorne, Charles. *Creativity in American Philosophy*. Albany: State University of New York Press, 1984.

Helm, Bertrand P. *Time and Reality in American Philosophy*. Amherst: University of Massachusetts Press, 1985.

Hildebrand, David L. *Beyond Realism and Antirealism: John Dewey and the Neopragmatists*. Nashville: Vanderbilt University Press, 2003.

Hook, Sidney, ed. *American Philosophers at Work: The Philosophic Scene in the United States*. New York: Criterion, 1956.

Kaelin, Eugene F., and Calvin O. Schrag, eds. *American Phenomenology: Origins and Developments*. Dordrecht, Netherlands & Boston: Kluwer Academic, 1989.

Kasulis, Thomas P., and Robert Cummings Neville, eds. *The Recovery of Philosophy in America: Essays in Honor of John Edwin Smith*. Albany: State University of New York Press, 1997.

Krikorian, Yervant H. *Recent Perspectives in American Philosophy*. The Hague: Nijhoff, 1973.

Kuklick, Bruce. *A History of Philosophy in America, 1720–2000*. Oxford: Clarendon Press, 2001; New York: Oxford University Press, 2001.

Kurtz, Paul, ed. *The American Philosophers,* volume 2, *American Philosophy in the Twentieth Century: A Sourcebook from Pragmatism to Philosophical Analysis*. New York: Macmillan, 1966.

Lawler, Peter Augustine. *Postmodernism Rightly Understood: The Return to Realism in American Thought*. Lanham, Md.: Rowman & Littlefield, 1999.

MacKinnon, Barbara, ed. *American Philosophy: An Historical Anthology*. Albany: State University of New York Press, 1985.

Margolis, Joseph. *Reinventing Pragmatism: American Philosophy at the End of the Twentieth Century*. Ithaca, N.Y.: Cornell University Press, 2002.

Margolis. *The Unraveling of Scientism: American Philosophy at the End of the Twentieth Century*. Ithaca, N.Y.: Cornell University Press, 2003.

McCumber, John. *Time in the Ditch: American Philosophy and the McCarthy Era*. Evanston, Ill.: Northwestern University Press, 2001.

McDermott, John J. *The Culture of Experience: Philosophical Essays in the American Grain*. New York: New York University Press, 1976.

McDermott. *Streams of Experience: Reflections on the History and Philosophy of American Culture*. Amherst: University of Massachusetts Press, 1986.

Morris, Charles. *The Pragmatic Movement in American Philosophy*. New York: Braziller, 1970.

Mounce, H. O. *The Two Pragmatisms: From Peirce to Rorty*. New York: Routledge, 1997.

Muelder, Walter G., Laurence Sears, and Anne V. Schlabach, eds. *The Development of American Philosophy*. Boston: Houghton Mifflin, 1960.

Mulvaney, Robert J., and Philip M. Zeltner, eds. *Pragmatism: Its Sources and Prospects*. Columbia: University of South Carolina Press, 1981.

Murphy, John P. *Pragmatism: From Peirce to Davidson*. Boulder, Colo.: Westview Press, 1990.

Murphy, Nancey C. *Anglo-American Postmodernity: Philosophical Perspectives on Science, Religion, and Ethics*. Boulder, Colo.: Westview Press, 1997.

Myers, Gerald E., ed. *The Spirit of American Philosophy*. New York: Capricorn, 1971.

Neubert, Albrecht. *Semantischer Positivismus in den USA: Ein kritischer Beitrag zum Studium der Zusammenhänge zwischen Sprache und Gesellschaft*. Halle (Saale): Niemeyer, 1962.

Passmore, John Arthur. *A Hundred Years of Philosophy*. London: Duckworth, 1957.

Passmore. *Recent Philosophers*. London: Duckworth, 1985; La Salle, Ill.: Open Court, 1990.

Peterfreund, Sheldon Paul. *An Introduction to American Philosophy*. New York: Odyssey Press, 1959.

Pütz, Manfred, ed. *Nietzsche in American Literature and Thought*. Columbia, S.C.: Camden House, 1995.

Rajchman, John, and Cornel West, eds. *Post-Analytic Philosophy*. New York: Columbia University Press, 1985.

Reck, Andrew J. *The New American Philosophers: An Exploration of Thought since World War II*. Baton Rouge: Louisiana State University Press, 1968.

Reck. *Recent American Philosophy: From Puritanism to Pragmatism*. New York: Pantheon, 1964.

Rescher, Nicholas. *American Philosophy Today, and Other Philosophical Studies*. Lanham, Md.: Rowman & Littlefield, 1994.

Restaino, Franco. *Filosofia e post-filosofia in America: Rorty, Bernstein, MacIntyre*. Milan: Angeli, 1990.

Romanell, Patrick. *Toward a Critical Naturalism: Reflections on Contemporary American Philosophy*. New York: Macmillan, 1958.

Rorty, Amélie, ed. *Pragmatic Philosophy*. Garden City, N.Y.: Anchor, 1966.

Rosenthal, Sandra B. *Speculative Pragmatism*. Amherst: University of Massachusetts Press, 1986.

Roth, Robert J. *American Religious Philosophy*. New York: Harcourt, Brace & World, 1967.

Roth. *British Empiricism and American Pragmatism: New Directions and Neglected Arguments*. New York: Fordham University Press, 1993.

Ryder, John, ed. *American Philosophic Naturalism in the Twentieth Century*. Amherst, N.Y.: Prometheus, 1994.

Sauer, Ernst Friedrich. *Amerikanische Philosophen: Von der Puritanern bis zu Herbert Marcuse*. St. Augustin: Kersting, 1977.

Schneider, Herbert W. *A History of American Philosophy*. New York: Columbia University Press, 1963.

Schneider. *Sources of Contemporary Philosophical Realism in America*. Indianapolis: Bobbs-Merrill, 1964.

Sellars, Roy Wood. *Reflections on American Philosophy from Within*. Notre Dame, Ind.: University of Notre Dame Press, 1969.

Shahan, Robert W., and Kenneth R. Merrill, eds. *American Philosophy from Edwards to Quine*. Norman: University of Oklahoma Press, 1977.

Singer, Marcus, ed. *American Philosophy*. Cambridge: Cambridge University Press, 1985.

Smith, John E. "The Course of American Philosophy," *Review of Metaphysics*, 11 (1957): 279–303.

Smith. *The Spirit of American Philosophy*. New York: Oxford University Press, 1963.

Smith, ed. *Contemporary American Philosophy: Second Series*. London: Allen & Unwin / New York: Humanities Press, 1970.

Thayer, H. S. *Meaning and Action: A Critical History of Pragmatism*. Indianapolis: Bobbs-Merrill, 1968.

Townsend, Harvey Gates. *Philosophical Ideas in the United States*. New York: American Book Company, 1934.

Vacher, Laurent-Michel. *L'empire du moderne: Actualité de la philosophie américaine. Essai*. Montreal: Herbes rouges, 1990.

Van Wesep, H. B. *Seven Sages: The Story of American Philosophy*. New York: Longmans, 1960.

Werkmeister, W. H. *A History of Philosophical Ideas in America*. Westport, Conn.: Greenwood Press, 1981.

West, Cornel. *The American Evasion of Philosophy: A Genealogy of Pragmatism*. Madison: University of Wisconsin Press, 1989.

White, Morton. *Pragmatism and the American Mind: Essays and Reviews in Philosophy and Intellectual History*. New York: Oxford University Press, 1973.

White. *Social Thought in America: The Revolt against Formalism*. London & New York: Oxford University Press, 1976.

Whittemore, Robert C. *Makers of the American Mind: Three Centuries of American Thought and Thinkers*. New York: Morrow, 1964.

Zoll, Donald Atwell. *The Twentieth Century Mind: Essays on Contemporary Thought*. Baton Rouge: Louisiana State University Press, 1967.

Contributors

Michael Allen . . . . *Columbia, South Carolina*

Alexander Bird . . . . *University of Edinburgh*

Jeff Buechner . . . . *Rutgers University*

Curtis L. Carter . . . . *Marquette University*

Stephen Cox . . . . *University of California, San Diego*

Philip B. Dematteis . . . . *Saint Leo University*

James H. Fetzer . . . . *University of Minnesota, Duluth*

Roger F. Gibson Jr. . . . . *Washington University, St. Louis*

Philip T. Grier . . . . *Dickinson College*

Lance P. Hickey . . . . *Rose-Hulman Institute of Technology*

John Howie . . . . *Southern Illinois University at Carbondale*

Jennifer Hudin . . . . *University of California, Berkeley*

Angelo Juffras . . . . *William Paterson University*

Thomas Krettek . . . . *Marquette University*

Ernest Lepore . . . . *Rutgers University*

J. P. Moreland . . . . *Biola University*

Walter W. Ross . . . . *Lexington, South Carolina*

D. Seiple . . . . *New York, New York*

George W. Shields . . . . *Kentucky State University*

Robert B. Talisse . . . . *Vanderbilt University*

Stephen L. Thompson . . . . *William Paterson University*

Willem A. deVries . . . . *University of New Hampshire*

Kathleen A. Wallace . . . . *Hofstra University*

William G. Weaver . . . . *University of Texas at El Paso*

Takashi Yagisawa . . . . *California State University, Northridge*

Cumulative Index

Dictionary of Literary Biography, Volumes 1-279
Dictionary of Literary Biography Yearbook, 1980-2001
Dictionary of Literary Biography Documentary Series, Volumes 1-19
Concise Dictionary of American Literary Biography, Volumes 1-7
Concise Dictionary of British Literary Biography, Volumes 1-8
Concise Dictionary of World Literary Biography, Volumes 1-4

Cumulative Index

DLB before number: *Dictionary of Literary Biography,* Volumes 1-279
Y before number: *Dictionary of Literary Biography Yearbook,* 1980-2001
DS before number: *Dictionary of Literary Biography Documentary Series,* Volumes 1-19
CDALB before number: *Concise Dictionary of American Literary Biography,* Volumes 1-7
CDBLB before number: *Concise Dictionary of British Literary Biography,* Volumes 1-8
CDWLB before number: *Concise Dictionary of World Literary Biography,* Volumes 1-4

G

Hochhuth, Rolf 1931- DLB-124

Hochman, Sandra 1936- DLB-5

Hocken, Thomas Morland
   1836-1910. . . . . DLB-184

Hocking, William E. 1873-1966 . . . . .DLB-270

Hodder and Stoughton, Limited. DLB-106

Hodgins, Jack 1938- DLB-60

Hodgman, Helen 1945- DLB-14

Hodgskin, Thomas 1787-1869 . . . . DLB-158

Hodgson, Ralph 1871-1962 . . . . DLB-19

Hodgson, William Hope
   1877-1918 . . . . .DLB-70, 153, 156, 178

Hoe, Robert, III 1839-1909 . . . . DLB-187

Hoeg, Peter 1957- DLB-214

Højholt, Per 1928- DLB-214

Hoffenstein, Samuel 1890-1947 . . . . DLB-11

Hoffman, Charles Fenno 1806-1884. . . DLB-3, 250

Hoffman, Daniel 1923- DLB-5

Hoffmann, E. T. A.
   1776-1822 . . . . DLB-90; CDWLB-2

Hoffman, Frank B. 1888-1958 . . . . DLB-188

Hoffman, William 1925- DLB-234

Hoffmanswaldau, Christian Hoffman von
   1616-1679 . . . . DLB-168

Hofmann, Michael 1957- DLB-40

Hofmannsthal, Hugo von
   1874-1929 . . . . .DLB-81, 118; CDWLB-2

Hofstadter, Richard 1916-1970 . . . . . .DLB-17, 246

Hogan, Desmond 1950- DLB-14

Hogan, Linda 1947- DLB-175

Hogan and Thompson DLB-49

Hogarth Press DLB-112

Hogg, James 1770-1835 . . . . DLB-93, 116, 159

Hohberg, Wolfgang Helmhard Freiherr von
   1612-1688. . . . . DLB-168

von Hohenheim, Philippus Aureolus
   Theophrastus Bombastus (see Paracelsus)

Hohl, Ludwig 1904-1980 . . . . DLB-56

Holbrook, David 1923- DLB-14, 40

Holcroft, Thomas 1745-1809 . . . . DLB-39, 89, 158

Preface to *Alwyn* (1780) DLB-39

Holden, Jonathan 1941- DLB-105

"Contemporary Verse Story-telling" DLB-105

Holden, Molly 1927-1981 . . . . DLB-40

Hölderlin, Friedrich 1770-1843 DLB-90; CDWLB-2

Holdstock, Robert 1948- DLB-261

Holiday House DLB-46

Holinshed, Raphael died 1580 . . . . DLB-167

Holland, J. G. 1819-1881 . . . . .DS-13

Holland, Norman N. 1927- DLB-67

Hollander, John 1929- DLB-5

Holley, Marietta 1836-1926 . . . . DLB-11

Hollinghurst, Alan 1954- DLB-207

Hollingsworth, Margaret 1940- DLB-60

Hollo, Anselm 1934- DLB-40

Holloway, Emory 1885-1977 . . . . DLB-103

Holloway, John 1920- DLB-27

Holloway House Publishing Company . . . DLB-46

Holme, Constance 1880-1955 . . . . DLB-34

Holmes, Abraham S. 1821?-1908 . . . . DLB-99

Holmes, John Clellon 1926-1988 . . . .DLB-16, 237

"Four Essays on the Beat Generation" DLB-16

Holmes, Mary Jane 1825-1907 . . . . . DLB-202, 221

Holmes, Oliver Wendell
   1809-1894 . . . . . . DLB-1, 189, 235; CDALB-2

Holmes, Richard 1945- DLB-155

The Cult of Biography
   Excerpts from the Second Folio Debate:
   "Biographies are generally a disease of
   English Literature" Y-86

Holmes, Thomas James 1874-1959. . . . . DLB-187

Holroyd, Michael 1935- DLB-155; Y-99

Holst, Hermann E. von 1841-1904 . . . . . . DLB-47

Holt, Henry, and Company DLB-49

Holt, John 1721-1784 . . . . DLB-43

Holt, Rinehart and Winston. DLB-46

Holtby, Winifred 1898-1935 . . . . DLB-191

Holthusen, Hans Egon 1913- DLB-69

Hölty, Ludwig Christoph Heinrich
   1748-1776 . . . . DLB-94

Holub, Miroslav
   1923-1998 . . . . DLB-232; CDWLB-4

Holz, Arno 1863-1929 . . . . DLB-118

Home, Henry, Lord Kames
   (see Kames, Henry Home, Lord)

Home, John 1722-1808 . . . . DLB-84

Home, William Douglas 1912- DLB-13

Home Publishing Company DLB-49

Homer circa eighth-seventh centuries B.C.
   .DLB-176; CDWLB-1

Homer, Winslow 1836-1910 . . . . DLB-188

Homes, Geoffrey (see Mainwaring, Daniel)

Honan, Park 1928- DLB-111

Hone, William 1780-1842. . . . . .DLB-110, 158

Hongo, Garrett Kaoru 1951- DLB-120

Honig, Edwin 1919- DLB-5

Hood, Hugh 1928- DLB-53

Hood, Mary 1946- DLB-234

Hood, Thomas 1799-1845 . . . . DLB-96

Hook, Sidney 1902-1989 . . . . .DLB-279

Hook, Theodore 1788-1841 . . . . DLB-116

Hooker, Jeremy 1941- DLB-40

Hooker, Richard 1554-1600. . . . . DLB-132

Hooker, Thomas 1586-1647. . . . . DLB-24

hooks, bell 1952- DLB-246

Hooper, Johnson Jones
   1815-1862 . . . . DLB-3, 11, 248

Hope, Anthony 1863-1933 . . . . DLB-153, 156

Hope, Christopher 1944- DLB-225

Hope, Eva (see Hearn, Mary Anne)

Hope, Laurence (Adela Florence
   Cory Nicolson) 1865-1904 . . . . DLB-240

Hopkins, Ellice 1836-1904 . . . . DLB-190

Hopkins, Gerard Manley
   1844-1889 . . . . DLB-35, 57; CDBLB-5

Hopkins, John (see Sternhold, Thomas)

Hopkins, John H., and Son DLB-46

Hopkins, Lemuel 1750-1801 . . . . DLB-37

Hopkins, Pauline Elizabeth 1859-1930 . . . . DLB-50

Hopkins, Samuel 1721-1803 . . . . DLB-31

Hopkinson, Francis 1737-1791 . . . . DLB-31

Hopkinson, Nalo 1960- DLB-251

Hopper, Nora (Mrs. Nora Chesson)
   1871-1906. . . . . DLB-240

Hoppin, Augustus 1828-1896 . . . . DLB-188

Hora, Josef 1891-1945 . . . . . .DLB-215; CDWLB-4

Horace 65 B.C.-8 B.C. DLB-211; CDWLB-1

Horgan, Paul 1903-1995 . . . . . .DLB-102, 212; Y-85

Horizon Press DLB-46

Hornby, C. H. St. John 1867-1946 . . . . . . DLB-201

Hornby, Nick 1957- DLB-207

Horne, Frank 1899-1974. . . . . DLB-51

Horne, Richard Henry (Hengist)
   1802 or 1803-1884 . . . . DLB-32

Horney, Karen 1885-1952 . . . . DLB-246

Hornung, E. W. 1866-1921 . . . . DLB-70

Horovitz, Israel 1939- DLB-7

Horton, George Moses 1797?-1883? DLB-50

Horváth, Ödön von 1901-1938 . . . . . DLB-85, 124

Horwood, Harold 1923- DLB-60

Hosford, E. and E. [publishing house] DLB-49

Hoskens, Jane Fenn 1693-1770? DLB-200

Hoskyns, John 1566-1638 . . . . DLB-121

Hosokawa Yūsai 1535-1610 . . . . DLB-203

Hospers, John 1918- DLB-279

Hostovský, Egon 1908-1973 . . . . DLB-215

Hotchkiss and Company DLB-49

Hough, Emerson 1857-1923 . . . . DLB-9, 212

Houghton, Stanley 1881-1913 . . . . DLB-10

Houghton Mifflin Company DLB-49

Household, Geoffrey 1900-1988 . . . . DLB-87

Housman, A. E. 1859-1936 . . . DLB-19; CDBLB-5

Housman, Laurence 1865-1959 . . . . DLB-10

Houston, Pam 1962- DLB-244

Houwald, Ernst von 1778-1845 . . . . DLB-90

Hovey, Richard 1864-1900 . . . . DLB-54

Howard, Donald R. 1927-1987 . . . . DLB-111

Howard, Maureen 1930- Y-83

Howard, Richard 1929- DLB-5

Howard, Roy W. 1883-1964 . . . . DLB-29

Howard, Sidney 1891-1939 . . . . . . .DLB-7, 26, 249

Howard, Thomas, second Earl of Arundel
   1585-1646 . . . . DLB-213

Howe, E. W. 1853-1937 . . . . DLB-12, 25

Howe, Henry 1816-1893 . . . . DLB-30

Howe, Irving 1920-1993 . . . . DLB-67

Howe, Joseph 1804-1873 . . . . DLB-99

Howe, Julia Ward 1819-1910 . . . . DLB-1, 189, 235

I

M

Metcalf, J. [publishing house] DLB-49

Metcalf, John 1938- DLB-60

The Methodist Book Concern DLB-49

Methuen and Company DLB-112

Meun, Jean de (see Roman de la Rose)

Mew, Charlotte 1869-1928 . . . . DLB-19, 135

Mewshaw, Michael 1943- Y-80

Meyer, Conrad Ferdinand 1825-1898 . . . DLB-129

Meyer, E. Y. 1946- DLB-75

Meyer, Eugene 1875-1959 . . . . DLB-29

Meyer, Michael 1921-2000 . . . . DLB-155

Meyers, Jeffrey 1939- DLB-111

Meynell, Alice 1847-1922 . . . . DLB-19, 98

Meynell, Viola 1885-1956 . . . . DLB-153

Meyrink, Gustav 1868-1932 . . . . DLB-81

Mézières, Philipe de circa 1327-1405 . . . . DLB-208

Michael, Ib 1945- DLB-214

Michael, Livi 1960- DLB-267

Michaëlis, Karen 1872-1950 . . . . DLB-214

Michaels, Leonard 1933- DLB-130

Michaux, Henri 1899-1984 . . . . DLB-258

Micheaux, Oscar 1884-1951 . . . . DLB-50

Michel of Northgate, Dan
circa 1265-circa 1340 . . . . DLB-146

Micheline, Jack 1929-1998 . . . . DLB-16

Michener, James A. 1907?-1997 . . . . DLB-6

Micklejohn, George
circa 1717-1818 . . . . DLB-31

Middle English Literature:
An Introduction DLB-146

The Middle English Lyric DLB-146

Middle Hill Press DLB-106

Middleton, Christopher 1926- DLB-40

Middleton, Richard 1882-1911 . . . . DLB-156

Middleton, Stanley 1919- DLB-14

Middleton, Thomas 1580-1627 . . . . DLB-58

Miegel, Agnes 1879-1964 . . . . DLB-56

Mieželaitis, Eduardas 1919-1997 . . . . . . DLB-220

Mihailović, Dragoslav 1930- DLB-181

Mihalić, Slavko 1928- DLB-181

Mikhailov, A. (see Sheller, Aleksandr
Konstantinovich)

Mikhailov, Mikhail Larionovich
1829-1865 . . . . DLB-238

Mikhailovsky, Nikolai Konstantinovich
1842-1904 . . . . .DLB-277

Miles, Josephine 1911-1985 . . . . DLB-48

Miles, Susan (Ursula Wyllie Roberts)
1888-1975 . . . . DLB-240

Miliković, Branko 1934-1961 . . . . DLB-181

Milius, John 1944- DLB-44

Mill, James 1773-1836 . . . . DLB 107, 158, 262

Mill, John Stuart
1806-1873 . . . . . . DLB-55, 190, 262; CDBLB-4

Millar, Andrew [publishing house] DLB-154

Millar, Kenneth
1915-1983 . . . . .DLB-2, 226; Y-83; DS-6

Millay, Edna St. Vincent
1892-1950 . . . . DLB-45, 249; CDALB-4

Millen, Sarah Gertrude 1888-1968 . . . . . DLB-225

Miller, Andrew 1960- DLB-267

Miller, Arthur
1915- DLB-7, 266; CDALB-1

Miller, Caroline 1903-1992 . . . . DLB-9

Miller, Eugene Ethelbert 1950- DLB-41

Miller, Heather Ross 1939- DLB-120

Miller, Henry
1891-1980 . . . . . . DLB-4, 9; Y-80; CDALB-5

Miller, Hugh 1802-1856 . . . . DLB-190

Miller, J. Hillis 1928- DLB-67

Miller, James [publishing house] DLB-49

Miller, Jason 1939- DLB-7

Miller, Joaquin 1839-1913 . . . . DLB-186

Miller, May 1899- DLB-41

Miller, Paul 1906-1991 . . . . DLB-127

Miller, Perry 1905-1963 . . . . .DLB-17, 63

Miller, Sue 1943- DLB-143

Miller, Vassar 1924-1998 . . . . DLB-105

Miller, Walter M., Jr. 1923- DLB-8

Miller, Webb 1892-1940 . . . . DLB-29

Millett, Kate 1934- DLB-246

Millhauser, Steven 1943- DLB-2

Millican, Arthenia J. Bates 1920- DLB-38

Milligan, Alice 1866-1953 . . . . DLB-240

Mills and Boon DLB-112

Mills, Magnus 1954- DLB-267

Milman, Henry Hart 1796-1868 . . . . DLB-96

Milne, A. A. 1882-1956 . . . . . DLB-10, 77, 100, 160

Milner, Ron 1938- DLB-38

Milner, William [publishing house] DLB-106

Milnes, Richard Monckton (Lord Houghton)
1809-1885 . . . . DLB-32, 184

Milton, John
1608-1674 . . . . DLB-131, 151; CDBLB-2

Miłosz, Czesław 1911- . . . DLB-215; CDWLB-4

Minakami Tsutomu 1919- DLB-182

Minamoto no Sanetomo 1192-1219 . . . . DLB-203

The Minerva Press DLB-154

Minnesang circa 1150-1280 . . . . DLB-138

Minns, Susan 1839-1938 . . . . DLB-140

Minor Illustrators, 1880-1914 . . . . DLB-141

Minor Poets of the Earlier Seventeenth
Century DLB-121

Minton, Balch and Company DLB-46

Mirbeau, Octave 1848-1917 . . . . DLB-123, 192

Mirk, John died after 1414? DLB-146

Miron, Gaston 1928- DLB-60

A Mirror for Magistrates DLB-167

Mishima Yukio 1925-1970 . . . . DLB-182

Mitchel, Jonathan 1624-1668 . . . . DLB-24

Mitchell, Adrian 1932- DLB-40

Mitchell, Donald Grant
1822-1908 . . . . DLB-1, 243; DS-13

Mitchell, Gladys 1901-1983 . . . . DLB-77

Mitchell, James Leslie 1901-1935 . . . . DLB-15

Mitchell, John (see Slater, Patrick)

Mitchell, John Ames 1845-1918 . . . . DLB-79

Mitchell, Joseph 1908-1996 . . . . . .DLB-185; Y-96

Mitchell, Julian 1935- DLB-14

Mitchell, Ken 1940- DLB-60

Mitchell, Langdon 1862-1935 . . . . DLB-7

Mitchell, Loften 1919- DLB-38

Mitchell, Margaret 1900-1949 . . DLB-9; CDALB-7

Mitchell, S. Weir 1829-1914 . . . . DLB-202

Mitchell, W. J. T. 1942- DLB-246

Mitchell, W. O. 1914- DLB-88

Mitchison, Naomi Margaret (Haldane)
1897-1999 . . . . .DLB-160, 191, 255

Mitford, Mary Russell 1787-1855 . . . .DLB-110, 116

Mitford, Nancy 1904-1973 . . . . DLB-191

Mittelholzer, Edgar
1909-1965 . . . . .DLB-117; CDWLB-3

Mitterer, Erika 1906- DLB-85

Mitterer, Felix 1948- DLB-124

Mitternacht, Johann Sebastian
1613-1679 . . . . DLB-168

Miyamoto, Yuriko 1899-1951 . . . . DLB-180

Mizener, Arthur 1907-1988 . . . . DLB-103

Mo, Timothy 1950- DLB-194

Moberg, Vilhelm 1898-1973 . . . . DLB-259

Modern Age Books DLB-46

"Modern English Prose" (1876),
by George Saintsbury DLB-57

The Modern Language Association of America
Celebrates Its Centennial Y-84

The Modern Library DLB-46

"Modern Novelists – Great and Small" (1855),
by Margaret Oliphant DLB-21

"Modern Style" (1857), by Cockburn
Thomson [excerpt] DLB-57

The Modernists (1932),
by Joseph Warren Beach DLB-36

Modiano, Patrick 1945- DLB-83

Moffat, Yard and Company DLB-46

Moffet, Thomas 1553-1604 . . . . DLB-136

Mohr, Nicholasa 1938- DLB-145

Moix, Ana María 1947- DLB-134

Molesworth, Louisa 1839-1921 . . . . DLB-135

Molière (Jean-Baptiste Poquelin)
1622-1673 . . . . .DLB-268

Möllhausen, Balduin 1825-1905 . . . . DLB-129

Molnár, Ferenc
1878-1952 . . . . .DLB-215; CDWLB-4

Molnár, Miklós (see Mészöly, Miklós)

Momaday, N. Scott
1934- DLB-143, 175, 256; CDALB-7

Monkhouse, Allan 1858-1936 . . . . DLB-10

Monro, Harold 1879-1932 . . . . DLB-19

Monroe, Harriet 1860-1936 . . . . DLB-54, 91

Monsarrat, Nicholas 1910-1979 . . . . DLB-15

N

Cumulative Index

Pitter, Ruth 1897- DLB-20

Pix, Mary 1666-1709 . . . . DLB-80

Pixérécourt, René Charles Guilbert de
1773-1844. . . . . DLB-192

Plaatje, Sol T. 1876-1932 . . . . DLB-125, 225

Plante, David 1940- Y-83

Platen, August von 1796-1835 . . . . DLB-90

Plath, Sylvia
1932-1963 . . . . DLB-5, 6, 152; CDALB-1

Plantinga, Alvin 1932- DLB-279

Plato circa 428 B.C.-348-347 B.C.
. . . . .DLB-176; CDWLB-1

Plato, Ann 1824?-? DLB-239

Platon 1737-1812. . . . . DLB-150

Platonov, Andrei Platonovich (Andrei
Platonovic Klimentev) 1899-1951 . . . DLB-272

Platt, Charles 1945- DLB-261

Platt and Munk Company DLB-46

Plautus circa 254 B.C.-184 B.C.
. . . . DLB-211; CDWLB-1

Playboy Press DLB-46

Playford, John [publishing house]. DLB-170

Plays, Playwrights, and Playgoers DLB-84

Playwrights on the Theater DLB-80

Der Pleier flourished circa 1250 . . . . DLB-138

Pleijel, Agneta 1940- DLB-257

Plenzdorf, Ulrich 1934- DLB-75

Pleshcheev, Aleksei Nikolaevich
1823?-1893. . . . . .DLB-277

Plessen, Elizabeth 1944- DLB-75

Pletnev, Petr Aleksandrovich
1792-1865. . . . . DLB-205

Pliekšāne, Elza Rozenberga (see Aspazija)

Pliekšāns, Jānis (see Rainis, Jānis)

Plievier, Theodor 1892-1955 . . . . DLB-69

Plimpton, George 1927- DLB-185, 241; Y-99

Pliny the Elder A.D. 23/24-A.D. 79 . . . . . DLB-211

Pliny the Younger
circa A.D. 61-A.D. 112. . . . . DLB-211

Plomer, William
1903-1973. . . . . DLB-20, 162, 191, 225

Plotinus 204-270 . . . . .DLB-176; CDWLB-1

Plowright, Teresa 1952- DLB-251

Plume, Thomas 1630-1704 . . . . DLB-213

Plumly, Stanley 1939- DLB-5, 193

Plumpp, Sterling D. 1940- DLB-41

Plunkett, James 1920- DLB-14

Plutarch
circa 46-circa 120 . . . . . .DLB-176; CDWLB-1

Plymell, Charles 1935- DLB-16

Pocket Books DLB-46

Poe, Edgar Allan 1809-1849
. . . . DLB-3, 59, 73, 74, 248; CDALB-2

Poe, James 1921-1980. . . . . DLB-44

The Poet Laureate of the United States
Statements from Former Consultants
in Poetry. Y-86

Pogodin, Mikhail Petrovich
1800-1875. . . . . DLB-198

Pogorel'sky, Antonii
(see Perovsky, Aleksei Alekseevich)

Pohl, Frederik 1919- DLB-8

Poirier, Louis (see Gracq, Julien)

Poláček, Karel 1892-1945. . . DLB-215; CDWLB-4

Polanyi, Michael 1891-1976 . . . . DLB-100

Pole, Reginald 1500-1558. . . . . DLB-132

Polevoi, Nikolai Alekseevich
1796-1846. . . . . DLB-198

Polezhaev, Aleksandr Ivanovich
1804-1838 . . . . DLB-205

Poliakoff, Stephen 1952- DLB-13

Polidori, John William 1795-1821. . . . . . DLB-116

Polite, Carlene Hatcher 1932- DLB-33

Pollard, Alfred W. 1859-1944 . . . . DLB-201

Pollard, Edward A. 1832-1872 . . . . DLB-30

Pollard, Graham 1903-1976 . . . . DLB-201

Pollard, Percival 1869-1911 . . . . DLB-71

Pollard and Moss DLB-49

Pollock, Sharon 1936- DLB-60

Polonsky, Abraham 1910-1999. . . . . DLB-26

Polonsky, Iakov Petrovich 1819-1898 . . . .DLB-277

Polotsky, Simeon 1629-1680 . . . . DLB-150

Polybius circa 200 B.C.-118 B.C. DLB-176

Pomialovsky, Nikolai Gerasimovich
1835-1863 . . . . DLB-238

Pomilio, Mario 1921-1990 . . . . .DLB-177

Ponce, Mary Helen 1938- DLB-122

Ponce-Montoya, Juanita 1949- DLB-122

Ponet, John 1516?-1556 . . . . DLB-132

Ponge, Francis 1899-1988 . . . . DLB-258

Poniatowski, Elena
1933- DLB-113; CDWLB-3

Ponsard, François 1814-1867 . . . . DLB-192

Ponsonby, William [publishing house] DLB-170

Pontiggia, Giuseppe 1934- DLB-196

Pony Stories DLB-160

Poole, Ernest 1880-1950. . . . . DLB-9

Poole, Sophia 1804-1891 . . . . DLB-166

Poore, Benjamin Perley 1820-1887. . . . . . DLB-23

Popa, Vasko 1922-1991 . . . . DLB-181; CDWLB-4

Pope, Abbie Hanscom 1858-1894. . . . . . . DLB-140

Pope, Alexander
1688-1744. . . . . . DLB-95, 101, 213; CDBLB-2

Popov, Aleksandr Serafimovich
(see Serafimovich, Aleksandr Serafimovich)

Popov, Mikhail Ivanovich
1742-circa 1790. . . . . DLB-150

Popović, Aleksandar 1929-1996 . . . . DLB-181

Popper, Sir Karl R. 1902-1994 . . . . DLB-262

Popular Library DLB-46

Poquelin, Jean-Baptiste (see Molière)

Porete, Marguerite ?-1310 . . . . DLB-208

Porlock, Martin (see MacDonald, Philip)

Porpoise Press. DLB-112

Porta, Antonio 1935-1989 . . . . DLB-128

Porter, Anna Maria 1780-1832 . . . . . DLB-116, 159

Porter, Cole 1891-1964 . . . . DLB-265

Porter, David 1780-1843. . . . . DLB-183

Porter, Eleanor H. 1868-1920 . . . . DLB-9

Porter, Gene Stratton (see Stratton-Porter, Gene)

Porter, Hal 1911-1984 . . . . DLB-260

Porter, Henry ?-? DLB-62

Porter, Jane 1776-1850 . . . . .DLB-116, 159

Porter, Katherine Anne 1890-1980
. . . . . .DLB-4, 9, 102; Y-80; DS-12; CDALB-7

Porter, Peter 1929- DLB-40

Porter, William Sydney
1862-1910 . . . . .DLB-12, 78, 79; CDALB-3

Porter, William T. 1809-1858 . . . . DLB-3, 43, 250

Porter and Coates. DLB-49

Portillo Trambley, Estela 1927-1998. . . . . DLB-209

Portis, Charles 1933- DLB-6

Posey, Alexander 1873-1908. . . . . .DLB-175

Postans, Marianne circa 1810-1865 . . . . . DLB-166

Postgate, Raymond 1896-1971 . . . . .DLB-276

Postl, Carl (see Sealsfield, Carl)

Poston, Ted 1906-1974. . . . . DLB-51

Potekhin, Aleksei Antipovich 1829-1908 . DLB-238

Potok, Chaim 1929- DLB-28, 152

A Conversation with Chaim Potok Y-84

Potter, Beatrix 1866-1943. . . . . DLB-141

Potter, David M. 1910-1971 . . . . .DLB-17

Potter, Dennis 1935-1994. . . . . DLB-233

The Harry Potter Phenomenon Y-99

Potter, John E., and Company DLB-49

Pottle, Frederick A. 1897-1987 . . . . .DLB-103; Y-87

Poulin, Jacques 1937- DLB-60

Pound, Ezra 1885-1972
. . . . DLB-4, 45, 63; DS-15; CDALB-4

Poverman, C. E. 1944- DLB-234

Povich, Shirley 1905-1998 . . . . .DLB-171

Powell, Anthony 1905-2000 . . . DLB-15; CDBLB-7

The Anthony Powell Society: Powell and
the First Biennial Conference. Y-01

Dawn Powell, Where Have You Been All
Our Lives?. Y-97

Powell, John Wesley 1834-1902. . . . . DLB-186

Powell, Padgett 1952- DLB-234

Powers, J. F. 1917-1999. . . . . DLB-130

Powers, Jimmy 1903-1995 . . . . DLB-241

Pownall, David 1938- DLB-14

Powys, John Cowper 1872-1963. . . . . DLB-15, 255

Powys, Llewelyn 1884-1939. . . . . DLB-98

Powys, T. F. 1875-1953 . . . . DLB-36, 162

Poynter, Nelson 1903-1978. . . . . .DLB-127

The Practice of Biography: An Interview
with Stanley Weintraub. Y-82

The Practice of Biography II: An Interview
with B. L. Reid. Y-83

The Practice of Biography III: An Interview
with Humphrey Carpenter Y-84

The Practice of Biography IV: An Interview with
William Manchester. Y-85

U

ISBN 0-7876-6023-X

90000

B
935
.A45

2003